STUDIES IN SCOTTISH
BUSINESS HISTORY

STUDIES IN
SCOTTISH
BUSINESS HISTORY

Edited by

PETER L. PAYNE

Senior Lecturer in Economic
History (Colquhoun Lecturer),
University of Glasgow

REPRINTS OF ECONOMIC CLASSICS

Augustus M. Kelley, Bookseller
New York 1967

First published in 1967 by
FRANK CASS AND COMPANY LIMITED
67 Great Russell Street, London WC1

Published in the U.S.A. by A. M. Kelley,
24 East 22nd Street, New York, U.S.A.

Congress Catalogue Card No. 67-20815

Printed in Great Britain

Contents

Acknowledgements

I wish to thank all those who have helped in the preparation of this book. The original idea for a collection of papers surveying Scotland's rich resources of economic and business records, combined with essays based on such archival material, emerged from a discussion that took place at the annual conference of the economists of the Scottish Universities at 'The Burn', Edzell, in 1961, when Professor S. G. Checkland and Professor Donald J. Robertson suggested that I should investigate the feasibility of producing such a symposium. Since that time I have received their constant support. Professor Checkland was the originator and organiser of the appeal for the Colquhoun Lectureship in Business History.

At various stages in planning and editing the volume I received the valuable advice of the late Professor Henry Hamilton, Professor R. H. Campbell, Professor S. G. Lythe, Mr. Malcolm Gray and Dr. Christopher Smout, the latter three of whom constituted an advisory committee. Throughout I enjoyed the ready assistance of the members of the Business Archives Council of Scotland.

For their contributions, for numerous ancillary suggestions and for their patience I must thank the authors of the various papers. I acknowledge permission from the Editor of the *William and Mary Quarterly* to reproduce the article by Professor Jacob M. Price.

Mrs. Margaret E. Davies and, latterly, Miss Margaret Marlow performed the task of typing many individual manuscripts with speed and efficiency. My wife, Enid, has helped with the proof-reading, the preparation of the index and with some of the charts. She has, moreover, provided great encouragement when editorial problems appeared almost insuperable.

Mr. Frank Cass and his staff have been unfailing in their patience and technical assistance.

PETER L. PAYNE.

The University of Glasgow,
September, 1966.

Business History

PETER L. PAYNE

Colquhoun Lecturer in Business History,
University of Glasgow

IN AMERICA BUSINESS HISTORY has been variously defined since the days when N. S. B. Gras was appointed to the Straus Chair of Business History at Harvard University in 1927,(1) but in Great Britain the discipline has been, and continues to be, regarded as an integral part of economic history.(2) Indeed, it could be argued that 'business history is simply that branch of economic history that finds its source material primarily in company records and takes as its starting point the entrepreneur and the firm rather than anything else'.(3)

Beginning in the United States as a 'study of the administration of business units in the past',(4) and concentrating almost exclusively on the discovery of 'the main lines of development in business policy and the chief results of business management' within the context of the individual firm, some scholars were soon 'approaching the issue of the history of business from a more theoretical base and focusing attention on the entrepreneurial function. Still others began writing biographies of businessmen in terms of the whole man—the entire range of his activities inside and outside business proper.'(5) Despite these occasional deviations, however, the emphasis on the internal affairs of the companies whose records were available for study secured for business history 'an independence which seemed at times to border dangerously on isolation'.(6) The reasons for this were complex, as Dr. Supple has made abundantly clear, but of crucial importance was the fact that during the 'thirties and early 'forties the intensive study of the businessman was not accorded a place of high priority among the many topics that called for detailed investigation in that unhappy period. Instead, American economists and economic historians largely devoted themselves to unravelling the problems of the trade cycle, macro-economic processes, income distribution and standards of living.

With the passing of the 'Depression Decade', and the end of the war, the nature of the problems exercising the social scientist has changed. The focus of study is now economic growth; and in their quest to understand this phenomenon, the economist has become increasingly empirical, marshalling historical cases and statistical series to comprehend the factors that have given rise to economic growth in the past, and the economic historian increasingly theoretical and statistically sophisticated. Among both groups, moreover, there has been a pronounced revival of interest in the rôle of the businessman as an historical agent of economic and social change.

Many of those who came to devote a significant proportion of their energies to the study of the businessman were dissatisfied with the scope of previous inquiries. They burst out of the confines of 'the company history' and addressed themselves to a host of themes that defy the imposition of any simple collective title. A representative cross-section of their studies were published, however, in that most stimulating of periodicals, *Explorations in Entrepreneurial History*. No journal has been more aptly named. The inquiries which found a place in *Explorations*, and the work of the Research Center in Entrepreneurial History, which encouraged and fathered many of them, 'may be said to have permanently broadened the base for further investigation'.(7) Business history was never to be the same again. Each attempt at a new definition of the subject touched off comments, rejoinders and rebuttals. At one stage of the debate the 'entrepreneurial historians' seemed to take up a position as far removed from the business historian as the latter had once been from the economic historian.

By 1961, after exhausting introspection on the part of the participants, a new synthesis appeared to be emerging. The effervescence died down. Business historians came to the conclusion that they were not company historians.(8) They developed an interest in 'the social environment of business; a concern with business ethics and their relation to the dominant themes of the culture; a curiosity about the sources and processes of change; and—on a different level—a willingness to go beyond the empirical evidence and speculate on the broader significance of the issues raised'.(9) At the same time, those scholars who previously had been prepared to accept the title of entrepreneurial historian, showed 'a disposition to assimilate the characteristic concern of business history with the internal organization of business units and, in the process, to remedy what was at one time a notable weakness: over-concentration on the social and economic environment and under-emphasis on internal functioning'.(10) Furthermore, both groups—the distinction between which was becoming increasing blurred—from repudiating any real connection with economic history,(11) had tentatively agreed that their chosen fields of study were, in fact, but aspects of this subject. In the course of this controversy the study of the entrepreneur has been reinstated as a major theme in economic history and the subject thereby considerably invigorated.

In Great Britain, meanwhile, there was little active debate on these lines. Those few persons interested in the study of business records never regarded business history as anything other than a branch of economic history.(13) There were several British contributors to *Explorations*—though significantly their papers were traditional in character, redolent of *The Economic History Review* —and a number of Englishmen participated in the activities of the Research Center in Entrepreneurial History at Harvard. Furthermore, there is no question that many British scholars learned much from the American discussions. However, the relatively few economic historians in this country devoting themselves to any significant extent to the study of business archives clearly believed that the spade work of the earlier American business historians was necessary before they became too actively engaged in the more exciting interdisciplinary studies being undertaken in the United States. Another factor that influenced the British approach was the rather limited pedagogical rôle accorded to business history in this country.(14) It was occasionally recognised that business history was capable of making a valuable contribution to economic theory, but I think it would be true to say that the majority of those who considered the function of business history at all saw its major value in establishing more surely the generalisations of the economic historian. This partially explains the notable lack of emphasis on administrative decision-making and the comparative rarity of the company history typical of the American pioneering days, for the British have never thought of their essays in business history as potentially valuable case material for the training of business executives. Indeed, only recently have we in this country thought in terms of *any* academic courses specifically designed for the training of businessmen, and even now, in the somewhat feverish attempts to set up business schools on the Harvard pattern, the provision of courses in business history is rarely mentioned.(15) Is this because in the initial plans to frame the curricula for the new schools any subject which *appears* to have no immediate utility has been jettisoned? If so, it may be salutory to recall the words of A. K. Steigerwalt, Professor of Business History in the Graduate School of Business Administration at the University of Michigan, to whom the major objective of history is that 'of finding significant relationships to explain and to understand the antecedents of the present and to understand the present itself. History develops the kind of intellectual orientation that makes the present more meaningful and the future understandable. This is eminently practical and useful to developing in potential business leaders that which will enable them to live maturely with change and uncertainty.'(16) It may well be, of course, that the promoters of the new business schools are sceptical of the historian who recounts the past but appears to ignore both the present and the future, the time dimensions most important to them. It is regrettable that the majority of British firms, while willing to permit the examination of their archives that pre-date the First World War, are extremely reluctant to grant access to their more recent records. In these circumstances, it is not entirely the historians' fault that their detailed analyses all too frequently terminate at 1914.(17) If the business community really wants penetrating and useful examinations of current economic problems to be conducted in the business schools being created, then it must be more liberal in throwing open its modern records for research. Until this is done many studies of such problems must have an antiquarian flavour.

The papers which make up the second and third sections of this book are typical of the British approach to business history; an approach which might have justified naming the collection 'Studies in Scottish Economic History'. 'Business History' was used in the title because the section on sources attempts to survey the business archives available for study in Scotland, many of the essays themselves were based on this material, and the rôle of the entrepreneur is given considerable emphasis.

Even a cursory glance at the section on sources will indicate the great wealth of Scotland's business archives. Many of the individual collections are capable of supporting full-scale histories of particular enterprises, valuable in providing the economic historian and even the economist with illustrative examples and quantitative data,(18) and the business schools with case studies sufficiently detailed to permit profitable discussion by management students.

It should be remarked, however, that I suspect that none of the essays in this volume emerged from conscious attempts on the part of their authors to produce case studies in business history or to fashion future footnotes for the economic historian, though several of them may well come to serve in such a capacity. To comment on the motives underlying the authors' choice of subject would be presumptuous, but I trust that a brief explanation of the context out of which there emerged the contributions of those of them who were graduate students at the University of Glasgow will not give offence. During the course of the Colquhoun inquiry(19) it became increasingly apparent that the majority of the collections of business archives that were coming to light were fragmentary; only rarely was there discovered a comprehensive set of records, covering every phase of a firm's past operations. Considered in isolation, the majority of these incomplete collections were of limited value and liable to be neglected, and the idea of using them to support a regional investigation of the West of Scotland promised to permit making the maximum use of these fragments. Early in the survey, a considerable number of pay books were unearthed (and the word could be employed literally!). They appeared to have survived in the shipbuilding, coal-mining, iron and steel and engineering industries, sometimes with little or no supplementary information. It was believed that the most fruitful use of these materials would be the construction of a series of wage indices and wage differentials for the nineteenth and twentieth centuries, and my colleague, Mr. A. Slaven began an exploratory investigation of the complexities of such a task, using as his starting point the Dixon colliery records. The work involved proved to be enormous, but enough was achieved before Mr. Slaven widened his field of operations to a general study of the coal industry of the West of Scotland, to indicate that this wage project is feasible. Work is therefore continuing, and it is hoped that eventually we will be able to produce meaningful statistical series of wages and earnings that may be employed in a comprehensive study of the economic evolution of the West of Scotland. Similarly, it may be possible to build up statistical series of prices, profits, capital expenditures, outputs, and so on.

For some sectors of the economy, the manuscript sources and the published house histories appear to permit systematic studies of entire industries; an investigation of the Scottish steel industry is already in progress and a history of Scottish shipbuilding is being planned. In fact, Mr. Milne's work on the Ben Line voyage books was originally conceived as the first stage of a historical analysis of Scottish shipping, and it was hoped that it would serve to indicate *inter alia* questions that a study of the prolific records of the Clyde shipbuilders might answer. Mr. Tyson's essay represents one aspect of his history of the ill-fated City of Glasgow Bank, the failure of which was so important to the economic development of Scotland. The point that I am trying to make is that the Glasgow inquiries are being conducted with a view to understanding more fully the economic growth and recent relative decline of Scotland. A conscious effort is being made to make each study intelligible in terms of what was happening in other comparable units, in other industries, and in the region as a whole.(20)

Professor J. R. T. Hughes has recently spoken of 'the new interest that seems to be building up in the use of the entrepreneur as a vehicle for the study and comprehension of American economic history and of economic development generally'.(21) Certainly a case could be made for such an approach to an understanding of the recent economic history of Scotland by using the entrepreneur as a focal point. Mr. Byres' essay—based on a much wider and comprehensively documented thesis—is abundant proof of this. Several years ago, Mr. W. I. French, then President of the Glasgow Chamber of Commerce, implied in his comments on the Chamber's Annual Report that native concerns were perhaps not so vigorous, so ready to grasp economic opportunities, as the illustrious Clydeside figures of the past. If this view is correct, what is the explanation? It is well known that industry in the West of Scotland is characterised by the family firm. Is it that the recent relatively poor economic performance of the region is to be partially explained in terms of a lack of entrepreneurial ability in the founders' successors or their having been educated in a scale of values which makes them prefer a life devoted to non-business pursuits? Are the findings of Mr. Byres' essay applicable to businessmen in the Glasgow region today? How much has depended on the accident of birth? What has been and is the rôle of the technically trained person in Scottish industry? It is hoped that detailed study of the business records listed in the first section of this volume will help to remedy our pathetically inadequate knowledge of these and related subjects.

This brief discussion has now turned full circle. May I therefore conclude by repeating a plea made elsewhere: a plea for the study of business records in terms not of the individual unit or of the industry (though such inquiries must be essential stages in the process) but in terms of the region.(22) It is not claimed that a regional approach is without its defects or its difficulties, simply that of all the alternative modes of utilising business archives it promises to be the one possessing the greatest potentialities. Scholars on both sides of the Atlantic have largely abandoned the concept of business history as the study of individual enterprises. With this I concur. I would prefer to define the subject as *the grass roots approach to economic history,* most capable of yielding significant results when it is attempted in a region context within an overall plan. By developing such a regional synthesis, business history will, I am convinced, attain a greater importance in the development of the social sciences.

NOTES

(1) Professor A. K. Steigerwalt has declared, in fact, that American scholars 'have been too preoccupied with defining what business history is'. *Business History in Graduate Schools of Business Administration*, p. 7, a paper prepared for the 11th Conference on Business History at the University of Indiana, 29th February, 1964.

(2) See, for example, T. S. Ashton, *Business History*, Business History, Vol. I, 1958-59, p. 2; P. L. Payne, *Business Archives and Economic History: The Case for Regional Studies*, Archives, Vol. VI, 1963, pp. 21-2.

(3) Payne, *op. cit.*, p. 22. The differences between the American and British approaches may perhaps be explained in terms of the use to which the subject has been put. See below, p. xiii.

(4) N. S. B. Gras and Henrietta M. Larson, Casebook in American Business History (New York, 1949), pp. 3, 17. For a brief, yet remarkably illuminating, account of the development of the subject in the United States, see B. E. Supple, *American Business History—A Survey*, Business History, Vol. I, 1959-60, pp. 63-76. It will be apparent that the subsequent paragraphs owe much to this perceptive essay. See also the papers, *Business History, Entrepreneurial History, and Business Administration*, by John G. B. Hutchins, and *Economic History and the New Business History*, by Herman E. Krooss, in The Journal of Economic History, Vol. XVIII, 1958, pp. 453-80.

(5) R. W. Hidy's *Comment* on an article by H. Klompmaker, *People or Circumstance?*, Business History Review, Vol. XXXVI, 1962, p. 463.

(6) Supple, *op. cit.*, p. 67.

(7) John E. Sawyer, *Entrepreneurial Studies: Perspectives and Directions, 1948-1958*, Business History Review, Vol. XXXII, 1958, p. 438. See also Ruth Crandall, The Research Center in Entrepreneurial History at Harvard University, 1948-1958: A Historical Sketch (Cambridge, Massachusetts, 1960).

(8) A. M. Johnson, *Where Does Business History Go From Here?*, Business History Review, Vol. XXXVI, 1962, p. 11.

(9) Hugh G. J. Aitken, *The Future of Entrepreneurial Research*, Explorations in Entrepreneurial History, 2nd Series, Vol. I, 1963-64, p. 8.

(10) *Ibid.*, p. 8.

(11) See, for example, A. M. Johnson, *Conference on the History of American Business: A Summary Report*, Business History Review, Vol. XXXIII, 1959, p. 209.

(12) A. M. Johnson, *Where Does Business History Go From Here? loc. cit.*, pp. 13-14. And see F. Redlich, *Approaches to Business History*, Business History Review, Vol. XXXVI, 1962, pp. 61-70; Supple, *op. cit.*, p. 76; and Hidy, *op. cit.*, p. 465.

(13) This attitude permeates the useful pamphlet on Business History by T. C. Barker, R. H. Campbell and P. Mathias, published by The Historical Association in 1960.

(14) In Australia, where there has been a considerable interest in business history for many years, the approach to business history has been more influenced by the British than the American attitude to the study. See A. Birch, *The Study of Business History in Australia*, Business Archives and History, Vol. II, 1962, p. 65.

(15) The need for, and rôle of, business historians in colleges of commerce

B

has, however, been mentioned in the Report of the Advisory Committee on Further Education for Commerce (1959), under the chairmanship of J. G. McMeeking, p. 22.

(16) Steigerwalt, *op. cit.*, p. 6. Clarence C. Walton, Associate Dean of the Columbia Graduate School of Business, has emphasised 'the importance to the businessman of *historical perspective*, breadth and flexibility of mind, and awareness of and ability to adjust to a continuously changing environment', in his paper delivered at the Business History Conference held at the Harvard School of Business Administration in 1961, by quoting this passage from the study by Robert A. Gordon and James E. Howell on Higher Education for Business (New York, 1959), sponsored by the Ford Foundation, Business History Review, Vol. XXXVI, 1962, p. 22. B. E. Supple, has provided an account of the part played by the course in *Business History at the Harvard Business School* in the Business History Review, Vol. XXXIII, 1959, pp. 575-79.

(17) See the point made in my paper *The Uses of Business History: A Contribution to the Discussion*, Business History, Vol. V, 1962-63, pp. 12-14.

(18) For this function see L. E. Davis, Journal of Economic History, Vol. XVIII, 1958, p. 484.

(19) See below, Chapter Three, pp. 42-46.

(20) Alongside this long-term plan to comprehend the mechanism of regional economic growth a concomittant study of urban history is being conducted in the University of Glasgow. See S. G. Checkland, *The British Industrial City as History: The Glasgow Case*, Urban Studies, Vol. I, 1964, pp. 34-54.

(21) J. R. T. Hughes, *Eight Tycoons: The Entrepreneur and American History*, a paper presented to the 11th Annual Conference of the Business History Association, held in March, 1964, at Indiana University. Explorations in Entrepreneural History, 2nd Series, Vol. I, 1963-64, p. 213.

(22) P. L. Payne, *The Uses of Business History* . . ., *loc. cit.*, pp. 16-17; *Business Archives and Economic History* . . ., *loc cit.*, pp. 27-29.

Part One: Sources

CHAPTER ONE

National Archive Sources
for Business History

JOHN IMRIE

Curator of Historical Records,
Scottish Record Office

MOST OF THE ARCHIVES mentioned below are preserved in the Scottish Record Office, H.M. General Register House, Edinburgh, which must be regarded as the main archive source in Scotland for the business historian. In the Register House there are lodged the national records of Scotland, administrative and legal, from earliest times to the present day; and, despite lamentable gaps in earlier series,(1) the public records do provide the continuity of material necessary for economic studies. But the Register House has now become more than a repository for the central public records, and the archive sources in the Scottish Record Office are fairly representative for the country as a whole.

Modern record policy in Scotland and other factors have brought in to the Scottish Record Office many local records, mainly of sheriff courts and burghs, and large collections of private archives, mostly family muniments but including the archives of a few business firms, societies and institutions.(2) Such collections contain much of direct interest for commercial and industrial development (*see* Appendix A). Moreover, town council minutes and other administrative records of the burghs are much concerned with the regulation of trade and industry. And, because of the wide civil jurisdiction of the sheriff courts, the legal records kept there (registers of decrees, processes and registers of deeds) complement the central legal records for business history, while possessing an interest of their own in small debt and sequestration proceedings and also in indentures of apprenticeship which are usually registered in sheriff courts. There is also other material in sheriff court records, which may be useful for the business historian: for example, registers of wills and confirmations from 1823 onwards;(3) records of workmen's compensation; and 'parliamentary' plans, especially railway plans which can be studied in association with the Scottish railway archives in the possession of the British Railways Board.

But the Scottish Record Office is not the only national source for the business historian, who may well commence his studies in the Department of Printed Books of the National Library of Scotland on Parliamentary papers and other printed series. The Library is also a national archive repository, although as a rule it does not hold the definite categories or long consecutive runs of records to be found in the Scottish Record Office. Nevertheless there is material for business history in such well-known collections as the Darien MSS. and also in a number of private collections deposited in the Library in recent years.(4)

The business historian will also find material, usually of a specialised nature, in the custody of other central bodies. The nationalised industries possess a quantity of pre-vesting records in addition to post-nationalisation records. For example, the Scottish Division of the National Coal Board has a number of pre-nationalisation colliery records, some of which have been deposited in the Scottish Record Office.(5) The Historical Records Department of the British Railways Board in Edinburgh has the archives of the five main Scottish railways up to the grouping of 1923 and of their earlier subsidiaries, together with the minute books of L.M.S. and L.N.E. Scottish boards and records of docks, canals and waterways belonging to the railway companies. The Scottish Gas Board and the South of Scotland Electricity Board, too, hold the records of a number of pre-vesting undertakings.

Although a scheme for the regular review and transmission of records to the Scottish Record Office has been accepted by the four major Scottish departments and certain of the smaller departments, modern departmental records are normally still in the custody of the departments concerned. Records transmitted to the Record Office so far are mainly archives of the eighteenth- and nineteenth century Boards and other bodies which existed before the modern departments. These include several well-known groups which may be useful for business history. The Board of Trustees for Manufactures instituted in 1727 was charged with responsibility for encouraging economic development on a wide front, and its records are particularly important for the linen industry, not only in showing the broad policies of the Board but also in providing detailed statistics as to output and information on experiments in industrial education. The Lord Advocates' papers (1839-1946) include reports and other papers relating to nineteenth-century legislation on trade and manufactures. Fishery Board records (1809-1909) include weekly fishing reports from the various districts. The files of Friendly Societies dissolved before 1920(6) (and dating back in some cases to the late eighteenth century) are less well known. These files cover Friendly Societies proper, Trade Unions, Building Societies and Industrial and Provident Societies. Like the Company files (*infra*) they provide a basic record with little detail,(7) which does, however, form a useful starting-point for research.

Most of the records still in the custody of the Scottish departments are very modern; most have not yet been reviewed and they will not be open to public inspection for many years. For these reasons any attempt at a detailed assessment of their value for research purposes would be premature. In general, however, modern departmental records should have much for the business historian in view of the increasing preoccupation of government with economic planning and the closer contacts with private enterprise.(8) Two groups of particular interest for business history may be mentioned. The census returns (from 1841) in the custody of the Registrar General for Scotland can be used to compile statistics on occupations and industries.(9) The files in the Companies Registration Office in Edinburgh provide formal information on particular companies,(10) which can also on occasions direct the researcher to the whereabouts of records of 'dead' companies.

The national records preserved in the Scottish Record Office fall into different groups, as they were produced by the various organs and departments of government.(11) They include the records of the main legislative and administrative organs of the old Kingdom of Scotland down to 1707—the records of the Scottish Parliament, Privy Council and Exchequer. (The latter survived the Union although it was reorganised on the English model.)

The Parliament and Privy Council series are largely in print, and their value for economic studies is well known. For business history the Privy Council records are particularly important since the Council was responsible for the practical working out of the general policies laid down by Parliament and exercised a close supervision and regulation of economic matters. The records of the Council contain much material for monopolies (cloth, wool, soap, cards, glass, tobacco, etc.) granted in great numbers in the first half of the seventeenth century and for the joint companies and 'manufactories' established during the second half of the century.

The records of the Scottish Exchequer are less well known, largely because they are still in course of arrangement.(12) It is clear, however, that there is a good deal to interest the business historian, both in the records prior to 1707 and in the post-Union series. The most important of the older records, the Exchequer Rolls, the Treasurers' Accounts and the Masters of Works' Accounts, have been published in part. Not only do they provide material for general economic studies, they also contain many references to individual merchants and craftsmen, as do the various accounts of expenses of the royal household. There are also Customs Books (arranged by ports) covering the periods 1498-1640 and 1662-1690, which although very incomplete can be used to show the main directions of Scottish overseas trade before the Union, particularly if taken with surviving business records.(13)

The development of industry in the second half of the seventeenth century is illustrated by petitions to the Exchequer for the erection of manufactories or for the admission of raw materials custom-free.(14) There are also papers relating to proceedings raised by manufacturers to enforce their privileges. The common good accounts of burghs include certificates of retail sales of wine, 1615-1634, and the excise accounts show duty paid on the brewing and retail sale of ale and include depositions by the retailers.

Many of the post-Union Exchequer series are more useful for general economic studies than for research on particular businesses. Excise revenue accounts and collectors' states of accounts, for example, only give a general picture of the volume of exciseable goods for the whole country and the particular localities, and it is not possible to trace individual businesses from them. Other series do refer to individuals but may be difficult to use. The judicial records of the Court of Exchequer, for example, contain many prosecutions by the Boards of Customs and Excise, but the only key is the court minute book. The massive series of quarterly customs accounts for Scottish ports, 1742-1830, not only give details of vessel, cargo and port of origin and destination, but also specify the consigner and consignee and it is possible (although laborious) to trace the activities of individual merchants and firms in both coastal and foreign trade. Records of tax assessments occasionally give incidental information about businesses,(15) and there is a Register of Recognizances by printers and publishers of newspapers, 1836-1855. The Exchequer records also show the operation of the official policy of encouraging Scottish industry, particularly by the payment of bounties, for example for herring and whale fishing.(16) For the Highlands the Forfeited Estates papers furnish material for the encouragement of manufacturers, particularly the linen and woollen industries.(17)

The public records of Scotland are not solely concerned with the governing of the nation; they also contain records of the rights of private individuals, since for centuries a prominent feature of Scottish law has been the power given to the individual to have his rights recorded in official registers. Such records of private rights continue in use to the present day and they form a particularly valuable source for the historian investigating the everyday legal and business activities of individuals or firms.

The Register of the Great Seal, which is the oldest public register in Scotland still current,(18) is mainly concerned with grants of lands and other privileges by the sovereigns of Scotland, but it also contains charters of incorporation to companies. Moreover, until 1853 separate patents of inventions were issued for Scotland under the Great Seal; and, while it became very common for English patents to be re-sealed in Scotland,(19) the records do show the spread of industrial ideas to Scotland.

The most important of the records of private rights is the Register of Sasines in which changes in ownership of land and heritable property have been recorded from 1617. From this record it is possible to see how successful businessmen invested in property from the seventeenth century onwards.(20) Again the Register of Sasines provides evidence of the acquisition of property for business or industrial purposes(21) or for the use of property to finance industrial projects.(22) And modern techniques of study seem to indicate that for property and property owners the Register can provide a fund of statistical information.(23) Leases, however, are not normally recorded in the Register of Sasines, and the Valuation Rolls (from 1855), which show owners and occupiers, should be used in conjunction with the Sasines for studies on the use of property for business purposes during the past century.(24)

Other important records of private rights need not be concerned with property. The records of the Court of Session, which was formally established in 1532, are most valuable for the business historian who may wish to investigate the litigation in which individuals or companies were concerned or to pursue specialised studies.(25) Sequestration processes in particular contain much useful information for business firms, but from the viewpoint of the business historian perhaps the most valuable feature of the records of the Court is that many business records, mainly of the eighteenth and nineteenth centuries, which were produced before the Court, have been preserved with the papers in the actions concerned (see Appendix B). From 1830 the Court of Session has exercised the original jurisdiction in all maritime civil causes. Prior to that year the records of the Court of Admiralty should be consulted for maritime and seafaring causes.

One branch of the work of the Court has produced a record known as the Register of Deeds, which has been kept from 1554 and in which are registered an infinite variety of documents, many involving merchants and craftsmen and throwing light on business transactions. From the late seventeenth century this record contains contracts of co-partnery which give formal details of the number of partners, the capital available, and the division of capital among the partners with the extent of liability. Down to 1811 protests on foreign and inland bills of exchange were recorded in the Register of Deeds, but thereafter a separate Register has been kept for protests.

One further public record concerned with private rights must be mentioned. Before 1823(26) wills and executries were dealt with by commissary courts, the records of which go back in some cases to the sixteenth century.(27) For the business historian the important element in each recorded testament is the inventory of 'goods, gear, debts and sums of money', which shows the stock-in-trade of merchants or craftsmen and includes the value of the various items. Some business papers of seventeenth-century merchants have survived because they were produced before the commissary court of Edinburgh in executry matters and are now preserved in a series of Miscellaneous Papers in the Record Office (*see* Appendix A).

NOTES

(1) The story of the vicissitudes of the records from the thirteenth century until they were transferred to the Register House at the end of the eighteenth century can be read in J. Maitland Thomson, The Public Records of Scotland (1922).

(2) In general *see* J. Imrie and G. G. Simpson, *The Local and Private Archives of Scotland*, Archives, vol. iii, no. 19, pp. 135-47; no. 20, pp. 219-30.

To date records have been received in the Scottish Record Office from the following sheriff courts: Cromarty, Cupar, Dingwall, Dunblane, Dunfermline, Dunoon, Edinburgh, Falkirk, Fort William, Haddington, Hamilton, Inveraray, Kilmarnock, Linlithgow, Paisley, Perth, Portree, Stirling, Stornoway, Tain, and Tobermory.

The following burghs have transmitted all or part of their older records: Ayr, Burntisland, Cupar, Dunbar, Dunfermline, Dysart, Elie and Earlsferry, Falkland, Haddington, Inverurie, Irvine, Linlithgow, Maybole, Montrose, Musselburgh, North Berwick, Peebles, Perth, St. Andrews, Stirling. The records of the Convention of Royal Burghs, which are particularly important for the study of the trading and industrial communities in the seventeenth century, are preserved in the Edinburgh City archives. For published burgh and Convention records *see* Handlist of Scottish and Welsh Record Publications (British Records Association, 1954), pp. 14-16.

(3) Before 1823 wills and executries were dealt with by the commissary courts (*infra*).

(4) *E.g.*, the Fletcher of Saltoun muniments contain papers relating to the Board of Trustees for Manufactures in Scotland, the South Sea Company, the British Linen Company, the woollen manufactory at Haddington and whale fishing at Campbeltown. A few company records have also been deposited, including the records of Alexander Houston and Company, Glasgow (general merchants), and William Wilson and Son, Bannockburn (tartan manufacturers).

(5) Fife Coal Company records, 1872-1952; Lochgelly Iron and Coal Company records, 1847-1953; Wemyss Coal Company records, 1889-1949. Others will be deposited in due course.

(6) Files of societies dissolved after 1920 and current files are with the Assistant Registrar of Friendly Societies (Scotland).

(7) The files are composed of rolls, accounts and documents dealing with dissolution.

(8) *E.g.*, statistics concerning the building and civil engineering industries in Scotland are collected by the Ministry of Public Building and Works.

(9) *See* R. S. Barclay, *Shetland Occupations*, The Shetland Times, 4 January 1957; Margaret C. Storrie, *The Census of Scotland as a source in the Historical Geography of Islay*, The Scottish Geographical Magazine, vol. 78, no. 3 (1962), pp. 152-65.

(10) *E.g.*, memoranda and articles of association, details of capital structure, details of directors and shareholders. In the case of public companies and non-exempt private companies there are also copies of the annual balance sheets and accounts. There are two separate alphabetical card indexes available—one relating to 'live', the other to dissolved companies.

(11) For full details of classes of records in the Scottish Record Office, *see* M. Livingstone, Guide to the Public Records of Scotland (1905); Scottish Historical Review, vol. 26, pp. 24-46 (list of subsequent accessions of public records down to 1946), and J. Maitland Thomson, Public Records of Scotland (1922). A list of main accessions is published each year in the October issue of the Scottish Historical Review. For official record publications, *see* H.M. Stationery Office, Sectional List, no. 24; for other record publications, *see* Handlist of Scottish and Welsh Record Publications (British Records Association, 1954).

(12) The section *Crown, Patrimony, Revenue, Exchequer and Treasury* in Livingstone's Guide to the Public Records of Scotland, pp. 28-76, is incomplete and suffers from defective classification. For the main records prior to 1707 *see* A. L. Murray *The Pre-Union Records of the Scottish Exchequer*, Journal of the Society of Archivists, vol. ii, no. III (April 1961), pp. 89-101.

(13) *See* T. C. Smout, *The Overseas Trade of Ayrshire, 1600-1607*, Ayrshire Archaeological and Natural History Collections, 2nd series, vol. 6 (1961), pp. 56-80; *The Development and Enterprise of Glasgow, 1556-1707*, Scottish Journal of Political Economy, vol. VII, pp. 194-212; and *The Trade of East Lothian at the End of the 17th Century*, Transactions of the East Lothian Antiquarian and Field Naturalists Society, vol. IX (1963), pp. 67-77.

(14) In terms of an Act of 1661 (Acts of the Parliaments of Scotland, VII, pp. 261-62).

(15) *E.g.*, window tax records, for counties and burghs, 1748-98; shop tax assessments, for various counties and burghs, 1785-89.

(16) Whaling bounty accounts for various ports, 1750-1831, give particulars of the catch for each ship.

(17) The Commissioners for the Annexed Estates also encouraged other industries, e.g., paper manufacturing, a tannery and brick works at Crieff, and a tannery and soap factory in Inverness. As well as supporting entrepreneurs, such as William Sandeman of Perth, to extend industry, the Commissioners, like the Board of Trustees for Manufactures and the Society in Scotland for Propagating Christian Knowledge, also instituted a system of apprenticeships in manufactures.

(18) The extant records of the Great Seal date from 1306.

(19) Of 177 patents recorded in Scotland up to 1847 only 47 were to Scotsmen.

(20) A number of Glasgow 'Tobacco Lords' bought estates. John Glassford purchased Dougalston in Stirlingshire in addition to his town house, Shawfield Mansion. Later industrialists, such as the Finlays and the Bairds, followed suit, as did those who made their money in the east, *e.g.*, Sir James Matheson who bought Lewis in 1844.

(21) *E.g.*, the growth of paper mills in the Edinburgh area in the eighteenth century (often by taking over existing corn mills); the expansion of large industrial concerns, such as the Carron Iron Company; or the process whereby companies acquired property for minerals in the nineteenth century.

(22) The extent to which the 12th Earl of Eglinton financed the building of Ardrossan Harbour by loans over his estate can be traced in detail in the Register.

(23) The Department of Social and Economic Research of Glasgow University have recently carried out from the Register of Sasines a sample survey of private houses in Scotland to find out how often owner-occupiers move and what prices they pay for their houses. Preliminary results indicate that houses change hands approximately every ten years and that there has been a fourfold increase in prices since the war.

(24) Considerable use has been made of the Valuation Rolls in recent years for such studies as the location and distribution of industry, the changing character of parishes, and the history of business firms not the owners of property.

(25) Indexes of pursuers only are available in the Scottish Record Office, but the printed Session Papers in the Signet Library, Edinburgh, are indexed not only by pursuers but also by subjects for the period 1713-1820. The subject index contains entries for such topics as: agency, apprentices, banks, bills of exchange, co-partnery, insurance, partnerships, patents, etc.

(26) Thereafter the confirmation of executors became a matter for the sheriff courts (*supra*).

(27) Indexes of persons (showing occupations) have been published by the Scottish Record Society for all Commissariots up to 1800. Typescript indexes for the period 1801-23 are available in the Scottish Record Office.

APPENDIX A

Business Archives in Scottish Record Office

The following list has been compiled from the inventories and hand-lists of business, private and local archives preserved in the Scottish Record Office. Uninventoried collections have not been included.

Abercairny muniments (GD 24)

Copy contract of co-partnership between David Drummond and Patrick Stewart on starting business as merchants, 1711 (No. 10).

Letters, accounts and other papers relating to the affairs of Mungo Graham, 1736-64, who, having been apprenticed to George Napier, merchant in St. Petersburg, traded from there to Persia and was killed in 1743 (No. 454).

Letters and papers regarding plantations in Jamaica, 1765-97 (No. 461).

Letters, accounts and other papers of John Drummond of Quarrell, merchant in Amsterdam, a director of East India Company, and commissioner for trade under the Treaty of Utrecht (1713), on business affairs including shipping to the Continent and East Indies, 1683-1745 (Nos. 464-99 and 829-30).

Dutch banker's day book, 1709-10 (No. 480).

Accounts, business papers and correspondence of George Drummond, merchant and provost of Edinburgh, 1715-65 (Nos. 833-51).

Papers relating to Queensferry Passage, 1809 (No. 919).

Railway papers, 1841-66 (Nos. 924-25).

Abercromby of Forglen muniments (GD 185)

Letter book of Douglas & Shaw, London, mainly on shipment of goods to New York, 1788-1806 (Box 38).

Submission and history of firm of Douglas & Shaw, 1823 (Box 40).

Account of cost of cotton mill at Newton Stewart. 1819 (Box 38).

Ailsa muniments (GD 25)

Contracts and accounts relating to linen manufactories at Culzean, Turnberry and Jamestoun, 1718-20 (Box 44).

Accounts of woollen manufactory at Maybole, 1749-51 (Box 44).

Tacks and other papers relating to coalworks at Altchealluly, Craigoch, Tradunoch, Dalzielily and Dalquherran, 1625-1812 (Box 46).

Airlie muniments (GD 16)

Letters, papers and accounts relating to estates of Kelty and Ferry Pen in Jamaica, 1812-73 (Sec. 27, Nos. 291 and 322).

Letters, reports and papers relating to Dundee and Newtyle Railway Company, Monkland and Kirkintilloch Railway Company, Newtyle and Glamis railway, Newtyle and Coupar Angus railway, Jamaica Railway Company, Scottish Midland Junction Railway Company, Great North of Scotland Railway, Alyth Railway Company, Erie Railway Company, Caledonian Railway Company, 1825-68 (Sec. 58, Nos. 77-87).

Airth muniments (GD 37)
Papers relating to export of coal, 1596-1619 (Nos. 312, 313 and 317).

Ayr burgh records (B 6)
Licensing records, 1785-1900.
Crafts and Guildry records: Wrights and squaremen, 1556-1724; Walkers (dyers and litsters), 1611-1853; Weavers, 1657-1792; Fleshers, 1661-1821; Dean of Guild, 1659-1825; Convener's Board, 1732-1904; Burgesses and Guildry minute books, 1817-1936.
Minute book of Committee of Undertakers for Coal in the Barony of Alloway, 1728-29.
Alphabetical List of Burgesses, *c.* 1760-1846.
Malt books, 1773-1811.
List of Magistrates and Councillors, 1686-1842 (including Register of Apprentices, 1691-1710).
Minute book of Magistrates and Council respecting the New Bridge, 1785-1831.
Ayr Bridge Trustees minute books, 1877-84.
Ayr Water Company minute book, 1835-48.
Ayr Merchant Company minute book, 1849-1907.
Fishing Company ledger, 1785-91.
Letter book and journal of Christopher Middlemass at Ayr, 1815-18.
List of Unfree Traders, 1840.
Documents relating to Incorporation of tailors in Ayr, 1614-1848.
Petitions to the dean of guild and guild council, 1745-82.
Letter to magistrates concerning Newton Coal Company, 1790.
Reports by Chamber of Commerce of Glasgow and case of the trading interest of Scotland relating to the Corn Laws, 1790.
Petitions to magistrates by weavers, etc., 1814.
Documents concerning mining operations of the Fort Colliery at Ayr, 1821-22.
Letter to the provost relating to coal working in the pit near the south quay of Ayr Harbour, 1826.

Baird of Saughtonhall muniments (GD 238)
Shipping papers, 1643-97.

Balfour-Melville muniments (GD 126)
Papers relating to Melville Hall estate, Dominica, and sales of sugar, rum, etc., 1760-1875.

Barcaldine muniments (GD 170)
Halbeath colliery and salt works accounts, 1798-1803.

Bargany muniments (GD 109)
Inventory of materials at Bargany coalheugh, 1762 (No. 3711).
Inventory of materials at Shalloch salt pan, 1762 (No. 3712).
Papers relating to lime craig on farm of Craighead in parish of Dailly, 1800-23 (No. 3768).
Note of Bargany coal journals, 1811 (No. 3791).
Report on lime quarries and copper mine (survey at Girvan for coal), 1819-22 (No. 3802).
Abstract expenditure on Bargany coalworks, 1822-23 (No. 3805).

Biel muniments (GD 6)
Papers relating to sugar works in Glasgow, 1671-75 (No. 1249).

Papers relating to coal and salt works of Innerwick and Thornton, 1678-1713 (Nos. 1251-66).

Blair of Blair muniments (GD 167)
Papers relating to Blair Iron Works, 1830-63 (Box 4).

Breadalbane muniments (GD 112)
Easdale Slate Quarry Company: Journals, 1745-74, 1792-1802 (12 vols.); Ledgers, 1792-94, 1796-1802 (10 vols.); Small slates books, 1793-1802 (5 vols.); Minute, remarks and observations, 28 August 1799; Letter books, 1818-20, 1823-47, 1860-70 (8 vols.); Bill books, 1825-49 (3 vols.); Accounts, 1817-62.

British Fishery Society papers (GD 9)
Minutes, ledgers, correspondence, accounts and other papers, including material on harbour construction (with letters and letter books of Thomas Telford), 1773-1877.

John C. Brodie, W.S., collections (GD 247)
Papers relating to copper mines at Currie, 1687-1771 (Box 13).
Letter book of W. H. Playfair, architect, 1830-33 (Box 100).
Letter books, accounts and other papers of Messrs. William Cunningham & Company, Glasgow, regarding trade with America, 1761-89 (Boxes 58, 59).
Plans of Melville Moor Coal, Pendrich Colliery, 1806, and Eldin Coal, 1820, and papers relating to Eldin Coal (Box 101).
Papers relating to Blair Adam coal. 1686-1800; letters to William Adam, architect, 1739-42 (Box 72).
Statements of produce of Prestonhall coal and related documents, 1810-13; papers relating to Prestonpans salt works, 1803-13, and Crichton Hope lime kilns, 1809-19 (Box 84).
Letter book, Brodie of Lethen to various correspondents on mercantile affairs, including trade in tobacco, salmon, etc., 1752-54 (Box 69).

Broughton and Cally muniments (GD 10)
Papers relating to Portpatrick Railway Company and Wigtownshire Railway, 1856-80 (Nos. 550-52).
Papers relating to Kirkcudbrightshire Mining Company and Cally Mining Company (copper and lead), 1845-58 (Nos. 1246-52).
Letters relating to Glasgow and South Western Railway, 1880-87 (No. 1418).

Bruce of Arnot muniments (GD 242)
Account current of linen manufactory and bleachery at Cupar, with list of proprietors, 1727-36.

Buchanan of Leny muniments (GD 161)
Shipping papers, letters and accounts of goods to and from Jamaica, 1736-40.

Bught papers (GD 23)
Papers relating to Brewery Company of Inverness, 1771-84 (No. D.198).
Papers relating to Clachnacuttin Friendly Society, Inverness, 1791-92 (No. D.215).
Letters and accounts on mercantile affairs of William Mackwerick and Gilbert Gordon, merchants in Inverness (skins, salmon, wine, tobacco, etc.), 1702-49 (App. I, Nos. 7-199).
Folio account book of Hugh Fraser, merchant in Inverness, for goods sold, 1723-49 (Additional, No. 521).

Burnett & Reid collections (GD 57)
 Papers relating to manganese mine at Grandhome, including valuation, 1808; statements of accounts, 1808-09; agreement for lease of mine, 1838; and tack of mine, 1840 (No. 358).

Burntisland burgh records (B 9)
 Guild Council book, 1617-1791 (including list of Guild Brethren, 1617-1828).
 Hammermen's minute book, 1648-1741.
 Documents relating to the Incorporation of Weavers, 1618-1864.

Campbell of Jura muniments (GD 64)
 Letters and papers on Jura Distillery, 1851-1904 (Nos. 122-130a).
 Papers concerning debt due by Robert Owen of Lanark Cotton Mills to Archibald Campbell of Jura and said Archibald's financial transactions with David Dale, merchant and manufacturer in Glasgow, including trust disposition by Robert Owen, rental of deceased David Dale's estate, memorial and queries for Archibald, minutes of trustees of David Dale, print of summons Royal Bank of Scotland and Stanley Cotton Mills Company, copy of contract of co-partnership of New Lanark Company, and miscellaneous correspondence, 1810-22 (No. 247).
 Draft memorial and queries for Archibald Campbell of Jura on management of his money matters by David Dale, and marriage of Robert Owen to latter's eldest daughter soon after sale of cotton mills to an English company, 1816 (No. 301).

Cardross writs (GD 15)
 Papers relating to coal and iron workings on Carnock estate, 1614-1806 (Nos. 895-904).

Carlops and Abbotskerse muniments (GD 65)
 Papers relating to Carron Company's lease of Carron harbour, Carronhall coal, and tracking on River Carron, 1765-1802 (Nos. 214, 230, 232, 242, 260 and 261).

Carron Company records (GD 58)
 Letter books, 1759-1807, 1836-62, 1878-81, 1884-85 (50 vols.).
 Account current ledgers 1786-1888 (26 vols.).
 Balance books, 1766-1891 (10 vols.).
 Abstract balance books, 1770-1815 (2 vols.).
 Invoice books, 1762-1813 (31 vols.).
 Stock books, 1768-69, 1772-93, 1798-1839, 1848-60 (16 vols.).
 Cash books, 1760-75, 1784-87, 1792-95 (10 vols.).
 Day books, 1764-69, 1779-81, 1794-97, 1802-16 (8 vols.).
 Weekly checks and oncosts book (coal and salt), 1760.
 Petty ledger, 1769.
 Inventories book (stock and effects), 1783-1802.
 Timber book, 1802-09.
 Stipends, etc., ledgers, 1833-46, 1860-69 (2 vols.).
 Bills payable ledgers, 1827-99 (2 vols.).
 Account book, 1852-1862.
 Wages book, 1879-96.
 Lands valuation books, 1897-1910 (2 vols.).
 Account book—household and personal of (?) Charles Gascoigne, 1757-64.
 Half-yearly accounts, 1877, 1896-1930 (72 vols.).

Reports on above, 1895-1922 (54 vols.).
Minutes of General Court, 1775-1940 (19 vols.).
Committee book No. 2, 1786-1813.
Record book (ironstone works), 1770-1810.
Drawing books, 1820-69, 1828-40 (2 vols.).
Designs, eighteenth-twentieth century (3 vols.).
Accounts and reports, 1759-1927.
Legal papers, 1756-1864.
Letters and statements relating to mineral fields (Quarrole, Cadder, Nether-croy), 1761-1890.
Articles of agreement and mineral leases, 1761-1833.
Contracts of copartnery, 1760, 1771.
Inventory of ballast, pig iron, etc., 1768.
Letter books, legal business, 1794-95, 1809-25 (2 vols.).
Inventory of goods at Carron Company's Leith Warehouse, 1827.
Journals and reports, 1827-60.
Letters, 1776-1868.
Minute book of Fifeshire Main Colleries Ltd., 1891-95.

Clerk of Penicuik muniments (GD 18)
Coal books, plans, cash books, ledgers, correspondence and other papers regarding Loanhead and Lasswade collieries, 1638-1909 (Nos. 988-1160, 2106, 2115).
Papers relating to Shotts Iron Company and minerals on Penicuik estates, 1869-1915 (Nos. 1155, 1161 and 1162).
Correspondence and memoranda relating to lease of Penicuik shale field to Midlothian Oil Company, 1883-1906 (No. 1157).
Papers concerning lease of bituminous shale deposits in Loanhead estate to the Clippens Oil Company, 1883-1910 (No. 1158).
Papers relating to lead mines in Dumfries-shire and Cornwall including papers on Craigtown Mining Company, 1712-1846 (Nos. 1163-1187).
Papers and letters concerning paper mill at Penicuik, 1707-67 (Nos. 889, 1317, 1320, 1323, 1324, 1328).
Letter books, account books, ledgers, stock books, and other papers of John Clerk, merchant in Paris and Edinburgh, 1627-76 (Nos. 2357-2567).
Accounts and papers concerning trading ventures, 1678-1720 (Nos. 2568-74).
Papers and letters relating to Wanlockhead lead mines, 1729-64 (Nos. 2633-83).
Letters and papers of Sir George Clerk as Under Secretary to the Home Department, Secretary to the Treasury, and Vice-President of the Board of Trade, containing papers on shipping, railways, banking, manufactures, printing, etc., 1823-48 (Nos. 3307-904).
Letters and circulation returns concerning Bank of Scotland, Union Bank of Scotland and Scottish banking system, 1857-59 (Nos. 3929-31).
Papers relating to Scottish banks, 1722-61 (Nos. 5873-84).
Papers on linen and woollen manufactures in Scotland, 1727-90 (Nos. 5889-951).

Closeburn writs (GD 19)
Contracts, inventories and valuations of Closeburn Limeworks, 1781-84 (Nos. 405-08).

C

Collins papers (GD 177)
Papers relating to Edward Collins & Company, paper-makers, Glasgow, from 1750.

Crail burgh records (B 10)
Craft minute books: Court books of Crafts of Crail, 1592-1743; Hammermen, 1588-1743; Cordiners, 1589-1743; Baxters, 1647-1743; Squaremen, 1668-1743; Tailors, 1684-1743; Coupars, 1690-1743; Weavers, 1694-1741.

Cunninghame Graham muniments (GD 22)
Papers relating to Culcreuch Cotton Company (spinning mill at Culcreuch and muslin manufactory at Glasgow), 1792-1802 (Sec. I, No. 219).
Papers relating to Edinburgh, Glasgow and Dumbartonshire Railway, and Forth and Clyde Junction Railway, 1845-59 (Sec. I, Nos. 591-5, Sec. II, No. 161).

Cupar burgh records (B 13)
Records of Incorporated Trades, 1650-1843. Guildry records, 1599-1838.

Dalguise muniments (GD 38)
Letters concerning William Creech, bookseller in Edinburgh, 1750-1820.

Dalhousie muniments (GD 45)
Papers of Earl of Dalhousie, as Vice-President and President of the Board of Trade, on railways, shipping, imports and exports, coal, etc., 1830-46 (Sec. 7, Nos. 1-76).

Dick-Lauder papers (GD 41)
Papers relating to copper mines at Currie, 1684-1757 (Nos. 242-46, 248, 431-42).

Dumfries burgh records (B 17)
Sederunt book of Company of Merchants in Dumfries, 1682.

Dunbar burgh records (B 18)
Licensing Court books, 1828-77.
Burgess books, 1691-1914.

Dundas of Dundas muniments (GD 75)
Papers relating to Bo'ness coal mines, 1738-41 (No. 530).

Dundas of Ochtertyre muniments (GD 35)
Papers relating to Glasgow Waterworks Company, 1846-53 (No. 226).

Dunfermline burgh records (B 20)
Dean of Guild Court minute book, 1753-78.
Accounts of coal work in the Muir of Dunfermline, 1671-74.

Dunglass muniments (GD 206)
Papers and letters (correspondents including George Stephenson) concerning construction of railway between Edinburgh, Berwick and Newcastle, 1838-47 (No. 63A/5).
Papers relating to coal mining at Cockburnspath and Dunglass, 1746-65 (Nos. 217-26).
Letters of Alexander Hall of East India Company on trade in Far East, 1749-64 (Nos. 499-502).

Dysart burgh records (B 21)
Burgess rolls, 1738-1927.

Edinburgh burgh records (B 22)
Register of Apprentices, 1583-1666.

Edinburgh and Leith papers (RH 9/14)
Papers relating to craft incorporations (*passim*).
Copy contract of copartnery for brewing, 1597.
Proposals to merchants of Edinburgh for setting up a factory for making woollen cloth and weaving silk stockings, 1681.
Proceedings against merchants of Edinburgh for importation of foreign manufactures, 1683 (53 docs.).
Papers relating to Merchant Company of Edinburgh, 1681, 1696.
Journal of voyage, Leith-Newfoundland, Barcelona, etc., by Edward Burd younger, merchant, Edinburgh, 1726-27.
Papers in action concerning Bank of Scotland and Bank Street, 1806-08.

Elibank muniments (GD 32)
Business correspondence of William Young, including papers on his agreement for supplying East India Company with opium, 1778-97 (Supplementary Bundles IV and VI).

Elphinstone muniments (GD 156)
Coal and salt grieves' books for Elphinstone colleries and salt pans, 1654-1719 (Box 11).

Falkland burgh records (B 25)
Minute book of Freuchie Equitable Co-operative Society Ltd., 1876-1912.

Forbes of Callendar muniments (GD 171)
Copper foundry wage books, 1778-90 (9 vols.); Letter book, 1778-82; Sale books, 1771-86 (9 vols.); Account books of stores supplied to various naval depots, 1777-90 (14 vols.); Metal books, 1777-85 (13 vols.); Order books, 1773-81 (12 vols.); Account book, Navy and Exchequer Bills, 1780-85.

Gordon Castle muniments (GD 44)
Miscellaneous papers relating to mines, 1726-1809 (Sec. 39).
Lochaber lead mines, 1756-57 (Sec. 39).
Papers relating to Ardonald lime works, 1796-1818, including pay books of lime workmen, 1803-06, and lime ledgers, 1802-07 (Secs. 39, 51, 52).
Letters relating to establishment of a mail coach on the North Road, 1777-1809 (Sec. 43).
Papers relating to Post Office mail coach tolls and acceleration of mails, 1838-44 (Secs. 42, 43).
Papers relating to Aberdeen Steam Company, 1840-41 (Sec. 43).
Railway papers, 1845-46 (Sec. 51).

Haddington burgh records (B 30)
Dean of Guild Court books, 1669-1818.
Burgess and Guild books, 1700-1887.
Craft minute books: Baxters, 1582-1684; Cordiners, 1605-1860; Fleshers, 1741-1836; Wrights and Masons, 1616-1807.
Papers and accounts relating to mainly Wrights and Masons, 1533-1915.
Apprentice register (Hume Donation), 1785-1869.

Hamilton Bruce muniments (GD 152)
Papers relating to East India Company, 1794-1813 (Nos. 36, 43-44 and 189).
Copy journal of voyage to East Indies, 1745 (No. 128).
Statistical survey of mining, agriculture, shipping, manufactures, etc., prepared *c.* 1842 (No. 161).
Letters regarding Bute Docks at Cardiff, 1825-55 (Nos. 196-98).

Hamilton-Dalrymple of North Berwick muniments (GD 110)
Memorials, etc., relating to rope manufactory at Glasgow, 1722-36 (No. 412).
Minute of court of directors of Royal Bank of Scotland, 1731 (No. 1149).
Lists (2) of names of adventurers in Bank of Scotland, 1730, 1734 [printed] (No. 1189).
Letters on various subjects including: letter from Alexander Dundas with memorial on appointment of agents for the South Sea Company at Barbados, 1721 (No. 1106); letters relating to Sir William Dalrymple's flax manufactory at Cranston, 1734-56 (No. 961); letters (4) from John Ross, secretary of Haddington Tarred Wool Manufactory, on its affairs, 1752 (No. 1023); letters and accounts concerning ship *Tamerlane* in which Sir Hew Dalrymple had a trading interest, 1752-55 (Nos. 633, 931).
Port book (in Dutch, with notes of many British shippers), 1718-21 (No. 1145).
Decreet arbitral relating to cargo of the *Providence* of Alloa, on voyage to Rotterdam, 1719 (No. 593).
Note of cost of freight to and from Bergen, N.D. (No. 1164).
List of brewers in and around Edinburgh, 1725 (No. 1147).
Papers relating to protest of Glasgow brewers against tax on beer, 1742-44 (No. 615).
Case of manufacturers and dealers in wrought silver plate, N.D. [printed] (No. 1209).
Papers relating to East Lothian and Merse Whale Fishing Company, 1756-57 (Nos. 636, 637, 1050).

Harwood writs (GD 53)
Papers concerning limestone quarry at Slitrighead, 1796-1800 (No. 237 1(e)).

Hay of Haystoun muniments (GD 34)
Papers relating to tobacco, plantations and cotton on island of Barbados, 1636-50 (Nos. 920-55).
Letter regarding shipping and fishing in Scotland, 1621 (No. 705).

Henderson muniments (GD 76)
Depositions in process concerning Clackmannan coal heuch, 1713 (No. 358).

Innes of Stow muniments (GD 113)
Letter books of George Innes, depute Receiver General, to James Douglas [later Douglas & Cockburn] in London, on remittance of land tax, window duties, etc., but also including correspondence regarding private financial transactions, 1747-76 (Nos. 86-89).
Account books of cashier of commissioners and trustees for improving fisheries and manufactures, 1728-80 (Nos. 152-74).
Balance books of Alexander Innes, teller of Royal Bank of Scotland, 1753-66 (Nos. 272-77).
Ledger of Alexander Innes as teller, 1748-80 (No. 278).
Letter books of George Innes as cashier of Royal Bank of Scotland, 1746-82 (Nos. 270-71).
Account book of Royal Bank ordinary and promissory notes, 1749-52 (No. 279).
Accounts current of William Alexander & Sons, merchants in Edinburgh, with Alexander Innes, teller of Royal Bank, 1752-61 (Nos. 280-281).

Progressive quarterly state of stock and profits of Royal Bank, with lists of proprietors of Royal Bank stock, 1764-89 (No. 283).

Cash book of miscellaneous expenses on Royal Bank affairs, 1755-60 (No. 284).

Letter books of Allan Whitefoord, merchant in Edinburgh, 1727-52 (Nos. 289-92).

Letter books of George Innes, deputy Receiver General, and cashier of Royal Bank, on public and private transactions, 1752-80 (Nos. 293-95).

Letter books, cash sales book, and ledgers of St. Christopher's Sugar Warehouse, Edinburgh, 1734-77 (Nos. 296-305).

Linen merchant's order book, eighteenth century (No. 323).

Merchant's notebook of accounts and memoranda, 1785 (No. 324).

Ship's book of the *Ann and Agnes*, containing accounts of expenses and freight charges on voyages to Europe and the Mediterranean, 1729-38 (No. 325).

Inverurie burgh records (B 36)
Licensing records, 1847-1912.

Irvine burgh records (B 37)
Dean of Guild processes, 1777-91.

Kinross House muniments (GD 29)
Papers of Sir William Bruce of Balcaskie as surveyor general regarding repair of Holyroodhouse, Bass, Dumbarton, Stirling, etc., 1671-79 (Nos. 92-103, and App. Nos. 1-5).

Letters from Edward Kennoway to his brother while an apprentice at Danzig, and trading in London, 1668-75 (Nos. 1959 and 2048).

Correspondence and other papers regarding trade with Mayne & Company, and Burn and Sons, both of Lisbon, 1784-97 (Nos. 2075, 2083 and 2085).

Letters from Thomas Graham, President of the Board of Revenue in Bengal, 1774-1818 (Nos. 2136-51).

Letters from John Graham on East India Company affairs, 1774-77 (Nos. 2121-35).

Kirkwall burgh records (B 44)
Dean of Guild Court book, 1672-1703.

Leith-Ross muniments (GD 186)
Account books (2 vols.) of George Ross of Clochan, merchant in Aberdeen, 1691-1705 (Box 12).

Leven and Melville muniments (GD 26)
Copy letter regarding weaving machines at Derby, *c.* 1718 (Sec. 13, No. 275).

Letter regarding method of manufacturing alkali from sea and rock salts, 1794 (Sec. 13, No. 287).

Papers and letters regarding Forth ferries, 1759-1841, and Fife roads, 1763-1846 (Sec. 12, Nos. 22 and 24).

Letters and papers regarding Cassingray, Carden, Prickhills, Markinch, Balgonie and Thornton coal works, Leven Iron Works, and Balgonie Iron Works, 1673-1823 (Sec. 5, Nos. 319-74).

Papers regarding the woollen manufactory at Newmilns, 1700-12 (Sec. 5, No. 675).

Lindsay muniments (GD 203)
Report on Cassingray and Belliston coal, 1790 (Sec. 11, No. 40).

Linlithgow burgh records (B 48)
  J.P. Court minute book, 1656-86 (including list of burgesses, 1665-1704).
  Craft Minute Books: Tailors, 1625-1847; Hammermen, 1749-87.
  Papers relating to Incorporation of Tailors of Linlithgow, 1744-1846.

Melville Castle muniments (GD 51)
  (Because of the wide scope of the material in this collection, only brief references can be supplied in this list.)
  Material relating to the East India Company and mercantile houses engaged in the East Indies trade, 1781-1860 (Secs. 3 and 4; Sec. 16, Nos. 83-86).
  Patronage, including applications from merchants, 1780-1882 (Sec. 6).
  Material relating to the following public undertakings: Glasgow New Gas Company, 1820 (Sec. 5, No. 104); Edinburgh Water Company, 1825 (Nos. 143, 146); Forth Ferries, 1808-26 (Nos. 576, 598, 599, 604, 613, 614); Glasgow, Paisley and Ardrossan Canal, 1813 (No. 582); Union Canal, 1817-19 (Nos. 585, 587, 591); Tay Ferries, 1819-30 (Nos. 594, 596, 619); Adrossan Canal Company, 1821 (No. 602); Leith Docks, 1824-36 (Nos. 607, 608, 610-12, 615, 617, 623); Johnstone-Ardrossan Railway, 1826 (No. 616); North British Railway, 1846-72 (Sec. 5, No. 627; Sec. 11, Nos. 136, 138, 153); suspension railways (Maxwell Dick, patentee), 1830 (Sec. 9, No. 489); Forth and Clyde Canal, 1789 (Sec. 5, Nos. 173-75).
  Material relating to the following trades, industries, manufactures and professions: banking, 1788-1875 (Sec. 1, Nos. 392, 394, 397, 401, 405, 414, 418, 428, 440, 447, 456, 457; Sec. 5, Nos. 83, 167, 170, 178, 179, 181, 183, 184, 189, 191, 202, 223, 231, 232, 234-38, 260, 275, 277, 284, 291, 296, 297, 299, 303, 310, 312, 317, 318, 320, 322, 331, 342, 343, 345-56; Sec. 9, No. 11; Sec. 10, No. 54); coal, 1784-1819 (Sec. 1, Nos. 356, 410, 411; Sec. 5, Nos. 168, 323, 326, 328; Sec. 11, No. 108); distilleries, 1793-1821 (Sec. 5, Nos. 192, 215-18, 224, 225, 227, 239, 245, 247, 248, 251, 253, 261, 263, 264, 272, 276, 283, 285, 288-90, 300, 301, 314, 316, 319, 321, 324, 327, 335, 336); fisheries, 1794-1843 (Sec. 1, Nos. 417, 437, 449, 452, 462; Sec. 5, Nos. 207-10, 233, 249, 257, 274, 279, 300, 340, 362); glass, 1793 (Sec. 1, No. 368); goldsmiths, 1818 (Sec. 5, No. 84); insurance, 1797-1811 (Sec. 1, Nos. 399, 400, 455; Sec. 5, No. 282); iron, etc., 1786-1819 (Sec. 1, Nos. 375, 450; Sec. 5, Nos. 241, 270, 271, 326; Sec. 10, No. 17); lime, 1809 (Sec. 1, No. 448); paper, 1807-60 (Sec. 1, Nos. 442, 449; Sec. 5, No. 155; Sec. 10, No. 52; Sec. 11, No. 122); pawnbrokers, 1792 (Sec. 5, No. 4); salt, 1791-1800 (Sec. 5, Nos. 182, 190, 201, 255, 259, 267); slave trade, 1792-1839 (Sec. 1, Nos. 363, 389, 391, 435, 441, 474; Sec. 5, Nos. 306, 355); sugar, 1792 (Sec. 1, No. 361; Sec. 5, No. 188); textiles, 1792-1868 (Sec. 1, Nos. 362, 376, 395; Sec. 2, No. 147; Sec. 5, Nos. 187, 212, 213, 265, 339; Sec. 11, Nos. 70, 152; Sec. 16, Nos. 23, 82, 89, 90); tobacco, 1775-90 (Sec. 1, No. 354; Sec. 5, Nos. 169, 174, 176); wine and spirits, 1795-1835 (Sec. 1, Nos. 463, 467; Sec. 5, Nos. 211, 240, 315, 337, 338, 344; Sec. 11, Nos. 33, 52, 64).

Mey muniments (GD 96)
  Letters and papers regarding quarries and shipping, 1858-87 (Box 24, No. 41).
  Papers regarding Caithness roads and railways, 1873-86 (Nos. 661-2).

Miscellaneous business records (RH 9/1)
  Ledger of Andrew Halyburton, 1492-1503.
  Shipmaster's memoranda book, 1589-1600.

Tailor's account book, 1598-1620.

Register and accounts of Tulliallan coal and salt works, 1643-48.

Accounts of Kincardine and Tulliallan coal and salt works, 1679-81.

Account books of George Dewar, vintner and wright in Edinburgh, 1673-77, 1691-1702.

Accounts of Torry coal and salt works, 1679-80.

Register of the coal works of Bonhard, 1701-02.

Miscellaneous deposits (GD 1)

Loch Etive Trading Company records, including tobacco accounts, 1720-89 (GD 1/2).

Shotts Iron Company sederunt and minute books, 1824-1936 (GD 1/3).

Letter books of James Hope, agent to Commissioners for making roads and bridges in Highlands, 1803-38 (GD 1/5).

Journals, day books, letter books and ledgers of William Macdonald, W.S., 1760-1816; account book and letter book of Grange estate, Jamaica, 1770-75; account books of Roderick McCraw, tailor in Edinburgh, 1757-73; Edinburgh's merchant's account book, 1764-74; Edinburgh whisky merchant's ledger, 1767-74 (GD 1/8).

Minute books of Ancient Fraternity of Free Gardeners of East Lothian, 1676-1953 (GD 1/10).

Minute books of Incorporation of Shoemakers of Haddington, 1707-1861 (GD 1/11).

Records of Incorporation of Tailors of Edinburgh, 1446-1881 (GD 1/12).

Documents relating to the Souters and Cordiners of Selkirk, 1535-1888 (GD 1/13).

Cordiner Craft minute books, Canongate, 1584-1773, 1843-52 (GD 1/14).

Documents relating to Cordiners Craft of Edinburgh, 1478-1760 (GD 1/15).

Specification by William Symington of Kinnaird for improvement of steam engine, 1802 (GD 1/17).

Shipping and trading papers, West Indies, 1738-88 (GD 1/32).

Minutes of Skinner Craft, Haddington, 1682-1801 (GD 1/39).

Records of Dean Orphanage, Edinburgh, 1733-86 (GD 1/40).

Papers relating to Capeldrae Colliery and to Westfield, Capeldrae and Bandrum minerals, 1869-1920 (GD 1/42).

Indentures for trades of blacksmith and shoemaker, 1822-39 (D 1/46).

Merchant's day book, 1659-84, and accounts of James Graham, merchant in Dundee, 1724-36, 1777 (GD 1/56).

Share books of East Linton Gas Company, 1848-1944 (GD 1/74).

Patent to James Morison, manufacturer, Paisley, for improvements in shawl-making, etc., 1836 (GD 1/108).

Invergarry Iron Works records, 1726-36 (GD 1/168).

York Buildings Society papers, eighteenth century (GD 1/170).

Subscription contracts for railway between Oban and Balloch, Scottish Western Railway), 1845 (GD 1/174).

Dissolution of co-partnery between Patrick Macleod and John Fraser of Bread Street, London, drapers and haberdashers, 1719 (GD 1/187).

Minutes of General Meeting of East Lothian Banking Company, 1822 (GD 1/265).

Letter book of Alexander Oliphant and Company, wine merchants, Ayr, 1766-71 (GD 1/306).

Patent to Joseph Swan, Glasgow, for invention of improvements in printing, etc., 1852 (GD 1/351).

Papers relating to Elphinstone Colliery, 1875-95 (GD 1/364).

Miscellaneous friendly society papers, 1794-1822 (GD 1/369).

Records of Irvine Incorporated Trades, 1646, 1756 (GD 1/374).

Papers relating to coalfields and coal mines in Newcastle area and in Bohemia, 1767-1952 (GD 1/378).

Bill book of Messrs. William Lambie, Moffatt and Aitken, architects, Edinburgh, 1859-81 (GD 1/412).

Papers in case J. M. Fraser and Company, Lisle, against Bell and others about Benjamin Bell's patented invention connected with furnaces and its use in France and Belgium, 1839-45 (GD 1/420).

Subscribers' agreements, etc., for Scottish railways, exchange, insurance and investment companies, 1845-68 (GD 1/421).

Miscellaneous papers (RH 9/18)

Company trading to Africa and the Indies: bonds by the partners; address by English Parliament to the King regarding the Company; printed list of subscribers, etc., 1695-98 (M.P. 5).

Spinning (wages) book, Anderson and Watson, Banffshire, 1757 (M.P. 11).

Account book of John Bredie, merchant, Saltmarket, Glasgow, 1670-82 (M.P. 23).

Papers of Andrew Brown, merchant, Edinburgh, 1688-1711.

Papers of Andrew Kemp, flesher, Edinburgh, 1696-1717.

Tailor's ledger used as a letter book by John Stewart, chirurgeon, Kinghorn, 1739-41 (M.P. 24).

Waste book and journal, 1728-34, with accounts, letters and other papers, 1720-40, of Edward Burd, wine merchant, Leith (M.P. 26-29).

Papers of Alexander Campbell, merchant in Edinburgh, and his brother, Dugald Campbell, merchant in London, 1661-1730 (M.P. 36-41).

Papers of John Charters, merchant, Edinburgh, 1674-90 (M.P. 53).

Papers of Arthur Clephane, seed merchant, Edinburgh, 1696-1730 (M.P. 54).

Part of co-partnery ledger of a colliery company, c. 1740 (M.P. 55).

Papers of James Craig, wigmaker, Leith, 1638-1740 (M.P. 59).

Papers of Andrew Downy, maltman, Burntisland, 1607-26 (M.P. 70).

Letters and accounts of James Elder, merchant, Aberdeen, 1747-68 (M.P. 71-72).

Bills, accounts and receipts, James Ewart, Royal Bank, Edinburgh, before 1760 (M.P. 74).

John Forrester, manufacturer in London—account books in London, 1742-43; in Cockspow, 1744-47; and in Stirling, 1748-49 (M.P. 82).

Papers relating to affairs of Andrew Gibson, sometime provost of Glasgow, 1705-19; Thomas Oswald, beltmaker, Edinburgh, 1671-88; and Robert Harris or Herries, merchant in Edinburgh, 1713-32 (M.P. 88).

Account books, memoranda books and other papers of John Hunter, merchant, Edinburgh, 1672-1710 (M.P. 133-35).

Business papers, letter books and account books of Robert Innes, writer in Edinburgh, 1650-1700, including papers of James Trumbull, watchmaker in London, James Reid, skipper in Leith, George and James Campbell, merchants in Edinburgh, and Andrew Brown, watchmaker, clockmaker to the King and to the town of Edinburgh (M.P. 136-54).

Journal and ledgers of James Ker, merchant, Edinburgh, 1688-93 (M.P. 162).

Papers of John and William Lamb, merchants in Edinburgh, 1625-1717 (M.P. 166-70).

Account book of Paul Lyll, merchant and 'customar' in Haddington, 1598-1602 (M.P. 174).

Papers of Alexander Pyper of New Grange, merchant, sometime in Montrose and afterwards in Edinburgh, 1656-1726 (M.P. 226-33).

Sederunt books of Newmilns Woollen Manufacturing Company, shareholders' receipt book, and other papers, 1691-1718 (M.P. 240).

Letters, accounts and other papers of Andrew Russell, merchant, Rotterdam, and his grandfather, John Russell, merchant burgess of Stirling, 1616-1702 (M.P. 258-65 and 380).

Papers of Sir James Stansfield relating to Newmilns Cloth Factory, Wanlockhead mines. Leith Glassworks, and Leith Brewery (M.P. 279).

Papers of John Hilston, merchant in Edinburgh, 1649-64 (M.P. 280).

Papers of James Wright of Loss including working of the mines at Logie and Loss, 1670-1769 (M.P. 292-96).

Account book, letters and papers of Thomas Young, merchant and provost of Dunkeld, 1633-1704 (M.P. 297-98).

Fife and Kinross Railway—subscription contract, December 1856 (M.P. 299).

Papers of George Mitchell, smith, Edinburgh, c. 1688 (M.P. 307).

Letters of William Caldwell, merchant, Leith, 1723-32 (M.P. 309 and 313).

Papers concerning Edinburgh Royal Exchange, 1700-04 (M.P. 311).

Papers relating to mercantile interests of Hog of Cammo, 1741 (M.P. 312).

Papers of John Trotter, elder and younger, merchants in Edinburgh, 1675-1716; John Blackie, merchant there, 1710-44; and glassworks at Morrison's Haven, 1709-16 (M.P. 316).

Letters and shipping papers of John Thomson. master of barque *Cingalese* of Glasgow, 1852-55 (M.P. 325).

Montrose burgh records (B 51)

Guild Court register of decreets, 1751-61.

Account Book of [Alexander] Erskine, merchant, 1704-52.

Morton muniments (GD 150)

Papers relating to roads and bridges, canals and ferries, 1718-1816 (Boxes 108-09).

Statements on export of wool and glass from Ireland and on iron trade between England and Ireland, N.D. (Box 110).

Papers relating to Longford coal works, 1798-1814 (Box 110).

Journals and account books of Dalachy Lime Works, Aberdour, 1792-1809 (Box 110).

Accounts and papers regarding Raw Camp Lime Works, 1791-1813 (Box 110).

Papers concerning oyster fishing in the Forth, 1735-93 (Box 115).

Yarn and linen account book, 1770-75 (Box 121).

Quarry accounts, 1787-93 (Box 121).

Papers regarding kelp, 1752-62 (Box 131).

Shipping papers, 1649-1848 (Boxes 132 and 143).

Company of Scotland trading to Africa and the Indies, 1669-1705 (Box 143).

Fishery papers, 1715-19 (Box 143).

Papers regarding the Distillery Bill, 1798-1811 (Box 144).

Carron Company papers, 1878-96 (Additional Box 29, **Bundle** 11).

Musselburgh burgh records (B 52)
Minute books of Fisherrow Harbour and Musselburgh and Dalkeith Water Trust, 1840-1900.
Craft Account Books: Wrights, 1668-1787; Hammermen, 1761-1827.

Perth burgh records (B 59)
Excise licences granted by J.P.'s, 1775-83.
Receipt books for wool and cloth, 1735-36, 1785-87.
Perth Steampacket Company minutes, 1822-25.
Guildry papers. 1600-1826.
Papers relating to Maltmen, Tailors, Glovers, 1701-84.
Papers relating to Perth Working Men's Building Society.
Note of cash lodged with Perth Banking Company, 1788-91.
Papers on Banking Companies in Perth, 1763-67.
Papers concerning Perth Printing Company, 1844.
Papers relating to ships *Eagle* and *Rose* of Perth, 1838-46.
Papers regarding navigation, 1724-1866.
Dyers' and merchants' book, 1703-50.
Papers on Scottish Central and other railways, 1845-60.
Papers regarding fisheries and manufactures of linen, 1726-1827.
Leather merchants' accounts, 1848-87.
Papers relating to Duff and Company, Bisset and Company, Morison and Company, merchants in Perth, late eighteenth-early nineteenth century.
Account book of Bailie Alexander Jamieson, merchant and shipowner, Perth, 1660-73.
Note of entries of burgesses and lists of guild brethren, 1684-1754.
Papers of John Glas, merchant, sometime provost of Perth, 1650-89.
Returns of the trades burgesses of Perth, 1832-33.
Contract of co-partnery of Central Bank of Scotland, 1834.
Prospectus and list of shareholders of Eastern Bank of Scotland, 1840-41.
Papers concerning Tailors' and Shoemakers' Incorporations, 1694-1835.
Papers regarding combinations of workmen, 1799-1803.
Contract of co-partnery, Caledonian Coach Company, Perth to Inverness, etc., 1825.
Stock books, Perth Stock Market, 1835-64.
Dean of Guild Court petitions, minutes, etc., 1772-81.

Reay muniments (GD 84)
Memorial regarding herring fishings, 1824 (No. 102).

Rollo of Duncrub muniments (GD 56)
Ledger of John Rollo, goldsmith, 1731-35 (No. V/1).

Ross muniments (GD 47)
Scheme for a linen manufactory, 1728 (No. 360).

Rosslyn muniments (GD 164)
Dysart colleries account book, 1776-80, and oncost vouchers, 1755-63.
Papers relating to production of salt, 1817.
Papers relating to Newhaven-Burntisland ferry, 1816-28.

St. Andrews burgh records (B 65)
Papers relating to salmon and mussel fishings, 1805-99.
Register of admission of burgesses, etc., 1766-68.
Returns of guild brethren, trade members, etc., 1818-43.
Dean of Guild court book, 1827-65.

Petitions to Dean of Guild, etc., 1762-1835.
Licensing Court Records, 1778-1908.
Guildry books, accounts and papers, 1604-1837.
Craft Minute Books: Seven Trades, 1594-1847; Maltmen, 1762-1849; Wrights, 1795-1869.
Papers relating to the Trades of St. Andrews, 1511-1884.
Harbour Trustees minutes, papers, etc., 1730-1895.

Scott of Raeburn muniments (GD 104)
East India Company papers, 1790-1800 (Box 14).

Seafield muniments (GD 248)
Papers relating to linen manufacture, 1727-54.

Seaforth muniments (GD 46)
Correspondence regarding Stornoway and Ness distilleries. 1818-35 (Sec. 1, Nos. 194-95, 198 and Sec. 13, Nos. 117-25).
Letters and papers on distilleries, timber, kelp, roads and railways, 1771-1853 (Sec. 1, Nos. 400-02, 453-539; Sec. 13, Nos. 1-51).
Papers relating to Muirkirk Iron Company, 1789-1827 (Sec. 2, Nos. 23-25 *and see* letter books below).
Papers relating to kelp (Sec. 13, Nos. 126-35).
Papers relating to fisheries (Sec. 13, Nos. 144-54).
Letter books. 1765-1829, containing correspondence on Muirkirk Iron Co., lead mines, kelp, coal mining, British Tar Company, fisheries, trade in U.S.A., Telford's offers on roads and bridges in Ross, open cast iron mine at Coltburn, wool trade, distilleries, harbours, etc. (Sec. 17).
Papers regarding East India Company, tea trade, and China trade, 1813-36 (Sec. 8).
Papers regarding Ceylon (coffee, machinery imports, etc.), 1824 (Sec. 9).
Papers regarding a fishing company (Lewis), 1631 (Additional).

Selkirk burgh records (B 68)
Craft Minute Books: Incorporations, 1717-1824; Cordiners, 1609-1835.

Shairp of Houston muniments (GD 30)
Papers regarding shale, coal and sandstone on Houston estate, 1866-1900 (Nos. 740-58).
Letters regarding trade in London and Holland, 1702-36 (Nos. 1552-54, 1578).
Letters from Walter Shairp, merchant in St. Petersburg and London, 1744-71 (No. 1583).
Letter on financial and estate affairs, including the African Company, 1708 (No. 1752).
Letters on roads, bridges, canals, and railways, 1672-1824 (Nos. 2149-74).

Skene, Edwards & Garson, W.S., collections (GD 244)
Letters and notes regarding granite and Rubislaw quarry, 1751-1829 (Box 5).
Report, Richard Whytock to James Skene, secretary to the Board of Trustees, on writer's visit to the Netherland's exhibition of arts and manufactures at Brussels, with pencil sketches of machinery, 1830 (Box 9).
Papers of Alexander Purdie, builder in Edinburgh, from 1798 (Box 15).
Papers relating to Lord Adam Gordon's engagements for Alexander Steven in building bridges in Roxburgh and Angus, 1778-85 (Box 19).

Executry papers of William Muirhead, merchant in Edinburgh, including inventories of his stock, 1789-93, and executry accounts, 1793-1801 (Box 36).

Sprot of Garnkirk muniments (GD 246)
Petty charges book of Garnkirk and Brodisholm Coal Company, 1847.

Stirling burgh records (B 66)
Licensing Court Book. 1759-1820.
Log Book of H.C.S. *Lady Melville,* 1819-21.
Dividend Book of Stirling Steam Boat Company, 1864-74, and papers relating to the Company, 1828-45.
Stirling Waterworks—estimates, contracts, accounts, etc., 1848-81.
Small account book of expenses in operation of a still, 1745-46.

Thomson, Dickson & Shaw, W.S., collections (GD 241)
Minutes and papers of North British Equitable Loan Company, 1824-27 (Boxes 11, 52-53).
Accounts of Conference sugar estate, Grenada, 1850-59 (Box 47).
Account of kelp manufacture, North Uist, 1808 (Box 51).
Executry papers of John Hunter, merchant in Leith, 1837-40 (Box 52).
Papers relating to affairs of Archibald Campbell, senior and junior, brewers in Cowgate and Chambers Street, Edinburgh, nineteenth century (Box 62).
Volume of disbursements for barque *Sir John Falstaff* for voyage U.K. to West Indies and back, 1853 (Box 62).

Tods, Murray & Jamieson, W.S., collections (GD 237)
Indentures, accounts of goods, letters, day book, cash book and ledger of Blackwood and Nisbet, merchants in Charleston, South Carolina, 1720-41.
Ledger of saddler in Edinburgh, 1780-95.
Papers concerning bankruptcy of Samuel and Francis Garbett and Charles Gascoigne, 1785.
Papers relating to Ludovic Grant and the Carron Company, 1777.
Company minutes of South Sugar House, Glasgow, 1777-79, and other business papers, 1736-72.
Sugar trading accounts of King Street Sugar House, 1768-69.
Legal papers and correspondence—Dixon & Co., Govan Colliery, Kilbagie Distillery, etc., eighteenth-nineteenth century.

Yule collection (GD 90)
Letters and shipping papers of John Adamson, shipmaster, Crail, 1661-1717 (Sec. 2, No. 88).

APPENDIX B

Business Archives in Court of Session Processes

The following list which is arranged under offices of the Court relates only to miscellaneous productions in the unextracted processes of the Court of Session and only to those items which have been identified with particular businesses. It may however be useful as showing something of the wealth and variety of material in the Court records for business history.

Adams Dalrymple
Bundles (24) of vouchers of account of John Nicol, cashier and manager for John Nicol and Company, contractor for the Glensheal, Rheabine, Dornie, Strathglass and Beauly roads, 1831-34 (Misc. Bundle 7).
Journal, ledger and letter book of Sibbald and Company, 1788 (Misc. Bundle 20/7).
Balance books and day book of Dumbarton Glass Company, *c.* 1831 (Misc. Bundle 22).
Waste books and ledger of Maxwell and Hunter, merchants in Dumfries (Misc. Bundle 24/4).
Cash books, ledgers and waste books of Dundas, Smith and Company, 1808 (Misc. Bundle 25/1).
Account book of R. H. Moncrieff and Company, 1851 (Misc. Bundle 25/2).
Waste books, journals, wages book and ledger of McCormick, 1790 (Misc. Bundle 26/1).
Plans: Cupar Waulk Mill (2), 1809; Grange Distillery, 1829.

Adams Mackenzie
Spirit order book of Allan and Company, 1797 (Misc. Bundle 15/2).
Shopkeeper's day books of David Crichton, 1793 (Misc. Bundle 15/3).
Merchant's account books of John McDonald, 1809 (Misc. Bundle 16/7).
Book of manifests of Union Shipping Company, 1816 (Misc. Bundle 17/4).
Journal of Thomas Webb and Company, 1810 (Misc. Bundle 17/6).

Currie Dalrymple
Ledger relating to Baberton Quarry, 1824 (Misc. Bundle 15/5).
Books of Cunninghame and Wallace, 1747 (Misc. Bundle 15/7).
Workmen's wage book—Caledonian Railway Company, 1854 (Misc. Bundle 16/4).
Account books of William and Robert Dalziel, Dumfries (Misc. Bundle 16/8).
Account books of Andrew Farquhar, merchant, Netherbow, 1765 (Misc. Bundle 17/5).
Account books of Glass Colliery, 1765 (Misc. Bundle 18/1).
Balance book of Samuel Garbett, 1797 (Misc. Bundle 18/4).

Order book of Glasgow and Ayrshire Railway Company (Misc. Bundle 18/5).

Account books, ledgers, letter books, etc., relating to the management by Jamieson, Lawson and Sample, Glasgow, of plantations in Maryland and Virginia, 1750-1817 (Misc. Bundles 19/2, 20/1, 21/1).

Minute Books in sequestration of Gavin Kemp and Company, 1785-86 (Misc. Bundle 22/1).

Account books of John and William Morrison, 1767 (Misc. Bundle 22/6).

Account books of James Milligan and Company, 1788-93 (Misc. Bundle 23/1).

Account book of Statute Labour Trustees of City of Glasgow, 1841 (Misc. Bundle, 25/8).

Log book of the brig 'Gem' of Peterhead, 1861 (Misc. Bundle 25/9).

Ledgers, journals, etc., relating to the Green Coal Company, 1795 (Misc. Bundle 26).

Minute book and ledgers in sequestration of Steven and Jamieson, 1851 (Misc. Bundle 27/7).

Minutes of directors of Edinburgh and Glasgow Railway Company, 1854 (Misc. Bundle 29/3).

Book relating to Woodlands Quarry, 1850.

Currie Mackenzie

Books relating to McDonald and Company, 1804 (Misc. Bundle 23).

Shields

Minute book of Wool Combers Society in Aberdeen, 1760 (Misc. Bundle 9/1).

Account book of Robert Baird, Rotterdam, 1708 (Misc. Bundle 9/4).

Spinning and reeling book of Douglas, Dale and McCall, 1800 (Misc. Bundle 10/3).

Books of James Elder, merchant in Aberdeen, 1760 (Misc. Bundle 11/1).

Books of David Henderson, tanner, Newburghshire (Misc. Bundle 13/3).

Volume relating to Ardrossan Canal Company, 1805 (Misc. Bundle 13/4).

Books of trustees of James Inglis, younger, merchant in Edinburgh (Misc. Bundle 13/6).

Volumes relating to Leadhills and Snarhead mines, 1840 (Misc. Bundle 15/3).

Account book of lead bought from George Lothian of Leadhills, 1716 (Misc. Bundle 15/6).

Books of Morrison, brewer, Dalkeith, 1794 (Misc. Bundle 17/1).

Notebooks and letters relating to sequestration of Norwich Bank, 1816 (Misc. Bundle 22/1).

Account book relating to the 'Providence' of Dundee, 1698 (Misc. Bundle 22/4).

Volumes in sequestration of Scott, Burt and Company, tanners in Kilconquhar, 1817 (Misc. Bundle 23/10).

Workmen's accounts in Shetland, 1821 (Misc. Bundle 23/11).

Ledger of Rainbow Coffee Room, 1829 (Misc. Bundle 24/1).

Volume relating to Tradeston Victualling Society, Glasgow, 1809 (Misc. Bundle 24/3).

Account books of John Wilson and Company, distillers, 1748-54 (Misc. Bundle 25/3).

Account books of David Young, merchant in Perth, 1758 (Misc. Bundle 25/6).

Plan: Sauchie Colliery, 1799.

Skene

Stock book of Forresters and Company, Glasgow, 1748 (Misc. Bundle 26/1).

Business books of Fairweather and Son, Dundee, from 1780 (Misc. Bundle 26/2).

Daybook of Messrs. Galbraith, 1797-98 (Misc. Bundle 27/3).

Daybook, ledger and wages book of Govan Dye Works, 1821 (Misc. Bundle 27/6).

Ledger of John Hunter, merchant, Edinburgh, 1810 (Misc. Bundle 28/4).

Day books of John Kerr, millwright, 1808-22 (Misc. Bundle 28/8).

Sederunt book of sequestration of Alexander McFarlane, cattle dealer, 1807 (Misc. Bundle 29/3).

Coal book of Milliken Colliery, 1839 (Misc. Bundle 29/5).

Account books of Andrew Meikle, tailor, Edinburgh, 1806-7 (Misc. Bundle 29/7).

Business books of Patrick Murison, brewer, Canongate (Misc. Bundle 30/1).

Letter book of Andrew Nimmo and Company, Grahamston Mills, 1805 (Misc. Bundle 31/1).

Sederunt book in sequestration of Robert Smith, merchant in Aberdeen, 1807 (Misc. Bundle 31/8).

Minute book of guild of wheelwrights and turners of Edinburgh from 1750 (Misc. Bundle 32/1).

Sederunt book in sequestration of William Young, coalmaster, Glasgow, 1827 (Misc. Bundle 32/5).

Books of Thomas Kennedy, stockbroker in Glasgow (Misc. Bundle 36).

Plan: Springfield Works, 1835.

Potts

Books of James Aitken relating to the carriage of goods between Edinburgh and Glasgow, 1800-8 (Misc. Bundle 12/2).

Books of Skein, Dewar and Company (Misc. Bundle 15/1).

Day book of James Jeffrey, draper, North Bank Street, Edinburgh, 1819-26 (Misc. Bundle 24/4).

Plan: Factory in Linktown of Kirkcaldy.

Drysdale

Sederunt book of sequestration of Balgonie Iron Company, 1812 (Misc. Bundle 16/2).

Books relating to Beauly Distillery, 1824 (Misc. Bundle 16/5).

Business books of Walter Henderson and Company, 1857 (Misc. Bundle 19/1).

Books relating to the 'Inverness Journal', *c.* 1832 (Misc. Bundles 33 and 34).

Plans: Mills of Perth, 1787; Salin Mill, 1857.

CHAPTER TWO

Historical Business Records in Private Hands Surveyed by the National Register of Archives (Scotland)

A. M. BROOM

*Secretary, National Register
of Archives (Scotland)*

A. ANDERSON

*Assistant Keeper of Historical Records,
Scottish Record Office*

THE NATIONAL REGISTER OF ARCHIVES (Scotland) was begun in 1946 to supplement the work of the National Register of Archives in London, established in the previous year under the auspices of the Historical Manuscripts Commission. The principal aim of the Scottish Register is to obtain details of manuscripts of historical interest in private hands in Scotland, and to compile a Register by which these details may be made available to research scholars.

The Secretary of the Register, who does the actual work of compilation, is responsible to a small Directorate representing Scottish record interests generally; and a close liaison is maintained with the Scottish Record Office, where the surveys of the Register are kept. The staff of the Record Office have been of great assistance to the Secretary in building up the Register to its present sizeable proportions.

Since 1946 a great deal has been achieved. Large quantities of material of value for historical research have been found and their particulars entered in the Register. Owners have been encouraged to give proper consideration to the storage of their records. And, most important, research scholars have been able to make good use of source material which might otherwise have been lost or destroyed. Generally, owners have co-operated willingly by allowing access to their records for research purposes, especially after assurances that there is no intention or desire to interfere with their rights of ownership. Moreover, they have come to realise that the Register, by dealing direct with enquiries about particular collections, can save them from a considerable amount of trouble and inconvenience. Similarly, scholars appreciate that an enquiry to the Register may save them from much fruitless searching for sources; and even when no information is available, they may rest assured that if material relative to their subject should turn up in any future survey, they will be informed of the fact by the Secretary.

Copies of the Secretary's biennial Report to the Directors, containing abstracts of all the surveys which have been prepared since the previous Report, are circulated to university libraries and learned institutions all over the world; while the full surveys themselves are available for consultation in the office of the Register in H.M. General Register House, Edinburgh. It is hoped to introduce a more comprehensive programme of publication in the near future.

For many years, the Register has concentrated almost exclusively on family muniments and the contents of law agents' strong-rooms, but now, in association with the Business Archives Council of Scotland, attention is being increasingly given to the private records of business firms. As a result, much important material for the economic historian will probably be revealed in the next few years. Details of business sources already reported on in the surveys of the Register are meanwhile shown in the Appendix to this note.

Further information about the Register will gladly be given by the Secretary, National Register of Archives (Scotland), H.M. General Register House, Edinburgh, 2.

Business Records Surveyed by the National Register of Archives (Scotland)

N.B. Enquiries for access to any of the material listed should be made in the first instance to The Secretary, National Register of Archives (Scotland), H.M. General Register House, Edinburgh, 2, and *not* to the owner or agent concerned.

Anstruther, Sir Ralph, of Balcaskie, Pittenweem, Fife
 Miscellaneous papers regarding stock in the woollen manufactory at Newmilns, 1680-95.

D

Plans of lands and colliery in Pittenweem, 1788.

Argyll, Duke of, Inveraray
Report and annotated plans of the coal deposits near Campbeltown, 1752.
Report by John Paton, overseer of the coalworks at Lightburn, on dis-coveries of coal in the Ross of Mull, 1753.
Report of a survey of the coal discovered in the Isle of Mull, 1757.
MS. 'An essay on Kelp, containing the rise and progress of that manufacture in the North of Scotland; its present state and the means of carrying it to a greater extent', 1788.

Askew, J., Ladykirk, Norham-on-Tweed
Letters and papers regarding East India Company's trade with China, 1787-1831.
Log books and journals of H.E.I.C. ships to Cape of Good Hope and China, 1802-21.
Letter book (copies) from merchants in Holland and London on Hopetown lead mines, eighteenth century.

Auchenharvie Estate per W. D. Kerr, Saltcoats
According to Mr. Kerr the estate papers give the history of Saltcoats harbour, the local coal pits and salt works.

Balfour of Balbirnie, Markinch, Fife
Coal-mining plans, 1752-1882.
Plan of Balbirnie Paper Mill and Wool Mill, 1905.
Railway plans, 1854-95.
Letters regarding Balbirnie Paper Mill with calculations of the cost of pro-duction, 1833.
Letters regarding Cadham and Auchmuty coal, 1833-34.

Bell-Macdonald of Rammerscales
Letters and accounts regarding the Western Bank, Glasgow, and its failure, 1850-63.

Bethune of Balfour MSS.—Mrs. Spicer, Ardtur, Appin
Minutes of barony court of Kilrynnie, mainly regarding the harbour and teind fish, 1625-75.
Rental of some mills in Tyre water, seventeenth century.
Memoranda and accounts regarding the interest of J. E. D. Bethune as partner in Perkins, Bacon and Co., 1850-53.

Blair, Sir James Hunter, Bt., Blairquhan, Maybole
Journal and ledger of James Hunter, bankers in Edinburgh, 1768-79.
Letters by William Logan and others relating to John Loudoun Macadam, 1778-86.
Letters and papers relating to the banking firm of Hunter & Co., Ayr, 1773-75.
Letters from Adam Smith, John Loudoun Macadam and others, 1774-86.

Blairs College, Aberdeen
Merchant's account book, 1689.

Bruce-Gardyne of Middleton, Friockheim, Forfar
Paper on Projected canal from Arbroath to Rescobie, 1788.
Papers regarding a lint mill and its water supply, 1775.
Papers regarding freestone quarry (with plans of 1840 and 1841), 1840-55.

Buccleuch, Duke of, Bowhill House
Tailor's account book, 1681-85.

Journal of mineral observations on Queensberry estate in Selkirk and Roxburgh, 1816.

Buccleuch, Duke of, Dalkeith House
Papers *re* financial administration of Charles Townshend, 1744-67. Papers relating to Scotland include returns of quantities of spirits distilled, 1744-57, and account of linen industry in Scotland, 1727-54.
Sheriffhall Colliery coal books, 1671-1805.
Coudon Cleuch Colliery coal books and cash books, accounts and other papers regarding Granton Harbour, 1712-41.
Map of projected railway between Berwick and Glasgow, 1810.
Plans relating to Granton and Granton Harbour, 1835-44.
Railway plans—Caledonian, Hawick and Carlisle, Glasgow and South Western Railways, Caledonian and Granton Junction, 1846-47.
Reports *re* Barrow Haematite Steel Co., 1865-84.
Reports, leases and letters *re* Dalkeith minerals leased to A. G. Moore & Co., 1903-23.
Canonby coal accounts, 1769.
Papers relating to Sheriffhall coal, 1694-1804.
Letters and accounts *re* Wanlockhead lead mines, 1823-63.
Letters *re* proposed railway from Hawick and Carlisle, 1852-53.
Letters, accounts and returns *re* Dalkeith Colliery, 1838-74.
Returns of Queensberry silver and lead mines, 1865-99.
Letters and accounts *re* Smeaton tile works, 1849-76.
Accounts of Dalkeith tile works, 1850-67.
Letters on affairs of Douglas Heron & Co., 1788-93.

Buccleuch, Duke of, Drumlanrig Castle
Wanlockhead lead mine accounts, 1723-75.
Account book and journal of above mine, 1748-56.
Burnfoot Colliery accounts, 1730.
Smelt book of bar lead raised and smelted at Wanlockhead, with accounts current, 1755-79.
Memorials, resolutions, minutes of directors, and other papers regarding the Darien Scheme, 1701.

Campbell of Dunstaffnage
Letters, account books and other papers regarding mercantile activities of Peter Cameron in H.E.I.C.S. on voyages to India, Malaya and China, 1806-27.

Campbell of Inverneill, Ardrishaig, Argyll
Register book kept by Mrs. James Campbell, spinning mistress at Inveraray, 1751-57.

Campbell, Sir George, of Succoth, Bt., Crarae Lodge, Inveraray
Forth and Clyde Canal letters and papers, 1769-1880.
Papers regarding mills on the river Kelvin, 1816-20.

Carnegie of Lour, Forfar
Memorial and queries for opinion of Counsel concerning the Dundee Banking Co. and the management thereof, 1802.

Carnegy-Arbuthnott of Balnamoon
Papers of a Cambridge draper's cash book, 1580.
Archives of the trading house of Carnegy and Shepherd, Gothenburg, Sweden, mainly trading in iron, timber and herring, comprising letter

books, letters, charter parties, accounts, order books, etc., 1771-79. A photostat copy is in the Register of a list of these papers with an index of correspondents. Papers are at present on temporary loan to Gothenburg.

P. R. Chalmers of Aldbar, Aldbar Castle, Brechin

Merchant's account book of Messrs. Cattenach, London, 1736-50.

Waste book, journal and ledger of Patrick Chalmers, London, with details of trading voyages to Jamaica, Antigua, Lisbon, etc., 1755; papers of Patrick Chalmers, merchant at London, and firm of Chalmers & Guthrie, merchants at London, including account book 1800-03.

Papers in process, Anderson and others, merchants in Dundee, against Chalmers & Guthrie, 1824-26, and including letters from James Bryce and James Ewing, Trinidad, on sugar, coffee and cocoa shipment, 1805; also Robert Fleming, Trinidad, on sugar, 1819; Francis Phillips, Manchester, on yarns for Russia, 1820. Thomas Inglis, India, on trade, 1809-27; and John and Robert Inglis, India and Canton, on trade 1826-41.

Christie of Bedlay

Bookseller's stock and account book, 1785-1810.

Account book of stock of John Christie (soap and candles), 1791.

Minute book of Bedlay Mill, 1807-42.

Cochran-Patrick of Ladyland

Merchant's account book (Irvine?), 1714-15.

Ledger, 1736, and waste book, 1741, of William Cochran of Ladyland, merchant in Irvine, dealing in linen and other fabrics, lead, leather, indigo, sugar and pimento. With another waste book, 1781, with notes of cargo to the West Indies, Philadelphia, etc.

Condie, Mackenzie & Co., W.S., Perth

Records of the glover incorporation of Perth.

Cumming, Sir William Gordon, Bt., Blairs House, Altyre

Memorial regarding copper mines, N.D.

Memorial regarding the mines of Scotland, N.D.

Payments to Adventurers to Canada, 1629.

Articles of agreement between Sir Robert Gordon and the makers of the sea pump, 1687.

Dalmeny Glebe per Hope Todd & Kirk, W.S.

Correspondence regarding Dalmeny Glebe freestone quarry outputs, 1879-1909.

Darroch, D., of Gourock, Swanston Cottage, Lothianburn, Edinburgh

Papers regarding water and gas supply, harbour and railway of burgh of Gourock, 1771-1884.

Volume containing invoices of goods shipped to Jamaica, 1779-81.

Minute book of coal committee for searching for coal in neighbourhood of Greenock, 1824-26.

Davidson & Garden, advocates, 12 Dee Street, Aberdeen

Aberdeen Herald

Minute books, wages receipt book, dividend receipt book, vouchers of accounts and papers concerning the legal and financial affairs of the Aberdeen Herald newspaper, 1833-77.

Bon Accord Distillery Co. Ltd.

Letter books, minute books, invoice books, day books and sales books from 1876.

Davidson and Co., Papermakers
Papers and accounts regarding Mugiemoss Paper Works from 1869.

D. Forbes (decd.), Migvie House. Aberdeen
Papers of Captain D. Forbes consisting of accounts and letters regarding trading voyages to the East, 1865-70, including letters from Alexander Matheson, and Matheson & Co., Hong Kong.

Gordon Paper Mills
Papers in liquidation of Gordon Mills Paper Co., 1810-95.

Alexander Hall & Sons, Shipbuilders, Aberdeen
Accounts, letters, plan of building yard and other papers from 1859.

Hay of Seaton
Letters and papers concerning the financial affairs of Bayne and Forbes, Calcutta, 1771-81.

James Keith's Trust
Papers regarding the North West Company and Hudson Bay Company, 1802-51.

Milne of Craigellie
Business correspondence, 1827-47.
Cash books, 1829-48, including note of goods landed on ships at Glasgow, 1840-41.
Letters on mercantile and shipping affairs, 1795-1827.

Morehead of Herbertshire
Papers regarding Stoneywood Paper Mill, 1801-09.
Plan of Herbertshire Printfield, 1815.

Pirie and Sons, Papermakers
Mainly legal papers but relating to Union and Woodside Paper Works, nineteenth-twentieth century, but including volume containing prices of machinery, notes on machinery, calculations regarding water supply, etc., 1818-21.
Stoneywood Paper Works invoice book from 1898.

Miscellaneous Papers
Contract of co-partnership of Edinburgh Life Assurance Company, 1823.
Papers in process Sir William Forbes, James Hunter & Co., bankers in Edinburgh, against the North British Insurance Co., 1830-31.
Trust volume of Josiah Maxton, saddler in Edinburgh, 1829-78, and trust volume of John Maxton, merchant in Leith, 1865-71, with his ledgers and letter books, 1843-64, and miscellaneous papers from 1820.
Account book of sale of cotton, indigo, pepper, hides, etc., from India, giving name of ship, freight and other charges, 1834-37. At Glasgow.
Ledger of David Stephen, merchant in Aberdeen, 1813-28.
Account book of David Robertson, druggist in Aberdeen, 1830-32.
Diary of journey to China and trading there, 1832-33.

Don-Wauchope of Edmonstone per Campbell & Don-Wauchope, W.S., Edinburgh
Papers and account books regarding Edinburgh and Dalkeith Branch Railway, 1819-58.
Papers regarding Niddry and Benhar colleries, nineteenth century.

Douglas, J. M. P., of Cavers, Midgard, Hawick
Abstract of the books of the African Company and state of the debt due the Company, early eighteenth century.

Dunbar, J. B., of Pitgaveny, Elgin
  Day books, letter books, account books, ledgers, ships' logs, correspondence and miscellaneous papers regarding trade by Brander and Co. with Portugal, France and Russia, 1770-1803.

Dundas of Arniston, Arniston House, Gorebridge
  Colliery account books of Newbyres, 1620-1770.
  Plans of Stobhill Colliery and coal seams, 1791-1802.
  Reports and letters regarding Stobhill Colliery and the branch railway to Newbattle and Dalhousie Mains, 1746-1833.
  Stobhill weekly coal account book, 1752-62.
  Stobhill Colliery, work book, 1770-75, cheque bill produce books, 1793-1804.
  Letters, reports and other papers regarding Polton and Largoward Colleries, 1847-84.
  Reports and plans of Arniston Colliery and Esperston Limeworks, 1851-88.

Dundee, Earl of, Birkhill, Cupar
  Papers (mainly printed) regarding failure of Douglas, Heron & Co.'s bank, 1788.

Dundee Guildry Records per J. Murray Wilkie, 27 Bank Street, Dundee
  Cash books, sederunt books, petitions and financial papers, 1696 to nineteenth century.

Dundee Weaver and Tailor Trades per J. A. Graham & Forbes, 2 Union Street, Dundee
  Weaver trade
  Locket books, 1557-1762.
  Minute books, 1760-1897.
  Account books, 1752-1951.
  Miscellaneous papers, 1592 to twentieth century.
  Tailor trade
  Minute books, 1764-1955.
  Account books, 1729-1880.
  Entry books, 1637-1735.
  Miscellaneous papers, 1556-1842.

Ewart Library, Dumfries
  Incorporated trades
  Minute book and accounts of the Seven Trades of Dumfries, 1612-1847.
  Minute books and accounts of fleshers, 1658-1848.
  Minute books and accounts of glovers and skinners, 1650-1848.
  Minute books of hammermen, 1703-1868.
  Minute books and accounts of shoemakers, 1658-1867.
  Minute books and account of wrights, 1725-1848.
  Minute book and accounts of tailors, 1732-1864.
  Minute books, accounts and day books of weavers, 1654-1890.
  Martin Mss.
  Business correspondence of John Martin, merchant in Dumfries, with correspondents in Scotland, England, and Ireland, 1648-93.

Findlay, Mrs. M. S., Carnell, Hurlford, Ayrshire
  Letters to Thomas Wallace, merchant in Glasgow, on legal, financial and business matters, some relating to trade with Guinea and the West Indies, 1720-43.

Papers relating to the Union Canal, 1818-22.
Papers relating to Hilderston Colliery, 1825-68.
General state of Hilderston coal, 1766.

Fletcher of Saltoun [now in National Library of Scotland]
Letters regarding the trustees for manufacture in Scotland, South Sea Company, British Linen Company (c. 1750), Woollen Company, Haddington (1755-59), and whale fishing, Campbeltown (1750's).

Gordon of Letterfourie
Business papers and letters of Gordon & Co., wine shippers, Madeira, including correspondence with Britain, Sweden, Holland, Denmark, Germany, the West Indies, and America, and copies of the firm's journal, 1760-88. The correspondence gives details of trade in various commodities (*e.g.*, iron and herring from Sweden) and contains references to trading conditions in the various countries.

Grant of Monymusk
Papers regarding Strontian lead mines, 1730-66.
Cash books, ledgers, invoice books and correspondence of Hassall & Wagstaffe, and Hassall & Walton, merchants in Jamaica, 1731-52.
Letters and papers on flax spinning, 1749-50.
Letters regarding whale fishing and the state of that industry, 1756-59. Also journal of voyage from Aberdeen to Greenland, 1756.
Report by Commissioner of Customs in Scotland on frauds in the tobacco trade; answers of Glasgow merchants; and observations on Gould's scheme for preventing such frauds, 1721.
Memorial on Scottish fisheries, eighteenth century.
Papers regarding British Linen Company, 1750.
Proposals for setting up a linen manufactory at Aberdeen, 1762.
Papers regarding the supply of wood to ironworks, 1762-68.
Papers regarding proposed ironworks at Monymusk, 1764-70.

Grant of Rothiemurchus
Letters and papers regarding manufacture of log water pipes from Rothiemurchus for London's water supply, eighteenth century.

Greenfield of Fascadale, Ardrishaig
Letters from Gillean Maclaine, founder of firm of Maclaine Watson & Co., Batavia, Java, early nineteenth century.

Hog of Newliston per Pearson, Robertson & Maconochie, W.S., Edinburgh
Newliston Shale Oil papers, late nineteenth-twentieth century.
Diary and book of business of Roger Hog as a director of the Bank of Scotland, 1770-71.

Hope, Sir Archibald, of Craighall, Pinkie House, Musselburgh
Cash book concerned with Sir Alexander Hope's interest in lead workings, transactions involving Lead Ore Company and the shipment of lead to Holland, 1662-71.
Papers relating to collieries at Wallyford, Pinkie, Newcraighall and Sheriffhall, from 1808.
Account books of salt making at Pinkie Pans, 1791-1856.

Hopetoun Trust, Hopetoun House, South Queensferry
A list was supplied by Dr. Smout of the Department of Economic History, Edinburgh University, of the lead-mining papers at Hopetoun House, 1625-1799. These include reports of visits to Leadhills, 1638-41; work

journals, 1641-52; contracts, correspondence and accounts regarding sale of lead in Holland, 1641-1789; account books of Alexander Tait, merchant in Leith, showing sales of ore to Holland, Dunkirk and to Scottish 'pig makers', 1649-76; wage books, 1662-1768; account of visit to lead mines in Flint and Derbyshire, 1688; report by R. E. Raspe on the Susanna vein at Leadhills, with drawings of winding equipment proposed, 1792; sketch map of the veins at Langcleuch, 1756; leases and other papers of the Scotch Mines Company, 1731-72; papers relating to social improvements at Leadhills, 1786-91; plans of mines, 1773-80; and Scotch Mines Company concession, 1817.

Hornel Library, Kirkcudbright
Journals of Wanlockhead lead mines, 1755-1811.
Merchant's letter and account book of goods shipped to and from Liverpool and Glasgow, 1781-89.
Kirkcudbright Trades Minute books and boxmasters' books:
Hammermen and Glovers, 1749-1825.
Shoemakers, 1770-1947.
Squaremen, 1734-1820.
Tailors, 1733-1897.
Weavers, 1756-83.
Incorporated trades, 1707-1927.

Lauderdale, Earl of, Thirlestane Castle, Lauder
Papers regarding coalheugh of Wolmet, 1633.
Plan and report on silver mine near Stirling, 1716-17.

Lindsay-MacDougall of Lunga, Ardfern, Argyll
Correspondence and accounts relating to trade in kelp in Scotland, England and Ireland after 1765.

McCash & Hunter, Solicitors, Perth
Court book, minute and account books of baker incorporation of Perth, 1679-1919.
Convener's Court of Perth minute books, 1628 to date.

Marshall, P., 140 Wedderlea Drive, Glasgow
Diary and letter books of Sir James Hope regarding lead exports to Holland from Leadhills mines, 1646-61.

P. Maxwell Stuart of Traquair, Traquair House, Innerleithen
Brown of Milnehead papers at Traquair include an interesting series of letters, 1704-21, to John Brown, merchant in Liverpool, about transactions in sugar, cotton, tobacco and other commodities. The letters originate in various locations, such as Virginia, Jamaica, Lisbon, Gothenberg and Dublin.

Meiklejohn, D., 16 Central Avenue, Grangemouth
Plans of Forth and Clyde Canal and Grangemouth and Bo'ness docks, 1761-1895.

Moray, Earl of
Papers regarding coal working at Kilrenny, Kelty, Cuttlehill and Bucklivie, 1583-1842.
Papers regarding railways: Great North of Scotland, Newcastle and Edinburgh, and Inverkeithing and Halbeath, 1833-46.
Report by Robert Stevenson on the opening of the valleys of Strathmore and Strathearn by railway or canal, 1822.

More-Nisbett, The Drum, Gilmerton, Edinburgh
Annual reports and other papers *re* railway companies, canal companies, Tontine Society, gas companies, etc., 1824-49.
Sketch of proposed railway to connect Upper Coal district of Lanarkshire with Glasgow, 1828.
Plan of canal from Glasgow Bridge to Campsie, 1836.
Papers regarding Cairnhill mineral field, 1859-84.
Statements of output from Kipbyre Colliery, 1871-72.
Statements of output from Dykehead, 1874-77.
Statements of output from Gartness, 1878-79.
Journal of No. 1 Bore, Dykehead, 1880.

Messrs. Neill & Co., Printers, Causewayside, Edinburgh
Most of the archives of this firm were destroyed by fire in 1916, and remainder consist of writs of subjects in Canonmills, 1641-1797, and a few accounts and letters regarding the business, 1759-1879.

Noble, Sir Humphrey, of Ardmore, Bt.
Agreement. letters and accounts regarding trading in lumber from Mississippi, 1776-78.
Papers of Sir Andrew Noble, 1st Bt. (1831-1915), chairman of Sir W. G. Armstrong & Co.

Pringle, J. W., 13a Market Street, Haddington
Minute books of the incorporation of hammermen of Haddington, 1627-1806.

Robertson-Aikman, W. H., The Ross, Hamilton
Ship log books and ledgers of E.I.C. ships, 1775-1837.
Accounts, letters and papers of John Aikman, merchant in Leghorn, 1737-63.

Scott, C., of Gala, Galashiels
Proposals for a [Scottish] Guinea trade, 1700.
Letters regarding proposed copper mining operations at Makerstoun, early nineteenth century.

Scott-Kerr, W. F., Sunlaws, Kelso
Letters from Lord Charles Murray regarding lead mines in Perthshire, 1726.

Scottish Australian Company, Sydney, New South Wales
Letters and letter books of correspondence with Aberdeen, Edinburgh and London, 1838-70.

Sempill, Lord
Papers regarding linen industry in Scotland, 1644-1760.

Shaw, David W., & Co., Solicitors, Ayr
  Lanemark No. II
  Papers relating to Lanemark Coal Co., including articles of association, minutes of meetings, contract of copartnery, reports on the colliery, coal and output statements, legal papers and correspondence, 1864-1909.
  Auchinleck
  Mineral leases and related papers, 1887-91.
  Papers *re* dispute with Glasgow and South-Western Railway, 1890-1901

Dalmellington Iron Coal Co. Ltd.
Lordship statement books of Sundrum minerals, 1898-1917.
Railways
    Papers regarding Ayr and Dunglass Junction Railway and branches, 1864-68, and Scroll minute book, 1864-65.
Shewalton (Earl of Glasgow)
    Papers re mineral leases, dispositions to Glasgow, Paisley, Kilmarnock and Ayr Railway, 1798-1893.
    Plan of ground to be taken for above railway, 1839.
    Plan of Eglinton Chemical Co. water supply, 1876.
    Plan of Sections of bores on Shewalton, 1860-61.
    Plan of General section of Kilwinning Main coal, N.D.
Miscellaneous
    Account book of coal produced and sold at Garlaft, 1840-43.
    Ledger of Samuel Brown, saddler, 1837-42.

Stair, Earl of
Letters and papers relating to Douglas, Heron & Co. (the Ayr Bank).

Stair Estates Ltd.—Oxenfoord Castle, Ford
Report re Cousland Limework, 1839.
Papers regarding coal including report and plan regarding coal and coal level in lands of Chesterhall, 1791.
Report on Newbattle coalfield, 1860.

Stirling-Maxwell of Pollok, Pollok House, Glasgow
Househill coal workings plan, 1836.
Plan of section of strata at Cardonald, Lochend, Dumbreck and Hagboose mineral field, 1847.
Plan, Ayr and Renfrew Railway, N.D.
Plan of section of minerals at Fitwood, N.D.
Plan, Gorbals Water Company, N.D.

Sutherland, Duke of
MS. vol., Mr. Farey's report on the minerals of Sutherland, 1812.
MS.—vol., 'Animadverto semidoctus naupegus or a Short Remark on our Compleat Shipwrights', 1707.
Railway plans: Inverness to Aviemore, Sutherland extension, and Sutherland and Caithness, 1869-77.
Plan of Brora coal workings, nineteenth century.
Memoranda regarding Brora coal-mine, 1813.
Report by Telford on Culgower harbour, 1805.
Report on Shiness marble quarry, 1813.
Bald's report on Sutherland coal, 1814.
Memoir on Buchan Fishers, and Wool manufactory, 1811.
Bills regarding erection of a coal engine at Brora, 1748.
Letters and papers regarding codfishing copartnery at Helmsdale, 1686-1719.

Todrick, T., Old Bank, Haddington
Minute books and papers of the incorporation of bakers of Haddington, 1551-1832.

Tods, Murray & Jamieson, W.S., Edinburgh
Royal Bank of Scotland
    Bank correspondence, 1804-08, and papers regarding John Thomson, agent in Glasgow, 1818-20.

Stewart of Stewartfield
Dutch and Dutch East Indies papers, including accounts and letterbooks, eighteenth century.

Trades Maiden Hospital, Edinburgh
Papers regarding the incorporation of skinners and furriers of Edinburgh, 1448-1701.

Trinity House, Leith
Minute books, statutes, rolls of skippers, cash books and other records, 1586 to date.

Wardlaw-Ramsay, Tillicoultry House, Tillicoultry
Accounts, letters and papers relating to coal works at Pendreich, Prestonhall, Hathorndean, and Tillicoultry, mid-eighteenth century to 1873.
Accounts, letters and papers regarding the brick and tile works at Musselburgh and Prestonpans, 1774-78, 1800-05.

Incorporation of Weavers, 4 King Edward Street, Perth
Minute books, accounts and indenture books, 1593 to date.

Wemyss, Earl of, Gosford House, Longniddry
Plan of section of engine pit at Stonnyhill Colliery, 1828.
Plan of Lord Wemyss' coal fields north of the River Esk, 1833.
Contract of copartnery and list of proprietors of East Lothian and Merse Whale Fishing Co., 1770.

CHAPTER THREE

Historical Business Records Surveyed by the Colquhoun Lecturer and the Business Archives Council of Scotland

PETER L. PAYNE

Colquhoun Lecturer in Business History,
University of Glasgow

IN 1959 THE COLQUHOUN LECTURESHIP in Business History in the University of Glasgow was founded from funds raised through an appeal sponsored by the Glasgow Chamber and Junior Chamber of Commerce. The lecturer's first task was to make a survey of the historical business records of Glasgow and the West of Scotland. It was originally expected that such an inquiry would take about two years; in fact, the search is still in progress and collections of business records are still being discovered.

Those embarking on similar regional surveys may find a brief account of the Colquhoun inquiry of some value. The author began with a major advantage: the very creation of the Colquhoun lectureship indicated that in the Glasgow region a considerable sympathy for the study of business history already existed. Initially, the method of inquiry that seemed most promising was to contact those firms who had contributed to the appeal fund. It soon became apparent, however, that a general appeal for records was virtually useless; it was imperative to write to each firm individually and to address oneself to a director of the firm. Company secretaries, with some noteworthy exceptions, were not prepared, and indeed were usually not in a position, to grant access to company records. It also became clear that the most fruitful results were achieved in those cases in which it had been possible to gain some prior knowledge of the history and organisation of the firm being approached,(1) and hence some idea of the sort of records that might have been kept. The more preliminary work of this kind that was possible the greater were the chances of a successful search, for it was helpful to give businessmen specific examples of what one was looking for.

Frequently, the records that members of the firm assumed to be of little or no value were those possessing the greatest significance for the economic historian.

Having gained access to a partner or director, it was found to be desirable to visit the company as soon as possible, explain fully the purpose of the survey and reassure the firm that no detailed investigation of the archives would be made without express consent. In Glasgow many companies were willing to grant access only to that material which pre-dated the First World War. Any definite decision on this (or some alternative) terminal date had to be accepted, though, of course, it was emphasised that the more modern the records open to examination the more value the records were likely to have in shedding light on current economic problems.

One significant question that required solution was what should be the ultimate destination of business archives. There are cogent arguments in favour of housing business records in a central depository. There they are both safe and freely open to qualified students. But many 'going concerns' are reluctant to allow their records to pass out of their own hands. This attitude should be encouraged, provided access for scholarly research is granted. Collections of business records are often characterised by great bulk (a glance at the list of manuscripts in the Baker Library, Harvard University, will make this abundantly clear,(2) it is costly to provide proper accommodation for them. But, of greater importance, often the contents of records can be more fully appreciated in what might be called their natural environment. In the works and offices there are often to be found persons who remember and understand both the method of past management procedures and the technical processes of manufacture. In the majority of cases, therefore, business records that are not more than a century old are probably best retained by the firms whose past activities created them. Only where destruction is contemplated should such archives be taken into safe keeping by a university or public body. Where the records are retained, however, it is advisable periodically to indicate a continuing interest in their survival, for fear that a change of officials may lead to their disposal.

Initially, then, the Colquhoun survey began by approaching firms who had contributed to the Colquhoun appeal. The results were encouraging but after some experience a change of plan seemed desirable. It was decided to work along industrial lines. The majority of firms originally contacted were prepared to co-operate, but many of them possessed scanty material. Sometimes, however, officials mentioned other firms *engaged in similar activity* that they believed might have material of historical interest and, in some cases, they were prepared to suggest names of persons in such firms who should be contacted. Since obtaining a sympathetic hearing often constituted half the battle, it seemed that the best way of creating such opportunities would be by exhaustively surveying an industrial group. This procedure possesses an additional advantage: detailed knowledge of the records of one firm often indicates the type of records that might be expected to have once existed in a similar firm.

It was while the author was working on these lines that the Business Archives Council of Scotland was established in 1960 by a group of businessmen, lawyers, chartered accountants, librarians, and university personnel. The number of persons actively interested in the preservation and study of business records in Scotland was not only multiplied by this step but support was enlisted from a wider geographical area than Glasgow and the West of Scotland. The Council's subsequent exhibition in the Mitchell Library, Glasgow, and the newspaper reports and the brief talks on the Scottish Home Service of the B.B.C. that were a direct consequence, brought the whole question of business archives before a larger audience.

At an early meeting of the Business Archives Council of Scotland, it was decided that a search should be made among the legal offices in the cities of Glasgow and Edinburgh. Sheer pressure of work has so far limited the Council's search mainly to Glasgow but already fruitful results have been achieved. Legal offices hold records of a different character from those of the firms themselves. Lawyers often have in their custody contracts of co-partnery, agreements, title deeds, leases, ground plans and the like: the sort of papers, in fact, that complement the ledgers, production and labour records of the business houses. Furthermore, archives held by lawyers tend to be somewhat older than those of going concerns. A beginning has recently been made on a survey of the holdings of chartered accountants, so often the major figures in liquidation proceedings and the fortuitous custodians of many records of firms long since disappeared.

Concurrent with these systematic explorations, a careful watch has been kept on the newspapers: no winding up or the movement of company and legal offices has taken place without an inquiry being made concerning the possible disposal of records.

The lessons to be learned from this experience may be summarised as follows. The best results are usually obtained by individual inquiries preceded by the acquisition of some knowledge of the firm to be approached. If a large-scale survey is to be made, then the systematic inquiry on industrial lines would appear to be the method promising the most rewarding results. Businessmen are basically sympathetic to any interest in their past records, it is therefore imperative to let the business community know what is being attempted by the publicity to be gained by articles in, and letters to, the Press, by radio talks, and by holding well-staged exhibitions. The Business Archives Council of Scotland has played a major rôle in establishing the 'respectability' of the study of business records, and its meetings have provided businessmen and professional people with an opportunity of expressing their opinions on what has been done and what might be attempted. Lastly, the ingrained and natural reserve of the businessman is not to be broken down without considerable effort. Those engaged on a search for business records must be prepared to be patient, not to give up at a first refusal, and to spend considerable time in building up goodwill.

The following list, then, represents the majority of the records so far tracked down during the Colquhoun and Business Archives Council of Scotland surveys, together with notes of the principal business archives in the Mitchell Library, Glasgow.(3) It is confidently believed that many more collections have yet to be discovered, and it is hoped that this represents only a first list. Others may be expected to follow. An attempt has been made to arrange the collections in a logical sequence. Beginning with agricultural pursuits and estate management, coal-mining follows, and the list continues with manufacturing industry, wood products and the timber trade, printing and publishing, civil engineering and building, transport, domestic and foreign trade, overseas enterprise, banking and insurance and professional services. Several of these groups have been sub-divided, the items in the most important of which, 'Manufacturing', have been arranged so that industries using raw materials of a vegetable nature come first, the metallurgical industries second, and chemicals third. Despite the weaknesses implicit in such a classification, it has been preferred to a simple alphabetical order. Each entry in the list contains the following information: name of the firm; dates covered by the collection; an indication of the quantity of material in the collection; a brief description of the material itself with dates of each item or series; and the name of the company or institution that either owns, or has custody of, the records. Where the basic description of the material fails adequately to indicate its contents or potential value, some brief comments have been added in those cases in which sufficient work has been done to permit such elaboration. Copies of the full surveys may be made available

for consultation at the Department of Economic History of the
University of Glasgow.

Finally, may I express my thanks to all those firms whose co-
operation has made the production of this list possible, to the many
officials who have given freely of their time both to help to locate
the records and to answer my questions, to the office-bearers and
members of the Business Archives Council of Scotland for their
support and detailed advice, and to my colleagues at the University
of Glasgow for innumerable hints leading to the discovery of
archives and for suggestions for their use.

NOTES

(1) In the author's case this preparation was greatly facilitated by the
questionnaires completed by firms in 1957 in connection with the compilation
of the commercial and industrial chapters of the Glasgow volume of the Third
Statistical Account of Scotland, ed. by J. Cunnison and J. B. S. Gilfillan
(Glasgow, 1958).

(2) List of Business Manuscripts in Baker Library, compiled by Robert
W. Lovett (Boston, Massachusetts, 2nd edition, 1951).

(3) These notes have kindly been supplied by Mr. C. W. Black, Glasgow
City Librarian, and Mr. Hepburn, the Mitchell Librarian.

List of Business Records

Inquiries for access to any of the material listed should be made to
Dr. P. L. Payne, Department of Economic History, the University
of Glasgow, and *not* to the company or agent concerned.

NURSERY PROPRIETORS AND SEED MERCHANTS

Austin and McAslan, 1841-1905

7 volumes

Ledgers, 1841-1905, and a letter book, 1879-81. Sometime proprietors of the
Little Govan Nursery, the firm of Austin & McAslan was established in
1717 and is almost certainly the oldest surviving business in Glasgow.

Austin & McAslan Ltd., Seed Merchants, Glasgow.

ESTATE MANAGEMENT

The Bedlay House Papers, 1740-1941

Accounts, business papers and letters of the Campbell and Christie families of Bedlay, Lanarkshire, 1740-1941, including Bedlay estate and rental books, 1817-34, memorandum of limestone quarries on the estate, 1843-50, and communications with the Baird Brothers relating to limestone leases, 1853-58.

The Mitchell Library, Glasgow.

The Brisbane Papers, sixteenth-nineteenth centuries

Family and estate papers of the Brisbanes of Bishopton and Largs, sixteenth-nineteenth centuries.

The Mitchell Library, Glasgow.

The Campbell of Shawfield Papers, 1691-1714

Letters and papers covering the business interests of Daniel Campbell, 1691-1714.

The Mitchell Library, Glasgow.

James Macdonald, 1747-62

2 volumes

Sederunt book of curatory for James Macdonald and his children, and book of accounts relating to this curatory, 1753-61. The estates of James Macdonald were situated in the Hebrides and the accounts indicate the great importance of kelping in the economies of the estates.

Thomson, Dickson & Shaw, W.S., and J. A. Campbell & Lamond, C.S., Edinburgh

MINING: COAL

William Dixon & Sons; William Dixon Limited: Govan Colliery, 1804-05, 1826-1938

287 volumes, 1 deed box

The major groups of records in this collection are as follows.

I. Account Books:

     (i) General ledger, 1804-05;
     (ii) Day books, 1857-92;
     (iii) Journals, 1849-58, 1863-1904;
     (iv) Account rendered books, 1853-1917.

II. Production, Stock and Sales Records:

     (i) Output and Sales Books, later called 'Abstract books', 1866-1923. These books contain *daily* statistics of coal, ironstone and fireclay production (by pits), and sales of these materials, together with the number of workers employed at each pit.
     (ii) Sales and Stock Books, 1898-1901, 1903-18.

E

III. Labour and Wage Records:

    (i) Wages books, 1826-1923. These 183 volumes, virtually complete from 1855 onwards, record wages paid to surface workers ('Oncost above ground'), Oncost workers below ground, and coal face-workers in each of the pits constituting the Govan Colliery. Since the face-workers were paid piece rates they provide detailed information on coal and iron-stone production.

    (ii) Funeral Fund Roll Books, 1841-c. 1880.

    (iii) Accident Report Books, 1905-20.

IV. Miscellaneous Papers:

Of the loose papers the most important are:

    (i) Copies of letters by or on behalf of William Dixon, 1842-45.

    (ii) Various inventories and valuations, c. 1900.

    (iii) Reports, correspondence and agreements concerning mineral leases.

    (iv) Papers concerning the establishment and subsequent re-organisation of William Dixon Ltd., 1873-1938.

University of Glasgow, gift of Colvilles Limited, Glasgow. Items IV (iii) and IV (iv) are in the custody of *Moncrieff Warren Paterson & Co., Glasgow.*

Forbes of Callendar Papers, c. 1855-1920

1 deed box

Papers concerning mineral leases on Callendar Estate. Falkirk, including output statements, 1855-1920.

A. J. & A. Graham, Glasgow.

Halbeath Colliery and Salt Works, 1785-1806

4 volumes, 1 box

Minute and account books, 1785-92; letter book, 1787-92; bill book, 1798-1806; two bundles of accounts, statements and letters, 1790-1803.

University of Glasgow, deposited on permanent loan by Thomson, Dickson & Shaw, W.S., and J. A. Campbell & Lamond, C.S., Edinburgh.

Whifflet Colliery, Coatbridge, 1852-83

1 deed box

Papers include output statements, 1852-83.

A. J. & A. Graham, Glasgow.

MANUFACTURING: FOOD AND DRINK

Bread and Biscuits

John Macfarlane & Sons; Macfarlane Lang & Co. Ltd., 1879-1938

40 volumes, 1 file

The more important records include minute books, 1904-38; ledgers, 1879-1928; cash books, 1879-1934; journals, 1879-1917; letter books, 1886-1938; stock books, 1884-93: inventory book, 1885-88; travellers' and agents' expenses and commissions, 1897-1907, and a collection of financial, production and wage memoranda, 1878-90.

Macfarlane, Lang & Company Limited, Victoria Biscuit Works, Glasgow.

Confectionary

John Buchanan & Brothers, 1858-59
1 volume
Day book, 1858-59.

University of Glasgow, gift of Buchanan (Confectioners) Ltd., Glasgow.

Edible Oils and Fats

Percy & Halden, Limited, 1901-55
4 volumes
See entry under 'Manufacturing: Lubricants'.

Brewing

J. & R. Tennent Limited, 1782-1859
6 volumes
Ale day book, 1782-84; sales accounts, 1806-10; rough books, 1829-46 (these include draft copy letters, 1839-46; production figures, 1837-41; and exports, 1832-33); packing book, 1859; book containing copies of feuing contracts and property conveyances compiled *c*. 1835, the original documents are dated 1798-1831.

The Tennent family is believed to have begun brewing on the present site of Wellpark about 1556. The firm of J. & R. Tennent was founded in 1745 and remained a private concern until 1901 when a limited company was formed to take over the assets of the company.

J. & R. Tennent Limited, Wellpark Brewery, Glasgow.

Distilling

William Teacher & Sons Limited, 1837-1912
13 volumes, 1 file
Shop results, 1860-1912; wages books, office staff and shopmen, 1865-1904, from 1899 the wages of the workers at Ardmore distillery are entered; shop drawings, 1863-92; miscellaneous legal agreements, licences, and papers, 1837-99.

William Teacher & Sons Limited, Glasgow.

MANUFACTURING: TOBACCO

Stephen Mitchell, 1839
1 volume
Account book of Stephen Mitchell, 1839. Stephen Mitchell was the founder of the Mitchell Library, Glasgow.

The Mitchell Library, Glasgow.

MANUFACTURING: TEXTILES

David & John Anderson, Ltd., 1828-1943

26 volumes, 1 file

The material includes minute books, 1911-28; ledgers, 1862-88, 1891-1911; trial balance sheets, 1880-1907; detailed sales records, 1908-43; letter books, 1828-34, 1838-42, 1897-1910; and a volume containing letters, copy agreements, investment data and testimonials, *c.* 1876-96.

University of Glasgow, gift of D. & J. Anderson, Limited, Atlantic Mills, Bridgeton, Glasgow.

The minutes books and the earliest of the ledgers and letter books are still in the possession of the company.

James Finlay & Company, Limited, 1789-1914

Approximately 75 volumes, 2 boxes, 6 files

This collection has two major components: (i) the records of James Finlay & Co. and (ii) those relating specifically to the company's cotton mills at Catrine, Deanston and Ballindalloch.

Material in the first group includes: minute books, 1845-83; ledgers, 1792, 1858-1914; journals, 1825-1914; balance books, 1789-1899; bill book, 1813-58; letter books, 1835-59; numerous papers and correspondence concerned with the firm's organization and structure; and a collection of letters written by Kirkman Finlay to his wife, 1814, and to his son, 1832-37. These records contain many details of the Catrine and Deanstone mills, but there are numerous archives relating specifically to these mills.

The most valuable of this second group of archives are a notebook entitled 'Statement and Calculations Relating to the Works', which contains data on wages, profits, capital employed, and expenditures at Catrine, Deanston and Ballindalloch, *c.* 1800-57; Catrine and Deanston memorandum books, 1911-16; Catrine Works journals, 1867-1906; 'Catrine Works: Annual State Book', 1857-64; Deanston Works journals, 1859-1908, and ledgers, 1872-1917; and two boxes of agreements, accounts, statements and testimonials, *c.* 1830.

James Finlay & Company, Limited, Glasgow.

Freemen Weavers in Carlton, Glasgow, eighteenth-nineteenth centuries

2 volumes

Abstract of the acts of the freemen weavers prior to 1786 and the minutes of their transactions, 1786-1872.

The Mitchell Library, Glasgow.

The Gourock Ropework Company, 1736-1873

3 volumes

Minute books, 1779-1873; letter book, 1736-46. Established in 1736, this is one of the oldest surviving Scottish companies; its records and those of its subsidiaries are virtually complete from the date of incorporation in 1903. The New Lanark Mills, associated with the names of David Dale and Robert Owen, are now owned by the Gourock Company.

The Gourock Ropework Company Limited, Port Glasgow.

Lanark Twist Company; Lanark Spinning Company; The Gourock Ropework Company; New Lanark Mills, 1799-1941

49 volumes, 1 bundle

Founded by David Dale and Richard Arkwright in 1784, the New Lanark Mills were purchased by the Lanark Twist Company in 1799 with Robert Owen as part-proprietor and sole manager. A number of records dating from the period of Owen's control have survived. They are:

(i) Report Book, 1802-08, containing monthly production reports from each of the three mills in operation. The volume, in perfect condition, is characterised by remarkable precision and detail.

(ii) Cotton Purchase and Order Books, 1811, 1814-20. These volumes give details of cotton ordered from the United States, *c.* 1811, together with general notes of the supplies needed at the mills; prices of various grades of cotton at different ports, weekly figures, 1814-20; and a detailed breakdown of the rove produced in No. 4 Room, No. 2 Mill, by each worker, daily, 1 June, 1812 to 1 September, 1812.

(iii) Day Book, Lanark Twist Co., 1804-08.

(iv) Sales Book, January, 1814 to May, 1815.

(v) Quarterly Balance Sheets, sixteen in number, variously dated, March 1818 to September 1823.

(vi) Letter book containing copies of letters sent from the continent, mainly St. Petersburg and Amsterdam, from J. H. Brink & Company and Allan Stewart & Company, 15 August, 1815 to 31 December, 1816.

(vii) Visitors' books; August, 1795 to October, 1799; June 1821 to September. 1824; October, 1824 to April, 1832.

(viii) Diary and notebook probably kept by Robert Owen, January, 1813 to May, 1822.

Other records relating to the New Lanark Mills include: cotton purchase books, 1860-1923; sales records, 1881-91; ledgers, 1910-34; letter books, 1902-04; 'Net and Banding Order Book', 1888-96; a Works Diary, 1879-1904, infrequently kept, occasionally contains items of considerable interest; a number of wage and employment records, 1810-1912, one volume of which provides statistics of the population of New Lanark, 1806-10, and the numbers employed at the mills in different capacities on 9 June, 1810, later pages reproduce the census statistics of 1841, 1851 and 1861; and a record of Births, Marriages and Deaths in New Lanark, 1818-53.

Gourock Ropework Company Limited, New Lanark Mills, New Lanark.

Robert Owen's notebook is preserved at the Company's Head Office, Port Glasgow.

John Lean & Sons, 1852-1951

160 volumes

Until 1960 John Lean & Sons manufactured cotton textiles mainly for the Indian and Middle Eastern markets and this collection is particularly noteworthy for its almost continuous series of letter books which record the vicissitudes of this export trade from 1852 to 1951. Other material includes ledgers, 1854-1932; indent books, 1893-1926; wage book, 1919-41; and, of considerable interest, a 'Hand Loom Materials Book', 1853-65.

University of Glasgow, gift of John Lean & Sons Limited.

Milton Printworks, 1828-64

6 volumes

Voucher books, 1828-31, 1840-64; invoice book, 1848-61. Miller & Mouter succeeded Patrick Mitchell as proprietors of this calico-printing works at Milton, by Dumbarton, in 1848.

University of Glasgow, gift of Professor A. M. Boase.

United Turkey Red Company Limited, 1845-1937

31 volumes, 4 files

The United Turkey Red Company was formed in 1898 by the amalgamation of the firms of William Stirling & Sons, founded *c.* 1723, John Orr Ewing & Co., *c.* 1830, and Archibald Orr Ewing & Co., *c.* 1830. In 1900 the firm of Alexander Reid & Sons was purchased. United Turkey Red was by far the largest firm in the bleaching, finishing, dyeing and printing industry in Scotland. In 1960 the company's assets were purchased by the Calico Printers' Association and the Alexandria Works closed.

The more important of the surviving records of the constituent firms are:

  (i) William Stirling & Sons, private ledgers, 1881-92, and journals, 1881-97.

  (ii) John Orr Ewing & Co., private journals, 1895-1927, the majority of the entries relate to United Turkey Red; letter book, 1868-90.

  (iii) Archibald Orr Ewing & Co., private ledgers, 1845-1901, and journal, 1845-97; account current book, 1845-98; 'Turkey Red Dyeing Calculation Book, Lennox Bank', gives details of dyeing costs, 1873-92.

  (iv) In addition there are a number of records whose origin cannot readily be identified. They include a wage book, 1845-47; production records, 1875-1910; purchase book, 1887-88; a pattern book with details of dyeing costs for each design, 1857-58; and a box of letters, statements and papers, 1867-1905, many relating to the Indian market.

Of the surviving records of the United Turkey Red Company itself the more noteworthy are: minute books ('Statements by Heads of Departments'), 1920-36; production records, 1898-1903; volume recording details of trade disputes, 1912-18; works letter books, 1909-17; and six volumes of reports by Bradstreets, Glasgow and West of Scotland Guardian Society, William Deacons Bank Ltd., Commercial Bank of Scotland, Royal Bank of Scotland, etc., on firms engaged in every aspect of the textile trade. The reports, dated 1921-37, provide a brief history of each firm and recommend maximum credit limits.

University of Glasgow, gift of The Calico Printers' Association Limited.

Rope and Sailmakers

The Dumbarton Rope Work Company, 1877

1 file

Copy contract of co-partnery to take over and carry on the business of rope and sail manufacturers previously owned by John Hamilton & Co. of Glasgow and Dumbarton, 1877; minute of agreement relative to this contract, 1877. The partnership is interesting in that its membership included David Croll of Amsterdam, and the senior partners of both Denny's of Dumbarton and A. & J. Inglis.

Business Archives Council of Scotland, gift of Colonel A. R. Cross, Mackenzie Roberton & Company.

Robert Douglas & Brittain Ltd., 1908-41

1 volume
Journal, 1908-41.

Robert Douglas & Brittain Limited, Plantation Sail Works, Glasgow.

John McFarlane & Co., 1840-47

3 volumes
Cash book, 1841-47; job books, 1840-42.

John McFarlane & McAlistair Limited, Glasgow.

MANUFACTURING: CARPETS

A. F. Stoddard & Company Limited, 1882-1940

46 volumes, 6 files
Arthur Francis Stoddard (1810-82), purchased the Glenpatrick Works in 1862. The firm became a public company in 1894 and in 1918 acquired the share capital of Ronald, Jack & Co. Ltd. and the Caledonian Carpet Company Ltd. The records include:

(*a*) A. F. Stoddard & Co.: minute books, 1894-1916; ledger. 1918-32; reports and accounts, 1894-1938; shipping and order books, 1920-36; price and quotation books, 1906-38; wage books, 1882-1940; a collection of letters concerning the company's acquisition of the shares of Ronald, Jack & Co. Ltd. and the Caledonian Carpet Company and notes on the amalgamation; and the minute book of the Patrick Bank Sick Society, later called the Glenpatrick Carpet Works Yearly Provident Society, 1853-68.

(*b*) Ronald, Jack & Co. Ltd.: minute book, 1909-33; journal and ledger, 1909-19; ledgers, 1919-33; balance sheets, 1899-1933; wage book, 1890-1908.

(*c*) Caledonian Carpet Co. Ltd.: minute books, 1899-1933; ledgers, 1898-1933; balance sheets, 1899-1933.

A. F. Stoddard & Company, Limited, Glenpatrick Works, Elderslie, Johnstone.

James Templeton & Co., 1876-1932

25 volumes, 3 boxes
Ledgers, journals and stock books, 1876-1932; production and sales records, 1879-1931; a private memorandum book, 1879-1907, contains copies of deeds of co-partnery, property conveyances, patents, etc.; wages books, 1912-23; collections of legal papers, biographical notes, and documents relating to the establishment of a carpet Union by H. E. Preen in 1889.

James Templeton & Company Limited, Glasgow.

MANUFACTURING: PAPER

The Clyde Paper Company Limited, 1877-1926
6 volumes
Minute books, 1890-1926; letter books, 1877-1926.

Clyde Paper Company Limited, Rutherglen, Lanarkshire.

Solomon Lindsay, paper and millboard manufacturers, 1864-1902

7 volumes, 3 bundles

Cathcart Snuff Mill account book. 1864-1902, and purchase book, 1878-1902; sales day book, 1875-1902; snuff sales ledgers, 1893-1902; paper ledger, 1895-1901; cash book, 1878-1902; miscellaneous papers, late nineteenth century.

A. J. & A. Graham, Glasgow.

MANUFACTURING: IRON AND STEEL

David Colville & Sons; Colvilles Limited, 1871-c. 1939.

Approximately 100 volumes, 10 deed boxes, numerous files.

This comprehensive collection of records covers almost every aspect of the formation and growth of the Colville group of companies from 1871, when David Colville built the Dalziel Ironworks, Motherwell, to the creation of Colvilles Limited as a public company in 1934.

In addition to the minute books of David Colville & Sons, 1895-1935, and the company's board meeting papers and agendas, ledgers and journals, the collection includes balance sheets from 1882 and innumerable letters, memoranda and legal documents. Of greatest significance, however, are the hundreds of accounts and papers relating to the establishment of subsidiary companies, and the amalgamations and purchases that resulted in the creation of the Colville group, the important iron, steel and coal complex that by the late 'thirties encompassed the Fullwood Foundry Co. Ltd., acquired in 1915; the Clydebridge Steel Co. Ltd. and the Glengarnock Iron & Steel Co. Ltd., 1916; Archibald Russell & Co. Ltd., 1917; the Clyde Alloy Steel Co. Ltd. and Smith & McLean Ltd., 1919; the Carnlough Lime Co. Ltd., 1920; the Clyde Ironworks and Calderbank Works of James Dunlop & Co., 1930; the Colville Constructional Co. Ltd., 1931; the Steel Company of Scotland Ltd. and the Lanarkshire Steel Co. Ltd., 1936.

There are extensive files of agreements, including the licence granted by Charles William Siemens to David Colville in 1880; financial papers, documents concerned with relations with the Ministry of Munitions, 1916-20; and newspaper cuttings. Of fundamental importance are the private papers and correspondence of Sir John Craig, who joined the company as office boy in 1888 and was chairman of the company from 1916 to 1956.

Colvilles Limited, parent company of the Colville Group of Companies.

David Colville & Sons Limited; Colvilles Ltd.: Glengarnock Iron & Steel Works, c. 1900-36

3 volumes, 1 file

Labour and wage records, 1913-36; statistical memoranda; album of photographs taken when the works were owned by the Glengarnock Iron & Steel Company, Ltd., c. 1900.

Colvilles Limited, Glasgow.

William Dixon & Sons; William Dixon Ltd.: Calder Iron Works, 1888-1914

2 volumes, 1 bundle

Collection of detailed analyses of the cost of making pig iron, 1891-1901;

an abstract of Calder iron works wages, 1888-91; stock book, 1907-14; and an 'index to Calder Leases'.

University of Glasgow, gift of Colvilles Limited, Glasgow.

William Dixon Limited, Dixon's Ironworks Limited: Govan Iron Works 1873-1958

64 volumes. 2 boxes

The major groups of records in this collection are as follows:

I. Letter Book:
    (i) Private letter book, 1873-1906.

II. Account Books:
    (i) Ledgers, 1932-52;
    (ii) Journals, 1931-52;
    (iii) Cash Books, 1934-47.

III. Production, Stock and Sales Records:
    (i) Pig iron production books, 1929-58;
    (ii) Sales and Disposals books (pig iron, coke and coke oven by-products), 1942-57;
    (iii) Pig iron stock book, 1907-14.

IV. Purchase and Receiving Records:
    Purchase ledgers and 'receiving books', 1929-52.

V. Labour Records:
    (i) Wages books, 1944-47, 1951-52;
    (ii) Time books, 1948-50;
    (iii) Minute Book of the Accident Prevention or Safety Committee, 1928-46.

VI. Technical Records:
    (i) Analyses of coals and coal Dusts, 1882-1925;
    (ii) Analyses of Samples from Sulphate Works, 1893-1938;
    (iii) Analyses of Pig iron, 1903-58;
    (iv) Analyses of Fuels, 1898-1926;
    (v) Analyses of Limestone, 1882-1958;
    (vi) Analyses of Blast Furnace Slags, 1908-58;
    (vii) Blast Furnace Report Books, 1927-58.

VII. Miscellaneous Papers:
    The most important of the loose papers are those concerned with the establishment and subsequent reorganisation of William Dixon Limited, 1873-1938.

University of Glasgow, gift of Colvilles Limited. The private letter book, 1873-1906, was the gift of Mr. and Mrs. R. R. Gardner of Bearsden. The collection of Miscellaneous Papers, Group VII, is in the custody of *Moncrieff Warren Paterson & Co., Glasgow.*

Lanarkshire Steel Company Limited: Lanarkshire Steel Works, 1889-1954

47 volumes, 3 files

Minute books of the board of directors, 1889-1954; ledgers, 1897-1957; journals, 1897-1957; analysis of capital expenditure, 1898-1954; and a loose leaf book, plus two roll charts, of annual statistics of almost every aspect of the company's activities, 1892-1944. Bound in the minute books are miscellaneous agreements, special resolutions, and other memoranda.

Lanarkshire Steel Company Limited, one of the Colville Group of Companies

Moses McCullock, 1875-78

1 volume

A time and wages book of a small family firm operating a foundry. The volume, 1875-78, contains notes of workmen's meetings held to discuss wages and working conditions.

The People's Palace, Glasgow.

Merry & Cunninghame, Glengarnock Ironworks, 1864-71

1 volume

Lease book, 1864-71.

Colvilles Limited, Glasgow.

James Beaumont Neilson, Hot Blast Trial Reports, 1841-42

2 volumes

(i) Report of the Case: James Beaumont Neilson and others, *v.* John Harford and others. This is bound together with a paper by Dr. T. Clark, Professor of Chemistry in the University of Aberdeen, read to the Royal Society of Edinburgh, 16 March, 1835, 'on the Application of the Hot Blast in the Manufacture of Cast-Iron'.

(ii) Report of the Action: James Beaumont Neilson and others *v.* The Househill Coal & Iron Company, 1842.

Bannatyne, Kirkwood, France & Co., Glasgow.

Smith & McLean Ltd., 1857-1941

7 volumes, 5 deed boxes

The more important records are as follows: ledger of Richard Smith, 1857-66; copy contract of co-partnery between Richard Smith and Charles McLean to take over the Clyde Galvanizing Company established by McGavin & Thompson at Mavisbank in 1852; minute books, 1895-1900; private ledgers, 1895-1916; stock book, 1906-11; letter book, 1895-1914; production and financial abstract, 1880-1935; reports and accounts, 1894, 1896-1941; papers relating to the purchase of Smith & McLean Ltd. by David Colville & Sons Ltd., 1919.

Smith & McLean Ltd., one of the Colville Group of Companies.
Richard Smith's ledger is the property of Colonel K. Barge, managing director of Richard Smith Ltd., Manufacturing Chemists, Glasgow.

Steel Company of Scotland, Limited: Blochairn and Hallside Works, 1872-1947

48 volumes, 2 bundles

This collection includes a complete series (20 volumes) of minute books of the board of directors, 1872-1947; the firm's first and fifth letter books, 1871-72, 1887-1909; copies of early legal agreements, including those with Charles William Siemens and Gilchrist Thomas for patent working, 1872-80; detailed weekly or monthly figures of output, costs, prices, deliveries, and stocks, 1898-1939; coal leases, 1906-32; and a collection of the firm's printed notices and forms, together with many press cuttings relating to the company, 1872-1934.

The Steel Company of Scotland Limited, one of the Colville Group of Companies.

MANUFACTURING: SHIPBUILDING

Denny Brothers, William Denny & Brothers, Leven Shipyard, Dumbarton, 1844-1952

131 volumes, 33 boxes
The major records in this comprehensive collection are: ledgers, 1844-1921; journals, 1844-1920, 1934-47; contract books, 1880-1921; contract envelopes, 1852-1940 (these papers, contained in 33 boxes, record prices, credit arrangements, tonnage and specifications, estimated and contract prices, charter parties and much other valuable material for almost every vessel built by Denny's between 1852 and 1940, the yard numbers being No. 39—No. 1351); cost books, 1875-1938; estimate books, 1872-1908; inventory book, 1871-79; bank books, 1917-52; wage abstract books, 1844-1940; and salaries books, 1879-1905.

Among other items the most interesting are a book entitled 'Particulars of Ships built by Various Shipbuilders', which contains details of Clyde-built ships launched between 1862-80; the Minute Books of the Awards Committee, Leven Shipyard, 1884-1931 (the firm was one of the first to make awards to workers for ideas by which output might be increased or made more economical, the scheme being introduced in 1880); newspaper cuttings, 1884-1908; and six jottings books, kept by William Denny containing notes of journeys made, work in progress in the shipyard and various observations, often of a religious character. They are variously dated, 1863-75.

University of Glasgow, made available by the joint liquidators of William Denny & Brothers, Limited.

John Elder and Company, The Fairfield Shipbuilding and Engineering Company, 1870-1916

1 volume
Private letter book, 1869-1916. The firm of John Elder & Company was established in 1870, it became the Fairfield Shipbuilding and Engineering Company in 1886.

The Fairfield Shipbuilding and Engineering Company Limited, Glasgow.

Antony and John Inglis, 1869-83

1 file
Minutes of agreement and co-partnery between Antony Inglis, John Inglis and John Inglis, Junior, 1868 (draft), 1873 (copy), 1877, 1883.

Business Archives Council of Scotland, gift of Colonel A. R. Cross, Mackenzie Roberton & Company, Glasgow.

James R. Napier, F.R.S., 1838-73

10 volumes, 1 box
James R. Napier, son of Robert Napier, was made a partner in his father's firm in 1853, but withdrew in 1857 to start business on his own account. A

few records have survived this short-lived venture: a cash book, 1857-61, a purchase book, 1858-59, a receiving book, 1858-60, and a letter book, 1857-59. In addition there are several personal records of James R. Napier: two volumes of private vouchers, receipts and accounts, 1848-57, a scribbling diary, 1860 (the major entries being references to his shipyard); a letter book, 1866-73; a collection of printed scientific papers and patents by himself and professional associates; and a book of lecture notes, calculations and exercises compiled by Napier in 1838 when he was a student at the University of Glasgow, attending the classes of natural philosophy and mathematics.

University of Glasgow, gift of Professor A. M. Boase.

Robert Napier & Company, 1834-45

1 volume
Cash book, 1834-45.

University of Glasgow, gift of Professor A. M. Boase.

Scotts' of Greenock, 1798-1908

12 volumes, 1 deed box
Ledger, 1851-54; journal, 1802-04; letter books, 1798-1800, 1802-06, 1810-18, 1833-50; tender book, 1905-06; wages book, 1903-08; miscellaneous letters and papers, 1879-1901. Founded in 1711 by John Scott, the surviving records cover the period when the firm was known as John and William Scott, John Scott & Sons, Scott and Company, and from 1904, Scotts' Shipbuilding and Engineering Company, Limited. By far the most important items in this small collection are the letter books which shed considerable light on the difficulties of shipbuilding during the Napoleonic Wars. A deed box contains many hundreds of balance sheets, monthly orders, patents, wage data, and correspondence of all kinds, c. 1875-85, of the Leeds Forge Company, in which members of the Scott family evidently held a powerful interest.

Scotts' Shipbuilding & Engineering Company, Limited, Greenock, Renfrewshire.

Alexander Stephen & Sons, 1848-1931

277 volumes, 5 deed boxes
The Stephen family has been associated with shipbuilding since 1750 when Alexander Stephen began building ships at Burghead in Morayshire. His descendants built ships at Aberdeen, Arbroath and Dundee before Alexander Stephen, grand-nephew of Alexander Stephen of Burghead, established the Kelvinhaugh shipyard on the Clyde in 1850. In 1870 the business was moved to the present yard at Linthouse. This remarkably comprehensive collection of records contains business and family papers of great value and interest. The major items are as follows:

I. Business: legal documents, including contracts of co-partnery and retiral, 1856-59, conversion of the firm into a public company, 1901, general agreements (mainly concerned with patent working), and patent specifications; minute book, 1892-94; ledgers, 1857-1921; journals, 1872-1928; stock and inventory books, 1863-1920; time and wages books, 1853-63; letter books (continuous series of 77 volumes), 1856-1931; and a large collection of notebooks and papers specifically concerned with drawings and specifications of ships, 1852-1922.

II. Personal:

Alexander Stephen (1832-99): diaries, 1859-99; notebooks, 1848-95; private letter books, 1859-99; letters to Alexander Stephen, c. 1845-90; copies of speeches made by Alexander Stephen.

John Stephen (1835-1917): diaries, 1862-67; private letter books, 1877-1917.

Alexander Edward Stephen (1861-1942): diaries, 1887-90; private letter books, 1903-16.

Frederick John Stephen (1863-1932): diaries, 1887-89; private letter books, 1890-1913; personal and business letters to F. J. Stephen, 1900-16.

Alexander Stephen & Sons, Limited, Linthouse, Glasgow.

William Simons & Company, 1893-1935

63 volumes

Abstract books, 1893-1914; ledger, 1907-09; personnel and apprenticeship records, 1897-1935; foreman's pay book, 1898-1900; wage rate books, 1922-35.

University of Glasgow, gift of G. & J. Weir Holdings Limited, Glasgow.

MANUFACTURING: HEAVY ENGINEERING

Dennystown Forge Company, 1854-1914

8 volumes

Ledger, 1854-66; cash book, 1854-66; cost book, 1885-96; letter books, 1854-58; 1886-90; record of stern frames manufactured, 1862-86; and forgemen's wages books, 1889-1914. Renowned for its large marine and engine forgings, the Dennystown Forge Company was established by James Denny, Alexander Tolmie and Andrew McGaan in 1854, later partners included Peter Denny and Walter Brock, leading figures in the firm of William Denny & Brothers, Arthur D. Wedgwood and Arthur Wedgwood.

Dennystown Forge Company Limited, Dumbarton.

Locomotive Building

Dübs & Company, 1865-1902

85 volumes

Locomotive cost books, 1872-1900 (these volumes give complete cost details of locomotives Nos. 547 to 4117, photographs of the locomotives are frequently included and summary cost break-downs and wage abstracts are provided); inventory books, 1865-1902; order books, 1870-73; 1882-84, 1890-91, contain details of locomotive fittings purchased from subcontractors.

University of Glasgow, gift of North British Locomotive Company, Limited, Glasgow.

Neilson & Company, Hydepark Locomotive Works, Springburn, Glasgow, c. 1850-1902

19 volumes

Inventory books, 1874-1902; order books, 1880-81 (fittings and materials ordered from other firms); cost and weight books, give detailed cost calculations, including a summary of the material and labour components, for six locomotives built in 1889-90.

There have survived two notebooks in which Walter Montgomerie Neilson, founder of the firm and eldest son of James Beaumont Neilson, has set down the 'Dates and Notes of the principal occurrences of my life', together with one of Neilson's diaries, intermittently kept, 1850-53.

University of Glasgow, gift of the North British Locomotive Company, Limited, Glasgow.

Walter Neilson's diary and notebooks are in the custody of Bannatyne, Kirkwood, France & Company, Glasgow.

North British Locomotive Company Limited, 1903-45

106 volumes

The North British Locomotive Company was formed in 1903 by the amalgamation of Sharp, Stewart & Company (founded in 1828, closed their Atlas Works, Manchester, in 1887, and moved to Glasgow on the acquisition of the works of the Clyde Locomotive Co., at Springburn), Neilson & Co. (founded in 1832), and Dübs & Co. (founded in 1864). The collection includes the following: locomotive cost books, 1903-09; cost day books, 1909-21; material cost books, 1915-46; cost and weight books, 1903-25; contract books, 1914-43 (these volumes provide details of contracts entered into for the supply of locomotives and give technical details, dates of quotations, acceptance and delivery, terms, and sometimes cost and profit figures); contract books for spare parts and additional fittings, 1915-45; and inventory books, 1903-22.

University of Glasgow, gift of the North British Locomotive Company, Limited, Glasgow.

Machine Tools

Hugh Smith & Company, 1876-1938

108 volumes

The material includes: minute book, 1903-35; ledgers, 1876-1935; sales ledgers, 1900-35; cash books, 1876-1935; and order books, 1893-1938; but perhaps the most valuable items in the collection are the time and materials books, which provide a minutely detailed record of the wage and materials costs involved in the construction of each machine turned out between 1876 and 1938.

Hugh Smith (Glasgow) Limited, Glasgow.

Marine Engines

The Greenock Foundry Company, 1870-76

1 volume

Journal, 1870-76.

Founded in 1790, the Greenock Foundry was acquired by John Scott (1752-1837), of the Greenock shipbuilding family, in 1825 and carried on as a separate but correlated concern under the title of Scott, Sinclair and Co. This engineering firm became The Greenock Foundry Company in 1859, and was merged with Scott & Co. to form Scotts' Shipbuilding and Engineering Company Limited in 1904.

Scotts' Shipbuilding and Engineering Company Limited, Greenock, Renfrewshire.

Tulloch & Denny, Denny & Company, 1851-1918

35 volumes, 1 file
Ledgers, 1851-1918; journals, 1851-89; copy contract of co-partnery between Peter Denny and John M'Ausland, 1862. Established by Peter Denny, partner in William Denny & Brothers, John Tulloch, engineer, of Greenock, and John M'Ausland, of Dumbarton, in 1850, the firm of Tulloch & Denny was formed to manufacture marine steam engines. Previously it had been necessary to have hulls built by Denny Brothers engined elsewhere. When John Tulloch retired in 1862, the firm became Denny & Co., with Peter Denny and John M'Ausland as co-partners.

University of Glasgow, made available by the joint liquidators of William Denny & Brothers Limited.

The contract of co-partnery was the gift of Colonel A. R. Cross, Mackenzie Robertson & Company, Glasgow.

Sugar Machinery

Duncan Stewart & Company Limited, 1881-1902

1 volume
Cost book, 1881-1902.

Duncan Stewart & Company, Limited, Glasgow.

The Mirrlees Watson Company Limited, 1900-36

20 volumes, 23 files
General letter books, 1915, 1936; letter books, sugar department, 1903, 1934-35; sugar estimating letter books, 1933-34; engine department, letter book, 1919; order book, 1916; quotation books, 1919-21; invoice books, 1900-02; and incoming letter files relating to the firm's business with India, 1926-36.

University of Glasgow, gift of The Mirrlees Watson Company Limited, Glasgow.

MANUFACTURING: AUTOMOBILE ENGINEERING

Albion Motor Car Company Limited, 1899-1964

Approximately 20 volumes, 4 files
Founded by T. Blackwood Murray and N. O. Fulton in 1899, this company is the oldest surviving vehicle manufacturing company in Scotland. Since 1951 the company has been part of the Leyland Group. Private car production ceased in 1913 and the firm has since specialised on heavy commercial vehicles. Among the surviving records are a continuous series of minute books since 1902, when the original partnership became a private limited liability company; several documents relating to the establishment of the firm including a copy contract of co-partnery, 1900; production and sales records, 1900-05; cost records, 1902-17; and three volumes containing photographs, annual statistical information on the number of models produced, capital, employees, etc., together with details of management, company structure and names of partners, and notes on contemporary events relevant to the development of the firm, 1899 to the present.

Albion Motors Limited, Glasgow.

MANUFACTURING: ENGINEERING

Sewing Machines

The Singer Manufacturing Company Limited, 1905-14

5 bundles
Virtually all the records of this company were destroyed by enemy action in 1941. The only notable pre-1914 records that have survived are detailed weekly production reports from 1910 to 1914, comparative summaries in these reports permit certain series to be constructed back to 1905.

The Singer Manufacturing Company Limited, Singer, Clydebank.

MANUFACTURING: CHEMICALS

Cassel Gold Extracting Company Limited, later (from 1906) Cassel Cyanide Company Limited, 1884-1927

6 volumes
Board minute books, 1884-87, 1889-1927.

Imperial Chemical Industries Limited, Mond Division, Widnes, Lancashire.

Halbeath Colliery & Salt Works, 1875-1906

4 volumes, 1 box
See entry under 'Mining: Coal'.

Charles Tennant & Company, St. Rollox Works, Glasgow, 1802-1914

7 volumes
A number of records of the St. Rollox Works established by Charles Tennant in 1797 are among the collection of historical material held by the Archives and Records Department of the Mond Division of Imperial Chemical Industries Limited. By far the most important item is a letter book of Tennant, Knox & Co., 1800-02, but there are also a number of letter books containing correspondence between St. Rollox and other constituent firms of the United Alkali Company, 1894-1914.

Imperial Chemical Industries Limited, Mond Division, Widnes, Lancashire.

The Tharsis Sulphur & Copper Company, Limited

83 volumes
See entry under 'Overseas Enterprise'.

MANUFACTURING: LUBRICANTS

Percy & Halden, Ltd., 1901-55

4 volumes
Minute book, 1909-52; journal, 1902-55; letter book, 1901-35; wage books, 1915-34. Founded in 1887, Percy and Halden Limited also manufactured edible oils and fats; in 1953 a subsidiary, Percy and Halden (Edible Products) Limited, was formed to take over these interests.

Percy & Halden Limited, Standard Oil Works, Glasgow.

MANUFACTURING: PAINT

Williamson Morton & Company, 1894-1924
5 volumes
Ledger, 1894-1924; balance book, 1895-1916; expenditures book, 1894-1903; stock book, 1909-14; wages book, 1909-14.
Federated Paints Limited, Glasgow.

MANUFACTURING: RUBBER

R. & J. Dick, Limited, 1908-14
2 volumes
Minute books, 1908-14.
R. & J. Dick Limited, Blackburn, Lancashire.

WOOD PRODUCTS AND THE TIMBER TRADE

Brownlee & Company Limited, 1863-1925
151 volumes, 1 deed box, 12 bundles
Ledgers, 1864-1914; journals, 1868-1925; cash books, 1863-1922; letter books, 1872-1901; contract record books, 1888-1909; timber costing books, 1891-1901; wage records, intermittent, 1873-1914; contract tenders, 1891-1905; and stock sheets, 1908-14.
Brownlee & Company Limited, City Saw Mills, Port Dundas, Glasgow.

Brownlie, Dunn & Company, 1859-98
27 volumes, 2 deed boxes
Ledgers, 1859-98; journals, 1860-98; cash books, 1859-77; bill book, 1881-86; a large collection of letters, vouchers, accounts, bills of lading, insurance certificates, and other papers concerning the purchase of timber in Canada and the Baltic and its shipment to Scotland, 1861-76.
The firm of Brownlie, Dunn & Co. was founded by Thomas Dunn, in 1836. The firm, subsequently J. S. Dunn & Co., became a Brownlee subsidiary in 1948.
Brownlee & Company Limited, City Saw Mills, Port Dundas, Glasgow.

The Clyde Cooperage Company Limited, 1884-1953
Loose-leaf minute book containing the minutes of the meetings of the board of directors since 1884; ledger, 1884-1953; balance sheets since 1884.
The Clyde Cooperage Co. Ltd., Glasgow.

Pollok Gilmour and Company, 1804-80
1 deed box
This large collection has two major components. First, there are many hundreds of letters, papers and accounts, dating from 1618 to 1887, relating
F

to the affairs of the Gilmour family of South and Easter Walton, Malletheugh, Montrave and Lundin. This group of documents contains, *inter alia*, sasines, deeds, marriage contracts, inventories, and receipted bills for repairs to property, supplies of grain, foodstuffs and ironmongery, servants' wages, taxes, etc. The second component consists of documents of fundamental importance in the evolution of the firm of Pollok Gilmour & Company, 1804-*c*. 1880. This firm, founded in 1804 by John Pollok, Allan Gilmour and Arthur Pollok, was established to trade in Scandinavian timber. Within a few years, however, branch houses were set up at St. John (Robert Rankin & Co.) and Miramichi (Gilmour Rankin & Co.), New Brunswick; Bathurst, Chaleur Bay (Ferguson Rankin & Co.); Montreal (Gilmour & Co.); Quebec (Allan Gilmour & Co.); New Orleans (Houghton Rankin & Co.); and Liverpool (Rankin Gilmour & Co.). The firm acquired extensive forest lands and was soon operating saw-mills on a large scale. Shipowning, which had begun on the Clyde with a fifty-ton coaster, became an important feature of the conduct of the business and the firm eventually owned a very large tonnage. The manuscripts include contracts of co-partnery, memoranda of retirals, miscellaneous agreements between the various partners and other concerns, several business accounts, a 'Memorandum on the Difficulties of the Square Timber and Sawn Lumber Trade in Canada', 1878, and a 'Memorandum by George Young, Writer, Glasgow, in relation to the history of the late firm of Pollok, Gilmour & Co., and Branch Houses', 1906.

University of Glasgow, on permanent loan from Anderson, Young and Dickson, Writers, Glasgow.

Robinson, Dunn & Company Limited, 1842-1910
22 volumes, 2 boxes
Established in 1838 by Samuel Wilson, Thomas and James Dunn as the Inchbank Saw Mills, the firm was reconstructed in 1842 under its present name by Wilson, Robert Robinson (Samuel Wilson's son-in-law) and James Dunn. The more important records include: ledgers, 1842-47, 1880-1904; journals, 1839-71; cash books, 1862-77; profit and loss accounts, 1851-72, 1874-80; letter books, 1880-1910; two notebooks kept by Robert Robinson, *c.* 1837-45, contain notes on bridge construction, travelling expenses incurred by Robinson as a surveyor, engineering sketches, and a note on the early days of the Inchbank or Partick Saw Mills. Among a collection of papers are contracts of co-partnery, 1877, 1902; letters from the Clyde Navigation Trust concerning timber dues, 1840-45; and price cards for timber and sawing, 1842-55. Thomas Dunn was the founder of the firm of Brownlie, Dunn & Company.

Robinson, Dunn & Co. Ltd., Temple Saw Mills, Glasgow.

PRINTING AND PUBLISHING

Blackie & Son, 1846-58
2 volumes
Binding shop wages books, 1846-58.
University of Glasgow, on loan from Blackie & Son Limited.

'The Glasgow Argus', 1833-47

1 volume
 Minute book of the finance committee of the proprietors of the *Glasgow Argus*, 1833-47, together with balance sheets and financial statements.

The Mitchell Library, Glasgow.

George Outram and Company, 1802-69

16 volumes
 Day books, 1820-25, 1835-37; cash books, 1818-20, 1828-55; and 'blotters' or advertising ledgers, 1802-03, 1825-69, relating to the publication of *The Glasgow Herald*.

University of Glasgow, gift of George Outram and Company, Glasgow.

John Ritchie and Company, 1817-c. 1914

75 volumes, 4 deed boxes, 9 bundles
 Although only one minute book (1868-81) appears to have survived, there are several loose minutes of the meetings of the original partners, 1817-c. 1828, together with a rough book and several bundles of papers containing statistics and financial jottings of the same period. Two volumes of balance sheets are interesting in that in addition to annual 'Abstracts of the Scotsman's Affairs', 1831-54, and 'Balance Sheets of J. Ritchie & Co., 1868-1913', they contain detailed observations on the financial state of the partnership, circulation figures, and significant trends in the affairs of the newspaper.

 Among the account books in this remarkable collection are journals, 1854-60, containing details of the advertising matter contained in *The Scotsman*; Contributor's Day Books, 1887-1918, and Contributor's Ledgers, recording the names of contributors to *The Scotsman*, 1872-1917, and the *Edinburgh Evening Dispatch*, 1886-1911, together with the subject of their articles, column inches and payments; 35 cash books, 1832-1913, and a 'Cash Book Analysis Book' giving monthly, and sometimes weekly, statistics of all items of income and expenditure, 1866-1939; and three wages books, 1838-69. Other records give details of book reviews, 1852-60, editorial and reporting expenses, 1852-60, and impression statistics of *The Scotsman* and *Semi-Weekly Scotsman*, 1855-66. One large volume, known familiarly to the executive staff as 'The Bible', gives daily figures of the number of advertisements, number of columns, credit and ready money income, total income, copies printed, and 'Remarks', plus monthly totals, average daily circulation for each month, average income per column and detailed breakdown of material costs involved in the publication of *The Scotsman*, *The Weekly Scotsman* and the *Edinburgh Evening Dispatch*. The period covered is 1866-1940.

 There are also several bundles of letters to John Ritchie; a most valuable collection of letters to Dr. Charles A. Cooper, editor of *The Scotsman*, 1880-1906; and a diary of John Findlay, a partner in the firm from 1868 to 1898 and associated with *The Scotsman* from 1842.

The Scotsman Publications Limited, 20 North Bridge, Edinburgh, 1.

CIVIL ENGINEERING AND BUILDING

Glasgow Workmen's Dwelling Company Limited, 1890-93
1 volume, 1 file
Memorandum of association, 1890; minute book, 1890-93.

University of Glasgow, gift of Mann Judd Gordon & Company, Chartered Accountants, Glasgow.

Kyle & Frew, Consulting Civil Engineers, Land Surveyors and Valuers, 1795-1890
20 volumes, 1 box, 30 maps
The firm of Kyle & Frew was founded in 1778 by William Kyle. Following William Kyle's death in 1837, his nephew Thomas Kyle succeeded to the business and carried it on until his death in 1862. Thereafter the business was conducted by a series of partnerships, the first of which consisted of John Frew and the trustees of Thomas Kyle, thus inaugurating the name Kyle & Frew. The collection includes: registers, 1845-47, 1855-59, 1864-67, these volumes record the work undertaken by the partners, the information includes descriptions of land surveyed, land values, land utilisation, feu duties, costs of construction of public works, and reports on the effects of railway construction on turnpike roads, existing properties, etc.; tracings, 1871-90, these volumes contain tracings made in conjunction with surveys and land conveyances, some tracings are of originals of a much earlier period; indexes of the plans in possession of William and Thomas Kyle, 1795-1857, the majority of the plans are lost but the descriptions are possibly of value in tracing land ownership and valuation; notebooks, containing jottings, calculations and field surveys, several relating to the River Clyde, 1804-42; book of plans and maps of Glasgow and the central valley of Scotland, *c.* 1820-40, showing canals, roads, railways, mineral deposits and iron works; collection of maps, framed or in single sheets, of Glasgow, Paisley, and railways between Edinburgh and Glasgow; letters addressed to Thomas Kyle, 1840-57, and miscellaneous reports, 1829-82.

University of Glasgow, gift of Mr. Alexander Frew, Jr. and Mr. Gordon Frew.

Incorporation of the Masons of Glasgow, 1603-1930
21 volumes
Minute books of the Master Court, 1603-1772, 1779-1805, 1813-1927; general minute books, 1603-1930; collector's account book, 1690-1737; roll books, 1760-1921; qualified roll books, 1888-1933.

Incorporation of Masons, Glasgow.

TRANSPORT: SHIPPING

Clyde Shipping Company, 1873-87
2 volumes
Minute books, 1873-87.

Clyde Shipping Company Limited, Glasgow.

The Clyde Steam Packet Company, Glasgow, 1852-71

Papers relating to the company, 1852-58; log books of the company's steamships, *Clyde* and *Petrel*, 1854-55; and papers relating to the founder, David A. B. Murray, 1857-71.

The Mitchell Library, Glasgow.

S.S. 'Haco', 1870-73

1 deed box

Master's Log book, 1871-72; chief engineer's log books; vouchers for captain's disbursements; wage sheets for all crew members; insurance certificates; correspondence concerning construction, outfitting and operation, 1870-72.

Scotts' Shipbuilding & Engineering Company Limited, Greenock, Renfrewshire.

William Thomson & Company: The Ben Line, 1844-1922

165 volumes

Voyage accounts of nineteen sailing vessels, 1844-98, and thirty-eight steamships, 1871-1922, owned or managed by William Thomson & Company of Leith and Edinburgh. The voyage accounts may be said to fall roughly into three groups: those of ships engaged in the North Atlantic trade, the Baltic trade and the Far Eastern trade. The general arrangement of the accounts, virtually identical throughout the series, is as follows: (*a*) outfitting expenses, followed in the case of the steamships by the costs of fuel; (*b*) William Thomson & Co.'s disbursements; (*c*) master's disbursements, (*d*) crew's salaries and wages; (*e*) earnings of each voyage; (*f*) 'gain on voyage', i.e. total earnings minus total disbursements; (*g*) division of the 'gain on voyage' into sixty-fourths, and its distribution to the partners.

William Thomson & Company, Edinburgh.

TRANSPORT: DOCKS, CANALS AND WATERWAYS

Burntisland Pier and Ferry Company, 1839

1 volume

Minute book, 1839.

University of Glasgow, on permanent loan from Thomson, Dickson & Shaw, W.S., and J. A. Campbell & Lamond, C.S., Edinburgh.

The River Clyde, 1810-35

2 notebooks, 4 plans

Notebooks containing surveys of the River Clyde, 1810, 1841-42; 'Longitudinal section of the River Clyde from the West End of the Broomielaw Quay to the Wear at Clydes Mill', *c.* 1825; 'Plan of the River Clyde from Glasgow to Port Glasgow', *c.* 1830; 'Map of the River Clyde', May, 1835; 'Plan of Part of the Clyde, West of Jamaica Street', *c.* 1830.

University of Glasgow, gift of Mr. Alexander Frew, Jr. and Mr. Gordon Frew. (See 'Civil Engineering and Building'.)

The Clyde Lighthouses Trust, 1757-1955

30 volumes, 3 deed boxes

Minute books, 1757-1804, 1850-1955; account of Cumbray [sic] Light dues collected at the Port of Greenock, 1835-38; return of dues payable to the Cambrae Lighthouse Commissioners, collected at Greenock, 1861-72; return of rates payable to the trustees of the Clyde Lighthouses, collected at Greenock, 1871-1916; three deed boxes contain titles, agreements, memoranda and precognitions for witnesses before Parliamentary committees, and newspaper cuttings; the collection includes a comprehensive set of the Acts concerning the Clyde lighthouses and the Clyde Navigation Trust, several volumes of annotated Parliamentary Papers relating to these Acts, and a number of relevant Provisional Orders and Board of Trade Inquiries.

The Clyde Lighthouses Trust.

Edinburgh and Glasgow Union Canal Company, 1833

1 bundle, 2 plans

Accounts and papers, relating principally to a loan from the Royal Bank of Scotland; two large plans of the proposed Edinburgh & Glasgow Union Canal, showing mineral deposits and coal workings, 1813-16.

University of Glasgow, on permanent loan from Mitchells, Johnston & Company, Glasgow. The plans are among the Kyle & Frew papers, see 'Civil Engineering and Building'.

The Monkland Canal Company, 1839-45

1 bundle

Statement of revenues and prospective income, 1839-45.

University of Glasgow, on permanent loan from Mitchells, Johnston & Company, Glasgow.

Port Glasgow Harbour, 1772-1867

1 file

Papers relating to the case of Anstruther against Pollok Gilmour & Company and the Port Glasgow Harbour Trustees, 1868. These include copies of Acts of Parliament relating to Port Glasgow Harbour, 1772, 1823, 1864; excerpts from the minute book of the Port Glasgow Harbour Trust, 1801-09; plans of Port Glasgow, 1792, 1810, 1867, and the harbour, 1793, 1815, 1831; minutes of an agreement to purchase land at Port Glasgow for the building of a wharf and wall, 1791-92; and precognitions in the case of Anstruther against Pollok Gilmour & Co., 1867.

University of Glasgow, on permanent loan from Anderson, Young & Dickson, Writers, Glasgow.

TRANSPORT: RAILWAYS

Ardrossan Railway and Ardrossan Harbour, 1823-1900

1 box

This collection of papers, mainly 1840-60, was extracted from that portion of the Eglinton Estate papers that was not incorporated in the main Eglinton collection at the Scottish Record Office. The records fall into two main groups: those concerning Ardrossan Harbour, and those concerned with railway companies in Ayrshire, Renfrewshire, Lanarkshire and Glasgow. The focus of interest is on the activities of Ardrossan Harbour and the Ardrossan Railway, and those records not directly resulting from the operations of these two undertakings usually have an important bearing on their prosperity. The following division is, therefore, somewhat arbitrary:

Ardrossan Harbour: abstracts of revenue and expenditure. 1852-62, 1878-81; cash balances, 1879-81; abstract of tack between the Earl of Eglinton and John Moffat, leasing the harbour to the latter, 1854; miscellaneous reports, accounts and papers, 1845-59; plans of Ardrossan Harbour, 1853, 1890; copy of Ardrossan Harbour Act, 1885.

Ardrossan Railway Company: reports, 1841, 1843, 1845, 1853-54; abstracts of accounts, 1847-49; traffic returns, 1844-52; agreements, memoranda and correspondence, 1841-53, including minutes of meetings concerning arrangements with other railway companies operating in the region regarding freight charges, extensions and possible sale or amalgamation.

Glasgow, Kilmarnock & Ardrossan Railway Company: reports and papers, mainly relating to the bill dissolving the company, 1846-52.

Other Railway Companies: other papers relate to the Ayr Railway, 1844-45; Garnkirk & Glasgow Railway, 1840; Glasgow & South Western Railway, 1883, 1898, 1900; Glasgow, Barrhead & Neilson Direct Railway, 1846; Kilmarnock & Troon Railway, 1823-48.

University of Glasgow, gift of Ayr County Council.

Edinburgh & Dundee Railway Company, 1836-37
1 volume
Minute book, 1836-37.

University of Glasgow, on permanent loan from Thomson, Dickson & Shaw, W.S., and J. A. Campbell & Lamond, C.S. Edinburgh.

Mitchells, Johnston & Company's papers, c. 1823-1911
54 volumes, 10 deed boxes
The legal firm of Mitchells, Johnston & Company, founded by Thomas Grahame, c. 1745, has been law agents to the University of Glasgow since 1776. In the third decade of the nineteenth century the firm became deeply involved with railway work. This was the major concern of James Mitchell, and, later, his cousin and partner, Alexander Oswald Mitchell. The firm was involved with many of the early lines subsequently absorbed by the Caledonian Railway and the North British Railway and, in acting as agents for these companies, amassed a large collection of papers relating to railway cases. These were presented to the University on permanent loan in 1963 and are as yet incompletely calendared. However, the contents of one deed box have been the subject of a study by Dr. J. R. Kellett entitled 'Urban and Business History from Railway Records in Solicitors' Offices', and it would appear that this part of the collection is typical of the whole. The papers in this deed box deal with the North British railway's Stobcross Docks extension line, 1864-72, and consist of the following types of document:

Memoranda and Precognitions for witnesses.
Valuators' reports, sometimes with tables of feu duties, mineral reports and maps.

Claimant's statement and proof.
Decrees arbitral.
Dispositions, certificates of rental.
Letters and newspaper cuttings.
Agreements as to accommodation works.
Detailed contracts.
Proprietor's Statement and Brief for Arbiters and/or Jury Trial.

Other papers are *mainly* concerned with the following railway companies:

Airdrie, Coatbridge & Wishaw Junction Railway, *c.* 1866-67. (Books of
reference; statements of advantages of the proposed line; traffic figures;
land valuations; way-leaves payable; notes of evidence, etc.)
Ardrossan Railway, *c.* 1854.
Ballochney Railway, *c.* 1826-48, including an early map, 1828, of the
original coal railway line built for William Dixon.
Edinburgh & Glasgow Railway, 1853-61.
Glasgow, Dumbarton and Helensburgh Railway, 1853-56.
Glasgow, Yoker & Dalmuir Railway, 1873-78, the papers include petitions
and letters by the principal shipbuilders, and drawings of Whiteinch and
other docks.
Glasgow & South Western Railway, *c.* 1854, 1905-11; the later papers show
the effects of the railway on the Kirktonhall Estate.
Monkland & Kirkintilloch Railway, 1845-48.
North British Railway, Coatbridge branch, 1865-68.
Slamannan Railway, 1845-48.
Wilsontown, Morningside & Coltness Railway, extension to Shotts, 1845-48.
Wishaw & Coltness Railway, *c.* 1844.

The collection also includes a series of fifteen ledgers, 1842-70, containing
accounts of fees for legal services in connection with work for railway
companies, thereby providing an invaluable chronological guide to railway
developments in Central Scotland and the nature of the legal problems
involved in railway promotions, extensions and amalgamations. In addition,
there are fifteen volumes of Acts of Parliament relating to Scottish railways, 1823-67; Parliamentary Papers, Callander & Oban Railways, 1864-
65, North British Railway, 1865-66; seven volumes of *Railway and Canal
Cases*, 1835-54; two editions of *The Law of Railways, Applicable to Scotland*, by F. Deas, 1873, 1897; Hodge's Law of Railways, 1888; bound
volumes of the *Railway Times*, 1843, 1845, 1847-48; the *Scottish Railway
Gazette*, Vol. I, 1845; and the reports of the directors of the Monkland
Railways (Monkland & Kirkintilloch, Ballochney and Slamannan Railways), 1848-65.

*University of Glasgow, on permanent loan from Mitchells, Johnston & Com-
pany, Glasgow.*

DOMESTIC TRADE

Archibald Arrol, c. 1833-90

1 deed box

Legal and executry papers of Archibald Arrol, merchant and commission
agent in Glasgow, *c.* 1833-90. Arrol also conducted business as a brewer in

Alloa and as a bottler in Glasgow. [These papers have yet to be calendered.]

University of Glasgow, deposited on permanent loan by Thompson, Dickson & Shaw, W.S., and J. A. Campbell & Lamond, C.S., Edinburgh.

P. & R. Fleming & Company, Hardware Factors, 1860-1913

2 files
Balance sheets, 1860-77; price lists and catalogues, 1875-1913.

P. & R. Fleming & Company Limited, Glasgow.

The Moir Papers, 1827-80

Letters to James Moir, tea merchant, Glasgow Bailie and donor to The Mitchell Library. The collection includes accounts and papers, 1827-80.

The Mitchell Library, Glasgow.

FOREIGN TRADE

The Bogle Papers, 1725-61

Family papers of the Bogles of Shettleston and Daldowie, and the Browns of Lanfine. Letter books and letters, 1725-31, 1729-42, 1759-61. Some letters deal with the Bogles of Glasgow and the tobacco trade in Virginia, other material deals with the fortunes of George Bogle (1746-81) in the East India Company.

The Mitchell Library, Glasgow.

D. Gavin, 1755-65

1 volume
Letter book, 1755-65, of a merchant trading mainly with France and the Netherlands.

University of Glasgow, on permanent loan from Thomson, Dickson & Shaw, W.S., and J. A. Campbell & Lamond, C.S., Edinburgh.

Glasgow East India Association, 1824-38

Printed and MSS. papers relating to trade with India, 1824-38.

The Mitchell Library, Glasgow.

The Lang Papers, 1760-1846

1 box
The bulk of this collection consists of the accounts and papers of Thomas Lang, a partner in Lang & Baine (later Baine & Johnston), merchants of Greenock, whose major trading interest was in shipping dried salt cod from Newfoundland to the European continent. Among the papers, mainly *c.* 1819-42, is a collection of letters addressed to Thomas Lang, including several from the United States, Canada, and Italy; bank receipts and accounts, 1830-43; factorial accounts and a rent book connected with house property in Greenock, 1819-40; and a number of papers of Thomas Lang's father, James Lang, and his uncle, John Russell, merchants and shipmasters of Greenock, 1760-85.

Business Archives Council of Scotland, gift of Miss E. Grieve, Grantown-on-Spey, Moray.

Adam Montgomerie, 1699-1702

1 volume

Copy-book of letters of Adam Montgomerie of Glasgow, 1699-1702; the letters are mainly from Stockholm and relate principally to Scottish commerce.

The Mitchell Library, Glasgow.

Alexander Sharp & Company, 1743-58

1 volume

Cash book, 1743-58, of merchants engaged in the trade with the West Indies and the American colonies.

University of Glasgow, on permanent loan from Thomson, Dickson & Shaw, W.S., and J. A. Campbell & Lamond, C.S., Edinburgh.

The Wylie Papers, 1809-40

9 volumes

Letter books containing copies of the business correspondence of John Wylie, a Glasgow merchant, with agents and firms in Bahia, Buenos Aires and Rio de Janeiro, together with copies of letters to English manufacturers and suppliers in Liverpool, London and Manchester, 1809-20; letter books containing copy correspondence of John Wylie and Wylie, Cooke & Co., of San Luis Potosi, to persons and business houses throughout Mexico, and to merchants and manufacturers in Britain and the United States, 1830-40. A noteworthy feature of these letters is the very high proportion of their contents devoted to discussions of contemporary political, social and economic issues in Mexico.

University of Glasgow, on permanent loan from Mitchells, Johnston & Company, Glasgow.

OVERSEAS ENTERPRISE

Netherlands India Dry Dock Company Limited, 1873-78

1 file

Three documents relating to the construction of dry docks at Batavia and Sourabaya, 1873-78. A firm of Glasgow merchants, Raalte Behrend & Co., contracted with Antonius G. Bosch, of Amsterdam, manager of the Netherlands India Dry Dock Company, to execute and supply docks, jetties, etc., at Batavia and Sourabaya. Raalte Behrend & Company then sub-contracted with Hanna Donald & Company, engineers and shipbuilders, of Paisley, for them to do the work. The capital involved was about £125,000. Troubles followed, the original agreement, 1873, was modified and in 1878 the Scottish firms had to take shares in the Dry Dock Company.

Business Archives Council of Scotland, gift of Colonel A. R. Cross, Mackenzie Roberton & Company, Glasgow.

The Tharsis Sulphur & Copper Company, Ltd., 1866-1964

83 volumes

The more important records include: minute books of the board of directors, 1866-1964; minute books of the Glasgow committee, 1920-37; reports of the directors, 1867-1964; reports of the proceedings at the annual general meeting, 1868-1939; 45 letter books, containing copies of correspondence, including reports by mining engineers and auditors, together with production statistics, sent from the company's mines at Huelva, Spain, to Glasgow, 1868-71, 1873-76, 1887-1919, 1921-39; Tharsis labour records, 1882-95; statistics of the shipment of pyrites from Huelva by mining companies other than Tharsis, 1875-84; copies of titles to property; collection of newspaper cuttings relating to the metallurgical industry, c. 1905-30.

The Tharsis Sulphur & Copper Company, Limited, Glasgow.

BANKING

The City of Glasgow Bank, 1840-82

30 volumes

The following records, mainly relating to the failure and subsequent liquidation of the City of Glasgow Bank, were among the papers of James Muir, a partner of Kerr, Anderson, Muir & Main (predecessors of Kerr, MacLeod & Macfarlan) and one of the liquidators of the Bank. The more important material includes: a volume containing the Contract of Co-partnery of the City of Glasgow Bank with supplementary contracts, special resolutions, certificates of incorporation, and resolutions for winding up and for appointing liquidators, 1840-78; official list of shareholders and trustees; excerpts from the minute books of the board of directors, 1857-78; directors' defence, reprint of 207 letters, 1872-78; newspaper cuttings, 1878; report by the investigators, 1878; resolution to wind up the Bank, 1878; four reports by the liquidators to the shareholders, 1878-82; report to the liquidators by James Muir on the history of the Bank's involvement with the Western Union Railroad Company of America, and the position in relation to these involvements, occupied by William Mackinnon, ex-director of the Bank, 1880; six appendixes relating to the case of the liquidators against William Mackinnon, containing proof for the parties, evidence taken in the United States, American railroad reports, 1859-79, details of the Bank's American investments, and correspondence, documents and accounts, 1857-80.

The legal firm of McGrigor, Donald & Co. also have copies of a number of the above records and, in addition, the following volumes: liquidation of James Morton & Co.'s liabilities from 1865 to 1878; directors' trial, prints of prosecution, Vol. II, 1878; report of the petition of William Muir and others for the rectification of the list of contributories of the City of Glasgow Bank, 1878; City of Glasgow Bank liquidation: evidence of William Morris, 1878; proceedings in Court of Session referring to the legal position of trustees of shares and other miscellaneous actions involving individual shareholders, 1878, nine volumes; prints of indictment, precognitions, correspondence, etc., in case against James Nicol Fleming, 1882.

Kerr, MacLeod & Macfarlan, Chartered Accountants, Glasgow; McGrigor, Donald & Co., Solicitors, Glasgow.

Commercial Bank of Scotland, c. 1824-60

2 deed boxes

Papers and letters, c. 1824-60. [These have yet to be calendared.]

University of Glasgow, on permanent loan from Thomson, Dickson & Shaw, W.S., and J. A. Campbell & Lamond, C.S., Edinburgh.

Dundee Union Bank, 1832

1 file

Deed of accession to the contract of co-partnery of the Dundee Union Bank, 1832.

University of Glasgow, gift of McClelland, Moores & Company, C.A., Glasgow.

The Savings Bank of Glasgow, 1836-1914

Approximately 390 volumes

The more important material in this comprehensive collection includes: minute books, 1836-1914; annual reports, 1836-1914; account and transfer ledgers, 1836-1900; investment ledgers, 1880-1914; declaration books, 1848-1914; letter books, 1836-1914; Penny Bank constitutions and reports, and the minute books of savings banks amalgamated with the Savings Bank of Glasgow, including those of Darvel, Hamilton, Kirkintilloch and Sanquhar.

The Savings Bank of Glasgow.

Western Bank of Scotland, 1832-72

1 deed box

With one exception, these records were presented to the University by Messrs. McClelland, Moores & Company, Chartered Accountants, a firm founded in 1820, one of the partners of which was involved in the liquidation of the Western Bank. They include: contract of co-partnery of the Western Bank of Scotland, 1832; first deed of accession to the contract of co-partnery, 1844; deed of alteration, 1857; lithographed facsimile of the minute book of the Glasgow committee of the directors of the Bank, 1847-49. The following papers relate to the liquidation of the Bank: six assignations, 1858-63; closed record of the action brought by the Western Bank and its Liquidators against Thomas Dunlop Douglas and others for payment and damages, 1860; papers relating to the ratification of the Liquidators' accounts and interim reports, 1861-63; discharge by the Liquidators of the Western Bank in favour of James McClelland as trustee, 1860; draft deed discharging the Liquidators, 1868; printed volume of the 'Debate *in causa* The Liquidator of the Western Bank against Mr. William Baird's Trustees', 1872; minute book of the Fund for the Relief of Shareholders, 1861-62.

University of Glasgow, gift of McClelland, Moores & Company, C.A., Glasgow.

The 'Closed record of the action brought by the Western Bank of Scotland . . . against Thomas Dunlop Douglas', 1860, is part of the Muir collection of Messrs. Kerr, MacLeod and Macfarlan.

INSURANCE

The Association of Underwriters and Insurance Brokers in Glasgow, 1818-1939

12 volumes, 1 file

The most important records are: the scroll of accession, 1818; minute books, 1818-1939; list of shipping registered in the different ports of Scotland, 1823; album of policies, from *c.* 1820.

Association of Underwriters and Insurance Brokers in Glasgow.

William Bennett & Browne, c. 1750-1831

4 volumes, 1 file
Insurance day book and ledger, 1795-98; cash books, 1805-10; bill books, 1795-1805, 1824-31; legal papers of William Browne, *c.* 1750; letters to James Browne, 1815-16; letters to William Bennett from Rio de Janeiro, 1808-09; legal documents concerning leases in Newfoundland, 1786-92.

Bennett, Browne & Company, Glasgow.

William Euing, c. 1790-1810
1 volume
Pocket ledger, *c.* 1790-1810.
William Euing & Company, Limited, Glasgow.

Glasgow Fire Insurance Company, 1803-11
1 file
The more important documents are: contract of co-partnery establishing the Glasgow Fire Insurance Society, 1803 (among the original partners were David Dale, James Buchanan, Kirkman Finlay, Archibald Grahame, John Scott); two deeds of accession, 1803; agreement to enlarge the scope of the business by engaging in insurance upon lives, 1803; agreement to invest in government securities, 1805; deed of dissolution and agreement to transfer the business to the Phoenix Fire Insurance Company, 1811; agreement between the directors of the Glasgow Fire Insurance Society and the directors of the Phoenix Fire Insurance Company, 1811.

University of Glasgow, gift of Professor A. M. Boase.

Seventh Friendly Society of Kilbarchan, 1909-60
1 volume, 1 booklet
Minute book, 1909-60; articles of the Society as revised in 1919. Instituted in 1803, the Kilbarchan Seventh Friendly Society's affairs were wound up in 1960.

University of Glasgow, gift of the Kilbarchan Seventh Friendly Society.

PROFESSIONAL SERVICES

Legal

Anderson Young & Dickson Papers, c. 1686-1876
1 deed box
Until this collection of papers has been calendared it will be impossible to list the bundles of related documents under more appropriate headings. The records include: Miscellaneous writs, *c.* 1686-1842; papers relating to bankruptcies, 1819-21; charter parties and marine insurance policies, 1838-51; estate papers, 1848-76; patent specifications and agreements relating thereto, 1839-40; and indenture agreements, 1809-41.

University of Glasgow, on permanent loan from Anderson Young & Dickson, Writers, Glasgow.

J. A. Campbell, C.S., 1821-22
1 volume
Letter book, 1821-22.

Thomson, Dickson & Shaw, W.S., and J. A. Campbell & Lamond, C.S., Edinburgh

J. L. Campbell, W.S., 1814-22
1 volume
Private ledger, 1814-22.

Thomson, Dickson & Shaw, W.S., and J. A. Campbell & Lamond, C.S., Edinburgh.

Mitchells, Johnston & Company, c. 1823-1911
54 volumes, 10 deed boxes
See entry under 'Transport: Railways'.

Medical

John Neil, Chemist, 1893-1944

23 volumes
Prescription books, 1893-1944. These records are of great potential interest to the student of the history of pharmacy.

University of Glasgow, gift of Cockburn & Co. Ltd., Glasgow.

Undertaking

Wylie & Lochhead, 1843-1914

Approximately 40 volumes
Robert Wylie and William Lochhead were already established as under-takers when in 1832 there was an outbreak of Asiatic Cholera in Glasgow; 6,000 cases were reported, half of which proved fatal. The civic authorities, as a result of the work performed by the partners during the epidemic, requested them to provide a complete funeral service by supplying the necessary ushers and bearers, hearses and catering arrangements. The earliest records of the firm's funeral department were lost in a fire, but there is a continuous run of ledgers giving detailed funeral accounts from 1843, with a single break in the 'nineties. The comprehensive service provided was the first of its kind in Scotland.

Wylie & Lochhead Limited, Glasgow.

CHAPTER FOUR

A Bibliography of Scottish Business History

W. H. MARWICK

Lately Lecturer in Economic History,
University of Edinburgh

SCOTTISH BUSINESS HISTORY, like Scottish local history, has been left largely to the amateur, in this case, often a partner or employee of the firm. Many such publications are compounded of anecdote and reminiscence, and lack documentation, or are compilations of technical detail, omitting most that is of interest to the economic historian. Some celebrate the centenary or other anniversary of the firm's foundation; the business expansion of the mid-nineteenth century is responsible for a large crop in recent years. The caption 'First Hundred Years' or 'Jubilee' appears with wearisome reiteration, occasionally varied by some flowery phrase. They vary very much in extent and quality; some of the better contain valuable background material; particularly surveys of economic conditions at the date of the firm's foundation. Latterly, there has been a trend towards commissioning a writer—often a journalist—to compose the volume, and admitting him to the company's records. The nationalisation of some enterprises after the late War encouraged this tendency. Only rarely as yet—notably in *Carron Company*—has the task been assigned to a professional expert.

Delimitation of sphere constitutes a special problem. In general, works relating to industry before the mid-eighteenth century have been excluded, but a few standard works such as W. R. Scott's *History of Joint Stock Companies* are excerpted, for their intrinsic importance as studies of Scottish industrial development. Some books concerned mainly with industry in England are included because of Scottish references. It is difficult to achieve a logical pattern of classification, as so many general works and individual histories overlap the categories adopted. Some firms undertake a variety of activities; occasionally, one has changed its main activity, for example, R. & J. Dick Ltd., from footwear to rubber belting. In such cases, to avoid duplication and cross references, the choice has been somewhat arbitrary. A suggestion that lists of periodicals be included has, on consideration, been rejected. Instead, articles of particular relevance are cited at the appropriate point, an example being the series on 'Clydeside Firms' which ran for some years in the *Journal of the Glasgow Chamber of Commerce.*

The system adopted is as follows. First, the principal bibliographies dealing with Scottish history are given. This section is followed by general and local histories, comprising a selective list of works on Scottish economic development (which may be supplemented by consulting the bibliographies in the previous section) and those dealing with the chief industrial towns and districts, plus several biographical compilations which include lives of business men. Biographies are relatively few; as Roy Lewis and Rosemary Stewart say in their recent study of *The Boss,* 'the biographical art has hardly been practised on the business man . . . Business men work in silence and in secret. Few leave diaries, documents or letters of any interest. . . .' The proportion of business men thought worthy of mention in the obituary column is tiny; so are the entries in the *Directory of National Biography* (one might add, in *Who's Who,* apart from those who obtain entry through receiving a title). Many memoirs are examples of family 'piety' rather than of informative presentation. There follow nine sections devoted to particular industries or forms of enterprise. In each case, a similar subdivision is utilised: works dealing with the 'industry' in general, histories of individual firms, and biographies of those concerned with it. The two final sections deal respectively with Co-operative enterprises and Fisheries. The latter has been compiled by Mr. Malcolm Gray, University of Aberdeen, and does not conform to the general pattern, partly because of the special nature of the 'industry'. After serious consideration, agriculture has been omitted.

I am indebted to the Editor and other members of the Editorial Committee, and to Mr. Ian MacDougall and Mrs. Margaret Swain, of Edinburgh, for suggesting additional items; and to several firms for presenting copies of their publications.

Bibliography of Scottish Business History

I. BIBLIOGRAPHIES

HANCOCK, P. D.   *A Bibliography of Works Relating to Scotland, 1916-50.* 2 volumes. (Edinburgh, 1959-60.)

KEITH, T.	*Bibliography of Scottish Economic History*. (Edinburgh. 1914.)
MARWICK, W. H.	'A Bibliography of Scottish Economic History', *Economic History Review*, III, 1931-32.
MARWICK, W. H.	'A Bibliography of Works on Scottish Economic History published during the last Twenty Years', *Economic History Review*, 2nd Series, IV, 1951-52.
MARWICK, W. H.	'A Bibliography of Scottish Economic History 1951-62', *Economic History Review*, 2nd Series, XVI, 1963-64.
MITCHELL, A. & CASH, C. O.	*A Contribution to the Bibliography of Scottish Topography*. 2 volumes. (Edinburgh, 1917.)
SALTIRE SOCIETY	*Scottish Books*. (Edinburgh, 1963.)
SCOTT, W. R.	*Scottish Economic Literature to 1800*. (Glasgow, 1911.)

II. GENERAL AND LOCAL HISTORIES
(i) *General Works*

BREMNER, D.	*Industries of Scotland*. (Edinburgh, 1869.)
CAMPBELL, R. H.	*Scotland from 1707: the Rise of an Industrial Society*. (Oxford, 1964.)
FOGARTY, M. P. (ed.)	*Further Studies in Industrial Organisation*. (London, 1948.)
HAMILTON, H.	*The Industrial Revolution in Scotland*. (Oxford, 1932.)
HAMILTON, H.	*The Economic History of Scotland in the Eighteenth Century*. (Oxford, 1963.)
HESS, A.	*Some British Industries*. (London, 1957.)
MARWICK, W. H.	*Economic Developments in Victorian Scotland*. (London, 1936.)
MARWICK, W. H.	*Scotland in Modern Times: A Survey of the Economic and Social Development Since the Union of 1707*. (London, 1964.)
OAKLEY, C. A.	*Scottish Industry Today*. (Edinburgh, 1937.)
OAKLEY, C. A.	*Scottish Industry*. (Edinburgh, 1953.)
SCOTT, W. R.	*History of Joint Stock Companies to 1720*. 3 volumes. (Cambridge, 1910-12.)
SCOTTISH COUNCIL OF SOCIAL SERVICE	*The Third Statistical Account of Scotland*. (Edinburgh & Glasgow, 1951 et seq.) (In progress.)
SILVERMAN, H. A. (ed.)	*Studies in Industrial Organisation*. (London, 1946.)

(ii) *Local Histories*

ALLARDYCE, J.	*Byegone Days in Aberdeenshire*. (Aberdeen, 1913.)
ANONYMOUS	*Falkirk: Official Guide*. (Falkirk, 1952.)
ANONYMOUS	*The Industries of Midlothian*. (Edinburgh, 1954.)
ANONYMOUS	*The Book of Airdrie*. (Glasgow, 1954.)
BARR, W. T.	*For a Web Begun: the Story of Dunfermline*. (Edinburgh, 1947.)

G

BRITISH ASSOCIATION	*Dundee Memorial Volume: Local Industries.* (Dundee, 1868.)
BRITISH ASSOCIATION	*Notices of Some Principal Manufactures of the West of Scotland.* (Glasgow, 1876.)
BRITISH ASSOCIATION	*Handbook on the Local Industries of Glasgow and the West of Scotland.* Ed. A. McLean. (Glasgow, 1901.)
BRITISH ASSOCIATION	*Glasgow, 1928.* Ed. J. Graham Kerr. (Glasgow, 1928.)
BRITISH ASSOCIATION	*Dundee and District, 1939.* Ed. R. L. Mackie. (Dundee, 1939.)
BRITISH ASSOCIATION	*Scientific Survey of South-eastern Scotland.* (Edinburgh, 1951.)
BRITISH ASSOCIATION	*The Glasgow Region: A General Survey.* Ed. R. Miller and J. Tivy. (Glasgow, 1958.)
CAMERON, J.	*Parish of Campsie.* (Kirkintilloch, 1892.)
FAY, C. R.	*Round about Industrial Britain.* (Toronto, 1952.)
GIBSON, W.	*Reminiscences of Dollar.* (Edinburgh, 1882.)
GORDON, T. C.	*Short History of Alloa.* (Alloa, 1937.)
GROSSART, W.	*Historic Notes of the Parish of Shotts.* (Glasgow, 1880.)
JOURNAL OF THE GLASGOW CHAMBER OF COMMERCE	*Clydeside Companies.* (Glasgow, 1953 et seq.)
LOTHIAN, J.	*Alloa and its Environs.* (Alloa, 3rd ed., 1871.)
MACARTHUR, W. F.	*History of Port Glasgow.* (Glasgow, 1932.)
MACKIE, A.	*An Industrial History of Edinburgh.* (Glasgow, 1963.)
MACLEOD, D.	*Dumbarton, Vale of Leven.* (Dumbarton, 1884.)
MACLEOD, D.	*Clyde District of Dumbarton.* (Dumbarton, 1886.)
MILLER, A.	*Rise and Progress of Coatbridge.* (Glasgow, 1862.)
MILNES, N.	*A Study of Industrial Edinburgh, 1923-34.* (London, 1936.)
MORGAN, P.	*Annals of Woodside and Newhalls.* (Aberdeen, 1886.)
MURRAY, R.	*Annals of Barrhead.* (Glasgow, n.d. [1942?].)
SCOTT, W. R. & CUNNISON, J.	*The Industries of the Clyde Valley During the War.* (Oxford, 1925.)
SMITH, R. MURRAY	*History of Greenock.* (Greenock, 1921.)
THOMSON, J.	*The History of Dundee.* (Dundee, 1847.)
WATSON, D .M.	'Early Manufactures of Hawick', *Transactions of Hawick Archaeological Society,* 1868, 1873.
WHAMMOND, A.	*Handbook and Directory of Motherwell.* (Hamilton, 1894.)

(iii) *General Biographies*

ANONYMOUS	*The Old Country Houses of the Old Glasgow Gentry.* (Glasgow, 2nd edn., 1878.)
ANONYMOUS	*Memoirs and Portraits of One Hundred Glasgow Men.* 2 volumes. (Glasgow, 1886.)
ANONYMOUS	*Some Local Men.* (Perth, 1907.)

ANONYMOUS	*Who's Who in Glasgow.* (Glasgow, 1909.)
JEANS, J. S.	*Western Worthies.* (Glasgow, 1872.)
MITCHELL, J. O.	*Old Glasgow Essays.* (Glasgow, 1903.)
MURPHY, W. S.	*Captains of Industry.* (Glasgow, 1901.)
NORRIE, W.	*Dundee Celebrities of the 19th Century.* (Dundee, 1873.)
STEWART, G.	*Curiosities of Glasgow Citizenship.* (Glasgow, 1881.)

III. INDUSTRIES AND TRADES

(i) *Coal and other Mining Industries*

(*a*) GENERAL

ANONYMOUS	Selections from the Auchenharvie Papers. *Ayrshire Archaeological & Natural History Collections*, 2nd Series, VI, 1958-60.
ASHTON, T. S. & SYKES, J.	*The Coal Industry of the Eighteenth Century.* (Manchester, 1924.)
BALD, R.	*A General View of the Coal Trade of Scotland.* (Edinburgh, 1808.)
BROWN, A. J. YOUNGSON	'The Scottish Coal Industry, 1854-1886'. (D.Litt. thesis, Aberdeen, 1953.)
CUNNINGHAM, A. S.	*Mining in the Kingdom of Fife.* (Dunfermline, 1913.)
CUNNINGHAM, A. S.	*Mining in Mid and East Lothian.* (Edinburgh, 1925.)
DRON, R. W.	*Coalfields of Scotland.* (Edinburgh, 1902.)
HAMILTON, H.	'Combination in the West of Scotland Coal Trade', *Economic History, Supplement to Economic Journal*, II, 1930.)
MEADE, R.	*Coal and Iron Industries of the United Kingdom.* (London, 1883.)
NEF, J. U.	*Rise of British Coal Industry, 1550-1700.* 2 volumes. (London, 1932.)
PORTEOUS, J. M.	*God's Treasure House in Scotland.* (London, 1876.)
SMOUT, T. C.	'The Lead Mines at Wanlockhead', *Transactions of the Dumfriesshire and Galloway Natural History Society*, XXXIX, 1962.

(*b*) HISTORIES OF FIRMS

CARVEL, J. L.	*A Hundred Years in Coal: The History of the Alloa Coal Company.* (Edinburgh, 1944.)
CARVEL, J. L.	*The New Cumnock Coalfield.* (Edinburgh, 1946.)
CUNNINGHAM, A. S.	*Fife Coal Company, 1872-1922.* (Leven, 1922.)
MUIR, A.	*The Fife Coal Company Limited: A Short History.* (Cambridge, 1951.)
PAYNE, P. L.	'The Govan Colleries, 1804-1805', *Business History*, III, 1961.

(ii) *Iron and Steel Industries*

(*a*) GENERAL

BYERS, T. J. — 'The Scottish Economy during the Great Depression 1873-96, with special reference to the Heavy Industries of the South-West'. (B.Litt. thesis, Glasgow, 1962.)

CAMPBELL, R. H. — 'Investment in the Scottish Pig Iron Trade, 1830-1843', *Scottish Journal of Political Economy*, I, 1954.

CAMPBELL, R. H. — 'Development in the Scottish Pig Iron Trade 1844-1848', *Journal of Economic History*, XV, 1955.

CAMPBELL, R. H. — 'The Growth and Fluctuations of the Scottish Pig Iron Trade, 1828-73.' (Ph.D. thesis, Aberdeen, 1956.)

CAMPBELL, R. H. — 'Statistics of the Scottish Pig Iron Trade, 1830-1865', *Proceedings of the West of Scotland Iron and Steel Institute*, LXIV, 1956-57.

CAMPBELL, R. H. — 'Fluctuations in Stocks: a Nineteenth Century Case Study', *Oxford Economic Papers*, new ser. IX, 1957.

CAMPBELL, R. H. — 'Early Malleable Iron Production in Scotland', *Business History*, IV, 1961.

FELL, A. — *The Early Iron Industry of Furness.* (Ulverston, 1908.)

GIBSON, I. F. — 'The Economic History of the Scottish Iron and Steel Industry, 1830-1880.' (Ph.D. thesis, London, 1955.)

GIBSON, I. F. — 'The Establishment of the Scottish Steel Industry', *Scottish Journal of Political Economy*, V. 1958.

RILEY, J. — 'On the Rise and Progress of the Scotch Steel Trade', *Journal of the Iron & Steel Institute*, II, 1885.

ROGERSON, T. B. & BUCHANAN, W. — 'Progress of Manufacture of Pig Iron', *Proceedings of the West of Scotland Iron & Steel Institute*, XXI, 1913.

ROWAN, F. J. — 'On the Iron Trade of Scotland', *Journal of the Iron and Steel Institute*, II, 1885.

SIMPSON, M. L. — 'Steel Works: a Twenty-one Years' Review', *Proceedings of the West of Scotland Iron & Steel Institute*, XXI, 1913.

WYLIE, W. — 'Malleable Iron Trade', *Proceedings of the West of Scotland Iron & Steel Institute*, XXI, 1913.

(*b*) HISTORIES OF FIRMS

ANONYMOUS — *Colville & Sons Ltd., 1871-1921: Souvenir Booklet.* (Glasgow, 1921.)

ANONYMOUS — *The Carron Company, 1759-1938.* (Glasgow, 1938.)

ANONYMOUS — *Shaw and McInnes Ltd.: One Hundred Years of Family Business.* (Glasgow, 1946.)

ANONYMOUS — *A Technical Survey of The Colville Group of Companies.* A Supplement to *The Iron & Coal Trades Review*, 1957.

BEALE, S. R.	*Crown Ironworks: L. Sterne & Co. 1874-1949.* (Glasgow, 1951.)
BIRCH, A.	'Carron Company, 1784-1822: the Profits of Industry during the Industrial Revolution', *Explorations in Entrepreneurial History*, VIII, 1955-56.
BOGLE, A. N.	*The Founding of Carron Ironworks.* (Falkirk, 1898.)
BORTHWICK, A.	*Ironfounders 1854-1954: Smith & Wellstood Ltd., Bonnybridge.* (Stirling, 1954.)
CAMPBELL, R. H.	'The Financing of Carron Company', *Business History*, I, 1958.
CAMPBELL, R. H.	*Carron Company.* (Edinburgh, 1961.)
CARVEL, J. L.	*Coltness Iron Company.* (Edinburgh, 1948.)
HAMILTON, H.	'Founding of the Carron Ironworks', *Scottish Historical Review*, XXV, 1956.
MUIR, A.	*The Story of Shotts: A Short History of the Shotts Iron Company Ltd.* (Cambridge, 1954.)
NORRIS, J. M.	'The Struggle for Carron—Samuel Garbett and Charles Gascoigne', *Scottish Historical Review*, XXXVII, 1958.
RITCHIE, P. M.	'The Romance of Wilsontown', *Journal of the West of Scotland Iron & Steel Institute*, XLVI, 1939.
THOMPSON, A. L. B. (ed.)	*Stewarts & Lloyds 1903-53.* (Stewarts & Lloyds Review, 1953.)
THOMSON, G.	'The Dalnotter Iron Company', *Scottish Historical Review*, XXXV, 1956.

(c) BIOGRAPHIES

MACGEORGE, A.	*Bairds of Gartsherrie.* (Glasgow, 1872.)
MACLEOD, W. H. & HOULDSWORTH, SIR H. H.	*The Beginnings of the Houldsworths of Coltness.* (Glasgow, 1937.)
OSBORNE, F. M.	*The Story of the Mushets.* (Edinburgh, 1952.)

(iii) *Engineering and Shipbuilding*

(a) GENERAL

BLAKE, G.	*Down to the Sea.* (Glasgow, 1937.)
CLEMENT, G. & ROBERTSON, R. H. S.	*Scotland's Scientific Heritage.* (Edinburgh, 1961.)
CORMACK, W. S.	'An Economic History of Shipbuilding and Marine Engineering.' (Ph.D. thesis, Glasgow, 1931.)
HARVEY, R.	*Early Days of Engineering in Glasgow.* (Glasgow, 1919.)
LYTHE, S. G. E.	'Shipbuilding at Dundee down to 1914', *Scottish Journal of Political Economy*, IX, 1962.
POLLOCK, D.	*Modern Shipbuilding.* (London, 1884.)
POLLOCK, D.	*The Shipbuilding Industry.* (London, 1905.)
SHIELDS, J.	*Clydebuilt.* (Glasgow, 1949.)

(b) HISTORIES OF FIRMS

ANONYMOUS	*Two Centuries of Shipbuilding by Scotts of Greenock.* (London, 1906; 2nd edn., 1930; 3rd edn., 1950.)
ANONYMOUS	*Dennys, Dumbarton.* (Dumbarton, 1908.)
ANONYMOUS	*Fairfield Shipbuilding and Engineering Works.* (*Engineering*, London, 1909.)
ANONYMOUS	*Development of Shipbuilding on the Upper Reaches of the Clyde: Barclay Curle & Co.* (Glasgow, 1911.)
ANONYMOUS	*Mavor & Coulson: Fifty Years of Pioneering.* (Glasgow, 1931.)
ANONYMOUS	*The History, Development and Progress of Barclay & Company Limited.* (London, 1933.)
ANONYMOUS	*Dennys, Dumbarton, 1844-1932.* (Dumbarton, 1933.)
ANONYMOUS	*A History of the North British Locomotive Company.* (Glasgow, 1953.)
ANONYMOUS	*The Story of Bruce Peebles, 1866-1954.* (Edinburgh, 1955.)
ANONYMOUS	*Within a Mile of Edinburgh Town: A History of Bertrams Ltd.* (Edinburgh, 1956.)
ANONYMOUS	*Fairfield 1860-1960: the Fairfield Shipbuilding & Engineering Co. Ltd.* (Glasgow, 1960.)
CARVEL, J. L.	*50 Years of Machine Mining Progress [Anderson Boyes & Co. Ltd.]. 1899-1949.* (Motherwell, 1949.)
CARVEL, J. L.	*Stephen of Linthouse: A Record of 200 Years of Shipbuilding, 1750-1950.* (Glasgow, 1951.)
CHAPMAN, D.	'The New Shipwright Building Company of Dundee, 1826-31', *Economic History Review*, X, 1939-40.
CUNNINGHAM, H.	*Sir Wm. Arrol & Co. Ltd. 1909-50.* (Glasgow, 1950.)
GRANT, A.	*Steel & Ships.* (London, 1950.) [A history of John Brown & Co.]
HOUSE, J.	*A Family Affair: the Story of Carlaws of Glasgow, 1860-1960.* (Edinburgh, 1960.)
HUME, C. W.	*One Hundred Years of Howden Engineering: A Brief History, 1854-1954.* (Glasgow, 1954.)
MORRIS, J. A.	*A Romance of Industrial Engineering: Glenfield & Kennedy.* (Kilmarnock, 1939.)
STEPHEN, M.	*A Shipbuilding History: Alexander Stephen & Sons, 1750-1932.* (London, 1932.)

(c) BIOGRAPHIES

BELL, D.	*David Napier, Engineer, 1790-1869.* (Glasgow, 1912.)
BRUCE, A. B.	*Life of William Denny, Shipbuilder, Dumbarton.* (London, 1888.)
DICKINSON, H. W.	*James Watt.* (London, 1936.)
MACKENZIE, T. B.	*Life of J. B. Neilson.* (Glasgow, 1928.)
NAPIER, J.	*Life of Robert Napier.* (London, 1904.)
NAPIER, J. D. D. (ed.)	*Autobiographical Sketch of David Napier, Engineer.* (Glasgow, 1912.)

NAPIER, J. R.	*Memoir of David Elder.* (Glasgow, 1866, 1891.)
PURVIS, R.	*Sir William Arrol.* (Edinburgh, 1913.)
RANKINE, W. J. M.	*Memoir of John Elder.* (Edinburgh, 1871.)
REID, J. M.	*James Lithgow, Master of Work.* (London, 1964.)
ROLT, L. T. C.	*James Watt.* (London, 1962.)

(iv) *Chemical Industries*

(a) GENERAL

CLOW, A. & N.	*The Chemical Revolution.* (London, 1952.)
MIALL, S.	*History of the British Chemical Industry.* (London, 1931.)

(b) HISTORIES OF FIRMS

TENNANT, E. W. D.	*One Hundred and Forty Years of the Tennant Companies.* (London, 1937.)
TROTTER, R. (ed.)	*Imperial Chemical Industries Limited and its Founding Companies.* Volume I. *The History of Nobel's Explosives Company Limited 1871-1926.* (London, 1938.)

(c) BIOGRAPHIES

ALLEN, J. FENWICK	*Founders of the Chemical Industry.* (London, 2nd edn., 1907.)
MACINTOSH, G.	*Biographical Memoir of Charles Macintosh.* (Glasgow, 1847.)
MURRAY, D.	*Paraffin Young.* (London, 1959.)

(v) *Textile Industries*

(a) GENERAL

BLAIR, M.	*The Paisley Shawl.* (Paisley, 1904.)
BLAIR, M.	*The Paisley Thread Industry.* (Paisley, 1907.)
CARRIE, D. C.	*Dundee and the American Civil War.* (Dundee, 1953.)
CAVALLO, A. S.	'Development of the Scottish Linen Damask Industry', *Business History Review,* XXXVII, 1963.
CHAPMAN, D.	'The Establishment of the Jute Industry', *Review of Economic Studies,* VI, 1938.
GASKIN, B.	'The Decline of the Hand Loom Weaving Industry in Scotland, 1815-45.' (Ph.D. thesis, Edinburgh, 1955.)
IRWIN, J.	*Shawls.* (London, 1955.)
LIVINGSTONE, P. K.	*Flax and Linen in Fife.* (Kirkcaldy, 1952.)
MCEWAN, R.	*Old Glasgow Weavers.* (Glasgow, 1916.)
MARWICK, W. H.	'The Cotton Industry and the Industrial Revolution in Scotland', *Scottish Historical Review,* XXI, 1924.
MITCHELL, G. M.	'English and Scottish Cotton Industries', *Scottish Historical Review,* XXII, 1925.

MORRIS, J. A.   *Art of Ayrshire White Needlework.* (Glasgow, 1916.)

OLIVER, T.   *Development of the Tweed Trade.* (Galashiels, 1921.)

PEEL, R. A.   'The Turkey Red Dyers of the Vale of Leven', *Journal of the Society of Dyers and Colourers,* LXVIII, 1952.

SINCLAIR, W. P.   'The Economic Background of the Tweed Valley Woollen Industry', *Yearbook of the Scottish Woollen Technical College,* Galashiels, 1950.

SWAIN, M. H.   *The Flowerers: History of Ayrshire Needlework.* (Edinburgh, 1955.)

THOMSON, D.   *The Weavers' Craft.* (Paisley, 1907.)

TURNBULL, G.   *A History of the Calico Printing Industry.* (Altrincham, 1951.)

TURNER, W. H. K.   'The Evolution of the Pattern of the Textile Industry within Dundee', *Institute of British Geographers, Transactions and Papers,* No. 18, 1952.

TURNER, W. H. K.   'Some Eighteenth Century Developments in the Textile Region of East Central Scotland', *Scottish Geographical Magazine,* LIX, 1953.

TURNER, W. H. K.   *The Textile Industry of Arbroath since the Early Eighteenth Century.* (Dundee, 1954.)

TURNER, W. H. K.   'The Textile Industry of Perth and District', *Institute of British Geographers, Transactions and Papers,* No. 23, 1957.

TURNER, W. H. K.   'The Textile Industries of Dunfermline and Kirkcaldy, 1700-1900', *Scottish Geographical Magazine,* LXXIII, 1957.

TURNER, W. H. K.   'The Significance of Water Power in Industrial Location: Some Perthshire Examples', *Scottish Geographical Magazine,* LXXIV, 1958.

WARDEN, A. J.   *History of the Linen Trade.* (London, 1864, 2nd edn. 1867.)

WHYTE, D. A. & SWAIN, M. H.   'Edinburgh Shawls', *Book of the Old Edinburgh Club,* XXXI, 1962.

(b) HISTORIES OF FIRMS

ALLAN, J. R. (ed.)   *Crombies of Grandholm & Cathal, 1805-1960.* (Aberdeen, 1961.)

ANONYMOUS   *Henry Ballantyne & Son, Walkerburn.* (London, 1929.)

ANONYMOUS   *D. & J. Anderson, Ltd.: Famous Fabrics.* (Glasgow, 1952.)

ANONYMOUS   *The Faithful Fibre: the Linen Thread Company.* (Glasgow, 1956.)

ANONYMOUS   *The Carpet Makers.* (Johnstone, 1962.) [A. F. Stoddard & Co. Ltd., Elderslie.]

ANONYMOUS   *Harrisons of Edinburgh, 1863-1963.* (Edinburgh, 1964.)

BARCLAY, J. F.   *Story of Arthur & Co.: 100 Years of Textile Distribution.* (Glasgow, 1953.)

CHAPMAN, D. 'William Brown of Dundee: Management in a Scottish Flax Mill', *Explorations in Entrepreneurial History*, IV, 1952.

DUNCAN, A. 'A Scottish Link with the Baltic', *Scottish Historical Review*, XXIX, 1950.

LYLE, J. E. *The Carpet House of Lyle*. (Glasgow, 1953.)

MUIR, A. *Nairns of Kirkcaldy, a Short History, 1847-1956.* (Cambridge, 1956.)

SCOTT, W. R. (ed.) *Records of a Scottish Cloth Manufactory at New Mills, Haddington, 1681-1703.* (Edinburgh, 1905.)

STEVENSON, A. E. C. *A. & J. Macnab Ltd. Dyers & Cleaners, Edinburgh.* (Edinburgh, 1960.)

(*c*) BIOGRAPHIES

CAVALLO, A. S. 'Joseph Noel Paton, Designer of Damasks', *Connoisseur*, 153, 1963.

COLE, M. L. *Robert Owen of New Lanark.* (London, 1953.)

LIVINGSTONE, J. *Alexander Morton, 1844-1923.* Ed. W. W. Morton. (Kilmarnock, 1960.)

PODMORE, R. *Robert Owen.* (London, 1906.)

(vi) *Consumption Goods Industries*

(*a*) GENERAL WORKS

Food, Drink, etc.

DEERR, N. *History of Sugar.* 2 volumes. (London, 1950.)

DUNNETT, A. M. *Land of Scotch.* (Edinburgh, 1953.)

HUTCHESON, J. M. *Notes on the Sugar Industry of the United Kingdom.* (Glasgow, 1901.)

LOCKHART, R. B. *Scotch.* (London, 1951.)

MACKENZIE, C. *Sublime Tobacco.* (London, 1957.)

SMOUT, T. C. 'The Early Scottish Sugar Houses 1660-1720', *Economic History Review*, 2nd series, XIV. 1961.

WILSON, R. 'The Scotch Whisky Industry', *Journal of the Royal Statistical Society*, Series A (General), 118, 1955.

WILSON, R. *Scotch Made Easy.* (London, 1959.)

Building, Furnishing, etc.

CAIRNCROSS, A. K. 'The Glasgow Building Industry, 1870-1914', *Review of Economic Studies*, II, 1934-35.

FINLAY, I. *Scottish Gold and Silver Work.* (London, 1956.)

FLEMING, J. A. *Scottish Pottery.* (Glasgow, 1923.)

FLEMING, J. A. *Scottish and Jacobite Glass,* (Glasgow, 1939.)

JEWETT, L. *Ceramic Art of Great Britain.* (London, 1883.)

KELLETT, J. R. 'Property Speculators and the Building of Glasgow, 1780-1830', *Scottish Journal of Political Economy*, VIII, 1961.

ROBERTSON, R. A. 'Scottish Domestic Glass', *Scotland's (S.M.T.) Magazine*, March, 1952.

SMITH, J. *Old Scottish Clockmakers, 1453-1850.* (Edinburgh, 2nd edn., 1921.)

Clothing, etc.

LUMSDEN, H.   *History of the Skinners, Furriers & Glovers of Glasgow.* (Glasgow, 1837.)

Vehicles

CASTLE, H. G.   *Britain's Motor Industry.* (London, 1950.)

MACDONALD, A. C. & BROWNING, A. S. E.   'History of the Motor Industry in Scotland', *Institute of Mechanical Engineers, Proceedings of the Automobile Division,* 1960-61.

ROBERTSON, D.   *Scotland's Motoring Story.* (Glasgow, 1960.)

Paper

ANONYMOUS   'Some Contributions to Scottish Paper Trade History', *World's Paper Trade Review,* 57-61, 1912-14.

CORMACK, A. A.   *Our Ancient and Honourable Craft, 1750-1933.* (London, 1933.)

WATERSTON, R.   'Early Paper-making Near Edinburgh', *Book of the Old Edinburgh Club,* XXV, 1945.

WATERSTON, R.   'Further Notes on Early Paper-making Near Edinburgh', *Book of the Old Edinburgh Club,* XXVII, 1949.

Rubber

ANONYMOUS   'The Rubber Industry in Edinburgh', *Transactions of the Royal Scottish Society of Arts,* XVII, 1924.

CROS, A. DU   *Wheels of Fortune.* (London, 1938.)

WOODRUFF, W.   *Rise of the British Rubber Industry.* (Liverpool, 1958.)

(*b*) HISTORIES OF FIRMS

Food, Drink, etc.

ANONYMOUS   *Fifty Years in the Baking Trade, 1872-1922: Bilsland Bros.* (Glasgow, 1923.)

ANONYMOUS   *Glenlivet Distillery, 1824-1924.* (Glenlivet, 1924.)

ANONYMOUS   *J. Smith & Sons, 1876-1926, Bakers, Edinburgh.* (Edinburgh, 1926.)

KEIR, D.   *The Younger Centuries: Wm. Younger & Co. Ltd., 1749-1949.* (Edinburgh, 1951.)

LAVER, J.   *The House of Haig: John Haig & Co. Ltd.* (Markinch, Fife, 1958.)

Building, Furnishing, etc.

ANONYMOUS   *100 Years of Building, 1848-1948: Robt. Gilchrist & Son Ltd.* (Glasgow, 1948.)

CARVEL, J. L.   *Alloa Glass Work.* (Edinburgh, 1953.)

HOUSE, J.   *Plumber in Glasgow: the History of the Firm of Hugh Twaddle & Son Ltd., 1848-1948.* (Glasgow, 1949.)

PARKER, W. M.   *Dobie & Son Ltd., Painters, Edinburgh, 1849-1949.* (Edinburgh, 1949.)

Clothing, etc.

CHALMERS, T.   *100 Years of Gutta Percha: R. & J. Dick, Ltd.* (Glasgow, 1946.)

REID, J. M.   *The First Hundred Years: Bayne & Duckett.* (Glasgow, 1958.)

Vehicles

ANONYMOUS   *Scottish Motor Traction Co. Ltd.: A Short History, 1905-1945.* (Edinburgh, 1945.)

Paper

ANONYMOUS   *A Century of Papermaking: Robert Craig & Sons, 1820-1920.* (Edinburgh, 1920.)

ANONYMOUS   *Young, Trotter & Son Ltd.: A Historical Account of Papermaking in Berwickshire.* (Chirnside, 1923.)

ANONYMOUS   *The Culter Paper Mills, 1751-1951.* (Aberdeen, 1951.)

ANONYMOUS   *Guardbridge Paper Co. Ltd.* (Dundee, 1951.)

ANONYMOUS   *George Waterston & Sons, Stationers, 1752-1952.* (Edinburgh, 1952.)

DARWIN, B.   *Robinsons of Bristol, 1844-1944.* (Bristol, 1945.)

Rubber

WOODRUFF, W.   'The American Origins of a Scottish Industry.' [North British Rubber Co.] *Scottish Journal of Political Economy,* II, 1955.

Others

ANONYMOUS   *Barr & Stroud Ltd.: A Souvenir Handbook.* (Glasgow, 1919.) [Scientific Instrument Makers.]

ANONYMOUS   *100 Years in the Timber Trade: Gilmour & Aitken Ltd., 1852-1952.* (Glasgow, 1952.)

ANONYMOUS   *Note it in a Book: the Story of Begg, Cousland & Co., Ltd., 1854-1954.* (Glasgow, 1958.) [Wire Weavers, Glasgow.]

ADAM, A. T.   *Bruntons, Wiremakers, 1876-1962.* (Musselburgh, 1962.)

CARVEL, J. L.   *100 Years in Timber: Brownlee & Co., City Saw Mills, 1849-1949.* (Glasgow, 1950.)

HOUSE, J.   *A Century of Box-making: Andrew Ritchie & Son, Ltd., 1850-1950.* (Glasgow, 1950.)

(c) BIOGRAPHIES

ANONYMOUS   *The Usher Family in Scotland.* (Edinburgh, 1956.)

BINNIE, T.   *Memoir of Thomas Binnie, Builder.* (Glasgow, 1882.)

FAIRRIE, G.   *The Sugar Refining Families of Great Britain.* (London, 1951.)

FLEMING, J. R.   *John Park Fleming.* (Glasgow, 1885.)

GALLOWAY, J.   *William Harley. A Citizen of Glasgow.* (Glasgow, 1901.)

(vii) *Transport*

(a) GENERAL

ACWORTH, W. M.	*Railways of Scotland.* (London, 1890.)
DOTT, G.	*Early Scottish Colliery Wagonways.* (London, 1947.)
DUCKWORTH, C. L. D & LANGMUIR, G. E.	*West Highland Steamers.* (London, 1935, 1950.)
GIBBS, C. R. V.	*Passenger Liners of the Western Ocean.* (London, 1952.)
HADFIELD, C.	*British Canals.* (London, 1950.)
HALDANE, A. R. B.	*New Ways Through the Glens.* (Edinburgh, 1962.)
HUNTER, D. L. G.	*Edinburgh's Transport.* (Huddersfield, 1964.)
LINDSAY, W. S.	*History of Merchant Shipping.* Vol. IV. (London, 1874.)
LUBBOCK, B.	*The China Clippers.* (Glasgow, 1916.)
LUBBOCK, B.	*The Colonial Clippers.* (Glasgow, 1921.)
MCQUEEN, A.	*Clyde River Steamers.* (Glasgow, 1923.)
NOCK, O. S.	*The Scottish Railways.* (London, 1950; revised edn., 1961.)
PRIESTLY, J.	*Historical Account of Navigable Rivers, Canals & Railways.* (London, 1831.)

(b) HISTORIES OF FIRMS

ANONYMOUS	*The Book of the Anchor Line, 1852-1931.* (London, 1932.)
ANONYMOUS	*The 'Vales' of Glasgow: Andrew Crawford & Co., Shipowners.* (Glasgow, 1955.)
BLAKE, G.	*B.I. Centenary, 1856-1956: the British India Steam Navigation Co.* (London, 1956.)
BLAKE, G.	*The Ben Line, 1825-1955.* (Edinburgh, 1956.)
BUCHANAN, E. G.	*Account of Glasgow & Garnkirk Railway.* (Edinburgh, 1832.)
CORMACK, I. L.	*Glasgow Tramways, 1872-1962.* (London, 1963.)
CORNFORD, L. C.	*The Sea Carriers, 1825-1925: the Aberdeen Line.* (Aberdeen, 1925.)
CUTHBERT, A. D.	*The Clyde Shipping Company Limited: A History.* (Glasgow, 1956.)
DOW, G.	*Story of the West Highland Railway.* (London, 1944.)
DOW, G.	*The First Railway across the Border.* (Edinburgh, 1944.)
DUNNETT, A. H.	*The Donaldson Line, 1854-1954.* (Glasgow, 1960.)
ELLIS, G. HAMILTON	*The North British Railway.* (London, 1955. 1959.)
HERVEY, M. BARCLAY	*History of Great North of Scotland Railway.* (London, 1940.)
INGLIS, J. L. & F.	*The Fordel Railway.* (Perth, n.d. [1946?].)
LAIRD, D.	*Paddy Henderson: Story of P. Henderson & Co., Shipowners, 1834-1961.* (Glasgow, 1961.)
MCILWRAITH, W.	*Glasgow & South Western Railway Co.* (Glasgow, 1880.)

MCLELLAN, R. S.	*The Anchor Line, 1856-1956.* (Glasgow, 1956.)
NOCK, O. S.	*The Caledonian Railway.* (London, 1962.)
OAKLEY, C. A.	*The Last Tram.* (Glasgow, 1962.)
PREBBLE, J.	*The High Girders.* (London, 1956.) [Tay Bridge.]
SMITH, J.	*Rise and Progress of the City Line.* (Glasgow, 1908.)
TAYLOR, G. RANKIN	*Thomas Dunlop & Sons, Shipowners, 1851-1951.* (Glasgow, 1951.)
THOMSON, G.	'James Watt and the Monkland Canal', *Scottish Historical Review,* XXIX, 1950.
VALLANCE, H. A.	*The Highland Railway.* (Dawlish, 1943.)
WILLIAMSON, J.	*The Clyde Passenger Steamers, 1812-1901.* (Glasgow, 1904.)

(c) BIOGRAPHIES

BRODIE, R.	*Reminiscences of a Contractor.* (Bristol, 1904.)
GIBB, A.	*The Story of Telford.* (Glasgow, 1935.)
HODDER, E.	*Sir George Burns.* (London, 1890.)
JONES, C. W.	*Pioneer Shipowners.* (Liverpool, 1935.)
MIDDLEMAS, R. S.	*The Master Builders.* (London, 1963.)
NICOLSON, J.	*Arthur Anderson, A founder of the P. & O. Co.* (Paisley, 1914.)
ROLT, L. T. C.	*Thomas Telford.* (London, 1958.)

(viii) *Wholesale and Retail Trade*

(a) GENERAL

ANONYMOUS	'Glasgow's Big Warehouses', *Glasgow Herald.* 24 December, 1936.
CHAMBERS, R.	*Edinburgh Merchants & Merchandise in Old Times.* (Edinburgh, 1859.)
COOK, A. S.	*Old Time Traders.* (Aberdeen, 1902.)
JEFFREYS, J. B.	*Retail Trade in Britain, 1850-1950.* (Cambridge, 1954.)
LIVINGSTONE, J.	*Some Edinburgh Shops.* (Edinburgh, 1894.)
WESTERFIELD, R. B.	*The Middleman in English Business.* (New Haven, U.S.A., 1915.)

(b) HISTORIES OF FIRMS

ANONYMOUS	*Royal Polytechnic Warehouse, Glasgow.* (Jubilee Volume, 1887.)
ANONYMOUS	*A Short Note on a Long History: John Smith & Son (Glasgow) Ltd., Booksellers.* (Glasgow, 1921.)
ANONYMOUS	*The House of Menzies.* (Edinburgh, 1958.)
GRIERSON, M. G.	*100 Years in Princes Street: Jenners, 1838-1938.* (Edinburgh, 1938.)
HALDANE, A. R. B.	*The Drove Roads of Scotland.* (Edinburgh, 1952.) [The cattle trade.]
MITCHELL, J. O.	*Two Old Glasgow Firms: Wm. Connal & Company; Crums of Thornliebank.* (Glasgow, 1894.)

(c) BIOGRAPHIES

LIPTON, T.   *Leaves from the Lipton Log.* (London, 1931.)

MACKAY, M.   *Memoir of James Ewing of Strathleven.* (Glasgow, 1866.)

WAUGH, A.   *The Lipton Story.* (London, 1950.)

WILSON, A.   *Walter Wilson, Merchant, 1849-1917.* (Glasgow, 1920.)

(ix) *Overseas Enterprise*

(a) GENERAL

ANONYMOUS   'The Rise of Glasgow's West India Trade, 1793-1818', *Three Banks Review*, No. 51, 1961.

BARKER, T. C.   'Smuggling in the Eighteenth Century; the Evidence of the Scottish Tobacco Trade', *Virginia Magazine of History and Biography*, LXII, 1954.

CRISPIN, B.   'Clyde Shipping and the American War', *Scottish Historical Review*, XLI, 1962.

DAVIDSON, J. &   *The Scottish Staple at Veere.* (London, 1909.)
GRAY, A.

MARWICK, H.   *Merchant Lairds of Long Ago.* 2 volumes. (Kirkwall, 1939.)

MACMILLAN, D. S.   'The Beginning of Scottish Enterprise in Australia: The Contribution of the Commercial Whigs', *Business Archives and History*, II, 1962.

ROBERTSON, M. L.   'Scottish Commerce and the American War'. *Economic History Review*, New Series, IX, 1956-57.

ROOSEBOOM, M. P.   *The Scottish Staple in the Netherlands.* (The Hague, 1916.)

SINCLAIR, G. A.   'The Scottish Trader in Sweden', *Scottish Historical Review*, XXV, 1928.

SOLTOW, J. H.   'Scottish Traders in Virginia, 1750-75', *Economic History Review*, New Series, XII, 1959-60.

YAIR, J.   *Account of the Scotch Trade in the Netherlands.* (London, 1776.)

(b) HISTORIES OF FIRMS

ANONYMOUS   *James Finlay & Co., 1750-1950.* (Glasgow, 1951.)

BROWN, P. L. (ed.)   *Clyde Company Papers.* 7 volumes. (London, 1941.) [In progress.]

BRYANT, A.   *100 Years under the Southern Cross: the Shaw Savill Line & Albion Company.* (London, 1958.)

CHECKLAND, S. G.   'Two Scottish West Indian Liquidations after 1793', *Scottish Journal of Political Economy*, IV, 1957.

GREENBERG, M.   *British Trade and the Opening of China, 1800-42.* (Cambridge, 1951.) [Jardine, Matheson & Co.]

INNES, C. (ed.)   *Ledger of Andrew Haliburton, 1492-1503.* (London, 1867.)

INSH, G. P.   *The Company of Scotland Trading to Africa and the Indies.* (London, 1932.)

LONGHURST, H.   *Borneo Story*. (London, 1956.) [British N. Borneo Co.]

MACKENZIE, C.   *Realms of Silver: One Hundred Years of Banking in the East*. (London, 1954.) [Chartered Bank of India, Australia and China.]

MACMILLAN, D. S.   'The Scottish Australia Co., 1840-50', *Scottish Historical Review*, XXXIX, 1960.

MACMILLAN, D. S.   *The Debtors' War, 1841-46*. (Melbourne, 1960.) [Scottish Australian Co.]

MILLAR, A. H. (ed.)   *The Compt Buik of David Wedderburne, Merchant of Dundee, 1587-1630*. (Edinburgh, 1898.)

RANKIN, J.   *A History of our Firm. Being some account of the firm of Pollock, Gilmour and Co. and its offshoots and Connections, 1804-1920*. (Liverpool, 2nd ed. revised, 1921.)

THOMSON, C. G.   *The Old Glasgow Family of Thomson*. (Glasgow, 1903.) [Colonial Merchants.]

WALLACE, D. R.   *The Romance of Jute; a short history of the Calcutta Jute Mill Industry, 1855-1927*. (London, 2nd edn. revised, 1928.)

(c) BIOGRAPHIES

BOLITHO, H. H.   *James Lyle Mackay, 1st Earl of Inchcape*. (London, 1936.)

CORMACK, A. A.   *Colin Campbell, 1686-1757, Merchant, Gothenburg, Sweden: a Scots-Swedish Study*. (Aberdeen, 1960.)

DAVIDSON, W. S.   *William Soltau Davidson, 1846-1924*. (Edinburgh, 1930.)

(x) *Banking, Insurance and Investment*

(a) GENERAL WORKS

BAIRD, W.   *The One Pound Note*. (Edinburgh, 1885; revised 1901.)

BAILEY, J. D.   'Australian Borrowing in Scotland in the Nineteenth Century', *Economic History Review*, New Series, XII, 1959-60.

DONALD, D. M. C.   'Scottish Investment Trusts', *Scottish Bankers' Magazine*, XLVIII, No. 188, 1956.

GASKIN, M.   'Note Issue in Scottish Banking, 1844-1953.' (M.A. thesis, Liverpool, 1955.)

GASKIN, M.   'Anglo-Scottish Banking Conflicts, 1874-81', *Economic History Review*, New Series, XII, 1959-60.

GILBERT, J. C.   *The History of Investment Trusts in Dundee, 1873-1938*. (London, 1939.)

GLASGOW, G.   *The Scottish Investment Trust Companies*. (London, 1932.)

GRAHAM, W.   *The One Pound Note in Scotland*. (Edinburgh, 1886.)

KERR, A. W.   *History of Banking in Scotland.* (Edinburgh, 1884); revised edition by F. H. Allan (Edinburgh, 1926.)

KERR, W. G.   'Scotland and the Texas Mortgage Business', *Economic History Review*, 2nd Series, XVI, 1963-64.

LAWSON, W. R.   *The Scottish Investors' Manual.* (Edinburgh, 1884.)

MACKENZIE, A.   *The Story of the Scottish Banks.* (*The Scotsman*, Edinburgh, 1963-64.)

REID, J.   *Manual of Scottish Stocks and British Funds.* (Edinburgh, 1842.)

SOMERS, R.   *The Scottish Banks and System of Issue.* (Edinburgh, 1873.)

STALKER, A. C.   'Scottish Insurance Companies', *Scottish Bankers' Magazine*, XLVIII, No. 189, 1956.

(b) HISTORIES OF FIRMS

ANDERSON, J. L.   *The Story of the Commercial Bank of Scotland Limited.* (Edinburgh, 1910.)

ANONYMOUS   *The Caledonian Insurance Co., 1805-1905* (Edinburgh, 1905.)

ANONYMOUS   *Records of the Glasgow Stock Exchange Association, 1844-1926.* (Glasgow, 1927.)

ANONYMOUS   *Our Bank: the Story of the Commercial Bank of Scotland Ltd., 1810-1941.* (Edinburgh, 1942.)

ANONYMOUS   *A Century of Progress, 1852-1952: the Scottish Legal Life Assurance Society.* (Glasgow, 1952.)

BOASE, C. W.   *A Century of Banking in Dundee.* (Edinburgh, 2nd edition, 1867.)

CAMPBELL, R. H.   'Edinburgh Bankers and the Western Bank', *Scottish Journal of Political Economy*, II, 1955.

FORBES, W.   *Memoirs of a Banking House.* (Edinburgh, 1859.)

GRAY, I.   *A Business Epic, 1885-1935: the General Accident Fire & Life Assurance Corporation, Ltd.* (Perth, 1935.)

GRAY, W. F.   *100 Years: A Chronicle of the Scottish Union & National Insurance Company, 1824-1924.* (Edinburgh, 1924.)

HAMILTON, H.   'The Failure of the Ayr Bank, 1772', *Economic History Review*, 2nd Series, VIII, 1956.

KEITH, A.   *The North of Scotland Bank.* (Aberdeen, 1936.)

KENNEDY, G. G. C.   'The Union Bank of Scotland', *Scottish Bankers' Magazine*, XLVII, No. 185, 1955.

KNOX, J.   *The Triumph of Thrift: the Story of the Savings Bank of Airdrie.* (Airdrie, 1927.)

HENDERSON, T.   *The Savings Bank of Glasgow: One Hundred Years of Thrift.* (Glasgow, 1936.)

HOUSE, J.   *The Friendly Adventure: The Story of the City of Glasgow Friendly Society's First Hundred Years.* (Glasgow, 1962.)

MALCOLM, C. A.   *The Bank of Scotland, 1694-1948.* (Edinburgh, 1948.)

MALCOLM, C. A.   *The British Linen Bank, 1746-1946.* (Edinburgh, 1950.)

MEIKLE, W.	*The Savings Bank of Glasgow: Its Origin and Progress.* (Glasgow, 1898.)
MUNRO, N.	*The History of the Royal Bank of Scotland.* (Edinburgh, 1928.)
MURRAY, D.	*The York Buildings Company.* (Glasgow, 1883.)
RAIT, R. S.	*The History of the Union Bank of Scotland.* (Glasgow, 1930.)
REID, J. M.	*The History of the Clydesdale Bank, 1838-1938.* (Glasgow, 1938.)
RICHARDSON, R.	*Coutts & Co., Bankers.* (London, 1900.)
SCHOOLING, W.	*The Standard Life Assurance Company, 1825-1925.* (Edinburgh, 1925.)
STEUART, M. D.	*The Scottish Provident Institution, 1837-1937.* (Edinburgh, 1937.)
WEIR, W.	*The First Hundred Years, 1851-1951: A Sketch of the History of the Glasgow Pawnbrokers' Association.* (Glasgow, 1952.)

(xi) *Printing and Publishing*

(*a*) GENERAL WORKS

MACLEOD, R. D.	*The Scottish Publishing Houses.* (Glasgow, 1953.)

(*b*) HISTORIES OF FIRMS

ALLAN, D. A.	'J. G. Bartholemew, Mapmakers, Edinburgh', *Scottish Geographical Magazine*, LXXVI, 1960.
ANONYMOUS	*Blackie & Sons Ltd.: Sketch of the Origin & Progress of the Firm, 1809-74.* (Glasgow, 1897.)
ANONYMOUS	*The Centenary of 'The Scotsman', 1817-1917.* (Edinburgh, 1917.)
ANONYMOUS	*The First Hundred Years.* (Glasgow, 1944.) [J. & J. Murdoch, Ltd.]
ANONYMOUS	*James Thin, 1848-1948.* (Edinburgh, 1948.)
ANONYMOUS	*Milestones: A Brief Review of 50 Years' Progress.* (Glasgow, 1950.) [Farquharson Brothers Limited.]
BLACKIE, A. A. C.	*Blackie & Son, 1809-1959.* (London, 1959.)
EWING, A. M.	*History of 'The Glasgow Herald'.* (Glasgow, 1949.)
HOUSE, J.	*The Romance of Murray; the Story of 110 Years' Achievement.* (Glasgow, 1952.) [Murray's Diaries.]
JUNOR, J.	*Footprints on the Sands of Time: the Story of the House of Livingstone, medical publishers.* (Edinburgh, 1963.)
KEIR, D. E.	*The House of Collins.* (London, 1952.)
MCLAREN, M.	*The House of Neill, Printers, 1749-1949.* (Edinburgh, 1949.)
MACLEHOSE, J.	*The Glasgow University Press, 1638-1931.* (Glasgow, 1931.)
MILLAR, A. H.	*'The Dundee Advertiser' Centenary Memoir, 1801-1901.* (Dundee, 1901.) ,
NEWTH, J. D.	*A. & C. Black, 1807-1957.* (London, 1958.)

H

SKINNER, R. T. — *A Notable Family of Scots Printers.* (Edinburgh, 1928.) [The Donaldson Family and 'The Edinburgh Advertiser'.]

TREDREY, F. D. — *The House of Blackwood.* (Edinburgh, 1954.)

(c) BIOGRAPHIES

BLACKIE, W. W. — *John Blackie, Senior, 1782-1874.* (Glasgow, 1933.)

BLACKIE, W. W. — *Walter Graham Blackie, 1816-1905.* (Glasgow, 1936.)

CHAMBERS, W. — *Memoir of Robert Chambers.* (Edinburgh, 1872.)

CHAMBERS, W. — *Story of a Long and Busy Life.* (Edinburgh, 1882.)

MURRAY, D. — *Robert and Andrew Foulis and the Glasgow Press.* (Glasgow, 1913.)

NICOLSON, A. (ed.) — *Memoir of Adam Black.* (Edinburgh, 1885.)

WILSON, D. — *William Nelson.* (Edinburgh, 1889.)

(xii) *Co-operative*

(a) GENERAL

BUCHAN, A. — *History of the Scottish Co-operative Women's Guild from 1892 to 1913.* (Glasgow [?], 1913.)

FLANAGAN, J. — *Wholesale Co-operation in Scotland, 1868-1918.* (Glasgow, 1920.)

HIMEIMY, A. — 'The Development and Organization of the Scottish Co-operative Movement.' (Ph.D. thesis, Edinburgh, 1955.)

JONES, B. — *Co-operative Production.* 2 volumes. (Oxford, 1894.)

LUCAS, J. — *Co-operation in Scotland.* (Manchester, 1920.)

MAXWELL, W. — *History of Co-operation in Scotland.* (Glasgow, 1910.)

(b) HISTORIES OF SOCIETIES

ANONYMOUS — *West Calder and its Co-operative Society.* (West Calder, 1865.)

ANONYMOUS — *Short Sketch of Glasgow Eastern Co-operative Society Limited.* (Glasgow, 1904.)

ANONYMOUS — *Souvenir of Paisley Congress.* (Paisley, 1905.)

ANONYMOUS — *History of Portobello Co-operative Society Limited, 1864-1934.* (Glasgow, 1934.)

ANONYMOUS — *Jubilee Souvenir of Gilbertfield Co-operative Society Limited, 1884-1934.* (Gilbertfield, 1935.)

ANONYMOUS — *Co-operation in Carluke, 1862-1962.* (Carluke, 1962.)

BATTISON, G. — *Wishaw Co-operative Society Ltd.: A Record of its Struggles, Progress and Success from its Inception in 1889.* (Glasgow, 1939.)

BULLOCH, R. — *A Century of Economic Striving.* (Glasgow, 1922.) [Larkhall Victualling Society, Ltd.]

DOLLAN, P. J. — *Jubilee History of the Kinning Park Co-operative Society, Glasgow.* (Glasgow, 1923.)

FLANAGAN, J. A. — *The Alloa Co-operative Society.* (Alloa, 1912.)

FLANAGAN, J. A. — *Memoirs of a Century, 1812-1912: Lennoxtown Friendly Victualling Society, Ltd.* (Lennoxtown, 1912.)

FLANAGAN, J. A. — *Co-operation in Lanark.* (Lanark, 1913.)

FLANAGAN, J. A. — *Co-operation in Sauchie.* (Sauchie, 1915.)

GORDON, T. C. — *History of Alva Co-operative Bazaar Society, Ltd.* (Alva, 1948.)

HUNT, W. D. — *The Story of the Century.* (Glasgow, 1961.) [Dunfermline Co-operative Society, Limited.]

LAWSON, W. E. — *A History of Clydebank Co-operative Society Limited.* (Clydebank, 1948.)

LAWSON, W. E. — *The Second Fifty Years of St. Cuthbert's Co-operative Association, 1909-1959.* (Edinburgh, 1959.)

MCALPINE, D. — *Centenary—Portobello Co-operative Society Limited —1964.* (Glasgow, 1964.)

MCWHIRTER, J. — *History of Barrhead Co-operative Society Limited,* Vol. III, *The Long View, 1937-1961.* (Barrhead, 1962.)

MARTIN, G. — *Ninety Not Out.* (Uddingston, 1951.) [Uddingston Co-operative Society Limited, 1861-1951.]

MAXWELL, SIR W. — *The First Fifty Years of St. Cuthbert's Co-operative Association, 1859-1909.* (Edinburgh, 1909.)

MURRAY, A. — *Fifty Years of Slamannan Co-operative Society Limited, 1861-1911.* (Slamannan, 1911.)

MURRAY, R. — *History of Barrhead Co-operative Society Limited, 1861-1911.* (Barrhead, 1911.)

MURRAY, R. — *History of Barrhead Co-operative Society Limited.* Vol. II, *1911-1936.* (Barrhead, 1937.)

MURRAY, R. — *Stirling Co-operative Society: A Historical Sketch, 1880-1930.* (Stirling, 1930.)

NICOLSON, J. — *Leith Provident Co-operative Society's 'Coming of Age'.* (Edinburgh, 1899.)

PAGAN, W. & YOUNG, R. — *Fifty Years of Service: A Historical Sketch of Broxburn Co-operative Society from 1879 to 1929.* (Broxburn, 1929.)

REID, W. — *History of the United Co-operative Baking Society Limited, 1869-1919.* (Glasgow, 1920.)

REID, W. — *Fifty Years of the St. George Co-operative Society Limited from 1870 to 1920.* (Glasgow, 1923.)

ROWAT, D. — *Jubilee Book of Paisley Provident Co-operative Society, 1860-1910.* (Paisley, 1910.)

STEVENSON, F. — *Jubilee Souvenir of Blantyre Co-operative Society Limited.* (Blantyre, 1933.)

STIRLING, T. B. — *History of the Vale of Leven Co-operative Society Limited, 1862-1912.* (Alexandria, 1915.)

SWAN, M. S. — *Jubilee History of Greenock Central Co-operative Society Limited.* (Greenock, 1930.)

TAYLOR, F. — *Jubilee Souvenir of Johnstone Co-operative Society Limited.* (Johnstone, 1916.)

WILLCOCKS, J.   *The City of Perth and Its Co-operative Society.* (Perth, 1892.)

YOUNG, J.   *Co-operation in Uddingston, 1861-1911: A Jubilee Book.* (Uddingston, 1911.)

(c) BIOGRAPHIES

MARWICK, W. H.   *Alexander Campbell.* (Glasgow, 1963.)

(xiii) *Fisheries*

ANSON, P. J.   *Fishing Boats and Fishing Folk on the East Coast of Scotland.* (London, 1930.)

ARBUTHNOT, J.   *An Historical Account of Peterhead.* (Aberdeen, 1815.)

BARRY, G.   *The History of the Orkney Islands.* (London, 1805.)

BERTRAM, J. G.   *The Harvest of the Sea.* (London, 1865.)

BIGGAR, W.   *A Short Account of the Herring Fishery in Scotland.* (Edinburgh, 1856.)

BUCKLAND, F. *et al.*   *Report into the Herring Fisheries.* (London, 1878.)

BUCHAN. P.   *Annals of Peterhead.* (Peterhead, 1819.)

CAUX, J. W. DE   *The Herring & the Herring Fishery.* (London, 1881.)

COWIE, R.   *Shetland, Descriptive & Historical.* (Aberdeen, 1871.)

CRANNA, J.   *Fraserburgh Past and Present.* (Aberdeen, 1914.)

DUFF, R. W.   *The Herring Fisheries of Scotland.* (London, 1883.)

EDMONSTON, A.   *A View of the Ancient and Present State of the Shetland Islands.* 2 volumes. (Edinburgh, 1809.)

EDMONSTON, E.   *Sketches and Tales of the Shetland Islands.* (Edinburgh, 1856.)

FEA, J.   *The Present State of the Orkney Islands Considered.* (Edinburgh, 1775.)

FRASER, R.   *A Review of the Domestic Fisheries of Great Britain & Ireland.* (Edinburgh, 1818.)

'A GENTLEMAN'   *An Exact and Authentic Account of the Greatest White Herring Fishery in Scotland.* (London, 1750.)

GIFFORD, T.   *An Historical Description of the Shetland Islands.* (London, 1786.)

GORDON, T.   *General Remarks on the British Fisheries.* (London, 1784.)

HERBERT, D. (ed.)   *Fish and Fisheries.* (Edinburgh & London, 1883.)

HOLDSWORTH, E. W. H.   *Deep Sea Fishing and Fishing Boats.* (London, 1874.)

HOLDSWORTH, E. W. H.   *The Sea Fisheries of Great Britain and Ireland.* (London, 1883.)

JOHNSTONE, J.   *British Fisheries.* (London, 1905.)

KNOX, J.   *A View of the British Empire, more especially Scotland.* (London, 1784.)

KNOX, J.   *A Discourse on the Expediency of Establishing Fishing Stations or Small Towns in the Highlands of Scotland.* (London, 1786.)

KNOX, J.   *Observations on the Northern Fisheries.* (London, 1786.)

LEVI, L.   *The Economic Condition of Fishermen.* (London, 1883.)

LOCH, D.   *Essays on the Trade, Commerce, Manufactures and Fisheries of Scotland.* 3 volumes. (Edinburgh, 1778.)

MCCULLOCH, L.   *Observations on the Herring Fisheries upon the North and East Coasts of Scotland.* (London, 1788.)

MILN, W. S.   *An Exposure of the Position of the Scotch Herring Trade in 1885.* (London, 1886.)

MITCHELL, J. M.   *The Herring: its Natural History & National Importance.* (Edinburgh, 1864.)

NEILL, P.   *A Tour Through some of the Islands of Orkney and Shetland.* (Edinburgh, 1806.)

O'DELL, A. C.   *The Historical Geography of the Shetland Islands.* (Lerwick, 1939.)

PITCAIRNE, G.   *An Essay on the Scots Fisheries.* (Edinburgh, 1785.)

PITCAIRNE, G.   *A Retrospective View of the Scots Fisheries.* (Edinburgh, 1787.)

PLOYEN, C.   *Reminiscences of a Voyage to Shetland, Orkney & Scotland.* (Lerwick, 1894.)

RAMPINI, C.   *Shetland and the Shetlanders.* (Kirkwall, 1884.)

SCOTT, W. R. (ed.)   *Rural Scotland During the War.* (Carnegie Economic & Social History of World War, London, 1926.)

THOMSON, J.   *The Value and Importance of the Scottish Fisheries.* (London, 1849.)

TUDOR, J. R.   *The Orkneys and Shetlands: their Past and Present life.* (London, 1883.)

WHITE, P.   *Observations upon the Present State of the Scotch Fisheries.* (Edinburgh, 1791.)

WHYMPER, F.   *The Fisheries of the World.* (London, 1883.)

WILSON, J.   *A Voyage Round the Coasts of Scotland and the Isles.* 2 volumes. (Edinburgh, 1842.)

Part Two:
Domestic Enterprise
and
Organisation

CHAPTER FIVE

Lead-mining in Scotland, 1650-1850

T. C. SMOUT

Reader in Economic History,
University of Edinburgh

'I regard mining as a very deep species of gambling, whereby there has probably been more lost upon the whole than gained.'
SIR WILLIAM FORBES, *Memoirs of a Banking House*, 1860, p. 39.

Introduction

The mining of lead is a very ancient activity north of the Border, yet it has never been among Scotland's leading industries: even when it reached its peak of prosperity at the beginning of the nineteenth century, lead workers and their families cannot have numbered more than 4,000 in a total population in excess of 1,625,000. Similarly, though lead has been worked in almost every Scottish county, the country has never provided more than a small share of the total lead production of the United Kingdom; in the 1820's, if contemporary estimates are right, Scotland accounted for less than five per cent of total British output,(1) and certainly far less than this later in the nineteenth century. Quantitively, then, it is unimportant.

Nevertheless, the industry provides many features of interest in the two centuries between 1650 and 1850 when it is most richly documented. It provides the first examples of large-scale English investment in any aspect of the Scottish economy, and perhaps the only example of widespread immigration of English labour into a native industry. It also provides some remarkable examples of foolish capitalists, for dubious mineral concerns were fatally attractive to the eighteenth-century instincts for gambling and amateur science. It is equally striking for its examples of successful industrial paternalism, evolved partly as a response to the isolation of the mining communities, and is in general an object lesson in the difficulties of running an industry in a very remote location. But before we can deal with these and other specific points, it is necessary to draw in broad outline the history of the industry in Scotland.

Lead-mining began early. The extraction of *galena* ores from the ground and their transformation into a ductile metal with innumerable practical and ornamental uses is one of the simplest processes of metallurgy, and was known to the Scots in the Middle Ages. There are several references among the scattered documents of medieval history, the earliest being to a mine on Crauford Muir granted to the monks of Newbattle in 1239: nearly all refer either to the seaboard of the western Highlands or to the Lanarkshire–Dumfriesshire border where the industry was later to have its greatest success.(2) The phrasing of an Act of Parliament of 1424 suggests that even then the Scots may have mastered the more difficult art of refining lead to extract silver.(3)

Nevertheless, the activities of miners before the sixteenth century were probably intermittent, their methods crude and their output very small. Then the pace quickened: prospectors of several nationalities, encouraged by bullionist governments, moved out over the hills in search of gold and silver—they found more of both than might reasonably be expected, but their only enduring achievement was to draw the attention of lively capitalists to untapped resources of the baser metal. From around 1550, lead began to be regarded with increasing interest; around 1570, fifty tons of ore a year were being dug from 'the kings mines'.(4) Twenty years later, Thomas Foulis— an Edinburgh goldsmith—began large-scale operations at what was already known as 'the leidhoillis' in south Lanarkshire: the attempt evidently bankrupted him, but the mine he started became profitable and famous in the hands of others.(5) On the eve of the Civil War, Leadhills *was* the Scottish lead industry—"the onlie of that natur within the kingdome': (6) it employed fifty workmen, produced 300 or 400 tons of ore a year, and went down twenty-four fathoms to the lead-bearing vein.(7) From 1638, when the mines came into the possession of Sir James Hope whose descendents own the lands at the present day, the 'business history' of the industry—in the sense of detailed written records of day-to-day administration—can be said to begin.

In the second half of the seventeenth century there were two major developments. Firstly, the temporary monopoly of the Hopes was broken in 1675, when Sir James Stansfield's prospectors reported favourably on certain deserted workings at Wanlockhead in Dumfriesshire, belonging to the Duke of Queensberry: (8) the mines subsequently sunk there were to prove hardly less important than the neighbouring ones at Leadhills, and the ore raised from the two estates together can never have accounted for less than 80 per cent of total Scottish production in any subsequent decade. Secondly, around 1690, smelting with charcoal was replaced by a very much cheaper process of smelting with peat (later, though perhaps not initially, with a small admixture of coal):(9) henceforth, an increasing proportion of the ore was smelted at the mines, and less was exported unprocessed to Rotterdam and elsewhere, though the foreign market for ore and bar continued to be more important than the home market until the nineteenth century. Shortly before 1700, the surface mines on Islay which had been operated in the sixteenth century and were to have a long future of intermittent exploitation in front of them, were also brought into operation.(10)

After the Union of 1707, there was a good deal of excitement about the potentialities of Scottish minerals reminiscent of the middle years of the sixteenth century: it was triggered off when Sir John Erskine discovered a rich pocket of silver ore on his lands at Alva in Stirlingshire, which was revealed to the government in dramatic circumstances after the Jacobite rising.(11) The subsequent publicity made many a laird look harder at his land, and one result was to bring to light in 1722 a very promising vein of lead at Strontian in western Argyll: it was soon rented (with disastrous results) by the York Buildings Company.(12) In 1741 an English baronet who had spent ten years looking for metals on the Breadalbane estate was rewarded by a strike of lead at Tyndrum in Perthshire,(13) and in 1763 a soldier engaged in road-building had similar luck at Minigaff in Kirkcudbrightshire.(14) All these mines were prolific for a time, and tempted intermittent activity for more than a century. The *Old Statistical Account* also mentions attempts to mine lead at about thirty other sites ranging from Orkney in the north to Wigtonshire in the south, but in hardly anywhere outside the six sites already mentioned were such attempts sustained for more than a few years.

The solid progress of the industry during this century can be measured by a few rough statistics based on the records of the larger mines. By 1720, the industry probably employed 200 workmen and produced 1,500 tons of ore, the deepest mine touching forty-five fathoms. Between 1740 and 1810, the workforce possibly approached 1,000, and annual production probably exceeded 5,600 tons of ore on several occasions: the deepest mine in 1800 was then at least seventy-five fathoms. The rapid expansion of Leadhills in mid-century and at Wanlockhead at the end accounts for this growth far more than the discoveries of veins in new localities, and

was stimulated partly by lucky strikes of ore, partly by rising demand under the influence of economic acceleration at home and
warfare abroad. The price of lead advanced from £12-£13 a ton for
smelted bar around 1720 and £13-£14 around 1750, to £15 in 1785,
£18-£19 in 1790 and finally under the press of the Napoleonic wars
to £32-£34 between 1803 and 1809.(15) At the same time technical
improvements in drainage made it possible to work at greater depth
than with the adits, gins and hand-pumps of the seventeenth century: the bab-gin, an economical and efficient method of harnessing
waterpower to a pump, was introduced into Wanlockhead in the
1720's,(16) and Watt's steam engine (quickly improved and made
more suitable for lead mines where coal was expensive by the
mine's own engineer and future pioneer of steam navigation, Andrew Symington) into the same concern in 1778:(17) both spread
quickly—Leadhills had three steam engines by 1782.(18) Carriage
from the main mines to Leith always remained expensive, but something at least was done to improve the cart-roads at the end of the
century. The mining communities were prosperous and the amenities of life were improving, at least until the end of the eighteenth
century.

The peace of 1815 marked the end of this phase of prosperity and
expansion. Lead prices, falling initially to £16 a ton, recovered to a
level of £24 or £25 until 1821, and then settled down to £18 or £19
until 1827. The import of cheap Spanish lead, facilitated by Huskis-
son's removal of protective tariffs, then brought prices down to £11
a ton(19) and caused a severe crisis, marked by unemployment
among the workers, several bankruptcies among the employers, and
the abandonment of steam-pumping in the mines as being too costly.
This persisted until the mid-1830's, and even then recovery was slow
and partial. Despite the opening of two new mines in Kirkcudbrightshire—at Carsphairn in 1839 and Cairnsmore in 1845, both of
which proved rich for a few years(20)—by the middle of the century
the industry was only producing 2,000 tons of ore a year with a
workforce of little over 500.

At this point the main series of business records give out, though
official statistics(21) provide information for a brief postscript.
Around 1860 more buoyant prices in the first instance, and large-
scale capital investment at Leadhills and Wanlockhead, assisted by
the coming of rail transport, provided a revival that lasted until
1896, with output rising to around 4,000 tons a year between 1878
and 1895. No less than 97 per cent of the ore raised in Scotland in
the second half of the nineteenth century came from these two
mines, but operations were also attempted at about twenty other

sites including most of those that had ruined their investors by previous disappointments—optimism died very hard. The years 1896 to 1906 were a decade of renewed depression, but a new boom started in 1906 and lasted until 1918: in a final flare of energy the lead mines raised 5,400 tons of ore in 1914—more than they had done at any time in the previous hundred years. Almost immediately after 1918 the industry succumbed again to postwar depression—this time with fatal consequences. By 1928, the industry had become extinct in Scotland, and attempts to revive it since the Second World War have not met with success. Not all the veins are exhausted, but the difficulties of working them at depth combined with modern labour costs and the ease of importation of foreign lead preclude any revival under normal circumstances. After seven hundred years, one small chapter in Scottish economic history appears to be finally closed.

The Business of the Lead Mines

The business of most Scottish lead companies between 1650 and 1850 consisted both of mining and smelting, carried out on the same site. A few concerns contented themselves with sending out ore unprocessed—a high proportion of Leadhills output in the seventeenth century and some in the eighteenth century reached Holland as pure *galena* or 'Potter's ore',(22) and the Mine Adventurers at Tyndrum in the eighteenth century sent the ore to their mills in Wales to be smelted:(23) a few very small concerns, like that at Morven in Argyll in the 1730's,(24) also exported ore because production was too small to justify smelting equipment. Smelting at the mine was generally advantageous. A ton of smelted lead in the eighteenth century often fetched twice the price of a ton of ore, and because the smelting process reduced the volume to be transported by about one third the saving in transport costs as a proportion of market price was therefore striking, sometimes in the region of 60 per cent. The refining of lead to extract the silver, which made the metal softer and more pliable as well as providing a by-product to be sold to Edinburgh goldsmiths, was less common, as few ores were rich enough to bear the cost, but it was carried on at intervals at Leadhills and Wanlockhead throughout the eighteenth century.(25) The process of manufacture was carried one step further by the erection of a shot-mill at Minigaff around 1780, and at Leadhills around 1830.(26)

To work a lead deposit satisfactorily it was therefore essential to have certain natural resources in addition to the ore: water, wood, peat and coal were all important. Water was quite indispensible—for working the bab-gins that drained the mines, for washing impurities from *galena* before smelting, and for turning the water-wheels that worked the bellows of the smelt-mill. Despite a high natural rainfall on the mountains, it was not always easy to obtain it in sufficient quantities in the right places. The construction of adit levels to drain the mines often had the accidental consequence of emptying surface streams that had been useful for motive power over a wide area: in 1747 it was said that one third of the useful water at Wanlockhead had disappeared down a new level at adjacent Leadhills,(27) and litigation in the first half of the nineteenth century over the use of the very limited surface water at Leadhills forced the main company from the field in 1860.(28) Small reservoirs in the hills were sometimes built to conserve it, but even where it was plentiful it was hard to control—for example Tyndrum smelt-mill was out of operation for eighteen weeks of the year in 1783-84, due either to frost or to the need to repair the wheel after bad weather.(29) Water was a bad servant, and there was very little to be done to control its vagaries.

Wood for the lead-mines fell into two categories: pit-props for timbering the workings, and charcoal (until around 1690) for use in the smelting hearths. In some mines, timbering provided no problem: Islay and Strontian, for example, were largely opencast and at Tyndrum abundant local supplies were available which the landowner permitted the lead companies to exploit free of all charges except felling and removing.(30) At Leadhills and Wanlockhead, however, the problem was much more serious. The immediate vicinity of the mining field was so desolate that Sir James Stansfield nearly abandoned his schemes at Wanlockhead in 1675 for want of 'timber for the groove as also for the hous and smidie: '(31) the valleys of Nithsdale and Annandale to the south were well afforested with natural oak, but in the hands of owners who knew their value and whose price had to be met. In 1676 John Maitland of Eccles in Nithsdale sold his wood 'to the use of the miners at Leadhills' and the cash thus realised formed the bulk of the estate handed on to his son; in 1691 Sir Alexander Gordon of Earlstoun sold his woods for nearly £1,300 sterling: there are many similar records.(32) The purchasers provided their own labour to cut and carry, selling the bark to tanners and the chips to country folk.(33) Contrary to the general belief, the demand from the lead mines helped to preserve the woodlands of the south-west, for, after allowing initial depredations, landowners began to take the trouble to fence in cut

woods for protection against grazing animals, and to treat timber as
a profitable crop rather than as a capital asset to be raided once and
for all.(34)

The adoption of peat and coal smelting after 1690 did much to
relieve the pressure on the lead mines, but demand for pit-props
continued to be met by Nithsdale and Annandale throughout the
eighteenth and earlier nineteenth centuries. Timber remained sufficiently dear to render even a rich vein unremunerative if it was
'soft'—by 1762 the Beltongraine Vein had been followed for 300
fathoms into the hillside at Wanlockhead, but 'the drift will not
stand unless it be well supported [and] it is doubted if the ore got
from it has fully defray'd the expense'.(35)

The peat used for eighteenth-century smelting was one resource
that was abundant in the neighbourhood of all the mines, free of all
charges save that of cutting it from the hillside and carrying to the
furnaces. Considerable quantities were needed: they were cut and
stored at the end of May, to dry, preferably for two years, before
use. Coal, however, was awkward to obtain: Islay, Strontian and
Minigaff could fetch it by sea, Tyndrum by a difficult route from
the Clyde, and Leadhills and Wanlockhead along mere tracks from
the mines at Sanquhar ten or a dozen miles away. There were two
basic ways of smelting in the eighteenth century. The reverberatory
air-furnace used eight times as much coal as the blast-furnace, and
utilised no peat: this added about 50 per cent to the expense of
smelting,(36) and made air-furnaces very unpopular unless there
was a chronic shortage of water to operate the bellows of a blast-
furnace. Normally, then, coal was needed only in small quantities
for smelting and the expense was not considered embarrassing
except at Tyndrum: the introduction of steam pumping at Leadhills
and Wanlockhead after 1778 much increased consumption and
could only be afforded while lead prices were high—after 1834,
drainage by water-power was again considered the only economical
way, since at that date no effective means of reducing the cost of
taking coal to the mines had yet been found.

Transport costs were bound to be something of a bugbear to the
main mines, situated as they mostly were, at high altitudes and far
inland. The final market for their product was often very distant—
apart from the paint manufacturers, plumbers and builders of Scotland, it lay mainly in Holland and England, with subsidiary markets
in France in the seventeenth century, in Russia in the late eighteenth
and in Germany in the nineteenth, with occasional cargoes to the
Mediterranean and apparently even to China.(37) The only concern
of the lead-companies, however, was to get it to the ports where

wholesale merchants took charge: only a small percentage was saleable at the mines. Minigaff was close to the Solway and in a good position to sell to either Chester or Liverpool.(38) Islay and Strontian, accessible by sea, sold to Glasgow—so did Tyndrum, but by a complicated route involving the dispatch of lead bars by horse down General Wade's road through Glen Falloch, whence they were loaded into boats and carried through Loch Lomond and the river Leven into the Clyde: either a drought, by blocking the Leven, or a flood, by carrying away the bridges in Glen Falloch, could and often did make the way impassable.(39)

Most Scottish lead, however, was produced at Leadhills and Wanlockhead, and exported through Leith: it was carted in two stages down the fifty-mile road through Biggar, a toll-free route that was carrying nearly 4,000 lead carts a year in either direction in the 1740's, but which could still be described as 'extraordinarily good in the summer months except when the season proves very wet.'(40) The route to Dumfries was shorter, but so badly maintained until the nineteenth century that it was little used by the lead-carriers. In 1770, it was calculated that the cost of transporting lead to the sea was fifteen times as much at Leadhills to what it was on Islay, but since lead in the form of smelted bar was valuable in relation to its weight, the price of cartage on a ton of the Earl of Hopetoun's lead was still only 10 per cent of the market price at Leith—or £1 10s. in £14 15s. The big lead mines could therefore be worked in a location unthinkable for an exporting colliery. As Adam Smith put it: 'The value of coal-mine to the proprietor frequently depends as much upon its situation as upon its fertility. That of a metallic mine depends more upon its fertility and less upon its situation.'(41) The majority of English lead-mines were sited equally badly, the Scots felt no serious competitive handicap from their isolation. Indeed, in one respect they had an advantage —throughout the eighteenth century English lead was liable to an export duty, while the produce of Leadhills and Wanlockhead left duty-free under an exemption conferred before the Union.

Given reasonable resources and tolerable access, the cost of erecting and maintaining smelting plant was a minor consideration. Washing, sorting and crushing ore were simple processes entrusted to boys who began work at the age of nine or later: sieves, shovels and hammers used in the open air or in rough wooden shelters were the usual equipment, though crushing mills worked by horses or by water-power were known in the eighteenth century and general in the nineteenth. The smelting equipment itself was also frequently very simple. The typical 'ore-hearth' of the eighteenth century was a small blast-furnace a few feet square used in a smelting mill with water-powered bellows; a few alterations would convert it from an ore-hearth (using clean dressed ore) to a 'slag-hearth' (using the wastes that had already passed through an ore-hearth).(42) The reverbatory air-furnace was less common but not much more sophisticated. Later, smelting equipment became more complicated and costly, involving water-wheels of thirty feet or more in diameter, roasting furnaces that prepared the ore before smelting, and (in the 1840's) elaborate flues running in a zig-zag through the hillside for five hundred feet or more. The workers in the smelting house were skilled men and highly paid, though short-lived, but there were not many of them : a dozen would be the maximum even in a large mine.

Inevitably, much greater costs were incurred below ground, in the actual business of mining. Driving the shafts and levels through hard rock was much more difficult than in coal mining, and usually involved the use of gunpowder: once the vein had been reached and followed, it was necessary to keep the workings free of water by means of adits and by bab-gins and steam-engines—'at great expense', 'with abundance of charge' were the usual comments of the engineers on making and maintaining their drainage system. Although the mines were normally free of gas, they still had to be ventilated by shafts running down to the level at frequent intervals, and these vertical openings were also used for winding: 'the cost of sinking these shafts would amount to no inconsiderable item in the expenditure', said the engineer of the company that took over Leadhills in 1861, 'as the total depth of the same is fully equal to the distances between them'.(43) Labour, if not as well paid as in the coal industry, was still expensive in relation to the value of the end product and the short working day of six hours, which was the longest practicable time for a man to spend below ground in a lead mine without fatal injury to his health.

Indeed, the speculative element so pronounced in lead-mining was largely compounded of the necessity to spend a great deal on sinking shafts, driving levels and maintaining drainage and ventilation, and the complete uncertainty as to whether the vein would prove productive. 'Tho' I wish a great deal, I dare not flatter myself too far', wrote one entrepreneur in Lanarkshire on receiving news of a strike, 'these things are very deceitfull'.(44) He who discovered his failure in time—like this Englishman—were fortunate in loosing little more than the cost of prospecting. A small initial success often proved a fatal lure: 'out of that hole I took fifty thousand pounds', Sir John Erskine used to tell visitors to Alva, 'and I put it all into *that* hole'.(45) Again and again a pocket of ore near the surface was

I

mistaken for a vein justifying extensive exploitation. Again and again a hitherto productive vein that had been followed for many years with varying success had to be abandoned because of unexpected failure: the common formation of the ore, occurring in productive knots between unproductive strings, accustomed miners to barren stretches in a vein and this encouraged them to continue working along a dead line in the vain hope of coming upon further rich knots. Again and again abandoned workings were reopened by optimists who believed themselves cleverer or more affluent than their predecessors. 'I suspect there is little chance of Tyndrum ever turning out to any profit, even if adventurers can be found disposed to speculate upon it', wrote a friend of the landowner in 1791:(46) one company had abandoned it in that year when the difficulty of mining raised the cost of production to nearly £20 a ton, yet in 1804, in 1812, from 1838 until 1862 and again in 1918, other adventurers did 'speculate upon it' with unanimous lack of success.(47) A similar story could be told at Islay, at Strontian and at several other sites. Only at Leadhills and Wanlockhead was there a reasonable certainty of workable mines continuing over a long period, and even there the landowners and companies kept a certain number of workmen constantly engaged in searching for new veins against the day the old ones gave out. Complacency about the future was about the last emotion justified in a lead investor. But who were the men rash enough to invest in lead?

The Capitalist

The financing of the Scottish lead industry between 1650 and 1850 was carried out by four main classes of investors—the Scottish landowners (generally those on whose land the mineral was located), the Scottish merchants (generally those who were engaged in the sale of lead to overseas consumers), those Englishmen who were already involved in lead-mining in the Pennines or Cumberland, and other Englishmen seeking an outlet for surplus capital in what was for them essentially a foreign speculation. Similarly, the investment was carried out in three main ways: through a capitalist acting alone, through a co-partnery composed of three to twelve adventurers, or through a larger joint-stock company acting under a royal charter. There was a tendency for each group to favour one method of investment rather than another: thus a capitalist acting alone was generally a Scottish landowner, the small co-partnerships were favoured either by Scottish merchants or by English lead interests,

and the chartered companies likewise by the general English specu-
lator—but there were a good many exceptions to these rules.

The attitude of the landowner on whose ground lead was discovered was, of course, crucial to future investment. Theoretically,
the news of a promising strike might lead him to sell the land outright to other capitalists, to ignore the good news entirely, or to
exploit it by leasing a mineral concession to others or by sinking a
mine himself. In fact, so far as can be discovered, only one landowner disposed of land as a consequence of lead being found upon
it, and very few brusquely turned their backs upon the possibilities
of exploitation without making some effort towards it. Optimistic action, and not indifference, was the almost invariable response
of an eighteenth-century landlord placed in this position.

The most sensible and cautious attitude was to grant a lease to
any who might be interested. Exceptionally, this would be a lease to
work minerals for a term of years in exchange for a fixed rent: thus
at Wanlockhead in 1675 the Duke of Queensberry was paid 1,000
merks Scots as tack duty for a lease to Sir James Stansfield and
partners, and in Orkney in the eighteenth century 'a company in the
south granted their obligation to the proprietor for 500 lib. a year
in order to obtain his permission to work them;' something similar
happened in Islay in 1680.(48) It was much more usual, however, to
grant a lease on a royalty basis, often combined with an entry fine
—the Scotch Mines Company paid £10,000 for a lease of 99 years
at Leadhills in 1772(49)—the proprietor taking a proportion of the
lead raised or its calculated equivalent in money. The fixing of this
proportion was a matter for negotiation: once a mine had been
proved prolific and put in reasonable running order it became traditional to surrender one bar in six to the landowner. When it was
just beginning, the proportion might be one bar in seven or eight,
or even as little as one bar in twelve if the opening of a new vein
entailed considerable capital expenditure—for example, the installa-
tion of steam drainage. In the depression of the 1830's, a sliding
scale was negotiated at Wanlockhead so that the landowner had one
bar in six only if output exceeded 14,000 bars, falling to one bar in
twelve if it was less than 10,000: at Leadhills in 1831 the landowner took one bar in six if the price exceeded £15 a ton, and one
bar in eight if it fell below that price.(50) Other clauses generally
safeguarded the landlord from neglect or abuse of the mines, ensuring that the leases kept a certain minimum of workers at the face,
and that they did not neglect the engines, the levels or the timbering
by 'robber mining' when the lease was about to fall in. In short, a
lead mine was regarded as a valuable asset, and the landowner who

was prepared to lease it stood a chance of some profit without being involved at all in the risk of loss.

The other common alternative was for the landowner to take part in financing the mine himself, accepting a risk in return for the chance of a greater profit. In a few instances, the landowner was the sole capitalist. The Hopes acquired the estate and mines of Leadhills by marriage in 1638, and for the remainder of the seventeenth century exploited the minerals without any assistance from outside investors, which amounted to carrying almost the whole lead industry on their own shoulders: in the eighteenth century they leased out more and more of the field, but as late as 1768 retained one of the richest veins in their own hands.(51) In the 1840's, the Duke of Buccleuch at Wanlockhead, the Marquis of Breadalbane at Tyndrum, and Colonel Cathcart at Carsphairn all took over the running of the mines at their own expense.(52) Nevertheless, this behaviour was very much rarer than in the Scottish coal industry, where the landowner as sole entrepreneur was a normal figure: the greater element of speculation in a lead mine presumably deterred him from shouldering the risk alone, especially as the usual proportion of one sixth of the gross product which he received as rent if he leased it was a good deal more satisfactory than the one tenth common in coal mines.(53)

The simplest way for the landowner to spread the risk was for him to enter a co-partnership. There were many instances of this. The Duke of Queensberry in 1709 signed a deed of co-partnership with the great English chartered concern, the London (Quaker) Lead Company, giving him a quarter share in the profits and expenses of the working of the Wanlockhead mines, in addition to his sixth bar as rent.(54) At one of the two mines at Minigaff, Patrick Heron of Heron in 1778 had three shares out of twenty-three in a partnership of eleven, mainly Englishmen, as well as his sixth bar.(55) In both cases the initiative was evidently provided by the companies, who probably felt it advantageous to involve the landlord a little more closely in their affairs, but the initiative could also come from the other side—as when the Earl of Cassillis persuaded his brother-in-law, James Hunter the banker, together with his partner Sir William Forbes and five others to join him in a partnership 'to ascertain whether we might reasonably expect to hit upon a productive vein of lead-ore or not'.(56) Much to Sir William's relief, the partnership collapsed after twelve months with the loss of only about £120 a head: he regarded it as a salutary lesson and a providential escape from greater folly.

There were also some landed Scots who invested in mines on

other people's estates as leasees. In the eighteenth century the agricultural reformer, Sir Archibald Grant of Monymusk, like five other Scottish landowners, had a share in the foundation of the Scotch Mines Company, and was also one of the twelve partners who took a lease at Strontian in 1724, contributing £225 to a nominal capital of £3,600.(57) His landlord there, Sir Alexander Murray of Stanhope, was a lead fanatic: he not only contributed £225 to this partnership and ran a mine on his own account on his own land at Lurga nearby, but also took leases for mines on Islay, Morven and Mull—he went bankrupt, and was forced to sell his right to the sixth bar at Strontian to Sir Archibald and a London merchant.(58) In the nineteenth century, the Marquis of Bute purchased all the shares in a co-partnership at Wanlockhead in the 1830's.(59) Such men were rather unusual, for the first priority for a landowner's capital was the improvement of his own estate, not the exploitation of others.

The other native class that played any considerable part in financing the industry was the Scottish merchants. They were not foolhardy or affluent enough to operate singly, and there is no proof they were ever much concerned as shareholders in the chartered companies. Their natural home was in a small co-partnership, a device with which they had long been familiar as shipowners, and which they had helped introduce into Scottish industry by their seventeenth-century investments in such things as sugar-refining and soap-boiling.

The most successful of the mercantile co-partnerships were those whose leaders had come to mining only after long years of experience in marketing lead. The Leith merchant Alexander Sherriff followed his father's footsteps as factor to the Earl of Hopetoun, and ultimately became a partner in a concession at Leadhills, in another in Ayrshire and in a cobalt mine at Alva: he was regarded as a leading expert in minerals, and only withdrew from these affairs when his partner at Leadhills (another Leith merchant) went bankrupt in 1773.(60) Similarly, Crauford and partners, who leased the mineral field at Wanlockhead from 1756 until the 1830's—'an enterprising and eminently successful company'—originated in a Scottish-Dutch family accustomed to disposing of native lead in the markets of Rotterdam.(61) Other merchants, who do not appear to have had much prior interest in lead, but who no doubt expected to use the produce of their mines to reinforce their general trade, were involved in partnerships in many places. Leith and Edinburgh names occur repeatedly: one of the more famous partnerships of the early eighteenth century was the Friendly Mining Society with a nominal capital of £10,000 and twelve partners, engaged unprofitably at Wanlockhead in the 1720's, and headed by Edinburgh's Dean of Guild, Robert Wightman;(62) in the nineteenth century, William Muir and Eagle Henderson, merchants of Leith, were leaders in a co-partnership that obtained a foothold at Leadhills in 1847, eventually taking over and reorganising the whole of that field after 1861.(63) Glasgow men were ubiquitous in the west, involved at Islay in 1720, at Strontian in 1724, at Tyndrum in 1749, and at Leadhills in 1847.(64) Two Ayr merchants took a lease of a mine on Sir John Kennedy's land at Maybole, Ayrshire, in 1718, a Dumfries merchant was involved in Heron's mine at Minigaff, and the abortive Caledonia Mining Company which planned to take over Tyndrum in 1803 had two Alloa merchants and one Stirling merchant as partners.(65)

In these partnerships, the merchants frequently associated themselves with other classes of investors—sometimes with landowners and Englishmen, especially other English merchants—and sometimes with other Scots from the professional or commercial classes. The harmless adventure of James Hunter and Sir William Forbes we have already noted, but another Edinburgh private bank, William Hogg and company, was drawn to its ruin in 1769 by backing a lead-mine.(66) Lawyers and tax-collectors were quite often associated: the Friendly Mining Society, for instance, contained an advocate (Duncan Forbes of Culloden), two writers to the signet and a collector of the cess.(67) Tradesmen describing themselves as 'plumbers' with an obvious connection with the industry were occasionally partners, but the general epithet 'manufacturer' was unknown among lead investors until a couple from Glasgow appeared at Leadhills in the 1840's.(68) Where these extraneous investors appear in mercantile partnerships, it is almost always in a passive rôle, with day-to-day administration done by a merchant.

Finally, no roll-call of Scottish lead entrepreneurs would be complete without a mention of Alexander Telfer, who was employing about 240 out of the 350-odd men at Wanlockhead in 1743, and whose father had been 'a common miner'. He held a lease there from 1735 to 1755, operated with more success than the other companies on that field at the time, and only gave up because of a quarrel with the landlord: apart from the fact that his relations were occasionally associated with him, it is not known how he obtained his capital—in his proletarian origins he remained a unique figure.(69)

Native investment in lead-mining then, though drawn as widely from Scottish society as any investment in the eighteenth-century economy, was not generally very successful—with the notable exceptions of the Hopes who made a fortune from Leadhills between 1650 to 1750, and Crauford and partners, who did well out of Wanlockhead between 1756 and 1830. It was, however, supplemented by streams of English capital not less optimistic and not always better directed.

The English investors might be broadly classified into those whose business was lead-mining, who often immigrated and generally worked in small partnerships, and those who were members of the general public looking for a promising speculation, who usually remained in the south and often preferred the anonymity of a chartered company. Investment over the Border had begun with the sixteenth-century gold seekers, with the flamboyant Bevis Bulmer the first to seek his fortune in person in the Scottish hills and the artist Nicholas Hilliard among the first to hope for it while staying comfortably at home in London.

English investment primarily for lead rather than for precious metals, however, did not begin until the 1670's, when Sir James Stansfield—an Englishman resident in Edinburgh—and two partners from the south began to prospect veins in Glen Lyon, Glen Esk and Wanlockhead.(70) The first half of the eighteenth century was the heyday of the English, and between 1700 and 1770 they were deeply involved in all the main mines—Leadhills, Wanlockhead, Islay, Strontian, Tyndrum and Minigaff, as well as in several minor ventures—as at Orkney, Glen Esk in Angus, New Cumnock in Ayrshire and Blebo in Fife. Thereafter their enthusiasm began to wane: there were no important new investments after 1810, and by 1840 virtually all English capital had been withdrawn.

A few of the Englishmen were solitary adventurers, almost on the romantic pattern of Bevis Bulmer. Captain William Thynne, for instance, took a lease at Islay in 1745 but backed out when the rising occurred, took another at Blebo in 1748 and then abandoned it all for a career in the West Indies.(71) Sir Robert Clifton was more persistent: an original member of the Strontian partnership in 1724, in 1730 he took an independent lease for thirty-eight years of all metals he might discover on the Breadalbane estates; he had no luck until 1741, when he found Tyndrum mine where he was soon employing 137 workmen; shortly afterwards he ran out of capital, despite a loan of £5,000 from the widow of Sir Thomas Lombe the silk manufacturer, and from 1745 until the lease fell in his family sublet to a series of English companies.(72)

It was much more typical to find the English involved in small partnerships, either alone or with Scots. Some of these were speculators out to turn a quick penny, like the Duke of Norfolk and General Wade, who contributed £1,350 and £225 respectively to the Strontian partnership.(73) More often they had some prior interest in the lead-industry either as mine-owners or merchants. In this case their intervention might be prompted as much by Scottish ignorance of technology as by shortage of native capital: for example, a Cumberland man, George Lothian, acquired a concession at Lead-hills after he had been working there under contract smelting the Earl of Hopetoun's ore,(74) and the Yorkshire family of Readshaw came to control Heron's mine at Minigaff after being interested in the potentialities of south-west Scotland by natives who valued their opinion on mineral strikes.(75) Such men usually came from the lead-districts of the north of England—the 'Rippon Company' at Tyndrum, the 'Cumberland Company' at Rusco, Kirkcudbrightshire, the 'Derbyshire Company' and the 'Yorkshire Company' at Lead-hills reveal their own origins.(76) Very often they were willing to try two or more sites in Scotland if their first venture misfired: the 'Derbyshire Company' headed by Antony Tessington took a con-cession at Langholm in Dumfries-shire and angled for one at Wan-lockhead while still working at Leadhills,(77) the Readshaws tried many places in the south-west,(78) and Patton and Richardson (a Chester partnership) removed from Tyndrum to Minigaff.(79) Such flexibility and persistence was rare with Scottish capital, more tied to local considerations.

Finally, there were four English chartered companies. The first to take up an interest in the north was the London (Quaker) Lead Company, formally known as 'the Governor and Company for smelting down lead with pit-coal'. They held a lease at Wanlock-head from 1709 to 1756,(80) and by driving adit levels and timber-ing they did much to benefit the mine but made little profit for themselves: later in the century they were involved in a small mine at New Cumnock in Ayrshire, and they also made trials in Orkney and were approached unavailingly by Sir John Sinclair to make trials on his lands near Thurso.(81) The Company of Mine Adven-turers of England were a similar professional concern who worked Tyndrum for fifteen years from 1745 to 1760, also without much success.(82) Both appealed to the Scottish landlords as ideal tenants: as the Earl of Breadalbane put it after dealing with Sir Robert Clifton, 'I am sure it will be upon the whole more beneficial and much safer to do with known reputable Company than with people who upon trial may perhaps be too late found unequal to the undertaking.'(83)

The same could not have been said of the York Buildings Company, who added a failure in lead-mining to a long list of notorious and shady fiascoes in Scotland: they held a sub-lease of Strontian from 1730, spent a large sum building a settlement there named New York, and ran through their funds so quickly that in 1735 the miners took possession of the ore in lieu of their unpaid wages.(84) From 1724 to 1731 they also attempted to mine in Glen Esk.(85) It was not to be expected that this concern, with its unique combination of incompetence and dishonesty, would add anything of value to the industry.

In contrast to these three companies, all, in different ways, disillusioned about Scotland's mining potentialities, it is refreshing to find an example of ambitious English investment that was accorded a measure of success—the important but almost forgotten Scotch Mines Company, incorporated by Royal Charter in 1729 under the title of 'the Governor and Company for working mines, minerals and metals in that part of Great Britain called Scotland', and wound up in 1861 with the return of its capital to the partners, after more than a century's activity at Leadhills. It originated in the fertile brain of Sir John Erskine of Alva, whose discovery of a silver-mine on his own lands had already led him in 1716 to create a partnership consisting of himself and a few Scottish and English merchants to prospect for minerals in Scotland:(86) in the next twelve years he personally collected seven different leases for copper, lead and silver in places ranging from Perthshire to the Pentlands, and ultimately he obtained a charter of incorporation for a group of southern capitalists who had offered to take them off his hands at terms advantageous to himself.(87) Despite Sir John's initiative, the new company was essentially an English investment, for it owed its whole being to the Sun Fire Office in London: throughout its existence its address was the same, its directors largely the same, and its shareholders mainly Londoners—the bulk of its surviving records reside today in the Sun building in Threadneedle Street. The source of the insurance office's initial interest must be sought in a group of London Scots headed by Robert Dalzell, William Hamilton and Thomas Watts, who gained control of Sun Fire in 1720 and no doubt still believed (as Scots will) in the economic possibilities of the land they had left behind.(88)

The Scotch Mines Company commenced operation with a nominal capital of £100,000, of which only £8,800 was paid up by seventy-five proprietors in the first instance.(89) At first, all went badly: six out of the seven leases conveyed by Sir John turned out to be worthless; the seventh, a lease at Leadhills from the Earl of Hopetoun renewed in 1730, looked promising and produced a great deal of lead-ore, but thanks to incompetent and dishonest management by the factors there made little profit. Sir John had been retained by the directors as their main agent in Scotland, but in 1734 he found it prudent to retire—'the Company's affairs were in great confusion . . . everything was in wretched order and a heavy debt contracted'.(90)

The company replaced him by a scholar and mathematician of European reputation, the brilliant James Stirling, whose withdrawal to live at Leadhills, as a mine manager, albeit at a fine salary of £220 a year, puzzled and intrigued his contemporaries. Stirling's régime, which lasted from 1734 until his death in 1770, placed the mines on an orderly and profitable footing which his successors maintained until the Napoleonic wars: (91) some indication of its fortunes can be gauged from the annual sums paid out in dividends —nothing before 1747, £880 in 1775, £4,400 in 1759, £7,000 in 1766, £10,000 in 1802, and then £4,000 from 1808 to 1830 (with the exception of 1816 when a dividend was withheld).(92) After 1830 the trading losses were considerable, and in 1840 the company assigned its rights to the then manager, William Borron, but the landlord refused to accept him as a tenant: as a consequence of low prices, rising costs, falling supplies of ore and protracted lawsuits over water rights, the company finally abandoned the mine in 1860, and was formally liquidated twelve months later.(93)

As it was described in its heyday around 1790, the company employed about 200 men at Leadhills and another fifty or so at Tyndrum, where it also had a lease from 1768 to 1792: it was financed by 100 shares of a nominal £1,000 each, and governed by a president, twelve directors, a secretary and a clerk sitting in the Scotch Mines room of the Sun Fire Office in London, receiving weekly reports from their resident manager at Leadhills.(94) It is the first instance in history, and the only one before the nineteenth century, of a Scottish business being entirely directed from London. That is should have been so successful for so long in such a notoriously speculative industry makes it an even more remarkable feat of entrepreneurship.

The Workers

Not the least of the practical difficulties facing the capitalist in Scotland was a shortage of skilled and disciplined labour to carry on a trade in which there was no native tradition and which, on account of its strangeness and danger, had little appeal to newcomers. In the seventeenth century, it seemed very likely that the lead proprietors would solve the problem in the same way as the coal and salt owners—by the forcible pressing of paupers and felons, and by instituting a form of serfdom to bind the worker to the mine for life and, effectively, to bind his children after him. Thus, in 1649, Sir James Hope obtained for the Leadhills mine all privileges already granted and to be granted in the future to the masters of coalheughs and saltworks, which if systematically implemented, would have depressed his men to the lowest levels of the eighteenth-century collier.(95) In 1695, however, Lady Margaret Hope explicitly repudiated this policy by an 'article for liberty' allowing her workers to leave 'upon any just consideration or where there are unjust grumblers about their wages'.(96) Others followed her lead, and in the eighteenth century the main lead mines gained a reputation for enlightened employment that was completely at variance with the legal tyranny of the coal mines.

The reason why the lead owners became liberal at a time when coal and salt owners were becoming harsher must be sought in the presence of increasing numbers of English lead-miners north of the Border, an invasion which solved the worst of the labour problem but which (as the employer was well aware) would not continue if the newcomers were to be subjected to an alien and degrading serfdom. Many of these welcome immigrants arrived in the train of English capitalists as the gold-washers and others had done in the sixteenth century: 'men may be had very fitt for [lead mines] either from Wales, Derbyshire or the North of England', Sir John Erskine told the London Directors of the Scotch Mines Company in 1729.(97) Others, even in the seventeenth century, made their way into Scotland on their own initiative, like the Englishmen who in 1660 arrived at Leadhills, 'upon a Setterday, and he says that he has wroght at lead mynes since he was ane boy, he had broght his wyffe with him, and he says that his brother-in-law is following him and will be heir shortly.'(98) He was neither the first of his fellow countrymen there, nor the last: Sir James Hope had spoken to two on his first visit to his new property in 1638, and by 1750 at least half the surnames on the wage-books of the Scotch Mines Company were English.(99) In the eighteenth century they penetrated into Orkney, Islay, Strontian and Tyndrum, as well as many other places, working with Lowlanders and Highlanders, occupying the more skilled jobs but training natives alongside them: 'John Lindsay English' and 'John Lindsay Scotchman' were carefully distinguished in the wage books of Tyndrum in 1763.(100)

The life-story of one of these workers, John Taylor, was the subject of an article in the *Scots Magazine*, because he claimed to be 132 in the year of his death. He was born at Alston in Cumberland of lead-mining stock, and moved first to a Quaker-owned mine at Blackhall in County Durham. Just before the Union he was sent by his employers to make trials of the Islay mines, then returned to Durham, and was again recalled to Scotland to make trials for Scott of Harden in the Ettrick Forest. From 1708 to 1730 he was employed as overseer of a large body of English miners on Islay, and on their failure spent two years at Strontian. In 1732 he worked both as a day-labourer in Glasgow and in the York Buildings Company silver-mine at Hilderstone in West Lothian. In 1773 he came to Leadhills and worked there until 1752 ('he was then about 114 years old'), dying in 1770. Apart from its improbable length, his career could probably be paralleled many times in other immigrants.(101)

The immigration of English miners came to an end before the closing decades of the eighteenth century, as a tradition of skill was created in the Scottish mines. By the mid-eighteenth century the men of Leadhills and Wanlockhead regarded themselves as very distinct from their English counterparts, though many of their names were still the same. Smelters, too, were almost invariably English until 1800, and mine managers were often English until 1850. English skill was thus at least as conspicuous as English capital in building up the eighteenth-century industry.

One of the internal details in which southern influence was most evident was in the changing system of paying wages. In the seventeenth century, payment in the Scottish lead-mines was like payment in the coal-mines—by day wages.(102) During the eighteenth century the miners went over to the English 'bargain-system', by which a partnership of anything from two to sixteen men (but usually four or eight) contracted either to raise ore for a stipulated price for a certain time, or to drive a certain distance of level for an agreed sum, the details being written down in advance by the overseer in a 'contract book' and signed by the men. The one system gradually supplanted the other: thus at Tyndrum in 1763 all the Scots were paid by the shift and the Englishmen 'John Knowels and partners' and 'George Shenkland and Partners' received bargains, but by 1775 the bargain system applied to both nationalities.(103) By the early nineteenth century all underground workers in the Scottish mines were working at bargains.

Payment was frequently related not to the quantity of ore raised, but to the final yield of metal from that ore—which might not be accurately known for as long as two years. In such cases the men were loaned a provisional sum or 'estimate' until the final reckoning. This might be justified as a means of ensuring a constant ratio between labour costs and output, and as a way of preventing the miners adulterating the ore, but it had the additional consequence of keeping the miners in debt to their employers and preventing them from leaving the mine too readily. Cash payments once a year or once every six months, combined with a company store where the men could get credit for meal and the necessities of their work— steel, candle and gunpowder—had a similar effect, though truck shops also fulfilled a very real economic need in these isolated settlements, generally many miles from other villages or retailing centres. An observer in 1853, commenting that few miners at Lead-hills escaped debt and condemning the whole system as an invitation to improvidence, went on: 'the debts thus recklessly incurred hang like a millstone round their neck till their dying day, trammeling their exertions, binding them still closer to the village, and adding another inducement to accept lower wages there from their inability to seek employment elsewhere'.(104) Miners in Scotland, of course, never possessed the liberty to mine and sell ore independently as the 'free miners' did in parts of England. They were always, in every sense, employees of the landowner or company with mining rights.

The key-note of industrial relations in the lead-mines from the seventeenth century to the nineteenth was paternalism—which may be defined as the maintenance by the employer of a strict fatherly discipline over his men's morals as well as over their work, combined with a measure of genuine benevolence and a real attempt to encourage self-help. Some such system was clearly necessary for the effective use of labour in very isolated and self-contained communities with a good deal of enforced leisure, where the constant temptation was to quarrel and to go on the bottle.

Different employers stressed different aspects of paternalism. It was at its worst where it was weakest. The Marquis of Breadalbane's administration of Tyndrum between 1838 and 1862 was paternalist only in the sense that the whole mine was designed as a system of public works to relieve crofter distress on his land. It was never really expected to show a profit and it certainly never did so, but the Marquis was of cheese-paring mentality and resented his losses sufficiently to avoid paying a living wage to the men he had uprooted and sent to the mine. His intervention in administration was capricious. He might send three bottles of wine and a supply of fresh meat from Taymouth Castle to a miner appallingly injured by an explosion that shattered his hip and one arm, and from whose suppurating wounds fragments of bone were extracted for weeks afterwards, but it worried him not at all that the men's houses were ruinous or that they had no surgeon or school. It was years before he discovered that the store-keeper was forcing 'the meanest labourer' to buy him drinks—'*he* never pays'—and when he found it out he appointed a man who was also dismissed after seven years in office for favouritism, drunkenness, overcharging and selling on the Sabbath—'being thus an involuntary wretched tool in the hands of a bountiful providence who wished to save the people from the torments of a Strathfillan sermon'. His German mine managers were appalled by the drunkenness and demoralisation of the men: 'it may look very well on the books, [but] it is only an illusion that a man will work with too low wages' said one; and another 'it is almost a religious point of every German miner to take care of the workmen and be kind to them, as it always turns to account'. Finally, one of them lost his temper and wrote a magnificent letter of resignation— 'And now, My Lord, please to allow me a few concluding words. You keep an emu and deer and pheasants and a museum and other remarkable things for your pleasure and not for any use. I am of the opinion that you have in the same way a mining officer, miners, a mine, a railway, a crushing mill, all *in majorem domini glorians.*'(105)

The Hope family in the seventeenth century at Leadhills exploited their mine in a very different spirit, and they would never have allowed their personal grip to slip so far as to permit this kind of abuse. Sir James Hope frequently visited the mine and explored the levels personally: his successors relied upon weekly reports from the managers, containing all kinds of *minutae*. Drunkenness was to be punished by corporal punishment and by fines—'if you neglect theis their guilt will be yors that should punish it', the manager was reminded; absence from the church established in the village in 1648 was punishable by the deduction of two shifts' wages, and a roll was kept of attenders; each day at 5.30 a.m. a bell was rung to summon the men to work; every month the manager was to call the most experienced workmen to counsel to discuss the running of the mines; grants were made for medical expenses to men injured in their work.(106) On the whole the emphasis was on discipline rather than on benevolence or self-help, but the mines were rich enough to afford tolerable wages and (except in the famine of 1696 to 1699) there were no indications of abject poverty like that of Tyndrum in the nineteenth century.

The Scotch Mines Company administration at Leadhills in the eighteenth century became, under the guidance of James Stirling and with the lively co-operation of the Earl of Hopetoun, the most per-

fect example of paternalism in the industry. Reform was sadly
overdue when the mathematician was appointed manager, for under
his predecessor discipline had gone to pieces: the men had become
'thoughtless and dissipated' and 'if they had high wages they could
hardly live on them'.(107) Stirling attacked the problem root and
branch:(108) discipline at work was re-established by a code of
rules governing the behaviour of each class of worker above and
below ground: control over morals was assisted by a system of
licensing ale-sellers and greatly reducing their numbers (there had
been twenty-one in the village in 1739 ministering to the 'odious and
abominable vice of drunkenness') and by the banning of spirits as
'little better than poison to people that wrought below ground';
benevolence established a schoolmaster in the village to attend to
their education and a surgeon to attend to their health and to recommend the correct diet. Above all, however, Stirling believed in helping the men to help themselves. With the landowner's permission,
the employee was encouraged to build his own house and allowed
to take in as much waste ground from the hillside as he needed for
a small-holding—this property he then owned rent-free, with liberty
to sell or bequeath as he wished. Arrangements were also made for
him to keep a cow for a small rent. A library was founded in 1741
with books given by Stirling and Hopetoun, but handed over to the
miners and run by them with great success: it was the first circulating library in Scotland, and still exists with a splendid collection
of eighteenth-century books ranging from theology and geography to
the art of gunnery and the novels of Smollet. Finally arrangements
were made for sickness and old age: there was a charity fund to
which the men, the company and the landowner all contributed and
a special pension fund run by the Earl, to which for instance one
of the workers successfully applied for admission in 1772 when he
reminded his lordship of his 'promise to do for me when I could not
do for myself'.(109) The main support, however, came from the
'partnership' system by which widows and old men were allowed
to take a share in the bargains of younger men. The consequence
of all this was a complete transformation both in the physical appearance of the village and in the manners and morals of the miners;
though the latter did not come about immediately. In 1784 the
chaplain found the workers 'in general a decent, intelligent, docile
people', but too many still employed themselves in 'sauntering
thro' the town, chatting in the smiddies, tippling in the ale-houses
and kissing the girls. During the few months I have been here I
have baptised more bastard children than for sixteen years before.'(110) A little later in the *Old Statistical Account*, he called

them 'the best informed and therefore the most reasonable common people I know'(111)—but in this there was undoubtedly an element of flattery not present in the earlier letter to the earl: the minister knew the miners could read as well as his Lordship.

Many of the characteristic features of the Scotch Mines Company's paternalism were copied by the other large mines, especially by the other concerns at Leadhills and Wanlockhead. Crauford and Company at the latter village favoured the same system of small-holding and house-building, with a pension fund, doctor, schoolmaster and minister, and also built a Miners Library (also still extant) in 1756.(112) The libraries soon became the most popular of all amenities for the men. An English sportsman visiting a small lead mine on the side of Ben Cruchahan, Argyll, in 1784, reported that the miners 'have taxed themselves in a moiety of their wages for the purchase of books and the gradual establishment of a library for their amusement in this sequestered situation'.(113) Similarly, when Colonel Cathcart opened a new mine at Carsphairn in 1839 he found that the workers were accustomed 'to the privilige of excellent libraries and regretted their separation from these means of entertainment and improvement', and he consequently felt obliged to provide books and a new school for the men.(114) The Royal Commission on the Employment of Children was told in 1842 that at Leadhills even the poorest miners who slept on heather mattresses and walked on earth floors generally owned a few books.(115)

Although down to 1750 the lead-miners were known for a somewhat turbulent and 'republican spirit'—there was, for instance, a strike at Leadhills as early as 1660, sabotage of the mine there in 1740, and a case of manslaughter following a drunken brawl in 1768(116)—by the late eighteenth century their reputation was improving, and by the nineteenth century all middle-class observers were unanimous in their opinion of the intelligence and sobriety of the men at Leadhills and Wanlockhead. The great Victorian temperance reformer John Hope opened his campaign in the villages, and set his seal to their reputation by sending poor town children for their holidays to Leadhills, because he was sure they could form no bad habits from the example of the miners.(117) Some other effects of paternalism did not so much recommend themselves to the leaders of the working class. 'They are what might be called a home-abiding people', the leader of the Miners Association of Great Britain said of the men of Wanlockhead in 1871, 'and live under the constant impression that to offend the manager would be to commit a very great wrong.'(118) Apart from an ill-advised strike at Leadhills in the middle of a depression in 1833—it was easily broken by blacklegs brought from the Highlands—the nineteenth-century lead-miner never showed the independent and aggressive spirit of his colleagues in the coal mines. As an employee of a small and declining industry he could hardly have done so had he wished.

The Standard of Life in the Lead Mines

The life of the lead workers in their isolated and unhospitable mountain valleys was bound to be a hard one, sweetened though it might be by the amenities provided by the employers in the larger concerns. Their health, for example, was constantly undermined by their occupation: 'Few of the miners live long', said a visitor to Wanlockhead in 1845, 'they are generally more or less attacked by pulmonary disease.'(119) It was not surprising, considering they habitually worked in a dust-filled atmosphere compounded of particles of rock, lead ore and gunpowder, sometimes with water up to their ankles and their clothes soaked from the dripping roofs. In mines that did not adhere strictly to the six-hour day for underground workers, the strain on the man was often intolerable, and at Leadhills even under Stirling the men had pallid unhealthy complexions suggestive of consumption.(120)

In fact, the health of the workers improved during the eighteenth century. Scurvy, a scourge in the lead mines in the 1740's when the villagers bought five times as many anti-scorbutic drugs as the other inhabitants of the Sanquhar district,(121) died out with the provision of a small-holding where potatoes and other vegetables could be grown. The horrible form of lead poisoning known as 'lead-brash', which Thomas Pennent in 1784 noted as being common among the miners as well as the smelters, bringing on 'palsies and sometimes madness, terminating in death in about ten days', and which caused most of the smelters to die 'either madmen or idiots' was almost unknown by 1862:(122) it had been eliminated by moving the smelt mills away from the settlements, by erecting tall flues to trap the poisonous fumes and by provision of a piped supply of unpolluted water—contemporaries also insisted that the restrictions on alcohol consumption had increased resistance to poisoning.

The accident rate in the mines was generally much lower than among the colliers, for there was little risk of choke-damp and none of fire-damp: on the other hand injury and death from collapsing rock, accidents with blasting and falls in the access shafts were only too frequent. Profit came before the safety of the employee—at Leadhills in the seventeenth and eighteenth centuries the men were

K

wound down on ropes with a harness round their waist, carrying a lighted candle in a ball of clay in one hand and fending off from the shaft with the other: this was considered safer, but slower and more uneconomical, than the ladders introduced into Wanlockhead and Leadhills in the nineteenth century.(123) It was certainly much safer than 'the wretched and dangerous manner of descent' described at Tyndrum by Raspe in 1789, 'by means of crooked branches or pieces of timber of every form and dimension . . . a miserly saving of expence'.(124)

The housing of the miners—in Leadhills and Wanlockhead largely built by the men after 1740, though in the latter village the Quaker company had built all the houses between 1709 and 1721(125)— probably altered little throughout the period. The type is recognisable in descriptions from 1603, 1740 and 1842—thatched, stone-built, low-roofed, with one living apartment that 'serves for both bed-room, sitting-room and kitchen, an arrangement inimical to neatness and cleanliness, and the advantages of which can be appreciated only by bearing in mind the wretched climate and the cost of fuel'.(126) Their haphazard arrangement over the hillside avoided the monotony and insanitary overcrowding of a collier-row. It was only after 1860 that the type began to change, thatched roofs giving way to slate and an extra room or two being added to the accommodation.

The best measure of the varying standard of living of the miners is probably their diet. One commodity—oatmeal—was their staple for two hundred years: it was upon oatmeal that the bulk of their wages was spent, and oatmeal was the main item in the companies' stores; in dear years the men fell into debt buying it on credit, and in cheap years in the seventeenth and eighteenth centuries they expended the surplus on meat, butter, cheese, ale and tobacco. Wages do not seem to have varied much between 1650 and 1750— 10d. a day seems to have been a fair average at Leadhills for skilled miners, and this would mean extreme deprivation only in periods of dearth like 1696-99, with 'many of them soe putt to it that they are lyke to starve'.(127) After about the middle of the century wages began to rise, and had almost doubled by 1791.(128) With reference, probably, to the 1750's it was said that the miners already 'ate more animal food than people of their station used to do at that time'(129) and old John Taylor who died in 1770 (but was a skilled and therefore a highly paid man) was reported to breakfast off porridge and milk and dine off flesh and broth—his hobby of trout fishing suggests another item to add variety.(130) By 1790 a village not only grew its own potatoes and other vegetables, and kept a herd of cows, but was also said to be plentifully provided with outside luxuries: both in intellect and income the miners regarded themselves as far superior to the agricultural labourers round about.(131)

By 1840, there had been very serious cuts in real wages and the standard of living. Money wages had advanced to nine or ten shillings a week (though some were as low as 4s. 6d.) but prices had risen and the differential with farm workers had been lost. Breakfast in 1841 was still porridge and oatcake, but dinner was also of oatmeal, or of potatoes and milk with an occasional herring and 'a bit of beef for a holiday treat'. The butcher had deserted the village for lack of custom and even in 1852 it was reported that 'meat is an almost unknown luxury'. 'The old men complain that advanced prices with which their wages have by no means kept up prevent their getting meat and butter as they did when a sheep was sold for four shillings and butter for fourpence per lib. Scots.'(132)

This deterioration was the consequence of the unemployment and depression that affected the whole industry after 1815, and especially after 1827. It was also seen in a falling off of library subscriptions and school attendance, and by extreme poverty in some of the households with 'floors of earth, beds of heath and an utter destitution of bed-clothes'.(133) But at both Leadhills and Wanlockhead the presence of small-holdings, the help of pension funds and the availability of domestic employment for the women of the family in the embroidery of muslin for Glasgow and Ayrshire manufacturers, kept families in lead-mining who might otherwise have left it for more flourishing trades and saved the majority from the extremes of destitution and demoralisation. It was otherwise at Tyndrum, with 'a set of people who are reconciled to their fate . . . satisfied if they have oat or peasmeal weekly, two sermons and whiskey' as one manager put it.(134) 'What is to be expected from a man who eats almost nothing?' asked another, 'he has no force and is sick in his work—it is not to be beheld without anger and desperation by the manager who wishes to see all going well.'(135)

At Leadhills and Wanlockhead, a real recovery of standards came after the end of our period—between 1850 and 1875. By the latter date the miners were enjoying an average wage of about 20s. a week, and were again eating butter, cheese and meat, and now even toast, tea and sugar, in their regular diet.(136) The minister was wondering if, after all, they had not all been happier when life was simpler: it had not escaped his notice that in one year the inhabitants of the two villages had spent £720 on tobacco, and only contributed £30 to the evangelisation of the world.(137)

Acknowledgements

It is a pleasure to be able to express my thanks to the many people who have helped me in my research. To the Marquis of Linlithgow, the Hope Trustees, the Duke of Buccleuch, Mr. James Stirling of Garden, the directors of the Sun Insurance Company and Mr. William Gilchrist of the Leadhills Library I am indebted for permission and facilities to examine the documents in their possession. To Dr. Michael Flinn I am indebted for reading the chapter through in typescript. The archivists of the Scottish Record Office, the National Library of Scotland, Edinburgh University Library and Dumfries Burgh Museum have, as always, rendered invaluable assistance. Many others have contributed help in various ways, notably Mr. P. G. M. Dickson, Mr. John Gladstone of Penpont, Mr. Basil Megaw, Mr. Douglas Menzies, Dr. P. L. Payne and Prof. Roy Campbell. To them all I am more than grateful.

A NOTE ON MANUSCRIPT SOURCES AND ABBREVIATIONS USED

HOPETOUN MSS.	Hopetoun House, West Lothian: Documents relating to lead-mining, catalogued by the author (in the care of the Hope Trustees).
QUEENSBERRY MSS.	Drumlanrig Castle, Dumfries-shire: Documents relating to lead-mining (in the possession of the Duke of Buccleuch).
BUCCLEUCH MSS.	Dalkeith House, Midlothian: Documents relating to lead-mining (in the possession of the Duke of Buccleuch).
GARDEN MSS.	Garden House, Stirlingshire: Documents relating to James Stirling (in the possession of James Stirling, Esq., of Garden).
SCOTCH MINES CO. MSS., EDINBURGH	Edinburgh University Library: folios relating to Scotch Mines Company at Tyndrum.
SCOTCH MINES CO. MSS., LEADHILLS	Leadhills Library: folios relating to Scotch Mines Company at Leadhills.
SCOTCH MINES CO. MSS., LONDON	Sun Insurance Office, London: folios relating to Scotch Mines Company (in possession of the Sun Insurance).
CLERK MSS.	Scottish Record Office: Clerk of Penicuik muniments.
AILSA MSS.	Scottish Record Office: Ailsa muniments.
BREADALBANE MSS.	Scottish Record Office: Breadalbane muniments, box labelled 'Mines' and associated folios.

STANSFIELD MSS.	Scottish Record Office: miscellaneous papers bundle 279, Sir James Stansfield's papers on lead-mining.
WALKER MSS.	Edinburgh University Library: paper on Wanlockhead mine sent to Rev. John Walker.
ERSKINE MURRAY MSS.	National Library of Scotland: Erskine Murray papers.
PAUL MSS.	National Library of Scotland: Paul papers.
KALMETER MSS.	Kunglig Bibliotek, Stockholm: manuscript diary of H. Kalmeter, 'Resa igenom England och Scotland', 1719-21.
DUMFRIES BURGH MSS.	Dumfries Burgh Museum: Chemist's accounts at Sanquhar, 1742-43.
CARRON MSS.	Scottish Record Office: letter books of Carron Company.

NOTES

(1) Buccleuch MSS., 'Memorial to the . . . Treasury from the Lessees of the Wanlockhead Lead Mines', 15th June, 1830, puts total British output at 60,000 tons of smelted lead.

(2) R. W. Cochran-Patrick, Early Records relating to Mining in Scotland (Edinburgh, 1878), *passim*.

(3) Acts of Parliament of Scotland, II, 5.

(4) Hopetoun MSS., IV, 114.

(5) Hopetoun MSS., IV, 114. Cochran-Patrick, *op. cit., passim*.

(6) Acts of Parliament of Scotland, VI, ii, 534.

(7) Hopetoun MSS., I, 2. 'Voyages to Leadhills', 1638-39.

(8) Stansfield MSS., Letters from William Blackett in 1675.

(9) Hopetoun MSS., II, 24/6. 'Mathew Wilson's commission . . . 23 April 1696'. Although this process was known earlier in England, it does not seem to have been practised in Scotland before this date.

(10) The Book of Islay (ed. G. G. Smith, 1895), p. 456 ff.

(11) Kalmeter MSS. See also Erskine Murray MSS., Paul MSS.

(12) D. Murray, The York Buildings Company (1883), pp. 68 ff.

(13) Breadalbane MSS.

(14) Old Statistical Account (henceforth cited as O.S.A.), VII, 54.

(15) Based mainly on Queensberry MSS., Hopetoun MSS., Breadalbane MSS.

(16) Walker MSS.

(17) New Statistical Account (henceforth N.S.A.), IV, 301; Carron MSS.; Bennet Woodcroft, A Sketch of the Origins and Progress of Steam Navigation, 1847, pp. 18-19.

(18) Clerk MSS., 1179; Carron MSS.

(19) Buccleuch MSS.

(20) N.S.A., IV, 274-81. Memoirs of the Geological Survey, Scotland. Special report on the Mineral Resources of Great Britain, XVII (H.M.S.O., 1921) (henceforth Report . . ., 1921), pp. 52, 55.

(21) Summarised in Report . . ., 1921. It may be noted that, in distinction to many English lead-mines production fell off at the end of the 'Great Depression' and not in the later 70's and 80's.

(22) Hopetoun MSS.; Kalmeter MSS.

(23) Breadalbane MSS., 1745-60.

(24) Sir Alexander Murray of Stanhope, True Interest of Great Britain (1741), plan of Loch Sunart dated 1733.

(25) Hopetoun MSS.; Queensberry MSS.; Kalmeter MSS.

(26) Clerk MSS., 1181. Joint Appendix of litigation in the House of Lords Scotch Mines Company v. Leadhills Mining Company and others, 1858 (henceforth cited as Joint Appendix).

(27) Queensberry MSS., 'Alexander Telfer's proposal', 1747.

(28) Joint Appendix.

(29) Scotch Mines Co. MSS., Edinburgh: 'Journal of the Mine, 1783-1788'.

(30) Breadalbane MSS., Mining leases.

(31) Stanfield MSS., letter from William Blackett, 9th Sept., 1675.

(32) J. Gladstone, 'The National Woodlands of Galloway and Nithsdale', Forestry, Vol. XXXIV, ii (1961), pp. 174-80.

(33) Kalmeter MSS.; Queensberry MSS., Tacks of woods.

(34) Clerk MSS., 2622; Queensberry MSS., Tacks of Woods.

(35) Walker MSS.

(36) This is based on a test made at Leadhills in 1735; Hopetoun MSS., III, 50/5.

(37) Hopetoun MSS.; Queensberry MSS.; Scotch Mines Co. MSS., London et al. For China see C. Gill: Merchants and Mariners of the Eighteenth Century (1961), p. 144.

(38) Clerk MSS.

(39) Scotch Mine Co. MSS., Edinburgh; Breadalbane MSS.

(40) Hopetoun MSS., IV, 84/1-5.

(41) The Wealth of Nations (Everyman edition, 1910), I, 153.

(42) The fullest description is given in Kalmeter MSS.

(43) Quoted in G. Vere Irving and A. Murray, The Upper Ward of Lanarkshire Described and Delineated (1864), III, 46.

(44) Clerk MSS., 1164; letter from Cuthbert Readshaw, Richmond, 25th July, 1755.

(45) Quoted in R. Chambers, Domestic Annals of Scotland (1861), III, 248.

(46) Breadalbane MSS.; copy letter from Mr. Campbell of Lochard, 6th Feb., 1791.

(47) Breadalbane MSS.; Report . . ., 1921. At the time of writing, news comes of a Canadian Company prepared to make yet another attempt to exploit the minerals of the area.

(48) Stansfield MSS.; O.S.A., XVII, 238; The Book of Islay, pp. 456-57.

(49) Joint Appendix, p. 8.

(50) Buccleuch MSS.; Joint Appendix, p. 87.

(51) Hopetoun MSS., IV, 57.

(52) Buccleuch MSS.; Breadalbane MSS.; N.S.A., IV, 274-75, 280-81.

(53) Adam Smith, op. cit., I, 153.

(54) Queensberry MSS. leases.

(55) Clerk MSS., 1184.

(56) Sir William Forbes, Memoirs of a Banking House (1860), pp. 38-39. The details given by Forbes from his own recollections do not quite accord with the records in Ailsa MSS., Box 46, which are followed here.

(57) D. Murray, op. cit., pp. 69, 81. The other landowners involved in the Scotch Mines Company were the Duke Queensberry, the Duchess of Buccleuch, the Earls of Arran and Buchan and Robert Dundas of Arnistoun: National Library, Paul MSS., 5160.

(58) D. Murray, *op. cit.*, pp. 69, 72, 81; Sir Alexander Murray, *op. cit.*; Book of Islay, p. 457.

(59) Buccleuch MSS.

(60) Hopetoun MSS.; Ailsa MSS., Box 46; Erskine Murray MSS.

(61) Buccleuch MSS., letter from Hugh Warrander, Edinburgh, 2nd April, 1815; N.S.A., IV, 301.

(62) Queensberry MSS., Deed of Settlement of the Friendly Society, 1722.

(63) Joint Appendix, p. 72.

(64) Book of Islay, p. 457; D. Murray, *op. cit.*, p. 81; Breadalbane MSS., 'Memorial for Mine Adventurers Company . . . against Andrew Brown . . . *et al.*', 1749.

(65) Aisla MSS., Box 46; Clerk MSS., 1166-68; Breadalbane MSS., 'Contract lease', 1804.

(66) Sir William Forbes, *op. cit.*, p. 24.

(67) Queensberry MSS.

(68) Joint Appendix, p. 72.

(69) Queensberry MSS.; Clerk MSS., 2656-57; Walker MSS.

(70) Stansfield MSS.

(71) Book of Islay, p. 458; O.S.A., XIV, 306.

(72) Breadalbane MSS.

(73) D. Murray, *op. cit.*, p. 81.

(74) Kalmeter MSS.; Hopetoun MSS.

(75) Clerk MSS., 1164-83.

(76) Breadalbane MSS.; N.S.A., IV, 383; Hopetoun MSS.; Joint Appendix.

(77) Buccleuch MSS.; Queensberry MSS.

(78) Clerk MSS., 1164-69.

(79) Breadalbane MSS.; Clerk MSS., 1173.

(80) The statement that the lease was given up in 1727 or 1731 (A. Raistrick, Two Centuries of Industrial Welfare: the London (Quaker) Lead Company, 1692-1905 (1938), p. 82, and Quakers in Science and Industry (1950), pp. 186-87) is incorrect, as is some of the information given there about the Friendly Mining Society.

(81) Raistrick, *ibid.*; Queensberry MSS.; Clerk MSS., 2622-57; Walker MSS.; O.S.A., VI, 99, XX, 537-39.

(82) Breadalbane MSS.

(83) Breadalbane MSS., 'Copy of my letter to Mr. Baillie about the mines', 16th March, 1747-48.

(84) D. Murray, *op. cit.*, pp. 70 ff.

(85) Clerk MSS., 1185.

(86) Kalmeter MSS.

(87) Paul MSS.: 5160/26 FF, Erskine Murray MSS., 5098/6.

(88) P. G. M. Dickson, The Sun Insurance Office, 1710-1960 (1960), especially appendix VI. All three were shareholders in the Scotch Mines Company.

(89) Paul MSS.

(90) Scotland and Scotsmen in the eighteenth century, from the MSS. of John Ramsey, Esq. of Ochertyre (Allardyce, 1888), II, 309-10 (henceforth cited as Ochertyre MSS). See also Hopetoun MSS., IV, 81.

(91) Ochtertyre MSS., II, 306-16. Garden MSS.; Stirling did not actually come to live in Leadhills until 1736.

(92) Scotch Mines Co. MSS., London.

(93) Joint Appendix, pp. 327-32; G. V. Irving, *op. cit.*, p. 46; Scotch Mines Co. MSS., London.

(94) Ochtertyre MSS., *ibid.*; O.S.A., VI, 511-12, XXI, 98-99; Breadalbane MSS.

(95) Acts of the Parliament of Scotland, VI, ii, 534.

(96) Hopetoun MSS., II, 23/2.

(97) National Library, Paul MSS., 5160/26.

(98) Hopetoun MSS., II, 2/10.

(99) Hopetoun MSS., I, 2; Scotch Mines Co. MSS., Leadhills.

(100) Breadalbane MSS., 'Wage book of Messrs. Patton and Richardson'.

(101) Scots Magazine, XXXIII (1771), 24-26. The accounts given in The Gentleman's Magazine, N.S., XXXIX (1853), 466 f. and elsewhere, differ only in detail but may have been derived from a different source.

(102) Hopetoun MSS.; Stansfield MSS.

(103) Breadalbane, MSS., 'Wage book of Messrs. Patton and Richardson'; Scotch Mines Company MSS., Edinburgh, 'Journal of the Mine, 1771-77.'

(104) Gentleman's Magazine, N.S., XXXIX (1853), 595.

(105) Breadalbane MSS., especially letters from S. Rechtendrop, 27th July, 1847, and H. Odennheimer.

(106) Hopetoun MSS., especially Ia, II 21/1, II 23/2, II 23/5.

(107) Ochertyre MSS., II, 310.

(108) Ochtertyre MSS., II, 306-26; Garden MSS.; Hopetoun MSS. III, 52/1. O.S.A., VI, 511-12; XXI, 98-99.

(109) Hopetoun MSS., IV, 64/6.

(110) Hopetoun MSS., IV, 9031.

(111) O.S.A.

(112) Queensberry MSS.; Buccleuch MSS. Even at Strontian in the 1720's Murray of Stanhope had obtained the services of a doctor.

(113) T. Thornton, A Sporting Tour through the Northern Parts of England and a great part of the Highlands of Scotland (1804), p. 241.

(114) N.S.A., IV, 281.

(115) Report from Commissioners on Children's Employment, Vol. III, P.P. 1842, XVII (henceforth cited as Report on Children's Employment), p. 863.

(116) Ochtertyre MSS., II, 324-25; Hopetoun MSS., II 2/14, 3/3; IV 57. Garden MSS., Letter from James Farquharson 22nd May, 1740.

(117) D. Jamie, John Hope, Philanthropist and Reformer (1907), Chapter XIX.

(118) Report from the Commissioners on the Truck System, Minutes of Evidence, P.P. 1871, c. 327, p. 168.

(119) Buccleuch MSS., II, 'Mr. Gibson's Report . . .', 5th June, 1845.

(120) Ochtertyre MSS., II, 321.

(121) Dumfries Burgh Museum MSS.; Sanquhar chemist's accounts, 1742-43, kindly analysed for me by Dr. Roger Buckett.

(122) G. V. Irving, *op. cit.* II, 36, III, 46 ff.

(123) Gentleman's Magazine, N.S. XXXIX (1853), 591.

(124) Breadalbane MSS., Letter from R. E. Raspe, 9th July, 1789.

(125) Clerk MSS., 2679.

(126) Report on Children's Employment, p. 863.

(127) Hopetoun MSS., especially II, 24/15.

(128) Hopetoun MSS., etc.

(129) Ochtertyre MSS., II, 311.

(130) Scots Magazine, XXXIII (1771), pp. 25-26.

(131) Ochtertyre MSS., II, 320 ff.

(132) Report on Children's Employment, especially p. 863. 'News of an Old Place' (attributed to Harriet Martineau), *Household Words*, V. (1852), pp. 537-42.

(133) Report on Children's Employment, p. 863.

(134) Breadalbane MSS., letter from S. Rechtendorp, 27th July, 1847.

(135) Breadalbane MSS., letter from Mr. Odennheimer, 8th June, 1839.

(136) J. Moir Porteous, God's Treasure-House in Scotland (1876), p. 114. Report from the Commissioners on the Truck System.

(137) J. Moir-Porteous, *op. cit.*, p. 263.

CHAPTER SIX

The Law and the Joint-Stock Company in Scotland*

R. H. CAMPBELL

*Professor of Economic History,
University of East Anglia*

THE LEGAL POSITION of joint-stock companies in Scotland is usually ignored by writers on economics and economic history. When recognised, it is too frequently dismissed perfunctorily, as by H. A. Shannon, by stating, in contrast with English law, that 'Scotch law was different and better'.(1) Some indication of the differences and the superiority is clearly warranted, but it also demonstrates, first, the way in which after the Union of 1707 the assimilation of Scottish law and practice towards English customs took place even when the Scottish position was superior, and, second, that even the superior legal position in Scotland was not a crucial determinant of business enterprise.

I

After the Union of the Crowns in 1603 increasing contact with England, and better administration, led the Scottish Parliament to institute a policy of encouraging long-term industrial growth, aimed especially at obtaining capital resources, frequently beyond the means of Scotsmen of the day, but necessary to remedy deficiencies in the country's economy. The statutory basis of Scottish industrial policy lay particularly in Acts of 1661(2) and 1681.(3) In 1661 two Acts confirmed a variety of privileges granted by an earlier statute of 1641(4) and, in particular, to remove the dearth of capital, permitted the formation of joint-stock companies in cases where an enterprise was beyond the resources of an individual, though to obtain such privileges it was necessary to apply to Parliament or to

* I am grateful to Professors A. E. Anton and M. Gaskin for their comments on this article.

the Privy Council. Subsequently, a few industrial concerns appeared, but most could continue only when they were given some degree of protection from foreign competition, through, for example, the grant of patents by the Privy Council. The provision of protection from foreign competition had a more general appeal, however, because it helped to conserve scarce supplies of foreign currency,(5) and so the Act of 1681 added a complete system to existing arrangements.(6)

Such encouragement did not long survive the Union because the law was soon affected by the famous Bubble Act, passed in 1719(7) by the Union Parliament. The Bubble Act did not, of course, prohibit incorporation, which could still be obtained by Royal Charter or by a special Act of Parliament, but opinion differs on whether the Bubble Act itself applied in Scotland.(8) Apparently in Scotland, as in England, there were few cases in which the Bubble Act was specifically cited. The first was in 1730 in *Masons of the Lodge of Lanark* v. *Hamilton*, in which the Lodge decreed that 'all members are discharged to receive, or be witness to the receiving or passing any mason within ten miles of the burgh of Lanark, except the benefit come to the Lodge, under the penalty of ten pounds' and sued some members for sums alleged to be due to it because of contravention of this regulation. The defence quoted the Bubble Act in support of the contention that the Lodge was an unlawful society, but the case was decided on the common law.(9) The second case came much later, during the revival of the Bubble Act just before its repeal. In *Macandrew* v. *Robertson* it was suggested on appeal by the Solicitor-General, for the defender, that a company floated in 1825 fell within the proscription of the Bubble Act because it was 'a joint stock formed by means of shares declared to be transferable without any limitation', and because 'the company had presumed to act as a corporation by means of office bearers'. But the courts were clearly reluctant to uphold the Act. Lord Balgray suggested that 'if we were to hold that this company fell under the Bubble Act, we would overturn all the extensive mercantile associations in Scotland. The criterion is whether it be of a nature prejudicial to the public; but it is absurd to say, that because the shares are transferable, ergo to associate is mischievous'. Lord Gillies was even more anxious to ensure that the Act did not apply. 'I think the restriction on the power of transferring is sufficient to take the case out of the statute. It is an act which, so far from having been beneficial, has, I think, been mischievous; and therefore we ought not to extend it to cases which do not fall within the letter of it.'(10)

Though these judgments indicate considerable reluctance to apply the Bubble Act, they do not indicate any belief that the Act was inapplicable in Scotland. The few specific references to the Bubble Act in Scotland may be taken, therefore, to indicate the Act's application in Scotland as much as its failure. In this respect Scotland's experience was comparable to England's. For that similar experience there are good reasons. First, applications for incorporation by Scottish firms in the eighteenth century are more meaningful on the assumption that the Bubble Act did apply in Scotland. Second, the charters of such companies, when granted, stated that their activities had not to contravene existing statutes, which was almost certainly a reference to the Bubble Act. Third, and perhaps most vital, applications for incorporation by Scottish firms were considered by the English law officers, so that English concepts of commercial law, as strengthened by the Bubble Act, were enforced in Scotland. When in 1728 an application was made for a charter for the 'Company for Working Mines, Minerals and Metals in that part of Great Britain called Scotland', the application was considered, and in effect granted, by the English law officers. The Lord Advocate was consulted only when doubts arose on whether the charter should or should not be issued under the Great Seal of Scotland.(11) Neither Scottish nor English law officers seemed aware that their separate legal systems required different interpretations of the Bubble Act.

Though the standing of the Bubble Act in Scotland may be a matter of dispute, there is greater certainty on how far subsequent company legislation, passed by the British Parliament, applied to Scotland. In the nineteenth century six acts were particularly relevant in laying the foundation of the modern statutory provision. Of these only the last, the famous Act of 1856, applied without qualification to Scotland; two others specifically did not; of the three others, two were certainly inoperative and the third, though its standing is more doubtful, was probably likewise. The legislative changes of the early nineteenth century were often aimed, therefore, at remedying the defects in English law.(12)

The first important change was the repeal of the Bubble Act in 1825.(13) While this was a necessary prelude for subsequent legislation, it also permitted the Crown to declare the extent of a member's liability on the grant of incorporation, a provision inserted in the hope, which was not fulfilled, that, since it represented a move away from the rigidly limited liability of members of incorporations, it would facilitate the granting of charters. Progress was continued by two acts: the Trading Companies Act of 1834(14) and the Chartered Companies Act of 1837,(15) which permitted incorporation by letters patent. The 1834 Act was the first general Act requiring the

public registration of members, but its failure to grant them limited
liability until three years after they had given up their shares restricted its usefulness, and so this particular defect was remedied by
the 1837 Act, which provided that the personal liability of members
might be limited to a stated amount in the letters patent. The Act of
1837 made the widespread adoption of incorporation and limited
liability possible, but, though a varied group of companies were
granted letters patent,(16) the Board of Trade did not wield its
powers freely. In Scotland the Faculty of Advocates could rightly
describe the Act as 'wholly inoperative',(17) because only the
Western Bank of Scotland and the Shotts Iron Company applied for
incorporation under it—both unsuccessfully. The next two major
developments in company law specifically did not apply to Scotland
except under certain special circumstances. The first, the Joint
Stock Companies Act of 1844,(18) provided for the benefits of
incorporation to become available on complete registration, with the
important exception that shareholders' liability remained unlimited
until three years after they had disposed of their shares. Two qualifications must be made to the general inapplicability of this Act to
Scotland. First, a Scottish company which had places of business
in other parts of the United Kingdom had to register under the Act
to obtain its privileges in them. Second, the right to sue, granted to
English banking partnerships more than sixty-five miles from
London, was repealed, and banks had to make special application,(19) a provision extended shortly afterwards to banks established in Scotland since 9th August, 1845.(20) The second major
act which did not apply to Scotland was the Limited Liability Act
of 1855,(21) which provided for the limited liability of members of
incorporations on registration. Thereafter it required only the Joint
Stock Companies Act of 1856(22) to consolidate these earlier attempts, to begin the modern statutory provisions, and to introduce
them in their modern form to Scotland.

II

Many of these statutes did not apply in Scotland, because there
was much less need for them there. Scots law already provided the
three chief attractions of incorporations even before they were provided by modern statutes: the transferability of shares, the separate
legal personality of the company, which enabled it to sue and to be
sued in its own name instead of in the names of individual members, and the limited liability of the shareholders.

Today, limited liability confers such privileges on shareholders that it is generally the prime reason why incorporation is sought and why limited liability is often assumed to be an essential element in incorporation, but in the eighteenth century the other advantages of incorporation, the right to sue and the right to transfer stock, were equally attractive. From the paucity of references to limited liability in applications for incorporation during the currency of the Bubble Act, it is easy to believe that in the early eighteenth century the desire to achieve limited liability was not the prime factor leading to efforts to obtain incorporation. On the other hand the absence of specific references to limited liability in applications for incorporation may be explained by the assumption that at that period incorporation automatically bestowed limited liability,(23) unless a provision to the contrary was inserted in the charter or act of incorporation. Liability may have been unlimited in the sense that a company could have taken action against its own shareholders to the extent of their individual fortunes in order to obtain the resources necessary to meet the claims of creditors, but that was rather an academic question as the attempt does not seem to have been made. For most practical purposes, incorporation, by Royal Charter or Act of Parliament, brought limited liability with it in the eighteenth century, but the chief incentive in taking the trouble to achieve incorporation lay either in the advantages of the transferability of shares or in the legal advantages of corporate personality in English law. By the late eighteenth century the growth of the unincorporated joint-stock company gave adequate facilities for the transference of shares, even though that was the practice the Bubble Act had tried to control, and so in England the great prize offered by incorporation was legal personality. The English law of partnership failed to recognise the distinct *persona* of the firm, so that, no matter how large an unincorporated joint-stock company became, legally it remained no more than an aggregate of individuals. Incorporation greatly facilitated litigation, and indeed frequently made it possible.(24) Only by the nineteenth century did the desire for limited liability begin to assume its modern primacy among the factors making for incorporation.

The position in Scotland was very different. Even if the application of the Bubble Act was common to both countries, the position of business enterprise, and especially the rights and privileges of partnership, were not. The law of Scotland favoured the business company in two ways. First, and less important, in spite of the Bubble Act, there were means of obtaining incorporation more easily in Scotland. Second, and more important, even where incorporation proved impossible, the Scottish law of partnership, which governed the affairs of unincorporated business companies, was much more liberal than in England, though it became progressively less so with the increasing infiltration of ideas derived from English commercial law.

First, a complete circumvention of the Bubble Act was possible through certain bodies continuing to grant charters of incorporation, even though it seems certain that the Bubble Act did not envisage any delegation of incorporating authority by either Crown or Parliament. In Scotland, as in England, the crafts in the burghs had obtained a 'seal of cause', which was regarded as equivalent to a charter of incorporation.(25) In the eighteenth century many of the burghs continued to grant these seals of cause, but some carried their powers even further and granted incorporation to what were in effect commercial concerns, and, more important, were joint-stock companies. In the second half of the eighteenth century the town council of Glasgow granted such seals of cause to a variety of different associations. Some were of the traditional type; the bonnet-makers in 1760, the gardeners in 1761, the painters in 1773, the porters in 1775, the sedan chairmen in 1775; others were charitable institutions; the Glasgow Shepherds' Society in 1762, Grahame's Charitable Society and the Glasgow Ayrshire Society in 1770; the Glasgow Dunbartonshire Society in 1771. At the very end of the eighteenth century more institutions were incorporated; Anderson's University, the Glasgow Lunatic Asylum, the Lock Hospital. Early in the nineteenth century, just before the repeal of the Bubble Act, but at a time when its revival brought renewed attention to its prohibitions, the tendency to move away from the granting of a seal of cause only to the more traditional type of association became even more striking. In 1820 the Town Council of Glasgow was authorised to construct a new street from Great Hamilton Street or Montieth Row to the Cross.(26) A joint-stock company was formed by Kirkman Finlay and others to persuade the council to delegate its authority to them, and especifically asked the council for a seal of cause 'incorporating them as a company'. After some negotiation the seal of cause was granted and the council 'did and do hereby create, erect, constitute and unite' the joint-stock company 'into a corporation or body politic', with, among other powers, the right to receive contributions, 'power to acquire, hold and sell heritages and goods in corporate name', and to have a common seal if thought fit.(27)

It would be wrong to regard these examples of incorporation as anything other than interesting survivals of a bygone age. No attempt was made to exploit this procedure on an extensive scale by company promoters. Since the Bubble Act never envisaged the delegation of power to incorporate, any retention of such power by bodies other than the Crown or Parliament would almost certainly have been rescinded if it had been used extensively to thwart the Act. On the other hand, it does not seem possible to suggest that the burghs were acting beyond their powers and that their actions were consequently illegal. In *Masons of Lodge of Lanark* v. *Hamilton* a grant of a seal of cause was asserted by the defence to be a legal means of incorporation.(28) In another case of a dispute on the validity of the rights and privileges of the Wrights of the Canongate the Lord Ordinary's interlocutor of 1772 held 'that the wrights, coopers, etc. of Canongate, are, by virtue of their seal of cause, charter and other units produced for them, a proper and regular corporation', a decision which was upheld in spite of the argument of a reclaiming petition that 'exclusive privileges of incorporation of any kind, as being contrary to liberty, and inconsistent with the true ideas of commerce and public policy, have, at later times, been by no means favourites of the law, which hath taken every opportunity of abridging and restraining them, and in several cases hath cut them off altogether, tho' sanctified by the most inveterate custom'.(29) The reclaiming petition's argument reflected an attempt to alter the privileges of incorporation because of changes in economic thought than in the law. In any case, whatever the legal validity of a seal of cause, those who applied for them, and those who granted them, believed that thereby the institutions were validly incorporated. To quote the application from the Gaelic Chapel Society in 1778, 'hitherto these matters were governed by the saids managers under such rules as occurred to them, without being erected by your lordships into a legal society, and observing that in time it may be necessary to have the sanction of an act of council or seal of cause, for enabling the petitioners and their successors in office to manage the said chapel and to be enabled to receive any donations, mortifications, gifts or subscription . . .'(30)

Such advantages as the business company retained in Scotland were, therefore, less through the retention of peculiar rights to grant incorporation as in the more tolerant and liberal attitude adopted by the law in Scotland towards unincorporated concerns. A minor confirmation lay in the greater toleration exercised towards bodies claiming corporate status, as in a plea in 1771 in *Wilson* v. *Jobson* that, though the Seceding Congregation of Dundee 'were no body corporate, they were, by the law of Toleration, a legal society, and as such entitled to the protection of the law, and to the enjoyment

of all their civil rights and liberties'.(31) Though the law of toleration failed to gain recognition of the corporate status for Seceding
Congregation of Dundee, it was virtually, though not explicitly, the
grounds for the recognition of the heritors and kirk-session of Dalry
as a body corporate in 1791.(32) Much more important in encouraging the growth of unincorporated joint-stock companies in the
eighteenth century was the superior nature of the Scottish law of
partnership, which governed the activities of all companies not
legally incorporated. Its advantages over English law become apparent by considering how far Scots law provided for the three
major advantages of incorporation: transferable shares, the right to
sue and limited liability. In England, as in Scotland, unincorporated
joint-stock companies had transferable shares, even during the currency of the Bubble Act, but the two other attractions of incorporation, were unobtainable for unincorporated concerns under the
English law of partnership. The notable difference in Scots law was
that the right to sue was always permitted, and at times limited
liability seems to have been possible too.

The position of the law on the right to sue is clear. The Scottish
common law maintained a distinctive position and today still re-
gards a firm as a separate *persona,* which can sue or be sued in the
firm's name.(33) Thus the Scottish partnership has always had in
effect one of the great advantages available to English concerns
only through incorporation. On this count a partnership could
operate as easily as an incorporation. The advantages of Scots over
English law in the matter of limited liability is less easily determined. The basis of the Scottish law of partnership were the principles of the Roman *societas,* as it had been developed by Dutch and
French jurists. In the same tradition France was able to graft on to
the *commenda* of the medieval Mediterranean world the modern
société en commandite, which distinguished the active from the
sleeping partners and gave limited liability to the latter. In Scotland
the recognition of the separate *persona* of the firm might well have
led to similar developments, especially since the courts were inclined
to give a liberal interpretation of the law of partnership. Though
English ideas were eventually supreme, and consequently arrested
growth in this direction, the change did not come quickly after either
the Union or Bubble Act, but only with the gradual permeation of
many aspects of Scottish life by English influences. Though an early
conception, that a partnership trading without reference to a capital
stock had limited liability, was surrendered, the possibility that the
shareholders in a joint-stock company might have limited liability,
even when the company was not incorporated by either Crown or

L

Parliament, was long recognised by Scots lawyers, and was enunci-
ated in Scotland as late as the early nineteenth century by Bell in his
Commentaries on the Law of Scotland. 'There is a clear distinction
between the case of a joint-stock company and that of a company
trading without relation to a stock: that in the former managers are
liable for the debt which they contract, while each partner is bound
to make good his subscription: that there is no ground of further
responsibility against shareholders, neither on their contract nor on
any ground of mandate beyond their share; the very meaning of
confining the trade to a joint-stock being that each shall be liable
for what he subscribes and no further.'(34) Bell's interpretation was
not accepted without question. A later editor of the *Commentaries*, McLaren, criticised his argument by suggesting that the
liability of shareholders was unlimited, unless there was an express
stipulation to the contrary in Royal Charter, Act of Parliament or
by registration under one of the Companies Acts. Though that is a
correct modern interpretation, Bell's rested on an earlier tradition
which, in the eighteenth century at any rate, had been accepted in
the Scottish courts.

The basis for Bells' argument was primarily the case, in 1757, of
Stevenson v. *Macnair*,(35) when the application of the Bubble Act
might have been expected. Since it was not applied, it may be held
that the Act was not applicable in Scotland, though, as has already
been suggested. this point of view is untenable; or that the Act was
simply forgotten, which, in view of the publicity attending it, is
improbable; or, most likely, that the court followed the more ancient
traditions of the Scots common law. Certainly the Bubble Act and
the doctrine of unlimited liability were both relevant to the case.

In 1752 Macnair and others had formed themselves into the
Arran Fishing Company, a joint-stock company with a capital of
£2,000 divided into transferable shares of £50 each. In the Contract
of Agreement, dated 1st January, 1753, the 17th Article gave powers
of regulation to the directors and to General Meetings of the Company, 'provided, nevertheless, that nothing herein contained shall
be understood to impart a Power to the Directors, or any general
Meeting, to compel any Partner or Subscriber to pay or contribute
any more Money to Stock than the Sum by him subscribed'. This
proviso confirmed the 6th Article, in which the possibility of the
directors 'binding subscribers in any debts was limited to the Extent
of their respective subscriptions'. In 1754 John Stevenson and Company of Port Glasgow brought an action before the magistrates of
Glasgow for £72 6s. 9½d., being the cost of ropes supplied to the
Arran Fishing Company, but named only some of its wealthier

partners in the action. The Bailies decided in Stevenson's favour and awarded £8 expenses. Thereafter the Arran Fishing Company took the matter to the Court of Session. Two pleadings were made. The first, the dilatory plea that all parties were not called, was sustained,(36) and the second, that the defenders were not liable in their private fortunes for the debts of the company, was not, therefore, decided at once. This particular judgment left the question of how to convene a company confused until 1841, when it was suggested that the citation of a company with three of the individual partners would suffice.(37) In *Stevenson* v. *Macnair* the more important judgment was on the second line of defence which in due course the Lord Ordinary repelled, finding the defenders liable, conjunctly and severally, for the debts.

This interlocutor was the subject of an appeal in which the Scottish law of incorporations was fully discussed. The pleadings of the Arran Fishing Company distinguished different types of partnerships: the *societas* of Roman law, 'a perfect Participation of all Rights and Goods of whatever Kind or Denomination' in which 'liability is complete'; copartneries, 'agreements for carrying on different Branches of Trade by joint-stocks, in which 'it would appear that, though in the Event of Bankruptcy of some of the Partners, the rest were bound to whatever Extent, yet till then they were bound only *pro rata*'; lastly, the important group in which the Arran Fishing Company claimed to fall, 'a new species of Copartnery in which those who have money to spare throw it by certain limited shares, forming a certain limited Capital, into particular Branches of Trade, which are to be managed by a few, in which the Subscribers contribute nothing but their Money; and in which they have no Concern further than to the Extent of that Money. . . . This Species of Copartnery took its Rise chiefly in Holland; it came afterwards to be known in France by the Name of *société en commandite*; and is at present received with Avidity in Scotland.' As to the liability of members of such an association, the pleadings were equally definitive. 'The very Essence of such a Partnership is that those concerned in it should not be bound beyond the Extent of their respective Shares. It is this Stock alone they put into Trade; it is this Stock alone they risk. And indeed if they were to be found further liable, such Partnerships, so beneficial to a Nation, and esteemed to be so secure to the Particulars concerned in them, might be attended with the most fatal Consequences. In such a Partnership, a Subscriber looks not, nor has a Power of looking into the Transactions himself; so that he would run all the Risks of an ordinary Partnership, and yet would not have the Power of avoiding them, nor of knowing how far he was dupt, as in the others he might have.' The chief plea of Stevenson in defence was a complete denial of the doctrine of limited liability. 'Trade and Commerce all over the World is principally carried on upon Credit. . . . It is the Faith and Credit of Individuals or of Societies that is followed in such Cases; and those who contract with the Company are understood to have the whole Partners of that Society jointly and severally bound to them; though it frequently happens that (in the present case) that when the Advances are made the Furnishers do not know all the constituent members of said Societies.' However, the cases cited in support of this doctrine were all instances of rejections of pleas of denial of liability because of a denial of responsibility for action by other partners.(38)

Macnair's petition succeeded because on 14th December, 1757, the Lord Ordinary's interlocutor was unanimously altered for reasons, which, though lengthy, should be quoted in full, as they indicate the decision on the different interpretations of liability advanced by the litigants. 'There is an obvious difference between the present case, and a Company trading without relation to a stock. In the latter case, each partner must be liable in *solidum* for the Company's debts, for there is nothing here to limit the credit; and if a partner be liable at all, he must be liable *in solidum*. In the present case the managers are liable for the debt they contract, and each partner is liable to make good his subscription. But upon what medium can he be made further liable? Not upon the common law; for he neither contracted the debt himself, nor gave authority to contract beyond his stock. The very meaning of confining the trade to a joint-stock, is, that each should be liable for what he subscribes, and no further. This is the very reason why joint proprietors of ships are never subjected beyond the value of the ship. With respect of equity, Grotius justly observes, L. 2, Cap. 11. f. 13, that it is not expedient to make partners further liable, because it would deter everyone from entering into a trading Company. To show the inexpediency, and even the absurdity of making each partner liable for the whole debts of a Company having a joint-stock, consider only the whale-fishing Company, composed of a vast number of partners for the subscription of £35 each. According to the interlocutor pronounced by the Lord Ordinary, any one partner, loaded with the whole debts of the Company, might be crushed to atoms in a moment.'(39) Other commentators were equally clear in the distinction drawn between the private partnership and the joint-stock company and the consequential limitation of the liability of shareholders in the latter. Lord Kilkerran reported the same judgment quite specifically: 'the parties are not liable beyond their subscriptions, and . . . the action has not been properly brought, and remit to the Lord Ordinary to proceed accordingly.' In this way Kilkerran confirmed the limitation on the liability of the shareholders which he had recognised, as far as direct action by a creditor was concerned, though not necessarily action by the Company against the shareholders, when he reported on an earlier case in 1741 that 'the creditor of a Company cannot pursue one of the partners for a company debt: his action lies only against the company'.(40)

Though the judgment in *Stevenson* v. *Macnair* gives the impression of clarity, the position was obscure in many ways. Whatever the earlier position may have been, the limitation of shareholders' liability seems to have rested by the mid-eighteenth century, first, on the existence of a joint-stock, and so was applicable only to unincorporated companies and not to straightforward partnerships, and, second, on the use of a descriptive name placing the company's credit with the public entirely, and without any possibility of misconception, on the joint-stock alone. In this way the use of a descriptive name became by the mid-eighteenth century a vitally important factor in obtaining limited liability. While this seemed clear in 1757, at the time of *Stevenson* v. *Macnair,* it became confused later after the failure of Douglas, Heron and Company (the Ayr Bank) in 1772. If a descriptive name was necessary to ensure limited liability, then Douglas, Heron and Company did not have it, as its shareholders knew to their cost.(41) On the other hand it commonly traded under the descriptive name of the Ayr Bank, which, it could have been suggested, gave the impression to many of its creditors that liability was limited. Above all else to modern eyes, it seems difficult to believe, if the mere adoption of a descriptive name would have obtained limited liability, that it would not have been done. In the eighteenth century the validity of such reasoning was not apparent. The privilege of limited liability was not then thought to be so important as it is today, at least not until it was too late, when the older tradition of Scots law, which accorded limited liability to unincorporated concerns, was becoming less evident as ideas of English commercial law infiltrated.

The case of *Stevenson* v. *Macnair* is important as the only definitive judgment on the liability of the shareholders of unincorporated companies. It confirms the greater liberality of interpretation by Scottish courts of company law in the eighteenth century and how 'it almost touched the doctrine of limited liability'.(42) If such an interpretation had not been arrested, Scots company law, already providing for transferable shares and an adequate right to sue, would have required in addition only some form of general registration to place it in a completely modern form. Unfortunately the move towards general limited liability was arrested and the decision made in *Stevenson* v. *Macnair* gradually ceased to provide the basis of the law, primarily because the question never arose for many years thereafter and so the judgment of 1757 was gradually but generally forgotten through the increasing influence of English decisions. When the acts granting general limited liability did appear in the mid-eighteenth century, the Scottish position differed little from the English on that point.

III

It seems certain, therefore, that, in Scotland, it was easier for a business to develop without running foul of the legal barriers which might have troubled a similar concern in England. The reason lay not in the inapplicability of the Bubble Act in Scotland but in the different legal standing of partnerships and unincorporated companies, which possessed transferable shares, the right to sue and be sued, and, perhaps for a time at any rate, something akin to limited liability. Since practically all the advantages of legal incorporation could, therefore, be obtained by other means, the restrictive clauses of the Bubble Act were irrelevant. However, the more favourable legal environment did not provide any conspicuous stimulus to economic growth in Scotland. It does not seem to have been a factor of any consequence in the formation of a number of unincorporated joint-stock companies in the late 1740's and, since they were indigenous in promotion and operation, they do not represent attempts by non-Scots to gain the advantages of Scottish legal principles, such as occasionally happened before 1707. In sum, there are no indications that business enterprise in Scotland in the eighteenth century was greatly helped or hindered by the state of the law. The law was not the determinant of the level of investment.

A comparative study of Scottish and English conditions is of greatest importance, therefore, as an illustration of the assimilation of the two systems with practically no reference to their respective merits. No matter how desirable it was to have a unitary system of law, nothing was gained by basing it on English practice. Yet, whatever benefits might have come from greater adherence to Scottish principles, it is not surprising that assimilation should have taken the form it did in this field. The Scottish economy was increasingly dominated by the English (by no means all to the former's disadvantage) and with the increasing importance of international decision in commercial affairs, the practice of the more dominant partner was inevitably followed. Approximation of the law of partnership has never been complete, but it has been sufficient for many to forget the differences. From the revival of the application of the Bubble Act in the early nineteenth century, when no one suggested that it did not apply to Scotland. the move towards the granting of general limited liability was common to both countries, but such differences as remained were more favourable to Scotland.(43) The assimilation was the consequence of the more pervading influence of the Union. It is, therefore, only one of several examples of the submergence of the Scottish tradition with no consideration of its merit, or, it should be stressed, without any attempt by Scots to retain it. Given such preference, by both English and Scots in the eighteenth century, the Bubble Act, far from being less effective in Scotland, was more so. It introduced principles unnecessarily hostile to incorporated bodies and principles inimicable to the Scottish legal system. To that system only insistence on registration had to be added to avoid the long-protracted struggle for general incorporation and limited liability.

NOTES

(1) H. A. Shannon, *The Coming of General Limited Liability*. Economic History Review, Vol. II (1931), p. 1, n. 2. This approach means that many general histories of company organisation and law are not applicable to Scotland without qualification. The differences between Scotland and England are recognised most extensively by A. B. Du Bois in his English Business Company after the Bubble Act, 1720-1800 (New York, 1938). The only attempt to deal with the issues covered in this article is a largely forgotten study by J. Robertson Christie, *Joint Stock Enterprise in Scotland before the Companies Acts*, The Juridical Review, Vol. XXI (1909-10), pp. 128-47.

(2) Acts of the Parliaments of Scotland, VII, 255, 261. (Hereafter cited as A.P.S.)

(3) A.P.S., VIII, 348.

(4) A.P.S., V, 497.

(5) J. M. Low, *A Regional Example of the Mercantilist Theory of Economic Policy*, The Manchester School, Vol. 21 (1953), pp. 62-84.

(6) For further details see R. Brown, Early Scottish Joint-Stock Companies (Glasgow, 1903); T. Keith, The Commercial Relations of England and Scotland, 1603-1707 (Cambridge, 1910); W. R. Scott, The Constitution and Finance of English, Scottish and Irish Joint-Stock Companies to 1720. 3 vols. (Cambridge, 1910-12.)

(7) 6 George I, c. 18 (1719).

(8) J. R. Christie held that the Act 'extended to Scotland . . . but prac-

tically it remained a dead-letter' (Christie, *op. cit.*, p. 137). G. C. H. Paton states that 'the statute was never enforced in Scotland'. G. C. H. Paton (ed.), An Introduction to Scottish Legal History (Edinburgh, 1958). Stair Society Publications, No. 20, p. 56.

(9) Lord Kames, Decisions of the Court of Session (Edinburgh, 1776), pp. 4-5.

(10) P. Shaw, Cases decided in the Court of Session, Vol. 6 (Edinburgh, 1828), pp. 950-55.

(11) British Museum, Additional MS. 36, 142.

(12) For an historical account of the English position see L. C. B. Gower, The Principles of Modern Company Law (London, 1957), pp. 21-58.

(13) 6 George IV, c. 91 (1825).

(14) 4 and 5 William IV, c. 94 (1834).

(15) 7 William IV and 1 Victoria, c. 73 (1837).

(16) British Parliamentary Papers, 1854, LXV, p. 611.

(17) Royal Commission on Mercantile Laws, B.P.P., 1855, XVIII, p. 102.

(18) 7 and 8 Victoria, c. 110 (1844).

(19) 7 and 8 Victoria, c. 113 (1844).

(20) 9 and 10 Victoria, c. 75 (1846).

(21) 18 and 19 Victoria, c. 133 (1855).

(22) 19 and 20 Victoria, c. 47 (1856).

(23) A. Smith, The Wealth of Nations (Cannan edition), Vol. II, p. 232. It is surprising that at this point Smith fails to distinguish the unincorporated joint-stock company which was increasingly common in both Scotland and England at this time. Since he failed to do so, it is not possible to follow Christie's interpretation of this statement to mean that Smith recognised the existence of limited liability in a joint-stock company in Scotland, whatever its origin. (Christie, *op. cit.*, p. 131.) Smith was probably not thinking of Scots law here.

(24) In England this was not wholly an advantage. The difficulty of suing a large unincorporated joint-stock company with many shareholders virtually gave it a form of limited liability in practice.

(25) W. M. Mackenzie, The Scottish Burghs (Edinburgh, 1949), pp. 117-19.

(26) 1 George IV, c. 88 (1820).

(27) Extracts from the Records of the Burgh of Glasgow, Vol. XI (1823-33) (Glasgow, 1910), pp. 37, 39, 45, 51, 53-54, 74-75.

(28) Kames, *op. cit.*, p. 5.

(29) Faculty Decisions, 1772-1774 (Edinburgh, 1782), XXXVII, pp. 96 ff.

(30) Extracts from the Records of the Burgh of Glasgow, Vol. VII (1760-80) (Glasgow, 1912), p. 521.

(31) W. M. Morison, The Decisions of the Court of Session (Edinburgh, 1811), 14, 555.

(32) *Ibid.*, 14, 557.

(33) A. McNeil and J. A. Lillie, The Mercantile Law of Scotland (4th edition, Edinburgh, 1949), pp. 274-75.

(34) G. J. Bell, Commentaries on the Law of Scotland, Vol. II (7th edition, Edinburgh, 1870), p. 517.

(35) The printed pleas of the case are preserved in the Signet Library, Edinburgh, Session Papers 56:59, F14:28. No records of the process could be traced in the Scottish Record Office. This case forms the basis of Christie's article, but he relied only on the reports of Kames, Kilkerran and Bell and does not seem to have used any of the original pleadings.

(36) Faculty Decisions, 1750-1760. (Edinburgh, 1765), LIV, pp. 87-88.

(37) A. Dunlop, Cases Decided in the Court of Session (Edinburgh, 1841), p. 1045.

(38) *Macleod* v. *Young*, 1665; *Johnston* v. *Sir William Binning and Neilson*, 1683 (reported in Lord Harcarse Decisions of the Court of Session (Edinburgh, 1757), p. 243); *Logie* v. *Durham,* 1697 and *Brand* v. *Warden and Buchanan*, 1698 (reported in Lord Fountainhall Decisions of the Lords of Council and Session (Edinburgh, 1749), pp. 806-07 and 815-16.

(39) Lord Kames, Decisions of the Court of Session (1752-68) (Edinburgh, 1780), CXXXV, pp. 191-92.

(40) Lord Kilkerran, Decisions of the Court of Session (Edinburgh, 1775), p. 518.

(41) Faculty Decisions 1778 to 1781 (Edinburgh, 1791), XXXIV, pp. 57-59.

(42) F. W. Clark, Treatise on the Law of Partnership and Joint-Stock Companies, according to the Law of Scotland (Edinburgh, 1866), p. 2.

(43) As was confirmed repeatedly before the Royal Commission on Mercantile Laws in 1855. B.P.P., 1855, XVIII.

CHAPTER SEVEN

The Savings Bank of Glasgow, 1836-1914[1]

PETER L. PAYNE

Colquhoun Lecturer in Business History,
University of Glasgow

WITH TOTAL FUNDS of over £153 millions, the Savings Bank of Glasgow is by far the largest trustee savings bank in the United Kingdom.[2] The history of this institution is a record of almost continuous growth and ingenious adaptation, and its officers have been among the leading personalities in the savings bank movement since the mid-nineteenth century. Because of the significant part the Bank has played in this movement, aspects of its story have been accorded a major place in H. Oliver Horne's standard work on the history of savings banks, where there can be found a detailed and cogent survey of the political, social and economic background against which these banks came into being and developed.[3] A systematic history of the Glasgow Savings Bank—the records of which are comprehensive and voluminous—would be a most rewarding undertaking.[4] This paper has more modest objectives. Its purpose is to shed some light on the question of the occupational and social composition of savings bank depositors in the nineteenth century; to indicate some noteworthy features of an analysis of the accounts of individual depositors; and to examine the factors that produced seasonal and annual fluctuations in small savings in the West of Scotland before the First World War. In short, it tries to produce answers to the following questions: Who were the savers? How much did they save? Why did their savings vary over time?

Since a proper understanding of these problems requires a basic knowledge of certain administrative developments (the scope and direction of which were greatly influenced by parliamentary legislation) it will be necessary to sketch in, at relevant stages in the discussion, the salient features of the history of the trustee savings bank movement and, more particularly, of the history of the Savings Bank of Glasgow. In so far as this is done, this essay does present, in effect, an outline history of the Bank in the nineteenth century, but this aspect of the paper does not pretend to be comprehensive.

I

The present Savings Bank of Glasgow was founded in 1836. There had been an earlier bank of this kind in the city but it had not prospered and no attempt was made to revive it when in 1835 the Act was passed which empowered Scottish savings banks to deposit their funds with the Commissioners for the Reduction of the National Debt.(5) Instead, at a public meeting held on 29th March, 1836, it was resolved to establish the National Security Savings Bank of Glasgow.(6) Among the gentlemen appointed to act as Trustees and Managers of the new institution were numbered the mercantile and industrial aristocracy of the city: James Buchanan, C. J. Tennant, William Collins, William Connel, Henry Dunlop, John Ewing, James Finlay, Charles McIntosh, Robert Napier, and John Wilson being among them. So enthusiastic were the promoters that within three months all the necessary preliminary arrangements had been made and, suitable premises having been secured in Hutcheson's Hospital, the Bank opened its doors on 30th July, 1836.

In accordance with the usual practice, the affairs of the Bank were placed in the hands of a committee of management, under the chairmanship of John Leadbetter, drawn from the body of Trustees and Managers. Initially, the permanent officials were five in number: Donald Smith, Treasurer, the Manager of the Western Bank; Alexander Gray, Actuary; Peter Scott, Cashier; and two clerks. Individuals were permitted to deposit, in sums of 1s. and upwards, to the extent of £30 per year until their principal amounted to £150. This was allowed to accumulate at compound interest until the total balance reached £200. The limit for charitable or provident institutions was £100 per annum, with a total of £300, and Friendly Societies, if duly enrolled, were permitted to deposit without limitation or restriction. The interest allowed to individuals was £3 6s. 8d. per cent, and to institutions and societies £3 8s. 5½d. per cent. Parents were permitted to deposit £30 a year for each of their children, as were Trustees on behalf of minors.(7) The deposits received were placed in the Western Bank (after the suspension of 1857, in the Bank of Scotland) and, when a large enough sum in excess of expected immediate requirements had accrued, transmitted to the National Debt Commissioners who credited the Bank with interest at the rate of £3 16s. 0½d. The difference between the amount the bank received in interest and the amount paid to depositors was used to cover the expenses of management.

In these basic matters the Glasgow Savings Bank was virtually identical to the 500 similar institutions existing up and down the Kingdom in 1836. The motives of the founders were everywhere the same. By affording 'a safe and beneficial place of deposit for the earnings of the industrious classes',(8) it was hoped that the burden of poor relief would be reduced and the moral and social condition of the working class improved. Speaker after speaker at the annual meetings of the Trustees and Managers felt that the attainment of the habit of thrift was an essential prerequisite for the work of the Christian evangelist.(9) Clergymen repeatedly avowed that: 'The working man with a little money in the Bank was generally a better workman, a better citizen, a better friend of religion and social order, than the working man who had not a farthing. The very act of laying past the money fostered those habits of sobriety, industry, providence, and carefulness that lie at the basis of all success and happiness in life.'(10) Those who failed to take advantage of the institution were apt to be lumped with the 'great hulking, pale faced, ill clad, dirty fellows', that Professor Gairdner told the 29th Annual Meeting that he saw every day, 'lounging at a close-mouth, doing nothing, and thinking of nothing in particular, but, on the contrary, blowing away their energies, their health, and their earnings in the form of a tobacco cloud.'(11)

Such sentiments exemplify the feelings of gentlemen who founded, conducted and supported savings banks elsewhere. Where the Glasgow institution was not representative was in the unparalleled success that attended the efforts of its Committee of Management and permanent officials. By 1870 the Bank had become the largest and most influential savings bank in the country.(12) Whereas, for several decades following the passing of Mr. Gladstone's Post Office Savings Bill in 1861, the trustee savings bank movement stagnated, in Glasgow the National Security Savings Bank was hardly touched by the new competition.(13) This success had its basis in 'the care taken by the Trustees to adapt their arrangements to the wants of the people'. William Meikle, the actuary from 1848 to 1895—a man 'who must be ranked as one of the outstanding figures of savings bank history in the nineteenth century'(14)—was never tired of preaching that 'The real secret of success of all Savings Bank management consists in *facilities*'.(15) These facilities and the advantages accruing to depositors were kept prominently before the public by the distribution of handbills and prize essays, and by placarding streets, workshops and factories with posters. The pro-

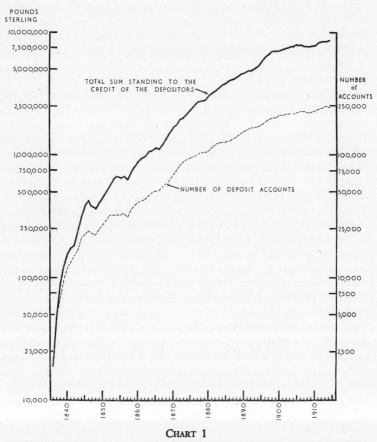

CHART 1

Number of accounts and total sum standing to the credit of depositors, Ordinary Department, Savings Bank of Glasgow, 1836-1914 (plotted on semi-logarithmic scale).

Source: Annual Reports of the Committee of Management.

gress of the Bank was immeasurably boosted by the opening of agencies and, later, branch offices in every major area in the city.(16) The officials fully appreciated that 'distance . . . militates against small depositors . . . working men [were] unwilling to walk a mile or two . . . in order to lodge a few shillings'.(17)

A significant rôle was played by the Penny Banks, the fostering of which was regarded as of the utmost importance in incalcating the

virtues of thrift in the young and very poor. Glasgow's first Penny
Bank was 'planted in one of the most degraded and necessitous
districts of the city—the Old Wynd'.(18) 'Convinced that it [was]
in the poorest districts that the greatest proportion of the earnings
of the people [were] mispent',(19) the Committee of Management
did everything in its power to encourage the establishment of these
ancilliaries. Clergymen once more took the lead, exhorting the
workers at mass meetings and from the pulpit to take their pennies
to the little banks that sprouted up all over the city. The Rev.
Gillan's address to a meeting of 3,000 workers in 1852 was greeted
with continuous cheers, especially that part in which he told a pipe
smoker who, 'If he had saved the money spent on this debauchery
between the ages of twenty and fifty . . . would have in the Savings
Bank £72 18s. 11d.; hard, heavy glittering gold instead of a nasty,
offensively smelling, muddlefying weed—for which, in the shape of
return, he gets smoke and fumes, as if his body was on fire and the
flames twisting out at the garret, and ashes, and blacked burned
pipes, with an unnatural precocity of parts, ending in premature
decay'.(20) With this frightening example before them, and remem-
bering the warnings that their indulgences maintained legions of
brewers, distillers and dramshop-keepers, the very small savers
flocked in their thousands to the thirty-six Penny Banks that had
been opened in and around Glasgow by 1860.(21) Within twenty
years of the opening of the Old Wynd bank, 102 banks had been
opened, at which 39,071 depositors had accounts.(22) These banks
—likened to the 'small pipes which conducted to the central reser-
voir the surface water which otherwise would have been evapor-
ated'(23)—steadily increased in number and scale of operations until
by 1881 the 60,000 depositors of the 213 Penny Banks in and
around Glasgow were transferring to the Savings Bank about
£20,000 a year, figures which had grown to 279 banks, 80,123 depositors, and transfers of £30,751, in 1914.(24)

Lastly, as William Meikle explained to the Select Committee on
Trustee Savings Banks in 1889, a major factor in the success of the
Glasgow bank, especially in relation to the poor showing of the
Post Office Savings Banks in the city, was that there was 'a kindly
influence constantly going on between the bank, that is to say, the
trustees and the officials, and their depositors. Poor people's affairs
constantly get involved one way or another, and they came to the
bank from time to time to ask advice, and it has been a great
pleasure to give that advice, and to keep them out of the hands of
pettifogging lawyers who fleece them greatly.'(25)

II

To assess the degree to which the trustee savings banks attained the high hopes entertained by their founders it is essential to discover how far these banks attracted a wage-earning clientele. Horne's verdict is emphatic: 'From the earliest days the savings banks were clearly securing the nest eggs of those people of small means for whom they were instituted.'(26) Yet two recent evaluations of the evidence have concluded that the impact of the savings banks upon the classes directly affected by the Industrial Revolution was meagre.(27) In 1864 Gladstone argued that 'if they took the artisans, mechanics, operatives and peasants of this country—he meant the fathers of families of the labouring classes—he very much doubted whether one in ten of those families throughout the country had any deposits in a savings bank. He might say, perhaps not one in twenty, and he was not sure whether the figures might not be placed lower.'(28) And, speaking of a period of twenty years earlier, Clapham was extremely doubtful whether much of the banks' total deposits had come out of wages or handicraftsmen's earnings.(29)

In classifying the occupations of new entrants, and providing figures broken down into occupational classes for the cumulative total of accounts opened, the Annual Reports of the Committee of Management of the Savings Bank of Glasgow for the period 1836-59 provide one of the most detailed insights into exactly who the patrons of these banks were during the very quarter century in which the material benefits of the Industrial Revolution began to percolate down to the working classes. In an average year, of every hundred new accounts, 28 were opened by mechanics (*i.e.*, wrights, masons, smiths, joiners, iron-workers, etc.), 13 by domestic servants, 11 by clerks and warehouse workers, 10 by minors (under 15 years old), 9 by labourers, carters and porters, 5 by shop-keepers and small traders, 4 by female warehouse workers and sewers, and 4 by factory operatives. The occupations of 7 per cent of the entrants were unspecified and the remainder constituted a miscellaneous group of professional persons, soldiers and sailors, those in agricultural employments, householders and lodging-house keepers. The percentage occupational distribution of new entrants is set out in Table 1. Perhaps the most surprising feature of this table is the remarkable stability of the proportional representation of the different classes, especially when it is remembered that the period embraces three full business cycles and two major crises, 1847 and 1857.(30)

TABLE 1

PERCENTAGE OCCUPATIONAL DISTRIBUTION OF NEW ENTRANTS, SAVINGS BANK OF GLASGOW, 1836–59

Year	Domestic servants	Mechanics	Factory operatives	Female warehouse workers and sewers	Dyers, bleachers, calico printers	Hand-loom weavers	Clerks and warehousemen	Shopkeepers and small traders	Labourers, carters and porters	Professional persons	Soldiers and sailors	Agricultural employments	Minors (under 15 years)	Householders, lodging-house keepers	Unspecified
1836	8·5	18·7	24·8	n.d.	n.d.	n.d.	n.d.	n.d.	n.d.	n.d.	n.d.	n.d.	8·4	n.d.	39·7
1837	17·5	27·7	13·1	n.d.	n.d.	n.d.	n.d.	n.d.	n.d.	n.d.	n.d.	n.d.	10·4	n.d.	31·3
1838	14·0	47·6	6·8	n.d.	n.d.	n.d.	n.d.	13·3	2·1	n.d.	n.d.	6·2	10·1	n.d.	—
1839	24·3	33·4	2·4	n.d.	n.d.	n.d.	n.d.	20·6	7·9	n.d.	n.d.	4·2	7·1	n.d.	—
1840	15·7	25·2	4·5	5·2	2·3	1·1	8·2	4·9	8·5	1·8	1·1	2·2	10·6	3·8	5·0
1841	15·0	26·2	4·8	4·4	2·0	0·5	8·0	4·5	12·7	1·6	1·4	2·1	9·9	3·1	3·9
1842	17·8	21·3	4·2	4·2	1·3	0·9	11·6	7·0	9·8	3·1	1·3	2·4	7·9	4·4	2·8
1843	13·8	22·9	5·3	5·0	2·1	1·7	10·8	4·8	8·2	2·3	1·4	2·4	11·8	4·6	4·8
1844	12·8	26·6	5·6	4·9	2·4	1·9	10·6	4·5	8·5	2·3	1·7	2·7	8·3	5·1	6·2
1845	11·8	28·6	5·0	4·3	1·7	2·0	10·3	4·1	10·1	1·3	1·4	2·7	9·5	4·1	4·6
1846	12·1	27·4	4·4	4·0	1·7	1·7	9·2	4·5	10·6	1·3	1·6	2·6	11·2	2·8	3·8
1847	12·4	25·4	3·3	3·9	2·0	1·3	11·2	4·0	9·5	1·5	1·5	2·6	10·8	3·3	5·3
1848	14·7	25·0	5·3	4·2	1·7	1·4	12·0	4·5	9·2	1·4	1·3	1·8	10·1	3·1	5·7
1849	11·7	25·7	4·0	4·5	2·0	1·3	10·9	5·6	8·1	2·0	1·3	1·8	8·8	1·8	9·8
1850	13·0		3·3	4·2	2·0	1·4	10·0	6·1	8·0	2·0	1·4	1·8	9·6	3·1	7·6
1851	11·9	31·3	3·3	5·0	—	—	10·2	5·3	8·2	2·3	—	1·8	9·5	3·3	6·6
1852	12·4	31·3	3·8	4·9	—	—	9·7	4·9	7·0	1·9	—	1·6	10·5	3·1	8·8
1853	10·0	31·7	3·7	4·7	—	—	10·1	5·0	8·3	1·9	—	1·5	10·3	3·6	9·2
1854	11·1	29·8	3·1	4·2	—	—	10·0	5·1	8·9	1·7	—	1·3	10·2	3·6	10·9
1855	12·2	29·2	2·5	4·1	—	—	10·9	5·2	7·7	1·8	—	1·6	10·8	4·5	9·5
1856	10·9	30·6	3·1	4·5	—	—	11·3	4·8	7·9	1·5	—	1·7	11·1	3·8	8·8
1857	13·5	29·5	3·5	5·4	—	—	12·1	5·4	7·6	1·7	—	1·3	6·6	4·4	8·9
1858	11·1	30·0	3·3	3·4	—	—	13·3	4·7	6·9	2·0	—	—	11·5	4·2	9·6
1859	11·1	32·1	4·6	3·8	—	—	13·0	3·8	7·3	1·7	—	—	11·2	3·6	7·8
1840–59 average	12·8	27·6	4·0	4·4	1·9	1·4	10·7	4·9	8·7	1·9	1·4	2·0	10·0	3·7	7·0

Source: Calculated from data presented in the Annual Reports of the Committee of Management.

New accounts do not, however, tell the whole story. Where the data are available, it is possible to calculate the occupational representation in the accounts that were closed each year. These figures reveal greater variability, but not to any significant extent. This means that at any time during the period the representation of any group in both the series of 'accounts remaining open' and the 'cumulative total of accounts opened' are fairly stable, although in the former series the representation of domestic servants fell and those of mechanics and minors rose over the period. Triennial figures are presented in Table 2.

In the year 1856—the last year for which the actuary calculated the number of 'accounts remaining open'—of every hundred active depositors, there were 15 domestic servants, 24 mechanics, 16 minors, 9 clerks and warehousemen, 7 labourers, carters and porters, 5 female warehouse workers and sewers, and 4 shopkeepers and small traders. Only 3 were factory operatives. It is at once apparent that Gladstone's estimate of the ownership of savings bank deposits does not do justice to the facts of the Glasgow situation. However, the applicability of Fislow's and Smelser's conclusions concerning the meagre impact of the trustee savings banks on the classes directly affected by the Industrial Revolution deserves further consideration. One thing is certain, during the first two decades of its existence, the Glasgow Savings Bank did fail to attract the factory operative.(31) Suspicious from the very beginning that the very organisation of the Bank—the Trustees and Managers being the most prominent industrialists in the city—would enable 'the masters to become acquainted with the savings of the workmen' (knowledge which would be used as a lever to depress wages),(32) and probably more subject to cyclical fluctuations of employment than other classes, barely one thousand of the depositors in 1856 were factory operatives. If to this number is added the 1,600 female warehouse workers and sewers who had active accounts in that year, it would appear that of the 60,000-70,000 workers in 'Textile, Fabrics and Dress' in the city only about one in twenty-five was a savings bank depositor.(33) Nevertheless, roughly one in four of the city's artisans and mechanics kept their savings in the Bank, and there is little question that this class was largely composed of persons whose occupations were called into being or profoundly influenced by the Industrial Revolution. Not so the domestic servant class, one in every three of whom entrusted their nest eggs to the bank.(34)

After 1859 no occupational tables are available and the time and labour involved in analysing the ledgers of the Bank to extract later occupational data assumes frightening dimensions. Indeed, the very

M

Table 2

Percentage Distribution of Accounts Closed, Cumulative Total of Accounts Opened, and Accounts Remaining Open, Triennially, 1841–59

Occupation	Percentage Distribution of																				
	Accounts closed							Cumulative total of accounts opened							Accounts remaining open						
	1841	1844	1847	1850	1853	1856	1859	1841	1844	1847	1850	1853	1856	1859	1841	1844	1847	1850	1853	1856	1859
Domestic servants	*No*	14·8	11·0	9·7	11·1	9·7	*No*	14·4	14·3	13·7	13·5	12·8	12·5	13·9	17·3	16·2	15·5	15·7	13·9	14·7	*No*
Mechanics	*data*	24·6	27·4	25·7	33·8	30·1	*data*	23·6	23·0	24·4	24·6	28·5	28·8	29·2	19·7	19·3	21·0	21·2	24·9	23·6	*data*
Factory operatives		3·7	5·0	4·8	4·1	3·5		6·0	5·6	5·2	5·0	4·6	4·2	4·2	5·3	5·2	4·5	4·3	3·8	3·2	
Female warehouse workers and sewers		4·5	4·9	4·7	3·8	4·2		3·9	4·2	4·2	4·2	4·3	4·3	4·3	3·8	4·8	4·4	4·5	4·8	4·7	
Dyers, bleachers, calico printers		1·8	2·3	2·1	—	—		2·0	2·0	1·9	1·9	—	—	—	0·8	1·9	1·6	1·8	—	—	
Hand-loom weavers		2·2	1·7	0·6	—	—		1·2	1·3	1·5	1·4	—	—	—	0·8	1·4	1·3	1·5	—	—	
Clerks and warehousemen		10·2	11·3	11·8	10·4	12·4		8·1	9·2	9·5	9·8	9·8	9·9	10·5	7·6	9·1	8·5	9·0	8·7	8·8	
Shopkeepers and small traders		4·8	4·7	5·8	5·0	5·7		3·9	4·4	4·3	4·6	4·7	4·8	4·7	6·5	4·1	3·8	4·4	4·2	4·1	
Labourers, carters, porters		9·2	11·2	13·9	8·0	8·3		8·1	8·4	8·9	8·8	8·4	8·4	8·2	6·8	7·4	7·9	6·3	6·8	6·6	
Professional persons		2·1	2·1	1·6	1·8	1·5		1·8	2·0	1·8	1·8	1·9	1·8	1·8	2·0	2·1	1·5	1·7	1·8	1·8	
Soldiers and sailors		1·9	1·5	1·7	—	—		1·0	1·1	1·3	1·3	—	—	—	0·9	1·0	1·2	1·1	—	—	
Agricultural employments		2·2	1·9	1·5	1·7	1·6		1·8	2·0	2·2	2·1	2·0	1·9	—	2·3	2·4	2·8	2·6	2·2	2·2	
Minors (under 15 years)		9·4	8·8	9·5	7·8	8·7		9·7	9·6	9·9	9·7	9·7	9·9	10·0	11·1	12·3	14·0	13·7	14·5	16·1	
Householders, lodging-house keepers		3·8	2·7	3·3	3·6	4·9		6·2	5·6	4·9	4·4	4·0	4·0	4·0	{ 15·3 }	5·6	5·0	3·7	5·5	3·5	
Unspecified		5·0	3·2	3·4	8·8	9·4		8·4	7·0	6·3	6·7	9·3	9·4	9·3		7·1	7·1	8·5	10·7	10·7	

Source: Calculated from data presented in the Annual Reports of the Committee of Management.

reason for the Bank's decision to abandon this feature of the annual report was the disproportionate effort involved. However, an attempt has been made to estimate the occupational distribution of the depositors who opened accounts in 1870 and in every tenth year thereafter from the Declaration Books of the Head Office and Bridgeton Cross branches.(35) Perfect statistical accuracy is not claimed for the result, but it is believed that the figures give a true impression of the occupations of new savers in the years preceding the First World War.(36)

The relative proportion of domestic servants opening accounts in each of the selected years falls off rapidly after 1859 (1859, 11 per cent; 1870, 5·9 per cent; 1900, 2·4 per cent); and the percentage of 'mechanics' was substantially reduced between 1859 and 1880, when their share of the total number of new entrants was stabilised at a figure roughly half of that of 1859 (1859, 32·1 per cent; 1880, 17·5 per cent).(37) Nevertheless, the Bank's continuous efforts to attract the factory operative—allied to the greater proportion of the city's workers finding work in the factories—eventually brought significant success, their number rising from some 4-5 per cent of the new depositors in 1859 to nearly 11 per cent in 1910. Even a few miners opened accounts though their number remained small, a speaker at the 1877 annual meeting remarking that he 'was surprised and sorry to find, when so many families were deprived of their bread-winners through the accident at Blantyre, that there was not a single instance of these colliers having a farthing in the Savings Bank'.(38) The ratio of female warehouse workers, dressmakers and shop assistants, nearly 4 per cent in 1859, declined, only to be restored to its former level towards the end of the century, when increasing numbers of shop assistants opened accounts, a similar trend being apparent in the class comprising clerks and warehousemen, travellers, salesmen and male shop assistants (1859, 13·0 per cent; 1890, 7·9 per cent; 1910, 12·9 per cent). Labourers, carters and porters retained their share of new savers throughout the period (approximately 8 per cent). Furthermore, all these classes would probably have secured a higher representation had it been possible to determine the livelihoods of those who entered the Bank via the Penny Banks. These savers, who were not obliged to sign the Declaration Book, were more likely to have been wage-earners, or the wives and children of wage-earners, than professional persons, shopkeepers and small traders and their families. Indeed, the great success of the Penny Banks in instilling the habit of thrift is strikingly demonstrated by the entries in the Declaration Books.(39) Even if it be assumed that many of the 'spinsters and widows' and a large proportion of the

TABLE 3

PERCENTAGE OCCUPATIONAL DISTRIBUTION OF NEW ENTRANTS, THE SAVINGS BANKS OF GLASGOW, DECENNIALLY, 1840–1910

Class	1840	1850	1859	1870	1880	1890	1900	1910
1	15·7	13·0	11·1	5·9	5·9	4·2	2·4	2·4
2a	11·2	n.d.	n.d.	9·4	7·7	7·9	5·6	7·2
2b	2·5	n.d.	n.d.	3·8	2·1	1·7	2·9	1·7
2c	5·4	n.d.	n.d.	4·6	2·0	2·3	2·3	3·2
2d	n.d.	n.d.	n.d.	1·4	2·0	1·4	1·4	1·7
2e	4·0	n.d.	n.d.	1·1	2·6	1·7	2·8	1·3
2f	2·1	n.d.	n.d.	1·5	1·1	1·2	2·1	1·5
2a–2f	25·2	25·7	32·1	21·8	17·5	16·2	17·1	16·6
3	4·5	4·0	4·6	9·1	8·3	9·7	9·1	10·8
4	5·2	4·2	3·8	2·7	1·8	2·7	3·2	3·6
5	8·2	10·0	13·0	8·6	9·9	7·9	10·8	12·9
6	4·9	6·1	3·8	9·9	6·9	5·1	6·2	6·1
7	1·8	2·0	1·7	2·4	1·5	1·2	2·1	2·7
8	n.d.	n.d.	n.d.	1·3	1·1	1·4	1·6	1·6
9	n.d.	n.d.	n.d.	0·9	0·6	1·3	1·2	0·6
10	8·5	8·0	7·3	7·5	8·3	7·6	8·3	7·0
11	1·1	1·3	n.d.	2·3	1·4	0·9	1·6	0·8
12	2·2	1·8	n.d.	n.d.	n.d.	n.d.	n.d.	n.d.
13	n.d.	n.d.	n.d.	6·0	8·9	7·7	9·7	11·1
14	10·6	9·6	11·2	12·6	12·0	10·9	7·6	8·3
15	—	—	—	3·8	12·9	18·5	17·1	13·0
16	12·2	14·1	11·4	5·3	3·0	4·4	2·3	2·4

Notes

Composition of the various classes: 1. Domestic servants, female. 2. 'Mechanics, artificers and their wives', this category is very broad and is known to have included the following groups (details of which are given where possible): 2(a). Blacksmiths, tinsmiths, boilermakers, iron-founders, iron moulders, engineers, machine makers and fitters, and, for 1900 and 1910, electricians; 2(b) Masons, bricklayers, plasterers, slaters, plumbers and housepainters; 2(c) Carpenters, joiners, cabinet makers, pattern makers, coopers; 2(d) Compositors, letterpress printers, bookbinders, and papermakers; 2(e) Shoemakers, tailors and potters; 2(f) Bakers, fleshers and millers. 3. 'Factory operatives and their wives', this class includes weavers, power loom tenters, calico printers, and many other grades of textile workers, plus the minor categories of gutta percha, leather and glass workers. 4. Female warehouse workers, milliners, dressmakers, needlewomen and shop assistants. 5. Clerks and warehousemen, salesmen and travellers, and, after and including 1900, typists. 6. Shopkeepers and small traders. 7. 'Professional Persons', *i.e.* clergymen, doctors, musicians, teachers, and chemists. 8. Employees of railway companies. 9. Miners. 10. Labourers, carters and porters. 11. Soldiers, sailors, policemen, firemen, seamen and fishermen. 12. 'Agricultural employments'. 13. Spinsters and widows. 14. Minors, these are children 'under 15' for the period 1840–59, and 'under 16' thereafter. 15. Depositors at the Glasgow Savings Bank who opened accounts through their Local Penny Banks, and whose occupations cannot be ascertained. The names of the Penny Banks cited in the Declaration Books indicate that many of these depositors were almost certainly factory employees or workers in ironworks and shipyards; it is also believed that large numbers were 'minors'; 16. Depositors whose occupations are either not given or constitute too small a category for separate classification over the period covered by the table. Lines 2a to 2f have been totalled to give a figure comparable to 'Mechanics' in Table 1, which always comprised these somewhat diverse categories.

Sources: 1. Glasgow, 1840, 1850 and 1859: as for Table 1. 2. Glasgow, 1870–1910: *These figures are estimates only;* they are based on random samples comprising 12·5 per cent of all new entrants opening accounts at the Head Office and Bridgeton Cross branches of the Bank during the years stated. My thanks are due to Miss J. Kalinowska for help in taking these samples, and to Mr. Lionel Needleman and Mr. Gerald Garton for advice on the statistical problems involved.

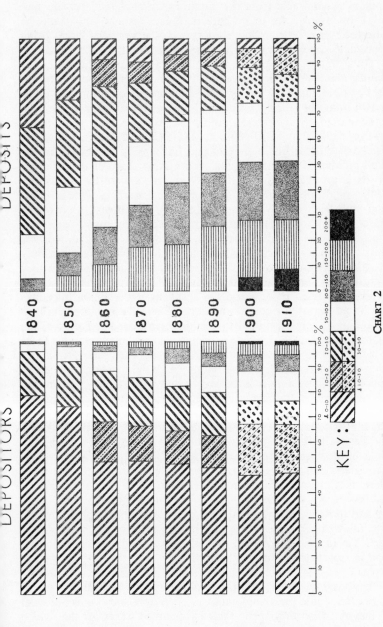

CHART 2

Percentage distribution of depositors and deposits by account size, Savings Bank of Glasgow, 1840-1910.
Source: Calculated from data presented in the Annual Reports of the Committee of Management.

'minors' were drawn from the families of professional persons and small tradesmen, the total share of the depositors who could be described as middle or upper classes was never very large, being represented on a scale roughly comparable with the 'mechanics'.

These figures corroborate the statement repeatedly made in the Bank's annual reports throughout the latter half of the nineteenth century that the great majority of the depositors continued to be drawn from 'the labouring classes'. It is arguable that this contention is supported by the great number of accounts that were in the £0-£10, £10-£20 and £10-£30 ranges (see Chart 2). It has frequently been asserted that the mere fact that but a small proportion of the total number of depositors held such a large share of the total deposits is proof enough that the trustee banks were the depository of the middle classes rather than the manual workers. This proposition must be treated with reserve. In Glasgow, at least, some of the larger balances were laboriously accumulated over many years, and there is no question that some skilled, and even unskilled, workers were the owners of substantial balances. The Trustees were certainly at pains to point this out, and there is no reason to believe that they were deliberately blinding themselves to the true state of affairs. William Meikle's reports and the speakers at the annual meetings are by no means solely self-adulatory. Where the Bank felt itself to be failing it rarely omitted to mention the fact. Furthermore, the managers repeatedly reminded themselves that 'much remains to be done. It is unfortunately too notorious that when labour is abundant and wages good, . . . in many cases the increased income is followed only by a more lavish expenditure, and the important duty of saving against the day of adversity is never thought of so long as the good times last.'(40) Members of the Church were always quick to point out that numerous though the transactions of the Bank and the Penny Banks had been 'they bore no proportion to the transactions of the dram-shops, pawn shops, and loan clubs in the city'.(41) The irrepressible Reverend Dr. Gillan calculated in 1863 that there were in Glasgow '120,000 individuals who might take advantage of Savings banks, but who do not'. From this number children under 10 and those aged beyond 60 were excluded, 'while a broad margin was allowed for those who could not possibly save a single farthing'. Yet in the High Street, the Saltmarket, Gallowgate, Trongate, and in Cowcaddens and Anderston,

'tens, and hundreds, and thousands are to be seen flitting out of or gliding into [drinking] haunts . . . Surely, they know not what they do when they spend their hard-earned wages for that which

is not bread, but—whiskey! Can they know that, instead of
savings banks they patronize wasting banks? Yes; within these
inviting retreats—these snug little boxes—these well curtained
parlours—these bright-blazing windows—within these retreats an
awful waste is incurred. There, when their uses are abused, your
capital is wasted; and then what becomes of your interest? There
your time is wasted, your health is, and at last your reputation.
Into such banks you consign what has the elements of material
usefulness and comfort; but instead of these, by such folly you
draw out vexation of spirit.'(42)

In 1876, when one in five of the city's population had an account
at the Bank, the managers felt constrained to point out that 'it is
painfully evident that a considerable proportion, perhaps even a
majority, of our adult population spend their whole earnings from
week to week, and lay by nothing'.(43) Even when the heroic efforts
to create new branches and expand facilities had resulted in two of
every five of the population having accounts at the Bank or in a
Penny Bank, the committee was disappointed to have to report
that the amount at the credit of depositors was 'not increasing in a
ratio commensurate with the growth of the city in population and
wealth'.(44)

In the light of these constant reappraisals of the clientele and
attainments of the Bank and the statistical evidence set out in
Tables 1-3, it is submitted that when the reports say that the majority
of the depositors and the bulk of the deposits belonged to the
working classes there is no reason to doubt that this represented the
true position. It would appear that those who have argued that the
trustee savings banks failed to achieve the high hopes of the founders
may well have been right if only *English* experience is analysed. In
the West of Scotland the Glasgow Savings Bank did attract and
retain the support of the manual workers.(45) In this matter Scottish
economic history appears once again to diverge from the so-called
'British' pattern.

III

As we have already noticed, it is commonly assumed that depositors with large balances were of the professional and middle
classes and that those with small balances were of the working class.
This assumption may be correct, but to use it to support the contention that the nineteenth century trustee savings banks were a

failure seems to be an example of the woolly thinking that has befogged many discussions of the rôle of these banks.

If the trustee savings banks were successful in achieving their primary object of benefiting the industrious poor, then we would *expect* to find that the bulk of the depositors held small balances; balances slowly built up and rapidly run down in the rent day quarters or when unemployment was rife. The motives of the savers are important in this context. The body of depositors always included 'a numerous and exemplary class of persons who [made] use of the Savings Bank not so much with a view to increase, as to safe custody and preparation against rent day and other periodical disbursements'.(46) This being so, the fact that about 70 per cent of the depositors possessed balances of £20 or less was used by the Glasgow officials as a potent argument in supporting their claim that the Bank was rendering important services 'to the very class contemplated by the legislature'.(47)

In 1890 80 per cent of the accounts were less than £50, and, it was stated, 'Of the larger balances the great majority are the happy result of industry combined with provident habits extending over a long course of years'.(48) This statement, in itself, does nothing to weaken the critics' case. It does not say that the holders of the larger balances were manual workers, but neither does it deny this possibility. Without more 'occupational evidence' one cannot say with any certainty exactly who were the holders of the larger balances.(49) It does remain true, however, that a small number of richer depositors were responsible for the bulk of the savings. But, with an upper limit of £200 and relatively attractive interest rates combined with absolute security, is this not precisely what might have been expected? The mere fact that in 1900, for example, 12 per cent of the depositors held 50 per cent of the funds does little to upset the Trustees' belief that the Bank was performing a valuable service to the working classes. Asked about the larger balances by the Select Committee on Trustee Savings Banks in 1889, Meikle argued:

'We aim at the encouragement of thrift in every possible way. We have to face a loss of £5,000 [on the accounts of 100,000 small depositors] but we counteract this by the larger profit we get from the larger balances. These larger balances are essential to the existence of an efficient saving bank.'(50)

The result of an analysis of the accounts of the individual depositors at the Glasgow Savings Bank is presented in Chart 2.

TABLE 4

OCCUPATIONAL DISTRIBUTION OF DEPOSITORS, WITH OUTSTANDING TOTAL
BALANCES AND AVERAGE BALANCE PER ACCOUNT, SAVINGS BANK OF GLASGOW,
19TH SEPTEMBER, 1848

Occupation	Number of active accounts	Total on deposit in each group	Average balance per account in each group		
		£	£	s.	d.
Domestic servants	3,575	48,822	13	13	2
Mechanics of all kinds, and wives	4,515	68,279	15	2	5
Factory operatives	930	12,414	13	6	11
Female warehouse workers and sewers	1,040	13,737	13	4	2
Dyers, bleachers, calico printers	357	5,122	14	6	11
Handloom weavers	293	3,774	12	17	7
Clerks and warehousemen	2,006	29,561	14	14	9
Shopkeepers and small traders	853	18,381	21	10	11
Labourers, carters, porters	1,649	26,541	16	1	10
Professional persons	333	6,803	20	8	9
Soldiers and sailors	251	6,110	24	6	10
Agricultural employment	646	12,519	19	7	6
Minors (under 15 years)	3,234	30,747	9	10	1
Householders, lodging-house keepers	988	21,192	21	8	11
Not specified	1,540	28,865	18	14	10
TOTAL	22,210	£332,867	14	19	8

Source: 13th Annual Report, 1848.

Note: George R. Porter, Progress of the Nation (London, New edition, 1851),
p. 616, gives figures for the Manchester and Salford Savings Bank for 1842,
which may be compared with the above. Overall the average balance in the
English bank was £27, and for each group the average balance was roughly
double the Glasgow figure. See also A. Fishlow, *op. cit.*, p. 35.

These bar diagrams are designed to portray the percentage distribution of depositors and deposits, classified by account size, at ten-
yearly intervals from 1840 to 1910. Thus, in 1840 the balances of
78·9 per cent of the depositors were less than £20 and their total
holdings represented 35·1 per cent of the total amount standing to
the credit of the individual depositors; by 1910 these figures had
fallen to 47·9 per cent and 3·7 per cent, respectively. At the other end
of the scale, only one in 200 depositors held more than £100 in the

Bank in 1840, yet this group held 5 per cent of the total funds.
These figures steadily rose until 1910, 11·9 per cent of the depositors
held balances in excess of £100 (£100-£150, 6·6 per cent; £150-£200,
3·9 per cent; and over £200, 1·4 per cent), and the sums standing to
their credit represented over half, 51·4 per cent, of the total sum
credited to individual depositors (£100-£150, 23·3 per cent; £150-
£200, 19·5 per cent; over £200, 8·6 per cent). It is submitted that the
statistical data embodied in Chart 2, reveal that the Bank was successful in attracting the small saver but that the richer depositors
always held a disproportionate share of the total funds; that they
are *capable* of supporting the contention that over time some of the
smaller savers gradually built up substantial balances; and that in
some degree they reflect the slow rise in the standard of living of all
classes in the West of Scotland during the nineteenth century.(51)
What these data do not show—and by themselves cannot show—is
any change in the character of the Bank's clientele. Only detailed
investigation into occupational classifications of depositors can do
this: those who employ simply account or deposit class statistics as
evidence of undue professional and middle class participation in
the trustee savings banks are arguing erroneously, correct though
their conclusions may be in the majority of cases.

IV

The factors operating on the annual volume of small savings
deposited in the Savings Bank of Glasgow in the nineteenth century
were manifold and complex. A number of influences appear to have
been of predominant importance: the availability of work, the wage
level of those employed, changing conceptions among the 'industrious classes' of the standard of living that they were entitled to
enjoy, the rate of interest that might be obtained, and certain psy-
chological factors bound up with the savers' notions of the degree
of security offered by the Bank. A complete explanation of the
fluctuations of small savings would have to take account of all these
plus an almost infinite variety of influences of an individual nature
affecting single persons or small groups rather than the complete
body of depositors.(52) Ideally, one would like to assess the impact
of each of these determinants, but they are inextricably intertwined
and the available data precludes any sophisticated analysis. We
must, therefore, content ourselves with some relatively crude judgements.

Throughout the eighty-year period under discussion it is apparent from occasional clues in the Annual Reports that there must have been a marked seasonal pattern in deposits and withdrawals. Unfortunately, the only monthly figures available are for a rather unrepresentative period embracing the abnormal crisis years of 1847-48. However, it seems probable that in the middle decades of the nineteenth century deposits were relatively high in December and were uniformly above average in June and the late summer months. March, April and May were, on the contrary, marked by low deposits. On the other hand, withdrawals were very high in May and November and substantially above average in June. Low withdrawals are recorded for the summer months. The amplitude of the fluctuations in withdrawals was greater than those in deposits. The net result—that is, the pattern of lodgements minus repayments—was that 'net savings' usually took place in December and the summer months (June to September), and that 'dis-saving' was a feature of the months of April, May and November.

Any explanation of these seasonal patterns is largely conjectural. This must be so in the current absence of adequate data on earnings in Glasgow, employment opportunities, and household expenditure on food, drink, lighting and rent. The high withdrawals and the net dis-saving in May and November are the features most easily explained. It was in these months that the rents payable at the Whit Sunday and Martinmas terms fell due. In 1871 it was estimated that withdrawals for rent and other termly payments in these months amounted to about £60,000, in 1880 to just over £100,000, and in 1902 to about a quarter of a million pounds.(53) An additional explanation for the high withdrawals in November is that interest was added to the accounts on the 20th of that month. Depositors would, it may be assumed, postpone non-essential expenditures until this date and then—having been credited with their interest—feel free to withdraw the funds they required.

The reason for the high net saving in the summer months is probably to be found in lower household expenditures on food, clothing, fuel, and lighting; this would reduce the need for withdrawals and permit the accumulation of savings at one and the same time. The relatively low net savings in the winter months might have been caused by a reversal of these conditions.(54) Statistical data for later decades in the century—were they available—would almost certainly reveal that these seasonal patterns changed in some degree as the century advanced. It might be expected that the influence of summer holidays, extraordinary hogmanay expenditures, and New Years' resolutions became progressively more important determinants of savings behaviour.(55)

These seasonal changes took place within a context of cyclical fluctuations and occasional crises. The impact of the trade cycle on the workers' ability and desire to save is perhaps most clearly seen in the chart of 'net savings' (*i.e.*, deposits minus withdrawals, Chart 3). Because the small saver is very concerned with the security of his money, the amounts deposited with, and withdrawn from, the Bank were highly susceptible to panics. Such was the case, for example, in 1847, 1857, and 1878. The high withdrawals and net dis-saving of 1847 was ascribed partly to 'the high price of pro-

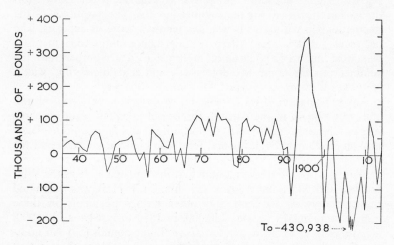

CHART 3

Annual 'net savings' (deposits minus repayments, including interest), Savings Bank of Glasgow, 1836-1914.

Source: Annual Reports of the Committee of Management.

visions consequent on the deficient harvest and failure of the potato crop in 1846. But above any other cause, it is to be attributed to the still prevalent pressure of a monetary crisis altogether unprecedented in this country's commerce.'(56) The other years, 1857 and 1878, were marked by runs on the Bank occasioned in the former instance by the suspension of the Western and City of Glasgow Banks, and in the latter by the failure of the City of Glasgow Bank.(57) The impact of these failures on the Savings Bank was only temporary. In Meikle's words to the Select Committee of 1889, 'There was nothing for it but just to stand to your work and pay the people; they usually recover their senses in a day-and-a-half'. The Bank did not insist on the twenty-one days' notice to which it was statutorily entitled. 'We paid at call,' said the actuary, 'but there is this good safety valve in the case of a large savings bank, that the small saver runs as well as the large depositor, and between them they crowd the office and little money suffices.'(58)

Of much greater influence on savings behaviour was the availability of employment and changes in earnings. There is a significant correlation of 'net savings' and employment throughout the period. National cycles are clearly reflected in the three main series —deposits, withdrawals, and 'net savings'—though the image is somewhat distorted by local enomonic conditions. This is what could be expected since the fundamental determinant of savings is the level of income,(59) and this in turn depended upon the availability of employment and on the level of earnings. The Strathaven branch reported in November, 1841, for example, that 'the past year, from the very depressed state of trade, has diminished the number and magnitude of deposits, and proportionally increased those of repayments. All must be aware, that during the past year several descriptions of labour have been both poorly paid and difficult to be obtained.'(60) More selective influences were at work in 1862 when a great increase in repayments took place

'in the class of sums under £5, . . . clearly traceable to the great depression of trade and scarcity of employment which have so long prevailed among cotton operatives, and other branches of business connected therewith. For several months past thousands of our working population have been under the necessity of having recourse to those small sums which they had wisely laid past for the day of trial and thereby have maintained that spirit of independence which so long characterised the working classes of Scotland. The pressure of the times has been severely felt by many, and has necessitated not a few to exhaust their entire savings, and close their accounts. . . . This adversity has . . . not overtaken the whole community, but only that portion of it which is more intimately connected with cotton manufactures. Other trades have been in fair employment and their lodgements have exceeded the withdrawals by the class referred to.'(61)

The prolonged depression following the collapse of the great boom of the 'seventies was characterised by years of 'scarcity of employment, and great depression of trade, aggravated by heavy failures. These events seriously affected the working classes, throwing many out of employment, and necessitating withdrawals from the savings of better times.'(62) During the mid-'eighties, too, there was 'little money to save, and the Bank was mainly useful to its Depositors in repaying money, thereby enabling many to ward off or mitigate the distress which has spread widely over the community',(63) and the reports told a similar tale in the latter years of the first decade of the twentieth century.

On the other hand, 'the abundance of employment and the cheapness of provisions, together with continued commercial prosperity'(64) produced high net savings in the early 'fifties and 'seventies. One speaker at the annual meeting commented in 1874 that 'whatever may be the experience of merchants, who, I have no doubt, have suffered severely, both in the rise in the value of labour, and the enormous and exorbitant rise in the value of coal, there can be no doubt that working men have received liberal pay and very full employment'.(65)

Such examples could be multiplied: they would simply emphasise the undeniable fact that savings fluctuate with income, itself largely dependent in this case upon employment. Other factors, however, were constantly influencing the small saver. The fluctuations in deposits, withdrawals and 'net savings' in the troubled years of 1847 and 1848 were explained in great detail by speakers at the annual meetings of these years. On 28th December, 1847, Sheriff Alison pointed out that: 'We had at the beginning of the year agricultural distress, amounting in some districts almost to a famine; at a later period we had commercial depression and embarrassment, unprecedented in magnitude in this country; and another matter of a still more depressing nature, was the engagement of a large proportion of the middle and humbler classes in rash and often questionable speculations, which have promised a larger return of interest than we could afford.'(66) The Very Rev. Principal MacFarlan felt it necessary to add another reason for the diminution of the Bank's funds, 'the effect of which has been powerful and extensive'. 'I mean the state of the health of the community. Thousands upon thousands of the working population have been for weeks and months during the last year stretched upon beds of sickness, and compelled to have recourse to those small sums which they had wisely laid up for the day of trial.'(67)

In 1848

'The well-understood causes which, in 1847, to some extent diminished the funds . . . continued to have a similar tendency until the month of June. . . . In addition thereto, throughout spring and summer, an extensive emigration from this city and district, occasioned numerous withdrawments of long-accumulated deposits, heavy in their aggregate amount. Subsequent to that period, the alarm which had for some time prevailed from thoughtless political excitement, gradually gave way before relative good sense to a healthful return of accustomed confidence. Partially reviving trade had again given employment to many steady and deserving workmen, who had, with their families, from months previous, been wholly dependent upon their Saving Bank's resources. There had subsided, also, much of that mistaken desire for lucrative investment . . . [This lead to] receipts exceeding repayments . . . from June.'(68)

Such factors were responsible for significant movements in deposits and withdrawals in later years. In 1852 the unusually large amount repaid was 'caused principally by withdrawals for the purposes of emigration. In the early part of the year, many hundreds of the most regular Depositors closed their connection with the Bank, and left the country, taking with them considerable sums which they had accumulated in the Bank.'(69) Large withdrawals by emigrants had a considerable impact on the funds in 1860, 1907 and 1910.(70) Of increasing importance was the depositors' growing awareness of more remunerative possibilities for their savings elsewhere. As early as 1839, however, the report stated that various sums were withdrawn for 'the candidly avowed purpose of being placed in the Commercial Banks of the city; the high rate of discount on bills having been in most instances mistaken for that of interest allowed on money deposited'.(71) In 1857, 1864, 1866 and in every year between 1899 and 1906, more attractive interest rates offered elsewhere were accorded a major place in explanations of falling deposits and heavy withdrawals. In 1902 W. B. Malcolm explained to the Select Committee on Savings Bank Funds that for the first fifteen days of the financial year ending 20th November, 1900, £181,239 were withdrawn to take advantage of the relatively high rate of interest—4½ per cent—offered by the Corporation. When asked if any of this sum had been replaced in the Bank, Malcolm replied, 'I really could not say definitely, but we did not offer to take it back. Our policy is not to accept money which is brought to us for interest only.'(72) The depositors who transferred their funds on this occasion were clearly those possessing relatively large balances. Malcolm was quite certain that the very small depositors—that is those with balances of less than £10—were little affected by changing rates of interest, though it was undeniable that they preferred the Bank to pay a fixed rate rather than one which fluctuated, presumably because changing rates influenced their conception of the security of their savings.(73)

One last point is worthy of mention. In the first decade of the twentieth century, only in 1901 and 1902 did deposits exceed withdrawals. Yet such was the magnitude of the annual interest payments that in only two years did the funds standing to the credit of depositors fail to rise. As Professor Ashton has observed, 'accumulation, which is the result of a mere refraining from spending part of one's interest is hardly the same thing as purposive thrift. In the main, the increase can be explained as due to the automatic working of compound interest.'(74) The net dis-saving of these years is not merely a manifestation of the owners of the larger balances transferring a portion of their funds to the Investment Trust or to more remunerative investments outside the Bank, but is evidence of a very real breaking down of the Victorian ideal of thrift under the erosive power of new interests and leisure opportunities.

The long run of good years was believed to have caused the workers to 'put aside the lessons of the past, and from a long continuance of regular employment and high wages they have become more self-indulgent in their habits and less careful to provide for a recurrence of bad times'.(75) In 1907 the Lord Provost, Sir William Bilsland, stressed the continued tremendous waste of money in connection with drunkenness and gambling, but added, significantly, that 'another evil that had been growing was the excessive amount of money spent by the public on music-halls and theatres every year . . . the total sum spent . . . amounted to £320,000 per annum . . . it was a serious drawback in the community that such a large proportion of the citizens were not taking a more serious thought of life'.(76) Other speakers at this time emphasised the disastrous effect on thrift of old-age pensions and the temptations offered to the working classes by 'the weekly half-holiday now enjoyed by assistant shopkeepers', the coming of picture palaces, the growing popularity of football matches, and the illustrated newspapers which, by giving an 'extraordinary unfair and unjust picture . . . of the apparent extravagances of the rich', encouraged workers to ape their betters.(77)

It was all very well to point to the fact that nearly a quarter of a million pounds had been added to the credit of the depositors in 1901, commented Lord Provost Chisholm, the truth was that £174,000 of this sum was interest credited by the Bank. The actual savings amounted to but 4s. per account. In view of 'the industrial conditions of the city and the current wages that had been going', this was not satisfactory.(78) In fact, the last year in which the excess of deposits over withdrawals was greater than the interest credited to accounts was in 1897. After that date there was not a single year in which 'interest credited' failed to exceed 'net savings' (*i.e.*, 'deposits' minus 'repayments including interest') during the period under consideration, the falling rate of growth in the total sum standing to the credit of depositors being clearly apparent in Chart 1. Even allowing for the transference of funds into the Bank's Investment Department (see below, Section V), it is hard not to agree with Sir William Arrol that the thrift of the working class was failing to keep pace with the prosperity of the city.(79) It would appear that a decline in the purposeful saving of the manual workers of Glasgow took place during the last decade of the nineteenth century. Before this date there seems to be no adequate reason to assume that the pattern of English experience—which has always pictured the clientele of Savings banks as mainly small shopkeepers, and by members of the professional and middle classes—is applicable to the West of Scotland. After the turn of the century it may well be that the typical Glasgow saver conforms much more closely to the English model; only detailed research into the Bank's later records will confirm this.

V

A major reason for the success of the Glasgow Savings Bank was undoubtedly its constant endeavours to cater to the wants of the depositors. It was this policy which led to the establishment of the investment department in 1870. The Glasgow trustees—like their far-sighted counterparts elsewhere—had, during the 'sixties, become increasingly irritated at the low limits of deposit, which successive Governments had shown no disposition to increase. William Meikle saw that an exceptionally clumsy clause in the Act of 1828, retained as Clause 16 in the Act of 1863, opened the way to the establishment of an investment department which would provide an outlet for the funds of those who had reached the statutory limit of deposit in what became known as the Ordinary Department of the Bank.(80) Furthermore, such a department—because it was capable of offering higher rates of interest—might act as a safeguard against the withdrawal of larger deposits seeking higher returns, and allow for a greater margin for expenses and for the building up of reserves. At the same time, the development of an investment department would constitute a significant competitive advantage over the Post Office Savings Banks, now the favoured child of the State.

N

The trustees rapidly acted on Meikle's memorandum. In the Annual Report for 1870, it was announced that the Committee of Management

> 'have agreed to open a separate Department for the accommodation of the older Depositors, who, having reached the maximum limit of deposit on Government Security, now find themselves debarred from lodging their further weekly savings. Under the new arrangement these Depositors may now open separate accounts, to which they may transfer a portion of their Savings, to be invested on Mortgages of the Glasgow Corporation Water or Gas Trusts, or in equally secure investments. In this way they will also participate in the higher rate of interest allowed by these Trusts, an advantage hitherto confined to capitalists.'(81)

By 1888 the Lord Provost, Sir James King, was able to claim that in this way the Bank had afforded to 'those whose means had been growing, and who had been attending to their business rather than learning the ways of the Stock Exchange, a safe and suitable local Investment for their savings. . . . About 3,000 of the Bank's earliest and most exemplary Depositors had availed themselves of this privilege.'(82)

Unfortunately, this facility was soon to be gravely impaired. Following the discovery of a series of frauds at the Cardiff Savings Bank in 1886, a Government Committee was set up to inquire into the conduct of the trustee savings bank. In the course of this inquiry the status and indeed the legality of the investment departments that had been set up by the larger banks following Glasgow's lead was seriously questioned. A principal official witness, Sir Charles Rivers Wilson, the Comptroller-General of the National Debt Office, felt that Section 16 of the 1863 Act—under which the departments had been established—was at variance with the whole spirit of savings bank legislation. 'He was clearly nervous about the growth of those . . . departments, over which the Debt Commissioners had no control and which were, in some banks, growing at the expense of the government department,'(83) and since an act passed in 1880 had created facilities for the purchase of consols, he felt the need for such departments no longer existed. Very able evidence was given to the Committee by William Meikle. He put forward a series of suggestions for the proper management of trustee savings banks, and stoutly argued in favour of the retention of the investment departments in their existing form. He pointed out that in Glasgow this department had 'been an advantage to the local

school boards, inasmuch as they get money from us at £3 7s. 6d.
per cent, while they pay £4 per cent to the Public Works Loan
Commissioners' and he emphasised that the Glasgow trustees took
'no money from the outside; they only take . . . transfers of money
already with us', confining their investments 'entirely to local securities which we know about, and where we know the gentlemen who
have charge of them'. Asked if it was strictly true to say that the
doors of savings banks were closed when the limit of £150 was
reached, in the words 'Persons can invest in consols, can they not?',
he replied:

'Yes; but there is a great drawback, especially in Scotland, to
consols; the people do not understand these securities, and you
cannot drive them into them. It is right to explain, however, that
the trustees in Glasgow opened their investment scheme ten years
before the Government allowed the people to invest in consols
through Savings banks, and the people of Glasgow are accustomed to, and highly pleased with, this mode of investment. It
is free from expenses for buying and selling, and it fits the habits
of the people much better than consols; they will get back the
money they put in.'(84)

Meikle's evidence strongly influenced the Committee and no
recommendation was made with regard to Section 16 of the Act of
1863. Nevertheless, the Act of 1891 did contain extremely serious
restrictions on the operations of special investment departments by
limiting the powers of investment to trustee securities. The 59th Annual Report of the Bank's Committee of Management explained the
impact of this change:

'The usefulness of the Investment Department has been seriously
crippled by the operation of the Savings Bank Act of 1891. . . .
Formerly such investments as loans to School Boards and Local
Authorities with Rating Powers were largely taken advantage of.
They were safe, profitable, and in all respects desirable investments; but now, . . . they are not permitted. . . . In these
circumstances Savings Banks, in conjunction with School Boards,
County Councils, and Local Authorities are promoting in Parliament a Bill to extend the investing powers of the Trustees. This
measure . . . will restore to Savings Banks the privilege so
greatly prized by the Depositors of investing in First class
Securities that do not fluctuate in value.'(85)

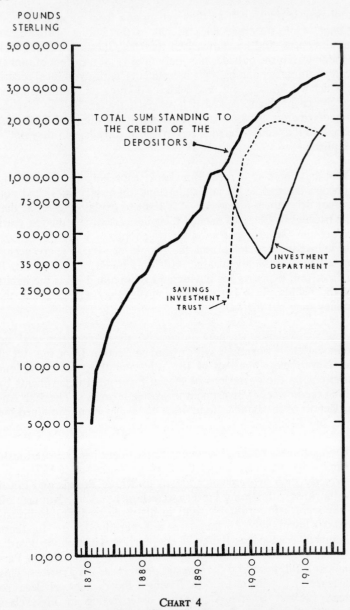

CHART 4

Total sum standing to the credit of depositors in the Investment Department and the Savings Investment Trust, Savings Bank of Glasgow, 1871-1914 (plotted on semi-logarithmic scale).

Source: Annual Reports of the Committee of Management and Reports of the proceedings of the Annual Meeting of Trustees and Managers.

The Government was unsympathetic. No concessions were to be made. The Glasgow trustees once more took the lead in seeking for a loophole. In 1896 they decided to transfer their special investment business to an Investment Trust, registered under the Companies Act, but conducted in association with the bank just like the old department before the Act of 1891. The move was very successful. By 1897 the Investment Trust had £641,500 to its credit and by 1901 just over £1½ million. The Trust took over all those mortgages which were ordered to be realised (*i.e.*, mortgages on rates, especially those for school boards), and temporarily performed all the Bank's investment business. The constitution of the Trust limited any single investor from investing more than £500 in addition to any sum transferred from the old investment department.(86)

The fluctuations in the funds of these two departments (see Chart 4) were much more erratic than those in the ordinary department, since the richer depositors were greatly influenced by alternative investment possibilities. In addition, the pattern of deposits and withdrawals was considerably distorted by the controversies over Clause 16 of the Act of 1863. The major determinant of the growth of the investment branch of the Bank was, however, the yield on such investments. The rate paid when the Investment Department commenced operations was £3 10s. This was reduced in May 1881 to £3 5s. on new accounts, though the old accounts were not similarly treated until November 1884. In March 1888 the rate offered to new investors was £3, a figure made uniform in November. In November 1894 and November 1896 two further reductions took place to £2 15s. and £2 10s. respectively. The effect of these changes is clearly visible in the rate at which the amount standing to the credit of the investors grew. The excess of deposits over repayments in 1881 was the lowest since the opening of the department; in the financial year of 1885, when the rate of £3 5s. was applied to all depositors, the increase by deposits over withdrawals was similarly very low, being just over £1,000. The next fall, occurring in the financial year of 1889, had no adverse effects on the accumulation of funds of the investment department, perhaps because even 3 per cent was substantially higher than the current yield on consols, but those in 1894 and 1896 brought the Bank's rates closer to this yield at a time of growing anxiety over the legality of the Bank's investment programme.(87) This combination of circumstances was instrumental in causing very heavy withdrawals.

The fact that from 1894 to 1903 repayments constantly exceeded deposits in this department is, however, largely a manifestation of the creation of the Savings Investment Trust in 1896, when large sums were simply transferred from the department to the new body. From the mid-'nineties, therefore, the true picture of the investing side of the Bank's activities can be seen only by combining the accounts of the old Investment Department and the Savings Investment Trust, statistics for which are not fully available until 1902, or but five years before it was decided to take advantage of the amendment to the Trustee Act for Scotland (passed in 1898) which made loans on the security of the rates permissible trustee investments in Scotland. This made it possible to wind up the Savings Investment Trust and amalgamate its accounts with the original Investment Department to form the Special Investment Department.(88) In 1907 the combined accounts showed a large net withdrawal, ascribed once more 'to the State of the financial market' which gave the investors an opportunity to obtain higher yields outside the Bank. In 1913, too, only the interest credited to the accounts enabled the total funds owing to the investors to increase.

It is clear that those 'most exemplary depositors' for whom the Investment Department was instituted in 1870 had, by the 'nineties, learned the lessons of thrift so well that they did not hesitate to transfer their funds to obtain the highest available yield. The fact that they were precluded from reinvesting their funds in the Savings Bank was apparently of little consequence to them.(89) The Bank had done its work; it had started them on the right path. 'You have a very considerable number of large accounts; is there any jealousy on the part of the great Scottish joint-stock banks against you upon such a matter as that?' Meikle was asked by the Select Committee of 1889. His answer was significant: 'I daresay there may be, but it is a very unfair jealousy, because we give off every year thousands upon thousands of trained depositors who form the best customers of the ordinary banks.' He might have added that the time chosen by the 'trained depositors' to sever their connection with the Savings bank was determined by the availability of more remunerative investment opportunities elsewhere.

VI

Little more than a piggy bank designed to reduce the burden of the poor rates and give a moral uplift to its clientele, the Glasgow Savings Bank had, by the eve of the First World War, become of considerable economic importance to the region, channelling the surplus funds of richer depositors to local authorities and, by reducing the small savers' fear of banks and bankers, increasing the working classes' propensity to save. Benevolent paternalism still existed but the active management was in the hands of astute and vigorous permanent officials who sought every legal opportunity to extend the Bank's power and influence. In Glasgow Gladstone's Post Office Savings Bank made little progress in the face of this well-established and economically operated Trustee Bank.(90) Its loans to school boards, police authorities, municipal water and gas under-takings and the like, were of great social benefit and by taking up public issues the Bank must have freed funds for investment in the region's industry and trade.(91) Trustee Savings Banks are rarely accorded more than a fleeting reference in economic histories: it is hoped that this paper will convince those who seek to reconstruct the economic and social history of the different regions of the British Isles that the records of local Savings Bank are worthy of greater attention.

NOTES

(1) This essay is based upon a paper first presented to the annual conference of Scottish Economists at Edzell, Angus, in 1961. I am indebted to Professor S. G. Checkland and to all those who joined in the discussion of the paper for numerous useful suggestions. My grateful thanks are due to the Trustees of the Savings Bank of Glasgow for granting access to certain of the Bank's archives and to Mr. J. D. Campbell, General Manager, Mr. W. B. McConville, Assistant General Manager, and other officials of the Bank for their unfailing assistance.

(2) On 20th November, 1964, the total funds of the four largest trustee savings banks were: Glasgow, £153,174,524; London, £133,559,019; York, £99,725,952; Belfast, £85,436,679. Trustee Savings Banks Year Book, 32nd edition, 1965.

(3) H. Oliver Horne, A History of Savings Banks (Oxford, 1947).

(4) Thomas Henderson's The Savings Bank of Glasgow: One Hundred Years of Thrift (Glasgow, 1936) is a brief, descriptive essay, almost wholly lacking in analysis, and William Meikle's pamphlet, The Savings Bank of Glasgow: Its Origin and Progress (Glasgow, 1898) merely highlights a number of significant developments in the bank's history.

(5) The affairs of the earlier bank—the Provident Bank of Glasgow—are briefly discussed by Alexander Gray, in his paper presented to the Literary and Commercial Society of Glasgow, subsequently published as a pamphlet entitled National Security Savings' Banks (Glasgow, 1836), p. 9. See also Horne, op. cit., pp. 50, 55. The Act was 5 and 6 William IV, Chap. 57.

(6) An account of this meeting is given in the second and subsequent editions of the pamphlet by Alexander Gray, op. cit., pp. 23-29. See also Henderson, op. cit., pp. 1-4.

(7) These rules were set out in detail in the 3rd Annual Report of the Committee of Management to the Trustees and Managers for the year ending

20th November, 1838. Subsequent references to the Annual Reports of the Committee of Management will be cited thus: '3rd Ann. Rep., 1838', where 1838 refers to the year ending 20th November, 1838.

(8) Principal MacFarlan, D.D., at the 3rd Annual Meeting of Trustees and Managers, 2nd March, 1838. Subsequent references to the Reports of the Proceedings at the Annual Meetings of Trustees and Managers will be cited thus: '3rd Ann. Meeting, 2nd March, 1838.'

(9) For example, the Rev. Alex. Raleigh to the 21st Annual Meeting: 'The habit of saving rendered important aid . . . in the attainment of that social amelioration which so many good men, in so many different ways, were trying to promote, and coalesced with the highest influences which could operate on the human mind, the influences of the gospel. . . . I hope we are all beginning to see better than we have done that the Christian evangelist had little hope among a famishing population. . . . I look upon it [the Glasgow Savings Bank] as a great breakwater against some of the most destructive vices, and a great vantage ground for the labours of the philanthropist and the Christian.' 21st Ann. Meeting, 5th January, 1857.

(10) Rev. James MacGregor, of the Tron. 29th Ann. Meeting, 9th January, 1865.

(11) 29th Ann. Meeting, 9th January, 1865.

(12) 35th Ann. Meeting, 3rd January, 1871. By 1867 the Glasgow Savings Bank had the largest number of depositors and by 1870 the greatest funds in the United Kingdom. It has never since lost its premier position in these respects. The growth of the Bank is shown in Chart 1.

(13) See below, p. 186, note (90).

(14) Horne, op. cit., p. 144.

(15) W. Meikle, op. cit., p. 14.

(16) By 1838 three branches existed at Strathaven, Kirkintilloch and Pollok Parish plus nine receiving agencies, that at Govan being regarded as a model of its kind. (See appendix to 3rd Ann. Rep., 1838, and Horne, op. cit., pp. 183-84.) Two years later two new branches and another eleven receiving agencies had been opened (3rd Ann. Rep., 1840). Receiving agencies always possessed a transitory character and when, in 1855, the four existing branches at Strathaven, Lochgilphead, Kirkintilloch and Hamilton severed their dependence upon the Glasgow Savings Banks and became autonomous, the Trustees immediately drew up plans to set up branch offices within the City, 'long regarded as a very desirable object' (20th Ann. Rep., 1855). The Branch Office of Anderston was opened in 1856, but not until the late eighteen-sixties was any systematic attempt made to 'cover' the city. By 1877 46 per cent of the lodgements and withdrawals were taking place at the branches in the northern, southern, eastern and western quarters of the city (42nd Ann. Rep., 1877), and this proportion grew when two further branches were opened in the 'eighties, and three in the 'nineties. By 1914 the Trustees were operating sixteen branches in addition to the head office at Ingram Street.

(17) Meikle, op. cit., p. 5.

(18) 15th Ann. Meeting, 30th December, 1850.

(19) 16th Ann. Rep., 1851.

(20) Savings Banks—Report of a Great Public Meeting held in Glasgow on 10th February, 1852 (Glasgow, 1852), p. 19. Part of this report is quoted by Horne, op. cit., pp. 138-39. Many similar—though somewhat less colourful —examples could be given from the reports of the annual meetings.

(21) 24th Ann. Rep., 1859.

(22) Report of the Penny Savings Bank Association of Glasgow, 1870. In

1871 William Meikle published an interesting pamphlet on the rules which should govern the operations of Penny Banks. See The Penny Savings Banks of Glasgow: Their Formation and Management (Glasgow, 1871).

(23) By the Rev. Dr. MacLeod at the 28th Ann. Meeting, 23rd December, 1863.

(24) 30th Report of the Penny Savings Bank Association of Glasgow, 1881, and 63rd Report, 1914.

(25) Report from the Select Committee on Trustee Savings Banks, 1889 (H.C. 301), Q. 897.

(26) Horne, op. cit., p. 98.

(27) N. J. Smelser, Social Change in the Industrial Revolution: An Application of Theory to the Lancashire Cotton Industry, 1770-1840 (London, 1959), pp. 358-75; Albert Fishlow, The Trustee Savings Banks, 1817-1861, Journal of Economic History. Vol. XXI, No. 1 (March, 1961), pp. 26-40.

(28) Quoted by Horne, op. cit., p. 205.

(29) J. H. Clapham, An Economic History of Modern Britain, 2nd edition (Cambridge, 1930), Vol. I, p. 592.

(30) Cf. A. F. Burns and W. C. Mitchell, Measuring Business Cycles (New York, 1946), p. 78.

(31) This failure is referred to, as is also the preference of 'the lower orders in Scotland' of placing 'their money in the public banks to placing it in establishments solely intended for their benefit [i.e. Savings banks]', by Archibald Alison in his Principles of Population and their Connection with Human Happiness (Glasgow, 1840), Vol. II, pp. 158-59. I am indebted to Dr. R. H. Campbell for this reference.

(32) Many examples are quoted in the Annual Reports. Apparently this fear long persisted, it was still being referred to in the eighteen sixties. See the Ann. Reports for 1838, 1839, 1840 and 1862. See also Fishlow, op. cit., p. 37, n. 15.

(33) Lack of precise information—particularly the terminological vagueness of the Bank's classifications—makes this estimate very crude, but it is probably of the correct magnitude. The Census of Scotland, 1861, gives the numbers engaged in 'Textile, Fabrics and Dress' as 26,349 males and 43,838 females. The other proportions given in the text have been made on the basis of the 1861 Census statistics.

(34) Despite the relatively good performance of the City's domestic servants, Strang wrote in 1861 of their 'daily increasing love of dress and ornament . . . which occasionally even surpasses which some might call the extravagance of their mistresses. [This] is, we fear, the rock upon which so many of our female domestics make shipwreck, thinking as they do only on present display, and never towards laying up a provision for future old age.' John Strang, Report on the Census of the Parliamentary and Municipal City of Glasgow (Glasgow, 1861), pp. 30-31.

(35) On opening an account at the Bank each entrant had to sign the Declaration Book and state his address and occupation. The data embodied in the columns covering the years from and including 1870 in Table 3 are calculated from this source, the figures being based on random samples of one in every eight new entrants; nearly 10,000 samples being taken from a total of 79,110 new entrants at the two branches in the selected years. To offset the possible professional bias of the Head Office 'declarations' a sample from the Bridgeton Cross branch, set in an industrial—predominantly textile and engineering—'working class' district were added in an attempt to provide a fairly representative mix.

(36) Indeed, much greater precision is probably precluded by the increasing propensity of depositors to describe their occupations in a way that invests them with an importance of social standing that is often fictitious. To give a crude but illuminating example, 'clerks' and 'typewriters', tend first to become 'secretaries' and then, 'company secretaries'!

(37) Comparing 1859 with 1910 the greatest relative fall occurred in group 2b, artisans connected with the building trades. It is interesting to compare the fluctuations in the proportion of new depositors drawn from this group with the fluctuations in residential building in Glasgow. See A. K. Cairncross, *Fluctuations in the Glasgow Building Industry, 1856-1914*, Home and Foreign Investment, 1870-1913 (Cambridge, 1953), p. 16.

(38) 42nd Ann. Meeting, 26th December, 1877, and see the Reports of H.M. Inspectors of Mines, for 1877. In Appendix No. 3 of Mr. Moore's Report for that year, it is stated that the explosion of firedamp at Blantyre Colliery, Rutherglen, on 22nd October, was responsible for the deaths of 209 miners.

(39) A typical entry of this kind would be, for example, 'Account Number 347016, Peter Graham, Linthouse Penny Bank'. No occupation is given, but Linthouse was the site of the shipyard of the famous firm of Alexander Stephen and Sons. This example is taken from the Head Office Declaration Book for 1880.

(40) 30th Ann. Rep., 1865.

(41) Rev. George Macaulay, of Stockwell Free Church, 30th Ann. Meeting, 8th January, 1866.

(42) Rev. Dr. Gillan of Inchinnan, 28th Ann. Meeting, 23rd December, 1863.

(43) 41st Ann. Rep., 1876.

(44) 67th Ann. Rep., 1902. See Chart 1.

(45) A similar statement could justifiably be made of the Savings Bank of Aberdeen. Despite certain difficulties in classification, tabulated statistics, using the groups employed in Table 3, demonstrate the great importance of working-class deposits in the Aberdeen Bank. These statistics, not reproduced here, were calculated from data kindly provided by Mrs. Margaret M. MacEwan, of the Aberdeen Savings Bank. For help in this matter, I am indebted to Mr. John Lowrie, Personal Assistant to the General Manager of the Savings Bank of Glasgow.

(46) 4th Ann. Rep., 1839.

(47) 6th Ann. Rep., 1841.

(48) 55th Ann. Rep., 1890.

(49) See Table 4, which summarises the situation in 1848.

(50) Report from the Select Committee on Trustee Savings Banks, 1889 (H.C. 301), Q. 859.

(51) If the conclusion of the previous section—that the majority of the Bank's clientele was drawn from the working classes—be accepted, then it is apparent that the credit balances of those working-class families who deposited their savings with the Bank rose steadily during the period under consideration. Certainly, the few random samples taken from the Bank's ledgers confirm the validity of this argument. Both Charts 1 and 2 indicate the growing size of the average account. The detailed statistics indicate that the average amount standing to the credit of the individual depositors rose from £8·17 in 1836 to £11·96 in 1840; the average account first exceeded £20 in 1856 (20·09); £30 was reached thirty years later (1886, £30·08); and in

1914 the average account stood at £35·08, somewhat lower than it had been in the years from 1902 to 1905 inclusive.

(52) The complexity of any analysis of the factors determining savings banks deposits was touched upon by John Towne Danson as early as 1848. See his Economic and Statistical Studies, 1840-1890 (London, 1906), pp. 86-93. I am indebted to Professor S. G. Checkland for this reference.

(53) See 36th (1871) and 45th (1880) Ann. Reports, and Report from the Select Committee on Savings Bank Funds, 1902 (H.C. 282), evidence of Mr. William B. Malcolm, one of the two accountants of the Glasgow Savings Bank, Q. 2227-31.

(54) Similar conclusions were reached in a study of the statistics of the Savings Bank of Baltimore by Professor Lance E. Davis and the author. See P. L. Payne and L. E. Davis, The Savings Bank of Baltimore, 1818-1866: A Historical and Analytical Study (Baltimore, 1956), pp. 58-64.

(55) This possibility is suggested by Professor T. S. Ashton's article: Fluctuations in Savings Bank Deposits, Transactions of the Manchester Statistical Society, Session 1929-30, pp. 89-91, 106.

(56) 12th Ann. Rep., 1847.

(57) 22nd Ann. Rep., 1857, and 43rd Ann. Meeting, 26th December, 1878.

(58) Report of the Select Committee on Trustee Savings Banks, 1889 (H.C. 301), William Meikle's evidence, Q. 852-54. A similar account of the 1857 panic is given in the 22nd Ann. Rep., 1857.

(59) See H. F. Lydall, British Incomes and Savings (Oxford, 1955), p. 164, and J. Lintner, Mutual Savings Banks in the Saving and Mortgage Markets (Boston, 1948), p. 106.

(60) From the annual report of the Strathaven Branch, appended to 6th Ann. Rep., 1841.

(61) 27th Ann. Rep., 1862.

(62) 43rd Ann. Rep., 1878.

(63) E.g., 50th Ann. Rep., 1885.

(64) E.g., 16th Ann. Rep., 1851.

(65) 38th Ann. Meeting, 5th January, 1874.

(66) The Scottish Guardian, 28th December, 1847, quoted in the 12th Ann. Rep., 1847.

(67) Ibid. At this time cholera was rife in Glasgow. Robert Robinson, the founder of Robinson, Dunn & Co., noted in his diary for 22nd December, 1848: 'In Glasgow, Cholera, 100 cases, 50 deaths.' Robinson, Dunn & Co.'s Archives.

(68) 13th Ann. Rep., 1848.

(69) 17th Ann. Rep., 1852.

(70) See 25th Ann. Rep., 1860; 72nd Ann. Meeting, 24th December, 1907; 75th Ann. Meeting, 20th December, 1910.

(71) 3rd Ann. Rep., 1839. The report added: 'About the same period . . . influences of a political nature were employed to excite distrust in the minds of depositors, but it was gratifying to your Committee to find the good sense of the working classes proof against those attempts.'

(72) Report from the Select Committee on Savings Bank Funds, 1902 (H.C. 282). Malcolm's evidence, Q. 2251-53.

(73) Ibid., Qs. 2343-46.

(74) T. S. Ashton, op. cit., p. 91.

(75) Report of the Annual Meeting of the Investment Trust Ltd., 24th December, 1903.

(76) 72nd Ann. Meeting, 24th December, 1907.

(77) See 73rd Ann. Meeting, 23rd December, 1908; 77th Ann. Meeting, 20th December, 1912; 78th Ann. Meeting, 23rd December, 1913.

(78) 66th Ann. Meeting, 24th December, 1901.

(79) 69th Ann. Meeting, 23rd December, 1904.

(80) This clause had already been used by the trustees of the Savings Banks of Exeter, Dundee and Perth for the investment of funds other than with the National Debt Commissioners. See Horne, *op. cit.*, 221-24.

(81) 35th Ann. Rep., 1870, and see Meikle's evidence before the Select Committee on Trustee Savings Banks, 1889 (H.C. 301), Q. 714.

(82) 53rd Ann. Meeting, 27th December, 1888. In this year over half a million pounds had been invested by the department in mortgages of the Glasgow and Govan School Boards, £432,680, the Corporation of Glasgow, £70,065, and various Parochial Boards, £11,200.

(83) Horne, *op. cit.*, p. 251.

(84) Report from the Select Committee on Trustee Savings Banks, 1889 (H.C. 301), William Meikle's evidence, Qs. 777-821.

(85) 59th Ann. Rep., 1894.

(86) See Report from the Select Committee on Savings Banks Funds, 1902 (H.C. 282), Malcolm's evidence, Qs. 2208-13, 2280, and Horne, *op. cit.*, p. 269.

(87) See Malcolm's evidence, *loc. cit.*, Qs. 2240-53, and T. T. Williams, *The Rate of Discount and the Price of Consols*, Journal of the Royal Statistical Society, Vol. LXXV (New Series), 1911-12, pp. 399-400.

(88) See Henderson, *op. cit.*, p. 32. Asked by the Select Committee of 1902 why the Savings Investment Trust was not immediately wound up following the passing of the Trustee Act for Scotland in 1898, Malcolm was evasive, but he clearly believed that the directors of the Bank were extremely concerned with the effect such a decision would have had on the confidence of the investors. *Loc. cit.*, Q. 2271.

(89) See above, p. 173.

(90) For example, in 1890 the total transactions of the Glasgow Post Office Savings Banks amounted to but £102,705, or barely $3\frac{1}{2}$ per cent of the comparable figure for the ordinary department of the Glasgow Savings Bank. The Post Office figures are given by J. Nicol, The Vital, Social and Economic Statistics of the City of Glasgow, 1881-1885 (Glasgow, 1885), p. 253, and 1885-1891 (Glasgow, 1891), p. 299.

In the late 'nineties the average cost of each transaction by the Glasgow Savings Bank was 4d. or 3s. 8d. per £100 of the funds, as compared with the average expenses of the Post Office Savings Department of $6\frac{1}{2}$d. per transaction, or 9s. per £100 of the funds. Quoted by Meikle, *op. cit.*, p. 16. At this time the Glasgow Trustee Bank held about £7,250,000 compared with the £170,000 held by local Post Office Banks. In the year ending 20th November, 1913, the average cost of each transaction by the Savings Bank of Glasgow was 4d. compared with the averages of 4·9d. for the whole of Scotland, 6·7d. for England and Wales, 1s. 2·1d. for Ireland, and 6·2d. for the United Kingdom as a whole. Trustee Savings Banks—Return of Expenses of Management, etc., 1914 (H.C. 347).

(91) It is perhaps to be regretted that the Trustee Savings Banks were, unlike their American counterparts, the Mutual Savings Banks, precluded from direct industrial investment. See L. E. Davis and P. L. Payne, *From Benevolence to Business: the Story of Two Savings Banks*, Business History Review, XXXII, No. 4 (1958), pp. 400-06.

CHAPTER EIGHT

Organisation and Growth in the East-Coast Herring Fishing 1800-1885

MALCOLM GRAY

Reader in Economic History,
University of Aberdeen

I

IN THE NINETEENTH CENTURY, fishing, an old and important activity in Scotland, grew sufficiently to keep its place within a more diversified and industrialised economy. The fishermen who most successfully adapted to changing conditions were those of the east coast. Each crew continued to engage in several different forms of fishing —for example, for cod and for haddock, the traditional main products—but it was a fishing which had previously existed on the east coast only in restricted and uncertain scale that was to dominate development: that for herring. Decade by decade, the indicators of activity—numbers of boats, value of capital, size of landings—rose. The herring came to dominate the life of the fisherman; and the whole system of activity which was set in motion every year for a few summer weeks came to rank as one of the main industries of the country. By the eighteen-seventies, on the east coast alone, some 30,000 fishermen and about the same number of shore workers would be thus employed. Herring, in addition, were caught on other coasts and at other seasons, often by the same men. But it was the summer fishing which pulled in the greatest number of men and boats and which, for most fishermen, overshadowed everything else in the fishing year. It is to this fishing, as pursued by east-coast fishermen, that the following discussion relates. In organisation it was largely separate from the other systems of equipment, fishing and marketing in which the same men were often engaged, and in this sense may be regarded as a separate industry.

The summer herring fishing, then, ran from about the third week in July till the middle of September and was pursued simultaneously at all active east-coast stations. Nearly all the fish then taken were cured by pickling and by far the greater part was exported. By the late 'seventies, there would annually be cured at the east-coast stations a total which swung between 600,000 and 1,000,000 barrels (each barrel containing about 800 fish, a weight of about 3 cwt.).(1) The activity which resulted in this great volume of produce had grown from the merest fragmentary beginnings in the last decades of the eighteenth century. The social foundations were solid, among the many scattered and old-established communities of 'white' fishers, which fringed the agricultural plain of the east of Scotland, but herring fishing, in 1780, was virtually new to these communities. For a few decades, then, landings grew by attracting the greater attention of men who previously had engaged only on haddock and cod, but even at this early time a new fishing population was brought into being in Caithness (not, before this time, of much account as a fishing region). From about 1820—when the existing fishing communities were already heavily committed to the summer herring fishing—the growth of the herring industry was effected largely by an increase, always within the existing villages and communities, of the total fishing population. No accurate figures can be given for the increase of fishing population up to 1850, but all accounts agree that fishing villages went through a period of particularly rapid growth between 1820 and 1850.(2) Since the whole of the active section of this population was drawn to the herring fishing the numbers engaged in the summer season showed at least a proportionate increase. From 1852 the Fishery Board gave annual figures of the numbers of fishermen and boys in each of the fishery districts. These figures include the non-resident men who were hired to help to work the boats at the peak of the season; but this is an advantage for it makes the figures more accurately representative of the numbers who were seasonally engaged in herring fishing. They show a fairly steady increase from year to year and, as a cumulative result, a 60 per cent increase between 1854 and 1884. Numbers of boats engaged in herring fishing and aggregate amounts cured in the summer season also increased in rough proportion. The number of herring boats in the Fraserburgh district increased by 152 per cent between 1835 and 1879 and by 66 per cent between 1855 and 1879;(3) for the east coast as a whole the number of first-class boats (which was virtually the number of herring boats) grew by 51 per cent between 1855 and 1886.(4) Increases in herring cured at east-coast districts were of the same order of size, about 84 per cent over the longer period, 65 per cent over the shorter.(5)

But the growth of the herring fishing required more than the simple increase of numbers within the existing social organisation. The upward swing of population and the parallel, and apparently easy, increase in the number of boats merely serve to conceal the problems of adjustment, organisation and equipment that lay behind. The fact that the social foundations were so strong and deep created its own problems, and forms of organisation had to be assembled which would fit a social order, which had grown into being around one type of fishing, to the very different technical and market requirements of the new activities. The older order was one of small and scattered groups—whether separate villages or sections of larger towns—at many of which, there being no harbour protection, boats had to be worked from open beaches. The boats—necessarily small because of these working conditions—and the gear were owned, in large measure, by the working crews, each member of which would have some property share; men would receive roughly equal rewards, both for their share in the danger and work and for a contribution to the boat or its equipment. The growth of physical capital depended largely upon the saving of the mass of working fishermen. The increasing grip of herring fishing on this old social order raised awkward new problems of organisation.

Firstly, activity now tended to concentrate and the focus to shift periodically from one region to the other; while the fishing population, though growing considerably in numbers, still continued to be drawn from communities which were scattered all along the coast in a pattern which better fitted the market and natural opportunities of the earlier forms of cod and haddock fishing.(6) It is true that the herring fishing did cast up a new fishing population around its first main centre of activity, in Caithness; but this region never contained more than about a quarter of the total east-coast working force and nearly all the remainder were drawn from the older communities to the south. Successful herring fishing depended very much upon natural features. One of the unshakable principles of the east-coast fishing was that the boats returned to land every morning with the night's catch. Since any herring fishing by drift-nets is designed to attack the moving mass of the shoals, the chances of a fishing depended upon the movement of fish that took these shoals within a few miles of the coast. Thus only where shoals approached fairly close to the shore, and did so year after year, was steady and successful fishing possible. During the nineteenth century, most sectors of the eastern coastline were able, at one time or another, to support such fishing for a number of years. But not all enjoyed the appropriate natural conditions all the time. Activity spread and receded; Caithness from being the dominating centre became one of many, and finally the fishing withdrew from the inner firths, leaving the projecting sectors of Caithness, Aberdeenshire and Berwickshire as the main centres. Thus, many sectors of coast—and among them some with a very dense fishing population—were left without a local herring fishing. Substantial seasonal movement of boats and crews was always necessary if every fisherman were to continue to have his chance at the herring fishing. In the main, this was a movement from south to north—from districts like Fife and the Lothians to the north-east—but complex local migrations also took place, for example from the western to the eastern reaches of the Moray Firth.

Secondly, the necessity of following the shoals was connected with a more gradual, but scarcely less relenting, pressure—the advantage of working at a few main centres rather than from the host of fishing villages in which the fishermen still lived. There was always perceptibly greater advantage for herring fishers in working in large groups than there was for white fishers. Herring fishing depended upon the accumulation of bulky stores and on the direct and speedy shipment of completed barrels of cured herring to the Continent; a harbour which could be entered by vessels drawing 11ft. of water was nearly an essential.(7) Again, where boats had to be unloaded every day it was of great advantage to avoid the laborious hauling of boats across open beaches, and to keep great numbers of fishing boats afloat needed an extensive as well as a reasonably deep harbour. Harbours to meet these needs could best be provided for large numbers of boats at a few centres and the tendency to concentrate on development at a few points was strengthened by legislation regarding harbour finance.(8) In a trade where sales were made throughout the season and where gain and loss might lie in taking advantage in momentary movements of what was a very sensitive and unpredictable market, it was essential to be at the points where the buyers—mainly the agents of German merchant firms—congregated; the advent of the telegraph merely emphasised this necessity. As boats grew larger—the inherent economies of herring fishing made for a larger type of boat than had been used at the beginning of the nineteenth century and the need to go to more distant grounds in the late 'sixties further forced increase in size(9)—so did the advantage of the established centre with an ambitious programme of harbour development lengthen. The tendency to concentrate was partly held back by the inadequacy of provision at even the best of the fishing harbours; some of the boats were forced out to the smaller places even near the end of the

'seventies.(10) But the pattern of landings was always appreciably
more concentrated than that of the communities in which the fishermen lived.(11) To the changing patterns of long-distance moves
were added the steadier seasonal congregation of the men of the
villages in their nearest main centre.

Thirdly, constant change and improvement of the equipment,
range and capacity of each boat was forced by natural changes. Not
only the exact location of the masses of herring but the ease of
operation from the shore and the return to fishing within the shoals
(once they were reached) varied, both capriciously from year to
year and in longer time phases. Until about 1870 they were to be
taken with reasonable regularity on some inshore grounds, with less
long-term certainty on others; but at all times an inshore fishing of
increasing scale and aggregate yield was possible. Yet within the
general boundaries of a slightly shifting inshore fishing the yield to
a given effort was continually diminishing. After 1870 there came
a more dramatic shift, for the inshore grounds were then yielding
so little that the boats were forced to more distant grounds.(12)
The crews managed the change by a sharp stepping up in the size
and comfort of the boats. Their reward was a fairly clear increase in
average takes. The upward step in yield, however, was less than
proportionate to the increase in capital cost.(13) One escape from
these crushing pressures was to improve equipment; another to
pioneer new grounds. The first device implied solid feats of saving
and expensive construction of physical capital; the second, investment in curing facilities and the intricate and accurate adjustment
of fishing capacity to such preparations. A controlling and adventurous mercantile hand could effect much.

Finally, new channels of trade had to be opened to carry off the
increased output. Fresh herring took only a small proportion of
landings and the home sale of pickled herrings tended to diminish
rather than increase with the improvement of internal transport and
with rising standards of living.(14) The traditional export markets
were the West Indies and Ireland and the new fishing and curing
system of the nineteenth century was set going to serve these
markets. But from both there came shocks that would have compelled readjustment even had there been no increase of output to be
sold. Emancipation instantly destroyed the West Indian market;
and the famines, in the immediate event, cut back Irish import and,
in the longer run, started a demographic and structural reshaping
that held the Irish market at a level lower than the pre-famine peak.
Compensation, and more, was found in the markets of Northern
Europe. Export thereto had started before the crises in the older

o

markets, but after 1850 the Continent took a larger and larger proportion of a broadly increasing export. Because of inflexibility and
secular decline in other markets this continental market had to take
nearly all the long-term increment of production and had to adjust
in the short run to changes of supply more than proportionate to the
variations in landings. The expansion of the Continental market
was due to some extent to outside influences; the market had been
left open by the autonomous decline of the Dutch exports (on
which for so long the whole commercial system had been shaped)
and for long after the Scotch cure was dominant, sales continued to
increase without drop of price, because of the independent factors
sustaining and increasing demand.(15) Much of the initial prospecting to bring Scotch herrings to Europe was done by German merchants and for long the German organisation penetrated Scotland
rather than the reverse. Nevertheless, there had to be a reshaping of
the Scottish processing and commercial methods, for the German
market was both different from, and more demanding than, the
traditional markets to the west. The Continent demanded a somewhat different type of cured herring than either the West Indies or
Ireland—tastes were adjusted to the old high-quality Dutch cure—
and was more discriminating and critical in seeing that the particular
quality was reached. Because of the influence of climate and geographical position herring had to be despatched with great speed
after packing. Further, merchants and producers had to adjust to a
market in which price might move suddenly, without warning, and
in unpredictable directions. Price on the Continent was indeed sensitive to a large number of external and changing factors—such as the
size of the Norwegian fishing, the success of the potato and grain
harvests, sometimes interruptions by military or blockade action—
and, most important of all, the course of the Scottish fishing itself
might lead to sharp movements of price.

II

The rising herring fishing depended, much more than the white
fishing which it was partly replacing, on an effective and separate
middleman organisation; and this, in itself, threatened some change
in the status and power of fishermen. But the fishermen remained a
separate, effective, and largely independent body. When the men of
this coast first took up herring fishing they were organised in firm
traditional schemes of ownership and of mode of operation. These
schemes had to be somewhat adjusted to meet the needs of the new

trade; but the organisation and social habits of the fishing villages altered to a surprisingly small extent. And the effectiveness of industrial response was much influenced by traditional features among the still independent body of fishermen.

In the main, the ownership by fishermen of boats and gear—and substantial independence in their use—continued to be a feature of the region. It is true that in parts of the north-east landlords had been accustomed to make some contribution to the purchase of boats and to draw a fixed rent from the crew;(16) but this had never interfered much with freedom of operation and by the 1840's, even where they had played a part, landlords were apparently retiring to leave the fishermen as full owners.(17) There were other threats to the independence conferred by unrestricted ownership of their boats. At one time in the 1840's debt threatened to turn ownership into an empty form, but although in Caithness many of the fishermen continued to be bound down by their obligations to the curers,(18) over most of the coast the threat passed and the fishermen were left substantially independent.(19)

The effective meaning of this independence was modified as time went on. The apparent structure of ownership did not change much. Each boat and its gear was owned by a compact group, composed of fishermen working in the boat—men who would often be close relatives and would in any case all be drawn from a close-knit fishing community, or even from one small concentrated section of such a community. These owning fishermen were aided during the herring fishing by hired men who came from other parts of the country and who were seasonal workers making no contribution to the equipping of the fleet. Thus each full-time fisherman made some contribution to the boat in which he worked; no one outside the boat had any permanent share in its ownership or its proceeds; the whole of the physical capital employed in fishing was owned by the working fishermen themselves; and each boat was worked as a completely separate unit.

The balance of property and of rights within the crew varied somewhat. Sometimes, as in Fife, it would be the custom for the skipper to provide the whole boat, while the remainder of the share fishermen provided nets and gear.(20) But much more commonly two or three sharing members would contribute both to boat and to nets.(21) There were clear traditional traces in these arrangements. It was expected that a man, to share with the rest of the crew, would provide some gear and the general custom was that all members provided equal shares—a custom which seems to have derived from the white fishing, where lines were far less expensive and where in effect all active members were equally rewarded while a smallish extra share went to the owner of the boat. Shares in the boat itself were less equally distributed even where it was common for all crew members to have some holding. The greatly increased expense of acquiring a boat was not accompanied by an increase in the proportion of the takings going to the boat, and the unequal property divisions were not fully reflected in the reward of the different crew members. Such a playing down of the rôle and reward of property had, of course, important implications for the incentives to building up the value of the fleet. The fishermen of the villages were thus placed in the position of making, all of them, some contribution to the purchase or equipment of the boat and of consequently drawing nearly equal shares in its proceeds. The coherence of the crew group as a permanent association of people working together and providing substantially, if not quite equally, to the equipment of a boat, was emphasised by the close blood relationships that often pertained between the members, by the fact that young lads taken on would be sons of the other fishermen(22) and by the initiation rites that sometimes symbolised entry into the fellowship.(23) How decisions would be taken within such a group is impossible to determine, but one man, the skipper, who might or might not have more property than the others, would have command at sea and would enter into engagements for the crew as a whole.

The wide dispersal of settlements and the fragmentation of ownership—the herring fleet was composed of upwards of 4,000 boats, each separately owned and most owned by two or three partners—were bound to render more difficult the tasks of capital provision and of effective operation. In fact the operations of the host of individual boats were brought into a more ordered design by the controlling hand of the curers. The instrument by which fleets were assembled and sometimes rearranged was the engagement.(24) On all stations north of Fife(25) most crews worked for the period of the herring fishing under engagement to a particular curer. This was based on a bargain made some time before the beginning of the season and it did not normally commit the crew beyond the season immediately in view. By such an agreement the crew had to fish from a particular station and to pass all the herring caught—up to a limit of 200 or 250 crans—to the one curer, being paid for each cran at a price agreed before the beginning of the season. If the limit of 200 crans (or 250 as the case might be) was not reached within a strictly defined period the agreement was then null, but if it was passed before the end of the season the crew was then free to negotiate a new price or to fish for an open market. This system had important implications for the manner in which curers carried on their business; it also, for the moment, limited the crew's freedom of action. Before engagements were fixed, the market—except for crews who were in debt—was largely an open one. Crews were free to choose between offers of different curers and at different stations. In practical terms the fisherman was faced with a range of possibilities, of fishing at various stations, often at rates which differed somewhat from one station to the other;(26) the extent and nature of this choice was determined by the initiative and valuations of curers seeking to engage crews. In entering an engagement with a particular curer the crew operated as an entirely free bargaining unit, with a flexibility and power determined by the number and eagerness of the curers seeking boats; in fact competition between curers to get boats was a normal feature of nearly all active stations.(27) A crew, unless bound for some particular reason, had a considerable range of choice in deciding where to fish; and each year might fish at a different station and for a different curer. A limitation on freedom of bargaining arose when a crew was in debt to a curer; they would then have to fish for their creditor until the debt was extinguished, in any case at a reduced rate compared with what might be obtained by the 'free' crews, and sometimes on 'general terms', that is at rates which would only be settled at the end of the season.(28)

III

The network of technical and market arrangements gave the middleman an expanding rôle in the herring industry as compared with earlier forms of fishing. The very fragmentation of control among the fishing host made the task of assembly and the articulation of operations more crucial and delicate; and the fishermen, still formally independent, was brought into an intricate system dominated by middlemen. The processing of the fish demanded the speculative gathering of expensive stores; if much of the capital for purchase of these stores and for payment of labour during the period of production came from outside lenders the existence of a known and credit-worthy body of specialist intermediaries was nonetheless essential. The selling of the fish demanded a close and knowledgeable attention to a market which was always in movement and which demanded quick disposal of cured fish. And the risks of the trade were such that some reserve of capital—even if it was only a reserve created by the goodwill of the banks—was needful to keep going for any period. The trade, then, thrust up its own new body of intermediaries—the curers: men who arranged the physical processing of the fish, who acted as the middlemen, standing between the steady price offered to fishermen and the day-to-day fluctuations of the market for cured herring, and who received short-term loans from outside the industry and to some extent transmitted them to fishermen for the equipment of the fleet. Fishermen, then, were in manifold dependence on curers; any dislocation or inefficiency in the curing section meant a breakdown of the immediate market of the fishermen and a stop to funds he might need for boats or nets. The manner in which curers operated was a matter of wide and keen interest.

The curers, then, formed the remaining section of the industry. They took possession of all the herring landed during the summer season and prepared most of it, by pickling, for further sale. Essentially the process of pickling was very simple. Immediately on landing—and not more than twenty-four hours after capture—the herring, after being lightly salted ('roused'), were gutted and sorted into three or four recognised grades; they were then packed in barrels of standard size and make, being laid tightly in layers, each of which was separated from the next by a controlled admixture of salt. After filling, the barrels were left open and upright for about two days, when the fish would have settled to leave an empty space in the barrel; this was filled with more fish, the barrels were closed and laid on their side, and after ten or twelve days the surplus pickle was run off (and the barrels topped up with fresh salt). They were now ready for despatch and generally would be speedily cleared from the yard (so that, in fact, many barrels would be on board ship for Germany within three weeks of being caught). To perform all these operations of gutting, packing and repacking girls were arranged in teams of three, each team being responsible for the whole sequence from the initial gutting. (Thus it came that each finished barrel was known as the separate work of a particular team.)(29)

The physical tasks of preparing and packing the fish were rudimentary, carried through on a simple plan of work, with little equipment and often in very small establishments. But for the curer, this work, concentrated in the fishing season, was merely the crown of the year; he was engaged in a year-long process of preparation and assessment. In his business, in fact, two types of task were articulated. For the greater part of the year the yard would be occupied only by coopers preparing the barrels for the coming season (and occasionally by labourers laying in the stores of salt that would be used). Then, during the active season a number of teams of gutters would be engaged, being specifically attached to one yard for the whole season, even though for most of the days there would be less than a full day's work to be done. The minimum size of business, then, was that which would keep a single cooper fully employed, for about nine months in the year, in preparing barrels. (During the season the cooper became a foreman supervising the girls.) This meant that about three or four teams of girls would have to be employed, a minimum of ten to fourteen labourers during the busy season. There were, however, certain advantages in going to larger size and most yards were substantially above this minimum. Whatever the size, the operations were sufficiently reduced to routine to make little call on managerial skills, although there were problems of judgement about how much salt and of what quality should be added, and some industrial discipline was necessary to ensure that, for example, the sorting was accurately done.

This simple sequence of activity was encompassed with great risks, which basically derived from an inevitable condition of the trade—the wide variations in scale of landings from day to day and from season to season. Large daily fluctuations meant either that capacity would be only partially used for most of the time, or that the heaviest landings would be beyond the capacity of the engaged labour force to pack in the short time allowed. More serious, however, was the danger that stores might be purchased which would not be used in the course of the season (and if borrowed money had been used for the purchase of the stores and payment of wages, it would prove difficult to find the funds for repayment). Or, if the season's landings turned out greater than expected, barrels and salt might have to be purchased at famine prices to deal with the herring (which, by the terms of his arrangements with the crews, the curer had to accept till the boats had fished their quota). But these risks were not likely to bring down a business. More lethal were the effects of price-fall. It was a heavy Scottish fishing that was most likely to bring down prices in Germany—in fact there is a definite inverse relation between prices and landings for the season—and curers dreaded a heavy fishing more than they did a short one.(30) The difficulty of accepting the shocks administered, either directly or through market effect, by varying landings was made greater by two special features of the Scottish curing trade. In the first place curers were committed to pay a fixed price for all fish landed from a given number of boats. Since these prices were often driven up to allow only a margin narrow even on a fairly optimistic view of prices, the slight downturn took all the profit out of curing. And the curer had no power of retraction or adjustment: he had to continue to accept fish—and pay for them at the stipulated price—even when it was clear that he was losing on every barrel cured. It was a trade, then, highly vulnerable to even small downward movements of price if they occurred after the engagements for the season had been made.(31) Secondly, much of the preparation for the season was carried out on money borrowed at short term. Repayment of these debts, which were contracted when both physical and financial results of a season were unknown, depended upon the autumn receipts from the sale of herring. The proceeds of such sales might well be far below the amount expended—and borrowed—on stores and labour and the amount due to fishermen and gutters for the season's operations.

The trade, then, had an unstable appearance. But it also had considerable resilience. The resilience stemmed from the fact that only small capitals were required to set up business, that no form of special skill seemed to be required and that there developed a strong social tradition in the fishing towns of people of varying background and occupation engaging in curing as a speculation; perhaps the high rate of failures and withdrawals that persisted year after year was partly due to the same reason. There was, however, one special source from which curers were drawn—the coopers who were brought up as wage-earners in the trade but who might well use their savings and skill to enter independent business. Indeed, in spite of the presence always of men from backgrounds and occupations quite unconnected with fishing, there becomes evident occasionally an underlying feeling that the only 'true' curers were those brought up as coopers.(32)

Comparatively little fixed capital was needed for curing.(33) The minimum equipment consisted of a broad rectangular trough—the 'farlin'—into which the herring were disgorged from the cart, and a number of tubs into which the herring were thrown after being gutted, in order to be carried to the empty barrels for the first packing. With such simple equipment, on an open space—which might well be hired for the season—curing of a sort could be carried out; but the curer, unless he was content to use purchased barrels and stores brought in precariously from day to day, would need a cooperage, a set of tools for each cooper, a salt store and preferably a barrel store. This was probably the commonest arrangement through the middle decades of the century—curing was done on an open and unprotected space with perhaps some temporary awnings to protect the gutters, but more permanent buildings, or sheds, would fringe the open yard. Yards, it is true, were becoming somewhat more elaborate in the last decades of the century. Permanent cover would be provided over the farlins, which would be arranged opposite a series of apertures in a continuous wall-face. An open-sided shed would be erected, too, for the packers and living accommodation would be provided for the gutters (who were normally girls from a distance). When it came to a curing at one of the out-stations of the West Coast or of the Shetlands a curer would build for himself a jetty within the natural anchorages from which such fishings were normally conducted and living accommodation would have to be run up for coopers as well as girls. A jetty cost about £200 but the increased cost in these respects was partly balanced by the fact that fairly flimsy wooden buildings were used. In any case, it was everywhere buildings rather than mechanical equipment that made expense and provision of fixed capital was a comparatively small part of the business problems of the aspiring curer.

Circulating capital posed a more serious problem. Much of the work for a season had to be done, if not paid for, before there was any return from the produce of the season; filled barrels did not begin to be shipped until the middle of August and before then many of the expenses of the season's working had been incurred; salt for the whole season would be in store, barrels would have been constructed up to the estimated need, fishermen would have received bounty money, and gutters would have been paid 'arles' on engagement. This was the gap that had to be filled—between the considerable pre-seasonal expenses and the receipts from the sale of barrels. About one quarter of the expense was incurred before the start of the season, but of course, the number of barrels produced, and therefore sold, might not nearly match the scale of these preparations; curers therefore needed, on this account alone, to have access to short-term capital probably averaging more than one quarter of the value of the barrels which they in fact sold. The remaining expenses—notably the payment to gutters, which was strictly a piece-rate, and the settlement with fishermen—waited until the end of the season when already some cash would be in hand from the sale of the barrels. The gap might be partly bridged by credit devices. Suppliers of salt and of timber might wait for payment. More important, however, were the advances made by the German merchants.(34) These advances were made against cured herring sold 'in blank', that is, a curer would undertake to sell at a prearranged price to a merchant a certain number of barrels from each boat he had engaged and would receive a proportion of that price immediately the contract was agreed (which might be some weeks before the beginning of the season). But in the end, the most important source of short-term credit was to be the banks. After about 1870 these—and particularly the North of Scotland Bank— became very free in their policy of supporting curers. Credits were granted not against goods already in existence but to meet the working expenses of a still hypothetical catch.(35) Moreover, they seem to have exercised little care about the business quality of the borrowers. It became possible for men, literally without capital at all, to set up as curers and there was little limit to the extension of business provided a man was willing to take a risk with the bank's money.(36)

Such ease in setting up business was not all gain, for it brought forward men without experience and sometimes without an understanding of ordinary commercial and accounting technique. Few of them, for example, kept any books beyond a day-book for the count of barrels.(37) The attraction of the trade lay not merely in the fact that a man of small capital might aspire to an independent business but also that the wide fluctuation of profits stimulated the gambling interest; there was always the chance of large profit on a very tiny capital. Inexperienced men of a gambling bent seemed rather a dangerous acquisition for a trade in which the risks were in any case unavoidably high. To some extent the lack of experience or even of judgement was softened by the routine nature of some of the decisions. There were some conventionally accepted rules of thumb to guide the proper preparation for a season's work. One team of girls, for example, would be engaged for every boat on a curer's list and the assembly of stores and barrels could be guided by taking the average results of past seasons. Further, the intricate business of selling was often done by the bank on behalf of the curer who in effect became an agent in charge of the processing side of the business.(38) But there remained a wide and important area in which prudence could keep a business going in face of the inevitable shocks; the quality and judgement of the men were important in determining how many would survive the time of stress. There were no rules to decide, for example, how far a man should go in engaging boats; he might engage large numbers with borrowed money—which would give a large profit if prices ran well but would mean disaster if they fell at the wrong moment. And to get boats he might so drive up the price to be paid to fishermen that a slight trembling of price would mean loss on each barrel. And in selling the completed barrels commercial shrewdness was needed and again might be a deciding factor. The quality of the men entering the trade did help to determine how far the industry would be racked by a constant succession of individual failures.

IV

The results of these factors was to shape a trade in which there was always, even in the smaller centres, an adequate number of competing units, although some of them were small and ephemeral. Every centre from which the boats operated would have its body of curers and the main centres would generally have fifty or more of them. It is difficult, however, to say how many firms were operating along the east coast. Many would have branches in several centres and to add together the numbers given for the different centres would involve a good deal of double-counting. Perhaps the total thus obtained should be reduced by about a third. If so, in 1859, there were nearly 400 curers in the business along the east coast.(39) It is certain that the influx to the trade and the ease with which capital could be raised normally created a market in which rates offered to fishermen were highly sensitive to the prices that existed in the Continental markets.(40) For the tentacles of the engagement system spread into every small village and every crew, however remote might be their place of residence from the seat of fishing, would have the advantage of curers competing for their services.

The structure and composition of the curing section can be followed in some detail in a particular district—that of Fraserburgh. The records derive from the regulation that anyone intending to cure herring had to give notice before the season to the Fishery Officer and had later to render a periodic account of the number of barrels cured.(41) There is no reason to suppose there to be serious gaps in these figures. The Fishery Officer was a practical man, who lived in his district and who could easily oversee the two or three places where curing was taking place; he would know, even without the returns, the number of curing ventures afoot in what were, even the largest of them, small and concentrated communities. Further, most curers would ask him to inspect some of their barrels in order to qualify for the official brand. And, there being no question of tax or, after 1829, of subsidy, no motive for falsification existed. The record, then, is continuous, complete and accurate.

At all times there was a considerable number of firms in the district, but more at the beginning of the century than at any time thereafter. The emergence of the district as a herring centre evidently threw up a host of curing firms, none of them large, most of them tiny, although some were evidently branches of larger firms in the south. The growth of the industry was accompanied by concentration. In 1830 there were 60 curers at work producing an average of 823 barrels.(42) The typical firm in that year produced between 500 and 1,000 barrels. (This would represent the output of four to eight boats and a labour force at the peak of the season of between fifteen and thirty.) Forty per cent of firms were in this range of size and only 6 per cent had an output of over 2,000 barrels, or employed more than sixty people, even for the two months of the summer season. By 1850 there had been a considerable concentration; forty-four firms accounted for a larger output and averaged 1,276 barrels. This rise in the average was mainly due to the overwhelming growth of a handful of firms. In fact the two firms which produced each more than 5,000 barrels—neither of them more than 10,000—accounted for 28 per cent of the total cure. On the other hand 69 per cent of establishments were each producing less than 1,000 barrels, and the proportion of firms producing less than 500 had even grown; but the typical firm could still be said to produce between 500 and 1,000 barrels, 39 per cent being in this group. Even in terms of output 35 per cent still came from such small firms. By 1870 there were still fewer firms but output had increased once more by a substantial amount. Average output had gone up to 3,603 barrels. This increase had come about by new entrants to the trade going quickly to a more considerable level of size than in the past; firms at all stages in the scale of age were larger than they had been. And a simple size distribution shows that the typical as well as the average firm was now a good deal larger. Whereas in 1850, 69 per cent of firms produced each less than 1,000 barrels, in 1870 only 19 per cent were in this lowest grade and 59 per cent produced each more than 2,000 barrels. By 1880 the tendency to reduction in the number of firms had halted; there were still forty-one firms in existence. But the increase of total output led to further increase in the business done by the average firm.

At least in the latter part of the period, then, the increasing size of firms—which is not fully measured by these figures, for more and more of them were doing substantial business on the West Coast and Shetland out-stations—is due more to the ease with which businesses could be built up than to the continuing increase of the older firms (although this does take place). It was, in fact, founded on the easy credit policy of the banks; on a movement of prices that allowed profits for ploughing back; and on an increase in physical yields that carried firms with a given number of boats under their control automatically to greater scale of operation. Thus the trade retains its character of containing many units which were just breaking into business. In 1870, 59 per cent of firms were less than ten years old, very much the same proportion as twenty years before, while the proportion of very young firms—of less than five years—had slightly increased in the twenty years. In output, the new, or newish, firms had a hold slightly less than proportionate to their numbers. In 1850, just 49 per cent of output came from firms less than ten years old, and in 1870, 45 per cent. Resilience, the fact that constantly new firms were emerging, plays an important part, then, in the working of the industry; the influence of young firms was much greater than the influence of the unstable (those which eventually were to have a short life). The personality and character of such firms makes an important imprint.

Resilience was accompanied by another feature which seemed to carry more danger for the trade—instability; the new firms that were constantly appearing on the lists were more than matched by the names which disappeared. In fact a very large number of people were in the business in the period of study and the business life of many firms was very short. Altogether over the sixty-year period there are 369 different business units, individuals or partnerships, on the lists. Equally evident is the great proportion of these firms that had only a short business existence. Thus, 244 out of 369 lasted for less than five years. (Sporadic appearances of particular names even at longish intervals of time are added together to give the total business life of the particular unit.) On the other hand, a handful of firms had a very long life, including one which lasted over sixty years. (One confusion is that certain firm names are carried on from generation to generation while in other cases the death of an individual leads to the natural succession of a son in what is really the same firm, but is now under a different name and therefore counted separately. Elimination of this inaccuracy would probably lengthen the real lives of some of the firms of medium and long durability but would not probably much alter the indicated length of life of the very ephemeral firms: in only a small proportion of cases would the shortness of life of such firms be due to death of the individual.)

The balance of importance as between short-lived and long-lived firms is not at all accurately indicated by these figures. Durable firms by definition continue in production for a larger number of years and on that account alone will bulk larger in the production record than their simple numbers imply. Again, the long-lived firms tended on the whole to be larger than the short-lived, although the relationship between the two groups is a somewhat changing one. Thus, in 1850, firms with a durability of over thirty years (durability being taken to include prospective life as well as age in that year) had an average output of 2,457 barrels, while the average of all firms was 1,276 barrels. There was also a fairly steady graduation in size of firm with the steps in the scale of length of life. In 1870 the same graduation was to be seen. Thus a disproportionate output came from the long-lived firms. In 1850 48 per cent of barrels cured came from the firms which were to have a life of over thirty years; by 1870 the proportion coming from this group had diminished to 34 per cent, but 54 per cent was accounted for by firms which lasted for more than 20 years. Thus, nearly half the fishermen would be engaged by solid and durable curing firms. On the other hand at the earlier date, 10 per cent of output, and at the later 7 per cent, came from firms which survived less than five years; and respectively 18 per cent and 14 per cent from firms which were to last less than ten years. The great bulk of the fishermen in other words, were dealing with curers whose record ultimately proved them to be fairly stable. Since so much of the business continued to be done by firms with a high capacity to survive, the influence of instability on the industry as a whole was fairly small.

V

Herring fishing grew and was shaped in a developing pattern of bargains between curers and fishermen; rates paid, numbers assembled at each station, the price at which cured herring was sold—these indicators and determinants were in constant intricate change. And on them depended the success with which the fishing was pursued, the numbers who gained a livelihood from it, the division of proceeds between the main sections. On the one side were the curers, a group constantly changing in composition but generally confident; on the other the fishermen, scattered through their villages, always willing to engage in the great gamble of the herring fishing however bad times might seem, but dependent on finding engagement with curers. The terms of the exact solution of these problems varied from year to year but certain outlines and continuing trends are evident.

Firstly, the curing section escaped any great disaster—in spite of frequent warnings that disaster was coming—until the collapse of 1884.(43) In a trade where fluctuations of price and of quantity were so great and where the curer was incapable of retrieving action once the season started the narrowing of margins seemed indeed highly dangerous; but serious failures were avoided for two reasons. In the first place, the movement of prices was normally upwards, by short steps, the downward swoops being greater but less frequent. This meant that in most years curers enjoyed some profit; losses in some years may have been severe but they were short-lived. Such losses would have been serious enough had it not been for a second feature. Banks showed themselves willing to carry over short-term debts and even to extend credit when debts were still outstanding.(44) They were indeed working to the assumption, justified till 1884, that the trade had merely to be supported for one, or at most two, years, before it would right itself, profits re-emerge and debts melt. The favourable price environment and the holding operation of the Banks protected the trade from any wave of failures in the long up-swing from the mid-'fifties till the mid-'eighties; and any gaps in the ranks were speedily filled by the press of new men (who also were helped by the easy credit conditions). Active and optimistic competition between curers to secure the services of boats was the normal condition.

Secondly, as a consequence, at least from the middle of the century onwards, curers or their agents went actively through the villages, seeking crews wherever they were to be found.(45) Thus, fishermen in the remotest creeks were brought into the main activity at the centre; virtually the whole of an increasing fishing population was sucked into the summer herring fishing. There were many small creeks, some of them far from any centre of herring activity, in which large boats would be kept drawn up on the beach for the greater part of the year, never operated at home, but always fitted out for herring fishing at a distant centre. They would receive a bounty for fitting out and would be certain of a given price for their catch even at a new and unknown centre. Some security was given for the seasonal migration, and curing capacity could be kept in line with the gathering throng of boats wherever it might move.

Thirdly, the intensity of competition among curers served to keep rates paid to fishermen highly sensitive to the price of cured fish.(46) This had its disadvantages to the fishermen: the downward marking of engagement rates on a fall, or anticipated fall, in the market was just as quick as the rise when the market seemed to improve. There was one period, in the late 'forties, when rates fell very low indeed. But rates were kept at levels which, on the normal expectations of a season, allowed no very great margin to curers. And when the long price-rise began in the mid-'fifties the rates paid to fishermen moved nearer to the price of cured fish. By the 'seventies, fishermen were taking a larger proportion of the price of the finished barrel than they had done in the first half of the century and rates were at least three times as high as they had been in the 'forties.(47)

On the whole, then, fishermen's incomes rose more than proportionately to price.

Lastly, the initiative of curers kept the quest for new grounds and stations going continuously. The geographical sweep of the industry was wide and the retreat from stations where the yield was flagging was carried through in good order without detriment to the fishermen of the particular area. Thus, activity at first swept southwards from place to place along the east coast from the activating centre in Caithness; by 1840, nearly every part of the coast had its seasonal herring fishing, with the exception of a patch immediately to the north of Aberdeen and southwards as far as Fife.(48) In the 'forties the early summer fishing of the west coast was first tried and in the 'sixties this was extended from the original centre in Lewis southwards to Barra. In 1861 Montrose emerged as a fishing centre(49) and in 1871, Aberdeen.(50) In 1865 the autumn move was begun to East Anglia.(51) Finally, in 1882, the east-coast herring fleet surged to the Shetland waters where, for a few years, the greatest takes of the nineteenth century were recorded.(52) Many of these fishings were in distant waters and some were additional to the home fishing in the summer months. But all were largely organised by east-coast curers and carried on by east-coast crews;(53) the herring were mainly prepared in the now traditional east-coast manner; and the problems of equipment and finance both for curers and for fishermen had to be considered in the context of more extended operations at a multiplicity of stations rather than as merely a two-months' effort in the summer.

VI

The interweaving problems of curer and fisherman did not end with the assembly and movement from place to place of a secure market framework. There was a constantly pressing need for technical adaptation and improvement. Partly this involved joint financial contribution by both fishermen and curers; but the system of ownership imposed the task of technical thinking and action largely on the fishermen.

For the greater part of the nineteenth century the herring fisherman had to struggle to master natural conditions of increasing difficulty; the shoals were becoming more elusive, more distant and less dense. Survival in the industry, let alone increased income, could only come by greater efficiency. The manoeuvres to escape from these limits were conducted within fairly narrow limits. On the fundamental points of method there was no change between the first emergence of the system in Caithness and the adoption of steam for propulsion just before 1900; herring continued to be caught in drift-nets, shot at night, from wooden-built sailing (or rowing) boats, and to be daily carried back for curing on shore. Yet the boats and the gear of the 1880's were very different from those of the 1800's. The changes came about by a long series of piecemeal changes. The decisions that carried on this change were made by the small groups of working fishermen, each responsible for its own boat and gear.

The central technical point concerned the area of nets that could be set, relatively to each man in the crew; and this in turn depended partly on the size of boat which a crew of given size could purchase or manage. A small boat was limited in the nets that could be carried because of their sheer bulk and because more fish might be captured than could be carried along with them. Another important point of technique was the range of the boats in making a daily trip to the fishing grounds. Larger boats had a greater turn of speed and therefore could reach more distant grounds within the given time-limits (although larger boats brought the disadvantage that they could not be rowed home in a flat calm). The readjustment of these variables never reached a final stop and for most of the century both the size of boat and the area of nets to be worked by a crew of given size were being forced up. It was, indeed, fairly evident from the early years of herring fishing that the boats—which in fact had been taken over from the different conditions of the white fishing—were too small for fullest efficiency. But the movement to a fishing unit which would be more effective in any conditions was slow, although sustained and, in the end, of decisive effect.

For long it was an article of faith with the Scottish fishermen that the open boat was a more economic, a more manageable and even a safer instrument of fishing than the various forms of decked boat that were suggested to him.(54) Thus he clung firmly to gradually enlarged versions of the traditional boats of the coast (sticking, for example, to local varieties of rig and hull shape). It was not lack of harbour space or lack of money that kept this traditional type in being, but the conviction of the fishermen. Still, there came slow enlargement of boats, in a traditional, but still open, design. On one station, for example, the size of the typical first-rate boat advanced in steps: 30 ft. keel in 1832; 35 ft. in 1848; 40 ft. in 1875; 45 ft. in 1879; 48 ft. in 1883.(55) Till 1860 the standard complement of nets was also being slowly increased. The pace of this adoption of larger boats and more extensive nets may have been partly controlled by

P

lack of funds. But it was also in part forced by the deterioration of yields which was constantly making some increase in net area—involving, of course, an accompanying increase in the size of boat—a necessity even of survival. The slow process of adding to physical capital, the autonomous revision of attitudes and the force of a worsening natural environment slowly pressed up the standard.

In the early 'sixties technical calculations were altered by a new factor—the machine-made cotton net. The superiority of the cotton over the hempen net was that, yard for yard, it weighed not more than half as much(56)—and consequently that on a boat of given capacity nets up to three times as extensive could be carried. The advantages of the new type of train were speedily and even eagerly, realised and in the mid-'sixties there followed a sharp stepping up in the effective area of nets carried by each boat. In the Fraserburgh district, for example, the average area of nets carried by each herring boat doubled between 1855 and 1870 and increased by another quarter between 1870 and 1875.(57) Such a change represented considerable investment, for the new nets were no cheaper, yard for yard, than had been the old; the cost of equipment increased in proportion to the size of the train. The rapid acceptance of the new material, then, seems to indicate that the old standard had not been held down by lack of funds; when the technical jump became possible the funds were forthcoming.

An even bigger step was to come in the early 'seventies—the change to decked boats, a change accompanied by continuing increase in the length of the boat. Again the switch was rapid and in less than ten years a fleet consisting of open boats, at the best of slightly over 40 ft. keel, was transformed to one in which nearly all boats were decked and the largest were being made up to 55 ft. keel.(58) Thus rapidly the fishermen gave up their most strongly held prejudice—the belief in the superiority of open boats. Yet they were not necessarily wrong in their first estimate; they had made a strong case for the open boat as the best instrument of inshore fishing. The revised valuations of the 'seventies may have been due as much to the necessity of fishing at a greater offing because the shoals had deserted the inshore grounds, as to a belated and independent change of mind. The change and accompanying continuous increase in the size of boats was hastened by the large catches returned by the first boats to reach the distant grounds;(59) for a number of years the profits both of curers and of fishermen were high and the funds were generated for rapid re-equipment (a continuing process as boats were being made ever larger). Yet since the large catches came from the use of large decked boats on the distant grounds the innovation can scarcely have been started by funds generated by good catches.

These were all decisions made and effected by fishermen in their capacity as independent business men. On the whole the record of change is not unimpressive. There was no long period of stagnation and at each stage, while the fleet from a retrospective view might seem to be composed of small and ill-equipped boats, the fishermen were able to put up a reasoned case for the boats they preferred. And when there were manifest reasons for change—and the means of raising the funds—the response was rapid and thorough. Certainly at the end the fishermen emerged as the owners and independent users of a fleet more numerous and far more powerful than that with which they had commenced the herring fishing eighty years before.

Most of the improvements of fishing method involved much addition to, or elaboration of, physical capital. Indeed a substantial rate of addition to physical capital was a minimum condition even of sustaining yields per head at a given level; growth of output demanded correspondingly greater additions—an increase either in the number of fishing units or in the effectiveness of each.

In the first place the number of boats was almost continuously on the increase, probably at all stations. A series is available for the Fraserburgh district from 1830 onwards.(60) The number of herring boats in the district increased in every year up to 1846; from then, numbers remained steady till the mid-'fifties. From 1855, the increase was resumed, to continue with an addition in every year to 1878, except for a decrease continued over two years between 1858 and 1860, and a relapse for one year between 1870 and 1871. At Eyemouth the numbers of first-rate boats increased from 1859 to 1868 and then slowly began to decline,(61) but at Buckie from 1855 till 1878 the increase was almost continuous except for two dips, one between 1859 and 1861, and the other between 1872 and 1873.(62) These boats, we have seen, were increasing in size as well as in numbers. And the addition to dimensions is itself an inadequate measure of the added expense and therefore the real effort of investment. Decked boats, for example, were far more expensive than open boats of equivalent size; it was not merely a matter of covering in an existing type of hull, but also of strengthening design and adding elaborate furnishings and equipment—bunks, a cabin, a winch. Thus, while at the beginning of the century a first-class boat would cost about £30,(63) by 1842 the cost had increased to about £60,(64) by 1865 to over £100,(65) by 1872 to about £200,(66) and by the early 'eighties to over £300.(67) Not only was the cost of new boats up to the best standards of the day continuously and substantially on the increase but also there was acceleration in the rate at which boats were scrapped—or sold second-hand—and replaced by new ones. In effect, the life of a boat was diminishing and gross annual investment was substantially greater than is indicated by the increase in the value of the capital stock. The boat's complement of nets, too, was on the increase, particularly in the 'sixties; the expense of nets increased almost exactly in proportion to the increase of area. The cost of nets, it is true, came to account for a diminishing proportion of the whole expense of fitting-out; but in absolute terms the increase was still considerable. Once a herring boat could be built and equipped for not much more than £50; by 1880 a boat with nets would cost over £500.

The effects of these changing standards are seen in the recorded total value of boats and gear: and in the increase in value relatively to numbers engaged on the boats. The first increase was more substantial than the second, but neither was small. Thus, for the east of Scotland as a whole, the value of boats and gear doubled between 1852 and 1866, and trebled between 1852 and 1878; altogether between 1852 and 1882 total value had multiplied fourfold.(68) On all the main stations—except Wick where there was a decline in numbers of fishermen in this period—value of equipment more than trebled in this 30-year period. Value of fishing capital, relative to numbers of owner-fishermen, might increase almost as much. Thus, at Fraserburgh, where the comparison can be made accurately, value of boats and gear, relative to each resident fisherman—this is, the body of people who owned the boats—increased nearly fourfold between 1855 and 1878.(69)

This stock of capital, growing in physical content and in value, was kept firmly in the hands of the general body of fishermen. In the final analysis then, it had to be financed by a general habit of saving diffused all through the fishing population. On the incomes normally earned by fishermen the burden of replacing and building up a fleet at the rates which were being achieved in the second half of the century would seem to be very heavy. The annual charge for maintaining the existing complement of capital unchanged was quite heavy because, apart from the possibility of induced obsolescence, boats had a fairly short physical life—certainly not more than ten years—and nets lasted for an even shorter period. The difficulty of this task of providing sufficient funds to maintain independence clearly changed much in the course of the nineteenth century. Before 1850, the rate of addition to capital, the value of existing equipment to be replaced, and fishermen's incomes, were all low;

and herring boats were used as such only for a small part of the year. A new boat with nets would cost about £135(70) and the crew would have to set by about £13 for depreciation: say £4 for each sharing member. This would come out of gross returns averaging less than £75 and individual incomes—from herring fishing—of less than £25. From about 1855—after a depression in which there was some disinvestment—fairly steep accumulation began and the value of a boat and its nets was carried to levels at which mere replacement of the existing stock became onerous; but at the same time the gross takings of the boats and the incomes of fishermen had substantially increased. By the 1870's it would probably take about £50 per annum to maintain the existing equipment and further additions were accruing at a rate of over 10 per cent per annum. But the takings of the summer fishing would now average about £200(71) and as much again might be added by herring fishings elsewhere—individual income from herring fishing would now be over £100, out of which savings of up to £20 would have to be made. But the problem is much complicated by the great inequality of takings as between different boats; the successful boats would take three or four times as much as the unsuccessful and the majority of the boats seem to have taken less than the average haul —some much less.(72) Moreover, the boats continued in the same ranking order year after year; luck did not even out the inequalities created by differences of skill. The takings of the more successful boats were not spread out to help the less successful; the difficulties weighing on probably the majority of crews were much heavier than the average figures suggest.

Fishermen, of course, did not act in isolation. The structure and daily working of the industry gave them contact with at least one outside source of finance. Curers, in fact, were called upon to help with the large payments for new boats, and nets might be purchased by use of the bounties that were given on engagement for the fishing season.(73) The borrowing of money—although it did not give the curer a direct share in the boat—carried with it certain severe restrictions on the bargaining power of the crew. They were bound to the creditor-curers for the duration of the loan; in this time they could not choose their fishing station and settlement was made at a lower rate than could be obtained by open bargaining.(74) Thus to be effectively independent for a large portion of the time fishermen had speedily to liquidate their debts. The use of advances from curers scarcely postponed and could not diminish the need for large savings from the fishermen to maintain their position. Little long-term help came from outside the industry. The only contact with a wider financial world was through the curers. They, of course, were often heavily in debt but almost entirely on account of short-term loans from banks or German merchants. Short-term help did release some of their own savings for aid to fishermen in acquiring their equipment, but on the whole the funds for investment had to be generated within one or other of the two sections of the industry.

The size of the funds available for investment in the industry depended upon the combined effect of varying levels of physical yield—to given amounts of equipment and effort—and of shifts in price of cured herring. The relationship between these two factors was a constantly changing and always complicated one, but at most times there was some rescuing feature which left just enough prosperity for the industry to hold its labour force and provide for adequate equipment. The independence of the fishermen and the retention of the traditional system of ownership depended in its turn not only on willingness by individual fishermen to save but also on a distribution of total proceeds of sale at least tolerably favourable to fishermen. In the earliest period, from 1780 till about 1815 prices were high and yields, even to small and ill-equipped boats, fairly good. It seems to have been the curers who most benefited from this conjunction, for rates paid to fishermen were low, whether considered as a proportion of the price of the finished product or compared with the rates that were to rule after 1850. Fishermen, probably, were able to maintain an independent position only because the necessary costs of acquiring and running a boat were low. In the next period, from 1815 till the early 'fifties, prices fell and remained low, and yields began to fall away. Curers' profits must have fallen drastically for the rates paid to fishermen were not reduced proportionately to prices. Even so, at the end, when prices were at their lowest in the late 'forties, perhaps a majority of fishermen were unable to make the full necessary contribution which would give them a place in an independent crew. The industry was rescued by a price-rise which began in the early 'fifties and lasted as an underlying trend till the 'eighties. At the same time the fact that rates paid to fishermen were driven hard up against the rising price of cured herring gave them the financial power fully to recover their independence. Finally, after 1870, rising yields, added to rising or steady prices, enabled fishermen to meet steeply increasing costs of equipment without increase of debt.

The industry was thus able to continue to offer a traditional independence for its members and to achieve a fairly good rate of technical improvement partly because of the continuing attitudes of fishermen; they were willing to devote much of their income to the improvement of boats. But also the complex of social and financial factors that led to the eager competition between the many curers played its part. And the external facts of natural and market environment—often individually adverse but never concertedly adverse for a long period—gave a reasonably firm support to the effort of a traditional society to adjust, without much internal change, to a changing and demanding world.

NOTES

(1) See the figures given for each fishery district in the annual reports of the Commissioners for the British Fisheries (a body which was to operate under three different nominal titles in the course of the nineteenth century, but which continued to perform substantially unchanged functions. It will be referred to hereafter as the 'Fishery Board').

(2) See, for example, the verbal comments attached to the retrospective tables given in the Census Report of 1851 and several parish accounts in the New Statistical Account.

(3) Fish. Bd. Rec., AF/24, 19-22.

(4) Fish. Bd. Ann. Reps., 1855, 1886.

(5)

Herrings Cured at East-coast Stations		Increase % since previous period
1835 (single year)	318,572 barrels	
1838-42 (annual average)	424,493	+11
1850-54 ,, ,,	472,657	+11
1880-84 ,, ,,	779,542	+65

Source: Fish. Bd. Ann. Reps.

This is not a full account of the herring landed by east-coast boats for they operated from other coasts and not all their landings were sold fresh. In fact, the increase in landings from such boats was considerably greater than the proportions indicated. But the figures give a fair account of the results of boats during the given summer period, for comparatively little was sent away fresh at this time and nearly all east-coast boats operated from east-coast stations during this season.

(6) See the detailed account of the fishing communities given in the Fish. Bd. Rep. for 1855 (Parl. Papers, 1856, XVIII). This may be compared with a similar account for 1886. In the first year there were 122 fishing communities listed, containing an average of 145 fishermen and boys (a slight overestimate because this last figure covers men hired for the fishing season); in 1886 there were 145 communities on the list and the average active population was now 110 fishermen and boys (the figures, in this case, relating to residents of the communities).

(7) The minimum necessary depth increased to 14 ft. when steam carriers came to be used after 1870. S.C. on Harbour Accommodation, Parl. Papers, 1884, XII, Q. 111.

(8) Loans tended to be granted under the Harbours and Passing Tolls Act (1861) only against the security of an existing harbour revenue. S.C. on Harbour Accommodation, Parl. Papers, 1884, XII, p. v. It is true that the Fishery Board attempted to reverse the tendency to centralise on large harbours, but the funds which they could use were too small for the success of this policy.

(9) See below, p. 191.

(10) For example, in 1879, herring fishing was carried on from twenty-nine stations to the north of Peterhead, but nearly 70 per cent of the boats operated from four stations. Peterhead Sentinel, 10th September, 1879.

(11) Compare figures such as those given in note (10) with the relative size and dispersion of the communities in which the fishermen lived. Fish. Bd. Rep., 1855, 1886.

(12) For example, Fishing Gazette, 30th August, 1878, 420.

(13) Detailed calculations of the relation between net area and catch, and between value of equipment (including boats) and catch, show that even the heavy catches of the 'seventies gave no increase in the return per unit of capital. In particular, the material for such calculations is to be found in the Fish. Bd. Ann. Reps. from 1852 on, and in Fish. Bd. Recs. AF/24, 19-22.

(14) See, for example, Fish. Bd. Rep., 1864, 2.

(15) S.C. on Herring Brand, Parl. Papers, 1881, IX, App. pp. 248-49.

(16) British Fisheries Society Records, 3.147 (1786).

(17) New Stat. Acct., Banffshire, 236.

(18) John O'Groat Journal, 18th December, 1846; 12th September, 1872; Committee of Sea Fisheries, Parl. Papers, 1866, XVIII, Qs. 30,443-453; 30,499.

(19) Fish Bd. Rep., 1873, 696; S.C. on Herring Brand, Parl. Papers, 1881, IX, p. vii.

(20) Fife Herald, 27th July, 1871; 24th August, 1871.

(21) Fife News, 6th April, 1872; 19th April, 1872.

(22) Fish Trades Gazette, 25th August, 1883.

(23) Peter F. Anson, Fishing Boats and Fisher Folk on the East Coast of Scotland (London, 1930), 54-55.

(24) Fisheries Exhibition Literature, Vol. IX (London, 1884): W. S. Miln, The Scotch East Coast, Orkney and Shetland, Lewis and Barra Herring Fishing, 19-23.

(25) Herring landed in Fife in summer were partly sold 'at the price of the day', partly under terms of engagement; in the Eyemouth district all were sold at the price of the day. But by far the greatest part was landed to the north of Fife under terms of engagement.

(26) Rates at which boats were being engaged were frequently reported in the various local newspapers and fishermen would thus know what was happening in other districts. Each engagement was, of course, a private bargain between crew and curer, the bargaining went on for weeks or even months at a host of sites, and the reports were not necessarily fully accurate; but there can be little doubt that most in the trade, whether curers or fishermen, had a clear picture of the going rates at the different stations.

(27) See below, pp. 201-206.

(28) Committee on Sea Fisheries, Parl. Papers, 1866, XVIII. Q. 30,444; S.C. on the Herring Brand, Parl. Papers, 1881, IX, Q. 2070.

(29) For descriptions of curing see John O'Groat Journal, 13th September, 1860; Miln, *op. cit.*, 11-18; R. J. Duthie, The Art of Fishcuring (Aberdeen, 1911), 6-32.

(30) A good price series for what was very nearly a standardised commodity can be constructed from quotations in the press and comparison with seasonal and annual landings is easy. An inverse correlation between price and quantity emerges.

(31) Local journalists and witnesses at official inquiries never tired of pointing out the danger of the system of bounties and pre-arranged prices. The actual experience of the predicted disaster came in 1884. A coherent account of this crisis, the worst in the history of the trade, is given in W. S. Miln, An Exposure of the Position of the Scotch Herring Trade in 1885 (London, 1886).

(32) S.C. on the Herring Brand, Parl. Papers, 1881, IX, Qs. 367, 591, 1299.

(33) For references see above, note (29).

(34) S.C. on Herring Brand, Parl. Papers, 1881, IX, Qs. 1198, 2995-3000.

(35) S.C. on Herring Brand, Parl. Papers, 1881, IX, Qs. 941, 3127.

(36) Fish Trades Gazette, 18th February, 1888, 6; 25th February, 1888, 7; Peterhead Sentinel, 31st January, 1888.

(37) See, for example, Peterhead Sentinel, 25th September, 1888, 6.

(38) Peterhead Sentinel, 25th September, 1888, 6; S.C. on Herring Brand, 1881, IX, Q. 3123.

(39) Fish. Bd. Rep., 1859.

(40) See below, pp. 205-206.

(41) The calculations which follow are based on Fish. Bd. Recs., AF/24, 95-113.

(42) Taking one year with another each boat would account for about 100 crans (which would make into slightly over 100 barrels of cured herring). Thus, 800 barrels represented the output of about 8 boats and since one team of girls (3) stood by for each boat such an average would represent the employment of between twenty-four and thirty persons during the height of the season.

(43) Peterhead Sentinel, 3rd August, 1870; Miln, East Coast Herring Fishing, 20.

(44) Fish Trades Gazette, 3rd July, 1886, 7.

(45) Peterhead Sentinel, 5th July, 1871.

(46) It is not possible to construct a complete series showing, year by year, the movement of the rates paid to fishermen since, in different cases, the rates were constructed on somewhat different principles (part of the payment being in a fixed sum before the beginning of the season, part in a pro rata payment for all herring landed, settlement being made at the end of the season). But there is ample evidence in press reports that rates did move sensitively and so as to press nearer to a price of cured herring that was, on the whole, rising. For a general statement see Miln, *op. cit.*, 20.

(47) By the 'seventies 20s. had become almost a minimum payment to which was added a varying bounty; at one time in the 'forties the rate per cran fell to 7s. without bounty.

(48) Fish. Bd. Ann. Reps.

(49) Committee on Herring Fishing, Parl. Papers, 1878, XXI, 246.

(50) Edmund W. H. Holdsworth, The Sea Fisheries of Great Britain and Ireland (London, 1883), 162.

(51) Fish. Bd. Recs., AF/19, 23-24.

(52) Andrew C. O'Dell, The Historical Geography of the Shetland Islands (Lerwick, 1939), 133-35.

(53) Duthie, *op. cit.*, 20-29.

(54) For a comprehensive statement of the fishermen's reasons for sticking to open boats, see a letter written by the Secretary of the Fishery Board. Banffshire Journal, 8th June, 1850.

(55) Fish Bd. Recs., Box 29, Reports on Harbours, 1883, Anstruther.

(56) Committee on Herring Fishing, Parl. Papers, 1878, XXI, 345.

(57) Fish. Bd. Recs., AF/24.

(58) Although, in the early 'eighties, most of the boats were still rather less than 50 ft. in keel, some had been built up to 55 ft. keel. See, for example, Fife News, 3rd December, 1881.

(59) Fish. Bd. Recs., AF/23, 20.

(60) Fish. Bd. Recs., AF/24, 19-22; 101-06.

(61) Fish. Bd. Recs., AF/23, 25-27.

(62) Fish. Bd. Recs., AF/21, 6-8.

(63) British Fisheries Society Records, 306/1 (1808).

(64) James Wilson, A Voyage round the Coasts of Scotland and the Isles (Edinburgh, 1842), II, 164.

(65) Committee on Sea Fisheries, Parl. Papers, 1866, XVIII, Q. 27,487.

(66) E. W. M. Holdsworth, Deep-Sea Fishing and Fishing Boats (London, 1874), 277-78.

(67) Fife News, 12th June, 1880.

(68) Fish. Bd. Ann. Reps.

(69) Fish. Bd. Recs., AF/24, 19-22.

(70) Wilson, *loc. cit.*

(71) In most seasons the average catch per boat at the summer fishing was now running at over 200 crans and rates were seldom below £1 per cran—and sometimes a good deal higher.

(72) Nearly always, in the final account of the fishing, there would be a few boats which had landed two or three times as much as the average, a majority of boats landed less than the average, and a few very much less than the average. Thus, there was always a great difference between the takings of the most successful and the least successful and the typical boat probably made rather less of it than the average figures suggest.

(73) Miln, East Coast Fishing, 3-6.

(74) See above, p. 195.

CHAPTER NINE

Earnings and Productivity in the Scottish Coal-mining Industry during the Nineteenth Century: The Dixon Enterprises

A. SLAVEN

Lecturer in Economic History,
University of Glasgow

IN VICTORIAN BRITAIN coal was basic to economic growth and its crucial importance is attested to by the numerous studies of the industry undertaken by both individuals and Royal Commissions.(1) Indeed, there is hardly an aspect of mining life that escaped investigation, but whatever the object of the separate studies, the influence of earnings and productivity on the general well-being of miners, and mining, is revealed again and again.

This paper is based on the surviving business records of William Dixon and Sons, prominent coal and iron masters, whose major undertakings during the second half of the nineteenth century were the Govan Collieries and the Govan Iron Works, near Glasgow. Their activities also extended to the operation of iron works at Calder and of numerous pits throughout the central Lanarkshire coalfield at Blantyre, Carfin and Lesmahagow, for example. The records comprise over four hundred bound volumes, nearly all relating to the Govan Collieries. These provide information on such factors as wages, output, employment, coal sales, accidents, rents and social organisation. In addition, there is material relating to mining equipment and operating costs, and the life-span of coal mines at various periods. However, the most complete information covers earnings, output and employment, and this paper is primarily an analysis of the labour component of the Govan Collieries with respect to its earnings and output over the period 1856-1913. Wherever possible the experience of the Govan Collieries is presented against the background of general Scottish conditions, and although it is probable that this single large concern is not completely typical, many of the differences between this and other Scottish coal-mining units are undoubtedly differences of degree rather than differences of kind. The study is presented in five parts: 'Earnings and Organisation'; 'Individual and Group Earnings'; 'Average Weekly Earnings'; 'Indices of Earnings' and 'Output and Productivity'.

The first section, 'Earnings and Organisation', deals briefly with the growth of organised labour in the Scottish mines, and the ways in which wage rates were negotiated. The system operating in the Govan Collieries is presented against this background. Section two, 'Individual and Group Earnings', is an analysis of the colliery's wage structure and it attempts to indicate how gross earnings differed from net earnings. The section on 'Average Weekly Earnings' outlines the method of calculating annual average weekly wages for the coal-face workers at Govan, and at this stage some attempt is made to measure the reliability of the wage figures. Section four, 'Indices of Earnings', examines the movement of the wage indices, for both coal-face and other underground workers in Govan, over the period 1856-1913. These movements are then related to what is known of similar movements for the whole of Scotland. Finally, section five, 'Output and Productivity', investigates the trend of output for all mines in Scotland over the same period, interpreting this in the light of more detailed information extracted from the Dixon Company records.

I

Earnings and Organisation

As the nineteenth century advanced the level of earnings of the Scottish collier was increasingly influenced by the power of the unions. Although the unions were always concerned with the matter of safety in the pits, most of their attention was directed toward the determination of what seemed to them to be adequate wage levels. The available material does not permit the reconstruction of a complete picture of either earnings or labour organisation, but rather provides a series of impressions through which runs a continuing thread of turbulence.

Between 1840 and the 1880's the Scottish coalfields were a great receiving ground of poverty-stricken Irish 'who are mobile and prevent effective organisation'(2) and who competed with the native

Scots for 'the lower kinds of employment',(3) and were effectively employed by coal and iron masters as strikebreakers. It is not surprising therefore that trade union organisation was weak and ineffective during this period. The Miners' Federation of Great Britain and Ireland was formed at Wakefield in 1841 and membership extended to Scotland during the following year; the indigenous Coal and Iron Miners' Association was formed under Alexander McDonald in 1855 and numerous loose district unions grew up from 1868.(4) The creation of nearly all of these was associated with upswings in trade but they collapsed in 1848, 1863 and 1879, respectively, all in times of poor trade when the mine owners would not meet their demands, wage cuts reduced their contributions and defections severely weakened their organisation. As Professor Youngson Brown has observed, 'the ebb and flow of trade unionism was directly related to the course of the trade cycle.'(5)

In these circumstances the negotiation of wage levels was left almost entirely to the initiative of men in the individual pits, and their efforts centred on the manipulation of the 'darg' or day's work. This device apparently originated soon after the repeal of the Combination Laws in 1824 when 'the whole of the colliers and miners in Lanarkshire with few exceptions, amounting to 16,000 men, . . . placed themselves under regulations as to the amount of their labour . . . for the maintenance of wages at a fair level; for their protection against overwork, and against overstocking of the market of labour, and the market of coal. These regulations [were] based on the principle of allowing no one man to do more work than another, of forcing into equality of earnings the young and the old, the strong and the weak, the industrious and the idle.'(6) In the eyes of the miners, this system of restricting their labour in order to keep down stocks of coal and therefore maintain prices and wages at a reasonable level 'arose originally out of a feeling, founded probably on common experience, that wages were not raised by masters in good times in proportion to the rise in the market price of coal'.(7)

Since the masters too attempted to control wage rates in accordance with the selling price of coal, it was inevitable that there should have been conflicts as both sides tried to gain an advantage over the other. Consequently, in the opinion of the owners, this restrictive 'darg' combination derived directly from the 'long observed evil results of ignorance among those densely crowded populations', and threatened to increase if 'two other evil consequences of great magnitude . . . Infidelity and Socialism'(8) were allowed to spread without control. More precisely, according to the masters, 'the darg combination restricts labour and therefore earnings by about one-third and forces iron and coal masters to build one-third more houses, keep one-third more horses and one-third more roadways underground, and one-third more of almost all kinds of standing stock in order to get the quantity of coal they require'.(9) The mathematics of the calculation are dubious, but nevertheless it was argued that as a result 'the nation annually loses vast sums by way of the colliers' restriction of labour'.(10)

Whatever the arguments for and against this system, the main principle was to keep wages up, coal stocks down, and the industry free from the effects of surplus labour. It is apparent that the application of the 'darg' was not very successful in attaining any of these objectives, and that by utilising cheap and plentiful Irish labour, the system eventually worked more to the advantage of the masters than the men. Nevertheless, it was the only weapon continuously employed by the men over this period, and the level of their earnings bears a direct relationship to the way in which they restricted their labour, and to the way in which the master distributed his returns from a fluctuating market. After 1888 the Scottish colliers replaced individual pit negotiation of earnings by a collective agreement with the owners, who were to adjust daily rates of pay by a sliding scale directly related to the selling price of coal. Earnings were to fluctuate between the limits of 5s. 3d. per day as a minimum, and 7s. per day as a maximum, or $31\frac{1}{4}$ per cent and 75 per cent above the 1888 base level of 4s. per day. In 1890 the limits were altered to 5s. 6d. and 8s. respectively, and were changed again in 1909 when the conciliation board arbitrated that the 'minimum wage of 50 per cent above the basis of 1888 shall be 7s. 5·45d. per ton'(11) and that wage rates would only be altered when the selling price of coal warranted an increase or decrease of $6\frac{1}{4}$ per cent in the prevailing rates.

Thus after 1888, the process of wage manipulation was removed from the hands of individual pits and entrusted to the trade unions, which between 1880 and 1913 made spectacular progress in organisation. This was possibly due to a combination of continuing fair trade, and therefore to the continuing ability of the men to pay union dues, and the growing stability of the mining communities where Irish and Scots were becoming integrated, and 'blacklegs' or cheap labour less easy to recruit as strike-breakers. This recrudescence of trade unionism was associated with the names of Keir Hardie and Robert Smillie, and the various local unions came together as the Scottish Miners' National Federation' in 1886, which was affiliated with the Miners' Federation of Great Britain in

1894.(12) Even then the negotiation of wage rates was not a smooth process, and abuses of the sliding scales led to continual, if sporadic, striking, notably the two great strikes of 1894 and 1912.

Even with a knowledge of the mechanisms of wage negotiation, it is not easy to construct a table of average earnings for the coal-face worker. Indeed, little is known with any certainty before 1850, and it is only after this date that more detailed, but still unreliable, data are available. After 1850 it is possible to estimate weekly earnings on the basis of the average daily rates of pay for coal-face workers. These figures have been assembled from diverse sources, such as newspapers, Royal Commissions, and other secondary material relating to mining in Scotland at that time, but at best they represent crude averages of numerous rates current in each year, and they

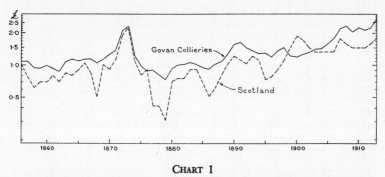

CHART 1

Average weekly earnings for coal-face workers in Govan and in Scotland.

are reliable neither as indicators of the daily earnings of Scottish colliers nor even of the wage rates in any one pit or coal seam. This unreliable figure has been multiplied by the number of shifts worked per week, an even more dubious value, to obtain the average weekly gross earnings of the coal-face worker. Throughout the nineteenth century, fragmentary evidence indicates a general working week of four or four-and-a-half days, increasing to five days in the first decade of the present century. The results are presented in Table 1. The resulting average is therefore based on very crude and unreliable estimates, and the levels of earnings indicated in this way must be treated with caution. In spite of the numerous inaccuracies embodied in these estimates, however, it is probable that they do provide a fair indication of the trend of colliers' earnings throughout Scotland.

TABLE 1

DAILY WAGE RATES, SHIFTS WORKED AND AVERAGE WEEKLY EARNINGS AT THE COAL-FACE (SCOTLAND)

Year	Rate/ day	Shifts/ week	Average weekly earnings	Year	Rate/ day	Shifts/ week	Average weekly earnings
	s. d.		s. d.		s. d.		s. d.
1856	4 6	4½	20 3	1885	3 0	4½	13 6
1857	3 6	4½	15 9	1886	2 6	4	10 0
1858	2 6	5	12 6	1887	3 0	4	12 0
1859	3 6	4	14 0	1888	4 0	4	16 0
1860	3 6	4	14 0	1889	4 6	4½	20 6
1861	4 0	4	16 0	1890	5 6	4½	24 9
1862	3 6	4	14 0	1891	5 0	4½	22 6
1863	4 3	4	17 0	1892	4 6	4½	20 6
1864	4 0	4	16 0	1893	5 6	4½	24 9
1865	4 6	4	18 0	1894	4 6	4½	20 6
1866	5 3	5	21 3	1895	3 3	4½	14 8
1867	3 9	4½	16 10	1896	3 6	4½	15 9
1868	3 4	3	10 0	1897	4 0	4½	18 0
1869	5 0	4	20 0	1898	5 0	4½	22 6
1870	4 0	4½	18 0	1899	6 0	5	30 0
1871	5 9	4	23 0	1900	7 6	5	37 6
1872	8 0	4½	36 0	1901	7 0	5	35 0
1873	10 0	4½	45 0	1902	6 0	5	30 0
1874	5 0	4½	22 6	1903	5 6	5	27 6
1875	4 0	4	16 0	1904	5 6	5	27 6
1876	4 6	4	18 0	1905	5 6	5	27 6
1877	2 9	3	8 3	1906	5 6	5	27 6
1878	2 6	3½	8 3	1907	7 3	5	36 3
1879	1 9	3½	6 0	1908	6 6	5	32 6
1880	3 6	4	14 0	1909	6 0	5	30 0
1881	3 9	4	15 0	1910	6 0	5	30 0
1882	3 9	4	15 0	1911	6 0	5	30 0
1883	4 0	4½	18 0	1912	6 6	5	32 6
1884	4 0	4½	18 0	1913	7 3	5	36 3

From Chart 1 it can be seen that the movement of this series is generally similar to that calculated for the Govan Collieries. The circumstances regarding wage negotiation in the latter were, however, somewhat different from those prevailing in Scotland as a whole. As the Mines' Inspector records: 'Since the repeal of the Combination Laws in the year 1824, combinations have become the mania of almost every class of workman. Those who are employed in the well-paid trades monopolise the trade to themselves,

to the total exclusion of every other person, thereby creating an evil
worse than the legislative enactments of which the working classes
complained. The workmen of Govan Colliery, deeply impressed
with a sense of the evil effects of combinations to restrict free
labour have resolved to form themselves into a Friendly and Free
Labour Society, for the purpose of supporting each other when
visited with sickness or accident, and for their legal and individual
protection from the threats and intimidation of the combined, while
exercising their just rights of working with whom [they please], and
on the terms considered best for their individual interest.'(13) In
spite of what the Mines' Inspector reports, it is almost certain that
it was Dixon himself, and not his men, who created this system, for
it conveniently excluded the influence of unionism, and forbade
combinations to restrict labour. The management of the Govan
Collieries maintained that this system did not in any way depress
wages, but gave rates 'generally 3d. per day higher than where
labour is restricted'.(14) This was achieved by the fact that when
Mr. Dixon 'regulates the price per cart according to the demand for
coal in the market . . . some . . . men will make an effort to put
out more'(15) coal in order to keep up the level of their earnings.

This system effectively eliminated the operation of the 'darg', or
restricted day's work, and for most of the nineteenth century, the
Govan colliers relied on the fairness of the owners in granting wage
increases. This was not always a harmonious arrangement and
between 1856 and 1888, the Govan Collieries experienced approximately forty-seven broken-weeks' work through strikes. All were
concentrated in three periods—1860; 1866, 1868 and 1870; and 1884
and 1887. These were all times when wage rates remained low, in
spite of slowly improving coal prices, and the men combined to
enforce wage increases. Needless to say, they were not successful.
After 1888 the sliding scale was in operation in Scotland, but the
Dixon records do not clearly indicate whether this new system was
applied, or if the Govan colliers were still tied to the company's
own sliding scale system. Even if the negotiated sliding scale was
not used in Govan the force of organised labour did make itself felt,
for when Dixons, in company with other owners, reduced their
wage rates in 1894, their colliers struck with the other Scottish
miners for almost five months. Again in 1912, the Govan colliers
also participated in the short and abortive minimum wage strike of
that year. This would seem to indicate that the Scottish sliding wage
scale also operated at Govan.

Apart from these irregular stoppages, the Govan Collieries present
a remarkably stable unit in the turbulent years of the second half

Q

of the nineteenth century. In the fifty-eight years from 1856 to 1913, no less than forty-three years were completely free from stoppages of any kind. Amidst the endemic strikes of the West of Scotland this was in no small way due to the operation of the Friendly Society, though other items contributed. The Govan Colliers were paid regularly each fortnight from as early as 1850, while many others were still paid irregularly for another twenty years; they did not suffer from the abuse of the truck shop after 1842, nor were their wages paid in the local public house. These had been part of the Govan system before Mine Inspection in the 1840's, but the management was quick to make alterations, and probably this had as much to do with stability as had the Friendly and Free Labour Society.

Whatever the cause, the colliers at Govan worked a twelve-day fortnight to around 1901, and thereafter one of ten days. Not all colliers worked full six days each week, but in comparison with the apparently broken and uncertain labour of colliers in many other mines, those at Govan were in an enviable position. Thus the criticisms levelled at the earnings calculated from daily rates do not apply to earnings calculated for the Govan Collieries. While these earnings cannot be regarded as fully representative of conditions throughout the West of Scotland, they are at least accurate and complete for one large mining unit, and throw much light on the make up and levels of colliers' earnings over this period.

II

Individual and Group Earnings

Within the Govan Collieries the earnings of the coal-face worker in the nineteenth century can best be considered in two parts, the first is the earnings of the individual, the second the earnings of the group. As far as the individual collier was concerned, his earnings at the end of the fortnightly payment period were made up of several components. The most important of these was that part of his earnings won by hewing coal, and for this he was paid, not by the shift, but at the current rate per cartload of output; initially this was a unit of twelve cwt., but after 1872 became a unit of one ton of twenty cwt. In the course of winning this coal the collier also produced varying amounts of dross, fireclay, and in some cases ironstone, and for each of these incidental products he was also paid a prescribed rate per cartload. These were payments received from the direct process of hewing coal; in addition, many colliers worked some extra time at various 'clearing' operations, and for these were paid the appropriate standard daily rate per shift, *i.e.*, an 'oncost' payment.

The individual collier's earnings were therefore made up of two elements, the 'piece rate' and the 'oncost rate', and while the earnings from the former fluctuated with the individual's productivity, the latter was a steady payment in respect of 'labour hours'. If oncost payments, which were usually marginal, are omitted, the individual collier's daily earnings largely depended on two factors; first his own productivity, and second, the cartload rate.

For the individual, there was no fixed rate of pay. A certain rate per unit of output might be maintained for several weeks, but this was directly related to the time it took to 'work out' any given section of the coal-face, where conditions remained the same. If these became easier, the individual's piece rate was immediately lowered; if he encountered difficult conditions, say through faulting, damp, etc., the rate was correspondingly increased. The individual's rate of pay not only varied with the operation, it also varied with the season and there was a tendency to pay a higher rate between the months of April and early November than during the remainder of the year. The differential was normally around 3d. per cartload.

The individual's gross earnings over the fortnightly payment period was influenced by the number of shifts he worked. Full employment was twelve shifts in the fortnight, and the usual number worked varied from nine to twelve. It might be expected that the man who worked the full twelve shifts would earn the most, and in some cases this was true; but in the majority of instances the individual who constantly worked nine to ten shifts per fortnight earned as much, and often more, than his twelve-shift counterpart. This was most likely to be a function of age, the younger man being capable of producing more per shift than the older man, who in compensation had to work a longer period for similar returns. Any 'equality of earnings' in Govan was more a function of hours of work and individual productivity, than the wholesale limitation of output, as was apparently the general case in Scotland at that time. This represents the structure of gross earnings for the individual, net earnings were quite a different matter.

From the collier's gross earnings, which represented his total earning capacity or inclination in any one fortnight, there were several standard deductions made at the end of each payment period. Collectively these were known as the 'offtakes' and comprised house rent, which varied from 2s. to 3s. or 4s. per fortnight, depending on the accommodation; contributions to the school at 6d. or 9d.; pick sharpening at 6d. or 9d. and occasionally 1s. 3d. depending on the industry of the individual and the hardness of the coal; the funeral fund at 6d. or 1s.; the surgeon at 6d., 1s. and 1s. 6d.; and sometimes 'fire-coal' at 3s. 6d. per ton. Of these only 'fire-coal' was not a regular fortnightly cost to the miner, and only house rent did not apply to all, since some lived in private houses. Thus, if a man living in a colliery house required coal, in that one fortnight there would be deductions of at least 7s. 6d. from his pay, and in ordinary fortnights a minimum of 4s. Throughout most of the nineteenth century this minimum would amount to at least 20 per cent of a single weekly wage packet and, in the poorest years of the 1870's, to some 40 per cent. Net earnings were therefore substantially lower than gross earnings and, as it is probable that similar deductions were made at all pits throughout Scotland, estimates based on daily rates of pay should also be regarded as gross earnings.

With these deductions made, the remainder should have been the net wage paid at the end of the fortnight. This, however, was not always the case. At times, several of the colliers could not sufficiently manage their incomes to make their funds last from one pay to the next, and thus these individuals had recourse to almost daily borrowing, or 'subs', from the management. At pay day, these were set against the collier's pay and also deducted, and thus one or two miners would receive only a few shillings, and others, mere pence. For a very few it resulted in a debt to the management which had to be cleared by a payment not yet earned, but this debt was apparently never permitted to grow to a large sum. There is no evidence in Dixon's books to suggest that colliers were encouraged to build up large debts to the owner. As late as the 1870's it was stated that some colliery owners used this device to tie down their labour force. The fact that so few men in Govan were burdened with debts of this sort would again seem to indicate that Dixon practised a form of enlightened management much earlier than many of Scotland's other colliery owners.

The second level at which earnings may be treated is that of the group. The variation of the individual collier's rate of pay over time was multiplied in the group, and this resulted in a surprising variation of rates among the colliers at any one time and in any particular seam. Some of the differentials between the men can undoubtedly be explained on the basis of a father/son partnership, but the majority escape this formula. The answer is to be found, not in the rates themselves, but in the gross earnings. If comparison is made of the gross earnings of men who have worked the same number of shifts, but at different rates, there was usually no great discrepancy in total wages paid, and often men on the highest rate would earn the lowest wages.

As can be seen from Table 2, men working eleven shifts at 2s. per ton earned roughly the same per fortnight, and men working eleven shifts at 2s. 2d. and 2s. 3d. per ton also earned comparable wages. However, those men on rates of 2s. 2d. and 2s. 3d. earned less than the men working for 2s. per ton. The solution appears to be that rates were not only varied with age and ability, but also according to the conditions of work. In order to have the coal worked systematically the owner obviously had to be prepared to make use of wage incentives in compensation for bad working conditions.

TABLE 2

COAL-FACE WORKERS—NO. 6 PIT GOVAN—SPLINT MAIN COAL: FORTNIGHT ENDING 11TH APRIL, 1891

Name	Shifts worked	Output		Rate/ ton		Gross earnings		
		tons	cwts.	s.	d.	£	s.	d.
Robert Geddes	11	36	11	2	0	3	13	1
Francis McGurk	12	37	18	2	0	3	15	10
Alex McGurk	11	33	1	2	0	3	6	1
Alex Bain	12	62	16	2	0	6	5	7
James Brown	9	21	0	2	2	2	5	11
John Stevenson	12	29	0	2	2	3	2	10
James Smith	11	27	18	2	2	3	0	5
Patrick Layden	11	23	0	2	3	2	11	9
John McQuilan	11	20	0	2	3	2	5	6
John Drew	10	24	11	2	3	2	15	9
Richard Waugh	10	22	18	2	3	2	12	0
Andrew Wilson	10	24	17	2	3	2	16	6
Daniel Drew	10	25	8	2	3	2	17	8
Mathew Purdon	8	27	3	2	3	3	1	8

But in spite of the conscious efforts of the colliery owner to 'standardise' the wages of his workers, there was often a large range of gross earnings within any one group, as Table 2 exemplifies. It was not unusual for a few men to make twice that of others in the same year, thus earning much above the group average. Since it was the colliery practice to manipulate rates to control advantage and disadvantage in working conditions, these large discrepancies must have come from ungovernable factors, such as age, illness and absenteeism. This, however, in no way detracts from the very high and sustained productivity of the top earners.

Although there were these variations within the group, the average earnings of the various groups working in both different seams and pits, were surprisingly comparable. The radical changes in the average earnings of the groups were not usually due to quick changes in productivity, as these seldom occurred, but were usually a result of basic changes in the level of the rate payments. As Dixon himself stated, this was dependent upon the level of prosperity of the coal trade, as measured by the selling price of coal.(16)

The group, being the sum of the individual earners, worked the same nine to twelve shifts per fortnight and also lost money by the usual deductions; but in addition it contributed, apparently voluntarily, some small part of its output toward the upkeep of an injured workmate, or for the benefit of his widow or mother when such an occasion arose. This practice is, of course, still common in the pits today.

At this level it is also possible to see that while the incidental payments for dross, ironstone and fireclay were common to both the individual and the group, the additional payment from oncost work was more a function of the individual. Not all colliers added this to their earnings, and in many cases, for those who did, it was at the expense of losing a day at the coal-face. Two other factors also influenced the final gross average wage of the group; these were holidays and absenteeism.

For the collier there were two main periods of rest in the working year. In January and July all work stopped for three days for the New Year and summer holidays. Added to this was the stoppage each Sunday. These breaks naturally reduced earnings but it is significant just how quickly the men resumed full production.

In an article on the earlier years of the Govan Collieries, Dr. P. L. Payne showed that at the beginning of the nineteenth century 'the average amount of coal raised on Mondays was . . . 60 per cent of the daily average and 55 per cent of the average daily output during the rest of the week, *i.e.,* Tuesday-Saturday'. From this he argued that 'while a proportion of this diminished output was perhaps due to the necessarily enhanced problems of getting the pits working smoothly again following the weekend . . . the weekend carousal did disrupt normal working and seriously hindered Wm. Dixon's efforts to meet fully the city's growing demands'. This led him to suggest that 'a possible means of dating the coming of a disciplined labour force is when the average Monday's production equals the average daily production'.(17)

Whatever may have been the case at this period (1804-05) things were vastly different by the 1850's. In spite of the common complaints of drunkenness, debauchery and laziness that colour the reports of the Commissioners on the coal trade at this time,(18) Dixon at least had established a disciplined labour force, as measured by Dr. Payne's indicator. Nowhere in the wage books is there any evidence of large scale absenteeism on a Monday; nowhere does output, and therefore earnings, fall significantly below the average of the rest of the week. In fact, higher productivity on the Monday after the weekend's rest would seem to be quite common. Earnings were therefore no longer lowered by the slow return to work so common at the beginning of the century. There is unfortunately no reliable way of estimating how general this quick return to work was, and therefore no way of indicating how the figures for daily rates of pay elsewhere may have been influenced by this factor.

The impact of annual holidays was slightly different. As has been said, twice in the working year the collier was allowed to remain idle for three days: in January and in July. Despite the loss in earnings implied by these 'holidays' it is apparent that many of the miners showed no inclination to return to work quickly, and this at least was characteristic of all miners in Scotland; many took at least another day, and some even stayed away for the whole week. What is significant, however, is that when they did return, there was again no period of slowly working into the job, and output and earnings immediately reached the weekly averages. Since it is unlikely that Govan was a vastly more efficient unit than all the other collieries in Scotland, the disparaging reports dwelling on the endemic laziness and drunkenness of the Scottish collier must be read with caution. Reports of all kinds too often only mention the worst and the best cases, and leave an ill-defined majority in between.

The other factor to be considered in the make-up of average earnings is absenteeism. When this occurred at Govan, it was apparently not the end product of a drunken weekend, but usually came some time in the middle of the week when the collier could judge what his earnings for that week were likely to be. If they were much above a personal average, many colliers felt that they could afford to take a day off and in this respect the second week was noticeably more vulnerable than the first in the fortnightly payment period. Much absenteeism was therefore deliberate and not involuntary. The amount of absenteeism varied: in 1860, 6·3 per cent; 1870, 2·5 per cent; 1873, 8 to 14 per cent; 1880, 7·9 per cent; 1890, 6·3 per cent; 1900, 6·9 per cent; 1910, 2·6 per cent; this absenteeism must have meant some reduction in personal average earnings to the individuals involved. In addition their depleted earnings must have reduced the average earnings of the group. Some of this absenteeism can also be attributed to the effects of illness and accidents.

The other significant group of earners was that represented by the men known collectively as 'Reddsmen' or 'Oncostmen' and this is a class of whom we know almost nothing for Scotland as a whole. It includes men classed as brushers, builders, bottomers, gaffers, drawers, and others, each charged with performing a distinctive duty. In this category the diversity of earnings was not within the group, but between the groups. To obtain the weekly earnings, the set daily rate of each grade was simply multiplied by the number of shifts worked per week. This was six up to 1908, and five thereafter. This method assumes full employment in respect of the average level of earnings, but does not affect the trend; in practice most oncostmen worked complete fortnights.

The average gross earnings of the oncostmen were also reduced by offtakes, which in their case were not so varied. Perhaps because of the constancy of their work, they did not take advances or 'subs' to the same extent as the colliers, and while the offtakes were elements which reduced their average earnings, one factor, overtime, raised them.

It is implicit in the earnings and output of the colliers that on occasion some of them worked longer hours than others, although the amount of overtime cannot be ascertained. Theoretically, for the men working under the widespread 'darg' system, no 'overtime' should have been possible, but the allocation of increases for 'sons' and children employed by colliers created an overtime surplus which is not included in the earnings estimated from daily rates. In many cases these estimates may be too low. In the cast of oncostmen, however, overtime was marked on the paybook. Surprisingly, it was neither a large nor a widespread element. Few men worked overtime, and those who did never exceeded fourteen shifts out of a twelve-shift fortnight; apparently the toil was arduous enough without extending it voluntarily. One extra shift, or thirteen in a twelve-day fortnight was the most usual, and unlike today, this was not paid at a higher rate, but was merely an extra day at the standard payment.

III

Average Weekly Earnings

In the construction of the average earnings of the coal-face worker, all men and their earnings were included, irrespective of how many days they worked. Only those whose names appeared in other coal seams or oncost groups were excluded, since then they were not solely colliers, but made a substantial part of their income from various other tasks. If these men were included, double counting would ensue and this would lower the average by giving the impression of very low earnings and high absenteeism. The annual average weekly wage was simply obtained by dividing the sum of the separate weekly average earnings by that of the average weekly employment. This is the average 'gross earnings' per week, or earning capacity per week of colliers in any given year. It is a figure not reduced by offtakes, but automatically takes account of such factors as age, illness, holidays and absenteeism, all of which tend to lower the maximum theoretical average, and overtime, which tends to increase the average. These factors tend partially to offset each other.

Just how reliable are these figures? A criticism which may be levelled at the series of figures established as average weekly earnings from daily wage rates (see Table 1) is that there is no indication of the scatter or variation of earnings around the average. If an average calculated from widely different results is to mean anything, then it must be accompanied by a measure of this scatter. For the averages calculated for the Govan Collieries, it has been possible to measure the general level of dispersion of both individual earnings around the average weekly figure, and the variation of the separate weekly averages from the annual weekly average.

The calculation of the annual weekly average involved two steps. First, the earnings of each individual collier were totalled for each payment period and the average obtained by dividing the total fortnightly earnings by the total number of coal-face workers employed in that period. This result was subsequently divided by two, to give a measure of average weekly earnings. Since a feature of the several hundred individual earnings each payment period was wide variation, several payment periods were chosen at random from the years 1857 and 1872. The first, 1857, represents an apparently normal year when wage rates remained reasonably stable; the second, 1872, was a year of rapid change, characterised by rising wages. The results obtained from the payment periods in both years were not greatly different. In 1857, for the week with the smallest range of earnings, 66 per cent. of the individual collier's wages fell within a range of plus or minus 6s. from the central average. In the week with the largest range of earnings in 1872, two-thirds of the men's wages fell within plus or minus 8s. of the central average. It is obviously necessary to treat the average weekly figures from which the yearly average is constructed with caution, since at any time allowance must be made for a range of roughly plus or minus 7s. from the central average to include 66 per cent of all the individual wages, and plus or minus 14s. to include 95 per cent of all the earnings.

The second step was to sum the averages for each payment period and divide by 52 to obtain the annual average weekly earnings per man at the coal-face. In this instance the dispersion of the weekly averages from the annual average was calculated for each decennial year from 1860 to 1910 inclusive. This sample included years which represented virtually all the conditions under which men worked during the latter half of the nineteenth century. The year 1860 is representative of years when earnings were badly affected by prolonged strikes: 1870 and 1880 are respectively representative of conditions at the beginning and end of marked booms. The year 1900 represents a period of slowly declining earnings, and both 1890 and 1910 are indicative of conditions when the trend of earnings was strongly upward. Table 3 indicates the results obtained for these years. In the very unsettled years of 1860, 1884 and 1894, when there was protracted striking at Govan, one must allow a range in the order of plus or minus 6s. from the annual average if two-thirds of the weekly results are to be included. On the other hand, in the remaining decennial years of varied, but relatively untroubled working conditions, it would seem that 66 per cent of the results will be included within a range of plus or minus 2s. to 4s. from the average. In all but very bad years, an allowance of, say, plus or minus 3s. from the average is likely to include 66 per cent of all results, and a range of plus or minus 6s. should include up to 95 per cent of all the separate weekly averages.

TABLE 3

RANGE OF GOVAN COLLIERS' EARNINGS FROM THE ANNUAL WEEKLY AVERAGE
FOR DECENNIAL YEARS 1860–1910

Year	Annual average earnings per week		Minimum range from the average to include 66 per cent of results		Range of earnings around average when 66 per cent of results included				Range of earnings around average when 95 per cent of results included			
	s.	d.	s.	d.	s.	d.	s.	d.	s.	d.	s.	d.
1860	19	9	5	7	14	2	25	4	8	7	30	11
1870	25	9	3	0	22	9	28	9	19	9	31	9
1880	18	4	4	2	14	2	22	6	10	0	26	8
1890	31	9	2	0	29	9	33	9	27	9	35	9
1900	24	4	4	2	20	2	28	6	16	0	32	8
1910	44	11	3	9	41	2	48	8	37	5	52	5

Thus, although the variability is marked, when its general limits have been defined, however roughly, the figures for the average earnings per week of each year in the Govan Collieries have a significance and measurable reliability far outweighing that of the figures calculated from daily rates for the whole of Scotland.

There is no necessity to calculate variation from the average of oncost earnings, since the only variation possible was by missing a shift, and this was a very irregular occurrence, or by overtime which, as we have seen, was not common. The averages for these underground workers are therefore acceptable at the given value.

IV

Indices of Earnings

An index of the average weekly earnings for Dixon's coal-face workers over the period 1856-1913 is presented in Chart 2 with the results presented in Table 4. The fluctuations of this graph of average earnings have also been smoothed and the trend represented by a nine-year moving average, centred on the fifth item.(19)

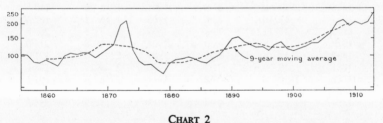

CHART 2

Index of average weekly earnings at coal-face in Govan Collieries.

The absolute movement of colliers' earnings in the last half of the nineteenth century was such that in the first third of the period the miner was raised briefly to a high pinnacle of prosperity, and thereafter plunged into a period of comparative stringency, this to be followed by years of progressive increase from the middle 1880's.

Between 1856 and 1886 the fluctuations in colliers' earnings moved in almost complete harmony with the broad movements of the whole economy, though thereafter there was considerable divergence as is indicated in Table 5. Up to the 1880's, coal was a com-

TABLE 4

ANNUAL INDEX OF COLLIERS' AVERAGE WEEKLY EARNINGS AT GOVAN COLLIERY
Average of earnings, 1862–68 = 100

Year	£	s.	d.	Index	Year	£	s.	d.	Index
1856	1	2	1	103·1	1885		18	10	87·1
1857	1	1	11	101·7	1886		18	4	84·7
1858		18	11	87·5	1887	1	0	3	93·8
1859		18	7	86·0	1888	1	1	9	100·6
1860		19	10	91·6	1889	1	6	4	121·9
1861		18	5	85·5	1890	1	11	9	147·3
1862		17	4	80·4	1891	1	12	11	152·7
1863	1	1	6	99·6	1892	1	9	8	137·5
1864	1	2	11	106·3	1893	1	7	9	128·6
1865	1	2	1	102·4	1894	1	6	6	122·6
1866	1	3	3	107·8	1895	1	6	8	123·3
1867	1	3	2	107·3	1896	1	4	6	113·4
1868	1	0	9	96·0	1897	1	7	11	129·4
1869	1	2	9	105·3	1898	1	9	9	137·8
1870	1	5	9	119·3	1899	1	5	3	116·9
1871	1	8	3	130·9	1900	1	4	4	112·9
1872	2	1	10	193·9	1901	1	5	9	119·3
1873	2	5	10	212·3	1902	1	7	1	125·4
1874	1	5	1	115·9	1903	1	9	0	134·6
1875		19	4	89·5	1904	1	9	5	136·1
1876		17	8	81·9	1905	1	12	6	150·5
1877		17	10	82·6	1906	1	16	1	167·3
1878		15	11	73·8	1907	2	4	5	205·8
1879		14	8	68·0	1908	2	6	8	216·0
1880		18	4	84·9	1909	2	1	3	191·0
1881		19	9	91·4	1910	2	4	11	208·2
1882	1	0	2	93·2	1911	2	2	6	197·1
1883	1	1	0	97·3	1912	2	4	11	208·3
1884	1	0	2	93·4	1913	2	15	2	255·6

modity whose sales were much influenced by the prosperity of other trades, e.g., iron working and railway building. From the mid-1880's, however, coal was less influenced by these demands and its prosperity was mainly affected by the fortunes of the export trade: this was a more direct influence than that of the prosperity of diverse industries. It may be that this extra vulnerability is at the root of the different fluctuations evident in the movement of the earnings in comparison with the cycles for the whole British economy. It is possible that while both Scotland and England were setting up heavy industry on the same basis of coal, iron and steam, there was no real possibility of the West of Scotland's economy pursuing a separate regional development. From the 1880's, however, as England diversified her industrial base more rapidly than Scotland, it might be that this allowed what would appear to be a distinct regional movement. However, since this is the evidence of only one colliery, it is also possible that this merely represents the idiosyncrasies of the unit and not of the West of Scotland as a whole.

TABLE 5

BRITISH CYCLES(1)		CYCLES IN COLLIERS' EARNINGS	
Trough	Peak	Trough	Peak
1855	1857	1858/9	1860
1858	1860	1862	1864
1862	1866	1865	1866
1868	1873	1868	1873
1879	1883	1879	1883
1886	1890	1886	1891
1894	1900	1896	1898
1901	1903	1900	1908
1904	1907	1909	1910
1908	1913	1911	1913

(1)A. F. Burns and W. C. Mitchell, Measuring Business Cycles (New York, 1947), p. 79.

The detailed movements of the index can be grouped in four broad periods: (1) 1850's-68, (2) 1868-79, (3) 1880-1900, (4) 1900-13.

1850's-68. In comparison with later movements, the period from 1856-68 was one of relative stability. With 21s. 6d. as the base, the range was from an index of 80 (17s. 4d.), to one of 107 (23s. 3d.) over a period of thirteen years. This reflected, and was indicative of, the level of prosperity of the trade. The industry would seem to have been in a phase of quiescence rather than one of marked expansion or contraction. It has been suggested that the movements in the early 1860's, with the marked dip in 1862, were related to the disruption of markets caused by the American Civil War and undoubtedly the down-turn owed something to this, though the general level of prosperity is probably better explained by conditions nearer home. During the 'sixties the Scottish iron industry, and therefore the coal trade, was feeling the impact of the new Cleveland iron industry in the North of England, with its cheaper ore, better coking coal and bigger and more efficient blast furnaces. In addition the best supplies of the native 'black band' iron ore were nearing exhaustion and technical progress in smelting techniques had been slow. The general level of earnings reflects this stagnation which seemed to grip the Scottish iron masters between 1850 and 1870.(20)

1868-79. Between 1868 and 1869 revival was fairly slow, the index moved only from 96 (20s. 9d.) to 105 (22s. 9d.) but thereafter the increase was rapid; between 1871 and 1872 it climbed by 63 points, and finally reached a peak of 212 (45s. 10d.) in 1873. The reasons for the expansion are well known and they were largely external to the Scottish economy. Greatest among them was the demand for railway iron, and therefore indirectly for coal, from America and Europe. The extent of the rise, however, 116 points in five years, is not wholly a function of rising consumption. The pattern was that even assuming almost full employment of labour and capital, the supply of coal was relatively slow to respond to sudden enlarged demands. The structure of the coal industry with its mixture of old and new pits, and large and small establishments was responsible for this, and hence the scarcity of coal raised coal prices, and colliers' earnings rose meteorically. The break in the boom came in early 1874, and with the glutting and collapse of overseas markets, this was sharply transmitted first to the selling price of coal, and immediately thereafter to the colliers' earnings.(21) From 212·3 in 1873, the index dropped to 115·9 (25s. 1d.) in 1874—a fall of 96·4 (20s. 9d.) in one year. The fall continued year by year to an index of 68 in 1879. In six years this represented a fall in money earnings from 45s. 10d. per week to 14s. 8d. per week. No compensating rise in real earnings could have mitigated the consequences of such a fall.

1880-1900. In this period it was not until 1888, fourteen years after the crash of 1873-74, that the index of earnings regained the level of the mid-1860's, roughly that of 100 or 21s. 6d. per week. Significantly, earnings had climbed to a new plateau and the index never dipped below 100 again. During the period, in spite of a marked boom and trough, the index at the end year had averaged an increase of five points, (1s. 0½d.) per year. In a time of continually falling prices, the increase in real wages must have been even more substantial than the money figures would indicate.(22)

Throughout the period the broad trend in earnings was upward, as is clearly indicated by the nine-year moving average, and in a way it was a time of transition. The slow climb was based on gradually rising coal prices; coal still fed the ironworks, but progressively shipping and the export trade were claiming a larger portion of the output (see Table 6). One local factor almost certainly contributed to this rise in earnings. The West of Scotland was already becoming an old mining area, and one of difficult conditions. The labour cost in mining therefore rose, and in comparison with the East of Scotland, the West Central District became a high wage rate area.

TABLE 6

CHANGING MARKETS FOR SCOTTISH COAL, 1870–1913

Year	Total output	Consumed in manufacture of pig iron	Exports	Used in bunkers
1870	14·9	3·0	1·4	N.A.
1880	18·2	2·5	1·9	N.A.
1890	24·2	1·5	4·3	1·1(1)
1900	33·1	2·3(2)	7·4	1·6
1910	41·3	2·6	9·0	2·2
1913	42·5	2·2(3)	10·4	2·9

Notes: All figures cited are in millions of tons. (1) Figure for 1893. (2) Figure for 1903. (3) Figure for 1912.

Sources: Royal Commission on Coal Supplies, 1905. Final Report, Part XI, Appendices, pp. 76–77, 86–89, 118; and Mineral Statistics of the United Kingdom of Great Britain and Ireland.

1900-13. In this period the trend in colliers' earnings was strongly upward, with a rate of increase reminiscent of the early 1870's. The root source was the growing demand of exports, and of fuel for shipping.

Unlike the 1870's, demand and supply moved closely together, and increased output, in total and per man shift at the coal-face, was reflected in the steeply climbing index of earnings. By 1908 it reached the peak level of 1873, with an index of 216. In money terms this represented an average weekly pay packet of 46s. 8d. as against 45s. 10d. in 1873. From 1908-12 the index fluctuated between 191 (41s. 3d.) and 208 (44s. 11d.), before rising to 255·6 in the peak year of 1913, an average earning of 55s. 2d. per week. Thus after thirty-five years money earnings were again on a level equivalent to the peak years of 1872-73, and in real terms the value was probably somewhat more.(23)

The increase during these years was spectacular in rapidity and in absolute terms. It was even more remarkable when it is realised that this was achieved with a ten-day fortnight from 1901 onwards. The increase, as will be shown later, came from rising personal productivity, rather than from extensions of the working week, and it was also in this period that Dixons installed much mechanical equipment.(24)

The movement of this index is, as has been said, generally paralleled by that series of figures based on the daily wage rates. However, the respective yearly averages are different and the former is a precise record for one large colliery. The fact that the trends are similar, however, makes it probable that the nine-year moving average calculated for Dixons represents the underlying trend of earnings for the whole of Scotland. With the exception of the marked peak and the succeeding slump in the 1870's, the movement is clearly one of slow but definite increase in earnings over the period, a phenomenon one would expect as adjustments were made to take account of slowly rising standards of living and regular profits from the sale of coal. This is only representative of colliers' earnings. There was another large body of underground workers; these were oncostmen, and as we have said, very little is as yet known about them.

The most characteristic feature of the colliers' earnings was their variability, with no two years showing the same level of earnings; in contrast, the relative stability of the earnings of men engaged in underground oncost tasks is very striking.

As shown in Chart 3, the series of oncost payments reveal three types of movement, two of which do not conform to the colliers' index. The first is the wage movement of the oversman. He was not a manual labourer, but exercised general supervision over the whole series of operations within one pit, or section of the pit. During the second half of the nineteenth century, the movement of his earnings would seem to be influenced by the prevailing state of prosperity of the industry, rather than by frequent changes which, in the case of colliers and other oncost men, were occasioned by short-term fluctuations in the selling price of coal.

Only once in sixty years did the oversman's earnings fall below a weekly average of 30s. and this was only for three months in 1863. In the great cycle between 1868 and 1873, in comparison with the collier, the oversman experienced a lag of three-and-a-half years before his earnings moved upwards. Almost immediately the level of colliers' earnings dropped sharply, and for the next two-and-a-half years, while colliers' earnings fell from an average of 45s. per

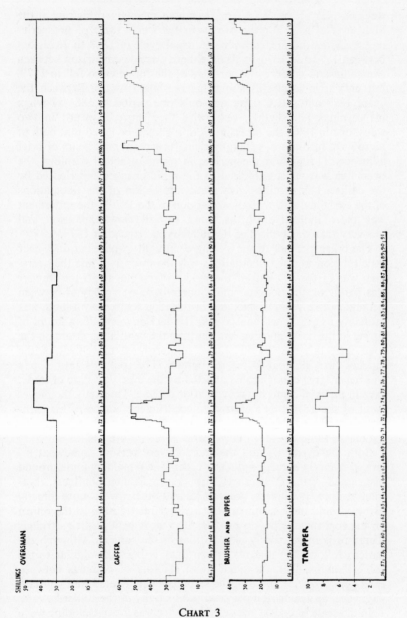

CHART 3

Average weekly earnings of oncost workers, Govan Collieries.

R

week to 17s. 6d. per week, the oversman maintained his rate at the high level of 45s. For the oversman the whole cycle of prosperity of the 1870's did not come in the usual cycle of 1868 to 1873, but between 1872 and 1876. In decline there was no comparison between oversman and collier: the earnings of the former also fell to 1879, but only to a level still above his pre-boom wages. Between the years 1879 and 1913, there was only one period in 1886-87 when his earnings fell slightly. Otherwise they moved upward in two steps, one in 1898, the other in 1906; it should be noted that both of these were in times of generally rising prosperity, not years of brief affluence. Throughout the period, in terms of actual earnings, the oversman was never subjected to the rapid changes experienced by the collier. His earnings give scant impression of the fluctuations of the economy and, with the exception of the 1870's, the movement was more indicative of the trend toward slow expansion and recovery that was typical of the industry at large after 1879.

The other member of the mining community whose earnings bear little relation to trade fluctuations was the trapper. While the oversman was at the top end of the ladder of employment, the trapper was barely on the bottom rung. Generally he was a boy of between ten and twelve years of age, and in the 1850's and early 1860's, was probably as young as eight years. His task involved long hours of sitting in the dark, opening and shutting the ventilating doors on the roadways; this was to allow the uninterrupted movement of the hutches carrying coal to the pit bottom. The trapper's rate of pay was never large enough to be affected by the everyday state of trade, save in times of rapid improvement or decline. Thus only the movement of the 1870's was clearly reflected in the course of his earnings. Elsewhere, stability was the main factor, his earnings remaining on the same level for many years.

Both the oversman and the trapper were persons somewhat removed from the direct productive tasks. The remaining underground oncostmen—gaffers, brushers, rippers, reddsmen, builders, bottomers, drawers, sinkers, brakers(25) and others, were more directly involved, and their earnings bear a closer relationship to the return on the coal they helped to produce; the movement of their earnings therefore is more closely akin to that of the colliers. Although the pattern followed by the oncost earnings is basically similar to the colliers' index, there is much more stability of earnings between each period of rise and fall, the stability being related to a constant day wage, as against the personal productivity of the collier.

In the scale of oncost earnings the gaffer was the outstanding wage earner. In level of pay, he compared favourably with the oversman, earning less in bad times, but substantially more in times of prosperity, Apart from this he, and all other grades of oncostmen, followed the same trend, only the level of earnings being different with the task involved. The general similarity of the oncost and collier wage movements is only interrupted once for a short period in 1900, when the former lagged slightly as wage rates fell in the slump of that year.

Thus it would seem that the earnings of the oncost worker moved in broad accord with those of the men at the coal-face. Both were directly affected by the prevailing state of the coal trade, the former earning less but having more stability and regularity of payment. While no complete representativeness can be claimed for these figures, it is probably not stretching the evidence too far to say that these are broadly indicative of the levels and movements of oncost payments in other pits. There is, as yet, little other available information from which it is possible to deduce how stable oncost employment was elsewhere in Scotland. However, there are numerous records now in the possession of the National Coal Board on which work of this nature could be pursued, and it must be hoped that corroborative evidence will eventually be obtained from these sources. It would seem, however, that oncost employment is unlikely to have fluctuated quite as erratically as that of the coal-face worker, for even when coal is not produced, maintenance of some kind, by oncostmen, is usually required.

The relationship between the earnings won at Govan and those gained elsewhere in Scotland is fairly definite. The general movement of wages has been established, and the fluctuations at least partly explained in broad terms. It is clear that there is a general sympathy of movement between the two graphs of earnings for colliers (Chart 1), and in Govan at least, the movement of oncost earnings follow the same general pattern. This would seem to indicate that the forces influencing earnings at Govan were similar to those experienced throughout Scotland. Further, it is possible that the average earnings for both colliers and oncostmen were broadly similar to those earned at the other large collieries, particularly when the range of earnings around the central average is utilised. It seems unlikely that, faced with common problems of geology, costs and market prices, the average weekly earnings of most colliers in Scotland would fall far wide of the range set by plus or minus 6s. around the average figure for Govan.

V

Output and Productivity

It has been customary to utilise statistics of output per man year,(26) as an indicator of the progress of the coal trade in the nineteenth century. Continuous and fairly reliable series of these figures are available from 1874(27) and the picture they present for Scotland is shown in Chart 4 and Table 7. This is amplified in Table 7A by a series of output figures for the West of Scotland from 1866 to 1886. These are based on total figures of "all minerals wrot', *i.e.*, including tonnages of coal, ironstone, shale, etc., and are therefore not strictly comparable with the later series. They do,

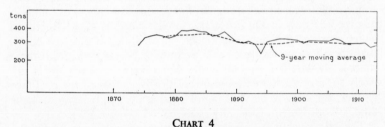

CHART 4
Output per man/year in tons all underground workers, Scotland.

however, help establish the trend of productivity between 1860 and the 1880's.(28) The trend indicated by the two series closely follows that for other mining areas in Britain and it has been argued that it indicates that the miner's efficiency reached a peak in the 1880's, and thereafter declined. The marked rise in productivity which the available series indicate between the 1860's and the 1880's is said to be due to a decline in the seasonality of the coal industry as its main consumers shifted from the domestic to the industrial field, therefore enabling a fuller use and less under-employment of labour and, more important, to the process of technical innovation. In these years there was a wider use of the steam engine to assist in pumping and raising the coal, the introduction of improved systems of ventilation, a fuller employment of safety lamps, and developments in mechanical underground haulage. This period also witnessed the beginnings of mechanical coal cutting.

TABLE 7

OUTPUT PER MAN YEAR IN TONS FOR ALL WORKERS
(SURFACE AND UNDERGROUND) SCOTLAND

Year	O.P.M.	Year	O.P.M.
1874	278	1894	233
1875	329	1895	306
1876	342	1896	318
1877	351	1897	326
1878	343	1898	328
1879	330	1899	324
1880	343	1900	318
1881	386	1901	303
1882	385	1902	313
1883	390	1903	314
1884	379	1904	314
1885	376	1905	313
1886	346	1906	328
1887	351	1907	321
1888	377	1908	296
1889	338	1909	297
1890	304	1910	299
1891	298	1911	301
1892	305	1912	275
1893	289	1913	287

TABLE 7A

OUTPUT PER MAN YEAR IN TONS, SCOTLAND: WESTERN
DISTRICT

Year	O.P.M.	Year	O.P.M.
1866	296·01	1876	310·12
1867	295·56	1877	318·47
1868	295·56	1878	312·02
1869	306·69	1879	310·76
1870	322·69	1880	312·42
1871	335·07	1881	330·31
1872	307·02	1882	329·19
1873	297·03	1883	338·08
1874	292·04	1884	336·03
1875	341·81	1885	338·39
		1886	333·08

The advances stimulated the working of deeper and larger mines and the renovation of many old ones. In fact, the general fluctuations in productivity have been regarded as 'the resultant of the opposing forces of the natural circumstances of the industry's existence on the one hand, and the ingenuity of the mining engineer on the other'.(29) If conditions at Govan were typical this explanation of the trend in productivity tends to obscure noteworthy changes in the disposition of the total mining force and masks a very real increase in the productivity of the coal-face worker.

Chart 5 reveals the fluctuations of the O.P.M. data for all underground workers in Scotland, similar but partial data for the Govan Collieries, and a more sophisticated series of figures, the O.P.M. of coal-face workers in Govan Collieries. Taking the first and

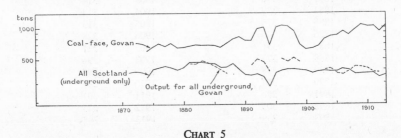

CHART 5

Output per man/year in tons for all underground workers, Scotland and Govan; output per man/year for coal-face workers at Govan.

second of these two series, it is clear that while the output for all Scotland and the output for Govan may not run at exactly the same levels, both the fluctuations and the output trends are similar. It follows therefore that productivity in the Govan Collieries, as in Britain as a whole, reached a peak in the early 1880's, and then began a progressive, if irregular, decline. However, the movements of the third series, that of the O.P.M. for the coal-face workers in the Govan Collieries, reveals a divergent and anomalous trend; that is, while O.P.M. for the whole pit was declining, that for the coal-face worker was showing a strong upward movement.

The best corroborative indicator of this trend would undoubtedly be the progress of output per man shift, but the sheer labour involved in calculating this very sophisticated index has made such a task impossible. Nevertheless, it has been possible to calculate

the average output per week for the coal-face workers at Govan
from 1856 to 1913, and the series is represented in Table 8 and
Chart 6. At first sight, this graph is erratic but in the earlier years
at least, there was a general periodicity of seven to nine years in
the movement, and accordingly a nine-year moving average (centred
on the fifth item), has been calculated to smooth out the irregulari-
ties, and indicate the trend. It is clear from Chart 6 that output per
week remained fairly stable between 1860 and 1880, but that this
period was followed by one during which a marked increase in
productivity took place. This continued until the late 1890's and
early 1900's, when the Govan Collieries suffered from a series of
labour disputes and the running down of one of the pits. Thereafter
the upward trend continues, at the very time when the O.P.M. data
indicates a general lowering of productivity.

CHART 6

Output per week in tons per man at the coal-face, Govan.

This phenomenon can be considered in more detail. Over the
thirty-six year period from 1876 to 1912 inclusive, it has been
possible on twenty-seven occasions to establish not only the average
weekly employment of coal-face workers, but also the numbers of
other underground workers. This information, together with total
employment underground, is presented in Table 9. This table reveals
an irregular diminution of the number of coal-face workers employed coupled with an increase in the number of oncost workers.
The ratio of the number of oncost workers to coal-face workers is
given in the fourth column. This shows that in 1876 there were two
face workers to every oncost worker, but by 1906 every two face
workers were serviced by three oncost-workers. It is apparent that
to utilise labour most efficiently the management must constantly
have made changes in what might be called the underground labour
ratio in order to cope with such factors as changing geological

TABLE 8

AVERAGE ANNUAL OUTPUT PER MAN PER WEEK IN TONS AT THE COAL-FACE: GOVAN

Year	Tons/week	Year	Tons/week	Year	Tons/week
1856	13·8	1876	13·7	1895	17·8
1857	13·6	1877	12·9	1896	19·3
1858	14·5	1878	13·6	1897	18·9
1859	13·6	1879	12·9	1989	17·6
1860	10·6	1880	12·5	1899	13·2
1861	12·9	1881	12·9	1900	10·8
1862	12·1	1882	13·7	1901	11·3
1863	13·9	1883	13·0	1902	13·6
1864	13·5	1884	13·1	1903	15·0
1865	13·4	1885	12·7	1904	15·6
1866	11·2	1886	12·5	1905	16·3
1867	12·5	1887	13·4	1906	17·4
1868	11·8	1888	15·3	1907	16·4
1869	12·2	1889	15·3	1908	18·2
1870	13·6	1890	14·5	1909	20·2
1871	13·5	1891	14·5	1910	20·5
1872	14·8	1892	18·6	1911	19·4
1873	12·9	1893	19·4	1912	18·7
1874	11·7	1894	16·9	1913	20·7
1875	12·7				

conditions, the efficiency of haulage and winding, and the introduction of mechanised coal-cutting. Over time these changes resulted in a growing proportion of the underground labour force being employed in oncost tasks. The face workers, whose own productivity was increasing with the introduction of coal-cutting machinery, required more servicing. In effect, this enhanced output had to be shared with a growing number of oncost workers, hence the crude O.P.M. figure had a downward tendency.

Without similarly detailed analysis of the records of other mines in the West of Scotland it is impossible to say whether the figures for the employment ratio at Dixon's Govan Colliery were typical of whether the output of the coal-face worker was increasing at other pits, to be similarly obscured in the overall O.P.M. figures by the need for more oncost workers to service the hewers. Certainly, efficient colliery management necessitated careful allocation of the total underground work force to keep labour costs per unit of output at a minimum and on occasions this must have resulted in conditions

TABLE 9

WEEKLY UNDERGROUND EMPLOYMENT AT GOVAN IN VARIOUS YEARS

Year	Number of coal-face workers	Number of oncost workers	Total workers	Ratio of oncost labour/ coal-face workers
1876	474	232	706	0·49
1878	402	194	596	0·48
1881	448	223	671	0·49
1882	425	228	653	0·54
1883	359	151	510	0·42
1884	384	190	574	0·49
1885	336	198	534	0·59
1886	349	228	577	0·65
1887	330	310	640	0·94
1891	288	245	533	0·85
1892	280	266	546	0·95
1893	260	292	552	1·12
1894	264	205	469	0·78
1896	219	240	459	1·10
1897	215	253	468	1·18
1898	248	197	445	0·79
1899	314	150	464	0·48
1903	248	239	487	0·96
1904	247	245	492	0·99
1905	209	276	485	1·32
1906	207	316	523	1·53
1907	210	252	462	1·20
1908	197	251	448	1·27
1909	202	318	520	1·56
1910	199	332	531	1·67
1911	209	371	580	1·78
1912	196	319	515	1·63

Note: Employment in the Govan Collieries slowly declined during the nineteenth century. In 1841, the work-force was 1,014; during the 1850's it was never far from 1,000, but by 1866 had declined to 800. The figures from 1876 onward give a fair estimate of the total work-force: the number of surface workers was always small.

in which the O.P.M. figures hide a very real increase in coal-face productivity. This theme deserves further examination, and if the findings of this paper, part of a broader thesis on which the author is currently working, stimulate further research into the surviving historical records of the British coal industry, many of which are being cared for by the National Coal Board, it will have served a useful purpose.

NOTES

(1) Between 1800 and 1913 there were no less than fifty-one separate government investigations of the coal industry. In addition some reports, like those of the early Commissioners, were published annually over a long period (see footnote 2).

(2) State of the Population, Education, and Schools in the Mining Districts. H. S. Tremenheere, Commissioner. Report of 1849, p. 16. Hereafter abbreviated to Reports on the Mining Districts.

(3) Reports on the Mining Districts, 1848, p. 14.

(4) R. Page Arnot, A History of the Scottish Miners (London, 1955), pp. 33, 34, 37, 40, 41, 46, 51, 66.

(5) A. J. Youngson Brown, The Scottish Coal Industry, 1854-1886, Thesis for the degree of D.Litt., University of Aberdeen, 1953, p. 208.

(6) Reports on the Mining Districts, 1844, pp. 31, 32.

(7) Reports on the Mining Districts, 1847, p. 15.

(8) Reports on the Mining Districts, 1852, p. 40.

(9) Reports on the Mining Districts, 1849, p. 18.

(10) Reports on the Mining Districts, 1852, p. 41.

(11) R. Page Arnot, op. cit., p. 110.

(12) R. Page Arnot, ibid., pp. 71, 91.

(13) Reports on the Mining Districts, 1844, p. 35.

(14) Ibid., p. 35.

(15) Ibid., p. 35.

(16) See footnote 15.

(17) Peter L. Payne, The Govan Collieries, 1804-1805, Business History, Vol. III, No. 2 (June, 1961), pp. 79-80.

(18) Reports on the Mining Districts, passim, 1844-59.

(19) A study of Chart 2 indicates that the general span of time from major peak to peak, or major trough to trough is eight or nine years. In his work on output in Scottish mining Professor Youngson Brown also found a nine-year moving average suitable. (See footnote 5.)

(20) See R. H. Campbell, in J. Cunnison and J. B. S. Gilfillan (eds.), Third Statistical Account of Scotland: Glasgow (Glasgow, 1958), pp. 156-57.

(21) Although the official sliding scale was not yet in operation, individual masters obviously used the selling price of coal to determine the collier's rate of pay—see footnote 15.

(22) A. L. Bowley, Wages and Income in the United Kingdom since 1860 (Cambridge, 1937), Table VII, p. 30. Bowley estimates that with 1914 as base year = 100, the cost of living index in Britain stood at 105 in 1880, fell continually to 83 in 1895 and 1896, and was 91 in 1900. Ibid., Table II, p. 8. Bowley estimates colliers' earnings index at a base of 100 in 1880, a low of 99 in 1886 and 1887 and 163 in 1900.

(23) Ibid., cost of living index estimated at 105 in 1880 and 102 in 1913. Table VII, p. 30. Colliers' earnings index 100 in 1880 and 163 in 1913, Table II, p. 8.

(24) The first mention of coal-cutting machinery appears in No. 5 pit in the fortnight ending 25th January, 1908. By 1910 there is evidence of at least five machines being used.

(25) Gaffers were group foremen, participating in manual labour, but responsible for the work of their own groups. Reddsmen (or roadsmen or

rippers), brushers and builders, all performed much the same task. The reddsmen blew down the roof to keep passageways open, the brushers cleared away the debris, and the builders rebuilt the material of the supporting walls on the roadways. Bottomers were the men responsible for the loading of the coal at the pit bottom, originally into baskets, and later by guiding the loaded hutches on to the cages ready to be raised to the surface. Drawers (and putters) were responsible for pushing the loaded hutches, originally direct from the coal-face to the pit bottom, and later from the face to the main roadways where often horses took over. Sinkers sank the shafts and often drove the roadways, and brakers worked on inclines where series of hutches moving under gravity had to be controlled to stop runaways. These are only some of the specialised tasks performed underground, all of which are necessary if the coal is to be delivered to the surface.

(26) Hereafter abbreviated to O.P.M.

(27) Mineral Statistics of the United Kingdom of Great Britain and Ireland.

(28) A. J. Youngson Brown, op. cit., Table XV, p. 52.

(29) A. J. Taylor, Labour Productivity and Technological Innovation in the British Coal Industry, 1850-1914, Economic History Review, Vol. XIV, 1961, p. 51.

CHAPTER TEN

Entrepreneurship in the Scottish Heavy Industries, 1870-1900

T. J. BYRES

Lecturer in Economics,
School of Oriental and African Studies,
University of London

1. Introduction—The Background to Scottish Entrepreneurship

Between 1870 and 1900 the outstanding characteristic of the Scottish economy was the rise to a position of hegemony of the heavy industries. These industries became the basis of Scottish economic growth and to study them is to get at the nerve-centre of economic developments in Scotland. The Census occupational statistics reveal(1) a significant decline in agriculture and textiles and an equally marked rise in heavy industry and chemicals. Agriculture dominated in 1871, employing 17 per cent of the total Scottish working population; textiles came second with 15 per cent; heavy industry(2) gave employment to 11 per cent; and chemicals to 1 per cent. In 1881 and 1891 the economy could be said to have assumed a more 'balanced' aspect (in the sense of having an even distribution of the working population among the different groupings); by 1901, however, 'heaviness' was the keynote. By then agriculture's labour force had declined to 11 per cent of the total and textile's to 10 per cent, while that of heavy industry had risen to 15 per cent and that of chemicals to just over 1 per cent.

Within the general advance of the 'heavies' there was growth and decline. The polyglot engineering industries(3) formed the largest group in both 1871 and 1901, increasing their share of the total over the period (from a third to not far short of half), and almost trebling their labour force (from 51,000 to 140,000). They were followed by coal, whose share remained fairly stable (30 per cent in 1871 and 34 per cent in 1901), its total more than doubling (from 47,000 to 102,000). A dramatic feature was the decline of both ironstone and iron manufacture, reflecting the depletion of the rich

Scottish ores and the demise of the pig iron industry: the former employed over 10,000 in 1881 and only 2,424 in 1901, and the latter almost 37,000 in 1881 and a bare 15,000 in 1901. Equally dramatic was the rise of the steel industry, which gave employment to 34 men in 1871 and to over 8,000 in 1901. Shipbuilding doubled its labour force (16,000 to nearly 35,000), while retaining its share of the total (10·6 per cent in 1871 and 11·4 per cent in 1901). These figures for shipbuilding certainly understate that industry's significance, since they do not include labour employed in marine engineering (which is not distinguished in the Census statistics). Even if these were added, however, the figures would not fully reflect shipbuilding's importance in the Scottish economy. It was, in fact, a 'leading' industry, in the sense that it 'set the tone' of the rest of the economy. Walter Dixon, speaking in 1911, recalled the 1890's: 'It is, I believe, taken as a truism in the district that when the Clyde is busy (*i.e.*, when the shipyards are fully employed) trade generally, and especially the iron and steel trade . . . is also busy. That has been, I believe, the universal experience of the past.'(4)

As these heavy industries came to dominate Scotland, so, with certain qualifications, they experienced a relative decline within the British economy. This can be demonstrated statistically,(5) except for engineering, where less exact evidence must be used.

In the case of iron ore, Scotland lost an important natural advantage as her supplies of rich blackband ironstone—the very basis of pig iron's strength before 1870—ran out. Between 1875 and 1900, Scotland's share of total British output fell from 34 per cent to 6 per cent. The coal industry presented a totally different picture. It retained, and, indeed, slightly improved its relative position, with 14 per cent of British production in 1870 and 15 per cent in 1900. Pig iron's share of British output fell quite markedly between 1870 and 1890, from 20 to 10 per cent, but recovered to 14 per cent in 1895 and 13 per cent in 1900. Unlike the other heavy industries, malleable iron notably increased its share of British production, from 8 per cent in 1870 to 20 per cent in 1895 and 18 per cent in 1900. This, however, is to be interpreted more as a sign of weakness than of strength—as an unwillingness to scrap in an industry rendered uneconomic by the advent of steel.

The Scottish steel industry went through three phases between the early 'seventies and 1900. In the first, from 1873 to 1879, the only large producer of open-hearth steel in Scotland was the Steel Company of Scotland, relying mainly upon the market for rails at a time when South Wales was the leading British producer of this type of steel. After 1879, with steel replacing iron as a material for shipbuilding, a number of Scottish malleable iron producers challenged the Steel Company's near monopoly of Scottish steel-making, and between 1881 and 1889 Scotland produced more open-hearth steel than any other region in Great Britain. It was about 1889 that this second phase came to an end, when Scotland was overtaken by the rapidly growing Cleveland area. In the last decade of the century Cleveland was the leading and the most efficient producer of open-hearth steel in Britain.(6)

Shipbuilding showed a relative decline between 1870 and 1900, and, as in the case of steel, the period can be divided into three phases. In the first, from about 1870 to 1876, the Clyde's share of gross tonnage launched in the U.K. was at its peak, varying from 34 per cent in 1872 to 49 per cent in 1876, and standing at 39 per cent for the whole period. In the second, from about 1877 to 1888, the share varied from 31 to 41 per cent, being 33 per cent for the twelve years. Finally, between 1889 and 1900 the Clyde's proportion was 29 per cent—varying from 26 to 31 per cent.

In the engineering industries, it seems likely that locomotive engineering, if it did not retain its relative position, at least did not lose it to any significant extent. South-west Scotland was the most important area in Britain in the early 1870's and remained so in 1900. In heavy machine-tools, but not in light, Glasgow seems to have improved her position over the period, though she stayed second to Manchester. Pipe-founding remained of considerable importance, but the manufacture of both sugar machinery and textile machinery declined absolutely and relatively. 'Bridges, roofs, and railway appliances' grew markedly, with the firm of Sir William Arrol and Company pre-eminent.(7) It would be rash to attempt to draw any sort of balance from such evidence, but more significant in the long-run than the changing relative positions of these *established* sections was the failure of the South-west of Scotland to develop the new branches, whose growth potential was great. The 1907 Census of Production revealed that 14 per cent of the value of output of U.K. engineering belonged to electrical engineering.(8) It was new and it was growing rapidly, and in Glasgow, further, Lord Kelvin was making, or had made, many of the basic discoveries in the field of electricity. Yet as late as 1912 it could be said that 'electrical engineering is . . . [a] vastly important branch of industry, although in Glasgow it is confined to the Corporation and some half-dozen firms'.(9) They were not, moreover, firms noted for their size. In the 'nineties, too, the production of cycles and motor cars increased rapidly in England.(10) Again, Scotland was behind. In the 1901 British Association Handbook, which purported to be a comprehensive survey of local industries in Glasgow and the south-west, there was no mention at all of cycles or of motor-cars. There were, in fact, at least nine attempts made to establish a motor industry in Scotland before 1900, and none was success-ful.(11)

Factors other than entrepreneurship were making for a relative decline in Scotland's importance in both the context of the British and world economies. The advantages that new areas have over an old one, the emergence of better—endowed competitors, the deple-tion of mineral deposits, and even the loss of an initial superiority in wage costs are factors over which entrepreneurs have limited con-trol.(12) Faced with such a situation, however, Scottish industrialists could have sought new sources of iron ore abroad, could have searched for and adopted cost-reducing technical processes, could have diversified or branched out into new activities where necessary, and so on. The rest of this essay attempts to estimate, in the heavy sector, at least, the nature of the Scottish entrepreneurs' response to the forces of change.

2. The Entrepreneurial Response—(a) Heavy Industry, Technical Progress and Technical Education

Professor A. H. Cole has suggested a method of evaluating the behaviour of entrepreneurs in relation to certain spheres of action,(13) in each of which there is a constant need for manage-ment, risk-taking, and innovation. They may be enumerated as follows:

(1) the acquisition of efficient plant and equipment and their revision as new conditions demand;
(2) the maintenance of efficient relations with labour;
(3) the securing and retention of adequate financial resources;
(4) the obtaining of a sufficient and steady supply of raw materials;
(5) the development of markets (home and foreign) for products, and the devising of new products to meet or anticipate con-sumer demand;
(6) the keeping of good relations with public authorities and society at large.

The field to be considered is so wide as to preclude a high degree of precision. Information on some spheres is readily available, while on others it is sparse. Only a full-scale assault on the increasingly abundant business records of Scotland can yield truly satisfactory answers.

The criterion easiest to document for the heavy industries is the first, which we can conveniently call 'attitudes towards technical progress and technical education'. In fact, this was probably the most important criterion of all during this period, when the heavy industries of the world were characterised by marked technical advance. To retain or improve a position in such a situation the entrepreneur must be prepared to make himself aware of any such progress and adopt improvements where possible. The heavy industries were requiring more and more technical knowledge as they grew in complexity, and countries like Germany and the U.S. enhanced their competitiveness by sponsoring institutions which specialised in technical education.

The *Scottish coal industry* had a mixed record in this respect. On the one hand, at the very beginning of the period, between 1871 and 1873, the coal-owners invested heavily in new plant, which resulted in increasing output per man in subsequent years;(14) and in the 'eighties and 'nineties minor improvements were adopted in the shape of smooth-running and powerful fans (which achieved better ventilation), washing, separating and picking appliances, and larger hutches.(15) Contrariwise, the coal entrepreneurs can be faulted on at least four important counts.

Firstly, they were backward in adopting haulage machinery. It is true that, compared with the 'fifties and 'sixties, the introduction of haulage machinery and the extended use of horses had done much to lessen the cost of conveying the coal to the shaft bottom. In 1883, however, it could still be remarked that 'it is astonishing . . . still to find not a few cases where the drawers have to convey their hutches containing no more than four or five cwt. of coal a long distance. I have come across instances, not long since, where the drawers had to travel with their hutches a distance of over two miles for each ton of coal produced.'(16) This was in marked contrast to practice in the North of England.

A second indication of deficient enterprise lay in a tardiness in introducing the new power of electricity. In 1881, Ralph Moore observed that electric light was to be fitted up at Earnock Colliery and that it was 'fast getting beyond the region of experiment'.(17) This was an isolated piece of enterprise, however, and, though between 1881 and 1891 there were stray references to the possibilities of electricity as a motive power, virtually nothing was done about it in the collieries of Scotland. By 1891 it had been proved beyond doubt to be more economical and less dangerous than any other source of power.(18) Before then, reluctance to invest in electrical plant could be excused because of the large sums involved and the uncertain results. After this, however, the reluctance shades into conservatism and a disinclination to take risks. Lip-service continued to be paid to the 'promise of electricity' up to 1900, but little was done about it in practice.

Allied to the reluctance to adopt electricity was, thirdly, the attitude towards coal-cutting machinery, which, had it been adopted, would have given Scotland a clear competitive advantage. In 1891 coal-cutting machines were in use in only eight Scottish collieries,(19) though it must be admitted that the rest of Britain showed similar conservatism.(20) It could not properly be pleaded that there were no satisfactory machines, since, from the 1870's on, there were many good and reliable models, which, driven by compressed air, could cut coal efficiently to a depth of $2\frac{1}{2}$ to 3 feet. By 1890, at least, it had been demonstrated that machinery could lead to significant reductions in costs if used in appropriate circumstances.(21) However, the heavy initial cost, allied to the fact that labour was comparatively cheap and plentiful in Scotland, meant that there was no compelling need to mechanise. Further the coal was still relatively easy to work. Nevertheless, it is difficult to avoid the conclusion that the reluctance to adopt coal-cutting machinery to even a minor extent was an indication of a lack of enterprise.

Finally, the inherent conservatism of the colliery owners is exemplified by their record on technical education. As far back as 1871, John Young, Professor of Natural History at Glasgow University, pointed out in a paper read before the Institution of Engineers and Shipbuilders in Scotland,(22) that although a mining engineer needed the specialised knowledge of a geologist, mineralogist, and civil engineer, there were no facilities in Scotland to provide such training. He spoke scathingly of the 'gross blunders of the so-called practical men',(23) and advocated qualified men, minimum standards, certified examinations, and the establishment of an appropriate school or college. Sweden and France had such facilities and there was the School of Mines in London. The latter could, in theory, be used by Scots, but very few took advantage of it. There was nowhere in Scotland where a proprietor, a manager, or a miner could obtain technical information about his work. The paper was fiercely opposed by the 'practical men', who were blind to the fact that what was being advocated was not complete reliance on theory, but a satisfactory combination of theory and practice. The first mention of technical education in the *Transactions of the Mining*

S

Institute of Scotland did not come until 1902, and even then re-luctantly.(24) It was not until this date, either, that there was talk of a lectureship in mining in Glasgow University—when those of marine engineering, civil engineering and naval architecture were already established.

In *malleable iron*, technical progress was non-existent. For thirty-five years after the industry's peak in 1880 there was no change of size, structure, or productive capacity. In the words of a contemporary: 'No new process having been introduced in the manufacture of puddled iron, the fundamental principles are just the same as have been in operation for fifty years or more.'(25)

In *pig iron*, the first point of criticism is the smallness of the furnaces. It was this which was largely responsible for Scottish output per furnace being smaller than that of any of the main pig-iron producing districts of the U.K.(26) It was argued that Scottish furnaces were traditionally small because of the nature of the Scottish splint coal and blackband ores which precluded too heavy a charge, for fear that the coke would be crushed and the free passage of gases interfered with.(27) This was certainly true from the 1840's up to the end of the 1870's, but thereafter less and less splint coal was used in Scottish furnaces and increasing use was made of imported Spanish ores. The reluctance to change, after the 'seventies, can be taken as a sign of conservatism. The Scottish pig iron industry was also backward in plant layout and furnace working. As late as 1913 'in Scotland the system of hand-filling [the furnace] with one or two exceptions prevails',(28) while to a very large extent it was done mechanically in England and abroad. Thirdly, the quality of the iron produced was low and markedly lacking in uniformity.(29) It was not until the mid-1880's that the industry started to produce significant quantities of the high-quality hematite pig required by the Scottish steel industry, which, until that time, was imported from Cleveland.(30) Symptomatic of the prevailing set-up, finally, was the neglect of pyrometry (or the measurement of high temperatures), which, Professor Sexton explained, was due to the fact that *'our managers are very conservative and do not care to introduce innovations'*.(31)

One redeeming feature was the successful introduction, in the 1880's and 1890's, of by-product recovery plant. In 1872 Scottish ironmasters were just beginning to utilise the hitherto 'waste' gases. By 1885, 'the persistent efforts of Mr. McCosh and his partners (of Wm. Baird & Company) to utilise the tar and ammonia contained in the furnace gas had just been crowned with success, and, encouraged by their example, several other works had begun to put down by-product plants. . . . Most of us can remember the very great interest they excited throughout the iron trade at the time.'(32) This gave the Scottish industry an important advantage over its rivals, and the plant became an indispensable part of the coal-fed blast furnaces of Scotland. Unfortunately, however, the advantage was short-lived. Competitors were quick to see the value of by-products and rapidly imitated the Scottish ironmasters.

Another progressive feature in Scottish practice was the increasingly effective use made of both ore and coal in Scotland, compared with England and Wales.(33) Between 1872 and 1896, Scotland, from being well behind England and Wales in the way she used coal, surpassed her, while between 1884 and 1896 she slightly increased her advantage in the use of ore.

These two redeeming features must certainly have saved Scottish pig iron from very serious decline, if not from virtual extinction, and they account for the industry's partial recovery in the late 1880's and early 1890's. Nevertheless, they pale into insignificance beside the 'black list' given above, and one is forced to conclude that the pig iron producers were largely devoid of drive, imagination, and enterprise for most of the period under consideration.

There was little integration between pig iron and steel, and this was serious in an industry where important economies could be realised by the location of the two branches in the same place. The malleable iron producers did not go in for steel until 1879, and the pig iron men were even more dilatory. It is true that by 1900, of the nine large concerns producing pig iron five also produced steel, but only two of these (Merry & Cunninghame and the Glasgow Iron and Steel Company) were fully integrated concerns. The other three (the Coltness Iron Company, James Dunlop & Company, and the Summerlee and Mossend) possessed steel works and blast furnaces, but they were on different sites.(34) The criticism, of course, applies equally to those firms which started primarily as steel-producing concerns (like the Steel Company of Scotland and David Colville & Sons) and which failed to move backwards into pig iron. As late as 1914 there were still only two fully integrated plants in Scotland.(35) The prosperous and expanding *steel industry* was, in fact, subject to conflicting pressures. Inefficient and stagnant pig iron pulled in one direction, and progressive and buoyant shipbuilding in the other—the result being a marked duality.

On the credit side, indicative of increasing efficiency, from about 1885 until the end of the century the capacity of smelting furnaces rose from 15-20 to 50-60 tons; handling equipment became more efficient, as heavier plates and slabs had to be dealt with; mechanical charging and clearing was started; cogging mills were introduced to replace steam hammers.(36) Nevertheless, the lack of integration prevented the adoption of hot-metal working in Scotland, though even where integration existed this process was not adopted; the practice of casting on cars was introduced in England but not in Scotland; the gas-engine was rejected by Scottish entrepreneurs in 1896; and the Scottish industry was reluctant to embrace the Gilchrist-Thomas process despite its obvious advantages.(37) More generally, it is to be noted that the Steel Company of Scotland was the only firm of importance producing steel in the country until 1879 and that even this firm was comparatively late in entering the field, starting to produce in 1873, nearly a decade after the Bessemer steel industry had been established in England. When the Scottish steel industry did arrive it utilised the open-hearth process; efforts to establish the Bessemer industry were few and unsustained.(38) It was not enough to argue that the quality of the pig was the stumbling block, for that could have been changed by a willingness to adjust plant to foreign, non-phosphoric ores. On balance, then, the steel entrepreneurs appear to have been less dynamic than they might have been. They were wary of the new, though once it was proven they went ahead. 'Safety-first' is not the formula for industrial supremacy, however, and the loss of the position as Britain's leading producer of open-hearth steel to Cleveland, from about 1890, finds part of its explanation in this attitude.

Closely related to Scotland's technical backwardness, and one of the reasons for it, was her neglect of technical education.(39) In almost all cases training for the iron and steel industry was still to be obtained only in the works. This old and simple method may have suited the needs of the 1850's and 1860's, but it was not appropriate to the age of rapid progress, advanced techniques, and keen competition, in which the industry now found itself. There was no satisfactory provision for such education in the universities, and the number of technical colleges was wholly inadequate. The works chemist did not receive the status and respect which he deserved, and the laboratory was more often than not located in some out of the way corner. For an industry whose work was largely chemical, this was most unsatisfactory. Professor Sexton pointed to the existence of the Glasgow and West of Scotland Technical College (where he himself held a chair), 'though it falls far short of what we would like to see it. When I look back on the record of this institution I can only wonder at the extreme apathy of the manufacturers of the district, especially the ironmasters, with reference to it.'(40)

In *shipbuilding and marine engineering*, in contrast to the other

Scottish heavy industries, the entrepreneurs were men of vision and enterprise, with the courage to experiment and the willingness to take risks. Shipbuilding may truly be said to have been an 'innovating' industry at this time, its success in world markets fully justifying the boldness of its entrepreneurs. Its loss of relative position, inasmuch as it was not the inevitable result of the growth of other shipbuilding areas, was probably due, in great measure, to the relinquishment of a considerable advantage in wage costs. Entrepreneurial initiative is seen in the rapid change from iron to steel, the development of triple- and quadruple-expansion engines, the adoption of the continuous cellular system, the increased use of machinery in the yards and a relatively favourable attitude towards technical education.

It was about 1876 that steel began to be seriously considered as a material for shipbuilding.(41) In fact, iron had barely established supremacy over wood, in the early 'seventies, when the advantages of mild steel began to be recognised. Lloyds issued their rules for steel vessels in 1877, and the price of steel plates on the Clyde fell from £20 per ton in 1876 to £9 10s. in 1879 (they were about £7 5s. per ton by 1885).(42) In 1879, the Clyde's output was 10 per cent steel and the U.K.'s 3 per cent. By 1884, the figures were 45 per cent and 18 per cent, and by 1886 69 per cent and 56 per cent.(43) The gap had disappeared almost completely by 1888, when steel was universally used in Britain, but the Clyde had shown a clear lead in developing the material and had derived therefrom a distinct competitive advantage. This was a tribute to the foresight of her shipbuilders, and especially to that of William Denny, who from 1876 was very active in his advocacy of the new material. It was his yard which in 1879 launched the first ocean-going steamer built of steel, the *Rotomahana,* and in 1884, out of the forty or so yards in operation on the Clyde, Denny's alone produced just under a fifth of the whole steel tonnage.(44)

Meanwhile, striking advances were made in engineering practice. Steel boilers made possible higher steam pressures and gave greater thermal efficiency. High pressures needed high ratios of expansion in compound engines, and in 1874 Alexander Kirk, then of John Elder and Company, developed the triple-expansion engine, and had it fitted aboard the screw-steamer, *Propontis.* It was not a complete success at first, however, and it was not until 1881 that it was adopted, this time on the screw-steamer, *Aberdeen,* with a reduction in fuel consumption, compared with previous practice, of 30 per cent. Thereafter its adoption was assured. Another step in the same direction was made on the Clyde in 1885, when Walter Brock, of

William Denny and Bros., developed a quadruple-expansion engine, which could sustain even higher pressures. By 1890 these were quite common.(45)

A third important development which originated on the Clyde was the modification in the structural arrangement of ocean-trading vessels known as the continuous-cellular system. Based on the principle of longitudinal construction, this gave greater structural strength, and meant increased security for vessels which made 'light' as well as 'loaded' runs. It had been advocated as early as 1854, but was never seriously considered until the Clyde builders recognised its value for water-ballast steamers, about 1878. Prominent among its advocates were John Inglis and William Denny, and by 1883 50 per cent of ocean-going steamers were fitted with cellular bottoms.(46)

William Denny was also to the fore in making increased use of machinery in the yards. This was made effective by the great extension of piece-work on the Clyde. Piece-work had long been in use for riveters and smiths, and in the late 'seventies was introduced for plate and bar fitters, joiners, and carpenters. It did not, as was forecast, lead to bad workmanship, and, partly as a result of its success, a variety of new machines were introduced to increase efficiency: machines for punching holes in the thickest plates at one operation, hydraulic presses to replace steam hammers, portable hydraulic riveters, woodwork machinery, and improved cranes for lifting heavy weights.(47)

Finally, the shipbuilders' attitude towards technical education was relatively favourable. In 1880, it was proposed to establish a Lectureship in Naval Architecture and Marine Engineering at Glasgow University, and the first lectures were given in 1881-82. Then, in November, 1883, the widow of John Elder, following her husband's wishes, gifted £12,500 for the endowment of a Chair of Naval Architecture, which was duly established. In 1884 Pollock could write:

'The appreciation and employment of scientific method and analysis in designing and building ships have at no previous time been greater than they are at present. This is already yielding benefits and ensuring successes which only a few years ago would have remained unachieved and ungathered . . . There is at last a proper regard for fundamental principles . . . [and] there has been progress in the pure science of naval architecture . . . [as well as] the practical application of scientific rules and principles to shipbuilding.'(48)

This happy state of affairs must certainly have been, in no small measure, the result of a due regard for technical education.

3. The Entrepreneurial Response—(b) Heavy Industry and Other Spheres of Action

Having explored, in some detail, one of the entrepreneurs' spheres of action, a number of the others will be examined in this section. There is not, outside the business archives, the same wealth of information on these themes. Technical progress and technical education were topics that came readily to the public gaze—subjects about which it was possible to generalise. Some of the other spheres of action, however, were less amenable to such treatment, requiring knowledge of individual firms which entrepreneurs were not ready to divulge. A full-scale analysis of entrepreneurship would require a far less jejune treatment of these spheres of action than is given here, and this can come only from an intensive search of the records of the firms.

One of the spheres of action noted was 'the maintenance of efficient relations with employees'.(49) In the western coalfields (though not in the eastern) and in the iron and steel industries such efficient relations rarely existed. Housing and working conditions were very bad, and in general the employers were completely opposed to the organisation of labour. The result was bad relations and frequent strikes, which must have meant considerably lessened efficiency. In shipbuilding, on the other hand, while there was a tradition of turbulence, relations were very much better. There was a sprinkling of enlightened views (notably those of William Denny and John Scott), organisation of labour came early and was effective and, in general, relations between masters and men were good.

Another sphere of action is the 'securing of adequate financial resources'. The period under review was one of movement towards the joint-stock company form of organisation, as capital needs became too great to be satisfied by private means alone. By 1900, however, coal, shipbuilding, malleable iron and engineering were still industries where more than half of the firms were privately financed, while pig iron and steel entrepreneurs had all but completely adopted the corporate form of organisation. This had varying implications for the different industries. There can be little doubt, first, that lack of financial resources among the small coal firms and the malleable iron producers proved a hindrance to growth. On the other hand, however, there is no evidence to suggest that this was true of either shipbuilding or engineering. Many of the firms in these industries apparently still found private sources adequate, though a speeding-up of the movement in the 1890's indicated that this was decreasingly true.

A further need is 'a sufficient and steady supply of raw materials', and the reaction of the pig-iron producers to the depletion of native ores provides a good example of an absence of enterprise. When it became obvious that ores would have to be imported, and that Spain was *the* source of imports, instead of establishing some sort of headquarters there or buying up mines, the pig-iron producers acted through agents, and very often could not be sure of the quality of the imported ores.(50) The ironmasters' adjustment to changed conditions was slow, fumbling, and uneasy. Later, with the advent of the Gilchrist-Thomas process, the steel producers could have freed the industry from its dependence on hematite ores, but they chose not to adopt the new method, despite its superiority, and so prolonged the problem. Not that the steel entrepreneurs went without a steady flow of raw materials. What they failed to obtain from Scottish ironmasters they obtained from England. Nor is there evidence of any of the other heavy industries experiencing difficulties in the acquisition of raw materials.

It has been posited that a task of the entrepreneur is 'the maintenance of good relations with public authorities and society at large'. In this sphere one can contrast the behaviour of the coalmasters in relation to the constantly recurring problem of waggon shortage and the shipbuilders with regard to the Clyde Trust and graving accommodation. Throughout the period, and especially at the peak of booms, the Scottish coal industry was plagued by a shortage of waggons to convey the coal from the pits to the ports or to their intended internal markets. This caused great inconvenience to the public ('society at large') and was the subject of bitter complaint.(51) Yet nothing was done by the coalmasters to improve the situation. On the question of graving dock accommodation, contrariwise, in 1872 the shipbuilders showed that by *straining* relations with a public authority—the Clyde Trust—results could be achieved. Prior to this date there was great need of a new graving dock on the Clyde. In 1872, despite pressure from shipbuilders and shipowners the Clyde Trust refused to act. Then, John Burns, a well-known shipowner, attacked the Trustees' position in a letter to the North British Daily Mail. This sparked off a heated controversy. There were frenetic denials by the Trust. Burns was ably supported by a number of letters from shipbuilders; and then 'at the meeting of the Clyde Trust it was curtly announced that the Trustees had agreed to make immediate application to Parliament for powers to construct a new Graving Dock'.(52) This was a complete 'change from the spirit which actuated the Corporation Trustees at their former meeting in their attempted justification of the existing state of affairs'. By spirited, independent action the shipbuilders attained their end.

Finally, an important sphere of action is 'the development of a market for products, and the devising of new products to meet or anticipate consumer demand'. In this respect, the coalmasters appear in more favourable light. They made successful inroads into export markets,(53) were active in developing new products like pea-coal and briquettes, and were persistent in their attempts to obtain a share of Admiralty contracts when these were being unfairly distributed.(54) The pig-iron producers, on the other hand, lost export markets to a dramatic extent,(55) and failed to produce the hematite iron necessary for the new steel industry. The steel entrepreneurs showed themselves quick to produce a material satisfactory for shipbuilding purposes, and were active in export markets.(56) The Clyde shipbuilders, finally, expanded foreign markets(57) and continually produced improved vessels (triple- and quadruple-expansion engines, the continuous cellular system, steel, higher and higher speeds, etc.). They are seen at work with regard to the granting of Admiralty contracts. Not content with the discrimination being shown against them,(58) they succeeded in having a Parliamentary Committee appointed to look into the matter. This Committee reported against the Admiralty and so led to some improvement in the situation.

On balance, then, the evidence considered in this section bears out the conclusions of the previous one. None of the industries was uniformly unenterprising, though pig iron came close to it (the one mitigating feature being the satisfactory record in securing financial resources); coal and steel had a mixed record; shipbuilding displayed characteristic drive; and very little is known about malleable iron and engineering. Before examining the entrepreneurs themselves, however, the failure to develop a successful motor-car industry in Scotland is worthy of note, inasmuch as it showed one branch of engineering, at least, to be inadequate in most of the spheres of action outlined. It provides an example, too, of Scotland's apparent inability to establish those very industries which, at the beginning of the twentieth century, had the greatest potential for growth.

In the 'nineties, Scotland 'with [her] widespread knowledge of steam and gas engines . . . was ready to take a sharp interest in the petrol engine and did so'.(59) Yet this interest was not translated into practical achievements (*i.e.*, a firmly-based industry) largely because of deficient enterprise. The most recent historians of the industry in Scotland, in considering the number of failures recorded, conclude that most of the factors at work 'could be summarised as plain bad management'.(60) Among those factors, they included primitive costing systems, inadequate capital investment, a mistaken belief that a mass market would not develop, neglect of the need for an after-sales service, and failure to appreciate the importance of overseas markets.(61)

4. *The Entrepreneurs of the Heavy Industries*—(a) *Coal*

The entrepreneurs themselves will now be considered—the individuals behind these collective generalisations—in order to glimpse some of the causes of deficient or dynamic entrepreneurship. A rigorous treatment would require some incursion into the fields of sociology and psychology and a degree of precision and detail not possible here. It is hoped, however, that some tentative hypotheses may emerge from what follows. About the individual malleable iron producers (other than those who went into steel after 1879) little is known. They were predominately small, and it was probably lack of capital that prevented many from starting as steel producers.

The Scottish coal industry during the period under consideration was characterised by a host of small enterprises in intense competition with one another. There were a few giants—mainly ironmasters—but they were exceptional.(62) They will be considered below. For the rest, information is meagre. Small men rarely wrote, or commissioned, biographies, or received mention in the press or technical journals. About them it seems safe to assert, however, that their size was both a cause and a result of lack of enterprise. Lack of capital (in itself a result of an absence of enterprise) meant that the small coalmasters were unable to adopt many of the results of technical progress. Coal-cutting machinery, the adoption of electricity, haulage machinery, or any positive step to further technical education, required relatively large sums of money. In an age tending increasingly towards large-scale units, the small enterprise was out of place.

There is, however, more precise information about some of the larger entrepreneurs (apart from the ironmasters, who are considered below). Thus, the Fife Coal Company, which owned and worked six mines in 1894, was founded in 1872, at the height of the boom of the early 1870's,(63) with a young mining engineer, Charles Carlow, as manager. He was to guide the company's fortunes throughout the period under consideration, and what is known of his management exemplifies the generalisations made about entrepreneurship in the coal industry. He was very active in both home and foreign markets. On the other hand, despite the trial of a coal-cutting machine in 1884, none was adopted, and there is no indication of electricity or modern haulage machinery being installed. Charles Carlow was born in 1849, the son of Charles Augustus Carlow, general manager of a group of collieries with headquarters near Dunfermline, attended Dunfermline High School, and studied mining engineering at both Glasgow and Edinburgh. At 19 he was assistant manager of a group of collieries in Midlothian, and was only 24 when appointed principal manager of the Fife Coal Company in 1873. Apart from his activities in this latter capacity, he was director of the North British Railway Company from 1894, member of the School Board at Leven for a number of years, and a director of the Royal Bank of Scotland, of the Edinburgh Collieries Company, and, from 1884, of the Shotts Iron Company, whose chairman he was for seventeen years. All his energies, then, could not have been centred on the Fife Coal Company. Membership of the School Board and four other directorships must have consumed a good deal of his time. Whether this was consistent with the full exercise of enterprise would require far more information. The question will be discussed in general terms, below.

Another firm about which there is some information is John Watson and Company, who were working six mines in 1894. John Watson, son of a coalmaster, began on his own account at an early age, with the help of some capital from his father. In 1877, twenty-seven years after he started his first major venture, he was the largest colliery proprietor (outside the ironmasters) in Scotland. It is obvious that in the years before 1870 he displayed unusual qualities as an entrepreneur. By 1872, however, he was very much caught up in political and social activities,(64) and this must have diverted much of his energies from the firm, to the probable detriment of enterprise.

The Wilson and Clyde Coal Company worked seven mines in 1894, and the controlling influence was John Wilson. In 1892, this son of a pioneer in the mining industry was in the prime of middle life and his family, the Wilsons of Wilsontown, had been working coal in Lanarkshire for about a century. In 1887 he joined his business with the Clyde Coal Company and thoroughly reorganised both the collieries and sales departments, with very successful results, doubling the output in a few years and making splendid returns to the shareholders. Drive and enterprise are obvious, but again serious inroads were made into the time of the entrepreneur. From the early 'eighties he took 'a keen interest in politics, having been, until the introduction of the Irish Home Rule Scheme, an ardent Gladstonian, but since then, as a Liberal Unionist, has used all his influence throughout the various divisions of the county in favour of Unionist candidates'.(65) In 1894 he was elected to the Town Council, and from 1895 until 1906 served as an M.P. A firm does not run itself, and Wilson, with such heavy demands on his time, could not have given his full attention to day-to-day matters in the coal industry. It is noteworthy that his keen interest and participation in politics first started about 1882, after he was well established as a man of wealth. There was not the same need to accumulate. Economic reorganisation had been achieved: a different kind of power and status was now being sought.

The career of James Wood, another prominent coalmaster (James Wood Ltd. worked six mines in 1894), showed similar characteristics. Born in Paisley, on leaving school he joined the Portland Coal Company, and while still in his 'teens, in 1860, struck out on his own account. Two years later he opened a coal depot in Renfrew, and so started a trade that was to reach huge dimensions. He had, at different times, leases in Armadale and in ten different estates in the counties of Fife, Stirling, Dunbarton, and Lanark, and offices in New York and London. Yet again, other interests came to drain some energy from the firm: 'Mr. Wood is also Chairman of the Pumpherston Oil Company . . . and of the Bryndu Coal and Coke Company . . . South Wales . . . and he . . . finds time to attend to public duties as a Commissioner of Supply, County Councillor, and Justice of the Peace for Linlithgowshire. . . . He is a leading Conservative in Linlithgowshire.'(66)

Another relatively big firm in the Scottish coal industry was James Nimmo and Company, with three mines in 1894, and by 1900 recognised as the largest producer of steam coal in Scotland. One of the partners, with a very important position in the firm, was James McKillop. Born in 1844, the son of a colliery manager, he gained experience as a miner and studied mining engineering and surveying at Glasgow University, before travelling in England and America to gain knowledge of mining methods. He subsequently became a partner with James Nimmo in the firm of Nimmo and McKillop, which eventually became the extensive concern of James Nimmo and Company. Like the other coalmasters studied, he became deeply involved in duties outside the firm. After many years of activity at parish and county level, he became an M.P. and as such was devoted to his constituents. 'No grievance has been too small for him to take notice of and endeavour to remedy. Through his importunity, many matters of interest to the people of Stirlingshire have been dealt with by the Government, and numerous complaints listened to and satisfied by Ministers, which would, in the hands of a less indefatigable member, have been buried in Government pigeon-holes.'(67) The Stirlingshire electors' gain must have been James Nimmo and Company's loss.

In 1894 the Alloa Coal Company worked four mines, and was run by Alexander Roxburgh.(68) He had been appointed accountant in 1870 and subsequently assistant manager, manager, and partner (in 1884). From the mid-'seventies he shared the burdens of management with Alexander Mitchell, until the latter's death in 1893. From 1893, until his own death in 1899, Roxburgh was the driving-force behind the company's activities. The careers of these two men are therefore of interest. Mitchell's father, William Mitchell, had helped found the Alloa Colliery Company in 1835 and was prominent in its management until he died in 1854. Thereafter, his sons, Alexander and Andrew, became partners, the former being most active in the direction of the company. Alexander Mitchell was a man of many interests. In addition to being a farmer, merchant, and ship-owner he sat on the County Council, the Alloa Commission Board, and the Burgh School Board, as well as commanding the local Volunteers (which he raised), and 'he was no mere passenger of any of these bodies'.(69) Roxburgh, born at Aberdour in 1834, the son of a coal salesman, had been with the Lochgelly Iron and Coal Company before joining the Alloa Coal Company. Like Mitchell he did not centre all his attention on the firm. In addition to the managing directorship which he eventually held, he was on the boards of the Lochgelly Coal Company, the Alloa Glass Works Company and the Scottish Mineowners' Defence and Mutual Assurance Association. He was, further, a member of the County Council and the Alloa Parish School Board, as well as being associated with many church, social and philanthropic organisations.

The Lanemark Coal Company(70) (one large mine in 1894) was founded in 1865 by John Hunter, James Paton (both connected with the iron industry), and Robert Brown, its management and control lying with the last named. Little is known of these three men's careers, but we do know that on Brown's death his daughter inherited the holding in the company, that in 1891 she married the Rev. William Granger, a minister at Ayr, and that he took over direction of the company. Carvel remarks that 'his background was hardly suitable for industrial management', and this is something of an understatement. He certainly did not have the time—apart from the requisite drive—to devote to the company's affairs: 'If his presence was urgently needed at Lanemark, he thought nothing of setting off from his manse on horseback or of taking out his bicycle. . . . Sometimes he did the journey out from Ayr and back in one day, but frequently he spent the night with his ministerial colleague, the parish minister of New Cumnock.'(71) He died in 1898, his management having been hardly of the heroic, Schumpeterian kind. While direction by a minister cannot have been typical of a Scottish coal enterprise, that it should have existed at all was symptomatic of the spirit in which the industry was carried on.

A noteworthy feature of the above survey is that of the nine men who controlled the seven concerns studied, six were at least second generation in the coal industry, one was a minister, and the backgrounds of the other two are unknown. Among the coalmasters of the period (and additional examples could have been given) there seems to have been a certain diversion of energies from the firm, as, with fortunes made, and a status in the community achieved, they sought power and status of a different kind. This could be obtained through participation in other industrial activities, or, more often, in local or national politics. These were time- and energy-consuming pursuits, and enterprise, it is postulated, was bound to suffer.

5. *The Entrepreneurs of the Heavy Industries*—(b) *Pig Iron*

The four giants of the pig-iron industry were the Bairds, the Dixons, the Houldsworths, and Merry and Cunninghame. Together with James Dunlop, they will be considered in this section.(72)

It was early in the nineteenth century that Alexander Baird, a farmer in the parish of Old Monkland, started working coal on a small scale.(73) By 1828 the Bairds had become extensive coalmasters, with the second generation, William (1796-1864) and James (1802-76) in control, and in that year they started erecting blast furnaces. The first two generations, and especially the second, showed exceptional qualities as entrepreneurs. They poured all their energies into the firm. Not that they took no part in outside activities. William was M.P. for the Falkirk Burghs from 1841 to 1846 and a director of the Caledonian Railway Company and the Forth and Clyde Canal; while James was M.P. for the Falkirk Burghs from 1851 to 1857 and also a director of the Forth and Clyde Canal. Their participation was not, however, excessive, and neither had a passionate interest in politics. It is to be remembered, also, that here were *two* men of outstanding ability in charge of one firm.

James died without issue, and none of William's large family appears to have been interested in the business. His second son, John, after being educated at Eton and Oxford, joined the 6th Dragoon Guards. He left the army in 1882, but retained a keen interest in military affairs. He was an M.P. from 1886 to 1906 and took 'a strong interest also in the public and charitable movements in Glasgow'.(74) The fourth son, Henry, after an identical education did not 'diverge into the paths of business, but . . . contented himself with the usual pursuits of a country gentleman'.(75) Management passed out of the hands of the Bairds, then, as the third generation conformed to the logic of 'Buddenbrooks dynamics'. Prominent among the men who later controlled the firm was Alexander Whitelaw (1823-79), son of Janet Baird (a sister of William and James), who looked after the commercial department of the business. He was 'a thoroughly public-spirited man',(76) very active in church work and in the field of education. Thus, in 1873, with the passage of the Education Act, he was elected member of the first school board of Glasgow, and, as Chairman, 'he at once threw himself into the duties with characteristic thoroughness and energy. Everything had to be planned [and] in every question involving statistics or arithmetical calculation it is surprising how much personal trouble he took. Every statement of the kind seemed to pass his independent verification. It became evident that the hours spent at the Board offices were only a small portion of the time which he devoted to the duties.'(77) The community at large must certainly have benefited from his unflagging zeal. But, in his capacity as entrepreneur, Whitelaw could only have worked at diminished efficiency. He died in 1879, when the pig-iron industry was approaching its nadir, and the year before his death William Laird was assumed as partner in the firm.

Born in Perthshire in 1830, Laird started his business career with a firm of lawyers and bankers in Blairgowrie. He left Blairgowrie for Edinburgh and, after a short stay there, came to Glasgow, where, in 1860, he took service with William Baird and Company. Once more there is evidence of an inordinate interest in affairs outside those of the firm. Laird was promoter and director of the Glasgow and Bothwell Railway, and of the Glasgow City and District Railway, a director of the Harbour Tunnel Company, a promoter of the Glasgow Subway Scheme, and one of the leading Conservatives in the West of Scotland.

The history of the second of the big iron giants, the Dixons,(78)

closely resembles that of the Bairds. The first Dixon was an Englishman who came to Scotland in 1771, with no capital or material
possessions, and soon set about making his fortune. Along with
David Mushet (discoverer of blackband ironstone) he set up the
Calder Ironworks, and, before his death in 1822, had opened coalfields in Govanhill, Wilsontown, and Fauldhouse. He was succeeded
by his son William (1788-1859), who provided the drive and ability
that made the firm so prominent in the Scottish pig-iron industry:
'He was astir early in the morning—by six o'clock he would often be
found at the pit-head . . . he was on the ground ready to superin-
tend the boring of a new pit, or give instructions as to machinery.
By ten o'clock he would always be found in the counting-house,
sketching out the business of the day. . . . His mental capacity was
great—his administrative powers were of a high order.'(79) Though
he took a lively interest in public affairs, he played no excessive
part in outside activities. He was active in the movement which
culminated in the Reform Bill of 1832, and an unsuccessful parliamentary candidate in 1847. Later, however, he appears to have lost
interest in politics.

William Dixon was married twice, leaving one son by his first
wife. He, William S. Dixon, changed the firm into a limited liability
company in 1872, but took very little active part in its management
—'a quiet, unassuming gentleman, who spends his time mainly
between his house in London and his delightful estate at Belleisle,
near Ayr'.(80) In the later history of the firm, Neil Robson, in 1891,
was taken on as partner, and he shared the management with I. R. J.
Logan. Robson was born in Glasgow in 1851, son of a well-known
civil and mining engineer, educated at school in Edinburgh and at
Glasgow University, and was with Merry and Cunninghame and
then on his own account, before joining Dixon and Company. Again,
a very active participation in outside affairs is seen, including
membership of the Kilmalcolm School Board for six years and of
the Renfrewshire County Council, as well as chairmanship of the
local Conservative Association for twenty years.

The third of the pig-iron dynasties, the Houldsworths,(81) was
founded by Henry Houldsworth (1774-1853), who, like the original
Dixon, was an Englishman attracted to Scotland. After a successful
sojourn in the cotton industry he had 'the true insight of business
genius' in seeing that iron was to become Glasgow's mainstay, and
he started the Anderston Foundry and Machine Works, before
opening, in 1837, the Coltness Iron Works. It is remarkable to note
that at the time of this step into a new venture Houldsworth was
62 years of age, and had been at work for 50 years. He was to con-

tinue working for another 17 years, helped by his three sons, Henry
(1797-1867), William (1798-1853), and John (1807-59). The second
son, William, was frequently away from the firm because of bad
health, and the third, John (who was in charge of the selling side),
had his attention diverted by municipal service. John was Provost of
Anderston, before that burgh was annexed to Glasgow, subsequently
entered the Glasgow Town Council, and eventually became Senior
Magistrate. Indeed, his uncle, Thomas, considered that too much of
John's time was taken up with the civic life of Glasgow for the
health of the firm.(82) The oldest son, Henry, did, however, give
most of his attention to pig iron, and old Henry, the father, who
was not long outlived by either of his younger sons, had one of the
faculties of the successful entrepreneur—that of *selection*. Early
staff difficulties sent him into Ayrshire in search of capable men, and
at Muirkirk he met James Hunter, a coalmaster on his own account,
of whom he had heard good reports. Hunter was persuaded to
become personal assistant to 'H. H.', was made a partner in 1853,
and it was under his forceful management that the firm reached its
most prosperous heights. Of the first two generations, then, it could
be said: 'They . . . always kept their minds open. If a branch of
trade seemed to languish they dropped it; if it promised to become
a success they rushed at it. And their sagacity and enterprise . . .
had their reward.'(83) With the addition of Hunter's drive this continued to be true, but the second phase came to an end in 1872.

Hunter, the only surviving member of the 1853 partnership, decided, in 1872, that his powers were waning somewhat and that he
needed some assistance in running the company. The company was,
accordingly, reorganised, and power seems to have resided with
Hunter (who died in 1886), with James Murray (who was influential
from the 'fifties into the 'nineties), later, on Hunter's death, with
James Hamilton (appointed general manager when Hunter died,
and holding that position until 1897), but predominantly with the
third generation Houldsworths—the three sons of the second Henry
Houldsworth, Walter, James, and Sir William. Of these men, Hunter,
as we have said, was less forceful than at his prime; Murray,
although he took a keen interest in the firm, lived in Manchester and
then London, communicated his ideas by letter, and made only rare
personal appearances; and Hamilton seems to have been dominated
by the Houldsworths. James and Walter were extremely cautious
about any change—the caution of the established 'third generation'
—and Sir William was the only one who showed any of his grandfather's qualities. He found it very difficult, however, to have any
of his proposals put into practice—perhaps because so much of his

T

time was taken up as M.P. for North-west Manchester from 1883 to 1906. For example, he wrote, in 1888, to his brother James: 'In order to carry on the Coltness Iron Company as a profitable concern either steel-making or some other manufacture must be added to, or substituted for, pig-iron making.'(84) James Houldsworth was opposed to the idea, and held that his brother was not close enough to the industry to know its trends. Accordingly, there was no radical change, though, in 1890, as a concession to Sir William's doggedness, a small steel-making plant was set up. The company was the first pig-iron producer to enter open-hearth steel and one of the only three to do so in the period 1870-1900. It was in the 'nineties, too, again as a result of pressure from Sir William, that the company began to concentrate more on coal and less on iron, Sir William believing, wisely, that it was a mistake to depend so exclusively on iron in a declining market. The difficulty which Sir William had in getting his ideas accepted by his cautious brothers illustrates the conservatism that pervaded the pig-iron industry. He must have been alone among its leaders in his attempts to force it out of its inertia.

Information on the firm of Merry and Cunninghame is more sparse.(85) It was founded by Alexander Allison (who retired in 1844), Alexander Cunninghame (who died in 1866), and James Merry. Merry was the only one of the original partners still alive in 1872, when the firm became a limited company. He appears to have contributed to the firm's early success by his shrewdness and enterprise, but latterly became involved in public duties—he was a Deputy-Lieutenant for Inverness-shire, Provincial Grand Master for the Middle Ward of Lanarkshire, and an M.P. in 1857 and from 1859 to 1874. Neither of his sons had any desire to go into business, but the Cunninghame line continued in the firm, with John Cunninghame, a son of the first Cunninghame, managing director of the newly constituted firm from 1872. Born in Edinburgh and educated at Harrow and Cambridge, he did impart a certain amount of progressiveness, and Merry and Cunninghame were one of the more enterprising of the pig-iron firms in the 1880's and 1890's, starting to produce steel in 1884-85 and having, by 1901, four Bessemer converters and three open-hearth furnaces. This enterprise was relative only to the extreme conservatism of the other pig-iron firms, however, and did not compare with the early record of the firm. The difficult conditions of the last thirty years of the nineteenth century demanded more time and attention than John Cunninghame was apparently willing to give. The list of his activities is quite staggering. He was a director of the Glasgow and South-western Railway Company and of the Standard Life Insurance Company; he served with the Renfrewshire Militia for twenty-eight years (1872-1900), and sat for two terms on the Renfrewshire County Council; he stood twice, unsuccessfully, for Parliament; he travelled widely in Europe, Australia, China, and Japan; he was active in rural affairs, running, personally, a sheep-farm on his 13,000 acre estate of Upper Foyers, carrying on two dairy farms with an average stock of 150 cows on another estate, in Wigtownshire, and gaining a reputation as a noted breeder of Clydesdale horses.

A final illustration of the careers of the ironmasters is afforded by James Dunlop, of the Clyde Ironworks.(86) These were founded by his uncle, Colin Dunlop, and what The Bailie said of him might have served as an epitaph for the pig-iron industry: 'like other men of that day [he] possessed a greater measure of individuality than has fallen to the lot of their descendants. We are probably more refined than they were . . . but we lack the power and eagerness which made them what they were.' James Dunlop, the second generation, was much preoccupied with politics, both national and local: 'No parliamentary election . . . has occurred in the city for fifty years in which James Dunlop has not taken an active part on the Liberal side.' Further, he was on the Town Council, a Justice of the Peace, and a Deputy Lieutenant, as well as being a director of the Western Bank, which failed in 1857. In this case the seeds were sown well before 1870.

In the first two of the pig-iron dynasties, then, the third generation opted out and men took over who were apparently over-preoccupied with outside affairs; in the third, the Houldsworths, the third generation retained control during the period, but, with one exception, were excessively conservative; the fourth and fifth were in the hands of second generations which engaged in manifold non-business pursuits.

6. The Entrepreneurs of the Heavy Industries—(c) Steel

The Scottish steel industry started with the founding of the Steel Company of Scotland in 1871, the Steel Company holding a monopoly of steel production in Scotland until 1879. In that year two malleable-iron producers, William Beardmore of Parkhead Forge and Williams and Company of Wishaw, started installing steel plant, to be followed, in 1880, by two other malleable-iron firms, the Mossend Iron Company and David Colville and Sons. By 1901, there were fourteen firms, of varying size, in the Scottish steel industry, and of these the three largest were the Steel Company of Scotland, David Colville and Sons Ltd., and William Beardmore and Company.(87) The pig-iron producers who had ventured into the open-hearth steel industry by 1900 (the Houldsworths, Merry and Cunninghame, and James Dunlop and Company) have already been considered and in this section attention is directed to the 'big three'.

It is significant that the enterprise and drive that went into the founding of the Steel Company of Scotland and so the Scottish steel industry came not from any of the established metallurgical industries but from chemicals.(88) The Tharsis Sulphur and Copper Company was finding itself, in the late 1860's, with a huge surplus of purple ore from the company's mines in Huelva, and Charles Tennant, of St. Rollox fame and a director of Tharsis, thought that it could be used in the production of steel. Along with some other businessmen of the south-west (including another Tennant, four others connected with Tharsis and St. Rollox, four of the Arrol family of constructional engineers, and Henry Dubs of the Glasgow Locomotive Works), and in conjunction with Siemens himself, inventor of the open-hearth process, Tennant had production under way by 1873. Most of the success from 1878, however, was due to the remarkably able management of James Riley, who was in control, as general manager, from then until 1894. Born in Halifax, the son of a porter, he started his working life as a millwright and engineer, and became manager of Sir William Siemens' Landore Steel Company of South Wales, before moving, in 1878, to the Steel Company. Under Riley's influence the Steel Company's products attained a high reputation for quality, a number of technical improvements were achieved, the company was run with great efficiency, and labour relations were good. The impact which he made upon his arrival was great: 'no one who was associated with him in the early days of the introduction of mild steel but admired him for his indomitable energy and the manner in which he impressed shipbuilders, boilermakers, and others as to the superiority of mild steel for all the purposes required in construction of ships. . . . He was rightly recognised . . . as the father of the mild steel trade in Scotland.'(89)

It was reported that when Sir Henry Bessemer visited the works in 1885, he remarked: 'I have not seen during the whole of my experience such excellent material and finished work as I see here today.'(90) Riley is seen at work in 1886, when the Steel Company was faced with the demand for a wage advance and the prospect of a strike. He met the men, showed himself to be sympathetic, but pointed out, by means of a month by month analysis of costs and prices, that the company could not afford to grant an increase at that moment. By his tact he averted the strike. His departure, in 1894, was a great loss and the Steel Company seems to have been less enterprising thereafter. It is noteworthy that in none of the numerous statements about Riley (obituary notices, vignettes, votes of thanks, etc.) is there any mention of participation in public affairs. He had the singleness of purpose of the successful entrepreneur. He stressed, above all else, the factor *personal management*, and with it 'constant vigilance, strict attention to details, and a thoroughly familiarity with all the various parts of the plant'.(91)

In 1901, the firm with the largest steel producing plant in Scotland and furnaces with the output record for Great Britain was that of David Colville and Sons.(92) Started as a malleable-iron works by David Colville, Senior, in 1872, it put down steel plant in 1879 and was producing in the following year. The man who guided the firm from relatively humble beginnings to a position of leadership in the Scottish steel industry was David Colville, Junior. He was born at Coatbridge in 1860 and educated at Hamilton Academy, and then his father, sensing the future importance of steel, had him enter the Steel Company of Scotland when he was 17. In 1880, at the early age of 20, he superintended the laying down of the steel plant at Dalzell, and undertook its management from the start. He visited America, Germany, and France, to make himself acquainted with methods there, and it was said of him that 'there was nothing in the industry with which he did not make himself fully conversant'.(93) As in the case of Riley, there is no record of participation in public affairs.

The third of the giants, William Beardmore and Company,(94) was the first of the malleable-iron producers to come into steel. William Beardmore, Senior, controlled Parkhead Forge from 1862, and under him it prospered. It was his son, however, also William Beardmore, who brought it to its huge proportions. Born in 1857, and educated at Glasgow High School and Ayr Academy, he entered the Forge at 15 years of age, served in each of its departments, and attended evening classes in mathematics and chemistry at Anderson's College. From there he went to the South Kensington School of Mines for two-and-a-half years, studying chemistry and metallurgy. During this period of apprenticeship his father died, but his uncle, Isaac Beardmore, carried on the business, and in 1880 young William Beardmore was taken into partnership. Six years later his uncle retired, leaving him in full control, and soon his enterprise became evident. His excellent grounding in theory, obtained through a rigorous technical education, was exceptional for the time, and stood him in excellent stead. Combined with a probing mind it produced 'a spirit whose activity and energy seem[ed] untiring'.(95) In 1886, on assuming full control, he was dissatisfied with the narrow range of the firm's activities. For example, he felt that Sheffield was not the only place in Britain where armour plates could be forged, and accordingly devised a patent of his own and set to with great success—soon supplying armour plates for the cruisers, destroyers, and battleships of the British Navy, and for the navies of Holland, Italy, and Japan. In 1900, Beardmore purchased the old-established shipyard and engineering works of Robert Napier and Sons, and founded an undertaking which in Britain 'occupied a position as a steel works, forge, and armour manufacturing establishment second to none'.(96) There is no doubting the ability and enterprise of William Beardmore, and nor is there any doubt about his singleness of purpose. All his energies went into the firm, and the only sign of any participation in public affairs which the Who's Who in Glasgow in 1909 (usually assiduous in its description of such matters) could adduce was that he was a J.P.

Each of the three major entrepreneurs in steel, then, had drive and imagination, allied to single-mindedness. There is no evidence of any of them taking on public duties except in the most minor way, and the 'safety-first' attitude of the steel industry, noted above, cannot be attributed to Riley, Colville, or Beardmore. It is to be noted that the Steel Company was far less go-ahead after Riley's departure (in 1894), so that by the 'nineties there were really only two outstanding firms in a total of fourteen. For the rest, the Springfield Steel Company, the Acme Steel Works and the Mount Vernon Steel Works were very small concerns, lacking the capital necessary for development. The Coltness Iron Company had only one furnace, while Merry and Cunninghame, though they had seven (four Bessemer and three open-hearth) furnaces, displayed no great drive in the steel industry. These two must certainly have had ample finance. It was enterprise that was lacking. The others—the Glasgow Iron and Steel Company, James Dunlop, the Lanarkshire Steel Company, the Clyde Bridge Steel Company, the Summerlee and Mossend Iron and Steel Company, A. and J. Stewart and Menzies—appear to have been undistinguished.

7. *The Entrepreneurs of the Heavy Industries*—(d) *Shipbuilding*

In 1870 there were forty-three firms contributing to total shipbuilding production on the Clyde, the leaders, in terms of tonnage launched, being Caird and Company, John Elder and Company, Barclay, Curle and Company, R. Napier and Sons, Alexander Stephen and Sons, the London and Glasgow Engineering and Iron Shipbuilding Company, J. and G. Thomson, A. and J. Inglis, Robert Duncan and Company, and William Denny Bros. By 1900 there had been little change in the total number of firms, and in the 'nineties about forty firms operated, the leaders, between 1891 and 1900, being Russell and Company, Connell and Company, Denny Bros., Stephen and Sons, Brown and Company (formerly J. and G. Thomson), Fairfield Company, Henderson and Company, Scott and Company, Caird and Company, and Barclay, Curle and Company.(97) These firms were in active competition throughout our period, and most of the important ones are included in the following analysis. Of the purely marine engineering firms that of James Howden and Company is considered.

The name most famous in Clyde shipbuilding and engineering in 1870 was that of Napier. By 1900 this may not have been true, but it was the Napiers, who, in the years up to 1870, did most to bring the industry from its small beginnings in the early nineteenth century to its position of greatness in the last three decades. It is fitting, then, to begin with the pioneers, especially since it was in the Napiers' yards that most of the men who later built up large and successful firms were trained.(98)

Robert Napier (1791-1876) and his cousin David Napier (1790-1869) were true pioneers, the former substantial and solid, the latter brilliant, and both contributing in almost equal measure to the development of Clyde shipbuilding. Of David Napier, Scott Russell said in 1841: 'We believe that from the year 1818 until about 1830 David Napier effected more for the improvement of steam navigation than any other man.'(99) He was important as one of the first to adopt marine engineering as a distinctive profession, and the improvements that stand to his name are legion.(100) In all the writing devoted to his career there is no single mention of participation in public affairs. David Napier left the Clyde, for London, in 1835, but Robert continued in mighty activity until 1853, numbering among his achievements the complete trust of the Admiralty (no mean feat), a prominent part in the inception of Atlantic steam navigation (he was closely connected with, and, indeed, stood behind Samuel Cunard), and the perception that iron shipbuilding was both possible and profitable. His biographer remarked of him that 'he never aspired to municipal honours'.(101)

Between them Robert and David Napier had trained the men who founded Denny Bros., J. and G. Thomson, John Elder and

Company, William Beardmore and Company, Smith and Rodgers (later the London and Glasgow Shipbuilding Company), Tod and McGregor, D. and W. Henderson, Aitken and Mansel, Shanks and Bell, Napier and Miller, Scott and Sons, Dunmuir and Jackson and G. L. Watson and Company. In addition, William Pearce (later the dynamic head of the Fairfield Shipbuilding Company), A. C. Kirk (inventor of the triple-expansion engine), and Walter Brock (developer of the quadruple-expansion engine), were trained or worked in Robert Napier's yards. He had, indeed, that most important of entrepreneurial qualities—the faculty of selection. He was succeeded by his two sons, James and John, the former leaving the firm in 1857. The firm continued to develop, though without such marked success as previously. A new phase started in the 'seventies.

In 1877 the firm came into new hands, when A. C. Kirk and John and James Hamilton took it over, with Kirk as senior partner. Under them the firm's fortunes revived, and in 1888 it was said that 'the widespread and longstanding renown of Messrs. R. Napier and Sons as engineers and shipbuilders . . . has not by any means been allowed to diminish during the past decade, for which period no one of the name of Napier has shared in the co-partnership. New lustre, indeed, has been conferred.'(102) Alexander Kirk was born in 1830 at the Manse of Barry in Forfarshire and educated at the Burgh School of Arbroath and the University of Edinburgh. After an apprenticeship with Robert Napier, he went to London and from there into the shale oil industry, working for Young's Paraffin Oil Works at Bathgate and West Calder and introducing many improvements in the apparatus used. In 1865 he returned to Glasgow as manager of James Aitken and Company's engine works, and in 1870, just before the death of John Elder, became manager at the Fairfield Engine Works, where he stayed until 1877 and where he developed his famous triple-expansion engine. After the move to R. Napier and Sons he was prominent in the introduction of steel as a material for shipbuilding. His partners, the Hamiltons, came of shipbuilding stock, their grandfather having been leading foreman to the Greenock firm of John Scott and Sons and their father a partner in the firm of Barclay, Curle, and Company. They were both educated at Glasgow Academy and served apprenticeships with Barclay, Curle and Company. The elder, John, was for some time a partner of Robert Duncan and when he came to Napier's took over the designing and commercial departments; while the younger, James, in the drawing-office of Barclay, Curle and Company until 1877, took over the shipbuilding department, attaining a reputation as a fine naval architect. In the late 'nineties, as these men declined in power, the business began to decline. Again, however, as the old became less efficient new blood was introduced and the business was bought by William Beardmore in 1900. There is no trace of a diversion of energy from the firm in the careers of Kirk or the Hamiltons.

A firm in which high qualities of enterprise were displayed throughout the period was that of John Elder and Company (or, as it was known from 1886, the Fairfield Shipbuilding and Engineering Company).(103) If Robert Napier was a Zeus-like figure in Clyde shipbuilding up to about 1850, John Elder inherited his mantle, from about 1860, and held it until his early death in 1869. Elder (1824-69) served his apprenticeship in Napier's yard, went to Bolton, returned to take charge of Napier's drawing-office and in 1852 joined the firm of Randolph, Elliot and Company, which soon became that of Randolph, Elder and Company. His father had worked for Robert Napier, and John Elder's work was marked by 'great scientific knowledge, originality, skill, and thoroughness, and possessed characteristics similar to that of his father, in the shape of wise and simple adaptation of means to ends'.(104) He effected numerous improvements (among them steam-jacketing, which James Watt had thought of but never successfully developed, and the compound engine, which resulted in economies of fuel of up to 40 per cent and made possible long voyages purely by steam propulsion) and allied to his great practical ability was a considerable commercial expertise. He was a distinguished marine engineer and a very successful entrepreneur and it is to his credit that after his death his widow carried out his wishes in adding to the endowment of the Chair of Civil Engineering and endowing the new Chair of Naval Architecture at Glasgow University.

Mrs. Elder inherited the property, but in 1870 a partnership was formed consisting of her brother, John Ure (an eminent civil engineer), J. L. K. Jamieson (formerly head draughtsman and later engine works manager), and William (later Sir William) Pearce, who had been shipyard manager of Robert Napier and Sons. The new firm was carried on along the lines laid down by John Elder until 1878, when Ure and Jamieson retired, and Pearce was left in sole control, which he retained until his death in 1888. Under his direction the firm became the leading shipbuilding establishment in the world. William Pearce was born at Brompton, in Kent, in 1835, and learned practical shipbuilding in Her Majesty's Dockyard at Chatham. He was in Government service until 1863, when he became surveyor to Lloyd's Registry in the Clyde district, and in the following year he was appointed general manager to R. Napier and Sons, where he stayed until his move to Fairfield. He was a true entrepreneur, full of drive and imagination, willing to take risks, with the rare power of selection and an eye for anything that furthered the company's fortunes: 'William Pearce was several times larger than life, a flamboyant character with the nose of a pirate and a wonderful eye for an opportunity. . . . His strength lay in choosing objectives. He looked around him, saw something that had never been done before, decided it could be done, and dragged his apprehensive associates after him. Usually he had three or four schemes in mind, mostly of a type which kept cautious men from their sleep.'(105) He reduced considerably the time for the Atlantic crossing (and so secured the business of the Cunard line) and also for the Channel crossing; he was noted for the speed with which he carried out orders; he employed outstandingly able men, like Alexander Kirk, Andrew Laing (the designer of the engines for the Atlantic and Channel crossings), and Richard White (who was mainly responsible for the rapidity of construction); and he is seen at work in 1887, when he was active in having a Parliamentary Committee appointed to look into alleged discrimination against the Clyde and other areas in the granting of naval contracts.

He was succeeded by his son, Sir William G. Pearce, who lacked his father's great ability, and by 1893 there was only one single vessel—and that a sailing ship—under construction in the yard. In 1894, however, with the arrival of Edmund Sharer as general manager, there was a rapid improvement. Sharer was born in 1857 at Sunderland, and educated at Greenock, where his father had moved to join Robert Taylerson, a shipbuilder of some note at the time. He served his apprenticeship in the yard of Robert Duncan of Port Glasgow, and in 1879 was appointed surveyor to Lloyd's Registry at Liverpool. A few years later he began business as a shipbuilder in Sunderland, eventually moving to Fairfield, in 1843. Thereafter, owing to his skill and energy, the Yard was kept fully employed. There is no denying the dynamism and imagination of John Elder, William Pearce, and, to a lesser extent, Edmund Sharer, nor the ability of men like Kirk, Laing, and White. In each case, energies were canalised into the firm. There is no evidence of any of these men taking part in public affairs.

When William Denny, a shipbuilder of some note in the early nineteenth century, died in 1833, he left seven sons, five of whom—John, James, William, Peter, and Alexander—became well-known in the Clyde shipbuilding industry.(106) John Denny succeeded his father at the Woodyard, while his brothers sought employment elsewhere. William proceeded to Belfast, and became chief draughtsman in the yard of Coats and Young; Alexander went to Paisley; and Peter and James stayed in Dumbarton. In 1841, William left Belfast to become manager of Robert Napier's yard, to be joined soon afterwards by Peter, though the latter stayed for only a few months, moving then to Paisley, to work with his brother, Alexander. In 1843, William left Govan for America, but returned in 1844, when he and Peter and Alexander Denny formed a company and began shipbuilding in Dumbarton. William Denny, in fact, was one of the most notable shipbuilders of his time. He was succeeded, as head of the firm, by his nephew and namesake the third William Denny (1847-87).

The third William Denny was the eldest son of Peter Denny, and without doubt the most progressive and enterprising shipbuilder on the Clyde from the early 'seventies until his death. Born in Dumbarton, he was educated at schools in Dumbarton, Jersey, and Edinburgh, showing little sign of the genius that later became evident. In 1864, he started to serve a five-year apprenticeship, his father having decided not to send him to university. Had he gone to university, the Clyde might well have lost an exceptional shipbuilder, for, about 1864, young Denny's thoughts were running in the direction of the Church. In 1868, at the age of 21, he was admitted a partner in the firm, and from the first engrossed himself in the work. The first subject to which he turned his attention was the adoption of piece-work, which operated with very successful results in the Denny yards from about 1870. He also introduced, again with success, a completely new system of administration, with rules and fines for the regulation of every conceivable process. On the 'labour question' he was far ahead of his time, frequently meeting his workmen in conference.(107)

His efforts were crowned with success. In 1883, for example, Denny's firm was the only one on the Clyde left unmolested by the Union of Iron Shipbuilders on the vexed question of apprentices; and in 1886 his men actually asked for a wage *reduction,* so that a steamer that was being built on speculation could be finished. He also instituted, in 1880, a successful awards scheme in his yards, to encourage inventiveness and improvements in machinery and enhance the cause of technical education, of which he was a passionate advocate. Denny was no less an innovator in the technical field. It was he who first established the practice of progressive trials of speed, over the measured mile, with models; he was a pioneer in the early employment of steel as a building material in the industry; he rendered a valuable service by his contributions to the easier calculation of stability; he introduced notable improvements in ship construction (for example, cellular double bottoms); and it was he who first made use of the experimental tank.

All of this great man's energy went into the firm. He wrote in 1886: 'I hope the day is not far distant in which an absentee employer will be looked upon with as much contempt as an absentee landlord.'((108) He died in 1887, but his ability to select men of high calibre for the various departments of his business ensured that efficiency would be maintained after his death. Walter Brock took over in 1887, and under his direction the firm 'developed into one of the largest and best-equipped marine engineering establishments on the Clyde'.(109) Born in Glasgow in 1836, and educated there, he served his apprenticeship with Robert Napier and Sons, completed his training at Brest and London, and returned to Napier's as manager. It was in 1871 that he joined Denny's and while there he gained a reputation as one of the foremost men in the marine engineering profession, being particularly famed for his development of the quadruple-expansion engine. There is no evidence to suggest that any of these men, who so successfully directed the fortunes of the Denny firm from the earliest days (William Denny, Senior, Peter Denny, William Denny, Junior, Walter Brock) ever involved themselves in public affairs.

A fourth firm of note was that of Alexander Stephen and Sons of Linthouse,(110) which in 1876 produced the highest tonnage on the Clyde, and which, throughout the period, was among the leaders in the industry. William Stephen (1690-1761) was a farmer at Kinnedar, and of his two sons, William (1720-99) and Alexander (1722-93), the former was also a farmer and the latter started shipbuilding in Burghead, about 1750. The second William's son, also William (1759-1838), served an apprenticeship with his uncle at Burghead, and then started on his own account at Aberdeen. Of his two sons, William (1790-1829) was a shipbuilder at Arbroath, and Alexander (1795-1875), a shipbuilder at Aberdeen, Arbroath, Dundee, and Glasgow. It was Alexander who started the Glasgow firm, in 1850, realising that the future of shipbuilding in Scotland lay in the southwest. He had three sons, William (1826-94), a shipbuilder at Dundee, Alexander (1832-99), and John (1837-1917). The last two, and especially Alexander, guided the firm's destiny throughout the period under consideration.

In the years before 1870 enterprise had been displayed in the move to Glasgow, and in the speed with which Alexander Stephen, Senior, started producing ships of iron. In the years after, no less drive was shown. The yard was kept constantly up to date, and the Stephens were aggressive in their quest for markets. They often visited the principal ports and shipowners in Britain, and frequently crossed to the Continent—to France, Belgium, Italy, and Scandanavia. Much business arose from such visits and there were periods when they had more foreign orders than three or four of their competitors together. In 1872, for example, when other firms were beginning to complain of dull times, orders came to Linthouse from Germany and Belgium. Alexander Stephen, unlike the shipbuilders studied above, did find time for an apparently full participation in public affairs: 'When school boards were established he became first chairman of the Govan School Board. . . . When the Glasgow and West of Scotland Technical College was formed, he was elected first chairman of the governors. . . . In 1881 he was elected Lord Dean of Guild of the City of Glasgow, being the first shipbuilder to hold that ancient office.'(111) It is to be noted, however, that he was backed by an extremely able man in his brother, who became chairman of the company on Alexander's death in 1899, and of whom there is no record of any attraction to public office or duty.

The firm of A. and J. Inglis(112) was founded in 1847 by Anthony Inglis and his brother John, who were, respectively, a smith and an engineer. They concentrated, at first, on land engines, but moved into marine engineering in the mid-'fifties and into shipbuilding in 1862. Until about 1867, Anthony Inglis was the driving-force, and throughout his career he took a keen interest in local affairs—being president and treasurer of the Anderston Savings Bank for many years, active in the Anderston Weavers Society, Deacon of the Incorporation of Hammermen, Deacon Convener of the Trades House, Clyde Trustee, and police commissioner and magistrate for the burgh of Partick. From 1867, control was in the hands of his son, John Inglis (1842-1918), who was born in Glasgow and educated at Glasgow Academy and Glasgow University. From his assumption of control the firm became noted for its river-steamers, and Inglis was the first shipbuilder on the Clyde to follow the practice of inclining vessels to ascertain their stability, one of the first to apply the correct method of estimating the longitudinal strains to which ocean steamers are subject in service, and along with William Denny followed the practice of testing new vessels over the measured mile. Under his control the firm grew markedly, and it is noteworthy that, unlike his father, he was not attracted to public affairs. It would not be unfair to say that under Anthony Inglis the firm was a notable one, while under his son, John, it became pre-eminent, and the difference may be traced to the relative energy that each put into its running.

James and George Thomson,(113) brothers who had been in the employment of Robert Napier, established the firm that bore their name in 1846. The first five years were spent in organising the engineering works, and then, in 1851, the shipbuilding yard was started at Clydebank. It was George (1815-66) who was most active in the management of the firm, and he 'devoted himself thoroughly to his business, and was little seen or known in public'.(114) He was succeeded by his two sons, also James and George, the former being the most active partner. In 1881 their yard launched the *Servia*, at that date the greatest ship ever built, and in the 'eighties the firm earned a high reputation as builders of swift Government cruisers and despatch boats. In 1886, indeed, when the rest of Clydeside was very deeply depressed, J. and G. Thomson completed besides other work, five twin-screw torpedo cruisers for the British Government, a torpedo vessel for the Spanish Government, a torpedo boat for the Russian Government, and two sets of engines for H.M.S. *Aurora*. It is noteworthy that of the thirty-two warships built for foreign countries on the Clyde between 1859 and 1899, eighteen (or 56 per cent) were built by this one concern, the yard with the next greatest number being Napier's, with six. This was, in all, a fine record, showing considerable entrepreneurial qualities. James Thomson found time to be a volunteer (first in the Highland Regiment, and then in the Dunbartonshire Rifles), a J.P., and a member of the School Board, but The Bailie was careful to point out—and this is the only occasion it took the trouble to do so—that 'all this, it must be borne in recollection is merely supplementary to his business career'.(115)

In 1885 James Caird, though 69, was still active head of the old Greenock firm of Caird and Company.(116) Born in 1816 and educated at the parish school, he served his apprenticeship with Caird and Company (being distantly related to the senior partner). From there he went to the St. Rollox Engine Works, and then to Randolph, Elliot and Company (forerunners of John Elder and Company) to return to Caird and Company in 1838, where he was, successively, head draughtsman, assistant manager, and head of the establishment. He was always prompt to take up any new ideas in his profession, and, indeed, was the first to adopt the inverted cylinder engine, which, by the 1880's was universal in the merchant service. In both local and national politics he had the interest that one might expect of any businessman, 'but his tastes never lay in that direction'.(117) By 1894 John Carmichael was manager of the yard. Born in Govan in 1858, he entered the Fairfield yard in 1873, to serve a seven-year apprenticeship, and when it was finished Sir

William Pearce appointed him head draughtsman and then assistant manager. He appears to have kept away from public affairs.

Perhaps the most prominent of firms specialising in marine engineering was that of James Howden and Company, founded by James Howden (1832-1913) in 1862.(118) Howden was born in Prestonpans in 1832, educated at the parish school there, and came to Glasgow in 1847 as an apprentice in the works of the engineering firm of James Gray and Company. He passed through the different departments with marked success, and before the completion of his apprenticeship was appointed chief draughtsman. Though the firm of James Howden and Company was not founded until 1862, Howden had struck out on his own account by 1854, after spells with Bell and Miller (civil engineers) and Robert Griffiths (a firm well known for work in connection with screw propellers). By 1862 Howden's name was securely established as one of the finest marine engineers on the Clyde, and from about 1871, when a larger works was constructed, he built marine engines for most of the steamer lines, and 'the character of the work executed, and the originality of the design, both of engines and boilers, along with the high standard of efficiency, economy, and durability attained, built up for the firm a world-wide reputation'.(119) Among Howden's many achievements were the devising of air surface condensers, a scheme for utilising the waste heat from the boiler fire gases, forms of water-tube boilers for high pressure, and, most famous of all, his system of forced draught. It was as early as 1862 that he first constructed and tried a boiler under forced draught, and he was to solve, thereby, the problem of satisfactory combustion. It was introduced into steamships in 1884, and its success was such that Howden retired from general marine engineering and concentrated exclusively upon the manufacture of forced draught apparatus. It became universal in steamships, and by 1898 the business had grown to such an extent that a new works again became necessary. Howden, whose contribution to Clyde marine engineering was substantial, was a lifelong Liberal, but took no part in either national or local politics, or, indeed, in public affairs at all.

Of the other firms, D. and W. Henderson,(120) of Partick, was controlled in the 'eighties and 'nineties by John Henderson who seems to have directed all his energies into the firm. Russell and Company(121) was run throughout by Anderson Rodger, under whose direction the firm for several years topped the annual tonnage launched list for the whole of Britain. Rodger was noted for 'his voracity for work and bargain driving skill', and, what is more, was a highly successful innovator. He 'saw that the enormous multiplication of sea-going craft, and the consequent lowering of freights, would compel owners to be content with a rougher and less costly article than the class of vessels sandpapered up to the gilt ball on the top of the main mast. Adopting this turn of the tide, Russell and Co. brought into the market a type of vessel that promised bigger dividends. The thing took. It met new demands and created more. Order after order was secured. . . .'

It is recorded that Rodger was a deputy chairman of the Harbour Trust, president of the Port Glasgow Choral Union, and an elder in the parish church—hardly positions which would have interfered significantly with his work. John Fullerton and Company(122) of Paisley was founded in 1867 by John Fullerton, controlled by him until about 1880, and subsequently by his son James, under whom it prospered. Of James Fullerton it was written in 1908 that he 'has been too busy a man to mix himself up to any large extent with the local affairs of his native town'. A smaller firm was that of Thomas Seath,(123) to whose enterprise the 'inland burgh of Rutherglen owed its position as a shipbuilding port', because of his constant and successful agitation for the removal of obstructions from the upper Clyde. He took 'an intelligent but not too prominent part in local affairs'.

It is clear that the entrepreneurs in shipbuilding and marine engineering possessed drive and enterprise. Their energies, almost without exception, seem to have been directed towards the firm. They may have been interested in local or national politics and in public affairs generally, but they were not, in the period 1870-1900, active participants in these fields.

8. *The Entrepreneurs of the Heavy Industries*—(e) *General Engineering*

The lack of information on the entrepreneurs engaged in general engineering makes generalisation impossible. Of four of them at least (Sir William Arrol, Walter Neilson, the Reids, and Sir William McOnie), however, we know something—enough to tell us a little about two successful branches ('bridges, roofs, and railway appliances', and locomotive engineering) and one branch that was declining (sugar machinery).

Sir William Arrol's life (1839-1913) is a classic story of industrial success achieved from humble beginnings, through high qualities of enterprise and technical ability.(124) Soon after his birth in the village of Houston, his parents (his father was a cotton spinner) moved to Johnstone, where he attended school until the age of 11. The family next moved to Paisley, in 1850, and the young Arrol began work in the bobbin department of J. and P. Coats. The work showed little prospect of advancement, and at 14 he was bound apprentice to a blacksmith in Paisley. At the close of his apprenticeship he left Paisley and gained experience by working in various towns in England and Scotland. In 1863, he became foreman in the boiler works of Messrs. Laidlaw and Sons, staying there for five years and gaining still more experience, until, in 1868, he set up on his own account, in very modest fashion. His capital—his life-savings, in fact—amounted to £85 and he bought his first engine and boiler for £43. It was from this that there arose 'the largest structural steel works in the United Kingdom, occupying about 20 acres, and employing, when in full operation, something like 5,000 men.'(125)

Arrol took to bridge-building, and his first important work—which laid the foundation of his career—was the construction in 1875, for the Caledonian Railway Company, of a viaduct over the Clyde at Bothwell. His great ability emerged clearly when 'he put into practice his idea of building the bridge on land, and then rolling it out over the water. Formerly bridges were riveted piece to piece in their place.'(126) The next important contract was the building of a long, multiple-span bridge over the Clyde at the Broomielaw, for the same company. This time he distinguished himself with the introduction of a new mechanical driller, which saved greatly on labour, and of his patent hydraulic riveter. Indeed, there were few difficulties which he did not overcome by some new device or other, and his inventiveness 'attracted the attention of leading engineers and made him ever afterwards a formidable competitor for all contracts of any magnitude'.(127) His greatest achievements were the building of the second Tay Bridge (completed in 1887) and of the cantilever bridge over the Forth (opened in 1890). Among his other works were the bridge over the Clyde at Central Station, the Redheugh high-level bridge at Newcastle, bridges over the Suir (in Ireland) and the Wear (at Sunderland), a bridge at Barrow-in-Furness, the steel work for the Tower Bridge, London, and bridges in Australia. Arrol was the first to advocate the substitution of steel for timber in the roofs of factory shops. His success was great, and for most of his working lifetime his energy went exclusively to building up the firm. In the 'nineties, however, there is evidence of a certain diversion of energy (after, that is, the firm was well estab-

U

lished and his great fortune created). He became a director of J. and P. Coats, of Stewarts and Lloyds, and the Union Bank of Scotland, and was an M.P. between 1895 and 1905.

At the turn of the century the leading firm in the locomotive trade in Europe was Neilson, Reid and Company.(128) The firm of Messrs. Neilson and Company dated back to 1837, first undertaking the production of locomotive engines as a separate line of business in 1845. Under the capable management of Walter Montgomerie Neilson (son of James Beaumont Neilson of hot-blast fame), it went from strength to strength, until in 1860 Neilson laid out at Springburn an entirely new works, on a large scale, exclusively for the production of locomotive engines. Neilson was a man of great energy, and thoroughly acquainted with the state of engineering skill in Britain and on the Continent. He was remarkable, also, for his fervent belief in technical education.(129) Neilson's only active participation in any public activity was the prominent position he held in the Masonic movement.

Neilson withdrew from most of the active work in the business in 1872 and retired altogether in 1878. Full control then fell to James Reid, under whose direction it grew to even greater strength. Reid's connection with the firm began in 1853, when he was taken on as engineering manager, and, after ten years in that capacity he became a managing partner, and eventually, in 1878, sole proprietor. He had four sons and all of them came into the business, being assumed as partners in 1889, twelve months before their father's death. In this case, the second generation showed no inclination to follow non-business activities, with the exception of Hugh, who was in the 'nineties a J.P. and a Deputy Lieutenant. Under the brothers' aegis the firm of Neilson, Reid and Company continued to grow at an impressive rate.

In 1900 one of the most prominent firms in the manufacture of sugar machinery was McOnie, Harvey and Company,(130) which emerged from an amalgamation, in 1888, of Robert Harvey and Company and W. and A. McOnie. The latter was founded by two brothers, William and Andrew McOnie, William having already been in business as an engineer in the firm of P. and W. McOnie (which later became Mirrlees, Watson and Company). It is interesting and significant to see William McOnie's time taken up increasingly in public affairs, though he remained in control of the firm. 'So long ago as 1867 he was elected to the Town Council. . . . Three years later he was appointed depute Bailie of the River and Firth of Clyde, and afterwards he sat on the bench as a Magistrate for the city from 1879 to 1883. All through these years he rendered excellent public service, especially in connection with departmental and committee work.'(131) In 1883 he became Lord Provost and remained so until 1886, and he was, also, chairman of the British and African Steam Navigation Company. There can have been little time left for the engineering industry.

9. The Rationale of Scottish Entrepreneurship

Between 1870 and 1900 the Scottish heavy industries, with the exception of shipbuilding, parts of the steel industry, and sections of engineering, lacked enterprise, and this was in marked contrast to the earlier years of the century. Faced with a situation of depleted ores, competition from England and abroad, and rising wage costs (except in coal), Scottish entrepreneurs were inadequate in their response.

The first and most satisfactory explanation of this defective enterprise is in terms of what happened within the individual industries. The original men in pig iron were full of drive, eager to build up their fortunes, and so achieve status and prestige in the community. Moreover, they were faced with a favourable situation—the invention of hot blast, plentiful supplies of high quality ore and coal at low cost, and low wages. They saw the opportunities, grasped them, and showed themselves to be dynamic entrepreneurs, in the process building very large successful businesses, and making substantial personal fortunes. All their energies had until this point gone into the firm. It was the prerequisite of success. Their fortunes made, and status achieved, they could either continue to accumulate more material wealth, via the firm, or seek new kinds of power and status. If the latter course were pursued, as it seems to have been by some of the ironmasters (and by men like Arrol and McOnie, of a later generation, in engineering), then the business could continue to expand, if circumstances remained favourable under the original momentum, but at a declining rate. It would more usually be their successors, however, the second and third generations, who would be interested, to a great extent, in matters outside the business. If this happened, then, collectively, the industry would lose most of its original impetus, and one might expect relative decline. The methods by which new kinds of power or status could be achieved were various—participation in other industrial activities, an active rôle in local or national politics, the purchase and management of large estates—all of them time- and energy-consuming. Enterprise was bound to suffer. If responsibility were delegated to managers, there does not seem to have been the same stimulus present. What was true of pig iron was true also of coal. All the large ironmasters were also coalmasters, and those coalmasters who were not in iron, and about whom there is evidence, seem also to have dissipated too much energy in outside activities.

In steel and shipbuilding the situation was different. James Riley, for example, stressed personal management; William Denny was contemptuous of absentee employers. Riley's attitude was apparently shared by the two other large steel firms, and so at least part of that industry was enterprising, while Denny's seems to have been typical of the great majority of shipbuilding entrepreneurs. These men had all one thing in common—singleness of purpose. The steel industry was new. Riley, of working-class origin, had the will to succeed; David Colville and Sons was founded as a malleable-iron firm as late as 1871, and so the drive for material success was present; William Beardmore, junior, was the son of a man who had come into the firm as late as 1861, and so also had the need to succeed. None of these men inherited a fortune. Each *had to succeed* as an industrialist if he wished to become a man of substance and prestige. The rest of the steel industry—the less enterprising part— was a mixture of small concerns (lacking the capital for development and the enterprise to get hold of such capital), one or two pig-iron producers (by nature conservative, for reasons already discussed), and former malleable-iron producers (whose origins were far back in the nineteenth century and who lacked enterprise presumably for the same reasons as the pig-iron men). Shipbuilding was also, in a sense, a new industry. True it was to be found in the early nineteenth century, but only on a small scale; equally true, Robert Napier was eminently successful in the years up to 1850, but he was exceptional. The conditions for large-scale growth did not come until the 'fifties, 'sixties and 'seventies, with the rapid increase in world trade and the opening of the Suez Canal. Slowly in the 1850's and increasingly thereafter, men trained in Napier's yards, who had started on their own account, were finding it possible to build up their firms. It was they and their sons who controlled the industry between 1870 and 1900. For the most part, they found themselves in the position that the ironmasters had occupied in the 'thirties, 'forties and 'fifties. To achieve status and power in the community they had to succeed in business. They found conditions favourable, or where unfavourable they changed them. They were dynamic, imaginative, and driving men.

NOTES

(1) A full treatment of the Census occupational statistics and of other points handled here in summary form will be found in my unpublished thesis, 'The Scottish Economy during the "Great Depression", 1873-1896', which can be consulted in Glasgow University Library. Hereinafter it will be cited as 'Thesis'.

(2) The grouping 'heavy industry', includes: coal, ironstone, iron and steel manufacture, shipbuilding, and engineering.

(3) These embraced iron and brass founding, boilermaking, machine tools, electrical engineering, sugar machinery, locomotive engineering, roofs and bridges and railway appliances, textile machinery and sewing machines, pipe-founding, sanitary, heating and lighting appliances, agricultural implements and machinery, instruments, and marine engineering.

(4) Journal of the West of Scotland Iron and Steel Institute, 1911, p. 36. Subsequently referred to as Journ. W.S.I.S. Inst.

(5) These statistics may be seen, in detail, in my thesis.

(6) Detailed statistics may be seen in my thesis. See also James Nicol, Vital, Social and Economic Statistics of the City of Glasgow, 1881-1885 (Glasgow, 1885), pp. 260-61, and British Iron Trade Association, Annual Reports, 1886 and 1887.

(7) British Association Handbook for 1876, Some of the Leading Industries of Glasgow and the Clyde Valley (Glasgow, 1876), pp. 103-09; British Association Handbook for 1901, Industries of Glasgow and the West of Scotland, edited by A. McLean (Glasgow, 1901), pp. 36, 44-50, and 66-72. These will be referred to hereafter as respectively, B.A. for 1876 and B.A. for 1901. See also, Transactions of the Institution of Engineers and Shipbuilders in Scotland, 1870, pp. 126-27, and Lord Aberconway, The Basic Industries of Great Britain (London, 1927), pp. 222-25. Subsequent references to the Transactions of the Institution of Engineers and Shipbuilders in Scotland will be cited thus: Trans. I.E.S. Scot.

(8) Census of Production of 1907, Final Report, 1912, pp. 125-27.

(9) Scottish Bankers' Magazine, Vol. IV, 1912-13, p. 214.

(10) W. Ashworth, An Economic History of England, 1870-1939 (London, 1960), p. 81.

(11) A. Craig McDonald and A. S. E. Browning, History of the Motor Industry in Scotland (paper presented to the Automobile Division of the Institution of Mechanical Engineers, Glasgow, 1961), pp. 3-5.

(12) All these factors are discussed at length in my thesis.

(13) A. H. Cole, An Approach to the Study of Entrepreneurship, in F. C. Lane and J. C. Riemersma (eds.), Enterprise and Secular Change (American Economic Association, London, 1953), pp. 181-95.

(14) Robert Moore, 1904 Presidential Address before the Mining Institute of Scotland, p. 63. With regard to output per man, over the period 1873-1900 it increased by 38 per cent in East Scotland (from 327 tons to 451), 37 per cent in West Scotland (304 to 415), and only by 9 per cent for the whole of the U.K. (351 to 382). See Report of the Committee on Eight Hours Working in the Mines, Part II, Appendix F, p. 141.

(15) On these points see Transactions of the Mining Institute of Scotland, Presidential Addresses: 1885, pp. 16-18; 1888, p. 18; 1891, pp. 15-20; 1894, pp. 230-34; 1897, pp. 246-48; 1904, pp. 71-72.

(16) *Ibid.*, 1888, p. 18.

(17) *Ibid.*, 1881, p. 23.

(18) *Ibid.*, 1891, pp. 214-17.

(19) Four in Lanark, and one each in Edinburgh, Haddington, Clackmannan, and Ayrshire (*ibid.*, Presidential Address, 1891, p. 4). At this date there were approximately 320 enterprises in the Scottish coal industry (see the Parliamentary Report, List of Mines in the United Kingdom . . . for 1894).

(20) In 1900, in Britain, there were only 311 coal-cutting machines in use, cutting approximately $1\frac{1}{2}$ per cent of all coal mined (Transactions of the Institution of Mining Engineers, 1901, p. 4).

(21) Transactions of the Mining Institute of Scotland, 1891, pp. 185-86.

(22) Trans. I.E.S. Scot., 1870-71, pp. 151-91.

(23) *Loc. cit.*, p. 152.

(24) Transactions of the Mining Institute of Scotland, Presidential Address, 1901, p. 54: 'In many trades much has been said about the need of technical education. That it is so much required in many trades, and ours among them, is not to be disputed, but the members must remember that for the most part the mine itself must be the mine manager's school and college.'

(25) Journ. W.S.I.S. Inst., 1901-02, p. 214.

(26) See thesis, pp. 614-16, for a detailed treatment of this point.

(27) See, for example, B.A. for 1901, p. 18.

(28) Journ. W.S.I.S. Inst., 1913-14, p. 22.

(29) *Ibid.*, Professor Sexton's Presidential Address, 1895, pp. 11-12.

(30) In 1882, for example, 40 per cent of total U.K. pig iron production was hematite, while Scotland produced negligible amounts (British Iron Trade Association, Annual Reports, 1883). In 1887, 61 per cent of total consumption of pig iron in Scotland in foundries and in malleable iron and steel was English (separate figures for the different categories are not available): while this had fallen to 34 per cent by 1889. (These figures are calculated from data in the monthly circulars of Wm. Connal & Co. The data can be seen in full in thesis, pp. 414-17).

(31) Journ. W.S.I.S. Inst., 1895, p. 7. Emphasis supplied.

(32) *Ibid.*, 1901, p. 203.

(33) Statistics of coal and of ore used per ton of pig iron made can be seen for both Scotland and England and Wales in thesis, p. 617.

(34) B.A. for 1901, pp. 16-23.

(35) Journ. W.S.I.S. Inst., 1913-14, p. 15.

(36) *Ibid.*, 1901-2, pp. 216-20, and 1913-14, pp. 45-57.

(37) *Ibid.*, Presidential Addresses, 1892, p. 13 and 1911-12, pp. 7-28; and 1913-14, p. 50.

(38) B.A. for 1876, pp. 36-7; B.A. for 1901, p. 25.

(39) Journ. W.S.I.S. Inst., Presidential Address, 1895, pp. 4-25.

(40) *Ibid.*, Presidential Address, 1894, p. 22.

(41) It had been tried as early as 1860, but its uncertain quality and high price effectively excluded it until the 1870's.

(42) David Pollock, Modern Shipbuilding and the Men Engaged in It (London, 1884), pp. 7-12 and 21, 24; British Iron Trade Association Annual Report, 1886, p. 141.

(43) Calculated from data in British Iron Trade Association, Annual Report, 1891.

(44) 24,016 tons of steel ships out of a total of 133,600. British Iron Trade Association, Annual Report, 1885, pp. 67-68.

(45) Trans. I.E.S. Scot., Presidential Address by Alexander Kirk, 1887, pp. 1-15 and 1906, pp. 430-32; Pollock, Dictionary of the Clyde, p. 219.

(46) Pollock, Modern Shipbuilding and the Men Engaged in It, pp. 12-18.

(47) Pollock, op. cit., pp. 129-48.

(48) Ibid., pp. 84-85.

(49) Because of the exigencies of space I have omitted documentation of this and the following paragraph. It can be found in my thesis, Chapter 6 (for labour), and pp. 262-70 and 650-56 (for the movement to joint stock).

(50) For an illuminating example, see J. L. Carvel, The Coltness Iron Company (Edinburgh, 1948), pp. 68-69.

(51) For example, during the 1870-73 boom: 'It is at present a well-known fact, and the subject of general complaint, that these coal waggons do not perform more than two-thirds of the work they should do' (North British Daily Mail, 3rd December, 1870). Or again in the boom of 1886-90: 'Vessels are occasionally experiencing detention in consequence of the limited supply brought to the loading cranes by the railway company' (Iron and Coal Trades Review, 10th September, 1886). Subsequently referred to as I.C.T.R.

(52) North British Daily Mail, 7th November, 1872.

(53) Between 1870 and 1896, for example, total Scottish coal exports increased three-and-a-half-fold (from 1,338,000 to 4,818,000 tons), much of the increase emanating from the east of Scotland, whose exports grew four-and-a-half-fold (from 832,000 to 3,863,000 tons) while those from the West of Scotland doubled (from 506,000 to 955,000—the figure for 1892 being 1,114,000). Not only this, but exports grew significantly in importance—from 9 per cent of total Scottish output in 1870 to 17 per cent in 1896. This time the increase derived wholly from the east, where exports rose from 31 per cent to 61 per cent of output. In the west the figure was 4 per cent in 1870 and 4 per cent in 1896. Production statistics are taken from the Royal Commission on Coal Supplies (1905), Part XI, Appendices, pp. 76-77, and those of exports from D. A. Thomas, The Growth and Direction of our Foreign Trade in Coal During the Last Half Century, Journal of the Statistical Society, September, 1903, Appendix C, p. 509.

(54) Transactions of the Mining Institute of Scotland, Presidential Addresses, 1885, p. 17, and 1894, pp. 230-34; Iron and Coal Trades Review, 16th September and 9th December, 1887.

(55) Pig iron exports stood at 389,000 tons in 1870, reached a peak of 617,000 in 1873 and had declined to 238,000 by 1890. Their diminishing importance to the industry is seen, further, in the fact that over the same years exports declined from 34 per cent of sales to 19 per cent. Sales statistics are taken from the monthly circulars of Wm. Connal and Co., and the earlier export ones from the same source. The figure for 1890 exports is from Vital, Social, and Economic Statistics of the City of Glasgow, 1885-91, p. 314.

(56) Between 1888 and 1896 total exports of Scottish steel varied from being 28 per cent of Scottish production in 1894 to 50 per cent in 1890. (Calculated from data in the British Iron Trade Association Annual Reports. The details can be seen in thesis, p. 440.)

(57) Between 1885 and 1892, for example, gross tonnage exported from the Clyde rose from 35,000 to 63,000 and was as high as 115,000 in 1889 and 123,000 in 1890. These statistics are drawn from annual reports in the Shipping World. For further details, see thesis, p. 439.

(58) William Pearce, President of the Fairfield Shipbuilding and Engineering Company commented: 'The firm with which I am associated had tendered

47 times during the last seven years and had been systematically ruled out'
(I.C.T.R., 18th March, 1887). It was a firm, moreover, noted for the quality of
its products.

(59) Macdonald and Browning, *op. cit.*, p. 3.

(60) *Ibid.*, p. 10.

(61) *Ibid.*, pp. 10-11. Macdonald and Browning, in describing these factors,
are discussing the years both before and after 1900. What they say certainly
had application in the 1890's, however. At least nine unsuccessful attempts
were made, before 1900, to start a motor-car industry in Scotland.

(62) In 1894 there were 512 mines working coal, owned by 318 firms. The
very large firms included William Baird and Company who owned 39 mines,
Merry and Cunningham (12 mines), the Houldsworths (25 mines), the Dixons
(7 mines). See List of Mines in the United Kingdom for 1894.

(63) This and the following information about the company is drawn from
Augustus Muir, The Fife Coal Company, Limited—A Short History (Cambridge, 1951), pp. 1-14 and 109-16.

(64) The Bailie, 31st October, 1877.

(65) *Ibid.*, 25th January, 1893.

(66) *Ibid.*, 25th January, 1893.

(67) *Ibid.*, 10th October, 1900.

(68) The information in this paragraph is drawn from J. L. Carvel, One
Hundred Years in Coal (Edinburgh, 1944), pp. 1-94, especially 81-94.

(69) *Ibid.*, p. 86.

(70) Carvel, The New Cumnock Coalfield (Edinburgh, 1946), pp. 25-30.

(71) *Ibid.*, p. 27.

(72) In 1872 there were thirteen large firms producing pig iron in Scotland
and a total of 154 blast furnaces, of which the 'big four' owned 58 per cent
(the Bairds 24 per cent, Merry and Cunninghame 13 per cent, the Houldsworths 13 per cent, and the Dixons 8 per cent). By 1900 the number of firms
of any size had fallen to nine and total furnaces to 101, of which the 'big
four' owned 66 per cent (the Bairds, 23 per cent; Merry and Cunninghame,
17 per cent; the Houldsworths, 14 per cent; and the Dixons, 11 per cent).
James Dunlop and Company owned six furnaces in 1872 (4 per cent of the
total) and five in 1900 (5 per cent). It is to be remembered that Merry and
Cunninghame, the Houldsworths, and James Dunlop all were producing steel
by 1900, while the 'big four' were also extensive coal producers. See North
British Daily Mail, 28th December, 1872, and B.A. for 1901, pp. 16-23.

(73) The following information about the Baird family is drawn from J. S.
Jeans, A Gallery of Western Worthies (Glasgow, 1872), pp. 78-87; 100 Glasgow Men, Vol. 1, pp. 13-20; The Bailie—29th July, 1874: 23rd February,
1887: 19th February, 1890: 30th August, 1893; Who's Who in Glasgow in
1909, p. 8.

(74) Who's Who in Glasgow, p. 8.

(75) The Bailie, 30th August, 1893.

(76) 100 Glasgow Men, Vol. II, p. 339.

(77) *Ibid.*, pp. 339-40.

(78) The information on the Dixons is drawn from 100 Glasgow Men, Vol.
I, pp. 103-5, and The Bailie, 28th November, 1877, and 29th July, 1903.

(79) 100 Glasgow Men, *loc. cit.*, pp. 103-04.

(80) The Bailie, 28th November, 1877.

(81) Their history is contained in John Carvel, The Coltness Iron Company
(Edinburgh, 1948). See also 100 Glasgow Men, Vol. I, pp. 165-66.

(82) Carvel, *op. cit.*, p. 23.

(83) 100 Glasgow Men, *loc. cit.*, p. 165.

(84) Quoted in Carvel, *op. cit.*, pp. 61-62.

(85) See North British Daily Mail, 21st August, 1872; The Bailie, 26th May, 1875; Who's Who in Glasgow in 1909, p. 55; B.A. for 1901, p. 27.

(86) The Bailie, 8th June, 1881.

(87) Nicol, Vital Statistics, 1885-91, p. 316; B.A. for 1901, pp. 25-29.

(88) The information on the Steel Company is drawn from The Bailie, 16th July, 1879; and 23rd January, 1884; 100 Glasgow Men, Vol. II, pp. 309-11; Who's Who in Glasgow in 1909, p. 205; Journ. W.S.I.S. Inst., Presidential Addresses, 1892, p. 16, and 1895, p. 5, and Volume IX, pp. 216-20, Volume XVIII, pp. 233-34, and Volume XXI, pp. 49-59; B.A. for 1901, pp. 25-28; I.C.T.R., 12th Nov., 1886. See also Charlotte Erickson, British Industrialists: Steel and Hosiery, 1850-1950 (Cambridge, 1959), pp. 13, 28, 50, 68, 169, and I. F. Gibson, *The Establishment of the Scottish Steel Industry*, Scottish Journal of Political Economy, 1958, pp. 22-39.

(89) Journ. W.S.I.S. Inst., Volume XVIII, p. 233.

(90) *Ibid.*, Presidential Address, 1892, p. 16.

(91) *Ibid.*, Presidential Address, 1894, p. 7.

(92) B.A. for 1901, pp. 27. The rest of the information on the firm is drawn from Trans. I.E.S. Scot., 1915-16, pp. 401-2, and Jubilee of David Colville and Sons Ltd., 1871-1921.

(93) Trans. I.E.S. Scot., *loc. cit.*, p. 401.

(94) W. S. Murphy, Captains of Industry (Glasgow, 1901); The Bailie, 12th February, 1902; B.A. for 1901, pp. 27-28; Who's Who in Glasgow in 1909, pp. 11-12.

(95) Murphy, *op. cit.*, p. 137.

(96) B.A. for 1901, p. 28.

(97) North British Daily Mail, 30th December, 1870; B.A. for 1901, pp. 96-98.

(98) The information on the Napiers is taken from James Napier, The Life of Robert Napier (London, 1904); David Bell, David Napier, Engineer, 1790-1869 (Glasgow, 1912); J. S. Jeans, Gallery of Western Worthies (Glasgow, 1872), pp. 143-51; 100 Glasgow Men, Vol. II, pp. 237-44; The Bailie, 29th April, 1885; Pollock, Dictionary of the Clyde, pp. 216-20 and 259, and Modern Shipbuilding and the Men Engaged in It, pp. 44; John Shields, Clyde Built (Glasgow, 1949), pp. 35-53.

(99) Quoted in Shields, *op. cit.*, p. 37.

(100) These included the introduction of surface condensers, steeple engines, feathering paddles, twin screws, and the designing of a rotary engine, a breech-loading gun and a steam carriage.

(101) Napier, *op. cit.*, p. 202.

(102) Pollock, Dictionary of the Clyde, p. 216.

(103) The information on John Elder and the subsequent history of the firm is drawn from 100 Glasgow Men, Vol. I, pp. 115-22; Who's Who in Glasgow in 1909, pp. 188-89; Trans. I.S.E. Scot., 1871, pp. 15-25: 1882, pp. 1-15; The Bailie, 2nd July, 1879: 12th December, 1883: 14th May, 1890: 15th February, 1893: 30th May, 1900; The Fairfield Shipbuilding and Engineering Works (London, 1908); Fairfield, 1860-1960 (Glasgow, 1960).

(104) 100 Glasgow Men, *loc. cit.*, p. 118.

(105) Fairfield, 1860-1960.

(106) The information on the Dennys is taken from Alexander B. Bruce, The Life of William Denny (London, 1889); The Bailie, 5th September, 1877: 12th January, 1882: 7th August, 1895; Trans. I.E.S. Scot., 1887, pp. 257-86: 1906, pp. 430-32: 1911, pp. 485-86; Pollock, Modern Shipbuilding, Preface, and p. 130, and Dictionary of the Clyde, pp. 101-06; Who's Who in Glasgow in 1909, p. 58; Shields, op. cit., pp. 104-06.

(107) See Bruce, op. cit., p. 122.

(108) Quoted in Trans. I.E.S. Scot., 1887, p. 264.

(109) Ibid., 1906, p. 431.

(110) See A Shipbuilding History, 1750-1932: Alexander Stephen and Sons of Linthouse (London, 1932); J. L. Carvel, Stephens of Linthouse, a Record of Two Hundred Years of Shipbuilding (Glasgow, 1950); The Bailie, 22nd June, 1881; 2nd July, 1902.

(111) A Shipbuilding History . . ., p. 85.

(112) See The Bailie, 3rd July, 1876, and 3rd January, 1895; Who's Who in Glasgow in 1909, p. 97; Trans. I.E.S. Scot., 1918, pp. 399-401.

(113) See The Bailie, 2nd March, 1881, and 1st March, 1905; 100 Glasgow Men, Vol. II, pp. 321-22; Pollock, Dictionary of the Clyde, pp. 272-73; Sir Allan Grant, Steel and Ships, the Story of John Brown's; Trans. I.E.S. Scot., 1908, pp. 14-39.

(114) 100 Glasgow Men, loc. cit., p. 322.

(115) The Bailie, 2nd March, 1881.

(116) For Caird and Company, see ibid., 3rd June, 1885, and 15th February, 1893.

(117) Ibid., 3rd June, 1885.

(118) For James Howden's career, see The Bailie, 3rd April, 1895; and Trans. I.E.S. Scot., 1913, pp. 665-68.

(119) Trans. I.E.S. Scot., loc. cit., p. 667.

(120) The Bailie, 26th June, 1895.

(121) Ibid., 1st August, 1894.

(122) Ibid., 8th July, 1908.

(123) Ibid., 9th April, 1879.

(124) The information on Arrol is drawn from Trans. I.E.S. Scot., 1912, pp. 472-75; Who's Who in Glasgow in 1909, p. 7; The Bailie, 22nd June, 1887, and 5th March, 1890; R. Purvis, Sir William Arrol—a Memoir (Edinburgh, 1913).

(125) Trans. I.E.S. Scot., loc. cit., p. 473.

(126) Who's Who in Glasgow in 1909, p. 7.

(127) The Bailie, 22nd June, 1887.

(128) For Neilson, Reid and Company's history see ibid., 22nd March, 1876, and 27th November, 1901; B.A. for 1876, pp. 105-06; and B.A. for 1901, pp. 66-67.

(129) The Bailie, 22nd March, 1876.

(130) See B.A. for 1901, pp. 64-65; and The Lord Provosts of Glasgow, 1833-1902 (Glasgow, 1902), pp. 405-08.

(131) The Lord Provosts of Glasgow, p. 407.

Part Three:
Scottish Enterprise Overseas

CHAPTER ELEVEN

The Rise of Glasgow in the Chesapeake Tobacco Trade, 1707-1775*

JACOB M. PRICE

Professor of History,
University of Michigan

THE MINISTERS, lawyers, teachers, artisans, the books, letters, ideas that made the ocean crossing from Scotland to North America in the eighteenth century went as freight in vessels bound upon other business. More often than not, these vessels were outward bound from the Clyde for the Chesapeake to bring home tobacco for all the North and West of Europe. It will thus not be out of place, in this issue devoted to the cultural relations between Scotland and America in the eighteenth century, to examine, if only briefly, those material relationships which facilitated, if they did not entirely account for, the other, less material, exchanges.

The importance of tobacco in the economies of colonial Virginia and Maryland is a truism. Its importance in the development of Scottish overseas trade is less well known. In 1772, tobacco accounted for 80 per cent of all Scottish imports from North America (at official values)!(1) Ten years earlier (1762), the proportion had been 85 per cent—or 74 per cent of imports from North America and the West Indies combined. In fact, in that year (1762), tobacco constituted 40 per cent of all Scottish imports from abroad (excluding England), or 47 per cent if Ireland is not treated as 'overseas'. On the other side of the ledger, the situation was comparable. Tobacco accounted for 81 per cent of Scottish re-exports of foreign produce in 1762 and for 52 per cent of all Scottish exports.(2) Other sectors of the Scottish economy could not have been unaffected, for in 1769 Virginia and Maryland received 83 per cent of all Scottish exports

* This paper is reprinted from the *William and Mary Quarterly*, Third Series, Vol. XI (April, 1954), pp. 179-99, by kind permission of the editor and the author.

to North America and the West Indies.(3) Eighteenth-century customs valuations are notoriously unreliable; allowing, though, for a considerable margin of error, one cannot but be impressed with the preponderant rôle played by a single commodity in the foreign commerce of this not uncommercial nation. For corroboration which avoids the problem of customs valuation, we may compare shipping data. Of all Scottish tonnage employed to North America and the West Indies in the three years from 1772 through 1774, Virginia and Maryland alone were the destinations of 49 per cent; if North Carolina were added to its neighbours, the proportion of the tobacco colonies would rise to 56 per cent.(4) Such a measurement, though, does not do full justice to the Clyde tobacco trade, for it was common practice to charter English and sometimes New England vessels in this trade. Neither do Scottish trade data do full justice to the commercial activities of the Scots, for there was a large colony of Glaswegians in London deeply involved in the Virginia trade of that city, and many Glasgow vessels carried their cargoes of tobacco to London—the Glasgow market, apparently, being too well known to be attractive to many a trading Scot.(5) These remoter fields of Scottish activity, however, we shall have to leave unexplored, and keep ourselves north of the border.

One of the most remarkable things about the Scottish tobacco trade proper was the rapidity and vigour of its growth. In the years immediately following the Union, imports averaged a mere 1,450,000 pounds per annum; this had only become 2,500,000 by the mid-'teens.(6) Shortly after, though, the first great spurt raised imports to six million in 1722, but this was followed by stagnation—to the Scots, politically induced. Eight million was not reached till 1741, but by then the heroic age had begun: ten million in 1743, thirteen million in 1745, twenty-one million in 1752, twenty-four million the next year, thirty-two million in 1760, and—the all time high—forty-seven million in 1771.(7) After the Scottish trade began its most imposing growth about 1740, the English trade ceased to grow significantly. As late as 1738, the Scottish trade had accounted for only 10 per cent of the British total. By 1744, this had become 20 per cent; 30 per cent was first reached in 1758 and 40 per cent in 1765. 1758 was also the year in which the Scottish imports first passed those of both London and the outports, making the Scottish sector the most important element in the national trade. This, as we shall see, also made Glasgow the first tobacco port in the realm. The Scottish trade attained its greatest relative importance in the three years from 1768 through 1770, when its share hovered about 50 per cent, the 51·8 per cent of 1769 marking the only occasion on which Scotland topped England (London and the outports combined) in the trade. In the glut years from 1771 through 1775, the Scottish trade did not grow as readily as the great bumper crops, and its share slipped to about 45 per cent, at which level the Revolution found it.(8)

Thus far we have been speaking of the Scottish tobacco trade; in effect, though, this was the tobacco trade of Glasgow—that is, of Glasgow city, Port Glasgow, and Greenock. The great merchants resided and transacted their business in the city of Glasgow, but little of the tobacco got farther up the Clyde than Greenock or Port Glasgow, for the improvers had not yet made the river navigable for ocean-going vessels. From the first, the Clyde's share in this trade was preponderant.(9) Of the mere 6,401,629 pounds of tobacco imported into Scotland between May 1, 1707 (the effective date of the Union), and September 29, 1711, 5,718,279 pounds, or 89 per cent, went to the port of Glasgow.(10) This pre-eminent position was never lost. The Clyde's share of the Scottish total was 91 per cent in the three years Michaelmas 1714 to 1717; 97 per cent in Michaelmas 1725-26; down to 80 per cent in Michaelmas 1730-31 and 79 per cent for the ten years Christmas 1737 to 1747; but 98 per cent in the ten years Michaelmas 1766 to 1776.(11) For all practical purposes, Glasgow was Scotland as far as the tobacco trade was concerned.

Here, then, are the formal measurements of the situation familiar to readers of the social history of Scotland and Virginia: in the Chesapeake, unpopular Scots factors engrossing the tobacco trade upon every river, in Glasgow, the scarlet cloaks of the tobacco lords —or Virginia dons—parading in awesome solitude along the pavement by the Exchange reserved by prescription for them alone.(12) But how did this come about? The logic of commerce is not perverse; nor do things just happen. To the Scots writers of that age, of course, there was no problem. 'So sensible', Gibson tells us, 'were the people of Glasgow of the advantages which they had procured by the Union, that no sooner was this treaty signed, than they began immediately to prosecute the trade to Virginia and Maryland; [lacking ships of their own] they chartered vessels from Whitehaven; they sent out cargoes of goods, and brought back tobacco in return.'(13) Gibson was not perplexed by the why and the how; nor were the writers who followed him; nor, it may be presumed, were his readers. The triumph of virtue and industry is seldom unexpected. Difficulties, of course, add lustre to the prize: lacking ships, the Clydesiders chartered those of Whitehaven; lacking capital and commercial connections in the colonies, their totally inexperienced captains and supercargoes bartered from ship side with willing planters.(14) Success followed in course, and their trade grew lustily.

Unfortunately, this pretty tale is too simple: truth was more paradoxical. Though the tobacco trade was cited in numerous pamphlets for and against the Union, the Union itself was *not* popular in Glasgow; on the contrary, it led to rather ugly riots there.(15) But the Glaswegians did not have to read pamphlets: they had a long experience of the tobacco trade, going back a generation or more before the Union. With other Scotsmen, they had been trading to and resident in the tobacco colonies since the middle of the seventeenth century.(16) The story of the Scots interlopers and their struggle against the Navigation Acts in the 1690's is too well known to need repeating here.(17) The anti-Union Glasgow merchant was familiar, too, with the European markets for tobacco. Following prices in the north of Europe carefully, he was used, when prospects seemed favourable, to buy tobacco speculatively in Whitehaven and Liverpool for shipment to Holland and Sweden.(18) Glasgow thus met the opportunities offered by the lamented Union with something more solid than industry and virtue and commercial sensibility. The rest of Gibson's picture must also be taken with a grain of salt. By the 1720's, there was already a significant Scottish mercantile element *resident* in Virginia, and Glasgow merchants were soliciting for, and receiving, consignment from the great planters.(19) It thus seems unlikely that the idyllic, creditless, barter-and-home-again commerce described by Gibson lasted as late as he would have it (1740), if it ever existed at all in an economically significant sense.(20)

To English competitors, and to some Virginians, the phenomenon of Scottish success was no great mystery: fraud, indulgence, collusion, corruption, and perjury accounted for it quite adequately. Logically it followed that if only the customs in Scotland were collected with the rigour with which they were allegedly collected south of the Tweed, then the distressing spectacle of prosperity along the Clyde would disappear along with the unfair advantages that nurtured it.(21) Such allegations started on the very morrow of the Union, to the discomfiture of Treasurer Godolphin, its architect.(22) His successors for three generations were, in varying degrees, similarly beset.(23) The diagnosis of the afflicted is not, however, always the surest guide to the nature, causes, or extent of the affliction. As a matter of fact, the produce of the tobacco duties in Scotland was disappointingly low, but it does not necessarily follow that either Glasgow or its greater merchants had therein any special advantage.(24) One will remember that this was an era in which inter-port rivalry was serious and bitter. Merchants who were accustomed to use the statute book to frustrate their foreign rivals were not unprepared to set the administrative machine to strangle indigenous competition. In the appointment of revenue officers, the merchants of each port were content for themselves with men who knew their interest but insisted for their neighbours on men who would know their duty. It was a complex game, in which the wails of fraud and ruin also counted for points.(25)

Viewed in retrospect, though, the most significant thing about Glasgow's rise in the tobacco trade—at least until the 1740's—was that it was simply part of the general shift of the trade to the North-west. Though duties were, in fact, collected rigorously at London, the lament of the metropolis at perfidy abroad was the more poignant because its own commerce (from high costs, etc.) was in these years falling behind.(26) Bristol cried with London, for Bristol, too, was (relatively speaking) standing still while Liverpool and Glasgow were booming. The South-west in general was undergoing a secular decline. At the beginning of the century, a dozen minor fishing havens in Cornwall, Devon, etc., could rank as tobacco ports of note.(27) By the end of the 1740's, however, the trade at Padstow, Truro, Fowey, Looe, Plymouth, Dartmouth, Exeter, Lyme, Poole, etc., was moribund while that at Barnstaple, Bideford, Falmouth, Penryn, and Weymouth was barely holding on.(28) Meanwhile, in the North-west new tobacco ports of eminence were emerging—south as well as north of the border. In the 1720's, Glasgow had passed Bristol, to become for the moment the second tobacco port in the land (after London), but in the late 'thirties its claim to that position was to be challenged by other northern ports.(29) Liverpool and Whitehaven had been significant in the tobacco trade from the late seventeenth century, but they came into eminence (as did Glasgow) only with the decline of the South-west. Liverpool, too, had passed Bristol by 1738, and Whitehaven did so in 1739. For a while, these three northern ports struggled for the honour of being second in the land (or first of the outports), but, when the dust settled, the emergent order, after London, seemed to be: Glasgow—second, Whitehaven—third, Liverpool—fourth, and Bristol—fifth. It will be noted that the sequence (first achieved in 1742) is from north to south.(30)

How can one explain this new order? What advantages, illicit or licit, did Glasgow and the other north-western ports have over their southern rivals? As noted above, the merchants of London and Bristol made much of the illicit or 'unfair' advantages which their

X

northern competitors enjoyed. These included the excessive susceptibility of the North British officers to corruption, the ignorance and sloth of the same officers, which made fraud easy without corruption or collusion, and the unfamiliarity of even the best officers with the correct English customs procedure, which resulted in excessive allowances and indulgences to the merchants. The earliest English complaints came to a head in 1722-23 and received the fullest consideration from the Treasury and Parliament. Despite the very active resistance of Glasgow's M.P., Daniel Campbell (himself once active in the trade), the opinion of the political public went against the Scots.(31) The South British victory was embodied in the statute 9 Georgii I. c. 21. This act established more stringent regulations for collecting the duties on tobacco and abolished the Union's separate board of customs for Scotland, fixing in its stead at Edinburgh a rotating sub-committee of the London board.(32) On the administrative level, this act was accompanied by a wholesale firing of native Scottish customs officers and their replacement by experienced English career men.(33) Though these changes caused great scandal at the time, it is really impossible to evaluate their long-range effects.(34)

In the 1740's, there was another great alarm in the South about the rise of the outports in general and Glasgow in particular.(35) Out of this came the Tobacco Act of 1751, which established a rigid system of controls governing the internal movement of tobacco.(36) Henceforth, unmanufactured tobacco could not change hands or be moved from place to place without a permit; through an elaborate central accounting system, special officers in London and Edinburgh had records of every pound of tobacco from the day it was imported to the day it was sold to the retailer.(37) This law, however, for all the intent of its London godparents, did not inhibit in the least the growth of Glasgow as the tobacco port. On the contrary, Glasgow flourished after 1751 as never before, and by 1758 was passing London to become the first tobacco port of the realm. The act seems, however, to have affected the lesser Scottish ports, for their share of the North British trade faded away to little more than nil in the years after 1751.(38)

If, now, it cannot be said that Glasgow and the other northwestern ports had any illicit advantage sufficient in itself to explain their startling rise, how, then, did they arrive? This never was an easy question. As late as 1768, President Nelson, the leading merchant at Yorktown, in Virginia, could write to John Norton, a London merchant of great experience, that he doubted that either of them knew all the elements which accounted for Glasgow's ascendency in the trade.(39) Some of these elements, though, we may at least guess at. First, it was noted above that the order of importance of the tobacco ports was their geographic sequence from north to south: Glasgow, Whitehaven, Liverpool, Bristol. The route north of Ireland was the shortest and quickest (by two or three weeks) to North America. A vessel could go from the Clyde to the capes of Virginia in the time a London man might be kept waiting at Portsmouth by contrary winds in the Channel.(40) Shorter sailing time meant that commercial intelligence could pass more quickly. This was particularly important to the Glasgow merchants, who generally traded on their own, in contrast to the Londoners, who were generally factors for the larger planters.(41) Then, too, the northern route about Ireland seems to have been decidedly safer in times of war. It was not until the Seven Years' War that enemy privateers penetrated this area in force.(42)

A second 'honest advantage' enjoyed by the Clyde tobacco trade may have been the financial and commercial facilities available at Glasgow. Brown tells us that 'the strength of the monied interest of the west of Scotland was embarked in it'.(43) We know from the correspondence of John Glassford the difficult straits the trade was put to when some of 'the monied interest' withdrew their money in 1761.(44) Since the three major banks in Glasgow were all dominated by 'tobacco lords', there could have been little difficulty in directing toward the trade when needed whatever outside wealth was sent into the city via the banking system. Before the first bank opened, in January, 1750, the situation was not too different, for persons desiring the service of a bank of deposit commonly left their money with a Virginia merchant—as the greatest and most prestigious type of foreign trader. By a fiction of the place, this was regarded as a special favour to the depositor.(45) The availability of such credit for the tobacco trade may also have been facilitated by a lack of competing areas of investment at Glasgow. Before the Revolution, the Clyde's West India trade was minor and its African trade non-existent—both inherently more highly capitalised forms of commerce than the tobacco trade.(46) Then, too, Glasgow was an important market centre for the light industries of the West of Scotland, many of which furnished products well suited to the Chesapeake trade. Defoe visited Glasgow in 1723, at the height of the furor over the tobacco frauds and the new customs policy. He took the side of the honest Glaswegians and scoffed at the notion that they had no fair advantages in trade. He gave a long catalogue of the native produce of the West of Scotland suitable to the needs of tobacco planters.(47) It was, perhaps, such financial and commercial facilities that gave Glasgow a particular advantage over Whitehaven, its closest competitor in the 1740's.

A third, and perhaps the most important, advantage enjoyed by the Clydesiders was that of low operating costs. President Nelson wrote to Samuel Athawes, a London merchant, in 1769, anent his fears that the Scots would monopolise the trade: 'certain it is they give more real money for Tob[acc]o here than can be had at your Market except for a few particular Crops. I know they have a vast Advantage over You by sailing their ships so much cheaper than you can do; and by having their Factors here, who are always buying against the Arrival of their ships, they make two Voyages in a Year; . . .'(48) The elements contributing to Glasgow's lower shipping costs were many—cheaper ship procurement, refitting, and labour, and better paying outward cargoes to America—but it was in coupling shipping costs and the factory system that President Nelson gave us the most significant key to the quantitative and structural development of the Glasgow trade.(49) The greatest expense in the tobacco trade, after the prime cost of the tobacco, was freight. In peacetime, freight was commonly about a halfpenny per pound (sterling), while the cost of the tobacco purchased in Virginia most commonly ran from a penny to three halfpence (sterling) per pound.(50) The strongest formative pressure upon the tobacco trade in mid-century was the drive to reduce these high freight costs by hook or by crook—by building larger ships or by changes in the institutional organisation of the trade. Shipping costs per hogshead varied inversely with the size of the ship but directly with the length of the voyage. The principal variant in the length of the voyage was the duration of the 'stay in the country'. Vessels were sometimes kept three or six or more months in the Chesapeake before they could obtain a full freight back. Where ships were on charter, catastrophic demurrage charges were often accumulated. Such considerations, while discouraging some from investing in the larger and more efficient vessels, encouraged Glaswegians and others to establish, at great expense, salaried and other agents in permanent stores in the tobacco colonies. Such agents purchased in advance cargoes for their employers' ships and thus reduced to as little as fifteen days the turn-around time spent in the Chesapeake. Because Glasgow agents were frequently more interested in buying in a hurry than in watching the price, they often drove up the price—to the great annoyance of the solicitors of consignments and the native buyers. (Oddly enough, later writers in the agrarian interest have been slow to give them credit for thus benefiting the planter.)(51) Contemporaries were fully aware of the crucial importance of shipping costs and turn-around time, and from them we can adduce a causal connection between such costs and the store system as it developed in the 1740's and after.(52)

The three explanations so far given do much to explain Glasgow's rise to the position of *prima inter pares* of the outports in the tobacco trade—a position she had attained provisionally in the 1720's and definitely by the mid-'forties. They do not explain the continued rise of Glasgow thereafter, a rise which, in 1758, brought her abreast of London and made her equal to all the English outports combined. For an explanation of this more startling development, we must look for something more fundamental and yet be content with something more hypothetical. Does it not seem that, in the generation or two preceding the American Revolution, there was manifest in Britain a tendency towards specialisation among the outports: Bristol in the West India trade, Liverpool in the slave trade, Glasgow in the tobacco trade? Might this not be associated with an incipient tendency towards the evolution of commodity markets of the sort later epitomised by the Liverpool cotton exchange? As long as Amsterdam remained the ultimate tobacco market in Europe, it did not matter where in Britain a given parcel of tobacco was landed and reshipped. In the seventeenth century, the little Cornish ports had specialised in this unloading-reloading business; in the eighteenth, for the reasons given above, Glasgow and Whitehaven took it over. (London and Bristol always dominated the domestic tobacco market, which was, however, much smaller than the foreign.) But when Amsterdam's hand began to slip, when French and German and other foreign buyers began to purchase directly in Britain, then the major markets attained a tremendous advantage over the minor. No one could expect the French Farmers-General to maintain buyers in every Fowey and Truro in the land; they did, of course, maintain them in London and Glasgow.(53) Which of these two ports would become ultimately *the* tobacco market was still undecided when the contest was called because of revolution. It seemed, though, that only London's position as the financial and communications centre of the land was withholding the decision which mere commercial economics would have given to Glasgow.

Growth not uncommonly is accompanied by change. As the Glasgow tobacco trade grew, it changed in its constitution and its constituent parts. Most strikingly, the individual firms that made up the trade became larger and fewer in number and more closely associated by ties of joint interest and kinship. Space enjoins any discussion of the details of kinship; they are a well-known phe-

nomenon in Scottish as in other social history.(54) The tale of
numbers is sooner told. In the four years from 1728 through 1731,
91 persons or firms entered tobacco for importation at Port Glasgow and Greenock. The number of actual firms was probably somewhat smaller, for several of the individuals named were undoubtedly
partners.(55) In 1773, however, when the Clyde trade was nine or
ten times what it had been in 1730 to 1731, it was handled by only
38 firms. (Many of these firms had partners in common.) In other
words, two-fifths as many firms handled ten times as much business.
The average firm in 1773 imported 1,157 hogsheads, or roughly
three shiploads! (The greatest had a fleet of 25.) The smallest im-
porter, one Ebenezer M'Nair, entered 16 hogsheads; at that, he was
a greater operator than all but a few of the 91 of the earlier period.
The two largest firms (Alexander Speirs & Company and John
Glassford & Company) together accounted for more than 25 per
cent of the importation, and the first seven firms together accounted
for well over half.(56)

These first seven firms were, for all practical purposes, only six,
for two of them—William Cuninghame & Company and Cuninghame, Findlay & Company—had several partners in common.(57)
If these two firms are considered one, the Cuninghame group, instead
of holding third and fifth place, would move to first place. Its internal organisation thus represents the fullest development of some
of the tendencies present in the Clydeside tobacco trade on the eve
of the Revolution and is well worth examination. The firm dated
back at least to the 1720's, when it consisted of Provost Andrew
Cochran, who had just come up from Ayr, and John Luke, scion
of an old Glasgow mercantile family.(58) In 1775, the firm, or
syndicate, embraced three firms: William Cuninghame & Company,
trading to Virginia, Cuninghame, Findlay & Company, and Cuninghame, Brown & Company, the last two trading to Maryland. The first
firm consisted of nine partners holding 229 shares between them, the
second of six partners holding 44 shares, and the third of three
partners holding 12 shares. William Cuninghame personally owned
64 of the 229 shares in the first, 10 of the 44 in the second and 6 of
the 12 in the third firm; Robert Bogle, of an old Glasgow mercantile
family, owned 48 shares in the first and 8 in the second; Robert
Findlay (a kinsman of Cuninghame) owned 8 in the second and 4
in the third. These three individuals were peculiar in the Glasgow
tobacco trade in not being personally involved in any of the Glasgow
banks. Virtually every other figure of note in the trade was a banker
—or at least a partner in a bank. (Because of the long-term American credits outstanding and the shorter term but heavier demands of

the customs, accessible credit was the lifeblood of the tobacco trade as it existed on the eve of the Revolution.) The firm did not, however, lack banking connections. The other major partners in the first, or Virginia, firm were Provost Andrew Cochran, its aged founder, and his brothers-in-law, Provost John and Peter Murdoch (whose mother was a Luke). The first two were founders and the third a prominent shareholder of the Glasgow Arms Bank, originally known as Cochran, Murdoch & Company. Moreover, a major partner in Cuninghame, Findlay & Company was Alexander Houstoun, founding partner in the Ship Bank (Dunlop, Houstoun & Company, the first bank in Glasgow) and great West India merchant, whose only known connection with the tobacco trade was this silent partnership.(59)

Of quite another order were the Cuninghame petty partners, like the David Walker who held two shares (out of 44) in the second firm, or the four persons who held from two to five shares each (out of 229) in the first. One of these, holding five shares, was James Robinson, 'the General Superintendent of the Company', who resided at Falmouth on the Rappahannock; the others were probably lesser employees of the company, resident either in Glasgow or America, who had likewise been allowed small shares in the undertaking as incentives to diligence.(60) The American resident partner was common to many firms, though in some of the smaller, he was a major rather than a minor shareholder.(61) In this, as in other aspects of its structure and staff, the organisation of the Cuninghame group was analogous to that of the Speirs and Glassford syndicates; it is to be doubted, however, that smaller houses found such elaborate organisation necessary, and, in particular, that they felt obliged to separate their Virginia and Maryland interests.(62)

The form of organisation assumed by the great Glasgow tobacco houses was peculiarly suited to the nature of the business conducted by these firms. It stood in marked distinction to that prevalent among the great London commission houses—which usually consisted of individuals acting alone or in partnerships of two or, at the most, three. Larger partnerships had been increasingly common at Glasgow since the earliest days of the trade. Such unions gave an opportunity to merchant-undertakers like Speirs, Glassford, and Cuninghame and their predecessors to unite into viable societies the diverse qualities and interests of poor but experienced ship-captains and factors and of inactive but astute monied and/or landed people, like Houstoun, the banker, or the Schaws of Greenock.(65) Such organisation was unnecessary in London, for the commission merchants did not employ factors in America and had to have sufficient capital *of their own* to deserve the reputation and attract the confidence which alone brought consignments; an unknown silent partner of the greatest wealth would do their reputations little service.

In America, too, the organisation of the great Glasgow firms expressed an adaptation to growing size. It was, nevertheless, relatively simple. A Scots factor was commonly a salaried employee. He was supervised by a chief factor, who might receive a percentage commission as well as a salary. Chief factors were sometimes partners in the employing firm. The subordinate factors were each in charge of a store or two, and assisting the factor in each store would be one or more storekeepers, clerks, or 'boys', commonly under contract or articles.(64) The architectural history of the stores tended to be an evolution from the barely utilitarian to the quite elegant. By 1775, many of the 'stores' were elaborate affairs, consisting of a brick residence with attached warehouses, shops, barns, etc. Some had home farms for domestic supplies, with slaves for farm and heavy work. The value of such establishments frequently ran upwards of a thousand pounds.(65) There was in all this, however, nothing basically new or peculiar to Glasgow. There had been stores and factors in seventeenth-century Virginia, and the stores kept for London Scots and Liverpool merchants in the 1730's and 1740's were essentially the same as those kept for Glasgow houses in the next decades.(66) The great Glasgow syndicates did, however, reach new extremes in the number as in the size of their stores. The Cuninghame interests had seven stores in Maryland and fourteen in Virginia. These were almost entirely in the newer regions away from tidewater, for it was from such areas that the great new additions to the colonies' tobacco crops were coming, and it was there that one found the smaller planters, who were the stores' usual customers.(67) As these newer areas were largely in Virginia, we find that the Glasgow trade was predominantly a Virginia affair—more so than one would suspect from the Cuninghame store distribution. Of the 43,970 hogsheads of tobacco imported into the Clyde in 1773, 35,035 came from Virginia, 7,298 from Maryland, and 1,637 from North Carolina.(68)

The factor, however, had not always been the primary representative of Glasgow's commerce in the Chesapeake. In the early days after the Union, as Gibson would have it, 'a supercargo went out with every vessel who bartered his goods for tobacco, until such time as he had either sold all his goods, or procured as much tobacco as was sufficient to load his vessel'.(69) Alas (for Gibson was writing in 1777), this circumspect method of doing business was abandoned and 'soon after the year 1740 a new mode was adopted in carrying on the trade to America; in place of the method of bartering, . . . factors were established in the country, who received the goods, and remitted the tobacco; these goods they gave credit of to the planters, on condition that they should receive their crops of tobacco, when ready for the market; for several years this method succeeded extremely well, and the payments were generally made in a reasonable time; but the trade, after the period of 1750, being exceedingly increased, and factors established in every corner of the country, the interests of these gentlemen began to interfere with one another; ambition for who should be possessed of the largest share of the trade took possession of them; they lent to the planters large sums of money, in order to secure them for customers, they gave them unlimited credits; and rendered the commerce with the people of America rather a speculative, than a solid branch of business.'(70) So much for the prudent Gibson. He is probably engaging in poetic license when he describes the earlier idyllic barter economy, but, chronology aside, his picture of the rise of the factories and the expansion of credit fits in with other contemporary evidence. All surviving correspondence between Scottish (or English) merchants and their American employees is but a variation on the theme of the near-bankrupt employer beseeching his extravagant representative to be less easy with credit in the future.(71) Most American writers from Jefferson onwards have drawn a picture in which the scheming British plutocrat instructs his minions to *entice* the unwary planter into the bottomless pit of debt irredeemable—debt which is to tie father and son as chattels to a house in London or Glasgow (phraseology after Jefferson).(72) Yet Jefferson, as a lawyer who frequently acted for merchants against reneging planters, must have known that most of the smaller and some of the larger planters felt no compunction in flitting from one store to another with their business—no matter how much they owed anywhere.(73) This myth has been a long time dying; one wonders that the subsequent agricultural history of this country should not have given some writers a keener insight into the credit needs of the colonial planter-farmer.

Look at it as one will, the credit advanced by Glasgow to the tobacco colonies and outstanding grew alarmingly in the generation preceding the American Revolution. During the Stamp Act crisis, John Glassford, testifying before a committee of the House of Commons, estimated that Glasgow had £500,000 outstanding in the Chesapeake, the greatest part of which was in small advances (under £30) to small men. He estimated that the average investment took four years to come back. The way trade was then ordered, he doubted if returns could be had in less than three years and had often known it to be five. Glassford alone had owing him £50,000.(74) In the next ten years, the debts outstanding did anything but contract. After the Revolution, the Cuninghame group submitted claims for £135,631 lost in Virginia and Maryland because of the war. Of this, £113,282 was for book balances due them (after deductions for bad debts)!(75) That figure probably represents a rather conservative picture of the credit extended by them in the last few years, for most of the firms are reported to have retrenched considerably in 1775.(76) The Cuninghame claim showed thousands of separate accounts in debt to them, the vast majority for small sums (under £10), with relatively few for as much as £100.(77) For the individual planters, this could hardly have been the irredeemable hereditary debt of which Jefferson spoke. The aggregate, however, is impressive for one firm. For the mid-eighteenth century, it was a fantastic sum.

In assessing the rôle played by the Glasgow tobacco trade in the development of Virginia and Maryland, first place must be given to credit. Glasgow may be said to have financed the Piedmont frontier. Such credit was seldom formal or long-term. A mortgage or bond was almost never taken, except to secure an otherwise dubious debt. The financial aid offered was usually in the form of a running credit on the books of a store. But it freed the planter's hand. In effect, it enabled him to divert to long-range projects cash and labour which otherwise would have had to be allocated to the needs of the hour: thus, he could speculate in land, buy slaves, clear land for cultivation, etc. This credit service and the market service effected by bringing the buying facilities of Europe to the Piedmont help to explain the continued expansion of tobacco cultivation in the eighteenth century—at a time when the older soils deteriorated, when the line of cultivation moved away from water navigable by ocean-going vessels, when the agricultural economies of Virginia and Maryland were becoming steadily, if gradually, more diversified, and when world-wide secular changes in prices were making grain cultivation once again more profitable *vis-à-vis* tobacco. In spite of all this, in 1775, tobacco was still king in the Chesapeake, and in the economy of North America it held a position it was never to enjoy again.(78)

The indirect, social results of the Glasgow tobacco trade in Virginia and Maryland are harder to assess. The number of factors and assistants could hardly have been large enough to form a quantitatively significant element in immigration. At the Revolution, most seem to have gone home. Their salaries were too limited to have enabled them to set the tone in circles of consequence in the colonies. They could hardly be considered extraordinarily accomplished in any sense. But they were there, and twice a year their ships came to them from the Clyde—ships as numerous as those from all Britain besides. For many a Virginian, this must have meant that mail, news, reading matter, ideas, religion, politics came to him via Glasgow. This could not have been without some effect.

In so far as the Glasgow element in the tobacco trade may be said to have had any distinctive influence on the evolving social structure of the Chesapeake colonies, its influence was negative. First, there was no place in the factory or store system for independent middlemen (nor for that matter was there very much of one in the alternative consignment system, used by the greater planters). Secondly, because of their skill, their resources, and their organisation, the Scots were terrible competitors for those who would pretend to be their rivals. The Glasgow chains of stores, one must remember, were both a remarkably rationalised and highly capitalised form of economic organisation for the commerce of those times. One has to turn to the great chartered companies for comparison. Thirdly, the factory system tended to drain the tobacco colonies of their ablest commercial talents. If a Scots factor were successful, he thought of returning to Glasgow and becoming a partner in a Virginia house there.(79) If he were a failure, he might stay in Virginia as an employee or a petty trader or, like so many, drift into planting. These conditions could not have failed to inhibit the development of a large indigenous mercantile element, such as existed elsewhere in North America.(80)

Thus, in the social sphere the very progressivism or rational efficiency of the Glasgow store system seems likely to have retarded the social diversification of Virginia and Maryland, as in the agricultural sphere it retarded the diversification of crops.

NOTES

(1) Customs 14/1B, Public Record Office (hereafter cited as P.R.O.).

(2) Customs 14/1A, P.R.O.; Customs Accounts I (1762-1763), 1, 3-5, 33, 37 ff., General Register House, Edinburgh.

(3) T. 1/469 fol. 131, P.R.O.

(4) T. 1/518 ff. 39-40, P.R.O.

(5) For examples of Glasgow vessels carrying tobacco to English ports, see C.O. 5/1349, 403, 415, 417, C.O. 5/1350, 99, 107, 110, H.C.A. 30/258/11, 13, 20, 21, 37, 128, P.R.O.

(6) T. 1/139/29, C.O. 390/5/13, P.R.O.

(7) T. 1/282/23, T. 36/13, T. 1/329 fol. 125, Customs 14, P.R.O.

(8) *Ibid.*; the London and English figures are from Customs 2, Customs 3, and Customs 17, plus T. 64/276B/328, 332.

(9) Daniel Defoe, A Tour thro' the Whole Island of Great Britain, ed. by G. D. H. Cole (London, 1927), II, 746.

(10) T. 1/139/29, P.R.O.

(11) C.O. 390/5/13, T. 1/282/23, T. 36/13, T. 1/329 fol. 125, P.R.O.; and British Museum Additional Manuscripts 8133B fol. 368. The slight drop in the Clyde's percentage in the 1730's and 1740's was probably due to a diversion of part of Glasgow's trade to the lesser Scottish ports, encouraged by the stricter customs enforcement at Glasgow, which followed events of 1722-1724.

(12) George MacGregor, The History of Glasgow (Glasgow and London, 1881), 352.

(13) John Gibson, The History of Glasgow, from the Earliest Accounts to the Present Time (Glasgow, 1777), 206.

(14) *Ibid.*, 206-07.

(15) Some Union pamphlets referring to tobacco are: [David Black], Essay upon Industry and Trade (Edinburgh, 1706), 23; [William Black], A Short View of Our Present Trade and Taxes ([Edinburgh, *c.* 1705-1706]), 6; [William Black], Remarks upon a Pamphlet, Intitled, the Considerations in Relation to Trade Considered ([?], 1706), 4-5; [James Donaldson], Considerations in Relation to Trade Considered ([Edinburgh], 1706), 23; A Letter Concerning the Consequences of an Incorporating Union, in Relation to Trade ([Edinburgh], 1706); John Spruel, An Accompt Current betwixt Scotland & England Ballanced (Edinburgh, 1705), 1-2. The riots are alluded to in Defoe, Tour thro' . . . Great Britain, II, 745; and Historical Manuscripts Commission (60), Manuscripts of the Earl of Mar and Kellie at Alloa House (London, 1904, 1930), I, 318, 322, 335, 340, 345, 346, 350-52, 357, 358, 363.

(16) Calendar of State Papers, Colonial Series: America and West Indies, 1661-1668 (London, 1880), no. 1340. Scots had a semi-legal entry into the colonies via residence in England. Cf. [George Ridpath], The Case of the Scots-men Residing in England (Edinburgh, 1703).

(17) Cf. Margaret Shove Morriss, Colonial Trade of Maryland, 1689-1715 (Baltimore, 1914), in Johns Hopkins University, Studies in Historical and Political Science, 32, no. 3, 117-20; Theodora Keith, *Scottish Trade with the Plantations before 1707*, Scottish Historical Review, VI (1908), 32-48. It is not commonly realised that the Scottish government took positive steps to encourage the importation of tobacco directly from the colonies. Cf. P. Hume Brown, ed., The Register of the Privy Council of Scotland, 3rd ser., VII (Edinburgh, 1915), 105, 210-12, 698; XIII (1932), 477, 538. Cf. also C.O. 5/1308/56 fol. 215 and T. 1/26/53 (ff. 209-12), P.R.O.; and Leo Francis Stock, ed., Proceedings and Debates of the British Parliaments Respecting North America (Washington, 1927), II, 195-96, 201. For a partial list of fifteen Glasgow merchants trading to the Chesapeake around 1696, cf. C.O. 5/714/1 fol. 6v., P.R.O. Some of the most prominent Glasgow mercantile names (e.g., Campbell, Bogle) are represented.

(18) Adam Montgomery letter-book, 9-10, 30, 31, 185-86, 188-89, 193, 196-97, 198, 200-01, 204, 205, etc. (I am indebted to Mr. A. G. Hepburn, of the Mitchell Library staff, for bringing this item to my attention); Samuel Hodgkin to Crosse & Lockhart, Sept. 7, 11, 1696, Steggall (Bogle) Manuscripts, XL. Both in Mitchell Library, Glasgow.

(19) Matthew Bogle to Capt. Newman Brokenbrough, Jan. 26, 1730, George Bogle to Matthew Bogle, Oct. 20, 1731, etc., Steggall (Bogle) Manuscripts, IV, Mitchell Library. About 1730, temporary Glasgow stores of a sort, established for a few months only, were a more or less common phenomenon in the tobacco colonies. These existed side by side with more permanent stores. Cf. Matthew Bogle to George Bogle, May 4, 1731, *ibid.*, XXXVIII. The Robert Carter letter-books in the Virgina Historical Society, Richmond (and at the University of Virginia) contain numerous references to the Scots in the 1720's, especially III, 75-80.

(20) Gibson, History of Glasgow, 206, 212.

(21) The Case of the Merchants Trading in Tobacco, at Whitehaven, in the County of Cumberland ([London, c. 1710]); Carter letter-book, I, 16-17, Virginia Historical Society.

(22) T. 1/121/39B ff. 33-34, P.R.O.

(23) T. 1/326/4, 17, 23, T. 1/332 ff. 70-71, T. 29/27, 158, P.R.O.; An Appeal to the Public; in Relation to the Tobacco *** [bill] (London, 1751); Reasons Humbly Offered for Regulating the Importation of Tobacco into this Kingdom ([London, c. 1722]).

(24) Because about 90 per cent of Scottish imports were re-exported, relatively small frauds at importation or exportation would have had an exaggerated effect on the duty-paying residue. In England, where only about 70 per cent was re-exported, the same frauds would have had a relatively less significant effect upon the duty-paying residue.

(25) Cf. Elizabeth E. Hoon, The Organisation of the English Customs System, 1696-1786 (New York, 1938), chap. 6; N. S. Jucker, ed., The Jenkinson Papers (London, 1949), 189, 208-09, 214-16; Josiah Tucker, A Review of Lord Vis. Clare's Conduct (Gloucester, [1775]), 1-3; The Undue Administration: or, the Usual Managements of the Customs Consider'd (London, 1718), for varying views on customs personnel procedure and politics.

(26) There was only the slightest addition to London tobacco imports between the 1720's and the 1760's. Customs 3, P.R.O.

(27) For the relative importance of the south-west ports at the beginning of the century, see the lists of tobacco bonds outstanding in Calendar of Treasury Books, Introduction to Vol. XI-XVII (London, 1934), ccccxxix, ccccxxxvi, etc.

(28) T. 64/276B/327, T. 38/363, T. 1/345 fol. 5, P.R.O.

(29) T. 1/282/23, T. 36/13, T. 64/276B/327, P.R.O.

(30) T. 1/329 fol. 125, T. 38/363, T. 1/345 fol. 5, P.R.O.

(31) For the standard exposition of the events of 1722 to 1723 as 'a terrible confederacy . . . against the trade of Glasgow', see Gibson, History of Glasgow, 207-09. Gibson was followed by James Denholm, The History of the City of Glasgow, 3rd ed. (Glasgow, 1804), 405-06. Also reflecting the Glasgow view were Defoe, Tour thro' . . . Great Britain, II, 746, and Robert Wodrow, Analecta (Edinburgh, 1842-43), II, 392. A special survey of the Scottish ports was made for the Treasury in 1722 by Humphrey Brent, a commissioner of customs in Scotland (T. 64/240, P.R.O.). It was printed as Report to the . . . Treasury . . . of Frauds in the Tobacco Trade, together with Answers by Merchants of Glasgow to the Report of Humphrey Brent . . . Concerning Frauds in the Tobacco Trade ([London], 1722). The latter was answered by London in Observations on the . . . Paragraph Delivered out by the Traders in Tobacco of Glasgow ([London, 1723]). Cf. also T. 1/236/4, T. 1/238/108, T. 1/239/2, T. 1/240/75, 91, T. 1/250/9, P.R.O., John Latimer, The Annals of Bristol in the Eighteenth Century ([?], 1893), 135; Stock, Proceedings, III, 451-52, 456-58, 460-69.

(32) Owen Ruffhead, ed., The Statutes at Large (London, 1763), V, 456-59.

(33) Gibson, History of Glasgow, 208-09; Historical Manuscripts Commission (67), Manuscripts of Lord Polwarth at Mertoun House (London, 1911-42), III, 249, 283. As early as Harley's time, it was being suggested that Scottish customs personnel be specially selected for these reasons. Cf. Historical Manuscripts Commission (29), Portland Manuscripts (London, 1891-1931), X, 160-63.

(34) See British Museum Additional Manuscripts 33,049 ff. 289v-90, for an adverse comment on the situation in 1754.

(35) T. 1/326/4, 17, 23, T. 1/332 ff. 76-78, T. 1/133 ff. 39-44, T. 1/334 ff. 1-2, P.R.O. Arents Manuscript 2918 (744,755) New York Public Library; An Appeal to the Public; in Relation to the Tobacco *** [bill]; An Essay on the Increase and Decline of Trade (London, 1749).

(36) 24 Geo. II. c. 41, in Ruffhead, Statutes at Large, VII, 375-85; Stock, Proceedings, V, 488, 493, 497-500, 506.

(37) Reports of these 'Registers-General' of tobacco can be found in Lansdowne Manuscript 661 ff. 51-150, British Museum, and T. 64/150, P.R.O.

(38) See note 11.

(39) Nelson letter-book, 83, Virginia State Library.

(40) Defoe, Tour thro' . . . Great Britain, II, 748. There are numerous references in the Carter letter-books and other correspondences to news arriving in Virginia from Glasgow before it came from London.

(41) 'Weekly arrivals, with cargoes from the [tobacco] provinces, so facilitated the intercourse, they seemed to be at no distance. The factors appeared to be as much under the eye of their employers at Glasgow, as the storekeepers were under them in the colonies.' Andrew Brown, History of Glasgow (Glasgow, 1795-97), II, 143.

(42) Defoe, Tour thro' . . . Great Britain, II, 748; Gomer Williams, History of the Liverpool Privateers (London, 1897), 36, 86.

(43) Brown, History of Glasgow, II, 143.

(44) Jamieson Manuscripts, I ff. 68-69, Library of Congress.

(45) [John Buchanan], Banking in Glasgow during the Olden Time, By Glasguensis (Glasgow, 1862), reprinted in Glasgow Past and Present (Glasgow, 1884), I, 463, 466-67, 470-75, 477-78. Cf. also ibid., II, 287.

(46) In 1775, when 57,143 hogsheads of tobacco were imported into Glasgow, only 4,621 hogsheads or so of sugar were imported and only 503 bags of cotton. Denholm, History of the City of Glasgow, 406.

(47) Defoe, Tour thro' . . . Great Britain, II, 747-48.

(48) Nelson letter-book, 111-12, Virginia State Library.

(49) Naval officers' reports show a very considerable proportion of Glasgow vessels were built in New England or the Chesapeake. Cf. C.O. 5/750, 1349, 1350, P.R.O. Some of these were built with Glasgow capital and under Glasgow supervision. Cf. Brice et al. v. Bryce ([London, 1740]), a printed brief in a House of Lords appeals cause. Defoe refers to the good, cheap ship-fitting at Greenock and Port Glasgow, and to the abundant supply of non-criminal emigrating labourers that made shipping from Glasgow so profitable. Defoe, Tour thro' . . . Great Britain, II, 746, 748.

(50) For examples of tobacco prices, cf. Ledgers A-S in Edward Dixon Manuscripts, Library of Congress. For examples of freights, cf. numerous accounts of sales in Carter-Keith Manuscripts and Custis Manuscripts in the Virginia Historical Society.

(51) William Lux to William Molleson, August, 1768, William Lux letter-book, New York Historical Society; T. 1/235/72, P.R.O.

(52) [Georges-Marie Butel-Dumont], Histoire et Commerce des Colonies Angloises (London, 1755), 260-65; H.C.A. 30/258/25, 33, 51, 54, P.R.O.

(53) All Glasgow correspondence is filled with references to the French buyers and their prices. Some Glaswegians made their purchases in America with the French market only in mind. Cf. Jamieson Manuscripts, I, 73-74, Library of Congress. For the French buyers, see Sir William Forbes of Pitsligo, Memoirs of a Banking House (London and Edinburgh, 1860), 9, 27-28, 44-48.

(54) For genealogical data on the 'tobacco lords', cf. Burke's Landed Gentry (any edition) and such works as The Old Country Houses of the Old Glasgow Gentry (Glasgow, 1870); Glasgow Past and Present; or Hardy Bertram McCall, Memoirs of My Ancestors (Birmingham, 1884).

(55) T. 36/13, P.R.O.

(56) James Cleland, The Rise and Progress of the City of Glasgow (Glasgow, 1820), 90; Denholm, History of the City of Glasgow, 406. The figures were slightly different for 1774. Then 46 firms imported 40,543 hogsheads. Six of the firms in the 1773 list are not in the 1774 list, and some 13 in the 1774 list are not in the earlier one. It is not possible to be too precise, however, for some firms seem to have changed their style, and others to have altered their personnel. *The overall situation as presented in the text stands unaffected.* Speirs, Glassford, and Cuninghame still headed the list in that order. Cf. James Pagan, Sketch of the History of Glasgow (Glasgow, 1847), 80.

(57) A.O. 12/56, pp. 292-93, 305-06, P.R.O.

(58) C. A. Oakley, Connal & Co., Ltd., 1722-1946 (Glasgow, c. 1946); T. 36/13, P.R.O.

(59) A.O. 12/56, pp. 292-301, 305-06, 307-08, P.R.O.; [Buchanan], *Banking in Glasgow* in Glasgow Past and Present, I, 470, 472-73. 482-83.

(60) A.O. 12/56, pp. 292-301, 305-06, 307-08, P.R.O.

(61) The Glasgow firm of John M'Dowall was formed in June, 1769, with a capital of £4,000. Hugh M'Mikin, the partner resident in America, held five-sixteenths; the Glaswegians John M'Dowall and James Brown (active in several firms) held one-fourth each, and one John Johnson held three-sixteenths. *M'Dowall et al.* v. *Ferguson* ([London], 1783), a printed plea in a House of Lords appeals cause.

(62) For Glassford, see A.O. 12/9, pp. 35-46; A.O. 12/55, pp. 46-61, 103-04; A.O. 13/30, P.R.O. For Speirs, see A.O. 12/9, pp. 49-55.

(63) A syndicate operating in Greenock before 1719, importing tobacco in its own ship, consisted of Lady Schaw (one-sixth), Robert Bontine the younger of Airdoch (five twenty-fourths), James Lees and Charles Crawfurd, merchants of Glasgow (each five twenty-fourths), and Thomas Fleming of Greenock, the manager (five twenty-fourths). George Williamson, Old Greenock (Paisley and London, 1886), 53.

(64) Cf. Baird & Walker to Allason, Dec. 21, 1756, William Allason Manuscripts, box 1, Virginia State Library; Jerdone Manuscripts, Ledger F letters, *passim*, William and Mary College Library.

(65) The Fredericksburg 'store' of the Cuninghame group was valued at £1,700. Of the 11 stores valued, the humblest was worth £200; together the 11 were worth £11,450, not including stock on hand, livestock, store furnishings, or slaves. The Shockoe or Richmond store of the firm was elegant, or, at least, spacious, enough to be described in 1787 as 'at present appropriated for the meeting of the Senate and House of Delegates'. A.O. 12/56, pp. 293 ff., P.R.O.

(66) For the seventeenth century, cf. Philip Alexander Bruce, Economic

History of Virginia in the Seventeenth Century (New York, 1895), II, 364-67; for the factor of a London Scot in the 1730's, cf. William Johnston's letter-book (Ledger F) in Jerdone Manuscripts, William and Mary College Library; for a Liverpool factor in Maryland in the 1740's, cf. Callister Manuscripts, photostats in New York Public Library and Maryland Historical Society; for the best example of a Glasgow factor around the 1760's, cf. Allason Manu-scripts in Virginia State Library.

(67) Cuninghame, Brown & Company's two stores were at Georgetown and Newport, Maryland; Cuninghame, Findlay & Company's five stores were at Port Tobacco, Chaptico, Leonardstown, Georgetown, and Bladensburg, Mary-land—all seven in the Potomac valley; the Virginia stores of William Cuning-hame & Company were at Richmond, Amherst, and Rocky Ridge, in the upper James valley, at Petersburg, Cabin Point, Mecklenburg Court House, Bruns-wick Court House, and Halifax, on the south side of the James River, at Dumfries on the Potomac, at Falmouth, Fauquier Court House, Culpeper, and Fredericksburg, in the upper Rappahannock valley, and at Caroline Court House A.O. 12/56, pp. 293 ff., 305-06, 307-08, P.R.O.

(68) Cleland, Rise and Progress of the City of Glasgow, 90. For all Scot-land, the ratio of the Virginia to the Maryland imports at this time was generally three to one or four to one. Customs 17/1-4, P.R.O.

(69) Gibson, History of Glasgow, 206.

(70) *Ibid.*, 212.

(71) E.g., H.C.A. 30/258/58, P.R.O.; Baird & Walker to Allason, Jan. 17, 1758, Allason Manuscripts, box 1, Virginia State Library.

(72) A. E. Bergh, ed., The Writings of Thomas Jefferson, XVII (Washing-ton, 1907), 58-59.

(73) J. P. Boyd, ed., The Papers of Thomas Jefferson, I (Princeton, 1950), 51-52.

(74) British Museum Additional Manuscripts 33,030 ff. 160v-62. A Glasgow manufacturer estimated in 1766 that the town had owing it in America near £1,000,000. Cf. Steggall (Bogle) Manuscripts, XCI (Journal of John Brown), I, 112-13.

(75) A.O. 12/56, pp. 286-88, P.R.O.

(76) David Macpherson, Annals of Commerce (London, 1805), III, 581.

(77) A.O. 13/29, P.R.O.

(78) In reference to diversification and new areas of cultivation, cf. Lewis Cecil Gray, History of Agriculture in the Southern United States to 1860 (Washington, 1933), I, 166-69, 233-34.

(79) William Cuninghame himself and many other great and small Glas-gow merchants served in humbler capacities in the Chesapeake in early life. A.O. 12/56, fol. 289, P.R.O.

(80) Public opinion in the tobacco colonies seems to have recognised that the indigenous firms were being held back by the Scots. At the time of the non-importation 'associations' of 1770, a merchant in Virginia wrote to his London correspondents to send some prohibited goods ordered by one such firm, for 'the Country seems inclin'd to indulge these Gentlemen as much as Possible as they are great Champions to oppose the Scotch Interest and it would be a Sin to leave them to combat on unequal Terms'. Thomas Adams to Perkins, Buchanan & Brown, June 16, 1770, Adams Manuscripts (N-Y), Virginia Historical Society.

CHAPTER TWELVE

Scottish Enterprise in Australia, 1798-1879

DAVID S. MACMILLAN

Archivist of the University of Sydney

THE ACTIVITIES OF SCOTTISH MERCHANTS, shipowners and investors in Australia, particularly in the sixty years after 1822, contributed greatly to the pastoral and commercial development of the colonies there. Indeed, Scotland's contribution in this respect was out of all proportion to its relative share of the population and resources of the United Kingdom. A study of Scottish commercial enterprise in Australia is particularly interesting for the way in which it reveals the contemporaneous workings of the Scottish economy. It is a story of experiments, failures and eventual success, especially in the evolution of efficient, economically-run investment companies, and it illustrates very clearly the growing confidence and expertise of Scottish projectors and entrepreneurs.

1. *Robert Campbell and the Beginnings of Australian Commerce*

The first Scottish commercial contact, if the word 'commercial' can be used of the new, primitive, penal settlement of New South Wales in the 1790's, where emancipated convicts, military officers and government officials traded and bargained for ships' cargoes, came with the arrival in Sydney in June, 1798, of Robert Campbell, a young Scot of twenty-nine, son of a Greenock lawyer with a small estate in Argyll.(1) Campbell was a partner in the Calcutta firm of Campbell and Clark (a concern founded in the 1780's by his elder brother, John Campbell) and his visit to Australia in 1798 followed on the partners' first unfortunate venture into the Australian trade two years earlier when their new ship, the *Sydney Cove,* had been lost off the south-east coast of the continent, on the shores of what is now Victoria. Robert Campbell's voyage was undertaken to clear

Y

up the business matters arising from this loss and to explore trading possibilities in Sydney. He sailed from Calcutta in another of Campbell and Clark's ships, the *Hunter*, with a cargo of Bengal goods and livestock.

By 1798 a large part of the import trade of the colony had fallen into the hands of a clique of military officers and officials, and Campbell's first important act was to attempt to sell his cargo directly to the small settlers (almost all of them emancipated convicts) instead of selling to the officers' syndicate at their artificially low prices. Despite the fact that he was eventually compelled to sell the goods to 'the ring', Campbell was so impressed by the potentialities of the settlement as a market for imports of all kinds and as a source of supply for whale-oil and sealskins that he returned to stay in February, 1800, setting up on a strategic waterfront site on Sydney Cove as the colony's first 'free merchant'.

Although Robert Campbell was not operating from Scotland in these vital early years when Australian commerce was born, and although his enterprises cannot therefore strictly be described as 'Scottish', his initiative and strength of character were largely responsible for freeing colonial trade from the officers' monopoly as far as the import trade was concerned, and from the equally restrictive East India Company monopoly which stifled the export trade in whale-oil and sealskins. As a 'free emigrant' and a man of property with respectable connections in Scotland and at Calcutta, Campbell was socially acceptable in the tight little group which made up colonial society. Few of his fellow merchants, being emancipists, enjoyed this advantage and so the young Scot was in a strong position in his struggle with 'the ring' during the Governorships of King, Bligh and Macquarie.(2) Under Governor Bligh in particular, the arch-enemy of the officers' monopoly, Campbell was in high favour, being appointed treasurer of the public funds, naval officer (a key position in the regulation of incoming ships and cargoes) and collector of taxes. By 1812, two years after the arrival of Governor Lachlan Macquarie, who suppressed the rebel 'provisional government' which had overthrown the Bligh régime, the last traces of the officers' trade monopoly had been expunged, and Campbell had played no inconsiderable part in bringing this about.

Even more significant for the future of Australian commerce, it was Campbell who organised the first large-scale exportation of sealskins direct to the London River in one of the Calcutta firm's ships, *Lady Barlow*, in 1805, in contravention of the East India Company's monopoly. It was not until the early 1830's that wool became the principal, staple export of the Australian colonies. In the earlier period sealskins, whalebone and oil, timber and bark extract (used in tanning) were the most important exports and by 1804 Campbell was 'the largest employer in the sealing industry'.(3) Before setting out in the *Lady Barlow* for London, with its cargo of 264 tons of sea-elephant oil, 13,730 seal skins and 3,673 solid feet of oak or beet-wood,(4) Campbell applied to Governor Philip Gidley King for permission to make the shipment. This was refused but so determined was Campbell to open up this new direct trade that he went ahead, writing to the Governor that, 'I duly understand that no responsibility for my sending the ship there can be attached to your Excellency'.(5)

The outcome of this expedition was almost disastrous for the Scottish merchant. His ship and cargo were seized on arrival in the Thames at the instance of the East India Company's directors, and only the intervention of Sir Joseph Banks, that influential London patron of the colony, prevented total loss. As it was, a compromise solution was worked out, by which the cargo was eventually landed and sold at the East India Company's sale for re-export, while the ship was permitted to return to India with a freight on account of the Company. The case was a classic instance of the workings of 'the Monopoly' in the last years of its application, and the feeling engendered in both the colony and in mercantile circles in London is exemplified by Governor King's assertion to the Secretary for War and the Colonies—'The proprietor and the whole Colony had flattered themselves that this first proof of their industry would afford pleasure to their native country and be favourably received. That it did not is to be regretted. It was four months before the restraint was taken off the cargo and then it was to land the skins and oil for export only.'(6)

In spite of this setback, Campbell, now resident in London, continued to press for the direct admission of produce from New South Wales without hindrance, and, through his representations to officials of the Board of Trade, the decision was reached in June and December, 1806, 'to prepare instructions for the future Government of the shipping concerns of the Colony on a plan suited to provide the inhabitants with the means of becoming by degrees less and less burdensome to the Mother Country'.(7) This statement clearly foreshadowed Parliament's cancellation of the Company's claims to monopolise the Australian trade in 1813, and Campbell's trial shipment of 1805 and the resulting case played a key part in freeing the trade. In 1815 Sydney was declared a free port, and its trade immediately increased.

This was not the only way in which Campbell played a vital part in the 'primitive' early colonial period. Between 1804 and 1812 he had contracts with the colonial government for the importation of livestock from India. His first large consignment arrived in February, 1803, in the *Castle of Good Hope*, of 1,000 tons, by far the largest ship to enter the vast harbour of Port Jackson up to that date. It consisted of 307 head of Bengal cows (now known as Zebus) and a number of donkeys.(8) In the six years before 1810, he imported altogether over 2,000 head of cattle—and thereby greatly added to the colony's resources, for in 1806 the entire cattle population had been only 3,264. Campbell also imported Arab blood horses from Calcutta, brought in shipwrights from the Thames to build sea-going ships for his sealing and whaling adventures and, in 1819, organised the colony's first savings bank which for long was known as 'Campbell's Bank'.(9)

It is not surprising that this resolute and adventurous man should have been known as 'King of the Wharf', a tribute not only to his financial power and acumen but to the fine wharf which he built on his waterfrontage, for years the only practicable landing place for goods in Sydney. By the year of his death in 1846, he was an extensive landholder in the interior as well as a merchant, and had served as a member of the Legislative Council from its inception in 1825 until 1843. Even his longest absence from the colony, from 1810 to 1814, has proved most fruitful historically, for in those years his Sydney agent, Charles Hook, carried on the trading, sealing and whaling ventures, and kept letter books which have survived to present the only full and dependable picture of such operations as conducted in the colony in its primitive phase.(10) The Hook letters are the very earliest of Australian business records to have survived and since the documentation of Australian history in its first fifty years is so largely governmental and legal, their value is great, not only for the light they throw on the sealing and whaling operations which provided the colony's chief exports, but also for the way in which they reveal the close connection between Campbell and the Calcutta mercantile houses.

It is not surprising therefore that Campbell's many-sided career should have attracted the attention of so many Australian historians in recent years, for he stands out as a resolute and remarkably enterprising individual in a small and very new community, the Scottish-Indian merchant turned Australia's first 'respectable' merchant and entrepreneur.(11)

2. *The Australian Company of Edinburgh and Leith*

It is hardly surprising that Campbell's career in the primitive settlement of the pre-Macquarie period failed to inspire other Scottish merchants. New South Wales was still an insignificant colony of slight mercantile importance and, after 1800, the energies of Scottish merchants were absorbed by the booming industrial and shipping developments of wartime, and by the new trades that were opening up in South America, in the West and East Indies and in the lucrative business of beating Bonaparte's Continental embargo in the Baltic and the Mediterranean. During the governorship of Lachlan Macquarie (1809-21), the Australian colony began to emerge as more than a mere penal colony, and its population increased under his rule from eleven thousand to thirty-five thousand. Even more important, the country began to be better known in Britain, and on the recommendations of Macquarie and of Commissioner Thomas Bigge (1822-23) its potentialities as an emigration field came gradually to be realised.

It was not until 1822, more than twenty years after Robert Campbell's arrival in Sydney, that a Scottish-based enterprise began to operate in Australia. This was 'the Australian Company of Edinburgh and Leith' or, as it was usually termed in the colonies, 'the Leith Company'.(12) Two factors brought about the establishment of this ambitiously conceived joint-stock shipping and trading company: the growing interest in Australia manifested in Scotland (as evinced by the sudden flow of middle-class emigration after 1820),(13) and the keen desire of the mercantile and shipping interests of Edinburgh and Leith for participation in some promising field of overseas trade.

Following Governor Macquarie's recommendation of 1815 that free settlers with capital should be encouraged to come out to New South Wales, the number of Scottish applicants for permission to settle and for grants of land rose significantly, reaching a peak of eighty in 1822. The yearly numbers of applicants for the period 1816-30 were:

1816 — 3	1821 — 66	1826 — 22
1817 — 4	1822 — 80	1827 — 26
1818 — 5	1823 — 61	1828 — 26
1819 — 8	1824 — 77	1829 — 10
1820 — 79	1825 — 32	1830 — 14

During this fifteen-year period Scots applicants made up roughly a quarter of the total. In the peak years 1820-24 about one-third of the applicants were Scots.

Until 1820 there were no direct sailings from Scottish ports to Australia, and Scottish emigrants had to make the difficult journey to London, the accepted port of departure, encumbered with their baggage, the range of chattels (household furniture, building materials and agricultural implements) recommended for settlers and, occasionally, with livestock. They also had to meet the heavy burden of expense involved in passages by smack or coach for their families, servants and other employees. This lack of direct shipping facilities from Scottish ports must have discouraged many from going to Australia, especially when it was comparatively easy and inexpensive to secure direct passages from the Clyde and the east-coast ports of Leith and Dundee to the North American colonies. In the first years of the emigration the sheer expense of going out to Australia was a considerable deterrent, for cabin passages to Australia were four times more costly than those to Halifax or Quebec, and steerage passages were relatively even more expensive.

Among the Colonial Office records, especially in the petitions and letters of application from intending emigrants in Scotland during this first phase of emigration to Australia in the period 1817-30, there is a preponderance of applications from the south-eastern part of the country, from the Lothians (especially from Edinburgh and Leith), from Fife, and from the eastern Border countries. The main occupational groups among the Scottish applicants during the four-teen-year period were: (14)

Farmers	94
Merchants	82
Half-pay Army and Naval officers	42
Craftsmen or 'mechanics'	34
Surgeons and physicians	26
Tacksmen	20
Landowners or sons of landowners	18
Lawyers	7
Shipmasters	7
Manufacturers	5
Distillers and brewers	5

These figures are interesting in that they reflect the economic problems of the country in the period after the end of the Napoleonic Wars, notably the increasing difficulty in finding farms to rent in the Lothians and Fife, the comparative decline of Leith's Baltic trade, and the difficulty experienced by many half-pay officers and young men of education in finding suitable employment for either their abilities or their limited capitals. Of the 438 Scottish applicants between 1817 and 1830 whose place of residence was specified, no fewer than 246 were domiciled in Edinburgh, Leith, the Lothians and Fife. Similarly, emigration from other areas, like Lochalsh, Mull, Caithness, Dunbartonshire, and Forfar,(15) indicate the decline of the black-cattle raising industry in the Highlands, the elimination of the tacksmen class, and the over-population of certain Highland and 'Lowland fringe' areas.(16)

It is significant that the first direct sailing from Scotland to Australia was from Leith. In June 1820 Captain James Dixon, a Whitby shipowner, set out from that port in his ship *Skelton* with fifty-seven Scottish emigrants, most of them Highlanders in the retinue of Major Donald McLeod of Talisker. In the course of the next two years, John Broadfoot, a Leith shipbroker and shipping agent, arranged for the dispatch of four further shiploads of Scottish emigrants from the port of Leith, the ships employed being London vessels, some of which had already made Australian voyages as convict transports. Nothing indicates the sudden growth of Scottish interest in Australian emigration during the early 1820's more than the numbers who went out from Leith under Broadfoot's auspices in 1821 (150) and 1822 (146). At the same time, the Scottish press and the widely-read periodicals, like *The Scots Magazine* and the *Edinburgh Review* were beginning to evince a remarkable enthusiasm for the hitherto despised Australian settlements. In 1814 Patrick Colquhoun, that influential and respected authority, had stated in his *Treatise on the Wealth, Power and Resources of the British Empire* that 'The British Population at New South Wales may be said to be lost to the nation. . . . The same population at the Cape of Good Hope or in North America would, on the contrary, be highly beneficial.'(17) The first sign of a change in attitude had come in 1817, when Captain Alexander McConochie, cousin of Lord Meadowbank, the Lord Advocate, had published in Edinburgh a book on the commerce of the Pacific in which he urged his countrymen to turn their interest to Australia and to 'cease regarding Canada as the best, or rather, the only outlet for our superabundant population'.(18)

By 1822, when James Dixon's *Narrative of a Voyage to New South Wales and Van Diemen's Land in 1820, with observations on the State of these Colonies* appeared in Edinburgh, enthusiasm for Australia was at its peak in the capital and its ancient port. Dixon presented a glowing account of the Australian settlement based on first-hand knowledge, and his praises were echoed in influential papers, like the *Edinburgh Evening Courant* and *The Scotsman*. It was Van Diemen's Land especially which attracted the attention of Scots emigrants in the 1820's. By 1822 a large part of the settlement's commerce was in the hands of Scots merchants, and in June of that year *The Scots Magazine* contained a lengthy article on the island colony, which was described as 'the favourite resort, within the last few years, of those who emigrate from this country'.(19)

It was against this background of enthusiasm that the Australian Company of Edinburgh and Leith was formed. To its promoters, a group of bankers, merchants and shipowners, all resident in either Edinburgh or Leith, both McConochie's picture of the Pacific as a great new field for trading enterprises and Dixon's more authoritative view of the potentialities of the Australian settlements seemed to offer a solution to a local problem that had become more acute since the end of the Napoleonic Wars. In 1814 the disastrous consequences of the 'Elbe Mania', when Leith and Edinburgh merchants had flooded Hamburg with unwanted goods, had led to many failures of established firms. The coastal trade of Leith was increasing, but its foreign trade was in comparative decline. More and more of Leith's traditional Baltic trade in wheat and timber was being channelled through the new rival port of Grangemouth by the Forth and Clyde Canal to the fast-developing industrial area around Glasgow. Not only did the Clyde ports control their traditional West Indian and American trades but they had taken the lead in the timber trade with the North American colonies and in the newly-opened Indian trade. Kirkman Finlay's *Earl of Buckinghamshire* sailed for Bombay in 1816, and it was not until 1827-28 that the first small Leith vessel made the voyage.

As well as stimulating Scottish industrial production, the Wars had led to a great increase in Scottish shipping, especially in the number of vessels of considerable tonnage. Some of these were absorbed in the new Canada trade, but by 1820 there was a great quantity of tonnage laid up or for sale. In these circumstances, and with the new emigration flow to Australia providing some guarantee of passengers and freights, it is not surprising that the mercantile and shipping interests of Edinburgh and Leith should have embarked upon an Australian venture. For years the Edinburgh Merchants' Company and the Chamber of Commerce, together with the Leith Merchants' Company (until 1811 'the Incorporation of Traffickers of Leith') and the Leith Trinity House had been pressing for the nomination of Leith as an outport permitted to participate in the Indian trade, but this did not come about until 1819. Furthermore, duties imposed on Baltic imports, especially wheat and timber, restricted the trade with north-eastern Europe. By October and November, 1822, the movement to form the Australian Company was well under way, and even that conservative Whig organ, the staid and widely-read *Edinburgh Evening Courant* was reporting that the first Scottish settlers were 'succeeding beyond their most sanguine expectations', and expatiating on the 'wonderful great iron deposits' of Van Diemen's Land and that island's very favourable prospects of a thriving trade in wheat with the Cape.(20) This optimism was reflected in the Australian Company's prospectus, which made fulsome references to the colonial produce which would provide return freights: 'The exports at present consist of cattle, sheep, wool, flour, corned meats, hams, tongues, hides, dried fish, tallow, barilla, bark for tanning leather seal-skins and oil, whale-oil and spars.' This statement showed a lamentable ignorance of colonial conditions for, far from being in a position to export many of these products, especially livestock and foodstuffs, the Australian settlements were importing them.

The composition of the promoting group, and of the original co-partnery is particularly interesting, for the Australian Company was launched by essentially the same group which had been responsible for the founding of the Commercial Bank of Scotland in 1810. This was the new bank which had been set up with the express aim of encouraging commerce and manufactures and of breaking the monopoly held by the private bankers and the three long-established chartered banks which they controlled. As Henry Cockburn, one of the original directors of the Commercial Bank described it, 'the Commercial, professing to be the bank of the Citizens . . . deeply and silently improved the conditions of our middle classes, on whose rise its effects have been more real than apparent'.(21) Most of the projectors of the Australian Company were Whig in sympathy, especially where the vital matter of Burgh Reform was concerned. Many had taken a stand against the East India Company's monopoly, and had fought staunchly over the years for better port facilities at Leith. Their leaders were James Wyld of Gilston, Leith wine-merchant and shipowner; Forrest Alexander of Oakfield, a prominent Edinburgh tanner who has been credited with the idea of founding the Commercial Bank;(22) Adam White of Fenns, Baltic and general merchant, and shipowner in Leith; John Hay, shipowner, and Master of the Trinity House of Leith; John Anderson of Gladswood, iron-founder in Leith, and John Clapperton of

Spylaw, merchant in Edinburgh, and a prominent Whig. At the head of the list of directors was Alexander Henderson of Press, Lord Provost of Edinburgh, a merchant and banker who, in 1825, was to take the lead in founding the National Bank of Scotland. No fewer than nine of the original directors of the Australian Company were directors of the Commercial Bank, and seven more of the original partners in the Company held directorships in the Bank. The promoters and partners were closely involved in many of the joint-stock concerns of the time, the fourteen directors holding a total of no fewer than forty-one other directorships in banking, insurance, shipping, iron-founding and other companies, and the ninety-two original partners (including the directors) holding a total of eighty-two such directorships.

The probative memorial of association entered in the Register of Deeds shows both the 'local' character of the Australian Company, and the occupational composition of the 'partnership'. Of the ninety-two partners, seventy were resident in Edinburgh or Leith, and the remainder in various parts of Central and South-east Scotland. There were small concentrations at Crieff, Dalkeith and Falkirk which were almost certainly due to the promotion of the company in these quarters by the local agents of the Commercial Bank. No fewer than five local agents or managers of the Bank's branches were listed among the partners. The largest occupational groups among the partners were merchants (28), who included the eight shipowners and others with shipping interests; manufacturers (12), lawyers (9), ministers of religion (4), and booksellers (5). Eight were engaged in banking and four were landowners. It was perhaps indicative of the growing importance of brewing and distilling at this time that the 'largest' recorded partners were Archibald Campbell, Edinburgh's leading brewer, and Robert More, distiller of Underwood near Falkirk, with shares of the nominal value of £3,000 and £2,000 respectively. The capital of the Company was set out in the contract of co-partnery, dated 31st October, 1822, as one million pounds. This was to be divided into shares of one hundred pounds. The initial paid-up capital was £55,000, and the average holding of the partners was six shares. The year 1822 was marked by a spate of company promotions in Edinburgh and Glasgow, but judged by contemporary standards, and in comparison with the other promotions of the time, this venture was extremely sound.

The prospectus of this first Scottish venture into the Australian trade was an imposing document, which showed the preoccupation of the promoters with the two problems of opening up a new overseas trade-outlet for their goods, and restoring Edinburgh and its port to their former importance as centres of overseas trade. The chief object of the promoters was to establish the first regular shipping service to Australia. Not even from London, which had always been the leading port in the Australian trade, were there regular sailings. By 1820 there were shipowners and merchants on the Thames whose vessels could justly be advertised as 'well known' or as 'regular traders' in the New South Wales and Van Diemen's Land trade, but no attempt had been made to organise the sailing at regular intervals of ships specially outfitted for the emigrant traffic. What the Australian Company's directors aimed at was a service every three or four months, entailing the employment of four fairly large vessels. As the contract of co-partnery put it, the aim of the Company was to 'effect the regular and speedy maritime conveyance of goods and passengers between Great Britain and these colonies'. To justify such a service it was essential that the emigrant flow from Scotland should continue at the rate it had reached by 1821-22. To provide the necessary employment for the ships on their return voyages it was equally essential that freights in the form of colonial produce should be available. Since the Company was also a trading concern, prepared to make advances to settlers on their produce, and to take colonial produce in return for the goods it sent out from Scotland, it was necessary too that there should be a British demand for colonial produce. None of these conditions, so necessary for the prosperity of the Company, obtained during the later 1820's.

The first two years of operations were full of promise, and the Australian Company rode the wave of prosperity and confidence that swept Scotland in the three years that preceded the financial crash of 1825. Three fine vessels were purchased and another, even larger, was specially built in Leith, in the yard of Robert Menzies, one of the partners. A warehouse and offices were built in Hobart, Van Diemen's Land, that was long to be the largest building in that colony, and an establishment was set up on the Sydney waterfront. Agents, office staff and storemen were dispatched to Hobart and Sydney to man these outposts of Leith and Edinburgh enterprise, and the colonial press gave a favourable reception to this new enterprise, which commended itself to many by offering to buy their produce, and by the fact that its directors made no claim for extensive land grants, unlike the two chartered companies which were being formed in London to develop the agriculture of the two colonies.(23)

In the nine years of its existence, the 'Leith Company' took out nearly seven hundred emigrants from Scotland to New South Wales and Van Diemen's Land. The number does not seem impressive

when compared with the emigration flow to North America in the
1820's, but when the slightness of the colonial populations is considered (about thirty thousand in New South Wales and seven
thousand in Van Diemen's Land) the importance of the influx is
apparent. The Company was responsible for taking out nearly three-
quarters of the entire Scottish emigration during this period, and by
setting up in Hobart and Leith registries where prospective employers and intending emigrants of the working class could enrol,
the Company launched the first workable scheme by which inden-
tured or 'bonded' artisans and mechanics could obtain steerage
passages. The lack of skilled craftsmen at this time was a serious
impediment to colonial development, and it was through this system
that several hundreds of Scottish artisans were introduced to Van
Diemen's Land. In April 1824, a number of the directors formed an
'Australian Emigration Society' to encourage artisans in Edinburgh
and Leith to avail themselves of the scheme. Altogether, the Company's ships, and vessels chartered by it, made sixteen round voyages, each averaging a year. Almost the entire seaborne trade
between Scotland and Australia was in its hands, giving Leith an
undoubted primacy in the trade. In the nine years of operations the
Company dispatched nearly seven thousand tons of shipping to the
colonies, two-thirds of the total tonnage that sailed from Scotland.
Its activities raised the proportion of Scottish tonnage participating
in the Hobart trade between 1823 and 1830 to more than a quarter
of the total, a remarkable proportion considering the relative
foreign-going tonnage of Scotland and the rest of the United
Kingdom.(24)

The aim of securing an outlet for Scottish manufactures and
produce was certainly achieved by the Company, at least until the
Hobart and Sydney markets came to be glutted with imports in the
later 1820's. Strong drink, especially Edinburgh and Leith ales,
whisky and rum, and imported wines bulked largest in the outward
cargoes, with ready-made clothing, foodstuffs (barrelled herrings,
butter and preserved meats), Baltic pitch, tar and timber, iron goods
and agricultural implements, and gunpowder also figuring prominently in the manifests. Livestock, paper, salt, glass, books, and
soap were also frequently consigned, and the few existent manifests
show clearly that those directors and partners who were engaged in
trade and manufactures availed themselves of the opportunity to
send out their goods. A critic of the Company in satirical vein
questioned the benefit of many of these imports, and pictured 'the
Australian youth, clothed in his blanket jacket and leathern in-
expressibles, seated at his log table in his bark hut, barbarizing

over one of the Company's smoked hams, with a bottle of their best Bell's ale, a cup of their real Glenlivet whiskey, a cool megrim of claret, and a bottle of true London particular Madeira, and one of the latest of Walter Scott's works'.(25) Had the emigration flow continued at the rate of 1820-22, if the colonial market had not become glutted with imports, and if markets had opened up in Britain for colonial produce like bark extract and timber, so well-conducted a venture as this would almost certainly have succeeded. In January, 1825, the *Scotsman's* stock list quoted the £100 shares of the Company, on which £40 had been paid up, at a premium of £10. By September, when the speculative boom was at its height, the premium had risen to £15. By this time, the Company was well-established in Hobart and Sydney, and its agents were held to be among the most influential men of affairs in both colonies. The high water-mark of the Company's fortunes had been reached, but with the bad years, 1826 and 1827, the decline set in.

The falling-off in emigration and the scarcity of return freights which made it necessary either to keep the ships lying at anchor in colonial ports seeking cargoes or to re-route them to India or the East Indies, dislocated the schedule of regular sailings. Increased competition in the trade from Leith, Greenock, London and Liverpool also made things more difficult, as did the glut of imports in Hobart and Sydney. In the latter port the return of vessels entering from the United Kingdom showed a steady increase from thirty-three in 1826 to sixty-two in 1829.(26) By the latter year these difficulties had made it impossible for the Australian Company's experiment to be continued. Gradually, the ships were diverted into the Canadian emigrant and lumber trade, or sold off. A general mood of disillusion with the Australian colonies succeeded the enthusiasm that had pervaded Edinburgh and Leith in the early 1820's. By 1833 the 'Leith Company's' ships and warehouse installations had been disposed of together with its headquarters at Ronaldson's Wharf, at the North Drawbridge of Leith. Within a few years the emigrant traffic revived, and wool became important as a marketable colonial product which would ensure return freights for ships in the Australian trade, but these developments did not come soon enough to save the first Scottish-based venture in the Australian trade. Although a peripheral activity, the Australian Company of Edinburgh and Leith showed a boldness of conception that was typical of the 'Commercial Whigs'. It was the depression of 1826-29 at home and the unsettled trading conditions in Australia, rather than faulty administration, which must be held responsible for its demise.(27)

3. *Shipping and Mercantile Contacts, 1830-42*

The introduction of assisted bounty emigration to Australia in the early 1830's did not immediately stimulate working-class emigration from Scotland, because, until 1837, the bounty emigration was controlled by a committee composed largely of London shipowners, and dominated by John Marshall, the leading operator in this field. In 1835, three years after the bounty scheme came into operation, John Broadfoot, the Leith shipping agent who had arranged the first sailings of emigrant vessels from Leith after Dixon's experiment of 1820, petitioned Lord Aberdeen at the Colonial Office for bounty privileges to be extended to emigrants sailing direct from that port.(28) But it was not until more than two years had passed that the London Committee was wound up and large-scale bounty emigration from the Scottish ports began. The first two government emigration agents were appointed at Leith and Greenock in April, 1834, and in 1836, Dr. Charles Boyter was appointed by the government of New South Wales as 'colonial agent for Scotland'.

It was the introduction of a 'Colonial Bounty' scheme in 1835, supplementing the scheme operated by the British Government, which led to the increase in emigration to Australia after 1836. The colonies had recovered from the depression of the late 1820's and the squatting movement was at its height. With wool exports growing at an enormous rate and land being taken up by purchase or by licence on an unprecedented scale, the need for shepherds and other agricultural workers became most urgent at the very time when destitution and depression were affecting the Highlands of Scotland. By 1837 efficient machinery at last existed for administering the bounty schemes and organising direct sailings, and Scottish shipowners and merchants with interests in the colonies, especially those who acted as agents for colonial firms and for settlers, quickly availed themselves of the opportunity of employing their vessels and supplying labour for their clients.

In 1837, the first year of large-scale operations, over 800 emigrants, many of them Highlanders, embarked at Greenock and over 300 from Dundee. In 1838 the total sailing from all Scottish ports rose to over 3,000, a figure that was maintained in 1839, increasing to nearly 4,500 in 1841, the year when the bounty emigration reached its peak.(29) After the demise of the Australian Company of Edinburgh and Leith in 1831, the shipping contact between Scotland and Australia had been maintained by its Leith rivals, the firms of George Young and Co., George Aitchison and Co. and

Buchanan and Davis. The only other firm to send out its ships regularly before 1837 was that of A. Alexander and Co. of Grangemouth, but the bounty scheme soon attracted several Glasgow, Greenock, Dundee and Aberdeen firms to the trade. Another consideration that drew owners to the trade was the growing consumption of Australian wool in the Border woollen manufacture. By the late 1830's more than four-fifths of the wool so required was imported and most of it came from Australia.(30) The foundation of the much publicised new colony of South Australia in 1836 opened up to the Scottish shipowners further prospects of outward and return freights, and by 1839 the flourishing Scottish mercantile houses of Elder and Co. had been established in Adelaide, its capital.

It was natural that Scottish merchants in the colonial ports should work closely in co-operation with merchants and shipowners in their native land in bringing out emigrants. Both sides in these operations benefited, the former getting labour for themselves and their clients, the latter obtaining the passage money that helped to make the long voyages pay. Colonial merchants involved in the business included Gilchrist and Alexander, Alexander Brodie Spark and Alexander Dick of Sydney. Gilchrist and Alexander had ties with the Glasgow firms of John Miller and Francis Reid, who selected emigrants suitably qualified for the bounty and arranged transport for them from their often remote homes to the ports of embarkation. The Port Phillip firms of Craig and Broadfoot and J. D. Lyon Campbell were other colonial operators who brought out considerable numbers of agricultural workers and craftsmen, almost invariably in Scottish ships. By 1839 Greenock and Glasgow shipowners were participating fully in the emigrant traffic, and the firms of Russell and Co., Gilkison and Co., McBrayne and McIndoe, John McLellans, Senior and Junior, Sempel and Co., Ross and Finlay, and Spencer and Wilson, all of Glasgow, Duthie's of Aberdeen, and Campbell and Anderson of Greenock, were regularly dispatching vessels for Sydney and Port Phillip.

If the bounty scheme had been in operation or if wool had been available as a return cargo when the Australian Company was struggling to survive in the later 1820's, it would almost certainly have overcome its difficulties. The last recorded act of its Leith manager, Robert Brown, was to petition the Colonial Office in 1835 on behalf of the partners, asking for some form of compensation for their losses on the unpaid passages of working class emigrants taken out in its ships before the bounty scheme came into operation. The plea was unavailing, and the verdict on the 'Leith Company' must be that it was premature.(31)

The emigrant traffic after 1837 provided the means of sending out cargoes of Scottish goods to the colonies. Spirits and woollens, linens and cottons continued to figure largely in the manifests, as in the 1820's, but foodstuffs were less in demand, for the colonies were producing their own supplies. The Scottish exports that became increasingly important in this later period of the 1830's were iron in all its forms, steam engines, agricultural machinery and implements of husbandry, and a wide range of ironmongery.

Renewed large-scale emigration and the consequent increase in shipping and commercial contacts were accompanied by a reappraisal of the colonies' potentialities, and by 1839 the interests concerned with overseas investment were turning their attention to this promising field.

4. *The Aberdeen Investment Companies*

With the onset of the depression in 1826 there was an almost complete cessation of Scottish interest in Australia, and emigration dwindled away to a mere trickle. Once again Scots regarded the antipodean colonies without enthusiasm; the writer of a letter from Sydney which appeared in the Edinburgh press in February, 1830, summing up the disillusion that was widespread among the Scottish settlers: 'With a sad heart I write from this place to which my hopes had turned in Europe. Distress is hardly less afflicting here, and vice and moral misery a thousand-fold more terrible. . . . Fatal resolution has flung me on these wretched shores. . . . The agricultural and commercial affairs of the whole of this vast continent seem smitten with a general curse. Nothing is heard but the voice of wailing, and worst of all, the ear is sore with daily tales of violence and murder. It is as usual for a gentleman to put a pistol as a handkerchief in his pocket.'(32)

It was not until 1837 that interest began to revive, largely because of the new flow of assisted emigrants under the bounty schemes conducted by the British and colonial governments. This was a widespread emigration and no part of Scotland, however remote, was unaffected by it. In 1833 only 253 emigrants had sailed from Scottish ports for Australia,(33) and even this figure fell to 134 in 1834 and to 114 in 1836.(34) In 1837 the number increased to 1,254, and in 1838 the bounty emigrants alone numbered 2,161. Between 1838 and 1846 about 12,000 Scots went out to Australia and, unlike the emigration of the 1820's, this efflux was largely made up of people of the working class.

This resumption in the flow of emigrants was accompanied by a surge of writings about Australia at all levels, from legal and economic treatises and philosophic essays through travel books to cheap pamphlets, 'emigrants' guides' and numerous magazine articles. In these circumstances, it was natural that commercial interest should also revive, and by 1837 Sydney, where Scottish merchants had been very few in the 1820's, boasted a colony of thriving merchants, some of them from the north-east, like Leslie Duguid, banking and steamship company promoter, and Alexander Brodie Spark, shipbroker and general merchant. A number of Scottish co-partneries had also been formed to participate in the growing pastoral industry, especially in the newly opened-up Port Phillip district (the present Victoria). A typical example was the Clyde Company, which was composed of Fife and Edinburgh landowners and capitalists, and of the Glasgow magnates, the Dennistouns. Members of the land-owning nobility, like the Marquis of Ailsa, also bought land and their sheep stations were managed by young men with farming experience, very often farmers' sons, sent out from the owners' Scottish estates.

It was partly through this north-east group, and especially through Duguid, an ebullient promoter, that the possibilities of the Australian colonies as fields for investment were brought to the attention of the capitalists and company promoters of Aberdeen. The city was still very much of a regional capital, unconnected by rail to the south until 1850. According to Henry Cockburn, the agricultural progress in the area since the beginning of the century had been more rapid than in any other part of the country, and cattle-raising for the southern markets, the linen, cotton and woollen manufactures, shipbuilding, iron-founding and a number of lesser industries, were putting capital funds into the hands of many people in the region. By 1838 the city was the headquarters of three banking and six insurance companies, and among its 'advocates' were some of the keenest and most enterprising men of business in the country, who were anxious to provide new channels of investment for the accumulations of capital held in the area.

As in the Edinburgh of the 1820's, these promoters were associated in groups which were related to the directorates of the various banks and insurance companies, and the most enterprising group was that headed by the advocate Alexander Anderson, who had played a major part in founding the North of Scotland Bank in 1836. In 1837 Anderson founded the first of the Aberdeen overseas investment companies, the Illinois Investment Company, which was to serve as a model for its successors.

Z

By the early months of 1839 confidence in North America as an investment field had been shaken by both the Canadian disturbances and the repudiations of several of the State legislatures of the United States. At the same time very favourable reports were reaching Aberdeen from emigrants who had recently gone out to Australia, especially to the Port Phillip district, and it was probably the glowing accounts of the agricultural potentialities of the country that induced Anderson and his associates, the advocates Alexander Jopp and Robert Shand, to launch their 'North British Australasian Company' in January 1839. Although the purpose of the Company as set out in the prospectus was the granting of loans (the rates of interest envisaged being from ten to twenty per cent) the 'chief business' of the concern was stated to be the acquisition of land 'either for resale, or for agricultural and grazing operations'.(35) The contract of co-partnery dated March, 1839, created a committee of management which consisted of Anderson and Jopp (both directors of the North of Scotland Bank), four more advocates and three local business men. The latter were William Annand of Belmont, a landowner; Thomas Blaikie, an iron founder with shipping interests; and David Chalmers of Westburn, a printer and the owner of the conservative Aberdeen *Journal*, founded by his family in 1748. As 'cashier and agent' Jopp was the leading spirit in the company in Aberdeen, and it was from his office, already the headquarters of several other concerns among which was an American investment company, that the North British Australasian was run. Anderson, who had probably conceived the idea for the venture, soon withdrew from active participation in it, no doubt because of his heavy commitments in so many other directions, but he remained a partner until at least 1857.(36)

Like the three North American loan companies which were being formed at the same time, the firm had a capital of £50,000, and the contract of co-partnery, obviously based on that of the Illinois Company of 1837, set out rates of commission for the manager in Australia on profits sent home. The rates envisaged were high, being as much as forty per cent and upwards.(37) Such great expectations were not unreasonable in the light of the statement made in the prospectus of an abortive 'Australian Loan Company of Scotland', which was being mooted in Edinburgh at this time, that the profits of settlers engaged in agriculture and grazing 'varied from 50 to 80 per cent',(38) but the whole outlook was over-sanguine and certainly not based on reliable information.

The records of this company are no longer in existence, but from the archives of its Aberdeen rival, the Scottish Australian Company, it is possible to trace its unfortunate career. Operations were commenced in Sydney towards the end of 1839, when the colonial land boom was at its height. Extensive estates were purchased at inflated prices, and shares in colonial joint-stock companies were taken up. The apparent success of the company led to the issue of an additional £10,000 of stock consisting of one pound shares at a premium of five shillings each in September, 1840,(39) and a rival group of promoters, headed by the advocate, Alexander Stronach of Drumallan, launched the second Aberdeen Australian venture in the weeks that followed. Stronach and his group were closely associated with the Aberdeen Town and County Bank, founded in 1825, and they had already matched the Anderson group in setting up a Marine Insurance Company in 1838 and a North American Investment Company (the Galena, Illinois, Company) in 1840.

The capital of Stronach's company was set at £100,000 in one pound shares, and the prospectus claimed that this new project was unique in character in that its aims were 'not confined to one particular species of business'. It was designed, so the promoters claimed, as a flexible concern, 'embodying in its constitution every principle of business which has proved successful in Australia'.(40) A combination of banking, insurance, and loan business was clearly intended, and high rates of profit were expected. The fact that the shares of the North British Australian stood at a premium of 25 per cent was noted in the prospectus, and everything was done to appeal to the potential investors, great and small, throughout the north-east. The result was heartening for Stronach and his colleagues. By 6th November, 1840, 348 people had intimated that they would subscribe over £29,000, and the company was constituted on the following day in the Royal Hotel.

The substantial number of small partners (223 holding fifty shares or less) reflects the widespread propensity for investment among the folk of the north-east at the time, but effective control of the company lay in the hands of some fifty large partners, who by February, 1841, held more than half of the shares allocated (25,950 out of 51,198 shares).(41)

Of the 416 original partners, 185 lived in Aberdeen and eighty-seven in Aberdeenshire. The remainder resided mainly in the shires of Banff, Moray, Inverness, Perth, Angus, and Kincardine, with a few in Fife, and the shires of Midlothian, Lanark and Renfrew. There was a group of seventeen large shareholders in Edinburgh, and only five of the partners lived outside Scotland, three in London and two in Hobart. The largest of the occupational groups among the partners were the merchants (51), the advocates, solicitors and writers (30), and the surgeons and physicians (22). Unmarried women figured prominently (37), as did farmers and landholders (90), artisans (44), ministers of religion (11), shopkeepers (36) schoolmasters (10) and married women and widows (18). However, almost every occupation in the community was represented, and the partners included university professors, ships' stewards, salmon fishers and coach guards.

The fourteen directorships were held by the promoting and controlling group. All were resident in and around Aberdeen, and they consisted of eight advocates, four merchants, a wine merchant and a druggist. Among them, they held nearly 6,000 shares and their families and relations held 4,000 more. In accordance with the custom of the time, there were fourteen 'extraordinary' directors, comprising influential landed gentlemen, ministers of religion and a university professor.

This second Aberdeen Australian Company was to prove much more successful than the first, and much of its prosperity can be ascribed to its manager, Robert Morehead. A brilliant and cultured young man, of an old Whig landed family, Morehead had served with James Finlay and Company before setting up on his own account as a shawl and zebra-cloth manufacturer in Glasgow. It was he who rejected the plans put forward by some of the Aberdeen directors for the company to engage in large-scale whaling ventures and who determined that the old colonial capital, Sydney, should be the Australian headquarters of the concern. Cautious, yet perspicacious, he quickly realised on his arrival in Sydney in July, 1841, that the time was opportune for a judiciously managed large-scale loan business, and in the next three years he conducted some brilliant business operations despite the vacillations of the board in Aberdeen, who swung violently from an advocacy of reckless profit-seeking in one despatch to an attitude of timorous caution in the next. The publicising of the high rates of interest (as much as sixteen per cent) obtained by Morehead also led to serious difficulties. The action of the Aberdeen directors in inserting extracts from the manager's confidential despatches in the circulars which they distributed all over the United Kingdom, some of which inevitably reached the colonies, greatly aggravated the usury controversy which was raging there. A powerful party of colonial landholders, many of them on the verge of bankruptcy, secured the passage of a bill limiting interest rates and Morehead entered the lists with an interesting statement of the Scottish investors' views, which reflected strongly the classical economic doctrines of Adam Smith and J. R. McCulloch.(42)

On the whole, however, Morehead was left remarkably free from interference by the Aberdeen directors. There was no local board of directors either to hamper him or to embarrass him with demands for loans to themselves, a practice that weakened the rival London loan companies, with their cumbersome machinery and restrictive charters, which precluded them from giving out loans on second mortgages. It was this line of business that brought in what Morehead called 'a rich harvest' during the years between 1841 and 1845, when the Australian colonies were experiencing the most serious economic crisis in their history. The fact that Morehead was allowed a comparatively free exercise of his own initiative was the distinctive feature of the Scottish Australian Company, and its success was to make it a model for many other overseas investment companies established in Aberdeen, Edinburgh and Glasgow. That Morehead himself appreciated this flexibility is revealed by his comment to Alexander Stronach in 1842: 'I find the greatest advantage to arise from the latitude of action allowed me, and much admire the sagacity which the originators of the company have shown in this part of its constitution'.(43)

The manager's own view of the company was well expressed when he wrote to Stronach, 'I consider that the village bears somewhat of the same relations to the city that this colony bears to the large and populous countries of the Old World, therefore a machine of the varied uses which our Company is capable of . . . a "Jack of All Trades", is most suited to the colony'.(44) By June, 1845, when this was written, the company had launched out into agency and exchange business, into property ownership, and into the making of advances on colonial produce, notably wool. Within another five years it would be concerned in the development of copper mines and coal fields, and would have entered the pastoral industry as a landholder. In 1852-53 the headquarters of the concern was moved from Aberdeen to London, to be near the markets for money and for wool and by 1862 the original capital of £100,000 had been increased to £600,000. Fortunate in the time when it was launched, this second Aberdeen Australian Company, still in existence in the 1960's, is perhaps the classic and most successful example of the overseas investment companies organised in the offices of the Aberdeen advocates of the 1830's.(45)

5. *The 'Australian Mania' and the Land Companies, 1852-79*

Although Australian historians have tended in recent years to take the view that the essentially pastoral economy of the country was established by 1850, and have played down the long-term, last-ing effects of the 'Gold Rush' of the early 1850's, there is little doubt that the stirring events of that time gave a new stimulus to emigra-tion from Scotland, which had fallen off since the onset of the depression in the colonies in 1841-42. As in the late 1830's, emigra-tion went with trade, and, in Glasgow particularly, there raged for a few years the phenomenon described over twenty years later by *The Bailie* as 'the Australian Mania'. Of the career of James Morton, Glasgow merchant and banker in those years, *The Bailie* wrote : 'Mr. Morton suddenly expanded into a full-blown Australian mer-chant. Not only did he export every known and unknown article of merchandise, from the traditional needle to the equally mythical anchor, but he also chartered ships, mixed himself up with other firms, and was generally recognised as one of the biggest specula-tors of that period of reckless speculators.'(46)

In 1857 the Australian bubble burst, with disastrous consequences for several Glasgow firms which had over-extended their credit, but in its earlier phase, the effect had been beneficial, especially to the shipping interest. In September, 1853, when the boom had been at its peak, a writer in the Glasgow *Scottish Review* had gone so far as to declare that 'Australia has saved the British shipowner from ruin',(47) and in the following year the same periodical, extolling Australia as 'the centre, and probably the seat, of the great Pacific empire which is to be', urged improved communications through the employment of larger steamships, operating regular services.

Certainly, men of James Morton's stamp were not discouraged from ventures in Australia and New Zealand by the collapse of the Glasgow 'Mania' in 1857, and the next thirty years were to see the flotation of numerous 'land companies', whose principal aim was to participate in pastoral and, to a lesser degree, in mining develop-ment. The brilliant success of the Scottish Australian Company was partly responsible for these promotions, for by 1866 this company had acquired numerous pastoral properties including the Bowen Downs complex of runs in Central Queensland, for long the largest sheep and cattle station in the world, and was extending its proper-ties to the shores of the Gulf of Carpentaria, where it was the first to take up land. This was the golden age of the great pastoral com-panies, when leases over great tracts of country were easily obtained and wool prices were high.

Morton and his associates maintained their Australian connec-tions, and strove to create a market in Scotland for a whole range of colonial products, especially for Australian tinned meat and hides. In the early 1870's Morton planned the New Zealand Land

Company. The stock of this company, which was designed to operate in Australia also, was held 'in enormous quantity' by the ill-fated City of Glasgow Bank. The collapse of the bank in 1878 led to the re-organisation of the New Zealand Company, whose headquarters were moved to Edinburgh, the centre of Scottish investment in Australia during the latter part of the century. By 1884, a writer in Blackwood's *Edinburgh Magazine* could comment that 'three fourths of the foreign and colonial investment companies are of Scottish origin. If not actually located in Scotland, they have been hatched by Scotch-men, and work on Scottish models.'(48) He listed nineteen overseas investment companies founded between 1860 and 1884 which were obtaining the bulk of their funds from Scotland. Five of these were operating in Australia and six in New Zealand. It was not surprising that he should observe that 'Scotland . . . does not pose before the world as a leader of commerce or a ruling centre of finance; but she has claims to both if she chooses to assert them'.(49) By 1875 the oldest and most conservative of the Scottish chartered banks, the Bank of Scotland, was acting as agent for the Bank of South Australia, the Australian and New Zealand Mortgage Company, and the New Zealand and Australian Land Company, and in 1878 it was to engage in the large-scale purchase of New South Wales Government debentures, the first departure from its time-honoured policy of confining its investments to the United Kingdom.(50)

The full story of Scottish investment in Australia in the latter half of the nineteenth century remains to be told, partly because the records of still-existent land companies have yet to be opened up for research. It is clear, however, that Edinburgh, still in 1966 the headquarters of one of the largest Australian companies, acted as an important organising centre for new projects to channel capital to the colonies. Apart from the actual capital sent out by land and investment companies, there was the contribution of personnel, managers, agents and, later, expert agriculturists and stock-breeders who figured largely in Australian commercial and agricultural development.

What are the conclusions that can be drawn from this brief survey of Scottish overseas enterprise? The early experiment of the Australian Company of Edinburgh and Leith was bold in its conception of a regular shipping service, sustained by large-scale trading activities and a regular emigrant flow. Its creation reflected the needs of the shipping, mercantile and manufacturing interests of the capital and its port for a new field of overseas trade, and an outlet for their manufactures. If it was premature, it nevertheless presented some novel features. The Aberdeen companies, with their wide appeal to investors of all classes in the north-east, also met a local need. The success of their flexibility and sound management set the pattern for later ventures into overseas investment. The years between 1822 and 1846 may, in fact, be regarded as an experimental period in which Scottish-based enterprise, after setbacks and failures, evolved a form of organisation in Australia that was to be employed in even wider fields.

NOTES

(1) Robert Campbell was the third and youngest son of John Campbell, Writer to the Signet and Ninth Laird of Ashfield. According to the great valuation roll of the Argyll estates compiled in 1771 the Ashfield Campbells were cadets of the more ancient house of the Campbells of Duntroon. C. E. T. Newman, The Spirit of Wharf House: Campbell Enterprise from Calcutta to Canberra, 1788-1930 (Sydney, 1961), p. 3.

(2) The fascinating story of Campbell's career, his tribulations and eventual triumph has been told at length and in detail by C. E. T. Newman, op. cit.; by J. K. S. Houison, Journal of the Royal Australian Historical Society, 1937, and in the booklet, Enter the Merchant (Melbourne, 1961), by David S. Macmillan.

(3) C. E. T. Newman, op. cit., p. 28.

(4) The Times, 17th July, 1805.

(5) Historical Records of Australia, Vol. V, pp. 232-33.

(6) Historical Records of New South Wales, Vol. VI, p. 101.

(7) Letter from the Commissioners of the Board of Trade to the Directors of the East India Company, 22nd December, 1806.

(8) Historical Records of New South Wales, Vol. V, p. 113.

(9) Sydney Gazette, 10th July, 1819.

(10) The valuable material contained in the Hook letter books, covering the period 1810-15, forms the basis of Chapters 15-18 in C. E. T. Newman's Spirit of Wharf House.

(11) Apart from the works cited in footnote 1 above, there is the thesis of Dr. Margaret J. E. Steven, of the Australian National University, Canberra, which incorporates new material relating to Robert Campbell's Scottish background and to his Calcutta connections, and her book, Merchant Campbell (Melbourne, 1965).

(12) The Australian Company was generally known in Sydney and Hobart as 'the Leith Company' because of the large number of Leith shipowners and merchants among its partners. The effective direction of the Company was also in the hands of Leith men, notably James Wyld of Gilston, wine-merchant and shipowner, who was described as 'Principal Director' of the Company. 'Journals of G. A. Robinson, covering his voyage to Van Diemen's Land in 1822-23', Mitchell Library, Sydney.

(13) Applications to the Colonial Office for permission to settle, and for land grants in New South Wales, were approved only when the applicants possessed sufficient capital (£500) to qualify. Successful applicants could take

out with them not only dependants but artisans, farm labourers and other agricultural workers, shepherds, and domestic servants.

(14) Of the 521 Scottish applicants in the period, 79 did not specify their occupation. Among the 'unspecified' there were probably many who were in the categories listed above.

(15) The number of applicants from these areas were Lochalsh, 8; Mull, 5; Caithness, 13; Dunbartonshire, 5; Forfar, 14.

(16) Colonial Office Records, Australia, C.O./201.

(17) Patrick Colquhoun, Treatise on the Wealth, Power and Resources of the British Empire, in Every Quarter of the World, 2nd edition (Edinburgh, 1815), p. 414.

(18) Alexander McConochie, Summary View of the Statistics and Existing Commerce of the Principal Shores of the Pacific Ocean, with a Sketch of the Advantages which would result from the Establishment of a Central Free Port within its Limits (Edinburgh, 1818), p. xvi.

(19) The Scots Magazine, New Series, Vol. 10, June, 1822, p. 772.

(20) Edinburgh Evening Courant, 18th and 23rd November, 1822.

(21) Henry, Lord Cockburn, Memorials of His Time (Edinburgh, 1856), pp. 252-53.

(22) James L. Anderson, The Story of the Commercial Bank (Edinburgh, 1910).

(23) The Australian Agricultural Company, founded in 1824, and the Van Diemen's Land Company, founded in 1825. It was proposed that the first should receive a grant of one million acres and the services of fourteen hundred convicts. The Colonial Office offered the Van Diemen's Land Company a block of a quarter of a million acres in the north-west of Tasmania, at a nominal price. By 1830 the Company had acquired 350,000 acres and a further 50,000 acres had been added to this by 1845. For the favourable reception given to the Company by the colonial press, see The Sydney Gazette, 21st January, 1824.

(24) The figures and proportions quoted refer solely to vessels engaged in the trade between Britain and Australia. Convict and military transports, whalers and sealing vessels, and ships proceeding to New Zealand and trading there only, are not included.

(25) Hobart Town Gazette, 9th April, 1824.

(26) Customs records, New South Wales, A. 279, Mitchell Library, Sydney.

(27) For further discussion of the Scottish background to the Leith Australian Company see David S. Macmillan, The Beginning of Scottish Enterprise in Australia: The Contribution of the Commercial Whigs, Business Archives and History, Vol. II, No. 2 (August, 1962), pp. 95-106.

(28) Broadfoot's Petition to Lord Aberdeen, 10th February, 1835, C.O. 384/39, f. 149.

(29) General Returns of Emigrants, C.O. 384/54, f. 284; C.O. 384/55, f. 234; and Statement of Bounty Emigrants, 1841, C.O. 384/70, f. 31.

(30) W. H. Marwick, Economic Developments in Victorian Scotland (Edinburgh, 1936), p. 109.

(31) Robert Brown to Lord Glenelg, 20th July, 1835, C.O. 384/39, f. 168.

(32) Edinburgh Evening Courant, 15th February, 1830.

(33) Customs returns of Emigrants, 23rd March, 1834 (Correspondence with the Colonial Land and Emigration Commissioners, C.O. 384/39, f. 77).

(34) Customs returns of Emigrants, 28th January, 1835, and February, 1837 (C.O. 384/39 and 43, ff. 72 and 109).

(35) Aberdeen Journal, 9th January, 1839.

(36) Share list of the North British Australasian Company, 9th September, 1857, Board of Trade Records, Public Record Office.

(37) 'Contract of Co-partnery of the North British Australasian Company', Aberdeen, 1839, p. 8.

(38) Aberdeen Journal, 13th March, 1839.

(39) Aberdeen Herald, 5th September, 1840.

(40) Draft prospectus, board minutes, Scottish Australian Company Records (subsequently cited as S.A.C.R.).

(41) Share-list, S.A.C.R., February, 1841.

(42) R. A. A. Morehead, Some Words for and to the Capitalists and Shareholders in Banks and other Moneyed Companies connected with the Colony of New South Wales (Sydney, 1843).

(43) R. A. A. Morehead to Alexander Stronach, January, 1842, S.A.C.R.

(44) Morehead to Stronach, 18th June, 1845, S.A.C.R.

(45) For an account of the early operations of the Scottish Australian Company, see David S. Macmillan, *The Scottish Australian Company, 1840-1850: The Origins and Growth of an Aberdeen Venture in Colonial Development*, Scottish Historical Review, Vol. XXXIX, No. 127, April, 1960, pp. 16-31. For a full and detailed account of the Usury controversy and the attitudes of the colonists and the Scottish investors to each other, see David S. Macmillan, The Debtor's War: Scottish Capitalists and the Economic Crisis in Australia, 1841-46 (Melbourne, 1960).

(46) The Bailie, No. 315, 30th October, 1878.

(47) The Scottish Review, Vol. 54, No. 455, September, 1853, p. 377; *ibid.*, Vol. 76, No. 467, September, 1854, p. 277.

(48) Blackwood's, October, 1884, p. 469.

(49) *Ibid.*, p. 469.

(50) Charles A. Malcolm, The Bank of Scotland, 1695-1945 (Edinburgh, 1947), p. 136.

CHAPTER THIRTEEN

British Shipping in the Nineteenth Century: A Study of the Ben Line Papers[1]

T. E. MILNE

Lecturer in the Department of Organisation of Industry and Commerce, University of Edinburgh

1. The Shipowners

The history of the partnership of William Thomson and Company is one of orderly progression and continuous adaptation to changing circumstances. Not the least remarkable feature of the firm is that it has been under the unbroken control of the same family for almost one hundred and thirty years. William Thomson, the founder, had two sons, both of whom proved able and willing to manage the maturing shipping line and to guide it through the difficult transition from sailing vessels to steamship operation. These two men had a number of children and four of their sons helped to carry the company through the problems of the First World War and the rigours of inter-war depressions. Of these, one, the present chairman, survived to supervise the rebuilding of the fleet necessitated by its almost complete destruction in the Second World War. In this formidable task he had the assistance of the son of a fifth brother who had preferred politics to commerce.

The partnership of which these men have formed a vital part, William Thomson and Co., controls the company called 'The Ben Line Steamers Ltd.', whose registered office is in Edinburgh.(2) That a limited liability company should be controlled by a partnership is perhaps curious, and is a reflection of the continuing family management of the firm. Before 1919 the majority of the shares in any venture were normally held by the partners, who managed the ships, but others were held by their relatives and occasionally, by outsiders.(3) When limited liability was introduced, however, the managing partnership was retained, although ship ownership was legally vested in the new company.

When William Thomson and his brother Alexander bought a minority share in the tiny ship *Carrara* in 1839, their idea was probably to further their business as marble cutters, the basis of their modest fortunes.(4) William must have had considerable commercial acumen for not only was he, in company with Alexander, in charge of the marble cutting and merchanting business, he was also an experienced ships' husband and auctioneer, selling cargoes of Canadian timber at Leith. The marble business had prospered with the building of the New Town of Edinburgh,(5) but the Italians, who controlled the source of the stone, were competing more and more strongly with the Edinburgh merchants at about the time that William and Alexander took control of the business.(6) In addition, the demand for marble for building was beginning to decline.

It was in order to strengthen themselves against the increasing competition, by controlling their own means of transport and improving their purchasing position in Italy, that the brothers acquired *Carrara*.(7) Following this first venture into shipowning, William apparently began to look for further trading opportunities elsewhere. In 1841 *Australia*, the second unit in the fleet to be managed and partly owned by William Thomson, ran aground on Sable Island in the mouth of the St. Lawrence.

The trade on which William had embarked was essentially simple. Alloa coal was shipped to Canada where it was sold on the ship owner's account. The responsibility for this sale was the captain's as was that of buying the cargo of timber to be auctioned by William Thomson on the Sands of Leith. The essence of this early trade was that the shipowner was his own merchant and the captain was his agent.

It was not until 1851 that William had an incentive to take his ships off the lucrative North Atlantic trade. With the discovery of gold in Australia he refitted *Wanderer* and despatched her on the emigrant run in 1851, while another branch of the family, in Alloa, despatched *Signet* on a trading venture of their own to Australia.(8) These enterprises were short lived,(9) but William Thomson's vision was widening. In 1851 he took delivery of *Araby Maid* from the builders and despatched her to Mauritius, and before the 'fifties were out his ships were plying in South American, Atlantic, Australian, and Indian waters; in short, anywhere that tramp vessels could secure cargoes.

By the mid-'sixties the company's trading pattern was largely established in Indian and Burmese waters, as well as on the original

North Atlantic trade, but so long as sailing ships remained there was always the occasional venture on other seas. At about this time the company's interests were extended to China and Japan. In the case of the former country this was made possible by the acquisition of increasingly larger ships which, if they could not compete with the clippers for the choicest cargoes of the tea trade, were still substantial enough vessels to obtain remunerative cargoes of that valuable commodity. Having ventured as far as China, it was an obvious enough step to try to gain a share of the nascent Japanese trade, and indeed the first call at a Japanese port was made as early as 1860.

Three events of the late 1860's were to set the course for the future development of the enterprise. The first was the abolition, in 1867, of the imperial preference on Canadian timber. This allowed the cheaper Baltic timber to compete for markets in Britain which, with the decline in the use of wood for shipbuilding, were in any case diminishing. Ultimately the disappearance of the Thomsons' Canadian trade occurred in the mid-1880's, through the sale or loss of the vessels thus employed, for they were not replaced. The decision to abandon the trade was probably taken before 1878, for it was then that the first steamers were received to inaugurate the Baltic trade. A thriving business developed which was brought to an end only by the Russian revolution.

The second of these three events was the opening of the Suez Canal in 1869. It now became possible for the steamship to demonstrate a clear commercial advantage on Far Eastern voyages, for the compound reciprocating engine, already established,(10) was capable of offering economies sufficient to show an advantage over the clipper ships. Probably the most important factor in favour of the steamship was the greater predictability of its arrival dates, which allowed it to charge more than the sailer for the same freight, and to pick up more valuable freights.(11)

The third point is that through the late 'sixties and early 'seventies William, senior, was gradually relinquishing his control of the company to his two sons. It is suggested that the assumption of power by the two younger men was important at this stage of the company's history because the record of ship acquisitions at the period is difficult to explain in any other way.

The Thomsons took delivery of their first steamship in 1871, which on its early voyages established clearly that, even in relation to its very much higher capital cost, it was more profitable than the sailing ships. Thereafter, however, four sailing ships were acquired, and the next steamer did not join the fleet until 1875, after William senior's final retirement. Even allowing that two of the sailing ships were large iron craft, and that in the state of knowledge of the early 1870's it was possible that these would be as profitable as steamships on the long haul to the Far East, the two others were small wooden vessels of the type that the company had always operated. It is difficult to see any explanation for this series of purchases except by reference to the control of the company.(12)

Until the turn of the century and up to the First World War the size and carrying capacity of the Far East fleet was steadily increased and ship costs rose, but not more than would roughly reflect the increase in tonnage and power of the new vessels. It is, perhaps, surprising that the fleet did not grow more swiftly, and two explanations may be offered for this. The Thomson brothers chose an inauspicious time to venture into steamship owning on the China run. In his study of the Blue Funnel Line, Professor Hyde has argued that: 'From 1875 to 1885 the profitability of the China trade was in itself a source of weakness for, in times of depression, shipping companies tended to transfer their unemployed tonnage from their normal trade routes to that between Britain and China. Thus the original trend towards excess of shipping space on offer at Chinese ports, which had been apparent since 1870, became subject to aggravation.'(13) Although the prosperity of Alfred Holt and Company's fleet was founded on very fast, high-class ships, which were only economic on the cream of cargoes, the conditions which Professor Hyde describes were equally detrimental to the Ben Line.

Notwithstanding their more vulnerable position, however, Blue Funnel acquisitions between 1865 and 1901 numbered no fewer than sixty-five vessels, compared with the Ben Line's thirteen between 1871 and 1901. The other likely explanation for the slow rate of growth lies in the system of ship ownership adopted by William Thomson and Company up to 1919.(14) The obvious drawback of this system was that profits distributed outside the partnership were not necessarily available for reinvestment at a later date. The change to a limited liability company in 1919 ushered in the largest expansion of the fleet in any decade in the company's history.(15) The change in the organisation undoubtedly contributed to the continued growth of the succeeding years.(16)

The First World War had relatively little effect on the company's prosperity. Despite overall increases in costs and high freight rates, the ultimate gains on voyages were little changed, relative to the increased investment required, from the levels prevailing immediately before the conflict. Thereafter the fleet continued to grow. Its tonnage was almost doubled in the 'twenties, but few acquisitions were made in the 'thirties, presumably because of depressed trade. In the Second World War the fleet had almost entirely to be replaced, chiefly because of losses through enemy action. In 1950, only one ship was of pre-war construction and nine out of a total of twenty-two were post-war vessels, the remainder being of wartime construction.

Certain aspects of this brief survey of the firm's history merit more detailed attention. The remainder of this paper is devoted to an exploration of three themes: competition in the Far Eastern trades, 1870 to 1914; profitability and fleet growth, 1870 to 1914; and the conflict of sail and steam.(17)

2. *Competition in the Far Eastern Trades, 1870 to 1914*

The evolution of company policy and organisation described above was the result of a continuing response to commercial pressures outside as well as within the firm, particularly the trading conditions prevailing on the Far Eastern run. Initially the Leith ships were small, even negligible, competitors of the Blue Funnel, P. and O., Glen, Castle and Shire lines.(18) These were big lines specialising in fast craft which could command the best freight rates for the choicest cargoes. On the outward journey they carried woollen and cotton goods and small manufactures, while tea, tin, tobacco, silk and bullion were typical homeward cargoes. Passengers, of course, made the voyage in both directions. These may be contrasted with typical Thomson cargoes in the nineteenth century of coal, timber, rice, jute and miscellaneous manufactures. The 'Bens' occupied a position somewhere between the liners and the windjammers. Their success was founded on offering high-quality ship accommodation at speeds slightly slower than the liners, thus operating more economically. At the same time, by offering regular sailing schedules, the Thomsons placed themselves in a better class than the orthodox tramp operators.

Until 1875, the Holt ships, having won the tea race from the clippers, were recognised as the most reliable carriers on the homeward voyage, while they were able to ship cotton piece goods from Manchester for their outward cargoes.(19) The opening of the Suez Canal, the growth in steamship trading to the Far East, and the impact of recession, coupled with a changing pattern of trade, all combined to increase competition and so lower freight rates and reduce profit margins. As a consequence, during the 'eighties and 'nineties the shipowners pursued a two-fold policy of reducing costs by technical improvements and of reducing competition by agreements of various kinds between rival businesses. The position of the Thomson concern, however, made it less vulnerable to the problems of high-cost operation than some of the other lines.

The combination of these forces depressed freight rates until in 1879 the main British lines (excluding the Ben Line) and the French *Messageries Maritimes* entered into agreement on equalising freight tariffs on both the outward and homeward trades, and instituted the technique of deferred rebate. It is interesting that the years 1880 and 1881 were the most profitable enjoyed by the Ben Line before the First World War. Increased profits were also earned by the Conference members, but it is difficult to saw how much of this was attributable to the Conference and how much to the trade cycle.(20)

The Ben Line did not represent serious competition to the Conference lines until the late 'eighties, but towards the end of that decade the company was able to muster sufficient tonnage to offer regular monthly sailings from the United Kingdom. After 1888 an intensive price war developed between the Conference lines and the China Shippers Mutual Company which, in partnership with the Mogul Line began a deliberate policy of rate cutting. The reduction in the profits of the Conference lines was such that, 'Had it not been for the changed attitude of the Holt managers in the early 1890's, the firm might have gone out of existence'.(21) Although the Ben Line, trading in a slightly different group of commodities, enjoyed good profits in 1889, these declined each year in succession from 1890 to 1893. During this period the Castle line went out of business and the remaining companies had to come together, along with the China Mutual, in an outward conference agreement which had little apparent effect on Ben Line profits.

The severity of competition for the China trade involved the leading competitors in large building programmes of new vessels to maintain marginal, but significant, advantages over rival ships. This itself had the effect of intensifying the chronic over-supply of tonnage in the China trade. The Conference agreements had little noticeable effect in improving profits in the face of this situation, and in 1903 Holts took over the China Mutual Company and between 1906 and 1911 Royal Mail Lines acquired direct or indirect control of the Glen and Shire lines, an interest which was absorbed in 1936 by Alfred Holt & Co. In this way the number of competing companies was reduced to a level where there was a reasonable chance of success for trade agreements. Only four British groups of any magnitude were trading to China and Japan at the outbreak of war, Blue Funnel, P. and O., the Glen-Shire grouping, and the Ben Line. Notwithstanding this grouping of interests, however, 1908 was the least profitable year in the company's history before 1914. With the approach of war, however, trade improved, and 1913 was the best year since 1881.

These company groupings, reinforced by the system of Conferences, may have been effective in helping to regulate a trade that initially contained elements which made for an unusual degree of instability. An example was the premium which some homeward cargoes such as tea placed on speed. To have survived such instability and at the same time to have evolved from tramp ownership to liner operation is a reflection of careful rather than of daring management, and of studied response to the changing internal and external business situation, rather than of dramatic innovation designed to shape the situation. Most of the other companies operating in the Far East had their moments of crisis when independent operation was jeopardised or brought to an end.(22) The Ben Line, however, by careful and conservative management, reduced their vulnerability to the violent fluctuations of the trade and, never overextending their resources, expanded their interests in orderly progression from owning a few tramps to operating a powerful liner fleet. Few shipping companies have even survived to tell their tale.

3. *Profitability and Fleet Growth, 1870 to 1914*(23)

The decision to increase the number of vessels in the fleet, or to replace existing vessels with faster or larger ones, was determined by a number of factors. In the case of the Ben Line before the First World War the most important of these appear to have been the availability of capital accrued from previous profits,(24) the anticipated profitability of the new unit, the current earning capacity of the vessel to be replaced, and the cost of the replacement. There is nothing very different in this from the general criteria determining decisions to add to the fixed capital of any business. From the voyage accounts it is possible to make an assessment of the relative importance of these factors in determining the timing and extent of fixed capital investment by the Thomson partners.

The growth in the carrying capacity of the fleet is shown in Chart 1. Carrying capacity depends upon the gross tonnage of the ship and its service speed. The former is known, but it has been necessary to make certain assumptions concerning the latter in constructing the index.(25)

During the phase of mature development there were no calls for

AA

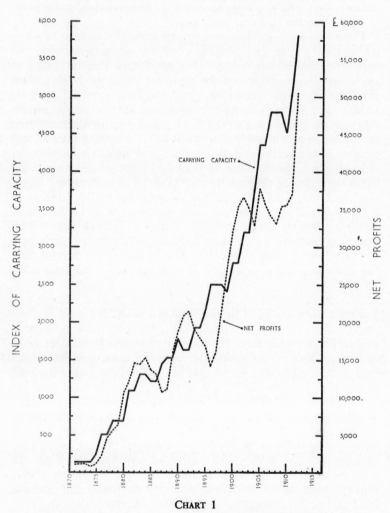

CHART 1

Carrying capacity and net profits earned, the Ben Line, 1870-1913 (six-year moving average). See text for calculation of the Index of Carrying Capacity.

capital except from the partners, their relations, and close associates. Indeed, it was never company policy to attempt to secure outside finance. It is, therefore, fair to assume that all growth was financed from accrued net profits, that is, the total net gain on all voyages preceding the acquisition of the vessel, less the depreciation allowance on preceding vessels. The voyage accounts indicate what these figures were, but it is impossible to estimate how much liquid capital, accrued from previous voyages, was available to finance a new ship. This is because such profits were immediately distributed to the shareholders on the conclusion of each voyage. Although a majority of the shares were held by the Thomson partners, a substantial minority were held by others. What proportion of such payments was used for administering the business, what proportion was treated as income, and how much was available for reinvestment is not known.(26)

The cost per gross ton of a new ship fell steadily from *Benledi*, 1871, to *Benlomond*, 1890, the former figure being about £17 and the latter some £13 10s. Thereafter the figure for most of the ships was £10 to £11 except *Bencleuch II*, in 1900, and *Benarty III*, in 1902, which cost some £13. These costs marked the beginning of an inflationary movement in new and second-hand ship prices. The records do not show any new ship bought after 1912, but *Benalder*, which had cost £30,550 in 1895, fetched £65,000 when sold in 1919. These price fluctuations, however, do not appear to have had any marked effect either on Ben Line purchases or on U.K. merchant ship launchings.(27)

There is a clear relationship between the age of a ship and the profits which it was capable of earning. The following analysis of seventeen steamers from 1871 to 1911 expresses profit at a particular stage of the ships' lives as a percentage of the new cost of the ships.(28)

TABLE 1

Voyage number	Number of ships	Average profit as % of new cost
1	17	13·0
5	17	9·3
10	17	6·4
15	15	6·8
20	13	2·8
25	8	4·5

Only one of these steamers remained in the company's service for thirty voyages. Of the four ships falling out of the calculation between voyages ten and twenty, three are accounted for simply by the records coming to an end, and one by the loss of the vessel, so that there was no policy decision to dispose of a ship before voyage twenty. Of the five disposed of between voyages twenty and twenty-five, three had been acquired by 1880 and so were fairly early designs, and were earning barely any gross profit in their last few voyages. Two of these were sold to Japanese owners, as were the remaining two, more modern vessels. These were earning fair profits even on their latter voyages, but they were the oldest units in the fleet when they were disposed of in 1903 and 1904. This was immediately before the very rapid acquisition of steamers that characterised the years 1904 and 1905. It seems probable that when the decision was taken to expand the fleet rapidly, about 1903, these two ships were sold to help pay for the new ones.

The decision to dispose of a unit might therefore be made either on the ground that the vessel was no longer profitable, or else to help pay for a new ship. In the case of the eight ships retained for more than twenty-five voyages, it is not clear whether the decision to sell them depended upon the purchase of new vessels, or whether the purchase of the new ships was decided upon because the old ones were no longer profitable. The former seems the likelier explanation in the light of the subsequent paragraphs of this section.

If profitability is defined as the gross profit earned per gross ton employed, the profitability of the whole Far East steamer fleet may be seen in Chart 2. This may be contrasted with the actual net profit earned by the total fleet (gross profit less a depreciation factor) plotted as a six-year moving average against the fleet carrying capacity in Chart 1. Since both graphs derive from the same data, they record basically the same information, but it may be observed that while Chart 1 does not really express the short-run relationship in time between the growth of the fleet and the growth in profits, Chart 2 illustrates the relationship between annual profitability of the Ben Line and the years in which they acquired their ships, which are indicated on the diagram. There is also apparently some relationship between U.K. merchant ship launchings generally and the Ben Line's profitability cycle. Examining the profitability time series, it may be seen that the usual time interval between troughs was six years (though on one occasion the interval was nine years and in two cases three years). This being so, it is possible to detect some pattern, albeit imperfect, in the timing of decisions to acquire new tonnage.

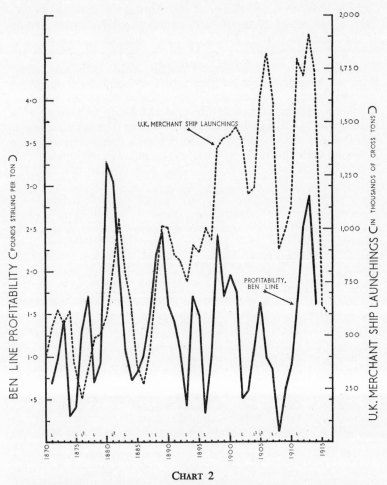

CHART 2

United Kingdom merchant ship launchings and Ben Line profitability and launchings, 1870-1914.

Years marked 'L' are years in which Ben Line ships were received.

Since a new ship normally earned the highest profits, it was in the owners' best interests to order near the bottom of the profitability cycle in order to take delivery of the ship on the upswing. In fact only twelve out of twenty-three ships were acquired at the bottom of the cycle or on the upswing. On an assumption, however, that the decision to purchase a vessel was made one year before the actual acquisition (all the vessels bought at this time came direct from the builders), then the years that are of interest are these 'decision years'. It is necessary to examine them to determine whether a decision taken then, in respect of a ship to be received in the following year, might reasonably have been taken in the expectation that the ship would go into service on a rising market. In the following table the 'decision years' are examined individually.

TABLE 2

Decision year	No. of ships	Comment on the likely course of the cycle, as it might have seemed to the managers at the time
1870	One	Apparently a low point in the market?
1874	One	A very low market. Upturn inevitable.
1875	Two	
1877	One	Top of the cycle—but the sudden downturn may have been unexpected.
1880	One	Top of an unexpectedly short cycle.
1882	One	Clearly a falling market.
1886	One	Beginning of a recovery.
1887	One	Market rising strongly.
1889	One	Cycle due to turn down.
1892	One	Third successive year's decline; recovery expected.
1894	One	Top of another unexpectedly short cycle.
1895	One	Downturn of same cycle.
1899	One	Market likely to turn down.
1901	One	A prolonged boom continuing, which may have given false encouragement. In any case, after the high profits of the previous three years, reserves must have been unusually high, especially bearing in mind the low rate of acquisitions in the 'nineties.
1903	Three	Apparently the beginning of another strong upturn in the market.
1904	Two	
1906	One	A falling market.
1910	One	Market rising strongly.

Note particularly the lack of activity between 1899 and 1903. It is as if the partners held off purchasing in the expectation of a recession which took a number of years to materialise. This was followed by a sharp bout of activity in time to catch the next recovery.

The present chairman of the company, Mr. E. G. Thomson, and his brother Mr. H. M. Thomson, have declared that the Thomson partners paid no attention to the trade cycle and that they made no attempt to forecast it in timing their investments. 'They contracted for new vessels when funds were available as a result of profits being made and when the other shareholders were willing to invest their money, and that was usually only when they had been getting regular dividends. About 1909 the leading outside shareholder threatened not to invest in any further tonnage.' In addition it is clear (see footnote 28) that it was likely that the decision to sell an old vessel would be made on the merits of the commercial performance of that ship, and that replacement would then be necessary, rather than that it would be decided to place a newer ship in service and then help to pay for her by sale of an old one.

It has also been stated that the acquisitions of the years 1902 to 1907 were made so that a regular fortnightly outward service might be maintained. The profits which financed these acquisitions had largely been earned in the prosperous period around 1900, which Mr. H. M. Thomson attributes to the Spanish-American, South African, and Russo-Japanese wars, the first and third of which enabled the Ben Line to obtain 'very lucrative time charters'.

Fluctuations in the family's personal fortunes undoubtedly had an effect on the availability of capital. In 1878, for example, William Thomson, senior, voluntarily decided to meet liabilities of between £80,000 and £90,000 as an executor of a trust involved in the failure of the City of Glasgow Bank, an obligation which with the assistance of his sons he met in full.

It is clear, therefore, that there were many more factors affecting the timing of investment than can be discovered from an analysis of the voyage accounts. It is equally apparent that the first determinant of that decision was whether capital was available. Such money might not always be so readily obtainable by shipping entrepreneurs in the East of Scotland as elsewhere, in Liverpool or London for example.

Nevertheless, the evidence of the voyage documents make it difficult to agree that this was the *only* determinant of the exact timing of a decision to buy a new ship. It seems unlikely that the partners necessarily decided to order a new vessel immediately adequate funds were available. The evidence for this lies in the period from 1899 to 1903 when the company was certainly enjoying great prosperity. The five new ships received in 1904 and 1905 were paid for out of funds accrued over a number of years. While it is possible that the United States Government was rather tardy in settling its account with the company for time charters, it seems more likely that in their counsels the partners were considering factors other than the simple availability of funds. This does not mean that the partners necessarily considered the possible future course of the trade cycle but they might, for example, have been influenced by technological trends, or the desirability of selling ships currently on time charter. Nevertheless, the degree of correlation between the record of U.K. launchings and the Ben Line's earnings cycle (Chart 2) provides *prima facie* evidence that ship ordering decisions were, however imperfectly, related to the trade cycle.

The reconciliation of the views of the past and present partners and the evidence of the voyage accounts may turn on the gestation period of a ship at any particular time relative to the length of the trade cycle. The businessman who ordered his ships when trade was prosperous would stand a strong chance of taking delivery of it on the downswing of the cycle. On the other hand, a company which only ordered as funds were available might find that by the time all their accounts receivable relative to the prosperous years had been paid the cycle would be on a downswing that would tempt them to hold off for a while, less on a basis of a prosperity cycle on a graph than on a good businessman's instinct that trade, for the present, was bad. Thereafter, of course, there would be the problem of longer delivery dates and possibly higher prices when the yards were busy, a time which frequently appears to have coincided with the periods of greatest prosperity for the Ben Line.

There is sufficient evidence to be derived from the voyage accounts to justify the argument that the precise timing of the investment decision depended upon a more or less complex conjunction of factors. Although the most important of these may have been the availability of funds, the desire to maintain a regular fortnightly outward service was of outstanding importance at one period and all the time the partners must have taken the state of trade into account, even if its prediction was more a matter of sound business instinct than any question of projections on a chart. It is suggested from the record of fluctuating profitability and the timing of their fleet acquisitions compared with launchings nationally that the Thomson partners' instincts in this respect were sounder than those of the average shipowner of the time, and that this may be one of the reasons for the continuing prosperity of the Ben Line.

4. Sail and Steam—1879 to 1888

For many years the Far Eastern trade was dominated by the carriage of perishable commodities, especially tea. Consequently there was an exceptional premium on speed which for some owners overshadowed the normal determinants of profitability, such as economic manning and safety. In response to this demand the China tea clippers were developed. These possessed great speed but were expensive to operate.

In the latter half of the 'sixties, when these vessels were at the peak of their success, Alfred Holt of Liverpool so developed the compound reciprocating steam engine that it was economically possible to work a steamship from Liverpool to China. His first compound-engined ship sailed from Liverpool in 1866, and by 1869 he had five such vessels in the trade. Although this was in many ways an experimental venture, it soon became clear that steamships of this type were capable of competing with the clippers on level terms, and, as propulsive efficiency increased, that they might be expected to improve their relative position.

With the opening of the Suez Canal, however, the balance tipped definitely in favour of the steamship. Nevertheless, the steamer, like the clipper, required 'luxury' cargoes on which high freights could be earned, for costs were much higher than those of the sailing vessel. For commodities such as rice or coal the sailing ship, although not the clipper, still had a firm place. About 1873 the conventional sailing ships began to give way to a new class of iron-built vessel, designed to handle bulk cargoes economically. These typically measured up to 2,000 gross tons and later were to be made much bigger. They were designed to carry a large payload and were the product of a growing realisation that, even with the Suez Canal, there was still a large area of trade in which the sailing vessel had a commercial advantage over the steamship.(29)

The Thomson partners were not alone in thinking that the sailing ship could co-exist with the steamer when they took delivery of two such ships in 1875 and 1876. Meanwhile they had taken delivery of one new steamer, *Benledi*, in 1871, which was trading successfully. In her first five voyages she earned a gross profit of £26,000, against her cost of just over £25,000. This was a much higher earning rate than could be achieved by a sailing ship, and for this reason it is surprising that the partners did not develop steamship owning more swiftly. They had, however, been unaccustomed to paying more than perhaps £6,000 for a sailing ship, and the steamer must have seriously depleted reserves. This acquistion was followed by two large iron sailing ships and two of the conventional small wooden ships, costing together almost as much as two steamers. Thereafter, only steamers were acquired. One possible explanation for this sequence of purchases lies in the retiral of William, senior, from the partnership in 1875. Perhaps he was unwilling to commit his firm entirely to a technology which had not been thoroughly tried under commercial conditions.

Whatever the explanation, it provides an opportunity to compare the commercial performance of two iron sailing ships and two iron compound-engined ships managed by the Thomson partners during the period 1879 to 1888. In making this comparison, however, it should be mentioned that the steamers were of more advanced design than the earlier Holt ships which established the steamer on competitive terms with the sailing ships, that the sailing ships involved were very different, technically and commercially, from both the China clippers and the conventional vessels of their era, and finally that even the sailing ship, however efficient, was meeting increasingly stringent competition from the steamers as propulsion economies were increased. This increasing pressure from better class ships was forcing more and more economies in sailing ship operation, and many innovations were adopted to help reduce the manning of sailing ships.

Of the four ships concerned, three were beginning their fifth voyage in 1879, and one, *Bengloe*, began her maiden voyage. Thus one would expect her profit record to be substantially better than that of *Benarty*, an expectation which is confirmed.(30) Some of the outstanding points of comparison are tabulated below. The period involved is the ten years 1879 to 1888.

TABLE 3

| | Sailing Ships | | Steamships | |
	Benan	*Bencleuch*	*Benarty*	*Bengloe*
Gross tonnage	1,416	1,418	1,724	1,854
First cost in £s	23,923	24,800	32,000	33,120
No. of voyages	11	10	15	16
Total operating costs in £s	43,939	43,896	156,309	173,755
Total revenue in £s	61,684	59,926	196,712	223,173
Total gross profit in £s	17,745	16,030	40,403	49,418
Operating costs as % of revenue	71	73	79	79

This table illustrates that the capital costs of the ships were of similar orders of magnitude. Indeed, the difference between a steamer and an iron sailing ship was less than that between an iron ship and a small wooden one. The current accounts were, however, vastly different, even allowing for the greater number of voyages which the steamers were able to log and despite the fact that the distance covered on each steamer voyage was generally much greater than for the sailing ship. Although both steamers easily recouped their first cost in ten years' trading, neither sailing ship was able to do so. Against this, however, must be set the fact that the steamer's margin of revenue over operating costs was smaller, and to the operating costs would have to be added the higher administrative and office charges ashore involved in the operation of powered vessels on longer and more complex voyages.

The difference between a profit and a loss was therefore smaller, and the magnitude of cash flows was very much greater in steamship operation. Indeed, in three of the steamship voyages included in this analysis, actual losses were recorded, while no sailing ship voyage resulted in a loss. Thus, while it is clear that more working capital and, possibly, greater reserves would have to be maintained to work steamers, there is no way of telling how important a factor this might have been in the managers' calculations. Although profits, expressed in both absolute terms and as a proportion of fixed capital, were greater in the case of the steamships, the smaller margin between working costs and revenue made the steamer an inherently more risky enterprise in the short run. This characteristic necessitated more sophisticated business judgements than had hitherto been required, a greater risk element was present, and much larger sums of money were involved. These factors may have accounted for the firm's unwillingness to acquire steamships more quickly.

*　　　*　　　*

The history of William Thomson and Company is the history of a group of men bound closely by family ties and commercial interest. This investigation of some of their decisions suggests that these men were disposed towards careful thought and studied action. In the course of their deliberations they did not always take the course that hindsight suggests they should have done. They acted with caution, and always ensured that they were in firm control of their undertakings.

Any attempt to analyse the motives of business men based solely on their company accounts and the visible results of their decisions without the supporting evidence of diaries or letters is hazardous. The results cannot be more than hypotheses to be tested by other studies. It is hoped that these will be forthcoming, but even in their absence the Ben Line's history is particularly interesting for the continuity that characterises it, and for the way in which a succession of managers, pursuing similar management precepts, have succeeded in developing an important and still-growing shipping company by reliance on internal resources.

NOTES

(1) I am deeply indebted to Messrs. William Thomson and Company of Edinburgh for placing the Ben Line papers at my disposal and for amplifying and commenting on the information contained therein. The interpretation of the facts and the conclusions drawn therefrom are, unless otherwise stated, entirely my own. In addition, I am most grateful to Dr. P. L. Payne for his careful reading of so many manuscripts and his many helpful suggestions.

(2) For the history of the company from its origins until 1955 see George Blake, The Ben Line, The History of a Merchant Fleet, 1825-1955 (London, 1956). The description of the company's development which forms the first part of this paper is based on this study. Since this description was written the legal form of the enterprise has been changed and the partnership wound up. This change is only significant for taxation purposes.

(3) The system of ship ownership adopted by the Thomsons was typical of much ship ownership of the time. Each vessel was divided into sixty-four shares which were held by a number of individuals a group of whom (in this case William Thomson and Co.) were managers of the ship. Each ship and each voyage were kept quite separate for accounting and legal purposes. The shareholders differed for each ship and occasionally changed between voyages. For an account of the evolution of this system of ship owning and management see Ralph Davis, The Rise of the English Shipping Industry (London, 1962), pp. 81-109.

(4) George Blake, *op. cit.*, p. 6.

(5) *Ibid.*, p. 6. The 'New Town' in Edinburgh was created broadly in the first forty years of the nineteenth century. The domestic architecture includes some of the finest in Europe, and almost a complete new town was built, a short distance from the ancient, crowded city, to house the newly affluent commercial and financial classes. Marble was widely used for decorative work in these homes.

(6) *Ibid.*, pp. 6 and 7. See also Dorothy Laird, Paddy Henderson (Glasgow, 1961), pp. 16 and 17. The Hendersons and Thomsons were connected by the marriage of Jemima, sister of Alexander and William to the oldest Henderson brother, Thomas, in 1833. Both Thomas Henderson and Alexander Thomson were engaged in business, including the marble business, in Leghorn. The companies were closely bound both in business and through the family ties. Like the Thomsons, Patrick Henderson's early ventures to the Mediterranean were by means of small sailing ships.

(7) The first Henderson ship was the brig *Tom and Jessie*, acquired in 1829 by George Henderson, the second brother, who had 48/64th shares while the remaining 16/64ths shares were held, till 1838, by Alexander Thomson. It is a matter for speculation whether there is any connection between Alexander Thomson's withdrawal from the Henderson enterprise, and the purchase of *Carrara* by the Thomson brothers in 1839.

(8) The Thomsons of Alloa, who were mine-owners, supplied the coal for the outward cargoes in William and Alexander's ships, as well as taking shares in the vessels.

(9) The history of P. Henderson and Co. makes an interesting comparison. In their case, such ventures became a mainstay of their trade for many years, in particular, the New Zealand emigrant trade. It is hard to explain why such firms as these were prepared to embrace one trade but let another, apparently equally as profitable, lapse after a few voyages.

(10) F. E. Hyde, Blue Funnel, A History of Alfred Holt and Company of Liverpool from 1865 to 1914 (Liverpool, 1956), p. 18.

(11) This point is amply illustrated from the Ben Line voyage accounts where it is apparent that while a sailing ship, with its greater economies of operation, almost invariably showed a small operating gain, sometimes after a protracted voyage, the figures on both the expenditure and income side of a steamship's account were always very much larger, with the result that there could be a very substantial profits as well as occasional losses on a voyage. See also below, Section 4.

(12) An analysis of steam and sailing ship accounts, derived from the voyage accounts, is contained in Section 4 of this paper. It should be borne in mind that William Thomson had operated sailing ships successfully on the North Atlantic trade long after steamers had successfully established themselves.

(13) F. E. Hyde, *op. cit.*, p. 34.

(14) See note 3 above.

(15) The following table, showing the fleet strength at ten-year intervals, illustrates the overall growth in numbers and tonnage.

| Date | Sailing Vessels | | Steamers | |
	Number	Total gross tonnage	Number	Total gross tonnage
January 1st				
1830	2	606	—	—
1840	5	2,493	—	—
1850	8	4,961	—	—
1870	11	9,037	—	—
1880	10	9,479	4	7,189
1890	2	2,381	7	15,748
1900	—	—	9	24,271
1910	—	—	12	43,049
1920	—	—	13	57,535
1940	—	—	20	110,319
1950	—	—	21	123,767
1960	—	—	22	159,575

(16) The change in organisation probably involved little change in the method of financing inasmuch as finance was always found from within the company's own resources. See note 24.

(17) These themes have been chosen because they cover aspects of shipping history which have been somewhat neglected, particularly the questions of timing and size of additions to the fleet. They also illustrate the analyses which may be conducted using such data as are provided in a ship's voyage accounts, and they provide an opportunity to try to assess the reactions of the company's managers when faced with some of the specific commercial issues which have been suggested in the foregoing survey.

The voyage accounts themselves consist of a number of volumes, each ship having a separate account, in which each voyage is treated as a separate entity. For each voyage all items of expenditure directly related to the ship are listed and, apart from some early ships, income from freight or passengers follows. The difference of these two leaves a net gain (or loss) on voyage which is then distributed to the shareholders with a small sum (or the loss) carried forward to the next voyage. The source for all the succeeding analysis in this paper is these voyage accounts unless otherwise acknowledged, and no further reference will be made to them as a source. The accounts, which are the property of the Ben Line Steamers Ltd., of Edinburgh, are at present on loan to the Department of Economic History of the University of Glasgow. An analysis of these accounts forms the subject of the author's B.Litt. thesis, University of Glasgow, 1965.

(18) The following fleet strengths, extracted from Lloyd's Register of Shipping for 1886, show the relative position at that date of some of the major competitors.

Company or Line	No. of vessels	Total gross tonnage
Blue Funnel Line	31	55,886
P. and O.	42	152,588
Castle Line	13	29,713
Glen Line	13	34,166
Messageries Maritimes	34	85,450
The Ben Line	6	11,738

(19) F. E. Hyde, *op. cit.*, p. 35.

(20) See Chart 2, p. 355.

(21) F. E. Hyde, *British Shipping Companies in East and South East Asia, 1860-1939*, a paper delivered in 1960 at the School of Oriental and African Studies, London University, to the Study Group on the Economic History of East and South-east Asia.

(22) A possible exception was the P. and O. Company, which had the advantage of a mail contract.

(23) The ideas put forward in this section and section 4 are intended to be tentative, for they are based on the records of only one firm, and should be regarded as hypotheses to be confirmed or denied by results which would have to be obtained from a large number of companies.

(24) In conversation with the author, a present partner in the company confirms that the investment policy has been to order a new vessel when there

are sufficient reserves to pay for her, rather than to anticipate an increase in trade and then borrow money to finance a new ship.

(25) The factor of service speed was always increasing, but in the absence of log books, trial records, or dates of actual port to port passages, it is difficult to ascertain the speeds of ships with any precision. Even when the mechanical data and dimensions of the ships are known (as they are in the case of the Ben Line vessels) unless the fineness of line is known at least, it is impossible to calculate the theoretical service speed. The following Ben Line speeds have in fact been calculated from adequate data and builders' records.

Vessel	Date	Service speed (knots)
Benledi	1871	$9\frac{1}{4}$
Benlawers	1887	$10\frac{1}{2}$
Bencleuch	1900	$9\frac{1}{2}$
Benlomond	1911	11
Benreoch	1921	$12\frac{1}{2}$
Benmacdhui	1948	$15\frac{3}{4}$

(For the analysis of the Ben Line fleet from which these figures are taken, see J. M. Murray, M.B.E., *Merchant Ships, 1860 to 1960* in Papers Presented at the Centenary Meeting of the Royal Institution of Naval Architects, 17th May, 1960.)

The list makes it clear that while progress in speed was not constant, speeds do appear to have increased from the order of $9\frac{1}{2}$ knots in the early 1870's to around 11 knots just before the First World War. In order to arrive at an index of the fleet carrying capacity, therefore, each vessel has been assigned an index number which has been determined by its gross tonnage multiplied by its estimated speed. This estimate has been arbitrarily chosen on a hypothetical assumption that the increment in speed between each vessel is constant from *Benledi*, $9\frac{1}{2}$ knots, to *Benlomond*, 11 knots. *Benlawers* and *Bencleuch*, are, of course, entered at their correct calculated speeds. The basis for such speed allowances is that they accord with the records of other lines and with the general Ben Line policy of fleet improvement. Furthermore, according to Murray, on known Ben Line data, speed was roughly proportional to the square root of the length of ships prior to the First World War, and length increased steadily.

(26) In a note to the author the present chairman has explained that the amount of capital available for reinvestment in shipping was influenced by a general family rule that about 50 per cent of all income should be invested and of the available sum 40 per cent should go into gilt-edged, 20 per cent into general investments, and 20 per cent into ships.

(27) See Chart 2.

(28) A former partner of the firm, Mr. H. M. Thomson, has explained to the author, 'It was recognised and later regretted that for many years every new "Ben" steamer ordered was on the small side and should have been 1,000 tons or so larger. This again, however, was mostly due to the difficulty over finance. As the size of ships was increasing slowly but constantly, the Ben Line vessels became uneconomic on account of size while they were still efficient in every other way and while a number of them were still under twenty years old.'

(29) The number of ocean-going square-rigged ships built in the United Kingdom in the years immediately before and after the opening of the Suez Canal was as follows: 1868, 138; 1869, 132; 1870, 51; 1871, 10; 1872, 14; 1873, 37; 1874, 109; 1875, 198; 1876, 119.

(30) Newer ships tended to earn higher profits. See above, p. 353.

CHAPTER FOURTEEN

Scottish Investment and Enterprise in Texas

W. G. KERR

*Lecturer, Department of Modern History,
St. Salvator's College, University of St. Andrews*

THE PRAIRIE CATTLE COMPANY LIMITED was the first large-scale joint-stock venture by British capital in cattle ranching in Texas. Edinburgh-based, it was founded in 1880. Two years after it began operations it paid a dividend of $19\frac{1}{2}$ per cent, followed by a payment to shareholders of almost 28 per cent in 1883.(1) The Prairie experience set off the Scottish-American cattle craze.

Since the Prairie was an Edinburgh company, American ranching ventures particularly captivated the Scotch investor. The Scottish connection with Texas ranching is well known.(2) Edinburgh and Dundee men were clamouring to form ranching syndicates. These two cities—Glasgow was never an organising centre for this business—accounted for eight out of the eleven British joint-stock ranching ventures organised between 1880 and 1885 for business in the Lone Star State. Among them were such legendary names as the Prairie, the Matador Land and Cattle Co. Ltd., the Texas Land and Cattle Co. Ltd., the Hansford Land and Cattle Co. Ltd., Western Ranches Ltd., and the Cresswell Ranche and Cattle Co. Ltd.(3) Dundee accounted for a disproportionately large percentage of Scottish investment in Texas ranching, having set up the Matador, and the Texas Land and Cattle and the Hansford Land and Cattle. The period 1882-84 was the high water mark.(4) Even those companies organised from London possessed substantial elements of Scottish organisation and capital. The Cattle Ranch and Land Co. Ltd. exemplifies this. It was a Scot, Lord George Campbell, who put the syndicate to the London market.(5)

London eventually caught the American ranch-craze infection, but never quite came down with the disease. Scotland did, Dundee in particular. Though Edinburgh-based, much of the capital for the Prairie was from Dundee. The reverse is not true for the

Dundee-organised ranches. They were largely locally financed. A rundown of the shareholders of the Prairie Cattle Co., at the inception of the company in May, 1881, shows the Dundee influence to have been so strong that there appears to have been a need for a two-city board. Out of a total of 12,500 shares issued and held by 104 owners, Dundee and environs controlled no less than 4,200 shares. These were in the hands of thirty-two shareholders. Dundee, therefore, controlled about one-third of the outstanding equity capital and of the remainder there were large holdings in the States. American holdings in this first issue of equity amounted to 2,500 shares, some of which were in the hands of Scots, trans-Atlantically removed. The Matador shareholder list for April, 1883, reveals that less than 10 per cent of the outstanding shares were held outside the Dundee region.(6) And it must be remembered that, although the Prairie was of Edinburgh, its first chairman was the Earl of Airlie,(7) whose roots, particularly in business, were in the Dundee area. William Lowson, a Dundee manufacturer and a director of the Scottish American Mortgage Co. Ltd., was also on the board.(8) These men held 500 and 400 shares in the Prairie respectively. Other Dundonians with large holdings in the Prairie at its inception were: Peter Moir Cochrane, merchant, 200 shares; Thomas Collier, merchant, 150; Thomas Hunter Cox, jute manufacturer, 200; other members of the Lowson family, 300 shares; the Gourlays, Alexander, Gershom and Henry, major Dundee engineers and shipbuilders, 250; James Stewart and Robert Grimman Kennedy, 200; William Mackenzie, company secretary, 200; Alexander Hay Moncur, manufacturer, and one of the organisers of the Texas Land and Cattle Co., 200; Alexander Henderson, another Texas Land and Cattle organiser, 100; Alexander Emslie, merchant, 150, and John Ogilvy, Kirriemuir manufacturer, and later a director of the Alliance Trust Company Limited,(9) 200 shares. Dundee's hold on the Prairie is therefore quite apparent, despite its Edinburgh foundations.(10)

The large returns yielded by the Prairie stimulated the organisation of other cattle and ranching enterprises.(11) In addition to the Matador, Texas and Hansford,(12) all organised in Dundee, largely because of the rousingly fat dividend reports of the Prairie, the Dundee investors had considerable holdings in the Arkansas Valley Land and Cattle Co. Ltd. and the Powder River Cattle Co.,(13) and minor interests in virtually every other cattle company organised in Britain during this heyday of American ranching ventures. These included, by the end of 1882, Texan and non-Texan ranches. Among them were the Missouri Land and Live Stock Co. Ltd., Cattle Ranche and Land Co. Ltd., Western Land and Cattle Co. Ltd.,

Maxwell Cattle Co., Western American Cattle Co. Ltd., and the United States Cattle Ranche Co. Ltd.(14) The list fails to indicate all the companies offered in Dundee, so numerous were the promoters 'with Ranches in their pockets' inundating the city.(15) Underwood, Clark & Co., largely in the person of Frank L. Underwood, who promoted the Prairie,(16) was successful in launching similar ranching ventures in Dundee. The Texas Land and Cattle and the Hansford, organised during 1881-82, were the result of his efforts.(17) Few American ranching promoters had the success of the firm of Underwood, Clark & Co. in inducing Scottish capital into Texas or western ranching. It was Alfred M. Britton of Fort Worth, Texas, who sold the Matador to Dundee interests for £250,000.(18) Both the Matador and the Hansford came into Dundee hands in 1882, somewhat later than the Texas Land and Cattle, whose articles of association were filed in December, 1881.(19)

The case for Dundee in the American cattle business does not obscure the powerful Edinburgh interests. Dundee had not cornered the market by any means, but *per capita*, its investment was probably heavier than Edinburgh's.(20) The Prairie was, after all, an Edinburgh combine, as were the Espuela and the Arkansas Valley, the Western Ranches Ltd., and such outfits as the Powder River, Missouri Land and Live Stock Co., Swan Land and Cattle Co. Ltd., and the Wyoming Cattle Ranche Co. Ltd.

Some of the soundest and most conservative names in Scottish business circles were caught up in the mania for American ranching. Robert Fleming, frequently referred to as the father of the investment trust movement, played a very active rôle in setting up the Matador, as well as being a substantial shareholder.(21) While not one of the original shareholders of the Prairie, Fleming did take a small stake in the first offering of Texas Land and Cattle.(22) The list of conservative business leaders who took the plunge into ranching shares would be too lengthy to enumerate, but a cursory glance reveals in addition to those already mentioned such names as Archibald Coats, of J. and P. Coats, Paisley, thread manufacturers; William Mackenzie, secretary of the Dundee Mortgage and Trust Investment Co. Ltd., and the Dundee Investment Co. Ltd.; William John Menzies, Writer to the Signet, Edinburgh, founder member of the Scottish American Investment Co. Ltd. All these were among the original shareholders of the Prairie.(23) In April, 1883, Matador shareholders included such figures as G. W. Boase, banker; George and David Carmichael, engineers, Dundee; William Ogilvy Dalgleish, Dundee; the Earl of Dalhousie; James Guthrie, banker, Brechin, later longtime Chairman of the Alliance Trust Co. Ltd.;

John M. Keiller, Dundee, confectionary manufacturer; John Leng, later an M.P., publisher of *The Dundee Advertiser*; William Mackenzie; James Pattullo, leading Dundee solicitor; John Sharp, spinner, Dundee, later also a chairman of the Alliance Trust.(24) Among the Texas Land and Cattle shareholders were G. W. Boase; George Carmichael; Joseph, Alexander, Dick and George Washington Grimmond, merchants and manufacturers, Dundee; David Grimond, flaxspinner, Blairgowrie; William Mackenzie, Dundee; James Pattullo; John Souter Baxter, jute spinner and manufacturer, Dundee; J. M. Keiller; John Leadbetter, merchant, Dundee.(25) This list is not meant to be comprehensive, and where names are repetitive, they are included only to show that with many of these business leaders, their holdings were not limited to one particular ranching venture. Multiple holdings were very common. The sample, largely based on Dundee, would bear a similar test put to places like Edinburgh. Men of considerable substance, like W. J. Menzies, Sir George Warrender, Thomas Nelson, R. Bruce Johnston, W.S., Duncan Smith, S.S.C., John Guthrie Smith, Sheriff of Aberdeen and Kincardineshire, Alexander Thomson, timber merchant, and a host of others were not just shareholders in ranching enterprises, but the leaders in the organisation of these syndicates.

In Edinburgh it was the mortgage and investment trust world which was largely responsible for establishing the ranching craze. The Scottish American Mortgage Co., was responsible for setting up the Prairie through two of its directors;(26) John Guthrie Smith, Scottish American Mortgage chairman, who succeeded to the chairmanship of the Prairie, following the death of the Earl of Airlie in September, 1881,(27) and J. Duncan Smith, Scottish American Mortgage's managing director. Duncan Smith established the initial contacts with Underwood, Clark, first for loans on mortgages, and later for the acquisition of the properties which formed the Edinburgh-Dundee Prairie syndicate.

The Scottish American Investment Co. Ltd., was also a power in ranching syndications, though its ranching promotions came somewhat later than that of its neighbour the Scottish American Mortgage Co. These two groups, with the Scottish American Investment under the control of W. J. Menzies, W.S., Sir George Warrender, Thomas Nelson, the publisher, and Edward Blyth, were the two most powerful 'money cliques' in Edinburgh.(28) Between them they sponsored many a North American investment, from coppermining syndicates to lumbering and ranching.

The cattle-ranching craze was short-lived and many companies came to grief between 1886 and 1887. There were notable exceptions, like the Matador and, to a lesser degree, the Prairie and the privately-owned JA Ranch, and, outside Texas, outfits like Western Ranches. But even these experienced hard times in the late 1880's and the 1890's. Before the crash, editorials in Dundee had warned of the pitfalls of putting too many eggs in one basket, while shortly afterwards *The Economist* editionalised on the shortcomings of ranching investment. Forty years later John Clay cogently set forth some of the other reasons for failure which had not been apparent to contemporary critics.(29)

The concentration of Dundee money in proliferating ranching promotions led to words of caution by the *Dundee Advertiser* early in 1882, virtually four years before this 'minor South Sea Bubble' burst.(30) The argument ran that in view of the remarkable success of a few companies 'in the early days of their career', it would not be wise to infer that those that followed would be 'equally successful'. As in all businesses, the early entries generally made the most profit, the writer felt, and where ranches had been judiciously purchased, and soundly managed, he did not doubt that future profits might be forthcoming. But, he warned, 'the Cattle Companies have had only a limited experience'. Even if there were a likelihood of success for all the syndicates yet planned, it seemed 'objection-able' that so many Dundee investors should tie up 'so rapidly' and 'so extensively' such an incredible amount of capital in new and really unproven ventures. Cattle company promoters spoke of this investment field, with good cause, as their 'happy hunting ground'. The distress signals were that these ventures were becoming specula-tions not just for the rich but for the ordinary investor.(31) In most instances cattle company shares were for £10 or £5, with from 10 per cent to 50 per cent called up, though in some instances, like the Cattle Ranch and Land Co., Western Ranches or the Hansford, the shares were fully paid.(32) In the early years, companies whose shares were not fully paid were in the great majority. This left the small investor in a difficult position if the companies were to call up the unpaid capital. This they were to learn by painful experience. The bounding enthusiasm of these early days tended to make the in-vestor oblivious of the fact that their uncalled share commitments might one day be in excess of their financial capabilities. In the late 1880's, this often happened.(33) 'The amount of money already called, and which has yet to be called on Companies recently con-stituted is so large that the possibility of raising it in Dundee would have been questioned not many years ago', commented one invest-ment critic in 1882.(34) His voice went unheard among Dundee in-vestors. His murmurings were drowned by the jubilant clatterings resounding from the trans-Atlantic cable, reporting bigger and better profits in American ranching. Further warnings against further speculation proved futile. These simply provoked 'wet blanket' reactions. *The Economist* commented in 1883 that most of the cattle companies introduced about that time 'dwelt upon the success of the Prairie Cattle Co. doubtless with the object of conveying the impression that they had but to transplant their shareholders' capital into the wilderness to realise like results.'(35)

While these warnings might have had the effect of limiting the number of companies floated in Dundee—no new ones were put on the market after the Texas Land and Cattle, the Matador, and the Hansford—it did little to stem the flow of new capital into these established ranching ventures. Figures for the twelve major companies at the end of 1882, based on a compilation made by the *Dundee Advertiser*, showed a total capital invested of £2,166,000.(36) The list is largely concerned with those companies in which Dundonians had invested heavily. Three years later a similar calculation for eleven companies,(37) the shares of which were heavily held in Dundee, showed the investment to have nearly doubled to £3,947,089.

This heavy influx of Scottish capital into ranching served to depress markets in some of the shares of well-established companies. These shares were often depreciated by the sales necessary to meet purchases of and, later, calls on partly-paid up shares in the cattle companies, not by any inherent loss in the investment calibre of the older investments.(38) This shift in capital investment indicates that the liquid position of many investors was under stress, a stress which was to increase in the late 1880's when the cattle companies, hard pressed after the bottom had fallen out of Western ranching, were to call up much unpaid capital.

While no new ranching ventures were set up in Dundee after the early months of 1883, such companies continued to be launched in Edinburgh and London until the mid-1880's. In fact, some of the largest ranching enterprises made their debut during 1883-85.(39) These three years were really the heyday of the cattle company craze. Although early in 1883 *The Economist* took comfort in the fact that 'had the Prairie Cattle Co. been a London instead of an Edinburgh concern, we should have had the nucleus of the speculation here', London was not immune to the contagion.(40) It spread south, largely with Scottish help, where some very large syndicates were floated.

Much of the dealing in cattle company shares was handled through the local stock market. Where organised north of the Tay, the organisers did not rush off to seek a quotation or a placing on the London market. In Dundee, the firm of Messrs. Andrew Ogilvie & Co. were active traders in this specialised market, while in Edinburgh it was brokers like Lawrie and Ker, who set the pace in dealing in these shares, as well as in those shares of other locally dominated and organised companies.(41)

The Dundee market was reasonably sophisticated by the 1880's. It was during the preceding thirty years, with the liberalisation of company law, that Dundee saw the beginnings of a market in largely locally controlled joint-stock companies,(42) mainly concerned with railways, banking, water, gas and shipping. The banks merged in the 1860's, the Eastern Bank with the Clydesdale in 1863, and the Dundee Bank with the Royal Bank of Scotland in 1864.(43) The capital involved was comparatively small. With the exception of two small gas companies in the vicinity of Newport and Carnoustie, the gas and water companies disappeared from the local list when they were taken over by the town of Dundee. By the 1880's, ten publicly-held shipping companies had a paid-up capital of £670,657, most of the shares being fully paid.(44) The Northern Marine was a local insurance company with a paid-up capital of £25,000, while there were substantial local holdings in the Northern Assurance, the Queen, the Royal, and others, which were estimated at £100,000.(45) All this investment was to look small after the surge of joint-stock company offerings of the decade beginning in the early 1870's.

The activities of Andrew Ogilvie, founder of the Dundee Stock Exchange,(46) exemplify this broadening of the equity market. He was an active participant in promoting the ranching boom in his native city. Until his death in 1898, Ogilvie was for more than fifty years a stockbroker in Dundee.(47) Born in 1814, he attended Glasgow and St. Andrews Universities, later studying law in the offices of his father, a prominent Dundee solicitor. Not being strongly attracted to the law, Ogilvie spent some time in the flax trade before entering the stockbroking business about 1850. The step from the law to stockbroking was not unusual in Scotland, where solicitors were actively engaged in advising clients on their finances and investments.(48) With the advent of mushrooming joint-stock ventures after the mid-nineteenth century, the opportunities were widely extended for public ownership and solicitors tended to devote more of their time to investment counselling. From there it was but a short step to stockbroking. Many a solicitor of this period, in London and in Scotland, was, but for the name, really an investment adviser, virtually a stockbroker. Two striking

Edinburgh examples at that time were the law firms of Graham, Johnston and Fleming,(49) Writers to the Signet, and Fraser, Stodart and Ballingall.(50) Partners in both these firms played a large part not only in the cattle companies but in the organisation of many joint-stock ventures geared towards North America. In Dundee a similar position was occupied by the legal firm of Pattullo and Thornton.(51) The Wyoming Cattle Ranche was organised in the offices of Graham, Johnston and Fleming in 1882. The prospectus for the Wyoming Ranche was issued by the same firm,(52) and one of its partners, R. Bruce Johnston, served on the original board of the ranching syndicate.(53) Fraser, Stodart and Ballingall were intimately connected with the organisation of the Swan Land and Cattle Co. Ltd.(54) Guthrie Smith and Duncan Smith, key directors of the Prairie, who served it as chairman and managing director, respectively, were lawyers.(55)

The legal profession in nineteenth-century Scotland was marked for the diversity of its operations. It developed great expertise in the field of investment. Scotch solicitors played a dominant rôle in launching the mortgage company and investment trust movement of Old Caledonia. Their English counterparts never became so thoroughly enmeshed in things financial. The Scottish-owned cattle companies of the 1880's in Texas and the American West were an outgrowth of those mortgage and investment trusts, which in large measure were organised by financial solicitors in Edinburgh and Dundee during the 1870's. This was a decade before the western cattle craze. In Edinburgh the field was led by companies like the Scottish American Investment Co. Ltd., founded in 1873, and the Scottish American Mortgage Co. Ltd., 1874, and on the banks of the Tay by the group of Dundee land and mortgage companies which were to amalgamate in the late 1880's to form the Alliance Trust Co. Ltd., and Robert Fleming's Scottish American Investment Trusts.(56) Mortgage companies and investment trusts in both these cities directed their activities towards the United States. Glasgow, a late comer to the field of mortgage and investment trusts, never took a really active part in the mania for American ranching properties.(57)

Scotland's passion for American ranching was not merely a question of Old Caledonia having the money and the "savvy" when it came to animal husbandry. Aberdeen possessed both these prerequisites. It was a question also of knowing the Trans-Mississippi West. In this Aberdeen was outdistanced by Edinburgh and Dundee, more so through their mortgage companies than through their investment trusts. North American-geared investment trust portfolios largely featured American railway bonds and government securities. Their transactions were mainly limited to New York and frequently they dealt in American securities through the London market. More often than not, their investment intelligence went no farther west than the American Northeast, only vicariously touching the Trans-Mississippi West. On the other hand, British mortgage companies, particularly those in Edinburgh and Dundee, were, by the late 1870's and the opening of the 1880's, funnelling most of their funds into western farm mortgages. They were on top of the developing ranching scene. It is hardly surprising, therefore, that they were so much a part of the ranching craze. Companies such as the Scottish American Mortgage and the Dundee mortgage companies had the best investment intelligence in Britain concerning the Trans-Mississippi West.

Aberdeen, like Glasgow, was not an entrepôt for western American ranching ventures. Indirectly the Granite City did in one instance enter the ranching field through its substantial financial backing of the Texas Land and Mortgage Co. (T.L. & M.). Though London-based, T.L. & M. was supported very largely by Scottish capital, most of which was from Aberdeenshire.(58) In the first few years following its organisation in 1882, T.L. & M. loaned considerable funds to Texas ranchers, and continued doing so in the case of the famed JA Ranch in the Texas Panhandle. T.L. & M.'s directors were predominantly Scottish and, as with many sister companies, they were mainly solicitors. In placing investment funds, Aberdeen's mortgage and trust investment companies were not similarly situated to those of Dundee and Edinburgh. Aberdeen played a leading rôle in the mortgage and investment trust movement, but where its interests were in North America, they were directed more toward Canada into companies like the North of Scotland Canadian Mortgage Co. Ltd. For this reason, the Granite City was not a major centre in spawning the numerous ranching schemes in the American West entered into by Scotch syndicates during the first half of the 1880's.

T.L. & M., which relied heavily on Aberdeen for its financial backing, found only one of its founder directors therein, J. Badenach-Nicolson. He was one of the promoters and directors of the North of Scotland Canadian Mortgage Company, which like many Scottish mortgage and trust companies, was founded in the 1870's. Texas Land and Mortgage's importance to the ranching movement in Texas lies only partly in the fact that it was the company which heavily backed the Anglo-American partnership of John Adair and the legendary cowman Charles Goodnight, in the famed JA Ranch. At one time the company had as much as £60,000 loaned to the JA.(59) Founded during the ranching craze in the winter of 1882, T.L. & M. also played a leading rôle in the Lone Star State by making loans to ranchers, among whom were the well-known Jot Gunter and J. S. Ikard(60) (the latter is often credited with introducing Hereford cattle to the state),(61) as well as to farmers and developers of urban and semi-urban property.(62)

Solicitors north of the Tweed also played a key rôle in T.L. & M. In addition to J. Badenach-Nicolson, two Midlothian solicitors, both directors of the Company, were instrumental in its success. These were R. Bruce Johnston, and A. D. M. Black, both Writers to the Signet in Edinburgh.(63) Johnston was an intimate of the Scottish American Investment Company's triumvirate of Menzies, Nelson and Warrender. He served as director of two promotions which had their strong backing: the Wyoming Cattle Ranche Co. Ltd. and the California Redwood Co. Ltd. In fact, it was Johnston's law firm, Graham, Johnston and Fleming, which served as secretaries to the Wyoming Cattle syndicate.(64) Johnston was also one of the organisers and a director of the Quebec Timber Co. Ltd.(65) He and his firm were a considerable promotional force north of the Tweed.(66) A. D. M. Black, partner in Mackenzie and Black, W.S., Edinburgh, was a director of the London and Canadian Loan and Agency Co. Ltd., Scottish board; Northern Investment Co. of New Zealand Ltd. and the Scottish Union and National Insurance Co. Ltd.(67) Both men, Johnston and Black, served as principal debenture agents for T.L. & M. in the Edinburgh area. Indeed, many Scottish lawyers played an active rôle in placing the debentures of similar companies and backed innumerable other Scottish financial ventures during this period.(68)

The lion's share of the credit for setting up T.L. & M. belonged to Arthur H. and Alfred G. Renshaw, financial solicitors, London.(69) They played the dynamic rôle in the launching and development of the T.L. & M., particularly Arthur, who virtually ran its operations and directed its fund raising. The Renshaws do not technically qualify as being Scottish. They were not born in Scotland. However, it was in Scotland that they made their headquarters and it was there that they made their money. Renfrewshire was the centre of much of the Renshaw family interests. The Renshaws were closely connected with one of the largest carpet manufacturing companies in Britain, A. F. Stoddard & Co. Ltd.(70) Sir Charles Bine Renshaw, elder of the brothers, was chairman and the largest stockholder in the company, while Arthur Renshaw served as vice-chairman. Arthur Renshaw at one time lived in Renfrewshire, and

Sir Charles Bine Renshaw, who owned large estates there, was Convener of the County Council, and for many years was M.P. for West Renfrewshire. He was made a baronet about the turn of the century. The eldest brother, Walter of Sandrocks, Sussex, was a Queen's Counsel.(71)

It was during a visit which Arthur Renshaw made to his friends, John Adair, and his wife, Cornelia, that he conceived the idea of starting T.L. & M. Adair and his partner in the JA Ranch, Charles Goodnight, sparked Renshaw's imagination with talk of the economic opportunities for investment in Texas cattle, land and mortgages, and he returned to London fired with the idea of launching the T.L. & M. There is little doubt that the Adairs influenced Renshaw personally, and Goodnight's commanding knowledge of the area and its opportunities clinched his decision.

The Renshaws were not new to overseas investment. Arthur's brother, Alfred George, an Oxonian with a keen interest in poetry(72) was also a director of J. W. Barclay's Colorado Mortgage and Investment Co. of London Ltd., and the Cape Stock Farming Co. Ltd.(73) Mexico, too, came under the Renshaw passion for diversified investment. In February, 1883, A. G. Renshaw wrote a letter from Mexico City to *The Economist*, which dwelt on the great future ahead for Mexico, and attempted to dispel the idea of excessive brigandage there as being 'exaggerated'. This was not Renshaw's first visit to Mexico. He had been there as early as 1876. He felt that much of Mexico's potential lay in the fact that railroads were opening the country to foreign markets. Alfred Renshaw served on the Committee of the Mexican National Railway along with Robert Fleming, the Scottish investment trust leader and promoter of American railway bond sales in Britain.(74)

As financial solicitors, Arthur and Alfred Renshaw, had splendid connections for floating T.L. & M. Among his wide and influential circle of friends, acquaintances, business associates and clients, Arthur Renshaw numbered people like Frederick Nettlefold, and Herbert Kitchener, later Lord Kitchener. He was not only Kitchener's solicitor and financial adviser, but an intimate friend. Kitchener was a shareholder in T.L. & M. and for a time sought a directorship in the Company.(75)

It was almost entirely at Arthur Renshaw's instigation that T.L. & M. was hurriedly organised in late October, 1882, to take advantage of the expanding ranching, farming and property boom in the Lone Star State. Aberdeen's financial backing of the company was striking. In the first offer of shares, 11,538 were allotted to eighty-four individuals, sixty-seven of whom were from Scotland

and no fewer than two-thirds of these were from Aberdeenshire. Seventy-four per cent, or 8,544 of these shares, were in Scottish hands.(76) James Meston & Co. of Aberdeen was responsible for much of the share placing of T.L. & M. north of the Tay, as well as for the company's success in placing its debentures.(77) James Meston, later Lord Meston, and a T.L. & M. director, though a cautious Aberdeen chartered accountant, had his dabble, like many others, in some of the less conservative Scotch speculations of the day. He held some Prairie Cattle shares and a sizeable holding of 700 shares in the volatile Arizona Copper Co. Ltd.(78)

While James W. Barclay's Colorado Mortgage and Investment Co. of London does not figure geographically as an integral part of this study, Barclay frequently figures in these events. His career illustrates the intimate nature of the Scottish financial community during the last quarter of the nineteenth century, when so many of the overseas pastoral ventures of the time were often directed by a coterie of men whose directorships interlocked. Significantly, Barclay personified the Scotchmen whose business activities oftentimes centred in London, but who raised much of their capital north of the Tweed. Barclay, who was M.P. for Forfar,(79) was a 'wheeler and dealer' in many of the leading overseas promotions of the day. Both Alfred Renshaw and C. Seale-Hayne of T.L. & M. were on the board of his Colorado Mortgage and Investment Co., while J. Badenach-Nicolson, also of T.L. & M., served under Barclay's chairmanship as a director of the North of Scotland Canadian Mortgage Co.(80) Barclay was also the chairman of the boards of the American Pastoral Co. Ltd., Arkansas Valley Land and Cattle Co. Ltd., British and New Zealand Mortgage and Agency Co. Ltd., Colorado Ranch Co. Ltd., Denver Mansions Co. Ltd., and the Platte Land Co. Ltd., and he was a member of the London board of the Hamilton and North Western Railway Co. Ltd.(81) His Colorado ventures caused him to interest the Dundee mortgage companies in first-class mortgages there.(82) An intimate friend of Lord Airlie, founder chairman of the Dundee Mortgage & Trust Investment Co., and of the Prairie Cattle Co., Barclay was with him at the time of his death in September, 1881, at Denver, Colorado.(83)

Though the Scottish mortgage and investment trusts were certainly instrumental in encouraging Scotsmen to participate in the western cattle craze because of their actual or vicarious knowledge of the Trans-Mississippi West, it was this knowledge which led the more experienced Scottish mortgage companies to lighten or liquidate their holdings and mortgages in the ranching boom before it burst soon after the mid-1880's. By the early 1880's the mortgage companies were becoming cautious of ranching loans, and were placing their funds largely in improved farm lands and urban properties. In the early 1880's T.L. & M. was willing to make advances on the security of mortgages on cattle with the collateral security of real estate.(84) They did so only as long as they could foresee the cattle market holding up. This does not mean that all T.L. & M.'s forays into ranching and cattle loans were a success. Most of them were, but some, like their loan to the large Texan syndicate, Curtis and Atkinson,(85) proved otherwise.

T.L. & M.'s directors were well aware of the pitfalls inherent in the nature of the ranching business. The board also realised the necessity of dealing in those things which ranchers could place as security. Early on T.L. & M. anticipated the deteriorating nature of the cattle market and in the autumn of 1884 the company shied away from excessive loans to ranching and cattle men. It diversified its portfolio of mortgages, placing considerable funds into urban North Texas loans, particularly in Dallas, as well as in loans to farmers.(86) Scottish mortgage companies with loans in Texas, like the Scottish American Mortgage, the Dundee Mortgage and Trust Investment Co. Ltd. and the Dundee Investment Co. Ltd., followed similar policies.(87) The latter two companies were one and the same, having virtually the same directors,(88) and the same illustrious secretary, the doyen of Scottish mortgage men, William Mackenzie. Mackenzie, who more than any other man was responsible for amalgamating the Dundee companies into the Alliance Trust Company Limited in November, 1889, was the highly successful architect of the companies' mortgage loaning policy. Mackenzie was the Alliance. In the early days when you cabled the Alliance in Dundee, the cable address was not 'Alliance' but 'Mackenzie'. 'Old Snasher', as he was affectionately known, was a contemporary of Robert Fleming.(89) They knew each other well. Had Mackenzie gone to London in the 1880's, as had Fleming, his mark on the City would have been substantial. Mackenzie chose to base his career on Tayside, but, like Fleming, laced it with frequent trips to the United States.(90) Both men qualified for dual citizenship on this score.(91)

Mackenzie was influential in inducing the Dundee companies to conduct business in Texas loaning in the early 1880's. He set up two agencies in the State, first at San Antonio (in 1882), and later at Fort Worth, and both were run at first by former Dundonians, W. J. Ballantyne Patterson, and William F. Sommerville, respectively.(92) Loans were balanced, and Mackenzie saw to it that despite the urge to rush funds into ranching in these hectic days of the early 1880's, diversification remained the central policy for investment.(93) One might push the Alliance acquaintance with Texas back two years earlier to 1880. It was then that the company, like the Scottish American Mortgage, first used the Kansas City firm of Underwood, Clark and Co. as an agent in placing its loans, some of which were earmarked for Texas.(94)

Scottish American Mortgage was very active in taking up Texan mortgage opportunities, even more so than were Mackenzie's Dundee companies. Diversification was also the mainstay of its investment policy. Following the collapse of the ranching business in the late 1880's, it successfully continued to operate in Texas. Scottish American Mortgage operated five agencies in the State. Geographically, they spanned a very wide area from San Antonio in the south to Paris in the north, and included Waco, Austin and Dallas.(95)

While success marked the rôle of the Scotch mortgage companies in Texas and the West during the fateful days of the late 1880's, little sunshine fell on the American ranching business during these years. Dundee, that citadel of British investment in American ranching, along with Edinburgh, philosophically looked at their cattle investments during the decade 1885-95 (and later for that matter) and spoke of them soberly over their port and nuts. Estimates of British investment in American ranching vary between £6,000,000 and £9,000,000.(96) British mortgage loans in Texas alone probably equalled if not exceeded this amount.(97) But, more strikingly, those Scottish mortgage companies who invested their funds largely in Western American mortgages not only did a significantly important job in bringing much needed capital to a credit-hungry country, but unlike the vast majority of British-American cattle companies, generally protected and enhanced the value of their shareholders' capital. British investment in American ranching was very much a one-sided affair. There is little doubt that it did much for the improvement of American ranching,(98) but the British investor, with few exceptions, reaped little or nothing. The operations of the mortgage companies and the investment trusts, however, proved mutually beneficial on both sides of the Atlantic.(99)

With the joint-stock cattle companies, successes were not the rule but the exception. The Matador had put in a stellar performance by the time it sold out to American interests in 1951.(100) The Prairie, also in Texas, eventually came through, but hardly as well. One of the other 'successes' often cited is Western Ranches.(101) Doubling one's capital, as Western Ranches did between 1883 and 1919, was a shoddy performance when considered in relation to the decline in the buying power of the pound sterling during those years.

Any of the Scottish mortgage or investment trust companies during the same period would have reported such an 'achievement' only with embarrassment. Yet, as one whimsical reporter commented, these companies could take some consolation in the fact that at least they '. . . give employment to many deserving Americans, and supply good beef at the lowest possible prices to the world at large'.(102) In many ways, over the long run, this whimsy largely proved to be true. The British investment in American cattle companies did much to lay the groundwork for the future rationalisation of the western cattle industry, but it proved a piece of involuntary 'philanthropy' on the part of the English and Scottish investor generally.(103) How it must have pained him in later years when he looked back at his mistake of straying from the successful path of the mortgage and investment trusts, in which an original investment of £1,000, in the Scottish American Investment Company Ltd., for example, had appreciated in fifty-seven years to be worth some £70,000.(104) The annual dividend alone had been £3,000. The records of the Alliance Trust, of T.L. & M. and of several other such companies were similarly successful.(105) There were consolations. The Scottish mortgage and investment trust shareholder generally had his cattle company fling too. He had his feet in both worlds. And what's wrong with a bit of 'philanthropy', involuntary as it was, if you were well invested in the Alliance or the Scottish American Investment Co.? It proved of substantial value to an 'emerging' American West.

NOTES

(1) The Economist, Vol. XLI (1883), p. 131; John Clay, My Life on the Range (Chicago, 1924), pp. 129-32.

(2) See the substantial study of British investment in American ranching by W. Turrentine Jackson which appeared in When Grass was King. Prof. Jackson's work appears with two other contributions on the western cattle business by Maurice Frink and Agnes W. Wright in a volume published in 1956 by the University of Colorado Press at Boulder.

(3) J. F. Rippy, *British Investments in Texas Lands and Livestock*, The South-western Historical Quarterly, 58 (1954-55), p. 332; Records of the Companies Office, Edinburgh; Prospectuses of the Stock Exchange, London; L. F. Sheffy, *British Pounds and British Purebreds*, Panhandle-Plains Historical Review, IX (1939), pp. 60-62; Clay, My Life . . ., p. 80.

(4) Stock Exchange Year-Books, 1880-1890, and the volumes of bound Prospectuses at the Stock Exchange, London, covering the same period. See also the Scottish Banking and Insurance Magazine, 1879-1886, and its successor publications, as well as: *Scottish Capital Abroad*, Blackwood's Edin-

burgh Magazine, CXXXVI (1883), p. 479. The Economist, XLI (1883), p. 131, and XLIV (1886), p. 365; L. F. Sheffy, The Life and Times of Timothy Dwight Hobart, 1855-1935 (Canyon, Texas), p. 246; E. E. Dale, The Range Cattle Industry (Norman, Oklahoma, 1960), p. 82; E. S. Osgood, The Day of the Cattleman (Chicago, Phoenix Books, n.d.), p. 365; J. Evetts Haley, The XIT Ranch of Texas and the Early Days of the Llano Estacado (Norman, Oklahoma, 1953) and Charles Goodnight: Cowman and Plainsman (Norman, Oklahoma, 1949); W. M. Pearce, The Matador Land and Cattle Company (Norman, Oklahoma, 1964); R. C. Cotner, James Stephen Hogg: A Biography (Austin, Texas, 1959) and H. T. Burton, A History of the JA Ranch (Austin, Texas, 1927).

(5) Cattle Ranch and Land Co. Ltd., Prospectus, Stock Exchange, London, and Jackson, op. cit., p. 156.

(6) Companies Office, Edinburgh, Prairie Cattle Co. Ltd., File No. 1003.

(7) Companies Office, Edinburgh, Prairie Cattle Co. Ltd., File No. 1003/ 1-2.

(8) Companies Office, Edinburgh, op. cit., File No. 1003.

(9) Directors' Report, The Alliance Trust Co. Ltd., April, 1899.

(10) The largest individual block of shares, 1,000, belonged to Messrs. Underwood, Clark & Co., of Kansas City and Muscatine, Iowa, who were the American promoters of the Prairie syndicate.

(11) Dundee Year Book, 1882, pp. 28-29.

(12) Stock Exchange Year-Book, 1887, pp. 556, 568, 589.

(13) Dundee Year Book, 1886, p. 28.

(14) Study of shareholder lists; Dundee Year Book, 1882, p. 29.

(15) Dundee Year Book, 1882, p. 28.

(16) Clay, My Life . . ., pp. 129-32.

(17) Companies Office, Edinburgh, Articles and Memoranda of Association, Texas Land and Cattle Co. Ltd., and the Hansford Land and Cattle Co. Ltd., Files No. 1075 and 1182.

(18) Companies Office, Edinburgh, Matador Land and Cattle Co. Ltd., File No. 1181.

(19) Companies Office, Edinburgh, op. cit., File No. 1075.

(20) All the Dundee-organised syndicates were in Texas.

(21) Companies Office, Edinburgh, op. cit., File No. 1181/6; Stock Exchange Year Book, 1887, p. 568.

(22) Companies Office, Edinburgh, op. cit., File No. 1075/4.

(23) Companies Office, Edinburgh, op. cit., File No. 1003/4.

(24) Ibid., File No. 1181/6.

(25) Ibid., File No. 1075/4. This sample is from the initial share offering.

(26) Companies Office, Edinburgh, Prairie Cattle Co. Ltd., Articles and Memorandum of Association, File No. 1003/1-2. In addition to John Guthrie Smith and J. Duncan Smith, other Scottish American Mortgage directors on the original Prairie board were William Lowson and Thomas J. Gordon.

(27) Dundee Mortgage and Trust Investment Co. Ltd., Minute Book, IV, p. 172; Stock Exchange Year Book, 1882.

(28) Clay, My Life . . ., pp. 14 and 91.

(29) Dundee Year Book, 1882, pp. 23-29; The Economist, XLI (1883), 131; Clay, My Life . . ., pp. 163, 171, etc.

(30) Dundee Year Book, 1882, p. 28.

(31) Dundee Year Book, 1882, p. 28.

(32) See Dundee Investments, and Public Companies, Dundee Year Books,

1882-1890; Stock Exchange Year Books, 1882-1890; in particular, see Dundee Year Book, 1886, p. 28.

(33) Dundee Year Book, 1890, p. 45; *ibid.*, 1891, p. 55.

(34) Dundee Year Book, 1882, p. 28.

(35) The Economist, XLI (1883), 131.

(36) Dundee Year Book, 1882, p. 29.

(37) Messrs. Andrew Ogilvie & Co., Dundee, published this analysis for the firm's clients in 1885.

(38) Dundee Year Book, 1882, p. 28.

(39) Clay, My Life . . ., pp. 172, 201. In London such companies as the Rocking Chair Ranche (1883), and the Cattle Ranche & Land Co. Ltd. (1883) were floated, while Edinburgh promoted the Swan Land and Cattle Co. Ltd. (1884). For example, the Espuela Land and Cattle Co. Ltd. and the American Pastoral Co. Ltd. appeared in 1884, and the Cedar Valley Land and Cattle Co., Capitol Freehold Land and Investment Co. Ltd., and the Cresswell Ranche and Cattle Co. Ltd., made their debuts in 1885.

(40) The Economist, XLI (1883), 131.

(41) Examination of minute books and dealing lists of the Dundee and Edinburgh Stock Exchanges.

(42) Dundee Year Book, 1882, pp. 23-28.

(43) Dundee Year Book, 1886, pp. 29-30; C. W. Boase, A Century of Banking in Dundee (Edinburgh, 1864); A. W. Kerr, History of Banking in Scotland (London, 1918), pp. 235; W. F. Crick and J. E. Wadsworth, A Hundred Years of Joint Stock Banking (London, 1936), p. 381; William Graham, The One Pound Note in the History of Banking in Great Britain (Edinburgh, 1911), pp. 125, 131-35, 177, 204, 244.

(44) Dundee Year Book, 1882, p. 25.

(45) *Ibid.*, p. 26.

(46) Interview with Thomas McLean, partner, Andrew Ogilvie & Co., stockbrokers, Dundee.

(47) Dundee Year Book, 1898, p. 82.

(48) J. D. Bailey, *Australian Borrowing in Scotland in the Nineteenth Century*, Economic History Review, 2nd ser., Vol. XII (1959-60), p. 268.

(49) Texas Land and Mortgage Co. Ltd., Minute Book, I (11th January, 1884), p. 98; Clay, My Life . . ., p. 158; Directory of Directors, 1885, p. 241.

(50) Scottish American Mortgage Co. Ltd., Minute Books; Clay, My Life . . ., p. 204.

(51) Dundee Mortgage and Trust Investment Co. Ltd. and Dundee Investment Co. Ltd. Minute Books; Dundee Year Books, 1903 and 1904, pp. 57-58 and 44, respectively.

(52) Prospectus, Companies Office, Edinburgh, Wyoming Cattle Ranche Co. Ltd.; Clay, My Life . . ., pp. 158-59.

(53) Interview with A. M. Anderson, partner in Graham, Johnston and Fleming, Edinburgh, July, 1961, and correspondence, Aug., 1961.

(54) Prospectus, Companies Office, Edinburgh, Swan Land and Cattle Co. Ltd.

(55) Directory of Directors, 1885, pp. 406-7; The Scotsman, Edinburgh, 22nd, 24th, 25th June, 1895.

(56) See J. C. Gilbert, A History of Investment Trusts in Dundee, 1873-1938 (London, 1939), and G. Glasgow, Scottish Investment Trust Companies (London, 1932).

(57) James Wright, *Investment Trusts in Great Britain*, Journal of Ac-
CC

countancy, Vol. XXXVIII (New York, 1924), p. 341, and W. T. Jackson, *op. cit.*, p. 156.

(58) See my article, *Scotland and the Texas Mortgage Business*, Economic History Review, 2nd ser., Vol. XVI (1963-64), 94.

(59) Texas Land and Mortgage Co. Ltd., Minute Book, I, 205. See J. Evetts Haley, Charles Goodnight, pp. 344-45. Under Adair and Goodnight the ranch at one time consisted of more than 1,000,000 acres and 65,000 head of cattle. See also H. T. Burton, A History of the JA Ranch.

(60) Texas Land and Mortgage (T.L. & M.) Minute Book I, 131, and II, 171.

(61) Haley, *op. cit.*, p. 318.

(62) T.L. & M. Minute Book, I, 121-308.

(63) T.L. & M. Prospectus, 1882, and Directory of Directors, 1890.

(64) John Clay, My Life . . ., 158-64; Stock Exchange Year-Book (London, 1888), p. 650; Companies Office, Edinburgh, California Redwood Co. Ltd., File No. 1261/1. Prospectus, Wyoming Cattle Ranche Co. Ltd.

(65) Memorandum of Association, Quebec Timber Co. Ltd., 1066/1; Directory of Directors, 1885, p. 241.

(66) Interview with A. M. Anderson, partner in Graham, Johnston and Fleming, Writers to the Signet, Albyn Place, Edinburgh.

(67) Directory of Directors, 1885, p. 44. Mr. Black's law partner, Colin James Mackenzie. was equally well connected with directorships, including the Arizona Copper Co. Ltd.; the Swan Land and Cattle Co. Ltd., of which he was chairman; the British Linen Bank; and the Florida Mortgage and Investment Co. Ltd.; he was also vice-chairman and chairman of the Scottish Mortgage Land and Investment Co. Ltd. and the Standard Life Assurance Co. Ltd.

(68) T.L. & M., Minute Book, I, 98; Bailey, *Australian Borrowing*, p. 268; A. K. Cairncross, Home and Foreign Investment, 1870-1913 (Cambridge, 1953), p. 89.

(69) Interview with G. A. Mitchell, Jnr., London. Mr. Mitchell and his father were both chairman and general managers of T.L. & M.

(70) Correspondence with Sir Robert A. Maclean, chairman, A. F. Stoddard & Co.; Interviews with Lady Winifred Renshaw, London. The Renshaws retained their interests in the carpet company until 1943.

(71) Interviews with Mrs. Thomas A. Renshaw, Eye, Suffolk. See also Dod's Parliamentary Companion, 1893, p. 329, and 1902, p. 338, as well as interviews with Lady Winifred Renshaw, and her son. Michael, advertising director of Thomson Newspapers.

(72) Interview with Horace Simpson, whose association with T.L. & M. dates back to 1908. He was for many years secretary of the company. See Poems by A. G. R., printed in 1892 at the Chiswick Press, London, and dedicated to John Young Sargent, Fellow of Hertford College, Oxford.

(73) Stock Exchange Year-Book, 1880, p. 199; Directory of Directors, 1889, p. 418; Stock Exchange Year-Book, 1889, pp. 465, 586.

(74) The Economist, 8th July, 1882, p. 848, as cited by Dorothy R. Adler in her penetrating but as yet unpublished Ph.D. thesis, British Investment in American Railways, 1834-1898 (Cambridge, 1958), p. 276.

(75) Letter in the possession of Thomas A. Renshaw, Eye, Suffolk, and also letters in the possession of Lady Winifred Renshaw, cited by Sir Philip Magnus in his Kitchener—Portrait of an Imperialist (1958), pp. 258, n., 230.

(76) T.L. & M. Minute Book, I, pp. 14-17.

(77) T.L. & M. Minute Book, I, p. 24.

(78) Scottish Banking and Insurance Magazine, 1884, pp. 23, 46-50.

(79) Dod's Parliamentary Companion, 1880, and 1892, pp. 167 and 187, respectively.

(80) Directory of Directors, 1880, p. 112; 1890, p. 496; Stock Exchange Year-Book, 1880, p. 199; North of Scotland Canadian Mortgage Co. Ltd., Minute Book, I.

(81) Directory of Directors, 1885, p. 23.

(82) Dundee Mortgage and Trust Investment Co. Ltd., Minute Book, IV, pp. 48-49, 82.

(83) Dundee Advertiser, 27th September, 1881; The Eighth Earl of Airlie, David Graham Drummond Ogilvy, was not a titled figure-head chairman as too often was the custom of the day. He took a leading and active part in his mortgage company and ranching participations. His son, Lyulph Ogilvy, went to Colorado as a young man, and with the exception of taking time out to serve in three wars, spent the rest of his life there. A colourful and capable Old Etonian, Lyulph came to Colorado in the days of the Old West. He is today revered as one of the State's legendary figures. See E. L. Howe, *Prince Hall Rides the Rockies*, Denver Westerners' Book (Denver, Colorado, 1961), pp. 241-78; correspondence with J. D. A. Ogilvy, Boulder, Colorado.

(84) T.L. & M., Minute Book, I, 67.

(85) T.L. & M., Minute Book, II, 171. See also Haley, Goodnight, p. 331.

(86) T.L. & M., Minute Book, I, 70, 131, 138-39, 308; II, 14, and *passim*.

(87) Scottish American Mortgage Co. Minute Book, II, 68, 73, 75 and 79; Dundee Mortgage and Trust Investment Co. and Alliance Trust Co., Account Books.

(88) See Prospectuses for Dundee Mortgage and the Dundee Investment companies.

(89) Conversations with old employees of the Alliance some of whose memories reach back over forty-five years.

(90) Interviews and correspondence with Mrs. Agnes T. Dean, London, daughter of William Mackenzie.

(91) See my article, *loc cit.*, pp. 97-98.

(92) Correspondence with Mrs. Ethel M. Sommerville, St. Andrews, Scotland; C. Stanley Banks, partner in E. B. Chandler & Co., San Antonio, Texas; Thomas Drought of H. P. Drought & Co., San Antonio; and Mrs. Agnes Dean, London. See also Dundee Land Investment Company, Limited, Minute Book, II, 119-20; Dundee Mortgage & Trust Investment Minute Book, IV, 208; V, 90-99; Fort Worth Gazette, Fort Worth, Texas, 11th December, 1890.

(93) Dundee Mortgage and Alliance Trust Account Books, 1884-87.

(94) Dundee Mortgage Minute Book, III, pp. 318-26, etc.

(95) Correspondence with Carroll W. Sturgis, Vice-President of the First National Bank of Waco, Manton Hannah, Prof. Guy Bryan Harrison and Rev. C. T. Caldwell, all of Waco, Texas; Thomas Drought and C. Stanley Banks, *op. cit.*, San Antonio; Mrs. Margaret Baker, Paris, Texas; Mrs. Marie Baldwin Webb, also of Paris, Texas, and her sisters, Mrs. Anna Baldwin Bywaters and Mrs. Adelaide Baldwin Bauer; Mrs. Egbert V. Smith and Mrs. Katherine Hart, both of Austin, Texas; S. L. Stumberg, dealer in cattle and sheep ranches, Sanderson, Texas; A. C. Robertson, former Kansas City manager of the Scottish American Mortgage Co. Ltd.; W. E. Thompson. land merchant, Houston, Texas, and Mrs. Carolyn Scott of Boulder, Colorado.

Scottish American Mortgage Co., Minute Books, I, pp. 281-82, 287; II, pp. 19, 62, 160, 190, 214; and the Report of S.A.M.'s 11th Annual General Meeting, p. 6.

(96) E. E. Dale, *Romance Rode with Development*, The Cattleman, Fort Worth, Texas, Vol. XII, no. 10 (1926), 19; Frink, Jackson and Spring, *op. cit.*, p. 223.

(97) British mortgage money in Texas by 1891 was estimated at between £6 million and £8 million by the knowledgeable British Consul at Galveston, Capt. James Boyle, Consular Reports, Parliamentary Papers, LXXXV, p. 8.

(98) Jackson, *op. cit.*, pp. 318-20.

(99) See Stock Exchange Year-Books, 1875 onwards; G. Glasgow, Scottish Investment Trust Companies (London, 1932); T. J. Grayson, Investment Trusts (London, 1928); J. C. Gilbert, Investment Trusts in Dundee, 1873-1938.

(100) See my article, *op. cit.*, p. 103.

(101) L. Atherton, The Cattle Kings (Bloomington, Indiana, 1962), 176-77; Jackson, *op. cit.*, p. 307.

(102) Dundee Year Book, 1890, p. 46.

(103) At the nadir of the decline in cattle company investment, it is interesting to look at the market value of some of its leading shares. Eight cattle companies, including the Matador, Texas, Hansford, Prairie, Swan, Cattle Ranche, Missouri and Western Ranches had a total paid-up capital of £2,070,076. By the end of 1889, the combined market value of their shares was but £394,456. In the following year, 1890, the same eight companies showed a difference of 76 per cent between the paid-up capital and its market value. The investment recommendation of the time for those companies with land as well as cattle, was to sit tight, stick to your properties and 'wait for the growth of the country'. Dundee Year Books, 1888, p. 149; 1889, p. 188 and 1890, pp. 45-46. Following the turn of the century, share values increased somewhat. See Rippy, *op. cit.*, pp. 335-41.

(104) Glasgow. *op. cit.*, p. 5.

(105) *Ibid.*, pp. 41-42, *et seq.*

CHAPTER FIFTEEN

Scottish Investment in American Railways: the Case of the City of Glasgow Bank, 1856-1881[1]

R. E. TYSON

Lecturer in Economic History,
University of Aberdeen

IN THE SECOND HALF of the nineteenth century Scotland was a considerable exporter of capital.[2] 'She welcomes any financial proposal to relieve her of her bank deposits and the contents of her old stockings by irrigating with them some undeveloped Goshen at the furthest ends of the earth.'[3] The Scottish banks appear to have played little part in the movement of capital. Nevertheless, two of them, the Western and the City of Glasgow, did invest overseas, particularly the latter, as was revealed when it failed in October, 1878. Among the holdings of this ill-fated bank were shares of the New Zealand and Australian Land Company, the Grand Trunk and Erie railroads, and considerable property in the Antipodes. But of particular interest was the bank's ownership of stocks and bonds of the Western Union Railroad, whose line ran from Lake Michigan to the Mississippi, and of the Racine Warehouse and Dock Company, with which the railroad was associated.[4] These were not merely speculative purchases, for most of the railroad's construction was financed by the bank, which at one period held the majority of stock and bonds. Lord Shand, a prominent Scottish judge, hearing a case involving the story of this connection, remarked: 'It strikes me that a Scotch Bank buying and working a railroad in America is about as startling a thing as one can well conceive.'[5] But if not typical of Scottish banking, the story of the City of Glasgow Bank's involvement with the Western Union does indicate some of the problems faced by British investors, particularly merchant bankers, in such concerns.

Founded in 1839, the City of Glasgow Bank had extended its business so rapidly that by 1857 it had eighty-eight branches in Scotland, a number exceeded only by the Western and Union banks, and it owned the Bank of Mona in the Isle of Man.(6) Not content with such expansion, early in 1857 the bank followed the example of the Western Bank and opened an agency in New York to 'Collect and Procure acceptances of Bills, Negotiate Coupons and Grant Letters of Credit'.(7) The agent chosen was Richard Irvin, brother of the bank's chairman and described later as 'the Scotchman of greatest eminence in the United States—as a merchant, and a man of honour'. But the bank had already become indirectly involved with the Racine and Mississippi Railroad, forerunner of the Western Union.

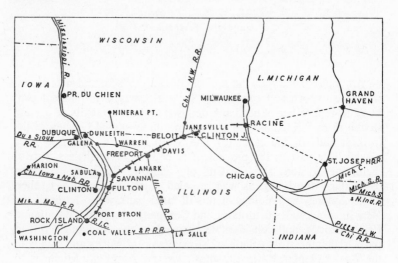

The Western Union Railroad and Connections, 1869.

This had been chartered with a nominal capital of $3,000,000 in April, 1852, to construct a line between Racine on the shores of Lake Michigan to Savanna on the Mississippi (see map). At first the undertaking was financed to a large extent by farmers and landowners along the route subscribing for the common stock, but instead of paying cash for their shares, they granted mortgages over their land. The railroad then disposed of these mortgages to the public as farm bonds, giving its guarantee as security for principal and interest, and purchased land and materials for the line.(8) By the autumn of 1855, sixty-eight miles of track had been built to

Beloit, and in order to complete the remaining seventy miles to Savanna the railroad issued 680 of its own mortgage bonds, each of $1,000 and bearing 8 per cent interest, over the road already made.

William Gemmell, partner in a firm of Glasgow wire-rope manufacturers, acquired 370 of these bonds at 80 per cent in the hope of selling them at par. In March, 1856, he wrote to Robert Salmond, manager of the City of Glasgow Bank, enquiring if the bank would be willing to hold the bonds, pay interest on them when supplied with funds, and grant temporary advances to the railroad on security of the bonds. The bank was offered 8 per cent interest for advances and a commission for other duties. Salmond agreed to the first two proposals, but refused to give advances directly. However, a series of credits was granted for the railroad to Gemmell and two associates, G. A. Thomson and Company, London stockbrokers, and Henry Watson and Sons, Glasgow merchants. The first, made on 15th April, 1856, was for £1,450 in favour of the New York agents of the railroad, on the security of 'the debentures which you already hold as the Company's property, and other securities you hold belonging to me [Gemmel]'. A year later the bank was appointed European bankers of the railroad.

In 1856 Gemmell had stated that the railroad had sufficient funds to reach Savanna, but in summer of 1857 it was obliged to issue $700,000 first mortgage bonds and $500,000 second mortgage bonds to continue the line to Freeport, about half way to the Mississippi. Instead of ending all transactions with the railroad, the bank authorised G. A. Thomson, who was about to sail to New York, to buy at his discretion the new first bonds using bills drawn upon Henry Watson and Sons. These were over the western division of the line, from Beloit to Freeport, to construct which the eastern division, from Racine to Beloit, had already been mortgaged. Thomson 'made a conditional contract to take them at 60 per cent, and as a temporary measure, to prevent entire stoppage of work on the line, I advanced 100,000 dols on the bonds at 50 per cent'. In return for this advance, H. S. Durand, president of the railroad, handed to Richard Irvin and Company a promissory note for £20,700, together with $163,000 of western division bonds. The contract, however, was cancelled as a result of the financial crisis of 1857.

At the outset of the panic Irvin informed Salmond that with some of the securities he held for the bank 'punctuality is not to be expected in times of such extraordinary difficulty and pressure'. He added that the Racine and Mississippi 'should have settled their credits with us today but have not done so'. Salmond, in remorse, replied: 'Perhaps as a rule it would be as well to decline in future railway securities in giving credits, or making advances on them of any kinds for they are hardly, at the best, of that strictly mercantile and legitimate character we would wish all our collaterals to be.' But his main anxiety was for the future of the bank itself.

The collapse of the Western Bank on 9th November produced so severe a run on the City of Glasgow Bank that it was unable to open on 11th November,(9) subsequent investigations revealing a deficiency of £77,577.(10) The bank resumed business on 31st December,(11) but not before the Edinburgh banks had insisted that among other precautions the New York agency should be closed. Irvin and Company were instructed to confine future transactions to liquidation. At the time of the bank's stoppage £117,508 had been advanced through various parties to the railroad, against which the bank held securities with a nominal value of £160,907 (see Table 4 for advances and nominal value of securities held).

It was apparent that the railroad would be unable to pay either the £20,700 due in April, 1858, or the interest on its bonds. Nevertheless, Irvin was optimistic about its future, placing his hopes on the construction of the line to Freeport, where it would meet the Illinois Central, and he asked the bank to forego interest for the time being. When the bill for £20,700 was protested, Thomson, who had returned to the United States at the bank's request, arranged for it to be handed back to the railroad in return for 194 western division bonds. Thomson, Gemmell, and Henry Watson were all embarrassed by the crisis of 1857 and were unable to meet their liabilities. In the autumn of 1858, therefore, Thomson and Watson relinquished all claim to their securities lodged with the bank in return for a discharge; Gemmell, more obstinate, was not discharged until the following year. The bank, apart from various worthless securities, now held 361 eastern division bonds of the Racine and Mississippi Railroad, 310 western division bonds, and $66,700 of farm mortgage bonds.

The stock of the railroad company was $2,717,541. There were also $1,380,000 of first mortgage bonds ($680,000 eastern division and $700,000 western), and $700,000 of second mortgage. By the autumn of 1857 ninety miles of track had been constructed from Racine to Davis at a cost of $2,930,335, and there it had languished for want of funds. After considerable difficulty Thomson gained access to the books of the railroad and recommended an immediate suit of foreclosure. This was instituted, but eventually the line was surrendered and an indenture executed on 10th May, 1859, under which the line was surrendered for five years to the Farmers' Loan and Trust Company of New York as trustees for the bondholders. The indenture provided for the redemption of the line in 1864, if the railroad was in a position to do so, for the deferring of interest on the bonds, and for the extension of the track to Freeport with funds provided by the bondholders. The old management, headed by H. S. Durand, was swept away, and Thomson and a certain T. B. Blackstone, who had practical experience of railroad affairs, became joint-managers. They had power to appoint a third manager and selected Marshall M. Strong, a Wisconsin lawyer. Within a short time, however, Thomson became president and sole manager.

Thus any hope of the City of Glasgow Bank regaining its advances was dependent upon what success could be achieved by G. A. Thomson in managing a railroad that had hitherto proved a failure. It was a formidable task. 'Over the level, fertile lands of the northwest central states railroads could be built cheaply in any direction. Only the Mississippi and Missouri rivers were natural obstructions. Consequently, advancing a railroad was like playing a game of chess. . . . Not only were parallel lines dangerous competitions, but each transverse line threatened to draw off traffic and shorten hauls. . . . Every rate had to be fixed with these complexities in mind.'(12) Although as a stockbroker Thomson had dealt in railway shares, this was not necessarily an advantage. Indeed W. Ackerman, a former president of the Illinois Central, wrote in 1884 that 'stockbrokers, as a class, do not make efficient railway managers. . . . Many have sought the position . . . for the express purpose of gaining an opportunity for speculating.'(13) But he was a man of great energy and considerable ability; furthermore, he had the support of Richard Irvin, who was an excellent adviser and well versed in the affairs of American railroads.

Both Thomson and Irvin were confident that the extension of the line to Freeport would make the railroad a profitable concern. After a visit to Racine, Irvin wrote:

'The country through which it passes is one of the finest I ever saw. For a hundred miles on each side the land is an uninterrupted track of finest wheat land, chiefly rolling prairie with oak openings here and there, abounding with the finest water. All the farms are under cultivation by respectable, industrious, and intelligent farmers. The country also is remarkably healthy, being free from the bad diseases so incident to early western settlements. The population wants only a completed railroad and good crops to make them highly prosperous.'

In fact, these same farmers were so far unable even to pay the interest on their farm bonds.

Irvin estimated that the cost of the extension would be $200,000, which would be raised by the bondholders advancing 12½ per cent on the amount of their bonds. However, this scheme collapsed when many of the bondholders refused to pay their proportion. The directors of the bank, anxious to secure the speedy realisation of their advances, agreed to finance the railroad to Freeport and advanced £51,410, which was secured by certificates granted by the Farmers' Loan and Trust Company. The line was opened on 1st September, 1859, but the results were disappointing. It had been built with the promise of considerable freight from the Illinois Central, which now preferred to use other lines to reach Lake Michigan.(14) Irvin, reporting on the position of the railroad early in 1860, now wrote: 'We cannot help feeling somewhat oppressed by the responsibility of dealing, under your general instructions, with an interest 1,000 miles from us, which requires more of your money than was contemplated, and its success as yet falling short of our expectations.'

Thomson's confidence in the enterprise remained unshaken and after a discussion with D. D. Williamson, president of the Farmers' Loan and Trust Company, he recommended that the railroad should be completed to Savanna as originally planned. In April, 1860, therefore, he travelled to Glasgow and proposed that the road should be built to the Mississippi, or at least to Cherrygrove, eighteen miles beyond Freeport. The directors rejected the idea, but accepted in principal a proposal that a new company, the Northern Illinois, should be formed to complete the line to Savanna, 'the advantage being that all monies spent would be unencumbered by old debts'. Irvin visited the area through which it would pass and reported that the new company would be profitable and would increase the receipts of the Racine and Mississippi by at least 50 per cent. Therefore, in November, 1860, the directors agreed to the formation of the Northern Illinois, but offered no financial support except any surplus funds of the Racine and Mississippi, of which the bank now held the majority of first mortgage bonds.(15)

'The magnitude of the advances already made by the Bank is such that the Directors however willing to encourage the new project, and however much they may be satisfied as to its expediency, feel that they would not be justified in sanctioning further increases to their present advances. Were they dealing with the question as a matter of their own they would have had less difficulty, but acting merely as trustees for others they feel that any failure in the anticipated results from an additional advance of this nature, might entail responsibilities which they do not see their way to risk.'

Despite this statement, however, the bank advanced £83,432 through Irvin for the construction and other expenses of the line to Savanna, receiving securities with a nominal value of $547,000. West of Freeport Thomson laid out the town of Lanark, selling 'a considerable quantity of lots, the price of which went to the credit of the Bank', while at Savanna the new company owned an elevator, workshops, engine-houses, warehouses and other property. The new line was worked by the Racine and Mississippi in return for 50 per cent of the receipts. Thomson was president and manager of both companies.

With the opening of the extension on 1st September, 1862, the Racine and Mississippi controlled 142 miles of track which was linked through neighbouring railroads with Chicago and Milwaukee. Moreover, in May, 1862, the Illinois Central allowed it the same privileges for the interchange of business as the Galena and Chicago Union. Other railroads in the area were now interested, particularly the Chicago and Northwestern, which in September, 1863, offered bonds and stocks with a nominal value of $3,550,000 for the two railroads. Both Thomson, who estimated the offer to be worth $1,575,762 in cash to the bank, and Irvin urged acceptance, the latter writing: 'The war, by closing the Mississippi, has given extraordinary traffic to the Western railroads, increasing their importance and selling price. A termination of the war, and the re-opening of river navigation, would probably bring down prices materially. The present disposition, strongly favourable to the Western railroads, might in a great degree abate.'(16)

A year earlier the directors of the bank would have sacrificed a few thousand pounds in selling the securities. Since then the position of the railroad had improved considerably, for as well as the increased traffic resulting from the war, there was also an abundant harvest in the summer of 1863. Thus Alexander Stronach, who had succeeded Salmond as manager of the bank in July, 1860, now wrote:

'At present the Racine and Miss. and Northern Illinois Companies seem in as good a position as the C. & N.W. The debt is greatly less per mile, and the Revenue Returns, according to Mr. Thomson's estimate, should yield as favourable return upon their

debt . . . The margin between the Bank's debt and the cash
value of the securities falling to them (as quoted by Mr. Thomson) is rather narrow, so that at the present rate of exchange
[$7 to the pound] the operation would involve a very heavy loss
which the directors do not see the necessity of incurring at the
moment.'

Since the bank's advances, including interest debited, amounted to
£354,000 by 1864, and as considerable expenses would have to be
met when closing the railroad account, the directors considered
£375,000 payable in sterling a fair price. But, as Irvin pointed out,
this was far too high a figure, for at the going rate of exchange it
would amount to over $2,700,000, nearly 40 per cent above the par
value of the securities. The Chicago and Northwestern then offered
either bonds and stocks (with a market value of $1,920,577) or
$1,800,000 in cash, but the former were rejected as 'suspect' and
the cash offer because acceptance would have meant an estimated
loss of about £60,000. Soon afterwards it amalgamated with the
Galena and Chicago Union, thus reaching the Mississippi at Fulton
and ending any necessity of negotiating further with the bank for
the time being.

Thomson now decided to strengthen the position of the Northern
Illinois, which had been weakened by neighbouring lines extending
across the Mississippi into Iowa. 'On looking down the Mississippi,
however,' he stated later, 'to Rock Island, Davenport, and the
immense works, coalfields, and large population there, and the fact
that a line down there would connect us with the [Union] Pacific
Line to San Francisco, I concluded there was great advantage in an
extension in that direction.' He therefore obtained a charter for the
Mississippi Railroad Company, which would extend the line thirty-
eight miles to Port Byron, at an estimated cost of $600,000. Work
had already begun on the first eight miles before the matter was
discussed by the directors of the bank.

In a letter to Richard Irvin setting out the views of the board,
Alexander Stronach wrote that although the extension might prove
a profitable investment, the bank would play no part in financing it.
'They have already advanced large sums with the object, as you are
aware, first of recovering the control of the property over which
the Bank's advances extended, and second, of placing that property
in such a position as would, according to Mr. Thomson's expectations at the time, speedily result in the return of all he invested in it.
We are far from blaming Mr. Thomson because these expectations
have not been realised.'

At the request of the board, Thomson came over to Glasgow in the autumn of 1864 to discuss the matter further. The directors agreed that the extension should proceed but still declined to make further advances. However, they did allow him to make use of any accrued interest from the bank's Northern Illinois bonds, 'which in consequence of the high rates of exchange, at present can neither be profitably invested otherwise nor remitted home', as well as the proceeds from the sale of $50,000 of Cleveland and Pittsburg Railroad bonds belonging to the bank. In all, Thomson received £8,699 from these two sources, and £10,000 ostensibly supplied by two directors of the bank, William Mackinnon and James Nicol Fleming, for the purchase of 800 tons of railroad iron.

These were the directors largely responsible for supervising the bank's interest in American railroads. Born in Campbeltown in 1823, Mackinnon had gone to India in 1847, where he became partner in the merchant house of Mackinnon, Mackenzie and Company. In 1856, however, he returned to Glasgow to promote the Calcutta and Burmah Steam Navigation Co. Ltd., which in 1862 became the British India Steam Navigation Co. Ltd.(17) 'He was marked as a rising man, and his Indian connection was already enough to attract the attention of bankers,'(18) particularly Robert Salmond, who invited him to join with others in speculating on behalf of the bank in foreign exchanges, Australian gold, and Indian Government stocks.(19) Although the principal banking account of his Glasgow house was with the Union Bank and he only became a shareholder of the City of Glasgow Bank in September, 1857, he was elected to a committee of shareholders who were to advise the bank during and immediately after the stoppage. In July, 1858, he became a director, but since his interests in India required long absences from Glasgow, he nominated James Nicol Fleming as a director of the bank in July, 1863, in order to obtain assistance with the railroad account. Fleming had recently returned from Bombay where he had made a fortune speculating in cotton, and now combined the life of a gentleman-farmer with that of a Glasgow merchant.(20)

Unknown to Thomson the £10,000 advanced for the purchase of railroad iron was in fact supplied by the bank. The likeliest explanation of this curious procedure of making a loan in the name of Mackinnon and Fleming is that the directors would have felt embarrassed if Thomson had been openly granted credits so soon after the refusal to make advances for the Port Byron extension. They may also have thought that he would be quicker in paying the railroad's debts if these were to individuals. Certainly it was a device used more than once in the next few years. In July, 1865, another such loan, for £25,000, was made in the name of Mac-kinnon, Fleming, and the London merchant house of Smith, Fleming and Company, and at the end of 1864 £10,000 was granted for the purchase of wheat. Thomson had suggested that he might check the usual falling off of traffic during the winter months by buying large quantities of wheat in Racine, thus raising the price and inducing farmers in the area to send their grain along the railroad to its eastern terminus. The scheme proved a dismal failure. Of 2,857,065 bushels of wheat carried by the railroad between April, 1865, and the end of 1866, over 2,000,000 were bought and sold by Thomson, at a loss of $46,441·59.

In September, 1864, when the agreement made with the Farmers' Loan and Trust Company came to an end, Thomson commenced a series of foreclosure suits to obtain possession of the Racine and Mississippi Railroad for the first bondholders. His aim, when this was accomplished, was to amalgamate it with the Northern Illinois and the Mississippi railroads and form one company, the Western Union. But considerable difficulty was experienced with the second bondholders, many of whom opposed the scheme. To assist the reorganisation, therefore, a 'combination', consisting of the six directors of the bank, Thomson, and a certain R. W. Smith, was formed to acquire bonds with credits supplied by the bank (which bought 184 first mortgage bonds on its own account). By April, 1865, the 'combination' had purchased 231 first mortgage and 699 second mortgage bonds for £41,580, and it acquired the one remaining second mortgage bond in May, 1866.

Although the extension to Port Byron was not completed until early in 1866, Thomson merged the Mississippi Railroad with the Northern Illinois in June, 1865, and this was amalgamated with the Racine and Mississippi into the Western Union Railroad in the following January.(21) Under an agreement of 1st February, 1866, the bonds, stock, and interest due of the Racine and Mississippi and Northern Illinois railroads were cancelled and replaced by the $4,000,000 first mortgage bonds and $2,705,693·33 of common stock of the Western Union. As security for total advances of £531,533, the bank now held $1,904,741·44 in bonds and $1,000,000 stock. The 'combination' received $359,058 in bonds and $705,693·33 of stock, and Mackinnon, Fleming, and Smith, Fleming and Company $430,000 in bonds (see Tables 1, 2, 3).

Both Irvin and Thomson were confident that the amalgamation would make the railroad a much stronger concern. 'The property', stated the latter, '. . . will cover much valuable territory, embracing sources of business which cannot but afford it ampler employment of a profitable character.' As for the directors of the bank, they regarded the reorganisation as a release from their troubles. In spite of all disappointments they were still full of hope and less prepared than ever to sell at a loss. Their views were summed up in a letter from Alexander Stronach to Thomson in December, 1865:

'I see no reason why the Bank should part with its interest in the security at a sacrifice, seeing that they have held on so long and are now apparently within sight of land. If any party were to come forward to relieve us at our own cost, with interest, we should, of course, be quite willing to treat; but in the absence of any such proposal or the prospect of it, I think we must calmly wait the result of the reorganisation, which, with a strong Board and a steadily increasing revenue, there should not be the same difficulties, as have hitherto stood in the way, of our relieving, to some advantage, our interest in that concern.'

Optimism, however, disappeared with the failure of Overend, Gurney and Co. in February, 1866. This firm, together with the bank, had largely financed the New Zealand and Australian land schemes of James Morton, and it was now left to the bank to bear this burden alone.(22) Moreover, in the financial crisis that followed the failure, it seemed unlikely that the bank's railroad securities could be sold without some considerable loss (estimated by Mackinnon in June at £50-£60,000). Nevertheless, the board sent Henry Dunlop, a former director of the bank with some experience of railway affairs, and J. M. Hall, an associate of Mackinnon, to the United States to negotiate the sale of the railroad. They returned to Glasgow in February, 1867, with an offer from the Chicago and Northwestern of $3,000,000 of 7 per cent bonds and $1,500,000 of stock, which together had a market value of $3,300,000. The total advances of the bank (including the credits for railroad iron, the 'combination' account, and interest debited) amounted to £613,313, in return for which, if the offer were accepted, it would receive bonds and stocks with a market value of $2,800,725 or £420,109.

Thomson believed that the offer was far too low, and declared that the financial position of the Chicago and Northwestern was by no means sound(23) and that there was strong indignation in Racine and the neighbouring countryside at that railroad attempting to establish a monopoly. 'This town [Racine] took $300,000 in the stock of the Racine and Mississippi which is wiped out, and all along, the towns and the people have suffered proportionately. I think they have some right to be considered.'

The directors were well aware that the offer was very low. 'But the state and suspense', wrote Alexander Stronach to Thomson, 'in which they have been kept for so many years, the disappointments they have met with from year to year in the net returns from the earnings of the Road, and the continuous drain upon them for fresh advances, particularly during the last year, may possibly make them more willing than they otherwise would be to avail themselves of the first opportunity of winding up the matter, even at a considerable sacrifice, and facing the loss.' Moreover, the main reason for the Chicago and Northwestern wishing to acquire the Western Union was to prevent it building a line from Milwaukee into Chicago under a charter acquired by Thomson early in 1866. This charter was due to expire in 1867, and if the offer were refused the Chicago and Northwestern would probably lose interest. 'The question', Stronach declared, 'is perplexing in the extreme'.

The letters received from Thomson about this time did little to restore the confidence of the directors either in him or the railroad. The business of the Western Union during the winter months had been worse than usual and large advances were required to meet expenses. The arrival of spring brought no relief, for traffic was so low as a result of what Thomson termed 'the general exhaustion of produce throughout the North-West', that instead of an estimated surplus of $80,000 or more in May and June, none was expected until after the harvest. Thus the bank had to advance $30,000 to pay bills. Early in 1867 the directors learned of the losses made by Thomson as a result of purchasing grain to stimulate traffic,(24) but worse was to come, for in February he informed the bank that he was heavily in debt as a result of becoming involved in the construction of a grain elevator.

The building of a grain elevator had been proposed as early as November, 1864, but nothing had been done until 1866. In August of that year Thomson wrote:

'It is a great misfortune that we have not the facility for accommodating at this point [Racine] one-fourth of the business which is ready to come to us, and it is absolutely necessary to make better arrangements with all possible expedition. We are entirely at the mercy of the C. and North-Western Coy., and if it was not for the energy we have already shown at this point, they would make it go very hard indeed with us. The old warehouses here are not capable of taking in the grain we bring to them, and we are obliged to send a large proportion of it over the Chicago and N-Western R.R., paying them for a quarter to half of the freight and losing the use of our cars for days. We cannot supply the cars to shippers of grain, hence discontent, threats, and indignation meetings all along our line. An Elevator of modern construction which will cost about $120,000 is our present necessity. The Railroad Coy. ought to own the Elevator, but if it is preferred a contract can be made which will induce outside parties to put it up.'

The directors preferred the latter course so Thomson, on his own initiative, ordered work to begin on the elevator and promoted the Racine Warehouse and Dock Company. Unfortunately, two of his partners withdrew, leaving him to bear the cost of the elevator, now estimated at $150,000, 'which I must meet promptly—or break down entirely'.

Hall was angered by this news and urged acceptance of the Chicago and Northwestern's offer. 'The contents of Thomson's letters are sickening. Every step foreward makes the bank's position more and more difficult. You get deeper and deeper into the mire. This constant drain should be—must be—stopped. How often have I said that already?' He proposed that the bonds and stocks received in exchange should be sold and the proceeds invested in United States bonds until the exchange rate rose, when the money could be remitted to Scotland without loss.

The directors were still undecided when Thomson arrived in June, 1867, to discuss the future of the Western Union and the construction of the grain elevator. 'After the most mature consideration of all the circumstances', wrote Stronach to Irvin, 'and looking to the disastrous consequences likely to arise to the prospects of the Railroad in the view of a rate to another Company, if the building were abandoned and discredit thereby thrown upon Mr. Thomson's position, the Directors most reluctantly came to the conclusion that the only course left for them under all the circumstances was to take over the concern and advance the necessary funds to complete it, in the hope that, while in the meantime the possession of such a building would have a tendency to improve the prospects of the Road itself, it could be disposed of quite readily to any party purchasing the Railroad interest.' In all the bank took up $200,000 of shares in the Racine Warehouse and Dock Company and agreed that the Western Union should supply the elevator with 2,500,000 bushels of grain a year for the next ten years or pay one per cent on every bushel under that figure not delivered. In return, Thomson promised to co-operate wholeheartedly in the sale of the Western Union. The board also decided to reject as too low the offer of the Chicago and Northwestern and authorised Irvin 'to negotiate,

DD

in conjunction with Mr. Thomson, the disposal of the property' to any party interested.

When re-elected a director in 1866, Mackinnon made it plain that he could spare little time for the affairs of the bank. But Stronach persuaded him to stay until the railroad account was settled. Early in 1867 Mackinnon suggested that, with the reorganisation completed and the prospect of a sale in sight, it might be advisable to conceal the bank's large stake in the Western Union by appointing some third parties outside the bank to negotiate in all matters concerning the railroad. The rest of the board agreed and a committee of bondholders was appointed, consisting of John Fleming of Smith, Fleming and Company, brother of James Nicol Fleming, J. M. Hall, and James Macdonald, manager of the General Credit and Discount Company. The secretary was C. S. Leresche, formerly partner in a Calcutta house which had failed in 1866, brother-in-law of James Macdonald, and a friend of Mackinnon. The duties of the committee, which met in London, were 'to exercise a general superintendance over the affairs of the railroad, to correspond from time to time direct with the president, the agents in New York, and any other officers of the company, when necessary, and generally to give these gentlemen . . . such directions and instructions as to them may appear requisite.' But the directors of the bank were anxious that the committee should not know too much. 'The committee', Stronach informed Thomson, 'although aware of the aggregate amount of indebtness on this side, do not know the extent of any one individual interest in the bonds or stock, nor is it proposed to furnish them with that information.' It did not begin to meet until September, 1867, and thus played no part in the negotiations with the Chicago and Northwestern.

The directors were cheered in the autumn of 1867 by news not only of a good harvest, but also of a dispute between the Illinois Central and the Chicago and Northwestern, which forced the latter to rely upon the Western Union for a connection to the Mississippi at Savanna. This change in fortune, together with the charter acquired by Thomson for a line between Milwaukee and Chicago, brought a number of offers from neighbouring railroads. Thomson, however, preferred to play one railroad off against the other, rather than make a sale as the directors wished. 'I am satisfied', he wrote to Irvin, 'our position improves with the discussion of the contending interests. If we work with the St. Paul and Milwaukee Coy. we control the business of the Upper Mississippi, and the North Western is cut off. The Illinois Central will not interfere at Dunleith and the North Western cannot do much at Fulton as they have not the arrangements necessary and their Fulton line is already overtaxed, while their Freeport line has no feeder. I think a few months' patience, it may be only two, will make a difference of $1,000,000 in the result. If immediate action is essential, a sale can be made on the terms offered last.' So exasperated were the directors by this policy that they offered him a commission (Hall called it a bribe) of 4 per cent if between $3,700,000 and $4,000,000 were realised within three months of 1st February, 1868, and 5 per cent if over $4,000,000. When this had no effect they sent C. S. Leresche to the United States with instructions to find a buyer.

Leresche arrived in July. Although impressed with the country through which the railroad ran, he was highly critical of Thomson's management, particularly his insistence that grain should not be carried to Chicago or Milwaukee. Thomson for his part found Leresche 'overbearing and inconsiderate'. No offer was received for the Western Union, but on his return home Leresche reported that Alexander Mitchell and some of his friends were interested in purchasing it. Mitchell, who was described by Irvin as 'a banker of great wealth and good standing, a countryman of yours who has resided many years at Milwaukee, a man of much sagacity, prudence, and closeness in business', was a former school friend of Alexander Stronach, president of the Milwaukee and St. Paul and a director of the Chicago and Northwestern. At a much later date he stated that the Western Union 'had a value to us for purposes of control apart from its intrinsic or moneyed value growing out of . . . the grain business of the upper Mississippi. It could destroy rates and it was important for us to maintain reasonable fair rates . . . it was very desirable that we should have it act in harmony with our road.' Thomson was opposed to any deal with Mitchell's party, for he distrusted them and believed Racine would suffer to the benefit of Milwaukee. He suggested that the bank should lease the railroad for ten years to Captain William F. Davidson, owner of a St. Louis-St. Paul steamboat line, in return for 25 per cent of the gross earnings. The directors, however, refused, preferring an outright sale.

Relations between the board and Thomson were now very bad. Not only was he an obstacle to the sale of the railroad, but he refused to surrender bonds purchased in his name with credits supplied by the bank, as the other members of the 'combination' had done. The board therefore decided to exclude him from all negotiations concerning the sale of the railroad. His mind was still set on further extensions, this time to Rock Island, which he estimated would require the creation of $340,000 of bonds. But the directors refused to consider the idea. 'The results, hitherto', wrote Stronach, 'in every instance of the same kind which he has undertaken have been unsuccessful and unsatisfactory. The estimate which he had got framed and put before us with due formality as to the probable cost have uniformly proved so very far under the actual expenditure that we never have been able to understand . . . what the use of such estimates could be at all, except to mislead himself and us.'

Early in 1869 a party headed by Angus Smith of Milwaukee and including Captain Davidson and Jesse Hoyt of New York, offered to purchase the stock of both the Western Union and the Racine Warehouse and Dock Company in return for $4,000,000 of first mortgage bonds and the expenditure of $852,000 on putting the track in first-class condition and building the extension to Rock Island. Although the offer was regarded as too low, Mackinnon was greatly heartened and wondered if Mitchell could be persuaded to join Smith. 'The time has some', he stated, 'when we must quit it [the railroad], and no effort must be spared to accomplish it.' In April Smith made a new offer, $3,500,000 of first mortgage bonds at 4 per cent for four years, and $500,000 in cash, with 7 per cent interest for four years. But it was opposed by an offer from Mitchell.

Alexander Mitchell met Mackinnon in January, 1869, before spending three months in Italy. He was unenthusiastic about the condition of the railroad and declared that his main interest in the Western Union was to prevent it falling into the hands of parties hostile to the Chicago and Northwestern and the Milwaukee and St. Paul. In April he proposed that he and his colleagues should purchase the common stock, increased to $4,000,000, for $650,000, the bank having the right to buy half for $325,000; that $1,000,000 of the $4,000,000 of first mortgage bonds should be cancelled and the remainder bear 3 per cent interest for three years from July, 1870, onwards and 7 per cent thereafter; and that the $441,755 of preference stock, issued since 1st February, 1866, in lieu of interest on the bonds, and of which the bank held $409,670, should be written off.

Irvin was extremely critical of these terms and wrote to Leresche that the offer of stock was deceptive, 'the astute and cunning managers here intending that it shall never be worth anything to you. They mean to swamp it, as they have done that of other roads they have purchased, directing all profits to their main line. Mr. Mitchell himself intends all right, but he takes no controlling part. His associates here are the real managers and schemers and the leaders of them just unscrupulous railroad speculators, utterly unreliable. One of them has already let out their design to destroy the W.

Union. . . . The Smith and Hoyt men are far more reliable, un-objectionable in character, and competent in resources.' Thomson, fearful for the future of Racine and in danger of losing his job, shared Irvin's views. Moreover he had just arranged with the Chicago, Rock Island, and Pacific Railroad for the Western Union to run trains into Rock Island, thus doing away with the need for an extension and increasing the value of the railroad, he estimated, by at least a million dollars. But their warnings were ignored. The directors had implicit faith in Mitchell, who denied that he had any intention of handing the railroad over to either the Chicago and Northwestern or the Milwaukee and St. Paul. 'Mitchell', declared Mackinnon, 'is undoubtedly the most reliable man to deal with, and the offers through Thomson [the revised offer of the Smith party], although an improvement, are not to my mind equal to Mitchell's.' On 27th April the offer was officially accepted. On 12th May the bank exercised its option and repurchased $1,999,000 of the stock for $325,000, although Mitchell was willing to take it back for $675,000. 'Such was the faith of the Directors in the future prospects of this common stock that, having got their heads out of the noose so far as to hold nothing but first mortgages, they voluntarily placed themselves in the trap by buying back the common stock to the cash value of $325,000 for the sake of speculating on the rise.'(25)

As soon as the sale was made Leresche sailed for New York, where Irvin and Thomson would surrender all the securities of the bank in their hands. The bank had agreed to pay off a loan of $190,000 made by Irvin and Company to the Western Union in return for the 326 bonds held as collateral and to give 80 per cent for the $82,272 of bonds owned by them. The directors had hoped that Irvin would accept a commission for his services of 1 per cent of the $325,000 received from Mitchell's party, 'especially as you must be aware the final clearing up of the account cannot but show a very considerable loss to us'. Irvin, however, refused to hand over the securities until he had received a commission of 1 per cent, $41,000, on all the securities held by the bank and his company. So disgusted were the directors by his attitude that they ended their connection with him, a connection begun early in 1857.

Thomson, who had resigned as president of the railroad on Leresche's arrival, was equally obstinate in his refusal to hand over the securities held by him, including his share of the 'combination' account. Towards the end of 1869 he came over to Glasgow to discuss the matter further and eventually surrendered the securities held in his name(26) for £26,000. He then became an iron manufacturer in Pennsylvania. In later life he wrote:

'In all these operations on behalf of the Bank, extending over a term of twelve years, I had many difficulties and much hostility to contend with. I endeavoured to conciliate the people [of Racine] by dealing with them liberally, and always justly, and in this I met with full success. I had to comply with the State Laws, to create Boards of Directors in my various organizations; and this was a very delicate matter to deal with, as the men I appointed, while merely nominees, might at any time have abused their legal power and ruined the interests I was working to preserve and protect. . . . I had devoted myself for many years to their service [the directors'], always anticipating being able to close up the business advantageously to all concerned.'

Leresche stayed in the United States for some time settling affairs with Mitchell, who assumed all litigation and claims for right of way against the railroad in return for $75,000 from the bank. As a reward for their services Leresche, who replaced Low as secretary of the bank in 1870, received £2,000 and the committee of bondholders $5,000 of first mortgage bonds.

Mackinnon resigned from the board in July, 1870, when the bank held $2,926,170 of first mortgage bonds and $1,992,340 of stock in the railroad, as well as $300,000 of stock in the Racine Warehouse and Dock Company. Total advances amounted to £600,696 and debited interest to £304,470; £905,166 in all (see Table 4). The directors had, in fact, surrendered control of the railroad for $325,000. In doing so they were convinced that they were 'housing it safely, and without the possibility of our ever requiring to look after it again'. But in April, 1870, Mitchell and his associates sold their $2,001,000 of stock to the Milwaukee and St. Paul for $1,507,500 of that railroad's stock, then selling at 76 per cent. When the directors heard of this, they offered the bank's holding of Western Union stock to the Milwaukee and St. Paul in the hope of similar terms, but the offer was refused, much to their annoyance.

Another complaint of the directors was that no dividends were being received on the stock. It was Mitchell's policy to control and regulate the traffic of the Western Union so that it produced enough to pay the interest on the bonds, thus preventing any threat of foreclosure from the bank, and to divert to the Milwaukee and St. Paul all other traffic 'for if we give a dividend on it, half of that will go to those who hold the minority of the small stock'. In fact there was a sufficient surplus left for a small dividend, but Mitchell, at a time when the Western Union owed the bank $100,000, used it towards the construction of the Sabula-Marion section of a feeder line in Iowa (the Sabula, Ackley, and Dakota) and to pay 7 per cent interest on the bonds of this railroad. The bank was offered bonds, but preferred to invest in the stock of the Milwaukee and St. Paul. The diversion of traffic was achieved by the construction of a line from Elkhorn on the Western Union to Eagle on the Milwaukee and St. Paul. Racine was badly hit by this action, which explains why Mitchell left the Racine Warehouse and Dock Company in the hands of the bank, although the agreement made with the Western Union in 1867 did not expire until 1877. Thomson later accused Mitchell of still further damaging Racine by removing a dredge, thus making it difficult for ships to enter the harbour.

But if Thomson's warnings had proved only too true, the bank nevertheless did gain considerable benefits from the association with the Milwaukee and St. Paul. The flow of advances from Glasgow ceased and the bank received an annual average return of £5 11s. 3d. per cent on its bonds between 1870 and 1878, £258,298 in all, despite a severe depression from 1873 onwards. Some of this money was brought home and some invested in Milwaukee and St. Paul stock. Under Thomson's management the Western Union had produced only £4,230 in cash for the bank. Moreover, in addition to constructing the Elkhorn-Eagle line, the Western Union purchased the line between Port Byron and Rock Island for $125,000 in 1872 and built a branch line, four miles long, from Watertown to the Hampton coal mines at a cost of $50,967. The increased traffic, together with careful management and improved track, produced profits which had eluded the railroad between 1857 and 1869 (see Table 5). The directors of the bank eagerly awaited the time when the railroad would pay dividends on the stock. 'Development of this road', wrote Leresche to Mitchell in May, 1876, 'has been a long wait for all interested here, but their patience will in the end, I trust, be rewarded.'

On 1st October, 1878, the City of Glasgow Bank closed its doors at the usual hour and declared its suspension. Five days later the directors decided to wind up the business and called a meeting of shareholders for 22nd October.(27) William Anderson, of Kerr, Anderson, Muir and Main, chartered accountants, and Dr. A. B. McGrigor of McGrigor, Donald and Company, solicitors, were instructed to prepare a report on assets and liabilities, which was published on 18th October. It revealed liabilities of £12,404,297 and assets of only £7,213,313, a far worse situation than anyone had imagined.(28) The directors, Robert Stronach, who had succeeded his brother Alexander as manager in 1875, and C. S. Leresche were immediately arrested. Leresche, however, was released and accepted as a witness by the prosecution. At their trial in January, 1879, the prisoners were found guilty of fraud, Robert Stronach and Lewis Potter, a director since 1858, receiving eighteen months' imprisonment, and the others, among them Robert Salmond, eight months.(29)

At the time of the stoppage the bank held $2,926,000 of bonds and $1,992,340 of stock in the Western Union, $300,000 of stock in the Racine Warehouse and Dock Company, which was owed $44,810 by the Western Union, and $407,300 of shares in the Milwaukee and St. Paul Railroad. The debit of the railroad account was now £1,016,000, an increase of £111,311 16s. since 1870, due to accumulation of interest charged in excess of interest earned on the bonds between 1870 and 1878. In order to find the market value of these stocks and bonds Anderson and McGrigor telegraphed Irvin and Company for further information and asked for an answer within twenty-four hours. Irvin, who could find no one who knew anything about the Western Union, finally went to the office of the Chicago, Milwaukee, and St. Paul. Mitchell was away, but he met the vice-president, Wadsworth, who said that 'the Western Union had been that year . . . doing a very losing business; that the next six months' interest would not, in all probability, be paid; that previous interest had not at all been earned, the coupons having been paid by help of large sums having been advanced by Mr. Mitchell himself. He would say $70 [per cent] a large price for the bonds, the stock he considered to have no value; the dock property might be worth $30,000.' Although surprised at these low figures, Irvin could not imagine that the Chicago, Milwaukee, and St. Paul would underrate property in which it had so large an interest, and based his reply to the investigators largely on Wadsworth's estimates. Thus Anderson and McGrigor valued the stock at £11,950, the bonds at £436,500 (less £90,000 which had been raised in May from the General Credit and Discount Company on $1,500,000 of bonds), and the stock of the Racine Warehouse and Dock Company at £6,000.

The liquidators of the bank decided to consult G. A. Thomson, who had returned to this country in 1877, and requested him to write an account how the bank had become involved with the Western Union. After considering this they invited him to become their representative in the United States, together with J. S. Kennedy and Company, investment bankers of New York, who were well known to two of the liquidators, John Cameron, secretary of the Clydesdale Bank, and George Auldjo Jamieson, a chartered accountant. The partners in this company were John S. Kennedy and

John S. Barnes, both of whom were associated with a number of railroads, including the St. Paul, Minneapolis, and Manitoba. This exchanged traffic with the Chicago, Milwaukee and St. Paul, which would be of use in dealing with Mitchell, the likeliest purchaser of the bonds and stock. Moreover Kennedy had been a partner in Morris K. Jesup and Company, who had been agents of the Racine and Mississippi Railroad until Thomson became president and manager.

In November, 1878, the *Chicago Tribune* reported that 'it is likely that the St. Paul Company will become the owner of all the Western Union Stock, for it is worth nothing to anybody else; and that the auxiliary road will come under the same ostensible, as it is now under the same actual, management; and that the fiction of two separate companies will eventually disappear.'(30) This eventually came true, but only after great difficulty was experienced with Mitchell.

In January, 1879, Thomson reported that Mitchell had offered 65 per cent, plus the February coupons, for the bonds, with the stock thrown in as worthless. Thomson's insistence on 90 per cent 'was received with a smile, which conveyed to us that the terms were far from what would be entertained'. Mitchell then defaulted on the coupons due in February, thus lowering the market value of the bonds, although the net earnings of the Western Union were sufficient to pay not only the interest on the bonds but also a small dividend on the stock. The liquidators therefore instructed Kennedy and Thomson to institute a foreclosure suit.

Nevertheless, some progress had been made in disposing of the bank's assets. The agreement between the Racine Warehouse and Dock Company and the Western Union Railroad in 1867 allowed the latter to purchase the property after 1877, but Mitchell did not take advantage of this until after the collapse of the bank, when he gave notice that the railroad wished to exercise its right. Arbitrators were appointed who valued the property at $41,933·33, and the $300,000 of stock was surrendered for this sum. Thomson considered the price 'entirely unfair' and estimated the land on which the elevator stood to be worth at least $45,000. But the elevator was of little use to Mitchell since the collapse of the grain market at Racine; his interest was in its site. Soon after this deal Thomson, who was not working harmoniously with Kennedy, came back to Britain, but the liquidators did not press him to return as they believed that their interests were safer in Kennedy's hands. Kennedy also realised the 4,073 shares of the Chicago, Milwaukee, and St. Paul Company, which the investigators had valued at 31 per cent

He himself was uncertain what they were worth. 'The stock', he wrote, 'is not only one that is speculative in itself, but the property is managed mainly by men who are notoriously speculative, and it is impossible to arrive at any intelligent conclusion from any facts that can be obtained as to what its intrinsic value may be.' He started to sell the shares in April, 1879, at 40 per cent and finished in September at 69 per cent, realising $203,500·17.

But his main task was to dispose of the Western Union bonds and stock. He was confident that the stock had some value and suggested that the 7 per cent bonds should be exchanged for the new 6 per cent bonds of the Chicago, Milwaukee and St. Paul. This appealed to the liquidators, who were anxious that a deal should be made with as little trouble as possible. 'If we had dealt with the Chicago and North Western Railway,' stated John Cameron, 'which was the only other road of any moment, we must have had to fight the St. Paul people through the whole of the foreclosure suit and the appointment of a receiver, and that would have been a matter of years.' The Chicago, Milwaukee, and St. Paul bonds were selling at nearly par compared with the 75 per cent of the Western Union's. Kennedy therefore travelled to Chicago and discussed the matter with Mitchell, who was beginning to extend the mileage under the control of the Chicago, St. Paul and Milwaukee, much to the annoyance of the Chicago and Northwestern.(31) Mitchell at first offered 5 per cent bonds, but eventually an agreement was reached in June by which the suit was dropped and the liquidators exchanged the $2,926,000 of Western Union bonds for a similar amount of Chicago, Milwaukee, and St. Paul 6 per cent bonds. They also received $15,000 of these bonds for the $1,992,340 of Western Union stock, $44,810·95 for the debt of the railroad to the Racine Warehouse and Dock Company, and $85,341·67 for the interest due on the bonds between February and July, 1879, making $3,081,000 of bonds and $152·62 in cash. The coupons due in February, $106,102·36, were paid in cash. The liquidators were disappointed at the stock being exchanged for so little, but Kennedy assured them that the settlement 'is one that you and we can both congratulate ourselves on having effected'.

The liquidators intended to sell these bonds as quickly as possible, preferably on the New York Stock Exchange where they would fetch the highest possible price. Kennedy, however, wrote that 'should you decide to realize "in block", we can arrange a syndicate here at very short notice that will take the bonds at once, and pay you the money for them in advance of the actual delivery of the bonds by the C. M. and St. P. Co.' The liquidators at first opposed this suggestion, but when John Cameron came over in September, 1879, he found 'that a change had taken place in the stock market between my leaving Glasgow and my arrival in New York, speculation was very brisk. The result was that it drew away money from permanent investments of the kind we had and people were inclined to look rather at things which would yield a larger return.' He therefore decided to follow Kennedy's advice and sell to a syndicate headed by Winslow, Lanier and Co., investment bankers, and including J. S. Kennedy and Co. After discussions with John W. Ellis of Winslow, Lanier and Co., Cameron disposed of the $3,081,000 of bonds for 98 per cent. The other members of the syndicate were Drexel, Morgan and Co., Kuhn, Loeb and Co., and Morris K. Jesup and Co., investment bankers of New York, the Scottish American Investment Company, George Readman, general manager of the Clydesdale Bank,(32) and a Captain Pavy, representing a London house who were customers of Winslow, Lanier and Co. Kennedy, who said that as an old Glasgow man he sympathised with the shareholders of the bank, handed over to the liquidators his share, about £4,000, of the syndicate's profits from the resale of the bonds, which fetched just over 103 per cent. As payment for their services, J. S. Kennedy and Co. received 10,000 guineas. 'If we had gone to realise in the ordinary market, it would have cost us . . . one per cent., and that would have been £6,000, and we also saved £4,000 by what Mr. Kennedy gave over to us.'

The liquidators estimated in October, 1879, that they would realise £687,299 on assets which the investigators in their report of a year earlier had valued at only £475,000.(33) They had, however, sold on a rising market and, unlike the directors of the bank, had nothing to fear from publicity, which enabled them to call Mitchell's bluff with a threat of foreclosure and make 'a far more advantageous arrangement than—with old bonds—they might even have been able to make in the course of years.'(34) Nevertheless, the sum raised was far short of the £1,016,478 at the debit of the railroad account or of the par value of the securities sold. Soon after the failure of the bank the liquidators had instructed James Muir of Kerr, Anderson, Muir, and Main to prepare a report on how it had become involved in the Western Union Railroad. The report was issued in March, 1880, and revealed the leading part played by William Mackinnon until his retirement in 1870. He was now head of a great shipping company which dominated the trade of the Indian Ocean and active in the exploitation of East Africa.(35) The other directors of that period who were not either dead or ruined clearly did not possess his wealth, so the liquidators decided to sue him for malfeance or breach of trust, under section 165 of the Companies Act, 1862. They argued that the interest which had been debited to the railroad account between 1858 and 1870 at rates varying from 5 to 10 per cent had been added to the amount of debt standing in the bank's books at the year balances, and then carried to the credit of the profit and loss account and paid out as dividend. They therefore demanded from Mackinnon that sum less the cash received from the railroad, £311,666 16s. 9d., on the grounds that it did not represent profits earned, but was in effect paid out of the capital of the bank.

The case was heard in the Court of Session, First Division, from 21st June to 6th July, 1881, and judgment given on 23rd December. The Court were of the opinion that the liquidators had no title to sue, that they were barred from sueing by the lapse of time since Mackinnon had retired from the board, and that the evidence heard had revealed that there was no fault or misfeance on his part. 'During his tenure of office', said the Lord President, 'it appears that the Respondent gave more of his time and attention to the management of the Bank's affairs than could well be expected from a man engaged in extensive mercantile transactions on his own account.'(36) The liquidators had also given notice that they intended to sue Mackinnon for £122,565 2s. 8d. with 5 per cent interest from October 1878, this being the difference between the sums advanced on the railroad by him and his co-directors and the amount which the securities realised in the course of the liquidation. The ground for action here was that the money was advanced on bad securities and without the exercise of necessary care. Mackinnon, however, argued that the securities were not bad and were worth a good deal more than the liquidators had realised on them. The Lord President refused to recognise any justice in calling upon Mackinnon to make good any loss as he had not been a director for over ten years and had played no part in the liquidation.(37) The liquidators therefore withdrew the action. Total costs borne by them amounted to £20,508.(38) 'It will probably be felt', commented *The Scotsman*, 'that a serious mistake has been made by the liquidators and that while there cannot be the slightest doubt of the strict integrity of their motives, they have given to their procedure something of the air of persecution.'(39)

Thus ended the unhappy involvement of the City of Glasgow Bank in American railroads. It is hard to disagree with the ironic comment of some anonymous clerk, who drew on the cover of a printed document connected with the case against Mackinnon a crafty Uncle Sam flanked by cornucopias pouring forth Scottish gold. The news that their money had been used to finance American railroads came as a complete surprise to the depositors of the bank, and public comment was made even more bitter by the low value placed upon the securities by the investigators in their report. Nevertheless, the directors of the bank inherited in 1857 a situation created by the incompetence of Robert Salmond and one which taxed even the ability of William Mackinnon to solve. Moreover, the American investments were only a minor cause of the bank's collapse in 1878. Much more important were the reckless advances by the directors, particularly after Mackinnon left, to themselves and their associates on what were often worthless securities. For example, the bank was owed £2,173,000 by James Morton, £1,968,000 by Smith, Fleming and Co., and £1,238,000 by James Nicol Fleming.(40) If, as Mackinnon had argued, the liquidators had delayed realising the railroad securities, there would have been no loss on them. This, however, was of little consolation to the shareholders of the bank, who were unprotected by any limited liability.

NOTES

(1) This essay is based upon records kindly placed at my disposal by Messrs. Kerr, MacLeod, and Macfarlan, Chartered Accountants, of Glasgow, which were among the papers of James Muir, a partner in the firm of Kerr, Anderson, Muir, and Main (predecessors of Kerr, MacLeod, and Macfarlan). They consist of James Muir, Report to the Liquidators of the City of Glasgow Bank upon the History of the Bank's Involvements with the Western Union Railroad Company of America, and the Position—in Relation to these Involvements—of Mr. William McKinnon, Ex-Director of the Bank (Glasgow, 1880); Report of Discussion in Note for the Liquidators of the City of Glasgow Bank against William Mackinnon (Glasgow, 1881); and six printed appendices relating to the case of the Liquidators of the City of Glasgow Bank against William Mackinnon, and containing proof for the parties, evidence taken in the U.S.A., American railroad reports, 1859-79, details of the bank's American investments, and correspondence, documents and accounts 1857-80 (including 954 letters).

(2) See W. H. Marwick, Scottish Overseas Investment in the Nineteenth Century, Scottish Bankers Magazine, Vol. XXVII, July, 1936, pp. 109-16.

(3) Anon., Scottish Capital Abroad, Blackwood's Magazine, October, 1884, pp. 468-69.

(4) Investigators' Report, City of Glasgow Bank, 16th October, 1878. Reprinted in W. Wallace (ed.), Trial of the City of Glasgow Bank Directors (Glasgow and Edinburgh, 1905), pp. 459-72.

(5) Report of Discussion . . . Liquidators of City of Glasgow Bank against William Mackinnon, p. 151.

(6) Report of the Select Committee on the Bank Acts and Causes of the Recent Commercial Distress. P.P. 1857-58, v (381), Appendix 27; Annual Report and Balance Sheet, City of Glasgow Bank, June, 1857.

(7) Glasgow Courier, 19th February, 1857.

(8) This was quite usual. Between 1850 and 1857 Winconsin farmers mortgaged their property for railroad stock for between $4,500,000 and $5,000,000. See Frederick Merk, Economic History of Wisconsin during the Civil War Decade (Madison, 1916), pp. 241-43, and G. R. Taylor, The Transportation Revolution, 1815-1860 (New York, 1951). pp. 97-98. For English merchant bankers in this area see R. W. Hidy and M. E. Hidy, *Anglo-American Mercant Bankers and the Railroads of the Old Northwest, 1848-1860*, Business History Review, Vol. XXXIV, No. 2, Spring 1960, pp. 150-69.

(9) Bankers' Magazine, 1857, pp. 1006-07; Glasgow Courier, 12th November, 1857.

(10) *Ibid.*, 10th December, 1857.

(11) *Ibid.*, 24th December, 1857.

(12) T. C. Cochran, Railroad Leaders, 1845-1890: The Business Mind in Action (Cambridge, Mass., 1953), p. 43.

(13) *Ibid.*, p. 81.

(14) For railroads in this area see G. R. Taylor and I. D. Neu, The American Railroad Network, 1861-1890 (Cambridge, Mass., 1956), with its map of the railways of Canada and Mid-Western States, 1st April, 1862.

(15) During 1860 the bank purchased forty eastern division bonds at between 35 and 40 per cent and one hundred western division bonds at between 20 and 25 per cent.

(16) For the effects of the war on the railroads between the Mississippi and Lake Michigan see Thomas Weber, The Northern Railroads in the Civil War, 1861-1865 (New York, 1952). pp. 83-93.

(17) Dictionary of National Biography, Supplement, Vol. III, pp. 127-28; The Times, 23rd July, 1893; The Bailie, 18th May, 1881; George Blake, B. I. Centenary, 1856-1956 (London, 1956), pp. 13-33.

(18) Anon., Clydeside Cameos (London, 1885), pp. 19-22.

(19) In all Mackinnon received £50,000 in credits for this purpose, of which £28,718 were current when the bank stopped on 11th November, 1857.

(20) The Bailie, 6th November, 1878.

(21) The final suit, for possession of the western division of the Racine and Mississippi Railroad, was not completed until March, 1867.

(22) Between June, 1865, and June, 1866, Morton's liabilities to the bank increased from £109,651 to £384,886. See David S. Macmillan, 'Scottish Enterprise in Australia, 1798-1879', above, pp. 340-41.

(23) Thomson claimed that of the 1,042 miles of line owned or leased by the Chicago and Northwestern, only 464 miles were profitable.

(24) See above, p. 396.

(25) James Muir, Report to the Liquidators, p. 231.

(26) These consisted of $121,018 of first mortgage bonds, $117,000 of preferred stock, $595,392 of ordinary stock (all Western Union), and $40,000 of stock of the Racine Warehouse and Dock Company.

(27) A. W. Kerr, History of Banking in Scotland (3rd edition, London, 1918), pp. 254-57.

(28) Investigators' Report, *op. cit.*

(29) A. W. Kerr, *op. cit.*, pp. 258-59.

(30) Reprinted in The Courant, 21st November, 1878.

(31) See Julius Grodinsky, Trans Continental Railway Strategy, 1869-1893 (Philadelphia, 1962), pp. 126-30.

(32) He was then visiting New York.

(33) Report of the Liquidators of the City of Glasgow Bank, 17th December, 1879.

(34) James Muir, Report to the Liquidators, p. 242.

(35) For Mackinnon's career, particularly in Africa, see R. Anstey, Britain and the Congo in the Nineteenth Century (Oxford, 1962); R. Coupland, The Exploitation of East Africa, 1856-1890 (London, 1939); M. J. de Kiewiet, History of the Imperial British East Africa Company, 1876-1895 (Univ. of London, Ph.D. thesis, 1955).

(36) Opinions of the Judges in Note for the Liquidators of the City of Glasgow Bank against William Mackinnon, 23rd December, 1881, p. 11.

(37) Ibid., pp. 15-16.

(38) Report by the Liquidators of the City of Glasgow Bank, 26th January, 1882, and 15th November, 1882.

(39) 24th December, 1881.

(40) W. Wallace (ed.), op. cit., pp. 64-65. I hope to deal further with the failure of the City of Glasgow Bank in a separate study.

TABLE 1

NORTHERN ILLINOIS RAILROAD SECURITIES EXCHANGED FOR WESTERN UNION RAILROAD SECURITIES, AS AGREED 1ST FEBRUARY, 1866

Held 1st February, 1866	Northern Illinois securities		Western Union securities received in exchange	
	Capital		Capital	
	First mortgage bonds	Common stock	First mortgage bonds	Common stock
	$	$	$	$
By bank	671,200.49	906,000.00	897,700.49	906,000.00
By public	779,000.00	94,000.00	802,500.00	94,000.00
TOTALS	1,450,200.49	1,000,000.00	1,700,200.49	1,000,000.00

Source: Appendix D (Liquidators City of Glasgow Bank v. William Mackinnon), p. 988.

TABLE 2

RACINE AND MISSISSIPPI RAILROAD SECURITIES EXCHANGED FOR WESTERN UNION RAILROAD SECURITIES, AS AGREED 1ST FEBRUARY, 1866

| Held by Bank | Racine and Mississippi Railroad Securities and Interest | | | | | Western Union Securities received in Exchange | | | |
| | Capital | | | | Past due interest | For capital of Racine bonds | | For past due interest on Racine bonds | |
Held 1st February, 1866	First mortgage bonds Eastern Division	First mortgage bonds Western Division	Second mortgage bonds	Receipts by Farmers' Loan and Trust Co.	To 1st February, 1866	First mortgage bonds	Common stock	First mortgage bonds	Common stock
By bank	$ 560,000.00	$ 436,000.00	$ —	$ 273,241.44	$ 798,069.67	$ 1,269,241.44	$ —	$ 315,956.34	$ 482,113.33
By 'combination'	50,000.00	185,000.00	700,000.00	—	164,946.67	515,000.00	1,000,000.00	16,920.00	148,026.67
By public	70,000.00	79,000.00	—	7,500.00	101,735.06	156,500.00	—	26,181.73	75,553.33
TOTALS	680,000.00	700,000.00	700,000.00	280,741.44	1,064,751.40	1,940,741.44	1,000,000.00	359,058.07	705,693.33

Source: Appendix D (Liquidators City of Glasgow Bank v. William Mackinnon), p. 989.

TABLE 3

BONDS AND STOCKS ISSUED BY WESTERN UNION RAILROAD COMPANY, AS AGREED, 1ST FEBRUARY, 1866

Held	First mortgage bonds	Common stock
	$	$
By bank	2,482,898.27	1,338,113.33
By 'combination'	531,920.00	1,148,026.67
By public	985,181.73	169,553.33
TOTALS	4,000,000.00	2,705,693.33

Source: Compiled from Tables 1 and 2.

TABLE 4

ADVANCES (INCLUDING INTEREST DEBITED) TO THE RACINE AND MISSISSIPPI, NORTHERN ILLINOIS, AND THE WESTERN UNION RAILROADS AND SECURITIES HELD BY THE CITY OF GLASGOW BANK, JUNE, 1858–JUNE, 1870

Year ending June	Advances, including principal and interest	Nominal value of securities held
	£ s. d.	$
1858	106,197 12 8	500,720.00
1859	128,119 5 11	758,528.54
1860	191,263 16 9	1,059,136.44
1861	214,615 12 7	1,458,473.58
1862	287,381 12 0	1,577,130.27
1863	336,503 10 0	2,288,008.42
1864	361,036 9 5	2,370,486.57
1865	425,913 3 10	2,449,964.72
1866	597,612 9 10	3,882,668.46
1867	656,401 1 5	4,068,755.60
1868	755,084 15 10	5,454,183.49
1869	801,248 15 4	5,661,507.60
1870	905,166 13 4	4,874,330.00

Source: Appendix D (Liquidators City of Glasgow Bank v. William Mackinnon), p. 1002.

TABLE 5

EARNINGS AND OPERATING EXPENSES OF THE RACINE AND MISSISSIPPI AND THE
NORTHERN ILLINOIS RAILROADS (COMBINED), AND OF THE WESTERN UNION
RAILROAD, 1858–78

Year ending	Gross earnings	Operating expenses	Net earnings
	$	$	$
May 10th, 1860	166,916.03	131,790.14	35,125.89
May 10th, 1861	220,850.04	152,411.48	68,438.56
May 10th, 1862	245,813.79	177,173.79	68,640.00
May 10th, 1863	344,769.20	260,929.48	83,839.72
May 10th, 1864	490,596.75	352,395.18	138,201.57
May 10th, 1865	600,799.59	487,827.42	112,972.17
January 1st, 1867	815,954.33	673,160.99	142,793.34
January 1st, 1868	775,075.59	610,423.64	164,651.95
January 1st, 1869	758,785.68	568,472.04	190,313.64
June 30th, 1869 (½ year)	319,629.92	279,819.33	39,810.59
January 1st, 1870 (½ year)	450,082.91	383,669.01	66,413.90
January 1st, 1871	766,937.85	617,982.51	148,955.34
January 1st, 1872	842,169.22	638,373.20	203,796.02
January 1st, 1873	847,111.21	702,960.18	144,151.03
January 1st, 1874	1,137,634.23	878,241.37	259,392.86
January 1st, 1875	1,123,107.81	768,164.21	354,943.60
January 1st, 1876	1,160,430.01	830,287.53	340,142.48
January 1st, 1877	1,047,915.40	799,369.42	248,545.98
January 1st, 1878	1,025,058.79	699,019.43	326,039.36
January 1st, 1879	1,061,731.44	753,775.70	307,955.74

Source: Appendix D (Liquidators City of Glasgow Bank *v.* William Mackinnon), p. 1024.

Note:

11th May to 1st September, 1859, road in operation to Davis, Illinois					90	miles
1st September, 1859, road opened to Freeport			for business		104	miles
1st October, 1861,	,,	,,	,, Lanark	,,	,,	124	,,
1st September, 1862,	,,	,,	,, Savanna	,,	,,	142½	,,
10th January, 1865,	,,	,,	,, Thomson	,,	,,	152	,,
10th August, 1865,	,,	,,	,, Fulton	,,	,,	159	,,
14th January, 1866,	,,	,,	,, Port Byron	,,	,,	181	,,

Index

N.B. The records preserved by the Scottish Record Office (pp. 11-29) and surveyed by the National Register of Archives (Scotland) (pp. 31-41), being listed alphabetically as Appendices to Chapters One and Two, are *not* included in this Index.